THE PAPERS OF
BENJAMIN FRANKLIN

SPONSORED BY

The American Philosophical Society
and Yale University

Lord Dartmouth

THE PAPERS OF

Benjamin Franklin

VOLUME 19   *January 1 through December 31, 1772*

WILLIAM B. WILLCOX, *Editor*

Dorothy W. Bridgwater, Mary L. Hart, Claude A. Lopez,
C. A. Myrans, Catherine M. Prelinger, and G. B. Warden,
Assistant Editors

New Haven and London YALE UNIVERSITY PRESS, 1975

Funds for editing The Papers of Benjamin Franklin *and
four similar publications have been provided by a grant
from the Ford Foundation, administered by the National
Historical Publications Commission under the chairman-
ship of the Archivist of the United States; the support of
the Commission and its Executive Director has been
indispensable. The Commission is also generously providing a subsidy to the Yale University Press, beginning
with this volume, to compensate for unrecovered publishing
costs.*

*Library of Congress catalog card number: 59–12697
International standard book number: 0–300–01865–7*

*Designed by Alvin Eisenman and Walter Howe,
and printed by Cambridge University Press.*

*Published in Great Britain, Europe, and Africa by
Yale University Press, Ltd., London.
Distributed in Latin America by Kaiman & Polon,
Inc., New York City; in India by UBS Publishers'
Distributors Pvt., Ltd., Delhi; in Japan by John
Weatherhill, Inc., Tokyo.*

Administrative Board

Advisory Committee

Since the appearance of the previous volume the Advisory Committee has been reduced, to our deep regret, by the death of three members: Samuel F. Bemis, the noted diplomatic historian; Clifford K. Shipton, who carried on *Sibley's Harvard Graduates* and was editor of the vast microprint collection, *Early American Imprints, 1639–1800*; and Sylvester K. Stevens, the well-known Pennsylvania historian and editor. The world of Franklin scholarship has also lost one of its most eminent figures in the death of Verner Crane, to whose meticulous work we owe a debt beyond expression.

Editor's Note

Esther Reiber, who for many years was the secretary, impeccable typist and transcriber, and general factotum of the editorial project, retired in 1974; and soon afterward Sara Turner left after two years as our hawk-eyed checker of citations. We deeply appreciated their services and miss them both.

W.B.W.

Contents

xiv

CONTENTS

List of Illustrations

Contributors to Volume 19

The ownership of each manuscript, or the location of the particular copy used by the editors of each rare contemporary pamphlet or similar printed work, is indicated where the document appears in the text. The sponsors and editors are deeply grateful to the following institutions and individuals for permission to print or otherwise use in the text of the present volume manuscripts or other materials which they own.

INSTITUTIONS

Académie des sciences, Paris
American Philosophical Society
Assay Office, Birmingham, England
Bibliothèque de Genève
British Museum
Buffalo and Erie Public Library
Central Library, Salford, England
Dartmouth College Library
Franklin Library, Franklin, Mass.
Harvard University Library
Haverford College Library
Historical Society of Pennsylvania
Library Company of Philadelphia
Library of Congress
Massachusetts Historical Society
New Haven Colony Historical Society

Newport Historical Society
New-York Historical Society
New York Public Library
Pennsylvania Hospital, Philadelphia
Public Record Office, London
Royal College of Surgeons, London
Royal Society, London
Scottish Record Office, Edinburgh
University of Pennsylvania Library
Henry Francis du Pont Winterthur Museum
Yale University Library

INDIVIDUALS

Mrs. Craig Barrow, Savannah, Ga.

Miss Louise B. Wallace, Los Angeles, Cal.

Method of Textual Reproduction

An extended statement of the principles of selection, arrangement, form of presentation, and method of textual reproduction observed in this edition appears in the Introduction to the first volume, pp. xxiv–xlvii. What follows is a condensation and revision of part of it.

Printed Material:

Those of Franklin's writings that were printed under his direction presumably appeared as he wanted them to, and should therefore be reproduced with no changes except what modern typography requires. In some cases, however, printers carelessly or willfully altered his text without his consent; or the journeymen who set it had different notions from his—and from each other's—of capitalization, spelling, and punctuation. Such of his letters as survive only in nineteenth-century printings, furthermore, have often been vigorously edited by William Temple Franklin, Duane, or Sparks. In all these cases the original has suffered some degree of distortion, which the modern editor may guess at but, in the absence of the manuscript, cannot remedy. We therefore follow the printed texts as we find them, and note only obvious misreadings.

We observe the following rules in reproducing printed materials:

1. The place and date of composition of letters are set at the top, regardless of their location in the original printing.

2. Proper nouns, including personal names, which were often printed in italics, are set in roman except when the original was italicized for emphasis.

3. Prefaces and other long passages, though italicized in the original, are set in roman. Long italicized quotations are set in roman within quotation marks.

4. Words in full capitals are set in small capitals, with initial letters in full capitals if required by Franklin's normal usage.

5. All signatures are set in capitals and small capitals.

6. We silently correct obvious typographical errors, such as the omission of a single parenthesis or quotation mark.

7. We close a sentence by supplying, when needed, a period or question mark.

Manuscript Material:

a. *Letters* are presented in the following form:

1. The place and date of composition are set at the top, regardless of their location in the original.

2. The complimentary close is set continuously with the text.

3. Addresses, endorsements, and notations are so labelled and printed at the end of the letter. An endorsement is to the best of our belief by the recipient, a notation by someone else.

b. *Spelling* of the original we retain. When it is so abnormal as to obscure the meaning, we supply the correct form in brackets or a footnote, as "yf [wife]."

c. *Capitalization* we retain as written, except that every sentence is made to begin with a capital. When we cannot decide whether a letter is a capital, we follow modern usage.

d. Words underlined once in the manuscript are printed in italics; words underlined twice or written in large letters or full capitals are printed in small capitals.

e. *Punctuation* has been retained as in the original, except:

1. We close a sentence by supplying, when needed, a period or question mark. When it is unclear where the sentence ends, we retain the original punctuation or lack of it.

2. Dashes used in place of commas, semicolons, colons, or periods are replaced by the appropriate marks; when a sentence ends with both a dash and a period, the dash is omitted.

3. Commas scattered meaninglessly through a manuscript are eliminated.

4. When a mark of punctuation is not clear or can be read as one of two marks, we follow modern usage.[1]

5. Some documents, especially legal ones, have no punctua-

1. The typescripts from which these papers are printed have been made from photocopies of the manuscripts; marks of punctuation are sometimes blurred or lost in photography, and it has often been impossible to consult the original.

tion; others have so little as to obscure the meaning. In such cases we silently supply the minimum needed for clarity.

f. *Contractions and abbreviations* in general are retained. The ampersand is rendered as "and," except in the names of business firms, in the form "&c.," and in a few other cases. Letters represented by the thorn or tilde are printed. The tailed "p" is spelled out as per, pre, or pro. Symbols of weights, measures and monetary values follow modern usage, as: £34. Superscript letters are lowered.

g. *Omitted or illegible words or letters* are treated as follows:

1. If not more than four letters are missing, we supply them silently when we have no doubt what they should be.

2. If more than four letters are missing, we supply them conjecturally in brackets, with or without a question mark depending on our confidence in the conjecture.

3. Other omissions are shown as follows: [*illegible*], [*torn*], [*remainder missing*], or the like.

4. Missing or illegible digits are indicated by suspension points in brackets, the number of points corresponding to the estimated number of missing figures.

h. *Author's additions and corrections:*

1. Interlineations and brief marginal notes are incorporated in the text without comment, and longer notes with the notation [*in the margin*] unless they were clearly intended as footnotes, in which case they are normally printed with our notes but with a bracketed indication of the source.

2. Canceled words and phrases are in general omitted without notice; if significant, they are printed in footnotes.

3. When alternative words and phrases have been inserted in a manuscript but the original remains uncanceled, the alternatives are given in brackets, preceded by explanatory words in italics, as: "it is [*written above:* may be] true."

4. Variant readings of several versions are noted if important.

Abbreviations and Short Titles

Académie des sciences, *Mémoires*	*Histoire de l'Académie royale des sciences... avec les Mémoires de mathématique & de physique...* (Paris, 1733–). Until 1790, when the title changed, the *Histoire* and *Mémoires* were paginated separately; our references, unless otherwise indicated, are to the second pagination.
Acts Privy Coun., Col.	W. L. Grant and James Munro, eds., *Acts of the Privy Council of England, Colonial Series, 1613–1783* (6 vols., London, 1908–12).
AD	Autograph document.[1]
ADS	Autograph document signed.
AL	Autograph letter.
ALS	Autograph letter signed.
Amer.	American.
APS	American Philosophical Society.
Autobiog.	Leonard W. Labaree, Ralph L. Ketcham, Helen C. Boatfield, and Helene H. Fineman, eds., *The Autobiography of Benjamin Franklin* (New Haven, 1964).
BF	Benjamin Franklin.
Bigelow, *Works*	John Bigelow, ed., *The Complete Works of Benjamin Franklin...* (10 vols., N.Y., 1887–88).
Board of Trade Jour.	*Journal of the Commissioners for Trade and Plantations... April 1704 to... May 1782* (14 vols., London, 1920–38).
Bradford, ed., *Mass. State Papers*	Alden Bradford, ed., *Speeches of the Governors of Massachusetts, from 1765 to 1775; and the Answers of the House of Representatives...* (Boston, 1818).

1. For definitions of types of manuscripts see above, I, xliv–xlvii.

Burke's Peerage	Sir Bernard Burke, *Burke's Genealogical and Heraldic History of the Peerage Baronetage and Knightage with War Gazette and Corrigenda* (98th ed., London, 1940). References in exceptional cases to other editions are so indicated.
Butterfield, ed., *John Adams Diary*	Lyman H. Butterfield *et al.*, eds., *Diary and Autobiography of John Adams* (4 vols., Cambridge, Mass., 1961).
Candler, ed., *Ga. Col. Recs.*	Allen D. Candler, ed., *The Colonial Records of the State of Georgia...* (26 vols., Atlanta, 1904–16).
Carter, ed., *Gage Correspondence*	Clarence E. Carter, ed., *The Correspondence of General Thomas Gage...* (2 vols., New Haven and London, 1931–33).
Chron.	*Chronicle.*
Cobbett, *Parliamentary History*	William Cobbett and Thomas C. Hansard, eds., *The Parliamentary History of England from the Earliest Period to 1803* (36 vols., London, 1806–20).
Coll.	*Collections.*
Crane, *Letters to the Press*	Verner W. Crane, ed., *Benjamin Franklin's Letters to the Press, 1758–1775* (Chapel Hill, N.C., [1950]).
Cushing, ed., *Writings of Samuel Adams*	Harry Alonzo Cushing, ed., *The Writings of Samuel Adams...* (4 vols., New York, 1904–08).
DAB	*Dictionary of American Biography.*
Dartmouth MSS.	Historical Manuscripts Commission, *The Manuscripts of the Earl of Dartmouth...: Eleventh Report*, appendix, part 5; *Fourteenth Report*, appendix, part 10; *Fifteenth Report*, appendix, part 1 (3 vols., London, 1887–96).
DF	Deborah Franklin.
Dictionnaire de biographie	*Dictionnaire de biographie française...* (11 vols. to date, Paris, 1933—).
DNB	*Dictionary of National Biography.*
DS	Document signed.

Duane, *Works*	William Duane, ed., *The Works of Dr. Benjamin Franklin*... (6 vols., Philadelphia, 1808–18). Title varies in the several volumes.
Dubourg, *Œuvres*	Jacques Barbeu-Dubourg, *Œuvres de M. Franklin*... (2 vols., Paris, 1773).
Ed.	Edition or editor.
Exper. and Obser.	*Experiments and Observations on Electricity, made at Philadelphia in America, by Mr. Benjamin Franklin* ... (London, 1751). Revised and enlarged editions were published in 1754, 1760, 1769, and 1774 with slightly varying titles. In each case the edition cited will be indicated, e.g., *Exper. and Obser.* (1751).
Gaz.	*Gazette.*
Geneal.	Genealogical.
Gent. Mag.	*The Gentleman's Magazine, and Historical Chronicle.*
Gipson, *British Empire*	Lawrence H. Gipson, *The British Empire before the American Revolution* (15 vols., New York, 1939–70; I–III, revised ed., N.Y., 1958–60).
Hinshaw, *Amer. Quaker Genealogy*	William W. Hinshaw, *Encyclopedia of American Quaker Genealogy* (6 vols. Ann Arbor, Mich., 1936–50).
Hist.	Historical.
Hutchinson, *History*	Thomas Hutchinson, *The History of the Colony and Province of Massachusetts-Bay*... (Lawrence S. Mayo, ed.; 3 vols., Cambridge., Mass., 1936).
Jour.	*Journal.* The citation "Jour." is of Franklin's MS account book described above, XI, 518–20.
Kammen, *Rope of Sand*	Michael G. Kammen, *A Rope of Sand: the Colonial Agents, British Politics, and the American Revolution* (Ithaca, N.Y., [1968]).
Larousse, *Dictionnaire universel*	Pierre Larousse, *Grand dictionnaire universel du XIXe siècle*... (17 vols., Paris, [n.d.]).

Ledger   The Franklin MS described above, XI, 518–20.

Lee Papers   Paul P. Hoffman, ed., *The Lee Family Papers, 1742–1795* (University of Virginia Library *Microfilm Publication* No. 1; 8 reels, Charlottesville, Va., 1966).

Lewis, *Indiana Co.*   George E. Lewis, *The Indiana Company, 1763–1798: a Study in Eighteenth Century Frontier Land Speculation and Business Venture* (Glendale, Cal., 1941).

LS   Letter signed.

Mag.   *Magazine.*

Mass. Acts and Resolves   Abner C. Goodell *et al.*, eds., *The Acts and Resolves, Public and Private, of the Province of Massachusetts Bay* (21 vols., Boston, 1869–1922).

Mass. Arch.   Massachusetts Archives, State House, Boston.

Mass. House Jour.   *A Journal of the Honourable House of Representatives of His Majesty's Province of the Massachusetts Bay...* (Boston, 1715[–75]). The title varies, and each session is designated by date. The Massachusetts Historical Society is republishing the volumes (Boston, 1919–) and has reached 1767; for later years we cite by session and date the original edition, which is most readily available in microprint in Clifford K. Shipton, ed., *Early American Imprints, 1639–1800.*

MS, MSS   Manuscript, manuscripts.

Namier and Brooke, *House of Commons*   Sir Lewis Namier and John Brooke, *The History of Parliament. The House of Commons 1754–1790* (3 vols., London and N.Y., 1964).

N.J. Arch.   William A. Whitehead *et al.*, eds., *Archives of the State of New Jersey* (2 series, Newark and elsewhere, 1880–). Editors, subtitles, and places of publication vary.

N.Y. Col. Docs.	E. B. O'Callaghan, ed., *Documents Relative to the Colonial History of the State of New York* (15 vols., Albany, 1853–87).
Pa. Arch.	Samuel Hazard *et al.*, eds., *Pennsylvania Archives* (9 series, Philadelphia and Harrisburg, 1852–1935).
Pa. Col. Recs.	*Minutes of the Provincial Council of Pennsylvania...* (16 vols., Harrisburg, 1851–53). Volumes I–III are reprints published in Philadelphia, 1852. Title changes with Volume XI to *Supreme Executive Council.*
Phil. Trans.	The Royal Society, *Philosophical Transactions.*
PMHB	*Pennsylvania Magazine of History and Biography.*
Priestley, *History*	Joseph Priestley, *The History and Present State of Electricity, with Original Experiments...* (3rd ed.; 2 vols., London, 1775).
Proc.	*Proceedings.*
Pub.	*Publications.*
Rev.	*Review.*
Sabine, *Loyalists*	Lorenzo Sabine, *Biographical Sketches of Loyalists of the American Revolution...* (2 vols., Boston, 1864).
Schofield, *Scientific Autobiog.*	Robert E. Schofield, ed., *A Scientific Autobiography of Joseph Priestley...* (Cambridge, Mass., and London, [1966]).
Sibley's Harvard Graduates	John L. Sibley, *Biographical Sketches of Graduates of Harvard University* (Cambridge, Mass., 1873–). Continued from Volume IV by Clifford K. Shipton.
Smyth, *Writings*	Albert H. Smyth, ed., *The Writings of Benjamin Franklin...* (10 vols., N.Y., 1905–07).
Soc.	*Society.*
Sparks, *Works*	Jared Sparks, ed., *The Works of Benjamin Franklin...* (10 vols., Boston, 1836–40).

Sutherland *East India Co.*	Lucy S. Sutherland, *The East India Company in Eighteenth-Century Politics* (Oxford, 1952).
Trans.	*Transactions.*
Van Doren, *Franklin*	Carl Van Doren, *Benjamin Franklin* (N.Y., 1938).
Van Doren, *Franklin–Mecom*	Carl Van Doren, ed., *The Letters of Benjamin Franklin & Jane Mecom* (American Philosophical Society *Memoirs*, XXVII, Princeton, 1950).
Votes, N.J.	*Votes and Proceedings of the General Assembly of the Province of New-Jersey...* (New York, Woodbridge, etc., 1711–). A separate volume was published for each session and is so designated, e.g., *Votes, N.J.* (Oct.–Dec., 1771).
W&MQ	*William and Mary Quarterly*, first or third series as indicated.
WF	William Franklin.
Wroth and Zobel, *John Adams Legal Papers*	L. Kinvin Wroth and Hiller B. Zobel, eds., *Legal Papers of John Adams* (3 vols., Cambridge, Mass., 1965).
WTF	William Temple Franklin.
WTF, *Memoirs*	William Temple Franklin, ed., *Memoirs of the Life and Writings of Benjamin Franklin, LL.D., F.R.S., &c.* .... (3 vols., 4to, London, 1817–18).

Introduction

The surface of Franklin's world was no more troubled in 1772 than it had been in 1771, but his life was packed with activity. Some of it was recreation: he found time to travel and visit friends in the country. Some of it was business: Pennsylvania silk was at last arriving in quantity, and the affairs of the Walpole Company suddenly brightened to the point where victory seemed within grasp. Much of his activity was scientific: his interests there were as varied as ever, but his central focus on electricity was more absorbing than it had been for years. His political involvement deepened, because a momentous dispute developed in Massachusetts between the Governor and the House; as the latter's agent Franklin was inevitably drawn in. Although coming events were beginning to cast their shadow, it did not yet have much effect on his day-to-day life, which was full but essentially tranquil. He must have looked back later on 1772, if he looked back at all, as one of the last years of serenity.

His personal life was presumably saddened by the loss of two old friends: John Canton died in London in March, and David Hall in Philadelphia on Christmas Eve. Franklin also endured a domestic upheaval in October, when Mrs. Stevenson moved from one house to another in Craven Street; but he escaped from this confusion to a country estate.[1] His penchant for travel took him on a summer tour of the north in company with Sir John Pringle, and he found much in the trip to intrigue him. He climbed a mountain in the Lake Country and went under the sea in a coal mine;[2] he and Pringle tried to calm Derwent Water with oil, and at Leeds called on Priestley when the chemist was making some of his most productive experiments.[3] The travelers were not exposed to new industries, as Franklin had been the year before, but otherwise the tour could scarcely have been more variegated.

His business interests in 1772, as they show through his papers,

1. BF to WF, Oct. 7, Nov. 3, and to DF, Nov. 4. This was his second country visit; in August he had been in Kent with his banker friend, John Sargent.
2. BF to DF, July 14.
3. Brownrigg to BF, June 12, and the headnote on BF to Priestley, end of July.

were more in silk than in land speculation. The embryonic, and eventually stillborn, Pennsylvania silk industry, of which he was the patron in England, has appeared in earlier volumes; but the first substantial sample of its produce did not reach him until 1772, and he made suitable provisions for publicizing its arrival.[4] In the affairs of the Walpole Company, on the other hand, he remained very much in the background; his unpopularity in governmental circles made him a liability for the promoters. Those affairs were still close to his heart and purse, however, and he could not have failed to rejoice when the Privy Council overrode the Board of Trade's opposition to the grant; but he had too much experience of fortune's wheel to be confident of the outcome.[5]

His scientific and technological interests, or at least those of his correspondents, ranged from the aurora borealis as a weather-predictor to marsh gas, speaking machines, and drill plows.[6] He was also becoming a chemist at one remove through his interest in Priestley's experiments, which were preparing the way for the discovery of photosynthesis.[7] But his central concern through the year was electricity in one form or another—diffused through the air, generated by a fish, and above all concentrated in lightning. Thomas Ronayne and William Henly reported to him their experiments in determining conductivity and electric charge in the atmosphere.[8] John Walsh, with his encouragement, embarked on an investigation that proved the torpedo fish, a form of ray, to be the piscine equivalent of a charged Leyden jar.[9] Another investigation, which concerned Franklin much more closely, grew out of the government's desire to protect its powder magazine at Purfleet against lightning. A committee of the Royal Society was appointed to consider the question. It included Franklin and Benjamin Wilson, and they differed categorically over the type of rod

4. BF to Evans, Feb. 6, and to the Managers of the Philadelphia Filature, under May 10.
5. See the note on the Company's rejoinder to the Board of Trade's report, under May 1, and BF to Galloway, Aug. 22.
6. For the first see Winn to BF, Aug. 12, and BF's comments that follow; for the second and third see Darwin to BF, July 18; and for the last Colden to BF, Nov. 30.
7. See the headnote on BF to Priestley, end of July.
8. In their letters, respectively, of Feb. 15 and Dec. 30.
9. See the headnote on Walsh to BF, before June.

to use; the resultant controversy lasted for several years. Franklin himself withdrew from it in December, but his friend and collaborator, William Henly, carried it on.[1]

Another friend, Jacques Barbeu-Dubourg, was collaborating in a different way, by translating Franklin's writings into French. Although the *Œuvres de M. Franklin* did not appear until the following year, much of it was finished in 1772; and it marked a new phase in the relationship between the two men. They had much in common: a broad and varied background, an eye for detail, and above all a voracious curiosity. The Frenchman discovered that close contact with Franklin's work opened numberless new vistas for his own speculation, and he was eager for whatever light the other could throw on the "multitude de questions qui s'offre en foule à mon esprit."[2] Franklin responded, often at considerable length; the exchange contained plenty of now tedious details, but its volume suggests that both men found it stimulating.

For Franklin the politician, the most gratifying event of the year was the appointment in August of Lord Dartmouth to the American department. His predecessor, Hillsborough, fell victim to the Walpole Company: as its ambitions gained acceptance in the Cabinet, his standing weakened to the point where he resigned. Franklin was unconvinced, and rightly so, that this development ensured the grant; what delighted him was the change that he foresaw in Anglo-American relations. Hillsborough was in his opinion as inimical to the colonies as Dartmouth was well disposed. Now that an enemy was ousted and a friend installed, a new era appeared to be dawning.

The appearance was misleading. Past controversy had left resentment on both sides of the Atlantic and, in New England, concrete reminders to keep resentment alive. Royal troops had been withdrawn from Boston, but a small garrison still held Castle William in the harbor. British efforts to curb smuggling angered the mercantile community, and in June the anger erupted in the burning of H.M.S. *Gaspee*. The Townshend duty on tea, retained

1. See the headnotes on BF to Dawson, May 29; on the committee's report, Aug. 21; on its letters to the Society, after Dec. 10, and to Pringle, Dec. 17.
2. To BF below, Feb. 12, 1773. For Dubourg's career see above, XV, 112–13. The *Œuvres* was not, as has sometimes been said, a translation of *Exper. and Obser.*; it contained a great many of BF's other writings, as well as extracts of the correspondence that Dubourg's questions evoked.

to assert Parliament's right to tax, was a universal irritant; and before the year's end the government opened negotiations with the East India Company that unintentionally converted an irritant into an explosive. In Massachusetts the issue of a royal salary for the governor and judges exacerbated the constitutional debate between the executive and legislature, and in November the Bostonians combined their grievances into what amounted to a sweeping denial of British authority.

Franklin's first extensive conversation with Dartmouth, late in the year, suggested the obstacles in the path of compromise. The interview may well have been disappointing to Franklin himself: he had placed high hopes in the new Minister, but got nothing from him except a plea to postpone a petition in which the Massachusetts House had insisted on its right to pay the governor's stipend. Though the agent agreed to the postponement, he offered no hope that his constituents would change their position.

With his letter describing the interview he sent Speaker Cushing the correspondence that soon became a *cause célèbre*, the letters from Hutchinson and Oliver to an English friend. Franklin's purpose, or so he said, was to mollify the Bostonians' resentment of British policy and give Whitehall a chance to amend it.[3] If this was his expectation, the effect was just the opposite—to add fuel to the controversy in Massachusetts and to start the chain of events that culminated in London, little more than a year later, in his political ostracism. He unwittingly contributed to that result in 1772, first by presenting his constituents' claim to pay royal agents and then by sending them material that inflamed them against those agents.

The pressure of developments, most of them outside his control, was making his role of mediator increasingly hard to maintain. As the gap between London and Boston widened, his attempt to straddle it was exposing him to the anger of both sides. He had no desire to cut himself off from either one, and it was several years before he consciously and overtly did so. But when he provided the Boston radicals with ammunition against Hutchinson and Oliver he crossed, without recognizing it, a personal Rubicon. The days of his usefulness in London were numbered.

3. The interview and the affair of the letters are discussed at length in the headnote on BF to Cushing, Dec. 2.

Chronology of 1772

January 21: Parliament reconvenes.

February 17: BF gives Richard Bache, who is about to leave for home, a joint power of attorney with DF.

March 22: John Canton dies in London.

April 15: The Board of Trade reports unfavorably on the Walpole Company's petition for a grant.

April 24: Richard Bache arrives in Philadelphia.

June 3: The *London Packet* prints BF's "Toleration in Old and New England."

June 9: Parliament adjourns; H.M.S. *Gaspee* runs aground near Providence, R.I., and during the night is attacked and burned.

June 17?–July 14?: BF is on a tour of the north, accompanied at least part of the way by Sir John Pringle; they visit Joseph Priestley at Leeds and William Brownrigg at Ormathwaite, and BF stays with the Baches at Preston.

June 18–20: The *London Chronicle* prints BF's "The Sommersett Case and the Slave Trade."

July 1: The Committee on Plantations of the Privy Council overrules the Board of Trade on the Walpole Company's petition.

Early July: At the request of the Board of Ordnance the Royal Society appoints a committee, of which BF is a member, to determine ways of protecting the Purfleet magazine against lightning.

July 14: The last session of the Massachusetts General Court at Cambridge is prorogued; the Court does not meet again until 1773.

July 31?–August 7: BF visits the Sargents at May Place.

August 7: BF and other members of the Purfleet committee inspect the magazine.

August 14: Lord Dartmouth succeeds Lord Hillsborough in the American department; the Privy Council accepts its committee's report on the Walpole grant.

August 15: Josiah Williams dies in Boston.

August 16: The Académie royale des sciences elects BF a foreign associate.

August 21: The Purfleet committee reports.
October 8–24: BF visits Lord Le Despencer while Mrs. Stevenson
moves to another house in Craven Street.
October 15: Pennsylvania reappoints BF as its agent.
October 28: BF is cordially received at Lord Dartmouth's first
levee.
November 2: A Boston town meeting creates the first committee
of correspondence.
November 4: BF presents to Lord Dartmouth, but agrees to with-
hold, the petition from Massachusetts against a royal salary for
the Governor.
November 26: Parliament reconvenes.
November 30: Sir John Pringle is elected president of the Royal
Society and BF a member of its council.
December 2: BF sends the Hutchinson letters to Speaker Cushing.
December 24: David Hall dies in Philadelphia.

THE PAPERS OF
BENJAMIN FRANKLIN

VOLUME 19
January 1 through December 31, 1772

From William Franklin

ALS: American Philosophical Society

Honoured Father,   Burlington Janry 6, 1772

The Session of the Assembly which ended the 21st. Ulto. and the Xmas Holidays since, have so engrossed my Time, that I have not been able to write you fully as I intended. At present I have taken up the Pen principally to acquaint you that I have had a very amicable Session, contrary to the Expectation of every Body, and indeed contrary to the Intention of most of the Members of the Assembly. I have carried two Points of great Difficulty, with which I suppose the M[inistr]y will not be a little p[leased.] One is the Supply for the Troops, and the other is, leaving out those Words in the Support Bill, which the Board of T. look'd upon as meant to establish the Assembly's Claim of the sole Right of appointing an Agent. This last, however, I suppose you [will] not be altogether pleas'd with. However, it really (*inter nos*) makes no kind of Difference, and yet will satisfy the M[inistr]y as it will appear to be a Point gained.[1] I will explain this in a future Letter.

I send you by this Opp[ortunit]y your Appointment duely certified, and the rough Draft of some Mes[sages] which I sent the Assembly, and Copies of their Answers. Further Particulars of the Session I must refer to my [next,] which shall be soon.

Messrs. Galloway and Foxcroft have informed me that they have wrote to you, Mr. Jackson, [and] Mr. Todd, fully with respect to the Grants said [to] have been made by the Government of Virginia, of Lands which will fall in the proposed New Colony. If the Accounts which those Gentlemen have received are just, we shall have very little worth our Attention unless the Bounds are considerably enlarged. But I can hardly believe that Lord Botetourt had any Authority to grant Land on the other side of the Allegany Mountains. The King's Proclamation of the 7th. of Octr. 1763 prohibited all such Grants.[2] It also seems improbable

1. For WF's long squabble with the Assembly, and the delicate issue of the agency, see above, XVIII, respectively 270 n and 218, 260–1. BF was displeased, as his son predicted, with the requirement that both houses and the governor should appoint the agent: to WF below, Jan. 30.

2. Galloway had written Richard Jackson, counsel to the Board of Trade; Foxcroft had written Anthony Todd, secretary of the Post Office. See below, Jackson to BF, Jan. 16; BF to Foxcroft, Feb. 4, and to Galloway, Feb. 6. The grants about which Galloway and Foxcroft were exercised were, we assume,

to me, that the Crown should, thro' Lord Botetourt, give the Virginians Leave to purchase of the southern Indians the very Land which the Crown had before purchased of the Six Nations, and vest them with a Right to the Lands so purchased, at the very Time there was a Negotiation on Foot for the Disposal of them to a Company in England.[3] I have several more Things to mention to you on this Head, but my Time will not permit.

Betsy joins me in wishing you many happy new Years. I am, Honoured Sir, Your ever dutiful Son   WM: FRANKLIN

Our Love to Mr. Bache, to whom I intend writing in a few Days. His dear Boy I have just heard is well, and quite free from all Apprehensions of the Small Pox. Please to forward the enclosed

---

those that Botetourt and his Council had authorized in principle in 1769; they were to the veterans of the French and Indian War whom Washington represented, and were based upon Gov. Dinwiddie's promise of 200,000 acres in his proclamation in 1754. Individual claims were submitted to and approved by Botetourt's successor, Lord Dunmore, and his Council in the fall of 1771. See Douglas S. Freeman, *George Washington: a Biography* (7 vols., New York, [1948–57]), III, 215–16, 239, 282–3. WF was mistaken in thinking that the Proclamation of 1763 permanently prohibited settlement west of the Alleghenies: the prohibition was intended to be temporary. Robin A. Humphreys, "Lord Shelburne and the Proclamation of 1763," *English Hist. Rev.*, XLIX (1934), 246–7, 249–50, 254; for the background and provisions of the Proclamation see also Gipson, *British Empire*, IX, chap. 3. In March, 1768, the Board of Trade had urged the prompt establishment of an Indian boundary by negotiation. *N.Y. Col. Docs.*, VIII, 19–31. The resultant treaties and revision of treaties, for which see the following note, were the background of Botetourt's and Dunmore's actions.

3. BF's correspondence in 1772–73 refers so often to Virginia's claims that the stages by which they evolved should be explained at this point. In 1768, at the treaty of Fort Stanwix, the Six Nations ceded to the crown "their" lands south of the Ohio and as far west as the mouth of the Tennessee. But not all of it was theirs to cede: from the mouth of the Great Kanawha the land belonged to the Cherokees, "the southern Indians," who almost simultaneously agreed, at the treaty of Hard Labor, to part with their hunting grounds east of a line running from the Great Kanawha southeastward. The Virginians were not satisfied. For a time the House of Burgesses dreamed of obtaining from the Cherokees everything north of the southern boundary of Virginia extended westward to meet the Ohio (it would actually have met the Mississippi); when the dream faded, in 1770, the House accepted a lesser cession. It was negotiated in a treaty at Lochaber the following October. The line, which was to run north from the confluence of the Holston and North Holston to the mouth of the Great Kanawha, parallel to the western border of the pro-

to the C. Justice with my Comp[liment]s and let him know that I receiv'd his Letter and shall write to him by the next Packet.[4]

To Sir Alexander Dick[5] ALS: New York Public Library

Dear Sir, London, Jan. 11. 1772

My last Expedition[6] convinc'd me that I grow too old for Rambling, and that 'twas probable I should never make such another Journey. 'Tis an uncomfortable Thing, the Parting with Friends one hardly expects ever again to see. This, with some occasional Hindrances, prevented my calling at Preston Fields after my Return from Glasgow: But my Heart was with you and your dear Family, and my best Wishes attended you all. Sir John Pringle rejoic'd with me on the Account I gave him of the Recovery of your Health, which I pray God may long continue. Pray present my respectful Compliments to Lady Dick, and to Miss Dick.[7] Many happy New Years to you and all yours. I am, with the sincerest Esteem, Dear Friend, Yours most affectionately B FRANKLIN

Sir Alexr Dick, Bart.

---

posed Walpole grant and well inside that vast tract, was never surveyed. It was almost immediately renegotiated, in 1771, to run northwest from the Holston to the Kentucky and along the latter to the Ohio; this revised line took the name of its surveyor, Col. John Donelson. Whitehall had been amenable to the Lochaber settlement, but refused until 1773 to extend it to the Kentucky. See John R. Alden, *John Stuart and the Southern Colonial Frontier...* (University of Michigan *Pub.*, History and Political Science, xv; Ann Arbor, 1944), pp. 276–80, 286–8, and the map on p. 102. There were thus, between 1768 and 1771, four successive proposals for demarcating Virginia's claims: the Hard Labor line, the line of the colonial border projected westward, the Lochaber line, and the Donelson line.

4. Richard Bache was about to sail for home and left in mid-February; his son had just been inoculated a second time for smallpox. Frederick Smyth, Chief Justice of New Jersey, visited England until late summer: 1 *N.J. Arch.*, X, 379.

5. BF's old friend, the president of the Edinburgh College of Physicians. For him, Lady Dick, and their home that BF mentions at Prestonfield House see above, VIII, 440 n.

6. His tour of Ireland and Scotland, which had ended some weeks before.

7. Probably the eldest daughter, Janet (1749–1806); see Margaret A. Forbes, *Curiosities of a Scots Charta Chest...* (Edinburgh, 1897), p. 185; *Scots Mag.*, LXVIII (1806), 488.

To Agatha Drummond[8]   ALS: Scottish Record Office

Madam,   London, Jan. 11. 1772
   I have lately received, in exceeding good Order, the valuable Present you have honoured me with, of Penn's Picture.[9] Please to accept my thankful Acknowledgments for the very great Favour, and for the abundant Civilities and Kindnesses receiv'd by me and my Friend[1] during our pleasant Residence under your hospitable Roof at Blair Drummond. My best Respects to Lord Kames and Mr. Drummond.[2] With sincerest Esteem and Regard, I have the honour to be Madam, Your much obliged and obedient humble Servant   B FRANKLIN

Mrs Drummond

To Joshua Babcock[3]

                ALS (letterbook draft): American Philosophical Society

Dear Sir,   London, Jan. 13. 1772
   It was with great Pleasure I learnt by Mr. Marchant, that you and Mrs. Babcock and all your good Family continue well and happy. I hope I shall find you all in the same State when I next come your Way, and take Shelter as often heretofore under your hospitable Roof. The Colonel, I am told, continues an active and able Farmer, the most honourable of all Employments, in my Opinion as being the most useful in itself, and rendring the Man most independent. My Namesake, his Son, will soon I hope be able to drive the Plough for him.[4]

   8. Lord Kames's wife. See above, XVIII, 251, where the subject of this note is explained.
   9. BF had originally asked, twelve years before, for the loan of the picture in order to have it copied. Whether or not the Kameses now intended to convert the loan into a gift, the portrait was never returned. See above, IX, 9.
   1. Henry Marchant, BF's traveling companion, who has appeared frequently in the previous volume.
   2. BF was probably referring to the Kameses' eldest son, George Home-Drummond (1743–1819).
   3. The ex-physician and storekeeper of Westerly, R.I., for whom see above, VI, 174 n.
   4. For Joshua's son, Col. Henry, and his grandson, Benjamin Franklin Babcock, see above, respectively, IX, 397 n; XV, 284 n.

I have lately made a Tour thro' Ireland and Scotland. In these Countries a small Part of the Society are Landlords, great Noblemen and Gentlemen, extreamly opulent, living in the highest Affluence and Magnificence: The Bulk of the People Tenants, extreamly poor, living in the most sordid Wretchedness in dirty Hovels of Mud and Straw, and cloathed only in Rags. I thought often of the Happiness of New England, where every Man is a Freeholder, has a Vote in publick Affairs, lives in a tidy warm House, has plenty of good Food and Fewel, with whole Cloaths from Head to Foot, the Manufactury perhaps of his own Family. Long may they continue in this Situation! But if they should ever envy the *Trade* of these Countries, I can put them in a Way to obtain a Share of it. Let them with three fourths of the People of Ireland, live the Year round on Potatoes and Butter milk, without Shirts, then may their Merchants export Beef, Butter and Linnen. Let them with the Generality of the Common People of Scotland go Barefoot, then may they make large Exports in Shoes and Stockings: And if they will be content to wear Rags like the Spinners and Weavers of England, they may make Cloths and Stuffs for all Parts of the World. Farther, if my Countrymen should ever wish for the Honour of having among them a Gentry enormously wealthy, let them sell their Farms and pay rack'd Rents;[5] the Scale of the Landlords will rise as that of the Tenants is depress'd who will soon become poor, tattered, dirty, and abject in Spirit. Had I never been in the American Colonies, but was to form my Judgment of Civil Society by what I have lately seen, I should never advise a Nation of Savages to admit of Civilisation: For I assure you, that in the Possession and Enjoyment of the various Comforts of Life, compar'd to these People every Indian is a Gentleman: And the Effect of this kind of Civil Society seems only to be, the depressing Multitudes below the Savage State that a few may be rais'd above it. My best Wishes attend you and yours, being ever with great Esteem, Dear Sir, Your most obedient and most humble Servant   B F

Dr Babcock

5. Rents raised beyond what tenants can reasonably be expected to pay.

To James Bowdoin

ALS: Massachusetts Historical Society; draft: American Philosophical Society[6]

In this letter, as in others later in the month, Franklin touched on a subject of crucial importance in the developing Anglo-American quarrel, the validity of the crown's instructions to colonial governors. The issue had underlain the wrangling the year before between Governor Hutchinson and the House of Representatives over matters in which he was bound by his instructions.[7] Challenging them struck at Franklin's idea that the centripetal force in the empire was allegiance to the crown, for the force would be vastly attenuated by eliminating the King's prerogative to govern through instructions. Franklin was no more eager than most of his countrymen to push the issue to that extreme, but he could not avoid the issue itself. It was a visible sign of the gap between the concepts held in Whitehall and in Boston of what the constitution was.

The British concept, because it is less familiar than the American, needs some explanation. It was a concept that had often been evaded and even violated with impunity, but the theory remained untouched by such practical considerations. The role that instructions played in it can be understood only in relationship to the two documents that were regarded as equally fundamental in the governing process, the charter and the governor's commission under the great seal. The charter, as long as it was in force, granted the colonists certain privileges, notably that of legislating for their own affairs. The crown alone could not revoke any part of the grant without the consent of the grantees or their successors; the only means of total revocation or alteration were either through the courts or by Parliament. The colonists in turn assumed certain obligations, notably that of adhering to limits on their self-government; for the powers granted them, being only those that the crown might confer, did not include the legislative independence that the General Court was beginning to claim. Its legislation might not contravene a Parliamentary statute or the principles of common law, or detract from the prerogative as exercised through the governor, or encroach upon the interests of another colony.[8] The Court was subordinate.

6. Substantial differences between the draft and the finished version are indicated below.

7. See above, XVIII, 121, 153, 173–5, 178–80.

8. George Chalmers, ed., *Opinions of Eminent Lawyers...* (2 vols., London, 1814), I, 29–32, 119–20, 189, 195, 252–3, 263, 296; II, 31–2, 62; John F.

The charter mentioned the governor's veto power and how he was to be appointed; but in British eyes it did not limit the office in the way the colonists claimed. The crown retained the right to create and define and fill the governorship, and did so through the commission and instructions. Each commission gave validity to the standing instructions that accompanied it, and to such further instructions as circumstances might dictate; these were binding on the governor provided that they did not violate the charter, colonial and Parliamentary statutes, or the principles of the common law. The standing instructions, for example, might order the governor in advance to veto certain kinds of bill or to follow certain legislative procedures; later instructions might further define the governor's sphere of action, as by ordering him to dissolve the Court under certain conditions. The charter, in short, reserved powers to the crown. Some remained there; some were deputed to the governor in his commission, and he then received specific instructions on how to exercise them so as to ensure the subordination of the legislature. The commission was never intended to contradict the charter, or instructions to contradict either one. All three were parts of what was conceived to be a unified body of law, through which executive authority operated.[9]

It was theoretically possible, however, for contradictions to arise. Improperly drafted instructions might run counter to provisions of the charter or the commission or the accepted corpus of law. If the governor violated any such provision without instructions, his act would presumably be void and he could be impeached. If he acted on improper instructions, he would be safe but his act would be unconstitutional. Here the right of petition became paramount. Whether or not a petition was effective, it was the one sure means of bringing to the sovereign's attention the constitutional grievances of individual subjects or an en-

---

Dillon, *Commentaries on the Law of Municipal Corporations* (5th ed.; 5 vols., Boston, 1911), I, 80–1; IV, 2727; Sir William Holdsworth, *A History of English Law* (6th ed.; 16 vols., London, 1938–66), IX, 49, 53–62, 65–7; XI, 55–6, 237–8, 248–9. Although we are solely responsible for this and other résumés of British constitutional theory in the present volume, we are grateful to Professor Ian R. Christie for reviewing them.

9. Thomas Pownall, *The Administration of the Colonies* (3rd ed., London, 1766), pp. 34, 39–40, 55–6; Chalmers, *op. cit.*, I, 190–2, 232, 244, 248–50, 260, 268–9, 276, 304–7, 316, 506; II, 29–32; Holdsworth, *op. cit.*, XI, 48–9, 56–7, 255–6; A. Berriedale Keith, *Constitutional History of the First British Empire* (Oxford, 1930), pp. 179–82, 251–2; Leonard W. Labaree, *Royal Government in America: a Study of the British Colonial System before 1783* (New Haven and London, 1930), pp. 8–11, 31–2, 99, 222, 226, 228, 442.

9

tire colony.[1] On this point, for once, the British and American views coincided: the right to ask for redress was crucial in the operation of the law.

But in every other respect Franklin's and the Bostonians' concept of the constitution was different from Whitehall's. They believed that the governor should obey only those instructions that conformed to the charter and to colonial law as both were interpreted in Massachusetts; otherwise he could and should ignore them. This belief rested on another, that the colonial legislature was autonomous within its own sphere, and might pass laws for the internal government of the province regardless of Parliamentary statutes or the royal prerogative. In this sense the General Court was in their view on the same footing as Parliament,[2] and Governor Hutchinson's proper role was to act as the House and Council told him to.[3] This concept was the seed of responsible government, whereby each colony conducts its internal affairs without interference from the crown's representative. The seed bore fruit in the nineteenth-century empire, but was far beyond the imagination of Lord North's ministry. Franklin suggested, and perhaps even believed, that the British would retreat from their position if opposed with spirit. Did he really expect them to adopt the American position, or did he realize that it was incomprehensible to them?

Dear Sir,   London, Jany. 13. 1772

I should very readily have recommended your Son to the Care of my Friend Priestly, if he had continued to superintend the Academy at Warrington: But he has left that Charge some time since, and is now Pastor of a Congregation at Leeds in Yorkshire.

I am much obliged to you for introducing me to the Acquaintance of Mr. Erving, who appears a very intelligent sensible Man.[4]

1. Sir William Blackstone, *Commentaries on the Laws of England* (11th ed.; 4 vols., London, 1791), I, 143; Chalmers, *op. cit.*, I, 191, 260, 304; Holdsworth, *op. cit.*, VI, 402; XI, 48, 100–1, 254–8. See also the headnote to BF's attack on Hillsborough below, under the beginning of August.

2. Pownall, *op. cit.*, pp. 30–2, 40–7; Holdsworth, *op. cit.*, XI, 57–8, 248, 250–1; Labaree, *op. cit.*, pp. 30–3.

3. See the headnote to Cushing to BF below, July 15.

4. In the preceding paragraph and this one, and in his subsequent references to *Exper. and Obser.* and, in the final paragraph, to the enclosures he had sent, BF is replying to Bowdoin's letters above, XVIII, 5, 23, 241–3. James Bowdoin, the son of the family, was studying in England; George Erving was his maternal uncle.

The Governing of Colonies by Instructions has long been a favourite Point with Ministers here. About 30 Years since, in a Bill brought into Parliament, relating to America, they inserted a Clause to make the King's Instructions *Laws* in the Colonies; which being oppos'd by the then Agents, was thrown out.[5] And I well remember a Conversation with Lord Granville, soon after my Arrival here, in which he express'd himself on that Subject in the following Terms; "Your American Assemblies slight the King's Instructions, pretending that they are not Laws. The Instructions sent over to your Governors are not like the Pocket Instructions given to Ambassadors, to be observed at their discretion as Circumstances may require. They are drawn up by grave Men, learned in the Laws and Constitutions of the Realm; they are brought into Council, thoroughly weigh'd, well-consider'd, and amended if necessary by the Wisdom of that Body; and when receiv'd by the Governors, are the *Law of the Land*; for the King is the LEGISLATOR of the Colonies." I remember this the better, because it being new Doctrine to me, I put it down as soon as I return'd to my Lodging.[6] To be sure, if a Governor thinks himself

5. The episode occurred in 1744. See Labaree, *op. cit.*, pp. 33–5, 439–40; Leo F. Stock, ed., *Proceedings and Debates of the British Parliaments Respecting North America* (5 vols., Washington, 1924–41), v, 187. The clause was apparently not thrown out, but died along with the bill when Parliament reconvened after the summer. By that time Granville (for whom see the next note) was no longer in the ministry, and his disappearance may have accounted for the dropping of his doctrine. It reappeared in 1748–49, and again was not adopted. *Ibid.*, pp. 313–20, 361–2, 365, 367; above, v, 28, 38. Inherent in the clause as worded was a major constitutional change: *all* instructions would have become binding, by the removal of the limitations upon them discussed in the headnote.

6. For John Carteret, first Earl Granville, see above, VII, 249 n and the *DNB*. As Lord President of the Council, 1751–63, he spoke with authority about the elaborate and painstaking process of framing instructions, for a description of which see Labaree, *op. cit.*, pp. 52–71. The Earl's statement is less explicit here, and in the closely similar wording in the *Autobiog.* (pp. 261–2), than in BF's third and most nearly contemporary version of it, which makes the king in council the legislator: when instructions "come there, they are the LAW OF THE LAND." Above, VIII, 293. An instruction certainly had the force of law, but only for the recipient; and in theory, as explained in the headnote, it might not be legally binding even on him. It was not a legislative act, and could not compel legislation in the colony. We can only conclude

oblig'd to obey all Instructions, whether consistent or inconsistent with the Constitution, Laws, and Rights of the Country he governs,[7] there is an End of the Constitution, and those Rights are abolish'd. But I wonder that any honest Gentleman can think there is HONOUR in being a Governor on such Terms. And I think the Practice cannot possibly continue, especially if oppos'd with Spirit by our Assemblies. At present no Attention is paid by the American Minister to any Agent here, whose Appointment is not ratified by the Governor's Assent: And if this is persisted in, you can have none to serve you in publick Character that do not render themselves agreable to that Minister;[8] those otherwise appointed can only promote your Interests by Conversation as private Gentlemen, or by Writing. Virginia had, as you observe, two Agents, one for the Council, the other for the Assembly; but I think the latter only was consider'd as Agent for the Province. He was appointed by an Act, which expired in the Time of Lord Botetourt, and was not revived.[9] The other I apprehend continues; but I am not well acquainted with the Nature of his Appointment. I only understand that he does not concern himself much with the general Affairs of the Colony.

It gives me great Pleasure that my Book afforded any to my Friends. I esteem those Letters of yours among its brightest Ornaments, and have the Satisfaction to find that they add greatly to the Reputation of American Philosophy.

In Ireland among the Patriots I din'd often with Dr. Lucas. They are all Friends of America, in which I said every thing I could think of to confirm them. Lucas constantly gave Mr. Bowdoin and the Boston Patriots for his Toast.[1]

---

with Keith (*op. cit.*, p. 180 n) that Granville, if BF was quoting him correctly and in context, held an aberrant view.

7. The draft here inserts "and can proceed to govern in that Train."

8. This point had become almost a cliché; see above, XVIII, 9–16, 153.

9. See *ibid.*, p.242.

1. The draft omits "often" in the first sentence of the paragraph; the concluding sentence reads "Lucas gave Mr. Bowdoin for his Toast." Dr. Charles Lucas, physician and reformer, was called the Wilkes of Ireland; he had died the previous November. *DNB*. He presumably knew of Bowdoin as one of the authors of the *Short Narrative* of the Boston Massacre, copies of which had been sent to the British Isles. Above, XVII, 160 n; *Sibley's Harvard Graduates*, XI, 527–8.

There is in the Governor's Collection of Papers relative to the History of the Massachusetts Bay, published 1769, a Copy of an Answer made by Randolph to several *Heads of Enquiry*, which I take to be the same with those I sent you. I shall be very glad to have an Account of the present Number of Rateables when you can obtain it for me. With sincere and great Esteem, I am, Dear Sir, Your most obedient humble Servant   B FRANKLIN

James Bowdoin, Esqr.

Endorsed: Dr. Benja. Franklin's Letter London Jany. 13. 1772, political, and important.

To Samuel Cooper

ALS: British Museum; draft: American Philosophical Society[2]

Dear Sir,   London, Jan. 13. 1772

I have now before me your several Favours of July 10, Aug. 23, and Nov. 5.[3] A long Journey I took in the Summer and Autumn for the Establishment of my Health, prevented my answering sooner the two first. I hope the State of your Health also is mended by your Retirement into the Country, as mine has sensibly been by that Journey.

You have furnished me with a very good additional Argument against the Crown's paying its Governors, viz. that the propos'd Independence is impolitic on the part of the Crown, and tends to prejudice its Interest, even consider'd separate from that of the People, as it will prove a strong Temptation to Governors to hold a Conduct that will greatly lessen their Esteem and Influence in the Province, and consequently their Power to promote the Service of the King. Indeed the making it a Rule among our selves that the Governor is to have his Salary from our Assemblies, tho' his publick Conduct should be wilfully and maliciously prejudicial to the Province, has the *same Tendency*; of which the Conduct of

2. A few words of the letter sent, lost in a later trimming of the margin, have been silently restored from the draft.

3. The first two letters survive, and explain the references below to the governor's salary, the customs commissioners, and Commodore Gambier: above, XVIII, 172–5, 211–13.

Governor Bernard while he was constantly and regularly paid by us, is a considerable Proof. And therefore, in my Opinion, if we would have our Power of granting the Support operate with any Weight in maintaining an Influence with the Governor, it should have been witheld from him, and we should withold it in part or in the whole, according to the Circumstances, as often as such a Conduct appears in any Governor. Otherwise the Power, if in such Cases it is not to be used, would seem of very little Importance. And since the Assembly have of late Years, and under such great Provocations, never attempted to abridge or withold the Salary, no Reason appears why the American Minister should now think it necessary or adviseable for the Crown to take the Payment of its Governor upon itself unless it be with an Intention to influence him by witholding it when he declines executing arbitrary Instructions; and then in such Cases the People should be sure to compensate him. As to procuring here any Change of this Measure, I frankly own to you that I despair of it, while the Administration of American Affairs continues in the Hands of Lord Hillsborough; and while, by our Paying the Duties there is a sufficient American Fund out of which such Salaries can be satisfied. The Failure of that Fund would be the most likely Means of demolishing the Project.[4]

The Attempt to get the Commissioners exempted from the Payment of their Taxes, by an Instruction to the Governor, is the most indiscrete Thing, surely (to say nothing of its Injustice) that any prudent Government was ever guilty of. I cannot think it will be persisted in. I hope it will never be comply'd with. If the Supply-Bill is duly offered without the Clause, I am persuaded it will not long be refused. The Publick must however suffer in the mean time by the Want of the Supply; but that will be a good Foundation for an Impeachment here. Your Reasonings against the Instruction are unanswerable, and will be of use in the Discussing that Business.[5]

4. BF is here repeating much of what he had written to Cushing the previous spring: *ibid.*, pp. 124–5.

5. For the taxing of the commissioners see *ibid.*, pp. 174–5, 177–80. In the APS draft the second clause of this sentence reads: "and shall appear here just before the Meeting of Parliament." BF's alteration suggests that he intended to publish Cooper's arguments and then changed his mind. But he clearly

I am glad that Commodore Gambier behav'd in so satisfactory a manner. His Uncle, Mr. Mead, first Commissioner of the Customs, is a particular and intimate Friend of mine, a Man of great Moderation and Prudence;[6] I knew that he gave his Nephew, before he went hence, a great deal of good Advice with regard to his Conduct among the People of Boston, for whom he has a great Esteem and Regard, having formerly commanded a Frigate stationed there; and he is happy to find by your Letter (which I communicated to him) that his Advice was so well followed. He gave also equally good Advice to your indiscrete Commissioners when they were sent out, but they had not Sense enough to follow it, and therefore have been the Authors of infinite Mischief. I wonder at the Invention of so improbable a Lye, as that I should desire a Place among them, who am daily urging the Expediency of their Dissolution. The other Calumny you mention, contain'd in an anonymous Letter to the Speaker, is so weak, that I believe you do not think I ought to take any Notice of it.[7] As to the Agency, whether I am re-chosen or not, and whether the General Assembly is ever permitted to pay me or not,[8] I shall nevertheless continue to exert myself in behalf of my Country as long as I see a Probability of my being able to do it any Service. I have nothing to ask or expect of Ministers. I have, Thanks to God, a Competency for the little Time I may expect to live, and am grown too old for Ambition of any kind, but that of leaving a Good Name behind me.

Your Story of the Clergyman and Proclamation is a pleasant one.[9] I can only match it with one I had from my Father, I know

---

meant to use them in a campaign against the government's policy, and may have dreamed that Hillsborough would be impeached; see the following document.

6. For Mead see above, x, 60 n; XVIII, 212 n.

7. "So improbable a Lye," which Cooper must have mentioned in his missing letter of Nov. 5, no doubt originated in a confusion of BF with Michael Francklin (for whom see above, XVIII, 88–9), whose name had been mentioned in Boston for a position as customs commissioner: Mass. Arch., XXVII, 92–3. For the anonymous letter to the Speaker see above, XVIII, 127, 213.

8. For the squabble about BF's salary see *ibid.*, pp. 153, 242, and Cushing to BF below, July 15.

9. The governor traditionally proclaimed a day of thanksgiving in No-

not if it was ever printed.[1] Charles I. ordered his Proclamation, authorizing Sports on a Sunday, to be read in all Churches. Many Clergymen comply'd, some refus'd and others hurry'd it through as indistinctly as possible. But one, whose Congregation expected no such thing from him, did nevertheless, to their great Surprize, read it distinctly. He follow'd it, however, with the Fourth Commandment, *Remember to keep holy the Sabbath Day*, and then said, Bretheren, I have laid before you the Command of your King and the Commandment of your God. I leave it to your selves to judge which of the two ought rather to be observed. With great and sincere Esteem, I remain, Dear Sir, Your most obedient and most humble Servant   B FRANKLIN

Revd Dr Cooper.

To Thomas Cushing

ALS: Public Record Office; incomplete draft:[2] American Philosophical Society

Sir,   London, Jany. 13. 1772
    I am now return'd again to London from a Journey of some Months in Ireland and Scotland. Though my Constitution, and too great Confinement to Business during the Winter, seem to require the Air and Exercise of a long Journey once a Year, which I have now practiced for more than 20 Years past, yet I should not

---

vember for the benefits that the inhabitants of Massachusetts enjoyed. One such benefit, "the continuance of our privileges," had been omitted from the proclamation after 1765 in deference to public opinion; on Hutchinson's restoring it in 1771, politicians encouraged the Boston clergy to refuse to read the proclamation in that form because privileges had been infringed. When the minister of Hutchinson's church did read it, many members of the congregation walked out. See Cushing, ed., *Writings of Samuel Adams*, II, 270–4; Frederick Tuckerman, ed., "Letters of Samuel Cooper to Thomas Pownall, 1769–1777," *Amer. Hist. Rev.*, VIII (1903), 325–6; Hutchinson, *History*, III, 249–50; *Boston Gaz.*, Nov. 11, 18, 25, 1771.
    1. It had been, a generation earlier. See William Knowler, ed., *The Earl of Strafforde's Letters and Dispatches...* (2 vols., London, 1739), I, 166, and for a more modern account Samuel R. Gardiner, *History of England...1603–1642* (10 vols., London, 1883–84), VII, 321–2.
    2. Significant variations in the draft are noted below.

16

have been out so long this time, but that I was well assured the Parliament would not meet till towards the End of January, before which Meeting few of the principal People would be in Town, and no Business of Importance likely to be agitated relating to America.

I have now before me your esteemed Favours of July 9, Sept. 25. and Oct. 2.[3] In the first you mention that the General Assembly was still held out of its ancient and only convenient Seat the Townhouse of Boston; and by the latest Papers from thence I see that it was prorogu'd, again to meet in Cambridge, which I [a] little wonder at when I recollect a Question ask'd me by Lord Hillsborough in Ireland, viz. Whether I had heard from New-England lately, since the General Court was return'd to Boston? From this I concluded Orders had been transmitted by his Lordship for that Removal: Perhaps such may have been sent, to be used discretionally.[4] I think I have before mentioned to you one of the Articles of Impeachment brought against an evil Administration here in former Times, that the Parliament had been caused to sit[5] *in Villibus et remotis partibus Regni*, where few People,

3. The draft adds June 24. Only that of Oct. 2 survives: above, XVIII, 223–4.
4. For the long quarrel over moving the General Court to Cambridge see above, XVIII, 121. The outcome of the quarrel can be briefly summarized. After the House, in June, 1771, reiterated in uncompromising terms its position that the Governor's instructions violated the constitution, Hutchinson successively prorogued it until he could learn Whitehall's response. By early March, 1772, he seems to have had word that he was to use his own discretion about the meeting place of the Court, provided that he did not yield on the constitutional issue. When the new legislature met in May, he privately assured members of the House that, if they did not raise the issue in their answer to his opening speech, he would allow them to return to Boston. In a more public gesture of reassurance he obtained the Council's agreement that he was authorized, on that condition, to make the move. The House then framed an answer that satisfied him, whereupon he moved the Court back after its three-year absence. Mass. Arch., XXV, 517–18; XXVII, 195, 246, 260, 277, 285, 305, 319–21, 342–4; Hutchinson, *History*, III, 250–1, 256. Hutchinson believed that the House had sustained a minor defeat (which increased its members' creature comforts), and that he had achieved the purpose of strengthening his position against future attacks on his instructions. He needed strength, for almost immediately the attacks were renewed on other grounds; see Cushing to BF below, July 15.
5. BF here touches for the first time on the constitutional implications of

propter defectum hospitii et victualium could attend, thereby to force *illos paucos qui remanebunt de Communitate Regni, concedere Regi quamvis pessima.* Lord Clarendon too was impeach'd for endeavouring to introduce arbitrary Government into the Colonies.[6] Lord H. seems by the late Instructions, to have been treading in the Paths that lead to the same unhappy Situation, if the Parliament here should ever again feel for America.[7] As there is something curious in our Interview in Ireland, I must give you an Account of it. I met with him accidentally at the Lord Lieutenant's, who happened to invite us to dine, with a large Company, on the same Day. He was surprizingly civil, and urg'd my Fellow-

---

moving the Court. The APS draft reads "against a bad Minister of a former King, 'That to work his Ends he had caused the Parliament to sit,'" etc. The quotation that follows is abbreviated from Thomas Gascoigne's account of the impeachment of the Earl of Suffolk in the reign of Richard II, as cited by Robert Cotton in "A Speech Delivered in the Lower House of Parliament Assembled at Oxford: in the First Year of the Reign of King Charles," J[ames] H[owell], *Cottoni Posthuma*... (London, 1651), pp. 279–80. For Gascoigne and Cotton see the *DNB*.

BF left two memoranda of the episode in his hand. One, now in the Library of Congress, differs little from the wording of this letter except for an addition at the end, "Sir Rob. Cotton's Speech." The other, now in the Public Record Office, has a different beginning: "Whatever the *Prerogative* may be, with regard to appointing the Place of Meeting for Parliaments and Assemblies, it should be used *only for the Good of the People.* Where it is made an Instrument of arbitrary Power, to enforce Ministerial Measures to the Prejudice of the People's Rights, such Use of it has justly been condemned. It was one Article of Impeachment against a former evil Minister, that to work his Ends (or the King's) he had caused," etc. At "evil Minister" BF appended a note: "Or a Charge against the King himself. I have not the Book by me from whence this Note was taken, but think it was some Minister of Hen. VI. Search the History." Neither of these memoranda is dated; Smyth mentions that the second one was attached to BF's letter to Cushing of June 10, 1771 (*Writings*, V, 328), but we are inclined to think that this was an accident of filing and that both were in fact the background for BF's passage in this letter.

6. Lord Clarendon's colonial policy played a minor role in the impeachment proceedings brought against him in 1667. See Leo F. Stock, ed., *Proceedings and Debates of the British Parliaments Respecting North America* (5 vols., Washington, 1924–41), I, 340–1.

7. Parliament of course did not, but the Continental Congress made moving the Court one of the articles against the King in the Declaration of Independence.

18

traveller[8] and me to call at his House in our intended Journey Northwards, where we might be sure of better Accommodations than the Inns could afford us. He press'd us so politely that it was not easy to refuse without apparent Rudeness, as we must pass through his Town of Hillsborough and by his Door; and as it might afford an Opportunity of saying something on American Affairs, I concluded to comply with his Invitation.[9] His Lordship went home some time before we left Dublin; we call'd upon him, and were detain'd at his House four Days, during which time he entertain'd us with great Civility, and a particular Attention to me that appear'd the more extraordinary as I knew that but just before I left London he had express'd himself concerning me in very angry Terms, calling me a Republican, a factious mischievous Fellow, and the like. In our Conversations he first show'd himself a good Irishman, blaming England for its Narrowness towards that Country, in restraining its Commerce, discouraging its Woollen Manufactury, &c. and when I apply'd his Observations to America, he said he had always been of Opinion that the People in every Part of the King's Dominions had a natural Right to make the best Use they could of the Productions of their Country: and that America ought not to be restrain'd in manufacturing any thing she could manufacture to Advantage; that he suppos'd she at present found generally more Profit in Agriculture; but whenever she found that less profitable, or a particular Manufacture more so, he had no objection to her persuing it; and he censur'd Lord Chatham for asserting in his Speech that the Parliament had a Right or ought to restrain Manufactures in the Colonies;[1] adding, that as he knew the English were apt to be jealous on that head, he avoided every thing that might inflame that Jealousy; and therefore tho' the Commons had requested the Crown to order the Governors to send over, annually, Accounts of such Manufactures as were undertaken in the Colonies, yet as they had not

8. BF's companion was Richard Jackson. Their host at dinner was Charles Townshend's elder brother George, Viscount Townshend, lord lieutenant from 1767 to 1772.

9. BF gave a quite different explanation of the visit in writing to WF below, Jan. 30.

1. Pitt, speaking on Jan. 14, 1766, made his celebrated statement that Parliament had this right, among others, but no right to tax the colonists without their consent. See above, XIII, 39–44.

ordered such Accounts to be annually laid before them, he should never produce them 'till they were call'd for.[2] Then he gave me to understand that the Bounty on Silk raised in America was a Child of his, which he hoped would prove of great Advantage to that Country; and that he wish'd to know in what Manner a Bounty on Raising Wine there might be contrived so as to operate effectually for that purpose, desiring me to turn it in my Thoughts as he should be glad of my Opinion and Advice.[3] Then he inform'd me that Newfoundland was grown too populous to be left any longer without a regular Government, but there were great Difficulties in the forming such a kind of Government as would be suitable to the particular Circumstances of that Country, which he wish'd me likewise to consider, and that I would favour him with my Sentiments.[4] He seem'd attentive to every thing that might make my Stay in his House agreable to me, and put his eldest Son, Lord Kilwarling, into his Phaeton with me,[5] to drive

2. For WF's report on New Jersey see 1 *N.J. Arch.*, X, 29–32, and for those of other governors Merrill Jensen, ed., *American Colonial Documents to 1776* (*English Historical Documents*, IX; London, 1955), pp. 418–23.

3. For the Parliamentary bounty on silk see above, XVI, 200; the Board of Trade, of which Hillsborough was president, had helped to promote it and to shepherd the enabling act through the House of Commons. *Board of Trade Jour.*, 1768–1775, pp. 51, 58, 60–1, 73, 87–8. A proposal for subsidizing viticulture in America is discussed in Huske to BF below, March 10, and BF's reply of Sept. 6.

4. The circumstances of Newfoundland were so particular that the creation of a regular government proved impossible. From the viewpoint of British commercial interests the purpose of such a government was to restrain the inhabitants from interfering with the annual fishing fleet, which came from Britain in the late spring and returned in the fall. But Whitehall, even if it had the will, had not found the means of effective restraint. The fishermen who constituted the bulk of the settlers were increasing rapidly in number, and had scant respect for the rights of their overseas competitors. The governor was merely the naval officer commanding the convoy, and he came and went with the fleet; in the long months of his absence the islanders lacked any authority worth the name. The government of Newfoundland, in Gipson's phrase, was "a figment of the imagination." *British Empire*, III, 262. See also A. H. McLintock, *The Establishment of Constitutional Government in Newfoundland, 1783–1832*... (New York and London, [1941]), pp. 9–12, and for a fuller discussion W. B. Kerr, "Newfoundland in the Period before the American Revolution," *PMHB*, LXV (1941), 56–78.

5. Arthur Hill, eighteen at the time, had the courtesy title of Viscount Kil-

me a Round of Forty Miles, that I might see the Country, the
Seats, Manufactures, &c. covering me with his own Cloak lest I
should take Cold: and, in short, seem'd in every thing extreamly
solicitous to impress me, and the Colonies through me, with a good
Opinion of him: All which I could not but wonder at, knowing
that he likes neither them nor me; and I thought it inexplicable
but on the Supposition that he apprehended an approaching Storm,
and was desirous of lessening beforehand the Number of Enemies
he had so imprudently created.6 But if he takes no Step towards
withdrawing the Troops, repealing the Duties, restoring the
Castle, or recalling the offensive Instructions,7 I shall think all the
plausible Behaviour I have describ'd, and the Discourse related,
concerning Manufactures, &c. as meant only, by patting and
stroaking the Horse to make him more patient while the Reins are
drawn tighter and the Spurs set deeper into his Sides. Before I
leave Ireland I must mention that being desirous of seeing the
principal Patriots there, I staid till the Opening of their Parliament.
I found them dispos'd to be Friends of America, in which Disposition I endeavoured to confirm them, with the Expectation that
our growing Weight might in time be thrown into their Scale, and,
by joining our Interest with theirs, might be obtained for them
as well as for us, a more equitable Treatment from this Nation.
There are many brave Spirits among them, the Gentry are a very
sensible, polite and friendly People. Their Parliament makes a
most respectable Figure, with a Number of very good Speakers
in both Parties, and able Men of Business. And I ought not to omit
acquainting you, that it being a standing Rule to admit Members
of the English Parliament to sit (tho' they do not vote) in the
House among the Members, while others are only admitted into
the Gallery, my Fellow-Traveller being an English Member was
accordingly admitted as such, but I supposed I must have gone

warlin: Namier and Brooke, *House of Commons*, II, 622–3. He eventually succeeded his father as second Marquis of Downshire.

6. The wish was father to the thought; BF hoped for a storm, but could
scarcely have foreseen the one that actually arose in Whitehall, over the
Walpole grant, and forced Hillsborough's resignation before the summer was
out.

7. For these grievances see above, XVII, 276–83; XVIII, 14–15, 147–53,
172–5, 177–80.

to the Gallery, when the Speaker having been spoken to by some of the Members, stood up and acquainted the House, that there was in Town an American Gentleman of Character, a Member or Delegate of some of the Parliaments of that Country,[8] who was desirous of being present at the Debates of this House; that there was a standing Rule of the House for admitting Members of the English Parliament; that he did suppose the House would consider the American Assemblies as English Parliaments; but this being the first Instance he had chosen not to give any Order in it without receiving their Directions. On the Question, the whole House gave a loud unanimous *Aye*, when two Members came to me without the Bar, where I was standing, led me in and placed me very honourably. This I am the more particular in to you, as I esteem'd it a Mark of Respect for our Country, and a Piece of Politeness in which I hope our Parliaments will not fall behind theirs, whenever an Occasion shall offer. Ireland is itself a fine Country, and Dublin a magnificent City; but the Appearances of general extreme Poverty among the lower People, are amazing: They live in wretched Hovels of Mud and Straw, are clothed in Rags, and subsist chiefly on Potatoes. Our New England Farmers of the poorest Sort, in regard to the Enjoyment of all the Comforts of Life, are Princes when compar'd to them. Such is the Effect of the Discouragements of Industry, the Non-Residence not only of Pensioners but of many original Landlords who lease their Lands in Gross to Undertakers that rack the Tenants, and fleece them Skin and all, to make Estates to themselves, while the first Rents, as well as most of the Pensions are spent out of the Country. An English Gentleman there said to me, that by what he had heard of the good Grazing in North-America, and by what he saw of the Plenty of Flaxseed imported in Ireland from thence, he could not understand why we did not rival Ireland in the Beef and Butter Trade to the West Indies, and share with it in its Linen Trade. But he was satisfy'd when I told him, that I suppos'd the Reason might be, *Our People eat Beef and Butter every Day, and wear Shirts themselves.* In short the chief Exports of Ireland seem to be pinch'd

8. The emphasis must have been upon "delegate": the rules were being stretched to admit BF as agent of four colonial legislatures, although he was not a member of any.

off the Backs and out of the Bellies of the miserable Inhabitants.[9] But Schemes are now under Consideration among the humane Gentry, to provide some Means of mending if possible their present wretched Condition.

I am much obliged by the very particular Account you have favoured me with of the general Sentiments of People in our Province on the present State of Affairs between the two Countries. They are for the most part the same with my own. I think the Revenue Acts should be repealed, as not constitutionally founded; that the Commission of the Customs should be dissolved; that the Troops (Foreigners to us, as much as Hanoverians would be in England, since they are not introduc'd with the Consent of our Legislature) ought to be withdrawn, and the Castle restor'd to its rightful Owners, the Government of the Province that built it; and that the General Court should be return'd to its ancient Seat, and the Governor's Salary put upon its ancient footing. But it is also my Opinion, that while the present American Minister continues, there is very little Likelyhood that any Change will be made in any of those particulars, that of returning the Court perhaps excepted: And yet I am also of Opinion that no farther Duties are intended, and that altho' the American Minister might wish to increase that Fund for Corruption, the other Ministers are not dispos'd to humour him in it, and would not consent to it. I may be deceiv'd in this Opinion, but I have Grounds for it. However, I think we should be as much on our Guard, and use the same defensive Measures and Endeavours as if we saw new Duties intended in the ensuing Session. And nothing can more effectually discourage new Duties, than the Diminution of the Revenue produc'd by Duties, from this most justifiable Measure, a resolute steady Refusal to consume the dutyable Commodities.

In complyance with your respected Recommendation, I introduc'd Mr. Story to a Secretary of the Treasury, who forwarded his Memorial; and he tells me he has obtain'd his Request relating to the Affair of Mr. Wheelwright's Debt. He now seems to wish for some Appointment in consideration of his Sufferings from the Mob. But I doubt whether it may be worth his while to attend here the Solicitation and Expectation of such Reward, those At-

9. BF had found answers, with a vengeance, to some of his questions about Ireland above, XVIII, 222–3. See also BF to Babcock above, Jan. 13.

tendances being often drawn out into an inconceivable Length, and the Expence of course enormous.[1] With the greatest Esteem, I have the Honour to be, Sir, Your most obedient and most humble Servant   B FRANKLIN

Honble. Thos. Cushing, Esqr

Private

Endorsed: Benja Franklin London Jany 13 1772[2]

To Samuel Franklin

ALS (letterbook draft): American Philosophical Society

Dear Cousin,   London Jan. 13. 1772
    I received your kind Letter of Nov. 8. and rejoice to hear of the continued Welfare of you and your good Wife and four Daughters:[3] I hope they will all get good Husbands. I dare say they will be educated so as to deserve them. I knew a wise old Man, who us'd to advise his young Friends to chuse Wives out of a Bunch; for where there were many Daughters, he said they improv'd each other, and from Emulation acquir'd more Accomplishments, knew more, could do more, and were not spoil'd by parental Fondness like single Children. Yours have my best Wishes, and Blessing if that can be of any Value. I receiv'd a very polite Letter from Mr.

1. For William Story's previous difficulties see XVIII, 223–4. BF had doubtless introduced him to his friend Grey Cooper at the Treasury, but to no avail: Story failed to get his appointment, and returned to Boston in the spring. He tried for help from Gov. Hutchinson, first by persuasion and then by threatening to divulge the contents of some letters from the Governor that he had seen in London. Hutchinson ignored the threat, and with impunity; but when his letters to Whately were published in Boston in 1773 Story was suspected of obtaining them. Despite the latter's denial, and the fact that he had left England six months before the letters did (see BF to Cushing below, Dec. 2), they may have been the basis for his attempted blackmail, and he may have alerted BF or his friends to their existence. See Hutchinson's letters in Mass. Arch., XXVII, 292, 349–52, 457–8, 564–5, 580, 584.
2. The endorsement is apparently in Cushing's hand. Another, added later, is in that of the loyalist Thomas Moffatt: the letter is "very remarkable and requires no Commentary." For Moffatt's part in the subsequent history of BF's correspondence with Cushing see above, XVIII, 120 n.
3. See *ibid.*, p. 245.

Bowen relating to the Print.[4] Please to present him my respectful Compliments. I am just return'd from as long a Journey as a Man can well make in these Islands, thro' Wales, Ireland, Scotland and the Northern Parts of England; and I find my Health much improv'd by it. I shall soon take some good Opportunity of letting you see one of the Books that were collected by your good Grandfather.[5] Sally Franklin presents her Duty to you and Mrs. Franklin, and Love to her Kinswomen.[6] I am, Dear Kinsman, Yours very affectionately   B FRANKLIN

S. Franklin

Per Meyrick

To [Catharine Greene][7]

ALS (letterbook draft; incomplete): American Philosophical Society

[January 13?, 1772[8]]

[*First part missing:*] I Send you a Copy of the Receipt, hoping that you may be a means of introducing so valuable a Manufacture into your Country;[9] the more valuable, as the Cream is saved, and thence the Farm affords more Butter; at the same time that the Cheese is of so much greater Value. The principal Cause of its Goodness is perhaps the Heating of the Milk, which I understand is not usual in our Method. After some Experiments I think you will succeed in it. Remember not to be discouraged by a few Disappointments at the Beginning. I send you a Piece of right Parmesan, that you may be acquainted with it, and know when you have hit it.

4. See *ibid.*, p. 244.
5. See *ibid.*, p. 176.
6. Sally (A.5.2.3.1) was a cousin of both BF and Samuel.
7. One of BF's oldest friends, who has appeared frequently in earlier volumes.
8. The date of the immediately following draft in the letterbook, that of BF to Ward below.
9. BF here deleted "and thro' you, Rhodeisland may become famous"; the deletion establishes to whom he was writing. For her interest in cheesemaking many years before see above, VI, 184.

Present my respectful Compliments to Mr. Greene and kiss the Girls for me.[10] My best Wishes attend you all. Believe me ever Your affectionate Friend   B Franklin

To the Massachusetts House of Representatives Committee of Correspondence

Reprinted from Jared Sparks, ed., *The Works of Benjamin Franklin...* (10 vols., Boston, 1836–40), VII, 543–5.

Gentlemen,   London, 13 January, 1772.

On my return from a late tour through Ireland and Scotland, for the establishment of my health, I found your respected letter of June 25th,[1] with the papers therein referred to, relating to the townships settled eastward of Penobscot River. I immediately waited on Mr. Bollan to consult with him, agreeably to your instructions, who informed me, that, in my absence, he had by himself thoroughly considered the same, having formerly had occasion to be acquainted with the whole affair, and he suggested to his constituents, the Council, a plan of accommodation to be proposed to government here, if they should approve of it; and that he hoped by the meeting of Parliament (before which, little public business is done here, so many of the Lords of the Council being out of town,) he might have their answer; and it would otherwise be to little purpose to attempt any thing sooner. I make no doubt but the proposal has been communicated to the House of Representatives, if they have since had a meeting, and that we may soon receive their further instructions thereon.[2]

10. For her husband William and for their daughters see William G. Roelker, ed., *Benjamin Franklin and Catharine Ray Greene, Their Correspondence...* (Philadelphia, 1949), pp. 4, 29–30.

1. Here and subsequently BF is replying to the committee's letters of June and July, 1771. That of July 9 is missing; for the others see above, XVIII, 138–44, 147–53, 179–80.

2. For William Bollan and his long experience with the problems of the eastern lands see above, XIII, 227 n; XVIII, 143 n. His proposal was an attempted compromise between the General Court's demand for complete jurisdiction over settlers in and grants of these lands and Whitehall's insistence on preserving the mast trees reserved to the King in the Massachusetts charter. The province should surrender its claim to the land that produced the

The town now begins to fill with members of Parliament, and great officers of state coming in daily to celebrate the Queen's birthday, and be present at the opening of the session, which is fixed for next Tuesday. It is given out, that nothing relating to America is likely to be agitated this session; that is, there is no purpose either to abrogate the old duties or lay new ones. For the first, I am sorry, believing as I do, that no harmony can be restored between the two countries, while these duties are continued. This, with the other aggrievances mentioned in your letters of June 29th and July 13th, your agents will constantly attend to, and take every step possible in their present situation, unacknowledged as they are here,[3] to obtain the redress, that is so justly your due, and which it would be so prudent in government here to grant.

In yours of July 9th it is mentioned, that the House desire I would annually send an account of the expense I am at, in carrying on the affairs of the province. Having business to do for several colonies, almost every time I go to the public offices, and to the ministers, I have found it troublesome to keep an account of small expenses, such as coach and chair hire, stationery, &c., and difficult to divide them justly. Therefore I have some time since omitted keeping any account, or making any charge of them, but content myself with such salaries, grants, and allowances, as have been made me. Where considerable sums have been disbursed, as in fees to counsel, payment of solicitors' bills, and the like, those I charge. But as yet I have made no such disbursements on the account of your province.[4] Please to present my duty to the

best trees, Bollan suggested, and promise its help in guarding them against trespassers; in return the crown should surrender its right to confirm the General Court's land grants elsewhere in the territory. Bollan had attempted the previous September to concert with BF on this scheme but, finding the latter absent in Ireland, had submitted it to the Massachusetts Council on his own. Mass. Arch., XXII, 581–8. He later consulted Dartmouth, who approved in principle. 6 Mass. Hist. Soc. *Coll.*, IX (1897), 311–14.

3. For the disputed status of the Massachusetts agents see above, XV, 196–8; XVIII, 9–16, 27–9, 153 n, 242 n.

4. Next March he charged Massachusetts and his other provinces a guinea apiece for the fee of an underling in the Board of Trade (Jour., p. 40), but his major disbursements were not until 1774. When he settled his agent's account with Massachusetts in Oct., 1775, it was more than £200 in excess of his salary.

House of Representatives, and believe me to be, with great esteem and respect, Gentlemen, &c.   B. FRANKLIN.

To Jane Mecom

ALS: Miss Louise B. Wallace, Los Angeles, California (1955); incomplete draft: American Philosophical Society

My dear Sister,   London, Jan. 13. 1772

I received your kind Letters of Sept. 12. and Nov. 9. I have now been some Weeks returned from my Journey thro' Wales, Ireland, Scotland, and the North of England, which besides being an agreable Tour with a pleasant Companion, has contributed to the Establishment of my Health; and this is the first Ship I have heard of by which I could write to you. I thank you for the Receipts; they are as full and particular as one could wish; but can easily be practis'd only in America, no Bayberry-wax, nor any Brasiletto being here to be had, at least to my Knowledge.⁵ I am glad however that those useful Arts that have so long been in our Family, are now put down in Writing. Some future Branch may be the better for it. It gives me Pleasure that those little Things sent by Jonathan, prov'd agreable to you. I write now to Cousin Williams to press the Payment of the Bond:⁶ There has been Forbearance enough on my Part; seven Years or more without receiving any Principal or Interest. It seems as if the Debtor was like a whimsical Man in Pennsylvania, of whom it was said that it being against his Principle to pay Interest, and against his Interest to pay the Principal, he paid neither one nor t'other. I doubt you have taken too old a Pair of Glasses, being tempted by their magnifying greatly.⁷ But People in chusing should only aim at remedying the Defect. The Glasses that enable them to see *as well*, at the *same Distance* they used to hold their Book or Work, while their Eyes

5. BF had requested the recipes in his letter to her above, XVIII, 187. The one for crown soap called for pure bayberry wax; the one for dyeing worsted undoubtedly called for brasiletto, a species of dyewood imported from Jamaica.
6. For the debt from Samuel Hall see BF to the senior Williams below, Jan. 13.
7. BF had sent her several pairs of glasses; see the letter to Jane cited above.

were good, are those they should chuse, not such as make them see *better*, for such contribute to hasten the Time when still older Glasses will become necessary. All who have seen my Grandson, agree with you in their Accounts of his being an uncommonly fine Boy, which brings often afresh to my Mind the Idea of my Son Franky, tho' now dead 36 Years, whom I have seldom since seen equal'd in every thing, and whom to this Day I cannot think of without a Sigh. Mr. Bache is here: I found him at Preston in Lancashire with his Mother and Sisters, very agreable People, and I brought him to London with me. I very much like his Behaviour.[8] He returns in the next Ship to Philadelphia. The Gentleman who brought your last Letter, Mr. Fox, staid but a few Minutes with me, and has not since call'd as I desired him to do. I shall endeavour to get the Arms you desire for Cousin Coffin. Having many Letters to write, I can now only add my Love to Cousin Jenny, and that I am as ever Your affectionate Brother

B FRANKLIN

Sally Franklin presents her Duty. Mrs. Stephenson desires to be affectionately remember'd.

PS. No Arms of the Folgers are to be found in the Herald's Office.[9] I am persuaded it was originally a Flemish Family, which came over with many others from that Country in Qu. Elizabeth's Time, flying from the Persecution then raging there.

Notation by William Duane: B Franklin to Jane Mecom, his sister London Jan. 1772.

8. See above, XVIII, 256–8.
9. Jane had, we assume, forwarded a request for the arms from Keziah Folger Coffin (B.1.4.2.2.2), who seems to have been much interested in her family's genealogy. See above, x, 397–9.

To Elizabeth Hubbart Partridge[1]

ALS (letterbook draft; incomplete): American Philosophical Society

Dear Betsey   London, Jany. 13, 1772

I received your *angry-a-little* Letter by Mr. Marchant,[2] written to me "tho' I had suffered a preceding one to remain two Years unanswered." If I did so, which I doubt, I was exceedingly to blame, and must desire you to excuse me in consideration of the many I have to write and the little time I have for Writing. I am sure I shall be the greatest Loser by a Failure of our Correspondence, since [*torn*] no Letters I receive afford me more Pleasure [*remainder missing.*]

Mrs Partridge

To Ezra Stiles

ALS: New Haven Colony Historical Society; draft: American Philosophical Society

Dear Sir,   London, Jany. 13. 1772

I receiv'd your Favour[3] by Mr. Marchant, who appears a very worthy Gentleman, and I shall not fail to render him every Service in my Power.

There is lately published in Paris, a Work intitled *Zend-avesta*, or the Writings of *Zoroaster*, containing the Theological, Philosophical and Moral Ideas of that Legislator, and the Ceremonies of Religious Worship that he establish'd. Translated from the original Zend. In two Vols. 4to. Near half the Work is an Account of the Translator's Travels in India, and his Residence among the Parses during several Years to learn their Languages. I have cast my Eye over the Religious Part; it seems to contain a nice Morality, mix'd with abundance of Prayers, Ceremonies, and Obser-

1. BF's stepniece. They had corresponded actively years before, but no letter between them is extant for more than a decade before 1772. She had married Capt. Samuel Partridge, shopkeeper and superintendent of the Boston almshouse: above, I, lix.

2. Henry Marchant had arrived in England in early autumn, and presumably delivered the letter when he joined BF in Scotland at the end of October.

3. See Stiles to BF above, XVIII, 144–7.

vations. If you desire to have it, I will procure it for you.⁴ They say there is no doubt of its being a genuine Translation of the Books at present deem'd sacred as the Writings of Zoroaster by his Followers; but perhaps some of them are of later Date tho' ascrib'd to him: For to me there seems too great a Quantity and Variety of Ceremonies and Prayers to be directed at once by one Man. In the Romish Church they have increas'd gradually in a Course of Ages to their present Bulk. Those who added new Ones from time to time found it necessary to give them Authority by Pretences of their Antiquity. The Books of Moses,⁵ indeed, if all written by him, which some doubt, are an Exception to this Observation. With great Esteem, I am ever, Dear Sir, Your affectionate Friend and humble Servant   B FRANKLIN

PS. Since writing the above, Mr. Marchant, understanding you are curious on the Subject of the Eastern ancient Religions, concludes to send you the Book.⁶

Revd Dr Stiles

Addressed: To / The Reverend Dr. Stiles / at / Newport / Rhode-island

Endorsed: Recd. Apr. 11. 1772

4. The work was translated by Abraham Hyacinthe Anquetil-Duperron, *Zend-Avesta, ouvrage de Zoroastre...* (3 vols., Paris, 1771). Anquetil sailed for India in 1755 to study Zoroaster's works; he returned in 1761 by way of England, where he was jailed as a prisoner of war, released at the intercession of friends, and remained to examine Zoroastrian MSS at Oxford. See George Sarton, "Anquetil-Duperron (1731–1809)," *Osiris*, III (1937), 193–223. BF lent the *Zend-Avesta* to Richard Jackson, whom it thoroughly annoyed; see his note to BF below, under Jan. 16.
5. The Pentateuch.
6. BF either obtained another copy or relinquished his own; Marchant paid him three guineas for it. Jour., p. 40.

To Samuel Ward[7]

ALS (letterbook draft): American Philosophical Society

Dear Sir,   London, Jan. 13. 1772

I thank you for recommending Mr. Marchant to me. I have had the Pleasure of a good deal of his Company in Scotland, and shall do every thing in my Power to serve him.

I condole with you on the Loss of your amiable Partner.[8] It must be a heavy one and hard to bear. I hope you will find Comfort in your Children. With great Esteem, I am, Dear Sir, Your most obedient humble Servant   B F.

Mr Ward, Govr

To Jonathan Williams, Sr. ALS: American Philosophical Society

Loving Cousin,   London, Jan. 13. 1772

Since my last, which I think was by Jonathan,[9] I have receiv'd yours of July 8, and 12. Aug. 5, Sept. 19. and Oct. 3.[1] My not answering sooner was owing to my Absence in Ireland and Scotland on a Tour of between 3 and 4 Months, by which my Health was much benefited: And since my Return this is the first Ship to Boston that I have heard of.

In yours of July 8. was the first Bill of Wheatly on Thornton for £100 which is pass'd to your Credit. In that of July 12 was Lemmer's Bill for 1000 Gilders or £90 which is likewise carried to your Credit. In that of Augt. 5. was Symmes's Bill on Bilboa (Gardoqui & Sons) for £100 with which you are likewise credited. In that of Sept. 19. were two more Dutch Bills, one for 975 Gilders, the other for 779 Gilders making £160 16s. 8d. [credited?] but

7. For the former Governor of Rhode Island see above, v, 504 n.

8. Anna Ward, Catharine Greene's sister, had died on Dec. 5, 1770. See *Correspondence of Governor Samuel Ward...Edited by Bernhard Knollenberg...and Genealogy of the Ward Family...Compiled by Clifford P. Monahon* (Providence, R.I., 1952), p. 214.

9. BF's letter of Aug. 25 (above, XVIII, 213–14), which seems to have been written after Jonathan, Jr., had left for America.

1. All but the first are in the preceding volume, where the remittances mentioned below are described.

32

not yet paid. When I have received this last Sum your Account with me will stand thus:

Ball. due to me at						
Settlement	£282	11s.	10½d.	By Bill 100	0s.	0d.
Jonathan had more	26	5s.	0d.	Do 100	0s.	0d.
Josiah	6	6s.	0d.	Do 90	0s.	0d.
more	21	0s.	0d.	2 Do 160	16s.	8d.
more	10	10s.	0d.			
more	21	0s.	0d.			
Paid Mr. Warren[2] per Order of Jona.	83	3s.	9½d.			
	£450	16s.	8d.	£450	16s.	8d.

Since which Josiah has had of me Forty Guineas more; and I shall continue to supply him with what he may have Occasion for during his Stay. He keeps his Health and Spirits, and I see him frequently.[3]

I am sorry to understand that the Bond is not paid.[4] I wish you to take all possible Methods to recover it speedily. There has been Forbearance enough on my part, it being now more than 7 Years.

It gives me Pleasure to hear that Jonathan is enter'd into Business, and has promising Prospects. I never had any Doubt of his

2. He was the relative of Francis Hopkinson who helped to start him in the woolen business in 1768: above, xv, 87. But our identification of him at that time was mistaken: we confused two brothers. Hopkinson's great-aunt on his mother's side, Anne Johnson Warren, had two sons, the elder a clergyman and the other a wine merchant. Ernest H. Pearce, *Hartlebury Castle, with Some Notes on Bishops Who Lived in It*... (London, 1926), p. 259. The younger son, who must have been in the cloth as well as wine trade, was James Warren; he lived on Craven Street and was involved at this time in BF's business affairs with Williams. *Kent's Directory*... (London, 1770); above, x, 360. For young Jonathan's debt to Warren see the following document.

3. The younger Williams brother, who was blind, was still studying music in London. His good health and spirits did not last long: he sailed for home at the beginning of April, and died of tuberculosis in August.

4. The bond was for Samuel Hall's debt, discussed above, XVIII, 16, 219–21; see also BF to Jane Mecom above, Jan. 13.

Success, Accidents of Fire, &c excepted. My Love to Cousin Grace and your Children. I am, Your affectionate Uncle

B FRANKLIN

Jona Williams Esqr

Addressed: To / Jonathan Williams, Esqr / Mercht / Boston

Endorsed: Jany 13. 1772

To Jonathan Williams, Jr. ALS: American Philosophical Society

Dear Jonathan, London, Jan 13. 1772.

I received yours of Sept. [*blank*] and Nov. 4. It gave me great Pleasure to hear of your safe Arrival and Entring on Business with such Appearance of Success. I wish you every kind of Prosperity.

Agreable to your Request after making a rough Sketch of the Account which I now send to your Father, I paid the Ballance appearing in my Hands £83 3s. 9½d. to Mr. Warren on your Account. He had call'd on me to know what he was to expect when the Bills should be paid, so imagining he might want the Money, I paid him the full that would be in my Hands; tho' before I paid it, Josiah had told me he should want 40 Guineas more: But this I chose to advance him on a new Account, rather than diminish so much the small Payment to Mr. Warren.[5] Your Uncle has never said anything to me of the £149. you desired him to pay me; and I have not ask'd him, understanding that he cannot at present spare it.[6]

All your Friends here rejoice to hear of your Welfare, and send their best Wishes. I hope you will adhere strictly to your Ready-money Plan, which in my Opinion is too good to be parted with, as leading directly to Success in your Business.[7] I am, Your affectionate Uncle B FRANKLIN

Addressed: To / Mr Jonathan Williams, junior, / Mercht / Boston

Endorsed: Doctr Franklin London Janry 13—1772

5. See the preceding document and Jonathan's reply to BF below, April 10.

6. For John Williams, the customs inspector, see above, XVII, 212 n. He seems to have been in perennial financial difficulties at this time; see BF's letter to him below, Aug. 15, 1773.

7. Although the two letters that BF was answering have disappeared, it

To John Winthrop

ALS (letterbook draft): American Philosophical Society

Dear Sir,   London, Jan. 13. 1772
  I have received by Mr. Marchant the 52s. you sent by him.[8]
I hope you received the Transactions for 1770. A new Volume is
expected soon, which I shall forward by the first Opportunity.
The enclos'd I have just receiv'd from Dr. Price, into whose
Hands I put your Paper, which he has now return'd to me.[9] Let
me know if you would have me give it to the Society. With great
Esteem I am, ever, my dear Friend, Yours most affectionately
                                                    B FRANKLIN
Mr Winthrop
Per Meyrick

From Anthony Tissington[1]

ALS: American Philosophical Society

Dear Sir   Alfreton 15th Jan 1772.
  I hope this will find you well in Craven Street, after a Summer
of rambling, in which I have been so unfortunate as not to see
you; in your first ramble thro' Derbyshire I was in Scotland; in
your last, at home, and sick of not seeing you.[2]
  I am my Self very well, my Wife yet poorly; wishes to hear that
Mrs. Stevenson holds stout; and yesterday sent a Turkey by
Clarks Wagon to the Ax in Aldermanbury; to regale you.[3] Our

---

seems clear that BF had recommended the plan; for Jonathan's discussion of it
see his reply cited above.
  8. Henry Marchant, who had arrived in England the previous August, had
presumably brought payment for the *Phil. Trans.* for 1770. This was Winthrop's usual method: above, XVII, 265; XVIII, 30.
  9. For Winthrop's paper on the transit of Venus, and the involved communication between him and Price via BF, see above, XVII, 264 n.
  1. See above, IX, 42 n, and subsequent volumes.
  2. BF had passed through Derbyshire the previous spring on his tour of
northern England, and again in November when returning from Scotland.
  3. Tissington had sent the same gift a year before, by the same carrier to
the same inn; see above, XVII, 309. BF put the turkey to good use, as indicated
in his acknowledgment below, Jan. 28.

best joint Complements with those of this season attend your self and Mrs. Stevenson and I am Dear Sir Yours Sincerely and affectionately ANTH TISSINGTON

Mr Franklin

Addressed: To / Benjamin Franklin Esqr / Craven Street Strand / London

From Hannah Walker[4]   ALS: American Philosophical Society

Most Honoured Sir   Westbury Jan 15. 1772

I Humbly beg Leave to Congratulate you on the Happy return of your Birth Day and wish you a great many returns in health and Happiness to the great Comfort of all your good Family and to all those as have felt the Effects of your Benevolent Hand as I my Self think I am bound in Duty to Congratulate So good a Friend on So happy occasion. My Family joyns me in begging the acceptance of all our Humble Duties and my Continual Prayers for your long Life and Happiness in as much Pleasure and Tranquility as you can wish from your most Humble and most obdient Servant HANNAH WALKER

Addressed: To / Docter Franklin / att Mrs Stevensons / Craven Street Strand / London

From Richard Jackson   ALS: American Philosophical Society

Southampton Buildings Thursday [January 16?, 1772[5]]

Dear Sir

I return you Monsr. D Anquetil's Voyage,[6] which I found reason to wish to read more attentively than I at first intended to have done.

4. BF's cousin, Hannah Farrow Walker, has appeared frequently in preceding volumes.

5. The Galloway letter that Jackson mentions was written on Dec. 2, 1771; BF had received it when he wrote Galloway below, Feb. 6. Hence this note enclosing it could not have been written before January or, because of the day of the week, after January: there was no Thursday in February before BF's letter to Galloway. Once the month is established, two plausible days can be determined by a process of conjecture described below; and our policy is to choose the earlier of the two.

6. See BF to Stiles above, Jan. 13.

The Evident carelessness and Ignorance of the Author in many Points and his palpable Malignity against the whole English Nation, in general, notwithstanding he is obliged to confess the Civility he received from Particulars, makes me doubt somewhat, every thing that depends on his Veracity.

This is the Day I was to have dined with you at the Mitre and I shall very well like to go; but as my first Intention was only founded on Dr. Mortons Invitation I do not feel in myself any Desire, to dine there, independent of that Invitation, or the Desire of your Company. Do not therefore call on me meerly to introduce me there. In case your Inclinations lead you to dine there, come to [me] and I shall like very well to dine there with you, but do [not] come on purpose. If Dr. Morton calls on me I will go, whether you come or not.[7]

I send you a Letter and some papers from Mr. Galloway and am Dear Sir Yours sincerely   RD JACKSON

Understand me; I have not the least reluctance to go, if it is agreable to you.

Addressed: To / Benjamin Franklin Esq

7. For Charles Morton, secretary of the Royal Society, see above, x, 71 n. He had invited Jackson to a meeting of the Royal Society Club at the Mitre Tavern, off Fleet Street; by rules adopted in 1766 any member might, with leave from the President or a majority of the members present, introduce not more than two guests at a meeting. Archibald Geikie, *Annals of the Royal Society Club* . . . (London, 1917), pp. 25, 93. Our conjecture is that Morton, planning to attend on a particular Thursday, invited Jackson but neglected to follow up the invitation. In that case Jackson was probably writing on Jan. 16 or 23, when the records of the Royal Society show that Morton did attend. The phrasing of the note, however, presents a mystery; for BF was not a member, but only a frequent guest. Unless the rules had fallen into abeyance, he could not have dined at the Club—let alone introduced Jackson —whenever he was so inclined. Neither man did in fact attend during January.

From Elizabeth Montagu[8]   AL: American Philosophical Society

Hillstreet Thursday [January?] the 16th [1772?9]

Mrs. Montagu presents her compliments to Dr. Franklyn, and is afraid he will think her troublesome in desiring the favour of his company on Sunday next the 19th, as well as on this day sennight. Mr. Bolton, who has promised to dine with Mrs. Montagu on sunday, will be best rewarded for his civility by meeting Dr. Franklyn, and so great an Artist as Mr. Bolton makes a grateful return to Philosophy by presenting it in forms and substances to the Beau monde which they are capable of admiring,[1] and therefore she flatters herself Dr. Franklyn will indulge him with his conversation.

Addressed: To / Dr Franklyn / at Mrs Stephensons / Craven street / In the Strand

From William Outram[2]   ALS: American Philosophical Society

⟨London, January 17, 1772: Has been commissioned by the Rev. Mr. Dunlap[3] to take care of buying and shipping a good armonica for Dunlap's son Benjamin, organist in his father's church in Virginia, and to ask Franklin where such an instrument might be

8. See above, XIV, 70 n.

9. BF's acquaintance with Mrs. Montagu, aside from a few casual meetings during his first English mission, began in 1767 at earliest (*ibid.*, pp. 70–1); and this invitation could have been issued at any time from then until his return to America in 1775. But the first evidence we have found of his visiting her is in 1772, an entry in his cash book (1772, 1778–80; APS) under Feb. 15. We are assuming, on no tenable grounds whatever, that she extended these invitations to him the month before.

1. Presumably James Bolton (*fl.* 1775–95), a self-taught Yorkshire naturalist and artist. *DNB*. He would have been a natural protégé for Mrs. Montagu, with her extensive Yorkshire connections.

2. A merchant captain, master of the Virginia vessel *Liberty*: 1 *W&MQ*, XX (1911–12), 209–10; Edmund and Dorothy S. Berkeley, "'The Ablest Clerk in the U.S.': John James Beckley," *Va. Mag. of History and Biography*, LXX (1962), 435.

3. William Dunlap, the husband of DF's niece and rector of the parish of Stratton Major; see above, XV, 24 n.

had; should be obliged to have the information addressed to him at the bar of the Virginia Coffee House.[4]⟩

Mrs. R. W. Viny[5] to Margaret Stevenson

ALS: American Philosophical Society

Editors now and then encounter a document that seems designed to train them in humility, and the one below is a case in point. The circumstances surrounding Mrs. Stevenson's and Franklin's projected visit to the Vinys are as obscure, thanks to the writer's prose, as they are insignificant. But the letter does throw some light on how acquaintances of humble station regarded Franklin, and for that reason we print it without venturing to explain it.

Mrs Stevens   new Cross[6] Jany 17. 1772

Not having oppertunity of Waiting on you in person; I have taken the liberty of directing my pen; by way of inquir'ry if any of my friends in Craven street, are offended. Mr. Viny, Called on wensday morning in the wheel on purpose to ask you how you did; and when it would be agreable to Doctr. franklin in this week; to favour us with your Company's; when he knocked at the door Miss franklin Came herself,[7] and with an Unpleasent Countenance; reply'd, here's no boody at home; Mr. Viny said it was such a damper; as hurt him greatly.

He Conclud'd I had misunderstood you, and that the Doctr. intend'd to favour us with his, and your Companys the last week; which if so; I am verry sorry for, and ask his pardon; there being no one; whose friendship expeirenc'd; we wish more to Cultivate then Doctr. franklin.

Mrs. Stevens; if our Conduct has appear'd inconsistant the whole fault is mine; for Mr. Viny did think the Doctr. talk'd of Comeing the wensday after we was; with you; but I said I understood him he Could not; and that you likwise replyed; twas out of

4. In Ball Court, Cornhill; see Bryant Lillywhite, *London Coffee Houses...* (London, [1963]), p. 628.
5. She was almost unquestionably the wife of John Viny, who has appeared briefly above, XVII, 72 n; her initials appear in a letter to BF from him and his family, May 21, 1783: APS.
6. A village not far from London and close to Deptford.
7. Sarah (Sally), who lived much of the time in Craven Street.

the question that week; as they were to go into the Country, to see mr. Beaches mother; I might not understand you wright;[8] however; I flatter myself from the generous sentiments; and great Candour of my worthy friend judgment in all things; that he will not Construe it slight, and disesteem; but intire misunderstanding; which I anxiously wish Clear'd up to our mutual satisfaction. From your much oblig'd friend   R: W: VINY.

PS: my best respects to the Doctr. and Son;[9] and we still hope to be favour'd with their Company at new Cross, when it shall be Convenient.

Addressed: To | Mrs Steevens. | Craven Street. | in the Strand.

From Miss Martin[1]   AL: American Philosophical Society

⟨General Post Office, January 20, 1772; a note in the third person. Asks Franklin to accept a copy of an Irish almanac which she has received that day. Mr. and Mrs. Jackson join her in compliments.⟩

8. How she could have understood "wright" is hard to imagine. BF had visited Mrs. Bache in Preston the previous autumn, and went again in the following June; he would scarcely have entertained the wild notion of traveling north in January.

9. *I.e.,* son-in-law, Richard Bache.

1. She has not appeared before, and no other correspondence of hers with BF is extant. We have discovered little about her except that she knew him reasonably well. Her connection with the Post Office we do not know, but it clearly brought her into contact with Charles Jackson, the comptroller of its Foreign Office. Her parents lived in Derby, and she arranged to have BF received there on his northern tour in the summer of 1772: on June 18 she wrote from the General Post Office to a Miss Rigale, presumably a relative or family friend, to ask that BF be introduced to her father as a particular friend of the Jacksons. In the surviving fragment of the letter (Hist. Soc. of Pa.) she promised that BF would make himself popular. "She is Certain the Doctor will be a Sincere Admirer of the Young Ladies but Miss Martin Vows Vengeance if they should prove Rivals." She had connections in Ireland as well as in Derby, as her gift of an almanac suggests. In June, 1772, BF paid her £3 2s. for "sundrys in Ireland"; the next spring she married the Rev. Henry Blacker, from Co. Tyrone. Jour., p. 42; *Gent. Mag.,* XLIII (1773), 202; Sir Bernard Burke, *A Genealogical and Heraldic History of the Landed Gentry of Ireland . . .* (10th ed., London, 1904), p. 38.

40

From John Hope[2]

ALS: Historical Society of Pennsylvania

Sir   Edinb 23d Janry 1772

I was honoured with yours of the 11th in Course of Post But defered acknowledging the Receipt of it till the box of plants arrived—which box came to hand yesterday and I hope I shall be able to save a few of them.

By an odd accident the medal has not been got ready and it may be still some weeks before it is. But as soon as it is ready, it shall be transmitted to you[3] meantime I request you will inform me what you paid for the freight of the box of plants to London and the re-shipping it at London.[4]

As soon as the medal is finished I shall write to Mr. Bartram to thank him for this present of the plants and avail myself of the permission you give of inclosing it under your Cover. I have the honour to be with much respect Your most obedient Servant

JOHN HOPE

From Sargent, Chambers and Co.[5]

AL: American Philosophical Society

⟨Mincing Lane, January 25, 1772, in the third person. The firm has received instructions by Mr. Bache to withdraw Franklin's account, which with interest amounts to £149 16s. 1d.; what does he wish to have done with the money?[6]⟩

2. The Edinburgh physician and botanist, who used BF as a go-between in communicating with John Bartram; see above, XVIII, 62. BF enclosed Hope's letter in his to Bartram below, Oct. 17. Both arrived, for George Bartram, who despite his name was John's son-in-law (above, XII, 16 n), later wrote on this one a note to the botanist on other business.

3. Hope had offered Bartram a gold medal in place of the £7 10s. still owed him for seeds; see William Darlington, *Memorials of John Bartram and Humphry Marshall* (Philadelphia, 1849), pp. 435–6. The medal was delivered to BF in October and forwarded by him four months later: BF to Bartram below, Oct. 17, 1772; Feb. 10, 1773.

4. Hope reimbursed BF 14s. 6d.: Jour., p. 39.

5. For the mercantile firm, formerly Sargent Aufrere, see above, IX, 359 n; XIII, 295 n.

6. The withdrawal was part of a present of £200 to Richard Bache, who was about to return to America. Jour., p. 38; BF to Sarah Bache below, Jan. 29.

From Jonathan Shipley

AL: American Philosophical Society

⟨Jermyn Street, January 25, [1772–75?[7]], in the third person and the Bishop's hand. Invites Franklin to dinner tomorrow.⟩

To Deborah Franklin

ALS (letterbook draft): American Philosophical Society

My dear Child, London, Jan. 28. 1772

I have written several short Letters to you lately just to let you know of my Welfare, and promising to write more fully by Capt. Falconer, which I now sit down to do, with a Number of your Favours before me.

I received the Box and Letter from Mr. Peter Miller, but if as you mention, Enoch Davenport brought it, I did not see him.[8] Perhaps he might call while I was absent in Ireland. I write by this Opportunity to Mr. Miller. What he sent me is a most valuable Curiosity.

I take Notice of the considerable Sums you have paid. I would not have you send me any Receipts. I am satisfy'd with the Accounts you give.[9]

I am much pleas'd with your little Histories of our Grandson, and happy in thinking how much Amusement he must afford you. I pray that God may continue him to us, and to his Parents. Mr. Bache is about returning. His Behaviour here has been very agreable to me. I have advis'd him to settle down to Business in Phil-

7. BF's acquaintance with the Bishop of St. Asaph and his family began, as far as we know, in the summer of 1771; we are therefore assigning this invitation to what seems to be the earliest likely date.

8. For John Peter Miller and his gift of the Ephrata Codex see above, XVIII, 130–1. Enoch Davenport, who is not listed in our genealogy in I, was BF's grandnephew, a son of Josiah Franklin Davenport (C.12.4). See *New England Hist. and Geneal. Register*, XI (1857), 20.

9. BF had written her an angry letter some nine months before about her finances, and in a missing reply she seems to have mollified him; see above, XVIII, 90–2, 207. The tone of this paragraph suggests that he thought she needed further reassurance.

adelphia, where I hope he will meet with Success. I mentioned to you before, that I saw his Mother and Sisters at Preston, who are genteel People, and extreamly agreable.

I receiv'd your young Neighbour Haddock's Silk and carried it my self to her Relations, who live very well, keeping a Linnen Drapers Shop in Bishop's Gate Street.[1] They have a Relation in Spitalfields that is a Manufacturer who I believe will do it well. I shall honour much every young Lady that I find on my Return dress'd in Silk of their own raising.

I thank you for the Sauceboats, and am pleasd to find so good a Progress made in the China Manufactury. I wish it Success most heartily.[2]

Mrs. Stevenson too loves to hear about your little Boy. Her own Grandson (my Godson) is a fine Child, now nine Months old. He has an attentive observing sagacious Look, as if he had a great deal of Sense, but as yet he is not enough acquainted with our Language to express it intelligibly. His Mother nurses him herself, for which I much esteem her, as it is rather unfashionable here; whence Numbers of little Innocents suffer and perish. His Name is *William*.

Mr. and Mrs. Strahan and their Family are well. We din'd there not long since. Yesterday Mrs. Stephenson, her Daughter Mr. Bache and my self, din'd at Mr. West's. They are well and their fine Boy.[3]

I am pleas'd that the Letters between me and the good Lady entertain'd you. But you ought not to have shown them to any body but Sally. Since my Return I receiv'd the enclos'd; but having too much to do, I could not accept the kind Invitation.

The Squirrels came safe and well. You will see by the enclos'd how welcome they were. A 1000 Thanks are sent you for them,

1. See below, BF to Rebecca Haydock, Feb. 5, and her reply under July 20. For Rebecca and her family see above, IV, 283 n; XII, 14 n.

2. The china was probably made in the new factory established by Gousse Bonnin and George Morris in 1769. BF's good wishes were in that case not fulfilled: the enterprise collapsed by the end of 1772. Harrold E. Gillingham, "Pottery, China, and Glass Making in Philadelphia," *PMHB*, LIV (1930), 115–18.

3. BF's godson was of course William Hewson; the Benjamin Wests' boy was Raphael.

and I thank you for the Readiness with which you executed the Commission.[4]

My Love to our dear Precious, to Polley Hunt, and all our kind enquiring Friends. Mrs. Montgomery's Health is I hope establish'd, as also that of our dear Friend Rhoads and his Family.[5]

The Buckwheat and Indian Meal are come safe and good. They will be a great Refreshment to me this Winter. For since I cannot be in America, every thing that comes from thence comforts me a little, as being something like Home. The dry'd Peaches too are excellent, those dry'd without the Skin; the Parcel in their Skins are not so good. The Apples are the best I ever had and came with the least Damage. The Sturgeon you mention did not come: but that is not so material.

I hope our Cousin Tyler will do well among us. He seems a sober well-inclin'd Man; and when I saw him at Birmingham, he appear'd to be well respected by his Relations and Friends.[6] An active, lively industrious Wife would be a good Thing for him.

I grieve for our Friend Bond's heavy Loss; and am sorry for poor Dr. Kearsley's Misfortune.[7]

I sent you from Ireland a fine Piece of the Holland of that Country. Capt. All, whom I met with there, found a Captain that he knew who promisd to take Care of it and deliver it safe. You mention nothing of it in your Letter of Decemr 2. when in the common Course you ought to have had it before that time, which makes me fear it is lost.[8] I wrote to you from Dublin; and from

4. BF's commission and the letter of thanks that he enclosed have vanished as completely as the squirrels, but the latter were undoubtedly designed for the Shipley daughters. See BF's epitaph on Mungo in his letter to Georgiana Shipley below, Sept. 26. We assume that the "good Lady" whose letters he had sent to DF was Mrs. Shipley, and that the enclosed invitation was also from her.

5. "Dear Precious" was probably Anna Potts; "Polley" was Mary Shewell Hunt, Isaac Hunt's wife. See above, XII, 168 n; XVII, 252 n. For Mrs. Montgomery's misfortunes see *ibid.*, p. 167 n. DF had mentioned in a missing letter, we assume, some illness in the family of Samuel Rhoads.

6. For DF's cousin, John Tyler, see above, XVIII, 208 n.

7. Dr. Bond's daughter Rebecca, the wife of Thomas Lawrence, had died the previous November: *Pa. Gaz.*, Dec. 5, 1771. For Dr. John Kearsley see above, V, 20 n; whatever his misfortune may have been, it was doubtless the cause of his death a few weeks before BF wrote: *Pa. Gaz.*, Jan. 16, 1772.

8. For Isaac All, who had married BF's niece, see above, XII, 31 n. The hol-

Glasgow in Scotland. I was in Ireland about 7 Weeks, in Scotland about 4 Weeks, absent from London in all more than three Months. My Tour was a very pleasant one, I received abundance of Civilities from the Gentry of both those Kingdoms, and my Health is improv'd by the Air and Exercise.

I have advis'd Mr. Bache to deal only in the Ready-Money way, tho' he should sell less. It is the safest and the most easy Manner of carrying on Business.[9] He may keep his Store in your little North Room, for the present. And as he will be at no Expence while the Family continues with you, I think he may, with Industry and Frugality get so forward, as at the End of his Term, to pay his Debts and be clear of the World, which I much wish to see. I have given him £200 Sterlg. to add something to his Cargo. My love to our dear Sally and to Ben concludes at present, from Your ever affectionate Husband   B FRANKLIN[1]

To Anthony Tissington

ALS (letterbook draft): American Philosophical Society

Dear Sir,   London, Jan. 28 1772
I received your very kind Letter of the 15th. together with the Turkey, which prov'd exceeding fine. We regal'd a Number of our Friends with it, and drank your and Mrs. Tissington's Health, which we wish'd sincerely. Mrs. Stevenson keeps about, but is ever ailing, like your Dame, with Rheumatic Pains that fly from

---

land, or unbleached linen, that he had had shipped went in all likelihood by the brig *Connolly*, Capt. Robert Miller; and she had a long and round-about voyage. After leaving Dublin in the fall, bad weather forced her into a Scottish port for a time, then drove her off the American coast to Antigua. BF gave her up for lost, but she reached Philadelphia in early April. See BF to DF below, March 19, May 5; *Pa. Gaz.*, Jan. 30, Feb. 27, April 9, 1772.

9. BF had probably given the same advice to Francis Hopkinson, and certainly had to Jonathan Williams, Jr.; see above, xv, 87; BF to Williams above, Jan. 13; Williams to BF below, April 10.

1. In the margin BF wrote, then deleted, "I have lately been chosen a corresponding Member of the Batavian Society at Rotterdam." His certificate of membership, dated June 11, 1771, is among his papers in the APS; in the previous April, it explains, he had been invited to join and had accepted. The Batavian Society of Experimental Science had been founded in 1769 and was the Dutch equivalent of the Royal Society and the Académie des sciences.

Limb to Limb continually. 'Tis a most wicked Distemper, and often puts me in mind of the Saying of a Scotch Divine to some of his Brethren who were complaining that their Flocks had of late been infected with *Arianism* and *Socinianism*. Mine, says he, is infected with a worse *ism* than either of those. Pray, Brother, what can that be? It is, the Rheuma*tism*!

I was a good deal mortified at not having it in my Power to call at Alfreton in my late Tours:[2] But I hope for the Pleasure of seeing you both in London this Winter. Mrs. Stevenson and Sally Franklin join in Wishes of every kind of Prosperity to you and yours, with, Dear Sir, Your oblig'd and affectionate Humble Servant

B Franklin

Mr Tissington

To Sarah Franklin Bache

ALS (letterbook draft): American Philosophical Society

Dear Sally   London, Jan. 29. 1772

I received your agreable Letters of Oct. 11. and Nov. 5. I met with Mr. Bache at Preston, where I staid two or three Days, being very kindly entertained by his Mother and Sisters, whom I lik'd much. He came to town with me, and is now going home to you. I have advis'd him to settle down to Business in Philadelphia where he will always be with you. I am of Opinion that almost any Profession a Man has been educated in, is preferable to an Office held at Pleasure, as rendering him more independent, more a Freeman [and] less subject to the Caprices of Superiors. And I think that in keeping a Store, if it be where you dwell, you can be serviceable to him as your Mother was to me: For you are not deficient in Capacity, and I hope are not too proud. You might easily learn Accounts, and you can copy Letters or write them very well upon Occasion. By Industry and Frugality you may get forward in the World, being both of you yet young. And then what we may leave you at our Deaths may be a pretty Addition, tho' of itself far from sufficient to maintain and bring up a Family. It is of the more Importance for you to think seriously of this, as you may have a Number of Children to educate. 'Till my Return you need be at

2. See Tissington's letter above, Jan. 15.

no Expence for Rent, &c. as you are all welcome to continue with your Mother, and indeed it seems to be your Duty to attend her as she grows infirm, and takes much Delight in your Company and the Child's. This Saving will be a Help in your Progress: And for your Encouragement I can assure you that there is scarce a Merchant of Opulence in your Town whom I do not remember a young Beginner with as little to go on with, and no better Prospects than Mr. Bache. That his Voyage hither might not be quite fruitless, I have given him £200 Sterling; with which I wish you good Luck. I hope you will attend to what is recommended to you in this Letter, it proceeding from sincere Affection, after due Consideration with the Knowledge I have of the World and my own Circumstances. I am much pleas'd with the Accounts I receive from all Hands of your dear little Boy. I hope he will be continu'd a Blessing to us all. Tho' I long to see my Family I am glad you did not come over,[3] as the Expence would have been very great, and I think I shall not continue here much longer. It is a Pleasure to me that the little Things I sent you prov'd agreable. I am ever, my dear Sally, Your affectionate Father   B FRANKLIN

To William Franklin

ALS (letterbook draft): American Philosophical Society

Dear Son,   London, Jan. 30. 1772
    I have now before me yours of July 3. Aug. 3. Sept. 3. and Nov. 5.[4] All but the last came in my Absence, which is the Reason they were not immediately answer'd.
    In yours of July 3. you mention some Complaisance of Lord H's towards you, that show'd a Disposition of being upon better Terms. His Behaviour to me in Ireland corresponds exactly. We met first at the Lord Lieutenant's. Mr. Jackson and I were invited to dine there, and when we came were shown into a Room, where Lord H. was alone. He was extreamly civil, wonderfully so to me whom he had not long before abus'd to Mr. Strahan as a factious turbulent Fellow, always in Mischief, a Republican, Enemy to the

3. See above, XVIII, 195.
4. Only two survive, one in fragmentary form: above, XVIII, 195–6, 217–19.

King's Service, and what not.[5] He entered very frankly into Conversation with us both, and invited us both to stop at his House in Hillsboro' as we should travel Northward, and urged it in so polite a Manner that we could not avoid saying we would wait on him if we went that way. In my own Mind I was determin'd not to go that way, but Mr. Jackson thought himself oblig'd to call on his Lordship, considering the Connection his Office forms between them. His Lordship dined with us at the Lord Lieut[enant]'s. There were at Table, the Lord Chancellor, the Speaker, and all the great Officers of State.[6] He drank my Health and was otherwise particularly civil. He went from Dublin some Days before us, and when we were on the Road, it was my Purpose to have turn'd off for Armagh on a Visit to Dean Hamilton,[7] let Mr. Jackson go to Hillsborough alone, and meet him at Belfast: But it so happen'd that where we were to have parted, no Post Chaise was to be had for me, nor any other to proceed with but that we came in, so I was oblig'd to go forward with Mr. Jackson to Hillsborough; and as soon as his Lordship knew we were arriv'd at the Inn he sent a Message over for us to come to his House. There we were detain'd by a 1000 Civilities from Tuesday to Sunday. He seem'd extreamly solicitous to give me and America through me a good Opinion of him. In our first Conversations he express'd himself as a good Irishman, censuring the English Government for its Narrowness with Regard to Ireland, in restraining its Commerce, Manufactures, &c. and when I apply'd his Observations to America, he agreed immediately that it was wrong to restrain our Manufactures, that the Subjects in every Part of the King's Dominions had a natural Right to make the best Use they could of the Production of their Country, and that Lord Chatham was extreamly wrong in asserting (as he did in his famous Speech), that England had a Right to forbid our manufacturing &c. and therefore, as he knew the Commons were apt to be jealous on that head, he never laid before them the Accounts, sent to his Office by

5. BF had in turn abused Hillsborough in writing to Cooper: *ibid.*, pp. 24–5.

6. Viscount Townshend was lord lieutenant; James Hewitt, Baron Lifford, was lord chancellor, and Edmond Sexton Pery was speaker of the House. See the *DNB*.

7. For Hugh Hamilton see above, XIII, 250 n. He had become Dean of Armagh in 1768, and was subsequently raised to the episcopal bench. *DNB*.

the Governors, of Manufactures in their Provinces,[8] unless specially called for, Being confident they would carry on none that were not more for their Advantage than Agriculture, and wherever that was the Case, they ought to be at Liberty to pursue them. He then told me the Bounty granted to America on Silk,[1] was a Child of his; and wish'd me to think how a Bounty on Wine could be granted so as to be effectual, and give him my Advice on that Head, or any other on which I thought he might be useful to the Colonies. In particular he wish'd me to consider the State of Newfoundland, and give him my Thoughts and Advice on the proper Form of Government to be establish'd there, that Country being grown too populous to be left much longer without a regular Government, &c. &c.[2] His Attentions to me in every Circumstance of Accommodation and Entertainment, were very particular, putting his own Cloak about my Shoulders when I went out, that I might not take Cold, placing his Eldest Son, Lord Kilwarling in his Phaeton with me, to drive me 40 Miles round the Country, to see the Manufactures, Seats, &c. and when we took leave, requesting that I would let him see me often in London, &c, &c. Does not all this seem extraordinary to you? I knew not what to make of it, unless that he foresaw a Storm on Account of his Conduct to America, and was willing to lessen beforehand the Acrimony with which the People and Friends of that Country might possibly pursue him. But as I do not yet find that any of his offensive Instructions are withdrawn, I mean those relating to the Sitting of the Assembly of Boston at Cambridge, the Exemption of the Commissioners from Taxes, the Possession of the Castle, the Appointment of Agents, &c. I begin to think he either fancies himself more secure, or had only a mind to amuse me.

I believe I wrote you a good deal of this before from Scotland, but as I have no Copy of that Letter I cannot easily avoid the Repetition. At Dublin we saw and were entertain'd by both Parties, the Courtiers and the Patriots. The latter treated me with particular Respect. We were admitted to sit among the Members

8. For Pitt's speech, the governor's reports, and other matters mentioned in this letter see BF to Cushing above, Jan. 13.

1. 9 Geo. III, c. 38.

2. BF reported this part of the conversation to Cushing at slightly greater length.

in the Commons house, Mr. Jackson as Member of the British Parliament, and I as Member of some English *Parliament* in America.[3] The Speaker propos'd it in my Behalf, with some very obliging Expressions of Respect for my Character, and was answer'd by the House with an unanimous *Aye* of Consent, when two Members, came out to me, led me in between them, and plac'd me honourably and commodiously. I hope our Assemblies will not fall short of them in this Politeness, if any Irish Member should happen to be in our Country.

In Scotland I spent 5 Days with Lord Kaims at his Seat, Blair Drummond near Stirling, two or three Days at Glasgow, two Days at Carron Iron Works, and the rest of the Month in and about Edinburgh, lodging at David Hume's, who entertain'd me with the greatest Kindness and Hospitality, as did Lord Kaims and his Lady.[4] All our old Acquaintance there, Sir Alexr Dick and Lady, Mr. McGowan, Drs. Robertson, Cullen, Black, Ferguson, Russel and others,[5] enquir'd affectionately of your Welfare. I was out three Months, and the Journey was evidently of great Service to my Health.

Mr. Bache had some Views of obtaining an Office in America, but I dissuaded him from the Application, as I could not appear in it, and rather wish to see all I am connected with in an Independent Situation, supported by their own Industry. I therefore advis'd him to lay out the Money he brought with him (£1000 Sterling) in Goods, return and sit down to Business in Philadel-

3. BF's fullest description of this episode was to Cushing.

4. See above, XVIII, 250.

5. Sir Alexander Dick and William Robertson have appeared frequently before. Joseph Black, William Cullen, Adam Ferguson, and James Russell were eminent faculty members of the University of Edinburgh, all of whom are in the *DNB*; see also Alexander Bower, *The History of the University of Edinburgh*... (3 vols., Edinburgh, 1817–30), II, 376–92; III, 7–12, 103–4, 110–19. McGowan is mentioned but not identified above, x, 146. He was undoubtedly John McGowan, an assistant solicitor for the excise and customs, who a few years later was dining with Sir Alexander Dick and James Boswell; he was famous for his good nature, conviviality, and skill in making rum punch. *The Edinburgh Almanack* (1771), pp. 122–3; Frederick A. Pottle, ed., *Private Papers of James Boswell from Malahide Castle*... (18 vols., New York and London, 1928–34), x, 256; XI, 25; XII, 74; XIII, 285; John Kay, *A Series of Original Portraits and Caricature Etchings*... (4 vols., Edinburgh, 1877), II, 416–17.

phia, selling for ready Money only, in which way I think he might, by quick Returns, get forward in the World. It would have been wrong for Sally to leave her Mother, besides incurring the Expence of such a Voyage.[6]

I cast my Eye over Goddard's Piece against our Friend Mr. Galloway and then lit my Fire with it. I think such feeble malicious Attacks cannot hurt him.[7]

The Resolution of the Board of Trade to admit for the future no Agents to appear before them but such as are appointed by "concurrent Act of the whole Legislature," will I think put an End to Agencies, as I apprehend the Assemblies will think Agents under the ministerial Influence that must arise from such Appointments, cannot be of much Use in their Colony Affairs. In Truth I think the Agents as now appointed, of as much Use to Government here as to the Colonies that send them, having often prevented its [?] going into mistaken Measures, thro' Misinformation that must have been very inconvenient to itself, and would have prevented more of the same kind if they had been attended to, witness the Stamp and Duty Acts. I believe therefore we shall conclude to leave this omniscient infallible Minister to his own Devices, and be no longer at the Expence of sending any Agent, whom he can displace by a Repeal of the appointing Act. I am sure I should not like to be an Agent in such a suspicious Situation, and shall therefore decline serving under every such Appointment.[8] Your Assembly may avoid the Dispute you seem apprehensive of, by leaving the Appointment of an Agent out of the Support Bill, or rather I should say the Sum for his Salary. The Money in my Hands will pay him (whoever he is) for two or three Years, in which the Measure and the Minister, may be changed. In the mean time, by working with a Friend who has great Influence at the Board, he can serve the Province as effectually as by an open Reception and Appearance.[9]

6. BF is here answering WF's comment on Sally above, XVIII, 195.

7. See *ibid.*, p. 196.

8. For the challenge to BF's New Jersey agency and the way in which WF met it see *ibid.*, pp. 218–19, 260–1, and WF to BF above, Jan. 6. BF must have abandoned his intention of not serving as formal agent under the new arrangement, for his papers contain ample evidence that he continued to be reappointed and to collect his salary.

9. BF's phrasing raises the question of whether he had thought the matter

I write a Letter, as you advise, to Mr. Jos. Smith, to receive for me the Salary hitherto allow'd me by your Assembly.[1]

I have heard nothing farther of the Slitting Mill Affair, and believe no Information has been given. If Lord H. was sincere in his Discourse to me, I do not see how he can well encourage it.[2]

I have not receiv'd the Letter you were writing to me on our Account.[3] Nor have you mention'd Parker's Affair. I suppose your Illness prevented. I rejoice at your Recovery, and hope your Health will be established by the salubrious Northwest Winter Winds. I doubt you use too little Exercise.

Our Friend Sir John Pringle put into my hand the other Day a Letter from Mr. Bowman, seeming, I thought, a good deal pleas'd with the Notice you had taken of his Recommendation.[4] I send you a Copy of it, that you may see the Man has a grateful Disposition.

Temple has been at home with us during the Christmas Vacation from School. He improves continually, and more and more engages the Regard of all that are acquainted with him, by his pleasing, sensible, manly Behaviour.

I have of late great Debates with my self whether or not I should continue here any longer. I grow homesick, and being now in my 67th. Year, I begin to apprehend some Infirmity of Age may attack me, and make my Return impracticable. I have also some important Affairs to settle before my Death, a Period I ought now

---

through. What money was in his hands? New Jersey had paid him, aside from his £100 salary for 1770, £200 for expenses during his agency (above, XVI, 255; XVIII, 218–19) but nothing more that we have discovered; there may or may not have been enough left of the £200 to employ another agent. If there was not, BF might possibly have been suggesting that money be conveyed to him unofficially for an informal agent, whom he would then put in touch with Richard Jackson, the counsel to the Board of Trade. In any case BF's essential point was that agents must henceforth be mere lobbyists, without status, until the government changed its tune. He had made much the same point about his Massachusetts agency in his letter to Cooper above, Jan. 13.

1. See BF to Smith below, Feb. 6; for WF's original advice see above, XVIII, 219.

2. For the slitting mill affair see *ibid.*, p. 217 n. Hillsborough's discourse was the one described earlier in BF's letter.

3. The letter eventually arrived, with enclosed comments on their accounts. The letter has disappeared; the enclosure is discussed in *idem*, p. 75 n.

4. For Bowman see *ibid.*, p. 74.

to think cannot be far distant. I see here no Disposition in Parliament to meddle farther in Colony Affairs for the present, either to lay more Duties or to repeal any; and I think, tho' I were to return again, I may be absent from hence a Year, without any Prejudice to the Business I am engag'd in, tho' it is not probable that being once at home I should ever again see England. I have indeed so many good kind Friends here, that I could spend the Remainder of my Life among them with great Pleasure, if it were not for my American Connections, and the indelible Affection I retain for that dear Country, from which I have so long been in a State of Exile. My Love to Betsy. I am ever Your affectionate Father

B FRANKLIN

A Memorandum about Lord Hillsborough

AD (draft): Library of Congress

[January, 1772?5]

When the Petition6 first came over, an Accident had happen'd to the Paper that made it unfit to be presented,

Therefore a Duplicate was waited for, being expected in some other Ship.

Before that arriv'd Lord Hillsborough was gone to Ireland.

On his Return B.F. waited on him 5 several times, or rather endeavoured to wait on him, but was always refus'd Admittance, or his L[ordshi]p was deny'd.

In the mean time hearing that his L[ordshi]p had declar'd the Minister who propos'd the Repeal of that Act would deserve to be hang'd, and also that his L[ordshi]p talk'd of resigning,7 thought it best to wait a little longer.   BF.

5. The earliest possible date, which we customarily assign, cannot in this case be far wrong. After returning from his tour of Ireland and Scotland at the end of November, 1771, BF made the five unsuccessful attempts that he mentions to see Lord Hillsborough. The second extract of BF to WF below, Aug. 19, makes clear that his attempts must have occupied at least the month of December. In early February, 1772, he sent a letter that is now missing, but of which this memorandum may well have been the basis, to the committee of correspondence of the Pa. Assembly: BF to Galloway below, Feb. 6.

6. The petition of the previous March from the Pennsylvania Assembly, urging total repeal of the Townshend duties; see above, xviii, 66.

7. Hillsborough was adamant against total repeal, but we have not heard,

From John Foxcroft

ALS: Historical Society of Pennsylvania

Dear Sir   Philada. feby. 2d. 1772

I have the happiness to acquaint you that your Daughter was safely brought to Bed the 20th. Ulto. and presented me with a sweet little Girl, they are both in good spirits and are likely to do very well.[8]

I was seized with a Giddyness in my head the Day before yesterday which alarms me a good Deal as I had 20 oz. of Blood taken from me and took Physick which does not seem in the least to have relieved me. I am hardly able to write this. Mrs. F joins me in best affections to yourself and Compliments to Mrs. Stevenson and Mr. and Mrs. Huson.[9] I am Dear Sir Yours affectionately

                                                    JOHN FOXCROFT

Mrs. Franklin Mrs. Bache little Ben. the Family at Burlington are all well I had a Letter from the Governor yesterday.   J. F

Addressed: To / Benjamin Franklin Esqr / at Mrs. Stevensons in Craven Street / Strand / London / J: Free: FOXCROFT

From Noble Wimberly Jones

ALS: American Philosophical Society

Dear Sir   Savannah 2d. Febry 1772

Not having had the pleasure for some time of a line from you, gives me great concern,[1] lest I by any Means have given offence, which if so can with truth assure you, must be without the least knowledge or intent as there is no Gentleman, with whom have only had the pleasure of a Written Corrispondence I do esteem more. We still remain as when I last Wrote, without a House of

---

as BF had, that he talked of resigning on that issue. A quite different one drove him from office five months later.

8. In the summer of 1770, just before the end of his leave in England, Foxcroft had married Judith Osgood, and BF had given away the bride. For that reason, apparently, she was referred to thereafter as BF's "daughter," which has generated the legend that she actually was; see above, XVII, xxviii n.

9. William and Polly Hewson.

1. BF's most recent surviving letter had been written the previous July, but we have no proof that Jones had received it. See above, XVIII, 158–9.

Representatives, what our Arbitrary Rulers mean by it am at a loss to conceive, unless to terrify weak-minded people into their measures, suppose however now, a short time will shew a part of their motives, as an Election begins to be talkcd off, whenever it be I trust you will be requested again to stand forth in behalf of the province, unless a set of timeserving creatures should compose the Majority which God forbid.[2] If not too much Intrusion on your valluable time it will extreemly oblige me if any thing occurs concerning the province in general or the Land recomended to you[3] to sollicit of a few lines from you. And am with the greatest Respect Dear Sir Your Most Obedient and Very Humble Servant.

N W JONES

Benjamin Franklin Esqr.

To Deborah Franklin   ALS: American Philosophical Society

My dear Child,   London, Feb. 3. 1772

I have written a long Letter to you, which goes per Capt. Falconer, who Sails in a few Days; but as I know you like to have a Letter by every Ship, I write this Line just to let you know I continue well, Thanks to God, as I hope this will find you and our Children. Mrs. Stevenson sends her Love to you all. Her Grandson grows a very fine Boy indeed.[4] Mr. Bache writes. So I only add that I am ever, my dear Debby, Your affectionate Husband

B FRANKLIN

Addressed: To / Mrs Franklin / Philadelphia / Per favour of / The Revd. Mr Coombe[5]

2. For the quarrel over the Assembly's choosing Jones as speaker, which had produced a dissolution in 1771, see above, XVIII, 158–9, 168–9. The quarrel was renewed with the same result when a new Assembly convened in April, 1772; see BF to Jones below, April 2. Until the following December Georgia had no legislature of more than a few days' duration; hence BF could not be reappointed as agent.

3. For Sir William Baker and the land claims of his estate see above, XVII, 139 n, 148–50; XVIII, 18, 158, 169–70.

4. William Hewson, Jr., then nine months old.

5. For Thomas Coombe, Jr., see the following document.

To William Franklin

ALS (letterbook draft): American Philosophical Society

Dear Son,   London, Feb. 3. 1772

This will be delivered to you by the Revd. Mr. Coombe, whom I recommend to your Friendship as a young Gentleman of great Merit, Integrity, and Abilities. He has acquir'd the Esteem of all that knew him here, not as an excellent Preacher only, but as practising the Morality he preaches. I wish him a good Settlement in his Native Country, but I think he would better have found his Interest in remaining here.[6]

I continue in Health since my Return from my Journey, and I hope yours is fully established. The Parliament has open'd with a Calm in Party Affairs, and Peace seems about to be restor'd between the Turks and Russians.[7] I write fully to you per Falconer who sails in a few Days. At present can only add my Love to Betsy, and that I am, as ever, Your affectionate Father

B FRANKLIN

Per Sparks

Memo Wrote also per Sparks a few Lines to Mrs. Franklin.

6. For Thomas Coombe's journey to England for ordination see above, xv, 286 n. He had taken holy orders in 1769 and become chaplain to Lord Rockingham in 1771, and had finally been ordained to the priesthood just before his return to America. He would have fully endorsed BF's good opinion of him. His ripening friendship with the older man he took as a tribute to his own success: "at my first coming here," he wrote of BF, "he appeared shy and cautious, but this wore away gradually, and upon observing the Attention which my Preaching gained me, and the Notice which was taken of me by some Men of Letters, he received me upon the Footing of a Friend." Coombe to his father, Aug. 4, 1770; Hist. Soc. of Pa. BF had repeatedly urged him to remain in England (see for example ibid., Oct. 3, 1769; June 6, 1770), but Coombe decided after considerable hesitation that the future looked more promising in Philadelphia. After his arrival there he became assistant minister of Christ Church and St. Peter's; in 1779, however, he returned to England, where he spent the remainder of his long career. DAB.

7. The London Chron. reported on Feb. 4–6 a rumor from Warsaw that preliminaries of peace had been signed between Russia and the Porte. The war actually continued for another two years.

From David Hall

ALS: Historical Society of Pennsylvania

Dear Sir,   Philada: February 3, 1772

Your last kind Letter to me, was dated June 11, 1770. in Answer to mine of the 17th. of March preceding.[8] What Money I have since received on our Company Account is as follows, viz.

For the Gazette, from February 17, 1770 to Jany. 28, 1772	£358 13s.
By Cash received for Work done, as credited in the Ledger, in the above mentioned Time	181 17s. 10½d.
	£540 10s. 10½d.

and I have paid on your Account to Mrs. Franklin the following Monies as by her Receipts and Orders will appear.

1771

Jany. 25.	For purchasing a Bill of Exchange for £30 Ster.	£50
Augt. 16.	By Cash paid Ballance of an Account from the Estate of the late Mr. William Branson[9] against you, by Order	7 19s. 7½d.
	By my Part of Eleven Years and three Quarters Gazette, discounted in Mr. Branson's Account against you	2 18s. 9d.
Octr. 18.	By Cash paid Mrs. Franklin	24
29.	By Ditto paid Robert Erwin[1] by Mrs. Franklins Order	7 12s.

8. Hall had written to try to get a settlement of their accounts, and BF had put him off; see above, XVII, 99–101, 172, and for the full accounts, XIII, 99–104. BF's reply below, March 20, brought the settlement no nearer.

9. A well-to-do Philadelphia merchant, who had been interested in mining and ironworks and whose son-in-law, Lynford Lardner, was the Penn's receiver general; see Thomas A. Glenn, "An Old Pennsylvania Coat-of-Arms," *PMHB*, XXIV (1900), 179; XXXIII (1909), 370–1; W. A. Newman Dorland, "The Second Troop Philadelphia City Cavalry," *ibid.*, XLVIII (1924), 282.

1. Presumably the same man who was a crony of Joseph Fox, BF's old political ally: Anne H. Cresson, "Biographical Sketch of Joseph Fox . . . ," *ibid.*, XXXII (1908), 191–2. He may or may not have been the Erwin identified above, VI, 375 n.

Novr. 29.   By Ditto paid Mrs. Franklin for
              the purchasing a Lot of Ground
              for you of Mr. Parker[2]   100
            By Sundries had in the Shop   6 13s. 2d.
                                               ——————————
                                               £199 3s. 6½d.
                                               ══════════════

I should be glad of the Pleasure of a Letter from you soon, and to know whether you can now fix the Time of your setting out for Philadelphia. I should be glad it was quickly, as Mr. Parker is now no more, and I want much to have our Partnership settled, as far as it can be done, and to endeavour to fall upon some Method, in order to get in the outstanding Debts, which must amount to a great Deal, if it was possible to get them anything like collected. It is an Affair, I think, worthy of your looking after and taking some Pains to accomplish.

My Family, at present, all in very good Health. My Wife as well as can be expected. I did not think she would have got over the Loss of our only, and much loved, Daughter; but it has pleased God to support her under that heavy Affliction; and I really think she is better in her Health now than she has been for Some Years past.[3] Mrs. Franklin Mrs. Bache, and Child, are all well; I suppose you will hear from them by this Packet. My Compliments to Mr. Bache. I am glad to know by those who have seen you lately, that you enjoy a good State of Health, the Continuence of which shall be always my most sincere Wish. You may beleive me to be, Dear Sir, Yours most affectionately,   DAVID HALL.

Benjamin Franklin Esqr.

Addressed: To / Benjamin Franklin Esqr. / At Mrs. Stevens's in Craven Street / London / By Pennsylvania Packet / Capt. Osborne / Q.D.C.

Notation: Letter from D. Hall to B. Franklin dated Febry 3d. 1772

2. See above, XVIII, 262–3.
3. For Mrs. Hall's ongoing ill health see above, XVII, 101. Her "only" daughter had been the only unmarried one, Deborah, who died on Nov. 1, 1770: Edward L. Clark, *A Record of the Inscriptions...of Christ Church...* (Philadelphia, 1864), p. 55.

To John Foxcroft

ALS (letterbook draft) and autograph extract: American Philosophical Society

Dear Friend,   London, Feb. 4. 1772

I have written two or three small Letters to you since my Return from Ireland and Scotland. I now have before me your Favours of Oct. 1. Nov. 5. and Nov. 13.[4]

Mr. Todd has not yet shewn me that which you wrote to him about the New Colony, tho' he mention'd it, and will let me see it, I suppose, when I call on him.[5] I told you in one of mine, that he had advanced for your Share what has been paid by others, tho' I was ready to do [it?] and shall in the whole Affair take the same Care of your Interest as of my own.[6] You take Notice that "Mr. Wharton's Friends will not allow me *any Merit* in this Transaction but insist *the Whole* is owing to his superior Abilities." It is a common Error in Friends when they would extoll their Friend, to make Comparisons and depreciate the Merit of others. It was not necessary for his Friends to do so in this Case. Mr. Wharton will in Truth have a good deal of Merit in the Affair if it succeeds, he having been exceedingly active and industrious in soliciting it, and in drawing up Memorials and Papers to support the Application, remove objections, &c. But tho' I have not been equally active (it not being thought proper that I should appear much in the Solicitation since I became a little obnoxious to the Ministry on Account of my Letters to America) yet I suppose my Advice may have been thought of some Use since it has been ask'd on every Step, and I believe that being longer and better known here than Mr. Wharton, I may have lent some Weight to his Negociations by joining in the Affair; from the greater Confidence Men are apt to place in one they know than in a Stranger.[7] However,

4. Only the letter of Nov. 5 has survived: above, XVIII, 243–4.

5. Galloway had written Richard Jackson in the same tenor as Foxcroft's letter to Todd; see the annotation of WF to BF above, Jan. 6.

6. BF is doubtless referring to his letter, now missing, of Dec. 3, 1771, which Foxcroft mentioned in his below of March 2.

7. Samuel Wharton was busily dissociating himself from BF, Thomas Pownall, and other promoters whom he considered, as friends of America, to be liabilities; and reports circulating in Philadelphia that neither BF nor WF had any influence with the administration were doubtless of Wharton's

as I neither ask or expect any particular Consideration for any Service I may have done, and only think I ought to escape Censure, I shall not enlarge on this invidious Topic. Let us all do our Endeavours in our several Capacitys for the common Service, and if one has the Ability or Opportunity of doing more for his Friends than another, let him think that a Happiness and be satisfied. The Business is not yet quite compleated, as many Things happen between the Cup and the Lip, perhaps there may be nothing of this kind for Friends to dispute about. For if no body should receive any Benefit, there will be no Scrambling for the Honour.

Stavers is in the Wrong to talk of my promising him the Rider's Place again. I only told him that I would, (as he requested it) recommend him to Mr. Hubbard, to be replac'd if it could be done without Impropriety or Inconveniency. This I did, and the rather as I had always understood him to have been a good honest punctual Rider.[8] His Behaviour to you intitles him to no Favour, and I believe any Application he may make here, will be to little purpose.

In yours from N York, of July 3. You mention'd your Intention of purchasing a Bill to send hither, as soon as you return'd home from your Journey. I have not since receiv'd any from you, which I only take notice of to you, that if you have sent one you may not blame me for not acknowledging the Receipt of it.

In mine of April 20. I explain'd to you what I had before mentioned, that in settling our private Account I had paid you the Sum

---

sowing. Peter Marshall, "Lord Hillsborough, Samuel Wharton and the Ohio Grant, 1769–1775," *English Hist. Rev.*, LXXX (1965), 726–7, 734. The reports, forwarded to BF, may have cooled but certainly did not destroy his admiration for Wharton, for which see above, XVIII, 75–6.

8. Bartholomew Stavers, who drove a stagecoach between Boston and Portsmouth, N.H., carried letters as a side line. To eliminate this illicit competition Tuthill Hubbart, the Boston postmaster, put him on salary; the mails that Stavers then carried amply paid for it. *Journal Kept by Hugh Finlay . . .* (Brooklyn, N.Y., 1867), p. 18. Finlay, writing in 1773, made clear that Stavers was at that time in the postal employ and gave no indication that he had ever been dismissed—if, indeed, that is what BF's wording implies. The postal rider had been in England in March, 1771, presumably sent by Foxcroft, to whom BF charged a payment of £600 to Stavers. Jour., p. 33; Ledger, p. 20; BF's bill of exchange, March 4, 1771, APS. At that time Stavers must have had the conversation that was the basis for his taking BF's name in vain.

of £389 (or thereabouts) in my own Wrong, having before paid
it for you to the General Post Office. I hope that since you have
receiv'd your Books and look'd over the Accounts you are satisfy'd
of this. I am anxious for your Answer upon it, the Sum being large,
and what cannot prudently for you [or] me be left long without an
Adjustment.[9] My Love to my Daughter, and Compliments to your
Brother.[1] I am ever, my dear Friend Yours most affectionately
                                                    B Franklin
Mr Foxcroft

To Thomas Bond   ALS: American Philosophical Society

Dear Sir   London, Feb. 5. 1772
    I received your Favour by Mr. D. Kuhn, but being then just
setting out on a Tour thro' Ireland and Scotland, I had not time to
answer it, Mr. Kuhn I believe went directly to Sweden. I shall, if
he returns hither while I am here, gladly render him any Service
in my Power.[2]

9. This financial imbroglio apparently went back six years. In 1766 BF paid
out of his own pocket £389 10s. 0½d. that Foxcroft owed the Post Office; the
next month he entered a payment from Foxcroft in the same amount; when
the two were together in England in 1770, BF paid him £389 0s. 10d.: Jour.,
pp. 9, 10, 24; Ledger, p. 20. The correspondence that followed these three
transactions suggests that in 1770 BF forgot the first one and hence believed
that the second, with which he had reimbursed himself, should instead have
been credited to Foxcroft's account with the Post Office; the third transaction, therefore, settled what he thought he owed his friend. He soon recognized his mistake, if our reconstruction is correct, and pointed it out in his
missing letter of Nov. 7, 1770, to which Foxcroft replied that he had taken
note and would credit the sum to him in their private account: above, xviii,
7. BF's letter of April 20, 1771, is also missing, but his reference to it here
indicates that he had not understood Foxcroft's acknowledgement. He returned to the matter in his letters to him below, Aug. 22, Oct. 7, and Dec. 2;
and the two did not reach a meeting of minds until BF's letter of March 3,
1773. Final settlement of their accounts was postponed until Oct., 1776:
Ledger, p. 11.
    1. For BF's "daughter" see Foxcroft to BF above, Feb. 2. Thomas Foxcroft,
the Philadelphia postmaster, has frequently appeared before.
    2. The Rev. Daniel Kuhn, who was on his way to the University of Upp-
sala, had carried Bond's letter to BF printed above, xviii, 164–7.

I suppose your Son Richard will spend some Time in London, where, by what I have heard, Physic and Surgery may be studied to as great Advantage as in any Part of the World, by attending the Anatomical Lectures and Hospitals, conversing with the most eminent Practitioners, and Reading under their Advice and Direction: And yet the general Run is at present to Edinburgh; there being at the Opening of the Schools when I was there in November last, a much greater Number of medical Students than had ever been known before. They have indeed a Set of able Professors in the several Branches, if common Opinion may be rely'd on. I who am no Judge in that Science, can only say that I found them very sensible Men, and agreable Companions.[3] I will endeavour to obtain Sir John Pringle's Advice in the Affair, as you desire. Every Wednesday Evening he admits young Physicians and Surgeons to a Conversation at his House, which is thought very improving to them. I will endeavour to introduce your Son there when he comes to London. And to tell you frankly my Opinion, I suspect there is more valuable Knowledge in Physic to be learnt from the honest candid Observations of an old Practitioner, who is past all Desire of more Business, having made his Fortune, who has none of the Professional Interest in keeping up a Parade of Science to draw Pupils, and who by Experience has discovered the Inefficacy of most Remedies and Modes of Practice, than from all the formal Lectures of all the Universities upon Earth. I like therefore a Physician's breeding his Son to Medecine, and wish the Art to be continued with the Race, as thinking that must be upon the whole most for the Publick Welfare.

When I was last at your House I observed that the Paint of the Picture you had was all cracked. I complain'd of it to the Painter. He acknowledged that in that Picture, and three others, he had made Trial of a new Vernish, which had been attended with that mischievous Effect; and offer'd to make Amends, if I would sit to him again, by drawing a new Picture gratis, only on this Condition, that the old one should be return'd to him. I wrote this to Mrs. Franklin, who should have acquainted you with it, but I sup-

3. BF had distinguished acquaintances in the medical faculty, among them Drs. Black, Cullen, and Russell; see BF to WF above, Jan. 30. Bond, in the letter just cited, had discussed medical schools where his son might study; but Richard stayed at home, and died soon afterward.

pose forgot it.[4] He was 5 or 6 Years in finishing it, having much other Business. If therefore you like the new one best, please to put the old one in a Box, and send it by the next Ship hither, as the Painter expects to have one or the other returned.

Mr. Small, an ingenious Gentleman, now gone to Jamaica, has bequeath'd to our Society some Journals of the Weather which he kept here with great Accuracy, which I shall send you as soon as they come into my Hands. With this you will receive a Circular Scheme for noting the Variations of the Barometer, and comparing them in different and distant Places, which he recommends to be used by the Members of the Society that inhabit different Provinces, as he conceives that some curious and useful Discoveries in Meterology may thence arise. I send also a Box from Mr. Ludlam,[5] containing some Books which he presents to the Society; a Parcel with some Books presented by Mr. Forster, another with two Volumes of the Philosophical Transactions presented to our Society by the Royal Society here,[6] in Return for the Volume you sent them. I inclose Mr. Forster's Letter, a Letter of Thanks from the Society of Arts, and a Letter from Mr. Ludlam. Dr. Smith, in a Letter which came with the Books, gave me to expect another Box with Copies for the learned Societies abroad; and a few spare ones for my Friends; but they are not yet come to hand; and I am often ask'd by the Curious how it happens that none are to be bought here. I hope soon to receive them, and have no doubt but it will procure us the Correspondence of those Societies.[7]

4. For the difficulties with Benjamin Wilson's portrait of BF see above, XVIII, 204.

5. BF here appended a marginal note: "Mr. Ludlum is a most learned Man and ingenious Mechanic. You will be so good as to communicate his Letter to Mr. Rittenhause." David Rittenhouse needs no introduction; for the Rev. William Ludlam see above, XII, 327 n, and for Alexander Small, IX, 110 n, and his letter below, April 13.

6. Ludlam's gifts were four books on astronomical observations and kindred subjects; the Royal Society sent vols. LIX and LX of its *Phil. Trans.*: APS, *Early Proceedings*... (Philadelphia, 1884), p. 72. For Forster's contributions see above, XVIII, 274–5.

7. William Smith, secretary of the APS, had sent BF some copies of the first volume of its *Trans.* for distribution to the Royal Society, the Society of Arts, and other recipients. He had promised more, primarily for European learned societies, but the second consignment was delayed for a year. See above, XVIII, 95, and Smith to BF below, May 16.

I thank you for the inaugural Dissertation, and am pleas'd to see our School of Physic begin to make a Figure. I know not why it should not soon be equal to that in Edinburgh. I am much obliged to the young Gentleman who has done me the Honour to inscribe his Performance to me. I wish him the Success his Ingenuity seems to promise him.[8]

My Love to Mrs. Bond and your Children. I condole with you both most sincerely on the great Loss you have lately sustained.[9] With the truest Esteem and Regard, I am ever, my dear Friend, Yours most affectionately   B FRANKLIN

The Parcels are in the Care of Mr. Bache.

Dr Thomas Bond

Notation: Dr Franklin's Letter to Dr Bond on divers Subjects Books from Ludlam Intended presenting our 1st Vol to the Learnd Societys, as Soon as recd from Dr Smith

To Rebecca Haydock

Extract: reprinted from *The Aurora*, August 24, 1802

London, Feb. 5. 1772.

I received my industrious young friend's parcel of silk, and should very willingly have taken any necessary care to see it manufactured agreeable to your directions; but your relation, Mrs. Foster, linen draper of Bishopsgate street, who appears a notable clever woman in business, called upon me for it; and informing me that she had a friend in Spitalfields a manufacturer, who would do it in the best manner, I delivered the silk with the pattern to her, and I dare say she will forward it to you by the first opportunity after it is finished.[1] I hope it will please you as much as I shall be pleased to see any of my young country women at my return dressed in silk of their own

8. For Jonathan Elmer's dissertation, dedicated to BF, see above, XVIII, 166 n.

9. The death of Bond's daughter, Rebecca; see BF to DF above, Jan. 28.

1. Mrs Sarah Foster (BF also spelled the name Forster) was a relative by marriage of Rebecca's mother. The silk was not finally finished until November, or sent until the following February; BF then forwarded it himself to Richard Bache. See below, BF to DF, Nov. 4, 19; to Rebecca Haydock, Feb. 14, 1773.

raising. I am, my good neighbor, Your assured friend and humble servant,   B. FRANKLIN.

My respects to your good father.

Miss Haydock

To John Morgan[2]   ALS: University of Pennsylvania Library

Sir,   London, Feb. 5 1772

I received your Favour of July 6. just as I was about setting out on a Journey thro' Ireland and Scotland, chiefly with a View to establish my Health by the Change of Air and daily Exercise. This prevented my Writing till now. I thank you for the inaugural Dissertations, and am pleas'd to see our College begin to make some Figure as a School of Physic, and have no doubt but in a few Years, with good Management, it may acquire a Reputation similar and equal to that in Edinburgh. I am oblig'd to Dr. Elmer for the Honour done me and my Son, by inscribing to us his ingenious Thesis:[3] I wish him Success in his Profession, and the Reputation and Advantages attending it when judiciously practis'd.

Please to present my Respects to Mrs. Morgan, and to good Mrs. Hopkinson and her Family, of whose Welfare I am always glad to hear.[4] With great Esteem, I am, Sir, Your most obedient humble Servant.   B FRANKLIN

Addressed: To / Doctor Morgan / Philadelphia / per / Capt. Falconer

Endorsed: from Mr Franklin Feby. the 5: london

2. The founder of the medical school of the College of Philadelphia; see above, IX, 374 n; XII, 203 n.
3. See BF to Bond above, Feb. 5.
4. Mrs. Hopkinson was Morgan's mother-in-law; for a sketch of her family see above, XII, 125 n.

65

From Mary Bache[5]

ALS: American Philosophical Society

[Dear] Brother   Preston Feby: 5 1772

I receiv'd your kind, and agreeable preasant, which gave us all great pleasure it is so like the original. You cannot imagine with what pleasure we look at it, as wc can perceive in it, the likeness of my Son, as well as your Self.[6] My daughter Marther told Mr. Atherton[7] that Doctor Franklin was come, the Next Morning he came down, and ask't wather the Doctor was up, and when you was produced, it made us all very Merry. You are sume times in the dineinroom, and other times in the parlor, ware we vew it with pleasure.

I think it is now time, to return my hearty thanks for it, and the oysters, you was so kind to send, they was very good and acceptable to us all.

My Daughters[8] Joyn with me in kind love and best respects to you, my Son, and good Mrs. Stevenson. [*Torn*] and Mr. Atherton, desiers to be kindly [remembered?] to you from Dear Brother Your affectionate Sister and humble Servant: MARY BACHE

Addressed: To / Benjamen Franklin Esq: / Craven Street / Strand / London

Endorsed: From Mrs Bache, Preston

5. The mother of BF's son-in-law, Richard Bache.

6. Probably one of the Edward Fisher mezzotints of Mason Chamberlain's portrait, for which see above, x, frontispiece; XIV, 215 n. For the resemblance between BF and Richard Bache see above, XVIII, 258.

7. Possibly Richard Atherton, who had been an alderman and was subsequently mayor of Preston: Henry Fishwick, *The History of the Parish of Preston . . . in the County of Lancaster* (Rochdale and London, 1900), p. 80. Richard and Harry Atherton were old friends of the family: Lydia to Richard Bache, April 10, 1759, APS. About Harry we know nothing.

8. Richard had four sisters living at the time: to BF below, Oct. 6. One was Martha, mentioned here; two others were Lydia and Anna Maria, who were alive five years later when their mother died: James Theobald to BF, Nov. 7, 1777, APS. Anna Maria was doubtless the Nancy Bache to whom BF gave a ring, costing £3 10s., in 1772: Jour., p. 43. Of the fourth sister we have as yet found no trace.

To [Stephen Crane⁹]   Copy: Yale University Library

Sir   London Feby. 6. 1772

After the Recess of Parliament the great Off[icers] of State generally go into the Country, and no publick Business except what may be immediately necessary, is done or taken into Consideration till the next Session brings them together again. Being much Confind to the town by business in the Winter I Usually take the Opportunity of the recess to make a Journey of two or three Months with [visits and?] Daily Exercise in the open air to recover and Establish my health. I was accordingly absent when your Respected Letter of June 22d. arrived here. I return'd just before the meeting of Parliament and take this first Convenient Opportunity of Acknowledging and Answering it.

I was much concern'd at the Disallowance of your paper Money Act, thinking the reasons against it not well founded and that it was impossible to conceive [of them;?] indeed I told their Lordships at the board of trade that the Parliament could never mean by their Restraining Act to Exempt the Treasurer of any Province or the trustees of the Loan office from being Oblig'd to receive and take [up their notes?] or Bills they had [emitted?].

Their answer was, that the words of the act were ag[ainst] the Bills being made a legal tender in any Case [what]ever and the business of the board was to follow the Letter of the act. They were not to Judge of the Meaning or Intention of Parliament. And I am now of Opinion that if a new act be framed and Passed without the 49th Clause which obliges the trustees to receive the bills in Discharge of the Mortgages, your Agent here may be able, Especially if it provides for the troops¹ to get [it] confirm'd tho there is in truth a rooted prejudice in the Board against paper money.² If I Should be here at the time when such an act is Presented for All[owance,] you may Depend on my Using my best

9. See Crane's letter above, XVIII, 134–6, where he deals at some length with the New Jersey affairs that BF is discussing in this delayed reply.

1. For the squabble over the troops see *ibid.*, p. 270.

2. BF is endorsing a suggestion that Crane had made in his letter. For a recent discussion of the controversy in New Jersey over paper money see Joseph A. Ernst, *Money and Politics in America, 1755–1775: a Study in the Currency Act of 1764 and the Political Economy of Revolution* ([Chapel Hill, N.C., 1973]), pp. 285–93.

67

Endeavours for the Service of the Province in that as well [as in] Every other wherein its Interest is Concerned.

I am Extreamly griev'd that any Misunderstanding Should arise between the Assembly and the Governor, but I hope the same is by this time Adjusted and the Harmony between you Restor'd. With great Esteem and respect for your Character I have the Honour to be, Sir Your most Obedient and Most Humble Servant

Endorsed: B Franklin Letter 1772   B: FRANKLIN

To Cadwalader Evans

Reprinted from Jared Sparks, ed., *The Works of Benjamin Franklin...* (10 vols., Boston, 1836–40), VIII, 3–4.

Dear Doctor,   London, 6 February, 1772.

The trunks of silk were detained at the customhouse till very lately; first, because of the holidays, and then waiting to get two persons, skilful in silk, to make a valuation of it, in order to ascertain the bounty. As soon as that was done, and the trunks brought to my house, I waited on Dr. Fothergill to request he would come and see it opened, and consult about disposing of it, which he could not do till last Thursday.[3] On examining it, we found that the valuers had opened all the parcels, in order, we suppose, to see the quality of each, had neglected to make them up again, and the directions and marks were lost, (except that from Mr. Parke, and that of the second crop,) so that we could not find which was intended for the Queen, and which for the Proprietary family. Then, being no judges ourselves, we concluded to get Mr. Patterson[4] or some other skilful person, to come and pick out six pounds of the best for her Majesty, and four pounds for each of the other ladies. This I have endeavoured, but it is not yet done, though I hourly expect it.

Mr. Boydell,[5] broker for the ship, attended the customhouse to obtain the valuation, and had a great deal of trouble to get it

3. The Philadelphia Managers had sent the trunks to BF and Dr. Fothergill the previous autumn: above, XVIII, 245–7.

4. The expert whom BF had consulted the previous summer: *ibid.*, p. 159.

5. Either Josiah or James Boydell, brokers of Abchurch Lane, Lombard Street. *Kent's Directory...* (London, 1770).

managed. I have not since seen him, nor heard the sum they reported, but hope to give you all the particulars by the next ship, which I understand sails in about a fortnight, when Dr. Fothergill and myself are to write a joint letter to the committee,[6] to whom please to present my respects, and assure them of my most faithful services. I am charmed with the sight of such a quantity the second year,[7] and have great hopes the produce will now be established. The second crop silk seems to me not inferior to the others; and, if it is practicable with us to have two crops, and the second season does not interfere too much with other business in the farming way, I think it will be a great addition to the profits, as well as to the quantity.

Dr. Fothergill has a number of Chinese drawings, of which some represent the process of raising silk, from the beginning to the end. I am to call at his house and assist in looking them out, he intending to send them as a present to the Silk Company. I have now only time to add, that I am ever, yours very affectionately,

B. FRANKLIN.

To Joseph Galloway
ALS: Yale University Library

Dear Sir,   London, Feb. 6. 1772

If I complain'd of your seldom Writing, the Case is now alter'd, and you may have more Cause to make the same Complaint of me: For I find before me your several Favours of Oct. 12, and 16. and Dec. 3. and 21.[8] The last indeed came to hand but this Evening.

The Ohio Grant is not yet compleated, but the Completion is every Day expected. When it is, I shall, as you direct, draw on your Brother to re-imburse me what I may pay for your Share. I have already advanc'd £25 but that I shall not trouble him with at present.[9]

6. The letter was long delayed, and eventually written by BF alone; see below, before May 10.

7. Only a sample had been sent in 1770: XVIII, 32.

8. Only the earliest of the four, a brief note, has survived: *ibid.*, p. 232.

9. The brother, we assume, was Thomas Nickleson (d. *c.* 1793), a merchant of Poole and the husband of Galloway's sister-in-law, née Elizabeth Growden: Charles P. Keith, *The Provincial Councillors of Pennsylvania*... (Philadelphia, 1883), p. 225 of second pagination. For the £25 assessment see Foxcroft to BF below, March 2.

Mr. Jackson has communicated to me yours of Decr. 2. with the Map and Observations. The present Ideas of the Ministry seem to be, that they have been drawn in to grant too much; they suppose it 25,000,000 of Acres. Yours is a very different Account, and may be of great Use in militating those Ideas. We are much oblig'd by your Remarks. But you have been misinform'd as to our Line from Sioto to the Allegeny Mountains. You suppose it a S.E. Line; but it is a South Line. This takes in a very large Gore of Territory that you imagine to be left out.[1] Mr. Wharton I understand will explain the Boundaries more fully to his Brother, to which permit me to refer you. He is better acquainted with the Virginia Grants than I am, and thinks them much less, and that we shall have no Difficulty about the Purchase made by that Colony.[2] What Addition we may be able to obtain hereafter one cannot say, but I think there is little Chance of obtaining any at present. If we were now to propose enlarging our Bounds, it would set us afloat, and we should have all the old Delays to go thro' over again.

I think you have chang'd Governors for the better. I like the manly Plainness of your Address.[3]

I thank you for your Admonition about Writing to the Com-

1. Jackson's letter is above, under Jan. 16. But the rest of the passage bristles with problems. In the first place, what were Galloway's map and observations? They may have been based on information supplied him by Thomas Hutchins, mentioned at the end of the letter, or by Robert Lettis Hooper, who had recently returned to Philadelphia from a survey of the area in question (see WF to BF below, Oct. 29), or by Hutchins and Hooper together. In the second place, why did Galloway believe that the western border ran southeast? Hooper provides a possible clue in a letter to WF ([March, 1772,] APS) enclosing a map, since lost, on which he had "altered the lower Line, and made it...nearly South"; Galloway could have seen the earlier version of that map. The line actually ran south from the Scioto to the Wasioto Mountains, then northeast and east to the Alleghenies. In their application for the grant (of twenty, not twenty-five, million acres) the Walpole associates used Onasioto for Wasioto: above, XVII, 8–11; for the inaccuracies of the map printed there see below, p. 123 n. The gore to which BF refers was the triangle bounded by the actual line, the line that Galloway imagined, and the Wasiotos.

2. BF was referring to Samuel Wharton and his brother Thomas. For the Virginia grants see WF to BF above, Jan. 6; the purchase was of the land ceded at Lochaber.

3. For the Assembly's address to Richard Penn, who replaced his brother as lieutenant governor in the autumn of 1771, see 8 *Pa. Arch.*, VIII, 6729–30.

mittee and enclose a Letter for them. If they would have me write freely they must not suffer Copies to be taken of my Letters, which will probably be sent hither.

I am glad you have declin'd the Business of your Profession, as I believe you will find your Health improv'd in consequence of that Step.[4] I wish you would now and then make long Journeys. You would find great Benefit from them. I imagine I should have fallen to pieces long since but for that Practice. The Dry Gripes are thought here to proceed always from Lead taken by some means or other into the Body.[5] You will consider whether this can have been your Case, and avoid the Occasion. Lead us'd about the Vessels or other Instruments us'd in making Cyder, has, they say, given that cruel Disease to many. Preparations of Lead us'd to sweeten prick'd[6] Wine have done the same.

My last Tour was thro' Ireland and Scotland. In Ireland I had a good deal of Conversation with the Patriots; they are all on the American side of the Question in which I endeavour'd to confirm them. The lower People in that unhappy Country, are in a most wretched Situation, thro' the Restraints on their Trade and Manufactures. Their Houses are dirty Hovels of Mud and Straw; their Clothing Rags, and their Food little beside Potatoes. Perhaps three fourths of the Inhabitants are in this Situation; and from a rough Calculation I am of Opinion, that tho' Ireland exports an amazing Quantity of Beef and Linnen, if every Inhabitant had Flesh once a Day in his Belly, and a Shirt for his Back, they could export neither Beef nor Linnen. In Scotland things make a better Appearance, and seem on the mending Hand. Yet half the People there wear neither Shoes nor Stockings, or wear them only in Church; No wonder that Scotch Stockings are imported into America. The Gentry in both Countries live extreamly well, are a hospitable Friendly People to Strangers, and very sensible in Conversation. In many Parts of England too, the Working Poor are miserably fed, clothed and lodged. In short I see no Country of

4. BF had hoped the previous summer that his friend would not abandon both his political career and his law practice: above, XVIII, 189. Galloway must have said in one of his missing letters that he had decided to give up only the second.

5. See BF's earlier correspondence with Cadwalader Evans on this point: XIV, 312–13; XV, 51–2.

6. Sour.

Europe where there is so much general Comfort and Happiness as in America, Holland perhaps excepted: tho' it may be, some Parts of Germany or Switzerland which I have not seen are as well provided as Holland.

I shall willingly subscribe for Mr. Hutchins's Map, and I think a Number of them will sell here; but People do not much care for Subscribing.[7] With sincere Esteem and Respect, I am, my dear, Friend, Yours most affectionately   B FRANKLIN

Private

Jos. Galloway Esqr.

To Joseph Smith[8]

Reprinted from Stan V. Henkels, Catalogue No. 1452 (April 9, 1931), pp. 4–5.[9]

[London, Feb. 6, 1772]

The Parliament has open'd with a Calm in Politics, which seems to promise a quiet Session, the Opposition appearing to be in a very Declining Way. There is not Talk of any Purpose to meddle with American Affairs, either by repealing the Present Duties or adding new ones. A Peace between the Turks and Russians is supposed to be nearly concluded,[10] and no present Probability of any new Rupture in Europe. So that it is to be hoped we may have a few years Quiet, and the Publick Debt be thereby lessened.

The Royal Family is at present in great Affliction. The dangerous Illness of the Duke of Gloucester, the imprudent Marriage of his

7. Thomas Hutchins (1730–89) was a military engineer and geographer; see above, X, 210 n, and for a fuller discussion of his career the introduction by Joseph G. Tregle, Jr., to Hutchins' *An Historical Narrative and Topographical Description of Louisiana and West Florida* (Floridiana Facsimile and Reprint Series, Gainesville, Fla., 1968), pp. [v-] xlviii. The map in which Galloway and BF were interested, we presume, was one that was not published until six years later, *A New Map of the Western Parts of Virginia, Pennsylvania, Maryland and North Carolina . . .* (London, 1778); it was accompanied by a topographical description.

8. The former secretary of the N.J. Assembly committee of correspondence; see above, XVI, 256 n.

9. The reprinted text omitted the place and date and the salutation.

10. See BF to WF above, Feb. 3.

Brother, the daily expected Death of the King's Mother and above all the Revolution in Denmark attended with the Imprisonment of his Sister, are such an Accumulation of Distress, that all good Subjects commiserate their Sovereign.[11]

I was much concerned to hear of a Misunderstanding between the Assembly and Governor, I hope it is amicably settled before this time, and that Harmony restored which has been so much to the Credit of your Province.[1]

I am inform'd that it is proper I should impower some Person to receive for me the annual Allowance made by the Assembly to their Agent. I beg leave to request you would take this Trouble in my Behalf, which I shall acknowledge as a Favour, desiring you would retain in your Hands what you receive, till you hear farther from me.[2]

If in any thing I can serve you here, it will be a Pleasure to me to receive and execute your Commands: being, with great Esteem Sir, Your most obedient humble Servant,   B. FRANKLIN.

Summons to Benjamin Franklin, with Memorandum by Him
ALS and ADS: American Philosophical Society

February 6–7, 1772

Benjamin Franklin Esqr. without Deduction being on Account of the purchase and Transportation of Forage for the Use of the forces Commanded by Genl. Braddock by Warrant dated 21st. June 1755[3]——£1000

11. William Henry, Duke of Gloucester, the King's brother, had been taken ill in Leghorn late in 1771, and at times his life was despaired of; see the *London Chron.*, Nov. 7–9, 1771, and subsequent issues. For the secret marriage of Henry Frederick, Duke of Cumberland, see above, XVIII, 252. The dowager Princess of Wales died two days after BF wrote. Her youngest daughter, Queen of Denmark and Norway, had become the lover of the man who dominated the government, Dr. Johann Struensee (above, XV, 226 n); in mid-January he was overthrown and later executed, and she was imprisoned. See Hester W. Chapman, *Caroline Matilda, Queen of Denmark...* (London, [1971]), chaps. xii–xvii.
    1. See WF to BF above, Jan. 6.
    2. For what happened to BF's salary see above, XVIII, 218–19.
    3. Braddock, just before his death, had sent the warrant to BF; *Autobiog.*, pp. 217-23. For the background and ramifications of BF's involvement in

Sir   St. Mary Axe 6th February 1772.
The Sheriffs of London and Middlesex have process come into
their hands against you for not passing your Accounts of the above
Sum, to which they are to make return to the Barons of the Exchequer to morrow Morning at Westminster Hall 10. oClock
when you will please to Attend the Court to give a reason why the
Accounts are not passed otherwise the Sheriffs will be obliged to
return Issues against you. I am Sir Your most Humble Servant
                                SAMUEL SMITH[4] late Undersheriff

Addressed: Benjamin Franklin Esq / Craven Street / Strand

[*In Franklin's hand:*] Memo. Feb. 7. 1772. This is the third Sum-
mons of this kind that I have received. After the first I went, (by
Advice of my Friend Grey Cooper and using his Name) to Mr.
Blyke, Deputy Auditor,[5] and left my Accounts and Vouchers with
him, he kindly undertaking to get the Business settled for me.
There is a Ballance due to me on the Account of about £30. This
Day I again waited upon him, finding by the Summons that the
Business still remain'd undone. He took me with him to the Court
of Exchequer, where I attended in Expectation of being call'd
upon, but was not, and the Court adjourn'd.   B FRANKLIN

Note, I never receiv'd any Commissions or Gratification for my
Services, nor is my Balance paid, and yet I am every now and then
vex'd with these Summonses.[6]

---

transport for the General's expedition see above, VI, 13–22 and *passim*; VII,
226; Whitfield J. Bell, Jr., and Leonard W. Labaree, "Franklin and the
'Wagon Affair,' 1755," APS *Proc.*, CI (1957), 551–8.
   4. The deputy usher of the Lower Exchequer and a deputy chamberlain of
its Tally Court; he died in 1774. *The Royal Kalendar...* (London, [1772]),
pp. 103, 110; *Gent. Mag.*, XLIV (1774), 47. For these two offices see Francis S.
Thomas, *The Ancient Exchequer of England...* (London, 1848), pp. 54, 118,
127–9; Hubert Hall, *The Antiquities and Curiosities of the Exchequer* (New
York, [1891]), pp. 72, 81.
   5. Richard Blyke (d. 1775) was an F.R.S. and deputy auditor of the Imprest
Office in Scotland Yard. See the *Royal Kalendar* just cited, p. 104; the *DNB*;
and, for the office, John E. D. Binney, *British Public Finance and Administration, 1774–92* (Oxford, 1958), pp. 195–9.
   6. BF was never reimbursed for his £30: Bell and Labaree, *op. cit.*, p. 558.
He was vexed with the summonses because he was caught in the slow, complex, and cumbersome machinery of governmental accounting. The normal

From David Hume

ALS: Harvard University Library

Dear Sir   Edinburgh 7 of Feby 1772

I was very glad to hear of your safe Arrival in London, after being expos'd to as many Perils, as St. Paul, by Land and by Water: Though to no Perils among false Brethren:[7] For the good Wishes of all your Brother Philosophers in this place attend you heartily and sincerely, together with much Regret that your Business wou'd not allow you to pass more time among them.

Brother Lin expects to see you soon, before he takes his little Trip round the World. You have heard, no doubt, of that Project: The Circumstances of the Affair coud not be more honourable for him, nor coud the Honour be conferd on one who deserves it more.[8]

I really believe with the French Author, of whom you have favourd me with an Extract, that the Circumstance of my being a Scotchman has been a considerable Objection to me: So factious is this Country! I expected, in entering on my literary Course, that all the Christians, all the Whigs, and all the Tories shoud be my

---

procedure, presumably followed with the General's accounts, was for the Treasury to authorize payment of the bills that Braddock drew on the Paymaster General, such as the warrant to BF for £1,000. But this was only the beginning. The Paymaster General's accounts were passed by the Controller of Army Accounts and then scrutinized by the government's auditors to make sure that all the persons concerned, in this case including BF, had presented the accounts and vouchers for their disbursements. Those who had not were subject to judicial action. They were assumed to reside in London or Middlesex, and therefore the agents for such action were the sheriffs, who were accountable to the Court of Exchequer. BF was first summoned to present his accounts and vouchers, whereupon he gave them to Blyke, who seems to have neglected to inform the sheriffs. Hence the threat in Smith's letter of "issues" against BF, which could in theory have landed him in the Fleet Prison if his evidence had not turned up. For the details of this arcane procedure see Binney, *op. cit.*, pp. 174–5, 189–216, 219.

7. II Corinthians 11: 26. BF's perils by water were in crossing from Ireland to Scotland between two hurricanes.

8. For Dr. James Lind (1736–1812) see the *DNB*. Joseph Banks had invited him to be one of the scientists on Capt. Cook's second circumnavigation of the globe, and Parliament had granted Lind £4,000 for the purpose. He, Banks, and their group withdrew from the expedition in May, 1772, and went instead to Iceland; John Reinhold Forster then became Cook's naturalist. Arthur Kitson, *Captain James Cook*... (London, 1907), pp. 228–9, 234–8.

Enemies: But it is hard, that all the English, Irish, and Welsh shoud be also against me. The Scotch, likewise, cannot be much my Friends, as no man is a Prophet in his own Country. However, it is some Consolation that I can bear up my Head under all this Prejudice.[9]

I fancy that I must have recourse to America for Justice. You told me, I think, that your Countrymen in that part of the World intended to do me the Honour of giving an Edition of my Writings; and you promisd that you shoud recommend to them to follow this last Edition, which is in the Press.[1] I now use the Freedom of reminding you of it.

Pray, make my Compliments to Sir John Pringle, and tell him how much I wish for his Company; and be so good as give him a Description of the House I reserve for him in this Square.[2] If you really go over to America, we hope you will not grudge us Sir John as a Legacy. I am Dear Sir with great Truth and Regard Your most obedient humble Servant   DAVID HUME

From Jonathan and Anna Mordaunt Shipley

AL: American Philosophical Society

⟨ Before February 9,[3] in the third person and the Bishop's hand. He and his wife invite Franklin to dinner next Sunday, February 9.⟩

9. The French author, like BF's letter that quoted him, seems to have vanished without trace. Hume's anger at his enemies, particularly the Scots, was greater than this cheery list of them suggests. He was never again going to expose himself, he told another correspondent a few weeks later, to "such factious and passionate readers as this country abounds in." John Y. T. Greig, ed., *The Letters of David Hume* (2 vols., Oxford, 1932), II, 255. The passionate readers were presumably those who supported James Beattie, a professor at Marischal College, who in 1770 had launched an attack on Hume that went through many editions and was widely acclaimed at the time. See Ernest C. Mossner, *The Life of David Hume* (Austin, Tex., 1954), pp. 577–82.

1. *Essays and Treatises on Several Subjects...* (2 vols., London, 1772). Hume's hope was disappointed: no American edition of his works appeared before his death in 1776.

2. Hume's new house on St. Andrew Square was entered from St. David St., which was supposedly renamed for him. See Mossner, *op. cit.*, pp. 562–3, 565–6, 620.

3. Feb. 9 fell on a Sunday during BF's second mission only in 1766 and 1772, and as far as we know he was not acquainted with the Shipleys until 1771.

To Richard Price
ALS and draft: American Philosophical Society

Dear Sir, Cravenstreet, Feb. 11. 1772

Permit me to thank you, not only on my own Account for the Book itself you have so kindly sent me, but in Behalf of the Publick for Writing it. It being in my Opinion, (considering the profound Study, and steady Application of Mind that the Work required, the sound Judgment with which it is executed, and its great and important Utility to the Nation) the foremost Production of Human Understanding that this Century has afforded us.[4] With great and sincere Esteem, I am, Dear Sir, Your obliged and most obedient humble Servant[5] B FRANKLIN

Revd Dr Price

Addressed: To | The Revd. Dr Price | at | Newington Green

4. Such hyperbole from BF was unusual. Any book of Price's that he had not already seen might have aroused it, but his wording seems to imply enthusiasm for something recently published. In that case there are two possibilities. One is a brief pamphlet, *An Appeal to the Public, on the Subject of the National Debt* (London, 1772), which was noticed at length in the *London Chron.*, Feb. 11–13; but why this highly technical defense of the sinking fund, couched in the author's usual heavy style, should have elicited such praise we cannot guess. A second and more likely possibility is *Observations on Reversionary Payments*..., of which two editions appeared in London within a few months of each other. Both contained Price's long letter to BF printed above, XVI, 81–107, which might explain the author's sending him a complimentary copy. The first edition appeared in the autumn of 1771 and created a sensation; reviewers emphasized, as BF does, the work's unique importance and utility to the nation. *Monthly Rev.*, XLV (1771), 303–17, 344–56; *Scots Mag.*, XXXIII (1771), 542. A second edition followed in January: *London Chron.*, Jan. 9–11, 1772. Price might have sent BF a copy of either edition, but the second would seem more likely.

5. The draft has a much less formal conclusion: "I am, my dear Friend, Yours most affectionately."

From John Alleyne[6]

ALS: Historical Society of Pennsylvania

Dear Sir   11 Febry 1772
Having often experiencd the Effects of your Benevolence and
Friendship, I am emboldened to request the Favour of the Loan
of £50 'till Monday next. The Occasion of my troubling You is a
desire to pay a Sum of Money which I cannot make up without
some Assistance before Monday. If you will be so good as to send
Me a Draught enclos'd in a Letter by the Bearer it will come safe,
and on the other Side I have made a Draught which being presented on Monday (the Day on which it is dated) will be certainly paid.[7] I have the Honor to be Your Friend and Servant
                                                              J ALLEYNE

p.s. I wo'd wait on You but am very much busied.
Addressed: Doctor B Franklin

From Thomas Ronayne[8]

ALS: the Royal Society

Sir   Cecil Street Feby. 15th. 1772
In conformity to the desire of some Friends, I have drawn up
the foregoing Observations on atmospherical Electricity,[9] which

6. The English friend whom BF had felicitated on marrying young: above,
XV, 182–3.

7. Alleyne had borrowed from BF before, £10 in November, 1769, and £25
in January, 1771; both had been repaid the following December. Ledger,
p. 40. This larger loan of £50 does not appear in BF's accounts; if it was made
and Alleyne kept his promise, however, such a short-term transaction would
doubtless not have been recorded.

8. An Irish electrical experimenter, with whom BF had been intermittently
in touch for more than a decade; see above, IX, 350–2; XIII, 247–50, 468–70.
Except for Ronayne's brief note below, March 27, this is the last extant communication between them.

9. With his own observations Ronayne included two in William Henly's
hand, which the latter had sent him; the two men were working in close co-
operation. Some one, presumably the Secretary of the Royal Society, noted
on the letter that it and the enclosed observations were received on Feb. 27
and read on April 30, 1772; all were printed in *Phil. Trans.*, LXII (1772),
138–46. Henly somewhat modified the apparatus and procedure that Ronayne
had used, and continued to experiment through the year; see below, his note
of Sept. 30 and letter of Dec. 30. Investigation of what are now called elec-

I beg leave to lay before you; and shall think the trouble I have had, in prosecuting the necessary Experiments, sufficiently compensated, if it shall appear to you that they contain any thing new or curious; in which case, you are at liberty to dispose of them in whatever manner you shall think proper. I am Sir, with very respectful consideration, Your most obedient Servant.

THOS. RONAYNE

Power of Attorney to Deborah Franklin and Richard Bache

DS: American Philosophical Society

⟨February 17, 1772. Franklin empowers Deborah Franklin and Richard Bache to request and receive payment of all debts due him in America, except those owed him by William Franklin, and to take all legal actions and whatever other lawful steps may be necessary for collecting from the debtors or their executors or administrators. Sealed, stamped, and delivered in the presence of William White and Sarah Franklin.[1]⟩

To Deborah Franklin

ALS: Franklin Library, Franklin, Massachusetts

My dear Child,   London, Feb 18. [1772]
    You will receive this Line, I hope soon by our Son Bache. I wish you Joy beforehand of his Return, to live with his Family in Philadelphia.[2]

---

trical fields in the atmosphere had begun in mid-century with Louis-Guillaume Le Monnier and been carried on by BF's friends, Beccaria and Kinnersley; see Priestley, *History*, I, 421–32. Although we are solely responsible for the editing of the scientific material in the present volume, we are most grateful to Professor I. Bernard Cohen for reviewing our annotation of this and many other documents.

    1. For William White see above, XVII, 246 n; Sarah Franklin was BF's young cousin, who lived in Craven Street.
    2. Richard Bache sailed in the *London*, Capt. Chambers, which after a two-month voyage arrived in New York on April 24; Bache reached Philadelphia at the end of the month. *Lloyd's Evening Post*, Feb. 17–19; *N.-Y. Gaz. and the Weekly Mercury*, April 27; *Pa. Gaz.*, May 7, 1772.

Supposing it would be agreable to you, as well as advantageous to our Interest in the collecting of our Debts, I have joined him in a Power of Attorney with you, for that purpose.[3]

Mr. Bache will tell you all about my Health. I wrote fully to you by Capt. Falconer, and therefore now only add my Love to our Children and Friends, and that I am ever Your affectionate Husband   B FRANKLIN

From Robert Rogers[4]   AL: American Philosophical Society

Thursday Eveng [February 20, 1772[5]]
Major Rogers presents his most respectful Compliments to Doctr. Franklin, informs him that his Petition for a Tour thro' the North American Continent,[6] comes on before the Committee of Council on Tuesday next, when he hopes for the Doctrs. Interest on that affair. At the same time requests the Doctr. will inform him where Govr. Pomlin lives.

Addressed: To Doctr. / Franklin / Craven / Street

3. See the preceding document.

4. For the famous figure of the French and Indian War see above, XVII, 134–5.

5. Rogers presented two petitions to the Privy Council on this subject, almost seven years apart. The first was heard in committee on Oct. 2, 1765, which was not a Tuesday, and the second on Feb. 25, 1772, which was. *Acts Privy Coun., Col.,* IV, 739; V, 316–17. The second petition was therefore the subject of this note, and the Thursday before "Tuesday next" was Feb. 20.

6. Rogers had in mind more than a "tour." His argument in both petitions was that a navigable Northwest Passage existed, and that the only way to discover it was by exploration on land. In 1772 he hoped to obtain support for his scheme not only from BF but from the Royal Society, to which he sent a copy of his petition, differing somewhat from the final version, with a request that the Society use its influence with the government. BF was presumably supposed to transmit the copy and request to the Society, but they are among his papers in the APS. The petition itself was referred by the Privy Council to the Board of Trade, which reported pessimistically, and was then passed on to the Treasury, where it seems to have been interred. *Loc. cit.;* VI, 417–19, 510.

From William Franklin

ALS: American Philosophical Society

Honoured Father,   Burlington Febr. 28th. 1772

In your Letter of the 20th. of April last you sent me enclosed your *London* Account against the Estate of Mr. Parker, and requested me to assist in securing the Debt. I gave the Account soon after it came to hand to Miss Parker, who promised to deliver it to her Mother, and to let me have a Copy of her Father's Account against you as it stood in his Books, which, however, I did not receive till lately. Enclosed is a Copy of it.[7] I likewise apply'd to my Mother to know what Bonds she had from Parker, and what Money she had receiv'd from him; when she delivered me two Bonds, which she said was all she had, and that she had given Receipts on the back of them for all the Money she received. But I can't yet find that she has kept any Account of the Money she has received, tho' she says she thinks she has, and Mr. Parker charges for several Sums sent and paid to her, for which no Receipt is given on the Bonds. If, however, he intended those Sums to be in Discharge of his Bonds, I wonder much that when he was at Philadelphia a little before his Death, he did not see that there was proper Receipts given on those Bonds. The only Receipt on the Bond for £65 12s. 0d. Sterling is wrote by himself (Janry. 25, 1766) and signed by my Mother. There are but two Receipts on the Bond for £178 18s. 0d., and they are both wrote and sign'd by her. But I need not be more particular here, as I have made a Memorandum on a separate Paper of every thing that occurr'd to me as necessary to enable you to state your Account properly against his Estate, which Paper is enclosed.[8] The sooner this is

7. Although the surviving fragment of BF's letter of April 20, 1771 (above, XVIII, 74–7) makes no mention of his claim on the estate of his old friend James Parker, he entered it on the same date in his books, to the amount of £327 6s. 10d.: Jour., p. 34; Ledger, p. 10. His "*London* Account" must have been that ending with the date of his letter, for which see above, X, 258. The task of settling Parker's affairs had devolved upon his daughter Jenny because of her mother's infirmity, as WF explains later, and dragged on for another year; see her letter to BF and his reply below, Feb. 2, April 9, 1773.

8. WF's memorandum, dated February, is among BF's papers in the APS; it adds little to what he says here, except queries about unreceipted payments and interest due from Parker. For the complicated accounting between BF and Parker see above, X, 257–60; XIII, 13 n. The two bonds in question are

done the better, as Mrs. Parker is very infirm and leaves all to the Management of Jenny, who is about marrying, or is married to a young Fellow not of Age, and Apprentice to a Lawyer.[9] Every Thing that I can do to assist in securing the Debt, when it is ascertained, you may be assured will not be neglected. Betsy joins in Duty with, Honoured Sir, Your ever dutiful Son

WM. FRANKLIN

From John Foxcroft

ALS: Historical Society of Pennsylvania

Dear Sir   Philada. March 2d. 1772

I am favour'd with yours of Decr. 3d by the Packet which Informs me of your having just return'd from a long Journey for your Healths sake and that you find it much Strengthened by it, on which Occasion give me leave sincerely to Congratulate you.

I am extremely obliged to you for your offer of paying the £25 advanced on the Ohio affair.[1] I wrote fully to Mr. Todd requesting him to shew it to you.[2] I must own I was rather fearfull on hearing the many things I did after I return'd to America concerning that grant, but Mr. Todds Letter dated the 4th. of Decr. which is very full and Satisfactory hath determined me to continue one of the proprietors[3] and have accordingly wrote him by this opportunity

---

printed above, x, 374–5; xII, 226–7. A third seems to have escaped WF's attention, perhaps because DF had forgotten about it: xIV, 151–2, 186.

9. The young man was Gunning Bedford, Jr. (1747–1812), who later achieved considerable eminence; see the *DAB*. He was not under age, and Jenny was not about to marry him; the wedding must have taken place by the end of 1770, for when Gunning graduated from Princeton in September, 1771, she attended the ceremonies with their baby. 1 *N.J. Arch.*, xxVII, 584. For an unscrambling of the several Gunning Bedfords see above, xIII, 379 n.

1. In the previous autumn the Walpole associates had agreed to contribute £25 for each share held, in order to finance the lobbying activities of Wharton and Trent. Peter Marshall, "Lord Hillsborough, Samuel Wharton and the Ohio Grant, 1769–1775," *English Hist. Rev.*, Lxxx (1965), 728.

2. *I.e.*, show the letter; see BF to Foxcroft above, Feb. 4.

3. Foxcroft had doubtless been concerned at hearing no word of development in the Company's affairs; Todd's letter may well have hinted at the forthcoming action in the Cabinet to precipitate matters. See below, p. 124. Another factor also influenced Foxcroft's decision: Robert Lettis Hooper, the surveyor, returned to Philadelphia from the Ohio with glowing

to continue to advance for me on that account the same as for himself, but At the same time if any thing should happen to come to my knowledge which appears to me, to clash with our Interests I shall think myself in Duty bound to advise you and Mr. Todd off it in order to lay it before the rest of the associators.

I was promised two Barrells of the best Flour which could be Mannufactored in this Province to come in Osborne from three different Houses all of which have disappointed me. I therefore Have by the advise of T. Wharton bespoken two Barrells of Mr. Reed who has great Connections in the lower Countries who has promised to put it up in a perticular Manner, and therefore you may depend on it's coming by the first Vessel which sails for London after osborne, I am sorry you have it not by him but indeed it was not my fault, as I depended on Mr. T. Smith Mr. Jonathan Smith and Ziekiel Lewis but they told me the People who had promised them had none which they could recommend to come to England.[4]

Yesterday we had the Little Stranger christened by the Name of *Sarah*. Mrs. Bache and Miss Parker Dined with us Mrs. F. pleaded the coldness of the Day. I will assure you She is a Sweet little Girl, you'll Excuse a father's fondness, but if you will not give me sufficient Credit, I dare say you'll allow your Grandson to be a good Judge and to have some taste, after Tea his Mamma after placeing him on the Carpet handed little Miss into his lap and desired him to Salute Her; which after doing he Exclaimed I do now love her Mamma.[5]

I can't help fanceying after reading the forgoing I hear you say

reports about the claim. "On my representation of the country," Hooper wrote, "Mr. Foxcroft has determined to hold his share . . . ." To wf, [March, 1772], APS. For Hooper see wf to bf below, Oct. 29.

4. Foxcroft may have been referring to either of the two Thomas Whartons, for whom see above, xi, 449 n. "Mr. Reed" was probably George Read, assemblyman and attorney general of Delaware (above, xiii, 32 n); the Smiths and "Ziekiel" Lewis we cannot identify. The *Pa. Packet*, Peter Osborne, cleared Philadelphia in early March: *Pa. Gaz.*, March 5. John's brother shipped the flour in May, and another consignment in October; see below, Thomas Foxcroft to bf, May 16, Oct. 23, and bf to him, Dec. 2. bf seems to have sold the first shipment, of two barrels, for £3 1s.: Jour., p. 42.

5. For Sarah's birth see Foxcroft to bf above, Feb. 2. "Miss Parker," we assume, was Jenny Parker Bedford; but was she for some reason keeping her marriage secret?

what an amazing alteration there is in about 18 Months in an use-
less half pair of Sheers.⁶ Mrs. F. and Brother joins me in sincere
Compliments to yourself and Mr. Bache and all Friends. I am my
Dear Sir your most obliged Friend and Affectionate humble Servant
JOHN FOXCROFT

From Jean-Baptiste LeRoy

ALS: American Philosophical Society

aux Galeries du Louvre ce 5 Mars. [1772]
Je demande Monsieur à tous les Anglois que Je vois de vos nouvelles. Je vis dernierement M. Ingelhausen qui me fit grand plaisir
en me disant que vous vous portiez toujours bien ainsi que M. le
Chevalier Pringle⁷ et je vous assurre que je m'entretins de vous
deux avec lui avec une grande joie. Mais dites moi mon cher
Docteur Est ce que depuis un an il ne seroit venu ici Aucun Anglois de votre connoissance que vous ne m'avez pas fait l honneur
de m'ecrire le plus petit mot? Quand vous me recommandiez des
Anglois j'avois un double plaisir d'apprendre par eux de vos nouvelles et puis de pouvoir obliger des personnes qui venoient de
votre part. En vérité vous me devez un petit mot pour me faire
connoître la cause de votre silence. Quoiqu'il en soit me confiant
toujours dans les sentimens que vous m'avez témoignés et que je
mérite bien par les sentimens sincères qui m'attachent à vous je
vous recommande le jeune homme M. De Bassue qui vous re-
mettra cette lettre.⁸ Cest un jeune homme très bien élevé et dont
l honneteté répond à l'Education and as we Say or rather as You
Say in English a gentleman born. Il sera très flatté d'avoir l honneur de vous connoitre et si vous ou Mons. le Chevalier Pringle
pouvez lui être utile je vous en serai infiniment obligé. J'ai l honneur d'être Monsieur avec les Sentimens d'estime et d'attache-

6. A bachelor, BF had remarked to John Alleyne, was as useful as "an odd
Half of a Pair of Scissars." XV, 184.
7. If our conjectural dating of an invitation from Pringle is correct, Dr. Ingenhousz had left London early in the previous December. See above, XVIII,
259.
8. In BF's reply below, April 20, the young man's name appears as Dazoux;
but regardless of what he called himself he has eluded us.

ment les plus distingués Votre très humble et très obéïssant
Serviteur   LE ROY

Quand vous me ferez l honneur de me répondre de graces man-
dez moi qui est M. West si c'est le Président de La Société Royale
et quelle est sa réputation dans Les Sciences.[9]
Pendant que Messieurs Banks et Solander vont courir les Mers
du pole Antarctique nous nous préparons à envoyer un Vaisseau
ou plutôt 2 Vaisseaux au Pôle Arctique éxactement au Pôle pour
faire toutes les Observations d'astronomie de Physique et d'histoire
Naturelle qu'on peut faire dans ces régions.[1] Si par hazard parmi
cette foule d idées si grandes et si ingénieuses qui vous passent par
la tête vous en aviez quelques unes à proposer à nos Nouveaux
Argonautes qui vont affronter ces climâts hyperboréens envoyez
les moi et je vous réponds que si la chose est possible on fera ce
que vous desirez. Ce voyage est presque décidé et les vaisseaux
doivent partir vers le quinze de May.
A Propos de Messieurs Banks et Solander j'ai tant de consideration pour les personnes qui comme eux affrontent les hazards et
les dangers et risquent leur vie pour instruire l'Univers tandis
qu'il y a tant de fous qui l'exposent si mal à propos que si vous
voyez ces Messieurs que vous connoissez surement je vous prie,
quoique je n'aye pas l honneur d'en être connu, de leur dire combien j'ai d'estime pour eux et je fais cas de leur courage.
Je vous prie de dire même à M. Banks que l'Académie a reçu par
M. De Lauragais qui la lui a fait tenir la lettre qu'il lui a envoyée.[2]

9. James West was indeed the President of the Royal Society, and had been
since 1768; he was, as BF pointed out in his reply, no scientist.
1. The investigation of a supposed continent in the Antarctic was the purpose of Captain, now Commander, Cook's second voyage, which began the
following July. Banks and Solander (above, XVIII, 209 n) were expected to
accompany him, but went to Iceland instead; see Hume to BF above, Feb. 7.
The French Arctic expedition was presumably that proposed by Louis-
Antoine de Bougainville (1729–1811), which was abandoned for lack of
funds; see Maurice Thiéry, *Bougainville, Soldier and Sailor* (London, [1932]),
pp. 258–60.
2. Banks's letter seems to have vanished; if it was intended for the *Mémoires*
of the Académie des sciences, it does not appear there. Its subject, we conjecture with some confidence, was Banks's previous voyage with Cook. That
expedition was much in the public eye at the moment, and Lauraguais was in
touch with Banks about publishing an account of it in Paris; see Edward

Vous entendez trop bien notre langue pour que je vous fasse des excuses de mon Griffonnage François.

Addressed: A Monsieur / Monsieur Franklin député / des Colonies Angloises, de la Société / Royale de Londres &c / a Londres

From John Huske[3]   ALS: American Philosophical Society

Dear Sir,   Paris 10th. March 1772
The enclosed Letter will fully disclose to you the Plan and the views of the Gentleman, who designs himself the honor of delivering you this. They, however crude and indigested from my hurry, pruned and dressed by your judicious Pen before they are presented, and your being so obliging as to accompany Mr. O'Gormand to Lord Clare on the occasion; I cannot but pursuade myself, added to the importance of the Subject to the whole British Empire, will produce in some mode, tho' perhaps not in ours, what every British Subject must wish to see put in train of Success.[4]

Smith, *The Life of Sir Joseph Banks...* (London, 1911), pp. 27–8. Louis-Léon-Félicité de Brancas, Comte de Lauraguais (1733–1824), was a member of the Académie but scarcely a scientist, or the sort of man who might be expected to be a messenger from Banks to LeRoy. The Count was an aristocrat with voracious curiosity, who was equally celebrated for his Anglophilia, his wit, and his love affairs.

3. A former merchant from Boston, Mass., M.P. for Maldon, protégé and secretary of the late Charles Townshend, economic adviser to BF on colonial trade, and a thoroughly unscrupulous adventurer. See above, XI, 444 n; XIII, 130 n; XV, 249–50; Namier and Brooke, *House of Commons*, II, 658–62.

4. Huske was introducing to BF Thomas O'Gorman, who had studied medicine in France, served in the French army against the British, and been made a chevalier. He was an antiquarian and genealogist by avocation, but his principal activity was exporting wine to Ireland from his Burgundian vineyards. Maurice Lenihan, "The Chevalier O'Gorman," 4 *Notes and Queries*, III (1869), 74–5; Richard Hayes, *Biographical Dictionary of Irishmen in France* (Dublin, 1949), pp. 231–2. The Chevalier's Irish connections were doubtless the reason why Huske wanted him introduced to Viscount Clare, a critic-turned-admirer of BF (above, XIII, 134 n; XIV, 123 n); Clare had been ousted from the Board of Trade four years earlier, but was a vice-treasurer of Ireland and a supporter of the ministry. O'Gorman clearly wanted to use him for an introduction to Whitehall, where he hoped to obtain a government subsidy to encourage wine-growing in the colonies. Two MS fragments

If the plan is relished by the Ministry so far as to give this
Gentleman encouragement to go to America, I have taken the
liberty to assure Him that you will favor Him with your best advice on the occasion, and oblige with Letters that will be of real
service to Him with your friends in Pennsylvania, N. Jersey,
Maryland and Virginia.[5]

I make no apology to you for this presumption, knowing you
have the subject at heart, as much as the proposer, or myself; and
shall finish with a confidence that you will afford all the assistance
in your power to so laudable an undertaking, and honor the
Bearer with your friendship; and not the Less so because He is
recommended to you by him, who has the happiness of being ambitious to approve himself, on all occasions, Dear Sir Your Most
Obedient and Very Humble servant   HUSKE

PS Write nothing to this Country on the occasion.[6]

Addressed: To Doctor Franklin

From William Neate[7]   AL: Historical Society of Pennsylvania

⟨St. Mary Hill,[8] March 11, 1772, a note in the third person. Hopes
Franklin will accept a dozen "New Town Pippins."[9]⟩

in BF's papers (APS) were presumably brought him by the Chevalier; one
describes the advantages of viticulture in America, and the other, in Huske's
hand, expatiates on O'Gorman's qualifications for directing the enterprise.

5. BF, in his delayed reply to Huske below, Sept. 6, concluded that the
project was impracticable in the existing colonies, but might succeed in the
new one that the Walpole Company was hoping to create.

6. Huske, when Townshend's secretary, had purportedly embezzled a
large sum from the Treasury. He had fled to France to escape prosecution,
and naturally had no wish to be traced.

7. An old merchant friend of BF, with connections in Philadelphia; see
above, IV, 115 n.

8. St. Mary-at-Hill is a street in the Billingsgate Ward of London.

9. In a letter to Mrs. Stevenson in the Hist. Soc. of Pa., Feb. 23, [1772?],
Neate had offered her the same gift of American apples.

To Lancelot Cowper[1]

ALS: Yale University Library

Sir   Cravenstreet London, March the 13th. 1772.

I was favoured by your Forwarding a Letter to me the 7th of last Month, which came in Capt. Spain, with a small Box; and you were so good as to say, the Box too should be forwarded when landed; but it is not yet come to hand. If it has been sent, I beg to know by what Conveyance, that I may enquire for it. If not I must request you would forward it by the first Opportunity, as it contains Seeds, and the Season is come for planting them.[2] Whatever Charges there may be upon it, I shall readily pay to your Order. Being Sir, Your obliged humble Servant

B FRANKLIN

Endorsed: B Franklen March 13th: 1772
Notation: To Lancelot Cowper

From John Alleyne[3]

ALS: Historical Society of Pennsylvania

Dear Sir,   17 M[arch?4] 1772

I am oblig'd to enquire in what Manner the People of Georgia usually transfer their Property in Lands, whether by the old mode of Conveyancing by *Feoffment* or by the modern Refinements of *Lease and Release, Bargain and Sale* &c.[5]

As I cannot obtain this Peace of Information from any of my

1. A Bristol merchant, for whom see Humphry Marshall's letter above, XVIII, 256.

2. Cowper had brought the box from Philadelphia with the letter just cited; the *Chalkley*, Edward Spain, cleared Philadelphia for Bristol in late December: *Pa. Gaz.*, Dec. 26, 1771. Tracing the box took time; it eventually turned up, but whether in time for the planting season BF did not say in his letter to Marshall below, Feb. 14, 1773.

3. See above, XV, 182–3.

4. This could, of course, be either March or May, and our policy is to choose the earlier.

5. The conveyancing of a freehold by feoffment, with livery of seisin, involved a public ceremony in which the donor, before witnesses, invested the donee with the land. The "modern Refinements" were later methods of transferring real property without such a ceremony. In Georgia a statute of 1768 recognized both feoffment and deeds of bargain and sale. Candler, ed., *Ga. Col. Recs.*, XIX, 96–9.

young Friends at the Temple, I trouble You with this Epistle, and shall think myself oblig'd by your Answer. I am Dear Sir Your most Obedient Humble Servant   J ALLEYNE

From William Canton[6]   AL: Historical Society of Pennsylvania

⟨Wednesday evening, March 18, [1772[7]], a note in the third person. His father, who is considerably worse than the previous Saturday, but because of laudanum in not quite so much pain, thanks Franklin for his kind inquiry.⟩

From Noble Wimberly Jones

ALS: American Philosophical Society

Dear sir   Savannah March: 18. 1772
Emboldened by the universal good Character of the bearer of this, Mr. William Stephens an Attorney at Law, a Native of the province (Grandson of a gentleman of the same name a former President of the Council here in the Trustees time) I make free to trouble you with this and to Introduce him to your kindness,[8] which I trust your goodness and regard for every worthy Man to excuse me for. Writs being Issued we have Elections going forward, Some over but whether they will be permitted to do business with any degree of honour to themselves cannot tell;[9] in case they do you'l no doubt hear from them, if not I shall again make

6. The son and subsequently the biographer of BF's old friend; see the *DNB* under John Canton.

7. Four days before John Canton's death. BF's cash book (1772, 1778–80; APS) shows that he had visited Canton, presumably for the last time, on March 5.

8. For the grandfather, a former governor of Georgia, see the *DNB*. About the grandson nothing seems to be known, at least during this period of his life; he later became attorney general of the new state, but during and after the British occupation was in trouble as a suspected Loyalist: Allen D. Candler, ed., *The Revolutionary Records of the State of Georgia* (3 vols., Atlanta, 1908), I, 119, 349, 377; III, 242, 560.

9. For the ongoing squabble between the Assembly and the executive see Jones to BF above, Feb. 2, and BF to Jones below, April 2.

free to trouble you in the Meantime a line will highly Oblige Sir With respect Your Most Obedient And very humble Servant:

N W JONES

Addressed: To | Benjamin Franklin Esqr. | Provincial Agent | for the Province of Georgia | London | per favour of | Willm Stephens Esqr

To Deborah Franklin

AL (incomplete): American Philosophical Society

My dear Child,   London, March 19. 1772
I received your kind Letters of Jany 5. and Feby. 3. and am glad to hear your Kingbird has gone thro' his second Inoculation.[1] Capt. Osborne is not yet arrived here. By this Ship I send the Curtains you write for. Mrs. Stevenson thought it best to have them made here. The enclos'd Letter to Sally will explain all. A new Bedstead is to be made with 4 Posts, not to fasten the Tester to the Cieling, which is never done here. The Toilet Cover, nicely drawn, is in the same [box with the?] Needles and Cotton to fill the Work. [I apprehend?] the Loss of the Ship and People, that I wrote from [Ireland by?]. My Love to Cousin All, who was in Luck [that he did?] not go in her.[2]
I wonder that the Picture could not [have been up?] stairs. I think it would have hung [very well in the?] Passage. It might have been more [*torn*]
I approve of your buying the [*torn*] it should be thought worth so much, [*torn*] upon it, if I remember right, in [*remainder missing*]
Addressed: To | Mrs. Franklin | Philadelphia | Via N York | per Packet | B Free FRANKLIN

1. There must have been a long delay in the second inoculation, which Sally had intended to have done as soon as her son had finished cutting teeth. See above, XVII, 153.
2. The ship was not lost but greatly delayed; for her adventures see BF to DF above, Jan. 28.

To David Hall

ALS: text, Yale University Library; cover with address, Haverford College Library.

Dear Friend,   London, March 20. 1772

I received your kind Letter of Feb. 3. containing a Note of the Moneys you have received on our Company Account since February 1770, and what you have paid to Mrs. Franklin. I am much obliged by your kind Attention to her in several Instances, and return you my hearty Thanks.

My Longing for home increases every Day, and you may probably see me, God willing, sooner than you imagine. Our Accounts, when we meet, may soon be adjusted. But tho' it is of Importance to us both to get in our Debts, I have no Conception how I shall be able to forward it; for I am persuaded you have done and are doing every thing that is practicable.[3]

I send you in a Box to Mr. Bache 6 of Dr. Priesly's new Work on Light and Colours. They cost me as a Subscriber One Guinea each, but are now sold here in Boards at a Guinea and half. Be so kind as to endeavour to sell them for me at the usual Advance. He is going on with the History of every Part of Natural Philosophy finding great Encouragement, what he has done being much approved. These are mark'd Vol. II. his History of Electricity being reckon'd Vol. I.[4]

Our Friend Strahan is grown a great Courtier as you may see by his Letters. But tho' we differ in some of our political Sentiments with regard to America, we continue our old Friendship.[5]

---

3. For Hall's ongoing and fruitless attempt to get BF to settle the accounts see the letter BF mentions of Feb. 3, above.

4. BF subscribed £22 for Priestley's *The History and Present State of Discoveries Relating to Vision, Light, and Colours* (London, 1772), and charged Hall £6 18s. for the six copies sent him, or £1 3s. apiece: *Jour.*, pp. 39–40; *Ledger*, p. 15. Priestley had hoped to write a comprehensive history of experimental philospohy (above, XVII, 155 n, 289 n), but discouragement over finances made him abandon the project; he was beginning instead his work on "airs" or gases; see his letters to BF below, June 13 and July 1, and Schofield, *Scientific Autobiog.*, pp. 108, 123–4.

5. Strahan was writing frequently to Hall, as BF obviously knew, but the letters that have survived from this period contain no sentiments about America to which BF could have taken exception. See "Correspondence

I rejoice to hear of the Health and Welfare of you and your Family. I sympathis'd very sincerely with you and Cousin Molly on the very great Loss you sustain'd in so amiable a Daughter.[6] My Love to her and your Children from Your ever affectionate Friend B FRANKLIN

This was intended to go per Capt. Loxley.

Mr D. Hall

Addressed: To / Mr David Hall / Printer / Philadelphia / via N York / per Packet /
B Free FRANKLIN

Endorsed: Mr. Franklin, March 20, 1772.

To Humphry Marshall

ALS: Yale University Library

Sir, London, March 20. 1772
    I received your obliging Letter of Nov. 27. It was forwarded to me from Bristol by Mr. Cowper, who mention'd on the Back of it, that the Box should be forwarded also as soon as it came on shore. Not receiving it in some time, I wrote to him about it, and had for Answer that it had been sent three Weeks since, and I should find it on Enquiry at Gerrard's Hall Basing Lane.[7] I have enquir'd there, and they know nothing of it; so I fear it is lost, which I am the more concern'd at, as your Observations were in it, which I am now depriv'd of. I shall however make some farther Enquiry, and write to you more fully per next Opportunity. In the mean time it is both Dr. Fothergill's Advice and mine, that you never send any thing for London by way of Bristol, that Conveyance being subject to such Accidents, but always directly hither. I am, Sir, Your obliged Friend and humble Servant

B FRANKLIN

---

between William Strahan and David Hall, 1763–1777," *PMHB*, XII (1888), 240–8.
    6. For Deborah's death see Hall to BF above, Feb. 3.
    7. For the lost box, containing seeds and Marshall's observations of sun spots, see XVIII, 255, and BF to Cowper above, March 13. Gerard's Hall was a tavern in the Cheapside area: Henry B. Wheatley, *London Past and Present...* (3 vols., London, 1891), II, 103–4.

Mr Humphry Marshal
Addressed: To / Mr Humphry Marshall / at West Bradford /
Chester County / Pennsylvania / Via NYork / per Packet / B Free
FRANKLIN

From Thomas Ronayne   AL: American Philosophical Society

Friday Morning. [March 27?[8] 1772]
Mr. Ronayne, at the request of Mr. Henly, informs Doctor Franklin that Mr. Henly wishes to see the Paper he wrote, on the effects
of Lightning on the Tabernacle, in order to render it more correct
for publication.[9]
Addressed: Doctr. Franklin

To Jane Mecom   ALS: American Philosophical Society

Dear Sister,   London, March 30. 1772
  I have this Day receiv'd your kind Letter by Mrs. Wright. She
has shown me some of her Work which appears extraordinary.
I shall recommend her among my Friends if she chuses to work
here.[1]

8. Henly wrote a paper, dated March 24, which was read before the Royal
Society on April 9; at some time between those dates he gave it to BF for his
comments and then, through Ronayne, requested its return. We are assuming
that BF received it on or about the 24th, a Tuesday, and was asked on the
following Friday to send it back.
  9. For the Tottenham Court Road Chapel, built by the Rev. George
Whitefield and commonly called Whitefield's Tabernacle, see Henry B.
Wheatley, *London Past and Present*... (3 vols., London, 1891), III, 502–3.
On March 22 the chapel was struck by lightning: *London Chron.*, March
21–4. Henly was immediately commissioned to protect it for the future with
lightning rods; he reported two days later on the damage done, and his report
was published in *Phil. Trans.*, LXII (1772), 131–6.
  1. Patience Lovell Wright (1725–86), a Quaker widow from New Jersey,
had established a reputation in the colonies for her wax models. In 1772 she
took her family to London, and promptly made a likeness of BF: *London
Chron.*, July 4–7. She later became friendly with the royal family, and during
the war acted effectively as a spy for the Americans. See Charles Sellers'
article on her in *Notable American Women, 1607–1950, a Biographical
Dictionary* (3 vols., Cambridge, Mass., 1971).

I will enquire for the Books Jenny[2] desires, and send them if I can get them.

As you are so curious to know something of Mr. Fox, I will see if I can find him out in St. James's Street. He never call'd after he left your Letter: tho' I requested he would, and told him I should be very glad to see him.

Mr. Bache is gone; and I hope near home by this time. I hope Josiah, who is on the point of going, will get safe and well to his Friends.[3] I send this Line by him, just to let you know that I continue well, and that I am ever Your affectionate Brother

B FRANKLIN

Addressed: To | Mrs Mecom | Hanover street | Boston | per Mr. Josa Williams | Q D C.

Endorsed: Dr Franklin

From Michael Collinson[4]   AL: American Philosophical Society

Manchr. Buildgs Monday [March?, 1772]
Mr. Collinson's very respectful Comp[limen]ts to Dr. Franklin and begs the favor of him to lay by Mr. Colden's Essay which Mr. C. will do himself the pleasure of calling for some Morning[5] there are also two little Volumes The Adventures of a Round headed

2. Jane's daughter, who was still unmarried.
3. Richard Bache had left some six weeks before. Josiah sailed in early April; BF's hope that he would arrive well must have been wishful thinking, for the young man died of tuberculosis five months later.
4. For Peter Collinson's only son see above, XIV, 214 n.
5. Although he was a theoretician of great note, Colden's theories were so abstruse that none of his friends could understand them, as BF had politely told him years before: above, III, 80–1, 90–1. But the old man was undeterred. This time he had sent BF a paper by way of Collinson, who acknowledged it in a letter of March 11, 1772, and explained to Colden that BF was still busy after returning from his tour of Ireland and Scotland. *The Letters and Papers of Cadwallader Colden,* N.-Y. Hist. Soc. *Coll.,* LXVI (1923), 218, where the letter is misdated 1774. We suspect that Collinson's explanation was inspired by BF as excuse for not reading what he had received, "An Inquiry in the Principles of Vital Motion," written in 1763 and still in MS today among Colden's papers (*ibid.,* p. 367); for more than a year later BF still could not make head or tail of it. To Alexander Colden below, June 2, 1773.

Indian which if Dr. Franklin can without any trouble lay his hand upon Mr. C will take with him at the same time if not, it is of no Importance in the least.

To Noble Wimberly Jones

AL (letterbook draft; incomplete): American Philosophical Society

Dear Sir,   London, April 2. 1772

I was in Ireland when your respected Favour of July 8. arrived at my House here. On my Return, which was just before the Meeting of Parliament I by a Line or two, acknowledg'd the Receipt of it,[6] intending to write more largely as soon as any Business should occur. I hoped the Petition relating to the controverted Lands[7] would have been brought forward long before this time, having been assured when it was presented that it should in its Turn come under Consideration; but such has been the Croud of more important Affairs, that the Council have as yet found no time to do any thing in it: Tho' I flatter my self, as no Solicitation is omitted, that it may be brought to a favourable Conclusion before the Season of Business is over.[8] [*Page or pages missing.*]

Your Account of the Governor's Trea[tment of] the Assembly and your self, determined me [not to?] wait upon him on his Arrival here, as [I could?] not but greatly disapprove his Conduct.[9] [And, as?] your Mode of appointing an Agent is by [an] Ordinance to which he must give his Assent, I think it not likely that I shall be continued in that Service for your Province. I shall nevertheless continue to render it every Good Office in my Power while I remain in England, which I think will not now be much longer.

The presenting of a Speaker to the King I suppose was origi-

6. For Jones's letter see above, XVIII, 167–70; it explains the second and third paragraphs of this letter. BF's first acknowledgment has not survived.

7. Claimed by Sir William Baker's estate; see Jones to BF above, Feb. 2.

8. His optimism was misplaced; see BF to Jones below, Aug. 3.

9. Sir James Wright, the governor, had sailed for England in July and had reached London by the end of August, 1771. See *The Letters of the Hon. James Habersham, 1756–1775*, Ga. Hist. Soc. *Coll.*, VI (Savannah, 1904), 155. An earlier editor has silently supplied missing words in this paragraph that differ from ours in brackets (Smyth, *Writings*, V, 390); the latter, we believe, are more probable.

nally intended that the King might know the Person from whom he was to receive the Sense of Parliament on every proper Occasion. To facilitate the Intercourse, it is probable, the Parliament might think it adviseable rather to chuse (other Qualifications being equal) a Person not justly obnoxious to the King; and then it was natural for him to compliment them by saying he approv'd their Choice. But from this it by no means follows, that without such Approbation the Speaker could not continue in his Office, as that if the House refus'd to chuse another, it would be a justifiable Use of the Prerogative therefore to dissolve them. I believe a King of England at this Day would hardly venture on such a Step; but Governors take greater Liberties, having naturally no Respect for the People, but abundance for Ministers. It is by the Arbitrary Proceedings of Governors and other Crown Officers countenanc'd by their Protectors here, that the Affections of the Americans to this Country are daily diminishing, and their Attachment to its Government in danger of being lost in the Course of a few succeeding Years.[1] As a Disunion [would?] be as Weakening to the Empire, and of course prejudicial to [*remainder missing*]

Noble Wimberley Jones, Esqr

1. In the letter to which BF is replying Jones had described the conflict between the Governor and Assembly over its choice of speaker: above, XVIII, 168–9. BF's analogy between the relationship of the King to Parliament and of a governor to a colonial legislature, however sound it may have been politically, was unsound in law, where the governor had the powers given him in his instructions. Wright and his predecessors had been instructed that the governor must approve a speaker; from the viewpoint of Whitehall, therefore, the Assembly's freedom of choice was circumscribed by a right of veto that derived from the king's prerogative. See George Chalmers, ed., *Opinions of Eminent Lawyers . . .* (2 vols., London, 1814), I, 222, 263–4, 296; II, 31; Leonard W. Labaree, *Royal Government in America: a Study of the British Colonial System before 1783* (New Haven, 1930), pp. 31–2, and *Royal Instructions to British Colonial Governors, 1670–1776* (2 vols., New York and London, 1935), I, 114. When the Assembly branded the exercise of the veto as a breach of privilege, the Governor met the challenge head on: before leaving for home he instructed James Habersham, the acting governor, to refuse whomever the Assembly first chose as speaker. Jones was chosen three times. The first two elections were vetoed, and after the third he withdrew; but the Assembly refused to rescind its action, and Habersham dissolved it. See William W. Abbot, *The Royal Govenors of Georgia, 1754–1775* (Chapel Hill, [1959]), pp. 155–9.

To [Jonathan Williams, Jr.]

ALS (letterbook draft; fragment): American Philosophical Society

[On or before April 2, 1772[2]]

[*Beginning lost*: sub]scribers they are now sold at a Guinea and half, and not under.[3] You will take such an Advance on them as you can get in reason, and pay the Money to your Aunt Mecom. My Love to her. Several Ships are arrived from Boston, without bringing me a Line from any Correspondent there.

Stick to the READY MONEY ONLY, and attend to the Printed Advice I enclose in this Letter; then there will be no doubt of your succeeding.[4] I am, Your affectionate Uncle   B FRANKLIN

To [Richard Wheeler]

ALS: Yale University Library

In November, 1771, just a year after the first sample of Pennsylvania silk had been sent to Franklin, the first consignment was dispatched to him for sale in London.[5] But this was not his only responsibility to the Managers of the Philadelphia Filature; they also wished his help in acquiring some land in the city, presumably for their establishment.[6]

2. The fragment immediately precedes, on the same page, the letter to Jones of this date.

3. BF was sending, via Josiah Williams, copies of Joseph Priestley's new work on color; see BF to Hall above, March 20, and Jonathan's acknowledgment of the books below, May 29.

4. The printed advice was from *Poor Richard*: *ibid.* Jonathan had already announced that he was selling his English broadcloths for cash only (*Boston Gaz.*, Nov. 25, 1771); for his complicated business affairs see his letter to BF below, April 10.

5. See BF to Evans above, Feb. 6.

6. We follow Jared Sparks in this assumption (*Works*, VIII, 4 n); although he gave no evidence, there is a considerable amount. BF sold the silk in April and credited the proceeds to the Managers, and at the same time he asked to be reimbursed for the smaller sum that the land had cost. To Evans below, under May 10, June 3. Instead the Managers drew upon him for the silk money and transferred it to Evans's account, leaving a surplus that represented the difference between what was paid for the land and received for the silk. Below, BF to James, June 3, and to Evans, Dec. 2. The only possible interpretation that we can see is that the Managers were assuming the cost of the land. The other evidence is that the surplus was later used to reimburse Wheeler for his services. BF to the Managers below, Jan. 6, 1773. The fact

Obtaining a clear title involved prolonged negotiations in London, and for these he retained Richard Wheeler, who was doubtless a solicitor but about whom nothing else is known. The deed was to be made out to Cadwalader Evans, and Abel James was also a principal in the deal;[7] they were acting, we believe, for their fellow Managers as well. The general outline of the negotiations is clear. A John Cook held the land, in the right of one John Stringfellow, and was offering it at a figure that more than tripled as time passed; some one named Philips, another unknown, was bidding against Evans and James.[8] Franklin here instructed Wheeler to buy at the asking price.

Sir,   Cravenstreet, April 3. 1772
   On Perusal of the Letter and Papers receiv'd yesterday from you I am of Opinion, that Cook should be agreed with. It is indeed a great Advance from £30 which he once offer'd the Right for, to £100. Sterlg. but since Dr. Evans supposes it worth £200 Currency, which is something more than £100 Sterling, I should think it adviseable to strike the Bargain, even if you find it necessary to give 10 or £15 more than Philips offers, but not to exceed 20. You will take care of the Particulars of Proof that Dr. Evans

---

that the lawyer, who as far as we know had nothing to do with selling the silk, was paid out of the proceeds strongly suggests that the two transactions were Siamese twins.

   7. See BF's letters to each of them below, June 3.

   8. The evidence, as so often, leaves much to be desired. When Philadelphia was founded, initial purchasers of land in the colony were guaranteed lots in the city. John Stringfellow, who held a 500-acre tract in Philadelphia County, received a city lot at the corner of Sixth and Vine, which by the 1740's was owned by John Cook. John Reed, ... *Map of the City and Liberties of Philadelphia with the Catalogue of Purchasers...* (facsimile republished by Charles L. Warner; Philadelphia, 1870); Nicholas B. Wainwright, "Plan of Philadelphia," *PMHB*, LXXX (1956), 164–5, 226. Cook held the 500-acre parcel as well, we presume, and BF was negotiating for the two together: Evans had the city lot surveyed (the penultimate stage in title-closing) on Nov. 2, 1772, and a year and a half later, after his death, the larger tract was surveyed in his name. 3 *Pa. Arch.*, XXIV, 13–14. The whole transaction bristles with problems. The filature is said to have been on Seventh, several blocks away from the lot in question: J. Thomas Scharf and Thompson Westcott, *History of Philadelphia...* (3 vols., Philadelphia, 1884), I, 262. Did the Managers intend to move their establishment? If so, why was the lot still in Evans' name in 1774? The records of the silk enterprise have disappeared, and the questions appear to be unanswerable.

says are requisite, and any Assistance I can afford shall be ready. I am, Sir, Your very humble Servant   B FRANKLIN

I return Dr. Evans's Letter inclos'd.

To ———   ALS (draft): American Philosophical Society

Dear Sir,   Cravenstreet April 3. 72

Yesterday we tapp'd the Porter, and found it excellent. To prevent its being wasted, we have bottled it off, having a safer Place for Bottles, and imagining that in our slow Draught it might not keep so fresh. So we are enabled Herewith to return the Cask.

How bountiful a Gratuity for half a Sheet of Paper!⁹ I can only say, that 'tis pity you are not in *fact* as in *Spirit*, a Prince.

Mrs. Stevenson joins in 1000 Thanks, and in requesting your Acceptance of some Sounds and Tongues just received from America. Her Directions for Dressing them are, to let them soak an Hour in warm Water, then (after pealing off the black Skins) put them into fresh Water and boil them as long only as would serve to boil an Egg.¹ They are to be eaten like salt Fish with melted Butter, or Egg Sauce, or Potatoes or Parsnips. That every kind of Prosperity may attend you, wishes sincerely Your much obliged humble Servant   B F

To Benjamin and Elizabeth West

AL: Yale University Library

⟨Before April 4, [1772?²], and in the third person. An invitation to dinner next Saturday, April 4.⟩

9. This slim clue perhaps justifies a conjecture about the recipient. BF could easily have replied on half a sheet to John Alleyne's inquiry about land tenure in Georgia (above, March 17), and been rewarded by the cask of porter; and Alleyne was on sufficiently good terms with the Craven Street household to account for the tone of this letter.

1. The sounds (air bladder) and tongues of codfish came from Mrs. Grace Williams, and the recipe was hers, not Mrs. Stevenson's; see above, XVIII, 263–4.

2. Between the artist's marriage and BF's return to America, April 4 fell on a Saturday in 1767 and 1772. Our predecessors did not print the invitation under the earlier date, and we are therefore assigning it to the later one.

From Jonathan Williams, Jr.

ALS: American Philosophical Society

Dear and honoured Sir   Boston April 10 1772

I am highly obliged by your Favours of the 13th and 14th Janry, with which I received the Gum, with the Amount of which please to charge my Father and I will pay him here,[3] as it will be needless to keep open 2 Accounts when one will be sufficient. After I have made the Rubbers I will take the liberty to inform you of their Success. I am obliged by your paying the Money to Mr. Warren, tho' I was afterwards sorry, I desired it fearing You would think I had taken too great a Liberty, but I did not intend you should have put the Money out of your hands, when you was in advance for my Brother; my Father will endeavour to remit you for him as soon as he can, with regard to my Uncles Money I only meant it should be so paid, in case he had offered it, and am glad you did not ask him for it.[4] I am fully convinced of the Advantages as well as Necessity of adhering to the ready Money Plan, which I am determined not to vary from, for it is certainly best, and I now feel myself happy that no Failures of Merchants can hurt me, and although it can't be expected that I should at first sell so many Goods as those who trade on Credit, I flatter myself it will in the End be more beneficial, for (as you have observed) tho' the Profits may not seem so much at First, they will finally be more, coming without the Deductions of Bad Debts, and supposing the Goods to fetch only the first Cost, (which may reasonably be supposed,) One has it in one's Power at any Time to pay all one's Debts, if there should be a pressing Occasion: but when I came from England with Goods, there was an Order from my Father on the Water, of a considerable Value, which came just after I had arived, and as neither of us knew of the others Intention, the Goods were not so well assorted, there being many Things of the same kind in both Orders, therefore I have been obliged to put of

3. Only the first of the two letters is extant; see above. BF had already, in the previous November, charged Jonathan's father with the gum: Jour., p. 37.

4. For the complicated transactions between BF, James Warren, and young Jonathan see BF to Jonathan Sr. and Jr. above, Jan. 13, and the latter to BF below, end of June and Dec. 26.

as many as I could by building a Brigantine, which is the only Instance wherein I have varied from the ready money Plan, and
which should not have done but for the above Reasons, but hope
it will turn out as well. I shall send her as soon as possible to
Champion & Dickason to be sold which if only at the first Cost,
will answer very well, as I put of the Goods for her at a good Advance. I mak a Remittance with her to them as I appropriated
only such Goods to the payment of her as came from them, and
not any of the proceeds of the Cloths.[5] Shipping I know is a precarious Business, which no person without a Capital of his own
has a right to enter into, and which I shall have no further Concerns with than I am obliged to, therefore shall get rid of the Brig
as soon as I can, and strictly adhere to the old Plan. I trouble you
with these Circumstances fearing, if you should hear of this Matter without knowing the Reasons, you would think I was sporting
with my Correspondents Property, and because I think myself
obliged to keep nothing from You, in consequence of your kind
reccommendation to Mr. Warren, whose Account is thus

Goods Received —
$£799$ $12s.$ $11\frac{1}{4}d.$ Dr — Cash you paid 82 3s. $9\frac{1}{2}d.$ Cr
Montagu's Bill 100 0s.
Sergants do 100
Bowers[6] — do 160

442 3s. $9\frac{1}{2}d.$
Ballance 357 9s. $1\frac{3}{4}d.$
$£799$ $12s.$ $11\frac{1}{4}d.$

5. Jonathan's difficulties were common at the time. A flood of British imports in 1771, after the collapse of the nonimportation agreements, glutted
the American market and brought drastic curtailment of credit the next year;
as British merchants called in their debts, their correspondents were hard hit
unless, like Jonathan, they had been trading largely on a cash basis. See R. B.
Sheridan, "The British Credit Crisis of 1772 and the American Colonies,"
Jour. of Economic History, XX (1960), 170–5; Marc Egnal and Joseph A.
Ernst, "An Economic Interpretation of the American Revolution," 3
W&MQ, XXIX (1972), 23–4, 27. Jonathan had departed from "the ready
money Plan" in regard to what he had ordered from Champion & Dickason,
the London merchants: he seems to have acquired the brigantine by bartering
the goods at a profit, in the hope of selling the ship and contents in England

(*Footnotes 5 and 6 continued on page 102*)

Which Ballance I shall pay as soon as I can; the greater part of what is already paid, is before the Term of Credit is expired, and I beleive the last Bill will be but a few Days after it, but he may depend nothing but want of Ability, shall occasion Delay, which I will do my utmost endeavours to avoid.[7]

We have had an uncommon hard Winter, by which Business has much suffered, our Streets have all the while been filled with Snow, and last Week we had as severe a Snow Storm as ever we had, near 5 foot of Snow fell and for some Days all Intercourse with the Country was prevented, at present we have fine Weather. We all expect Josiah has taken his Passage before this, therefore do not write him but please to give my love to him, if he is still with You, and tell him we are suprized that he should think my Father wished his longer Stay, as it seems so to appear by the Tenor of his Letter, it is so farr the Contrary, that we have been expecting him for some Time past, and my Father desires he would be as expeditious as possible in returning to his Friends, who are very anxious to see him.[8] I am with the greatest Respect Your dutifull and affectionate Kinsman JONA WILLIAMS

Doctr Benja Franklin

Addressed: To / Benja Franklin Esqr LLD / at Mrs Stevensons in Craven Street / Strand / London / per Calef

---

for enough to repay his creditors there. See his letters cited in the previous note.

6. The Montagu bill, we assume, was one that Jonathan had bought, drawn on the Navy Board by Rear Admiral John Montagu, the commander in chief on the American station. Sergant might have been either Epes or Daniel Sargent, father and son who were Gloucester merchants: Jules D. Prown, *John Singleton Copley* (2 vols., Cambridge, Mass., 1966), I, 113, 190–1. Bowers was perhaps Jerathmeel Bowers, a Bostonian who was involved in politics and is mentioned in Butterfield, ed., *John Adams Diary*, I, 313; II, 83.

7. He had managed to clear most of this debt by the year's end, but only to acquire a new one: to BF below, Dec. 26.

8. Josiah sailed within a day or two of when his brother was writing, and reached home in late May. See below, BF to Jane Mecom, April 13; Jonathan to BF, May 29.

To Thomas Cushing

Reprinted from Jared Sparks, ed., *The Works of Benjamin Franklin . . .* (10 vols., Boston, 1836–40), VIII, 7–8.

Sir,   London, 13 April, 1772.

I wrote to you in January last a long letter, by Meyrick, and at the same time wrote to the Committee, since which I have received no line from any one in Boston, nor has Mr. Bollan yet received the answer we wait for, respecting the eastern settlements on the crown land.[9]

The Parliament has been employed in the royal marriage bill, and other business; nothing of importance relating to America has been mentioned hitherto during the session, and it is thought that India affairs will fill up the remainder of the time, to the prorogation.[1] I have not met with Lord Hillsborough since my return from Ireland, seeing no use at present in attending his levees.[2] The papers mentioned his intention of moving something in the House of Lords relating to America, but I cannot learn there was any truth in it.[3]

9. Both BF's letters are printed above, Jan. 13, where the answer that he and Bollan were awaiting is explained; the letters went by the *Neptune*, Capt. Meyrick (Myrick, Mirick), whose arrival in Boston was announced in the *Mass. Gaz. and Boston Weekly News-Letter*, April 3, 1772.

1. The Royal Marriage Bill, provoked by the clandestine alliances of the Dukes of Gloucester and Cumberland, narrowly restricted the freedom of all descendants of George II, with a few exceptions, to marry as they chose; North pushed the bill through the House of Commons at the King's behest and in the face of strong opposition. "India affairs" came to the fore in March, when friends of the East India Company introduced legislation to reorganize the administration of Bengal; on the day that BF was writing, a select committee was appointed to look into the whole situation. See Alan Valentine, *Lord North* (2 vols., Norman, Okla., [1967]), I, 246–7, 276–7; Sutherland, *East India Co.*, pp. 230–2; Cobbett, *Parliamentary History*, XVII (1771–74), 383–6, 391–423, 454–63. BF was quite right: East India Company affairs absorbed the attention of Parliament until it was prorogued on June 10.

2. But BF had made five attempts to call on him; see his memorandum above under the end of January.

3. Neither can we. Hillsborough gave notice in March that he would soon introduce an important motion (*London Chron.*, March 28–31), but we can find no record of his doing so. On both sides of the Atlantic, however, rumors were rife that Parliament would deal with American affairs before the year was out; see Mass. Arch., XXV, 525, 535; XXVII, 283. Our guess is that

It is my present purpose to return home this summer, in which case, I suppose I am to leave your business and papers in the hands of Mr. Lee, which I shall do, if I do not receive other directions.

Upon the present plan here of admitting no agent, but such as governors shall approve of, from year to year, and of course none but such as the ministry approves of, I do not conceive that agents can be of much use to you; and, therefore, I suppose you would rather decline appointing any. In my opinion, they have at all times been of full as much service to government here, as to the colonies from whence they come, and might still be so, if properly attended to, in preventing, by their better information, those disgraceful blunders of government, that arise from its ignorance of our situation, circumstances, abilities, temper, &c., such as the Stamp Act, which too would have been prevented, if the agents had been regarded. Therefore I should think, that, if agents can be allowed here on no other footing than is now proposed, we should omit sending any, and leave the crown, when it wants our aids, or would transact business with us, to send its minister to the colonies. Be pleased to present my respects to the Committee, and duty to the Assembly, and believe me, with sincere esteem, &c.

B. FRANKLIN.

To Jane Mecom

ALS: American Philosophical Society

Dear Sister, London, April 13. 1772

I received your kind Letter by Mrs. Wright, and shall do her all the Service in my Power. I think I wrote to you by Cousin Josiah, who sailed in Acworth last Week, and I hope will get safe home to

Hillsborough attempted to precipitate a full-scale Parliamentary review of the colonial situation, aimed at far-reaching reforms. He had made a similar attempt in 1768–69, for which see Gipson, *British Empire*, XI, 234–5, 239–41. If we are right, he probably failed in 1772 for two reasons, lack of support in the Cabinet and the distraction of East India Co. affairs. Parliament contented itself at this time with two measures that specifically affected the colonies: in April the Felony and Dockyard Bills (12 Geo. III, c. 20, 24) received the royal assent.

his Friends.[4] I continue well, and purpose returning this Summer, God willing, and then may hope next Year for the Pleasure of seeing you, as 1773 is my Period for visiting Boston, having left it in 1723, and visited it in 1733, 43, 53, and 63. My Love to your Daughter, and best Wishes of Health and Happiness to you and all you love, from Your affectionate Brother   B FRANKLIN

From John Michell[5]   ALS: American Philosophical Society

⟨Tom's C. H.[6] April 13, 1772: Returns a book together with Winthrop's letter,[7] which he has ordered sent to Franklin. Is leaving town today and will not see him again until next winter unless, as Michell hopes, Franklin visits Yorkshire during the summer. If instead he leaves for America, wishes him a pleasant and prosperous voyage and happiness in his native country.⟩

From [Alexander Small[8]]

AL (incomplete): American Philosophical Society

Dear Sir   New York April 13th 1772
    Having soon dispatched all I could do in Jamaica, and having no Opportunity of returning soon to Britain from thence, I was

4. For Patience Wright and Josiah's return home see BF to Jane above, March 30.
5. The astronomer and clergyman of Thornhill, Yorks.; see above, VII, 357 n.
6. Tom's Coffee House, but which? For the three of the same name see Bryant Lillywhite, *London Coffee Houses* . . . (London, [1963]), pp. 583, 592–3, 595.
7. Doubtless the one on the aberration of light that BF had shown to Price; see BF to Winthrop above, Jan. 13.
8. Identified by the handwriting. For the Scottish army surgeon, chemist, and F.R.S. see above, IX, 110 n. He had recently been appointed co-chairman of the committee on chemistry of the Society for the Encouragement of Arts, Manufactures, and Commerce: *The Royal Kalendar* . . . (London, [1772]), p. 220. He had left England for Jamaica at the beginning of the year, was in New York in mid-April and then briefly in Philadelphia, and was back in London by early August: above, BF to Bond, Feb. 5, and DF to BF, May 14–16; BF to Evans below, Aug. 22.

tempted by a very ingenious Gentleman Mr. Shariff[9] to accompany him hither. As he purposes being in England some time this Summer, I shall give him a Letter of introduction to you.

As I gave you from Jamaica an Account of what occurred during our Passage thither, I shall now continue a Journal of our Voyage hither, which was a most disagreable one of forty six days, during which many cross Accidents happened.

As we came down from Kingston to Port Royal our Commander Mr. Tunis de la Fountanye informed us that being in Kingston harbour in the year 1764, he saw a Stream of fire descending from a small black Cloud upon Muskita Fort, which was succeeded by a Clap of Thunder, and by the Explosion of a large Magazine of Gun powder then lodged in the fort.[1] Mr. Shariff, who is much conversant in Electrical Experiments, said that when an electrical Machine is highly charged, and a Shock is then given with it, he had observed that the electrical fire proceeded in a streight line; and from thence concluded that when Lightning did any Mischief, it constantly proceeded in a streight line. I confirmed this Opinion by the instance of St Bride's Steeple.[2]

9. The only man of the name we have encountered is an implausible candidate: William Sheriff, of the 47th Foot, served in America from the beginning of the French and Indian War and eventually rose to be deputy quartermaster general and a lieutenant colonel: Worthington C. Ford, comp., *British Officers Serving in America, 1754–1774* (Boston, 1894), p. 92; William B. Willcox, ed., *The American Rebellion: Sir Henry Clinton's Narrative of His Campaigns, 1775–1782*... (New Haven, 1954), p. 557. Why he should be referred to as "Mr.," or be knowing about electrical machines, we have no idea.

1. Small's informant was undoubtedly Teunis la Mountanye, or Mountaine, master of the *Dispatch*, which cleared New York for Tobago in December, 1771, returned by way of Jamaica, and arrived the following April: *N.-Y. Gaz., and the Weekly Mercury*, Dec. 9, 1771; April 20, 1772. He had witnessed the explosion of the magazine in Fort Augusta on Mosquito Point, Sept. 14, 1763, which caused extensive damage and loss of life: *The Annual Register...for 1763* (1764), p. 113; Benjamin Wilson, *Observations upon Lightning*... (London, 1773), pp. 65–8. The "Stream of fire" appears to have been either ball lightning, a rare and mysterious phenomenon, or a stroke that hit and exploded the ball.

2. For the damage to St. Bride's in 1764 see Small's letter to BF above, XI, 544–5. Electrical experimenters had long been interested in whether lightning moved in a straight or crooked line, and from cloud to earth or vice versa; see above, IV, 256, 510.

When we were in the Latitude of 34 proceeding to the stormy Cape Haterass, a very fine Morning began at Noon to be over cast. While we were at Dinner, our Capt. started up and run upon deck to give the proper Orders. He had scarcely stept when we heard two Claps of thunder resembling two Cannons fired off quickly very near us, and then ceased instantly without that repetition of Sounds which is usual in thunder. This was succeeded by rain, and then a clear Sky. When the Capt. returned to make an end of his Dinner, we asked him the reason of his so suddenly starting up. He answered that he saw a flash of Lightning exactly similar to that which fell on Muskita fort. In the Evening Mr. Shariff and I being upon deck, observed a very black Cloud to the northward, and saw a great deal of Lightening in it, but were at too great a distance to hear the Thunder. We could evidently distinguish three different kinds of Lightning, viz: the common flash, which diffuses much Light, and is instantly gone. The next was the Zig-Zag kind which generally reached a considerable way along the Cloud. We observed one flash which darted along at least one quarter of the Sky. Does this account for the noise of the Thunders being heard for a considerable time, and lessening as it goes to a greater distance; as well as it does for our Cannon Shot the flash being then in a Spot? The third kind is that Stream of fire which our Capt. Saw. We saw a faint one in the evening, extended from the Sea to the Cloud; and in about a quarter of an hour, we saw another Stream of clear fire, reaching in the same manner; in a continuous fire. We did not see from which it took its rise.[3] From this dark Cloud, other Clouds extended themselves over the whole Sky, tho' on one Side, directly against the wind, with that mixture of light and darkness peculiar to thunder Clouds; and soon produced a total darkness especially as Night was approaching; but a darkness which was at times abundantly enlightened by almost continued flashes of Lightning. About eight O'Clock the Mate, who had the Watch on deck, called out with astonishment that a Stream of fire descended from the Sky to the Sea, as large he thought as his wrist. What between the Lightning, thunder, and luminous appearance in the Waves which broke every where

3. The three forms of discharge that Small is describing are now known as sheet, air discharge, and streak lightning. For BF's earlier speculations about lightning over the ocean see above, III, 367–71; IV, 257–8.

around us, I assure you the Night had a most tremenduous Appearance.

A few Nights after this Storm another, so violent, came on, that we could bear no Sail, but as the Sailers express it lay a Hull. This was not attended with thunder; but the Sea was in the most luminous state I ever Saw it, which our Capt. imputed to our approach to the Shore. The whole surface of the Sea being covered with breakers, appeared as if all on fire: and as the Sea broke over us every minute, and the Spray ascended on the Masts and Rigging, both Deck and rigging seemed to be constantly on fire, which gave so clear a light that a pin might have been picked up on the Deck. The Vessel and we appeared like Salamanders living in the midst of Flame.[4]

In these violent Storms there frequently appears a Phenomenon which the Sailors call a Comet, this is a ball or balls of fire or of some luminous Substance, which play up and down the Masts, and Sometimes remain Stationary at the Mast head. The Sailors observe that when they descend and disappear the Storm is on the decline. Our Capt. relyed so fully on this Circumstance that so soon as he saw the Comet descend and appear no more, he went to Sleep, being fully satisfied that no farther mischief would happen. Mr. Shariff and I differed in Opinion as to the Cause of this Phenomenon. There are in the Sea many gelatinous Substances which seem to be animals by their change of posture at pleasure. They have a peculiar luminous appearance in the Night, as several other fish have. He was of Opinion that the balls were some Animals of that kind which were thrown up by waves, and preserved their luminous appearance for some time. I alledged that if so, their Appearance would not cease but with the Storm; nor could it be the common luminous Substance, for its Shining ceases the Moment the Agitation of the Sea water ceases. Sub Judice Lis est.[5]

4. Small's vivid description of phosphorescence touched on a subject about which scientists had been speculating for more than a century. BF had put forward a theory and then disproved it himself; he had subsequently adopted James Bowdoin's explanation, which turned out to be the correct one, that luminous microscopic animals in the water caused the "sea light." See above, III, 367; V, 68, 113–15, 155.

5. Horace, *Ars poetica*, 78, which may be freely rendered as "the matter is still in dispute." Small had reason to disagree with Sheriff, who was confus-

I do not know that the perpendicular height of the Waves of the Sea has been yet ascertained by any Accurate Experiments. Our Capt. relates the following facts. On the Bar of Canso Bay⁶ there are four fathoms Water in calm Weather. Passing over the bar in a great Storm, he kept the lead going constantly, and found that when on the top of a Wave, he had five fathoms; and in the hollow between the Waves, he had only three. When we approached the Coast of your Country, and were got within Sounding, a Storm came on, which brought us to our bare poles. In this Condition a Vessel has little progressive Motion, and on that account, our Capt. had a fair Opportunity of ascertaining exactly the difference of depth between the top of a wave and the hollow between two. He took the lead line in his own hand, and found that when on the top of the Waves, he had forty four fathoms of water, and when in the hollows, scarcely forty. The Sea did not at this time run so high as in the former Storms, for it was not of so long continuance.

I was once in a gale of wind in the Bay of Biscay, and there [?] I keep greatly within truth when I say that the waves were at least a third higher than any waves I had seen during this passage and the distance between the Waves in a much greater proportion. The reason may be that the Waves on your Coast had a much less space to run, the Strongest Winds being generally off Shore. When in the Bay of Biscay, we met a Ship and when both were on the tops of the Waves, we could easily speak to one another. I cannot now be positive how many waves we were asunder, I think not above two, or three at most, but when both descended into the

___

ing phosphorescence with St. Elmo's Fire. BF had done the same thing years before, but had soon come to an explanation that was, like Small's, much nearer the truth: above, III, 473; IV, 143. The luminescence is produced by electric discharge from points on the ship, such as the masthead, in the presence of an electrified cloud, particularly when it is directly overhead. The phenomenon is in essence the same as that demonstrated by Henly in his experiment above, XVIII, 19–20. By the time the cloud is above the ship the wind and seas have moderated, and the worst of the storm is over; hence the appearance of St. Elmo's Fire has been regarded since ancient times as a good omen. See Sir Basil Schonland, *The Flight of Thunderbolts* (2nd ed., Oxford, 1964), pp. 47–50.

6. Canso, Nova Scotia, is on Chedabucto Bay, and the bar was presumably at the entrance.

hollows at the same time, neither of us could see the tops of one another's Masts.[7]

You See your Country gave us a very unkind Welcome, for we were Sixteen days from Cape Haterass to New York, and in almost continual Storms.[8] Your World is formed on a grander Scale than ours. Your Mountains are more lofty, your Lakes more extensive, your Rivers larger, and your Storms more violent than with us. The Truth of the latter we have abundantly experienced. Here we are cast a Shore in Wintery weather, the Snow lying on the ground, and no Signs of Vegetation yet appearing.

In Order to give the whole that related to Lightning together, I passed over a considerable part of our Voyage, during which, two remarkable circumstances occurred. When we had got to the West end of Cuba, we were Sensible that the Current carried us to the Northward, and, as we supposed, into the Gulph of Florida. When in the Latitude of 23, the Current made a difference in a day of twenty miles between our Log and Observation; and next day, a difference of 40, when we got beyond the lat: of Cape Florida tho' we steered both day to the S:E: against a strong Easterly wind, endeavouring to make the Island of Cuba. From thence we judged that [the] Current of the Gulph Stream had carried us into the Gulph without seeing the Island of Cuba. The next day we found we were carried still to the Northward more than our log gave. Next day our Observation and Log agreed; but the two following days we found by our Observations at Noon that we had rather lost of our Northing. This allarmed us, but we accounted for it by Supposing that we had got too near the American Shore, and so into an Edie formed by the Gulph Stream.[9] Luckily for us, we next day saw a Ship the Master of which informed us, that he had left Pensacola the day before and [*remainder missing*]

7. BF, as Small may well have known, had long been interested in the physics of waves and wind. See above, IX, 212–16; X, 93–4.

8. They were lucky to get through unscathed, for numerous ships did not. The papers were full of reports of those lost or damaged; see for example the *N.-Y. Gaz.*, and the *Weekly Mercury*, May 4.

9. Small undoubtedly knew that details of his voyage would be welcome because of BF's long-standing curiosity about the effects of the Gulf Stream upon navigation, for which see above, III, 67–8; X, 94; XV, 246–8.

To Jean-Baptiste LeRoy

AL (draft[1]): American Philosophical Society

Dear Sir,   London, April 20. 1772

I received your Favour of March 5[2] per M. Dazoux, and shall be glad of any Opportunity of doing him Service. It gave me great Pleasure to learn by him, that you are well and happily married, on which I give you Joy.[3] 'Tis after all the most natural State of Man.

Mr. West our President concerning whom you make Enquiry, is esteemed as a good Antiquarian, but has not distinguish'd himself in any other Branch of Science. He is a Member of Parliament, was formerly Secretary to the Treasury, and is very rich.

I am glad to hear that a Voyage is intended from France to the North Pole. The World owes much to the noble Spirit with which your Nation pursues the Improvement of Knowledge, and to the Liberality with which you communicate what you acquire to the rest of Mankind. I hope your Philosophers on that Voyage will be able to discover more clearly the Cause of the Aurora Borealis, and a Passage round the North of America.

I suppose Care has been taken to make their Ships very strong, that they may bear thumping among the Ice. My best Wishes will attend them, for their Success and safe Return.

Messrs. Banks and Solander, are to sail with two Ships in about a Fortnight, for the South. They expect to be out near 4 Years. They present their Compliments, and are pleas'd with the Notice you honour them with, in your Letter to me. Sir Jno Pringle continues well and presents his respectful Compliments to you. I am with the most perfect Esteem, Dear Sir &c.

M. Le Roy

1. We have silently supplied a few illegible words from Smyth, *Writings*, V, 393–4.

2. Above, where most of the matters mentioned in this letter are discussed.

3. Little is known about the marriage, or about the bride at that time. She mentioned in a later letter to BF (Jan. 1, 1778; APS) that her father was the comte de Milly: Nicolas-Christien de Thy, comte de Milly (1728–84), who after a distinguished military career retired to study science. [Louis M. Chaudon,] *Dictionnaire historique, critique et bibliographique...* (30 vols., Paris, 1821–23), XIX, 103. BF, during his French mission, saw a good deal of Mme. LeRoy; see Claude-Anne Lopez, *Mon Cher Papa: Franklin and the Ladies of Paris* (New Haven and London, [1966]), pp. 211, 213–15, 222–4.

William Temple Franklin to Jonathan Williams, Jr.[4]

ALS: American Philosophical Society

Dear Jonathan.   London, April 25th 1772
I am sorry I could not have the pleasure of writing to you before now, but I hope this letter will find you in good health. I go to Morrow to Mr. Hewson's to celebrate William Hewson's birth day;[5] he is one of the finest Boys imaginable. I have nothing more to say at present than that Dr. Franklin Mrs. Stevenson and Sally are well and join in best respects with your humble Servant
WILLIAM TEMPLE.

From Anthony Benezet

ALS: American Philosophical Society

The writer of this letter has hitherto appeared only incidentally. Anthony Benezet (1713–84), philanthropist and author, was born in France and educated in England, and became a Quaker as a boy; soon afterward he moved to Philadelphia, where he was first a merchant and then a teacher. From the 1750's until his death he labored to impress upon the world in general, and the Society of Friends in particular, the iniquity of the slave trade.[6] The opening sentence of this letter makes clear that he had already been in touch with Franklin; but none of the earlier correspondence has survived, and subsequent letters are few and far between.

Yet this relationship with Benezet was a factor, among others, in changing Franklin's attitude toward slavery. He had long been aware that the institution had grave disadvantages, but not that it was iniquitous. In his earlier years he had printed advertisements of slaves for sale and had bought them himself;[7] more recently he had published a de-

---

4. This is the earliest surviving letter between the two. They had become acquainted during Jonathan's stay in Craven Street; he was twenty-one at the time. WTF was probably twelve; see above, XIII, 443 n.

5. His first; see above, XVIII, 91.

6. DAB; George S. Brookes, Friend Anthony Benezet (Philadelphia and London, 1937); Arthur Zilversmit, The First Emancipation: the Abolition of Slavery in the North (Chicago and London, [1967]), pp. 74–5, 85–90.

7. For samples of advertisements see above, I, 186, 272, 378; for BF's slaves see VII, 203; VIII, 425; XII, 45 n. BF's objections to slavery in "Observations Concerning the Increase of Mankind" were partly economic, partly xenophobic: above, IV, 229–31, 234.

fense of American slaveholders and had campaigned in Whitehall for Georgia's slave code.[8] He had realized for a decade, however, that Negroes were not innately inferior human beings.[9] They were warped by slavery, and he was concluding that the institution should be gradually eliminated.[1] The process of conversion was under way that made him, at the end of his life, as convinced an abolitionist as Benezet himself; and in this process the Quaker played his part.[2]

Philadelphia, the 27th. 4th Month 1772
Dear Friend Benjamin Franklin
   Thy affectionate letter, by Capne. Falconer, gave me great pleasure. To hear of the welfare of a real friend and fellow traveller on a dangerous and heavy road, affords great comfort to a fellow pilgrim. The hopes of having soberly to converse in the winter evening on past dangers and better future prospects, affords an agreable sensation; but in the mean time, I am solicitous, that our present diligence may, as thou observes, furnish a comfortable reflection, that in the day time we did what we could, towards carrying on the great and good designs of the father of the family. Now as thy prospect is clear, with respect to the grievous iniquity practiced by our nation, towards the Negroes I venture to take up a little more of thy time, tho' with reluctance, being persuaded thou hast full business on thy hands, earnestly to request, thou would'st deeply consider, whether something may not be in thy power towards an effectual step, and a kind of basis lay'd for the removal in time (if not at present) of that terrible evil. When I sent the tracts on the Slave-Trade to thee I also sent to some of the most weighty of our Friends, in London vizt. Doctr. Fother-

8. Above, XVII, 37–44, 137, 203.
9. His work with the Associates of Dr. Bray had convinced him, as early as 1763, that Negro children were as promising as white: above, X, 395–6. Free adults were improvident and poor, he declared in 1774, only because they were uneducated: Smyth, *Writings*, VI, 222.
1. In 1769, when he reprinted his essay on population of 1751, BF made a significant change of wording that indicates a change of mind: slavery, and not nature, was responsible for the slaves' shortcomings. Above, IV, 229 n. His first attack on the institution itself was in "The Sommersett Case and the Slave Trade" below, June 18.
2. Along with other Friends who were working for the same goal as Benezet. See Arthur S. Pitt, "Franklin and the Quaker Movement against Slavery," Friends Hist. Assn. *Bulletin*, XXXII (1943), 13–31.

gill, Thos. Corbin, John Elliott, Mark Beaufoy &c and now to David Barclay, Thoms. Wagstaff &c[3] persons whom I thought might be men of the most interest, whom I requested to consider whether it might not be the duty of our Friends, either as a body or some particulars joining, to lay the iniquity and dreadful consequence of the Slave Trade before the Parliament, desiring a stop may be put to it: which I apprehend is more especially their duty, as the Members are their representatives, in the election of whom, many are active. But I am fearful least the fear of acting in so unpopular a cause or the prevelancy of that unfeeling disposition, for the miseries of others, which so much prevails, in this age, may prevent the matter's being sufficiently considered. Now dear friend what I would earnestly request is, that thou wouldst let, not only the deep sufferings and vast destruction of these our deeply distressed fellow Men; but also the corrupting effects it has on the hearts of their lordly oppressors, be, as the scripture expresses it, precious in thy eyes.[4] I will grant thou must expect to meet with dissagreable opposition, from too many, who sell their country and their God for gold, who laugh at human Nature and compassion, and defy all religion but that of getting money; but the testimony of a good Conscience; the favour of the great father of the family, for having, tho' under difficulties, endeavoured to relieve his Children from such horrible oppression, will afford on the Winters evening, a satisfaction and comfort beyond, even, the possession of Millions; and beyond what can be expressed. Nothing of this kind is so difficult but, thro' the divine blessing, it may succeed. As we are fully acquainted not only with the grievous sufferings and prodigious havock which is by this trade made of the human species, by means the most disgraceful afflictive and cruel, but also of its woful effects on their lordly oppressors, in corrupting their morals, and hardning their hearts, to that degree,

3. Fothergill and Barclay need no introduction; for the little that is known about Mark Beaufoy (1718–82), Thomas Corbyn (1711–91), John Eliot or Elliott (1734–1813), and Thomas Wagstaffe (1724–1802), all prominent London Quakers, see Brookes, *op. cit.*, p. 288 ns. Benezet may have showered them with the many anti-slavery tracts that he had written, but our guess is that among them were copies of his *Some Historical Account of Guinea . . . with an Inquiry into the Rise and Progress of the Slave-Trade . . .* (Philadelphia, 1771), which contained extracts of the work of others.

4. A reference, we assume, to 1 Sam. 26: 21.

that they and their Offspring, become alienated from God, es-
tranged from all good, and hastning to a state of greater, far
greater, and more deeply corrupt barbarity, than that from whence
our northern progenitors emerged, before their acquaintance with
Christianity, can we be, indeed, at the same time *Silent and innocent Spectators?* By a late computation there is now eight hundred
and fifty thousand negroes in the English Islands and Colonies;
and an hundred thousand more yearly imported, by our Nation;
about a third of this number is said to perish in the passage, and
seasoning, before they are set to labour; the remnant are mostly
employ'd to make up deficiencies, as noted at page 87. of the
treatise[5] or sold to the spaniards.

The People of the Northern Colonies begin to be sensible of the
evil tendency, if not all, of the iniquity of this trade. One of our
friends a Person of sagacity,[6] who not long since returned from
Virginia and Maryland acquainted us, that from what appeared to
him, of the disposition of the people there he thought ten or twenty
thousand people might be brought to sign a petition to Parliament,
for the prohibition of any farther import. And I am told the people
of New England have made a Law which nearly amounts to a
prohibition of importing them there, and have even gone so far,
as to propose to the Council, the expediency of setting all Negroes
free at a certain age.[7] Our friends at their several Yearly Meetings
have also had that Matter under their serious consideration; those
of Maryland did actually, last fall, sign a petition to their assembly
for a law to prevent any farther import, and I am told many

5. He was referring to his *Account of Guinea,* just cited, where he quoted a
statement that Barbados imported five thousand slaves a year in order to keep
the total at eighty thousand, and that the same proportion held for the other
British islands. The estimate of the total Negro population was based on a
survey supposedly made in 1762: Thomas B. Chandler, *An Appeal to the
Public, in Behalf of the Church of England in America . . .* (New York, 1767),
p. 57.

6. John Hunt; see Brookes, p. 286. Hunt was the London Quaker merchant
mentioned above as an emissary between the Friends in England and Pennsylvania: VII, 373 n; X, 107 n.

7. Benezet's hope was ahead of reality: the strong anti-slavery movement
in New England was not yet producing results. Although the Massachusetts
House and Council had passed a bill in 1771 forbidding the importation of
slaves, Hutchinson had vetoed it. Zilversmit, *op. cit.,* p. 101.

friends in Virginia have the same under their consideration:[8] so that if any publick step was taken in this weighty matter, perhaps one of the most weighty which ever was agitated, we should have the approbation and good wishes of many, very many, welminded people of all Countries and religious denominations. With love I remain thy affectionate friend   ANTHONY BENEZET

Excuse interlineations &c as time will not permit to write over my letter

Addressed: For | Benjn. Franklin Esqr | Agent for the Provce of Pennsylvania | in London

From a Committee of the Library Company of Philadelphia

> LS: American Philosophical Society; minutebook copy: Library Company of Philadelphia

Sir,   Philada. April 27th 1772

By order of the Directors of the Library Co. of Philada. we have the pleasure to acknowledge the receipt of your polite and friendly Letter of the 16th April 1771, and beg you to accept our Thanks for the good wishes therein expressed towards this institution as well as for the Services you have at many times and in different ways rendered it. An Account came to hand at the same time from which it appears that there was then due to the Company £87 18s. 6d.[9] Stg. exclusive of a Balance you apprehend due to you on a Settlement, a State of which remains in America: in order to

---

8. The Maryland Assembly gave the Friends a brusque reception: "read and rejected the petition of sundry people called Quakers." William H. Browne *et al.*, eds., *Archives of Maryland* (72 vols. to date; Baltimore, 1883—), LXIII, 20. Agitation in Virginia, on the other hand, had already been effective, although Benezet had apparently not heard the news. On April 1 the House of Burgesses had adopted an address to the crown against the importation of slaves into the province; a month later the Governor forwarded the address with a covering letter. Elizabeth Donnan, *Documents Illustrative of the History of the Slave Trade...* (4 vols., Washington, 1930–45), IV, 153–5.

9. The balance of the £150 that BF had received from the Company: above, XVIII, 69 n.

adjust this Account we have carefully examined our Papers and Minutes and under the 12th Decr. 1763 find you Sir, then a Director present, exhibiting an Account, with proper Vouchers, amounting to £18 16s. 1d. when it was *Resolved* "That an Order be drawn upon the Treasurer to settle said Account with Dr. Franklin, at the rate of 75 per Cent which was accordingly done." We applied to Mr. Joseph Morris,[1] then Treasurer, to see if he could assist us, from him we learn, that he paid you on the 14th. of May 1764 £32 18s. 2½d. Currency equal to the said Sterling Debt: his Accounts were examined approved and Signed by a Committee of six Directors, of which number you was one. Notwithstanding all which the Balance you mention may be that of some later Account however, this is all the Light we are able to obtain, therefore must refer ourselves to you for farther Information.[2]

We have also been favoured with yours of the 5th. of June, inclosing an Invoice of Books, shipped by Mr. Strachan [Strahan], amounting to £62 8s. which was executed to Satisfaction (except as in the Account below) and arrived in good order.

The Directors agree in Sentiment with you that £300 Stg. would be thought too much to lay out for the Transactions of the several European Societies, but as the French Encyclopaedia may probably contain Extracts from the most material parts of all of them, they intend to purchase the new, improved Edition, which you will be so good as mention to Mr. Strahan, that he directly on its publication may forward it.[3]

Your Assistance we farther request in procuring for us the inclosed Catalogue of Books which hope to receive so soon as possible.[4] By Falconer we intend a Remittance to pay for the Books

1. For Morris see above, VIII, 324 n.
2. BF must have mentioned in a letter, now lost, the sum that he thought was due him; he presumably concluded that it was not due, for it does not appear in his Jour. or Ledger.
3. BF had suggested purchasing the transactions of all European learned societies, but on Priestley's advice had dropped the idea; see above, XVIII, 69, 117.
4. The minutebook of the Library Company contains the list of items ordered (pp. 65–9), and most of it can be reconstructed. It indicates, by comparison with 1769, a great increase in the appetite of Philadelphia readers or the wealth of the Library, or both. The identifiable items requested three years before were forty-six (above, XVI, 27–9 n), whereas the present order contained ninety-eight. Three broad categories were emphasized in both:

now ordered. Wishing you every Happiness we remain very Respectfully Your most obedient humble Servants[5]

MATTH CLARKSON
FRAS. HOPKINSON
R STRETTELL JONES.

[*In Franklin's hand:*]
Not sent.

Ogilvies' Poems	£0 12s.
Potts on the Fistula	1s. 6d.
Gray on Inland Navigations[6]	1s.
	14s. 6d.

Dr Benja Franklin

Addressed: To | Dr. Benjamin Franklin | London. | per the Mary and Eliza[beth] | Capt Sparks

Notation: Dr B Franklin

---

current literature and art; politics, political theory, and law; and the Greco-Roman period, both through translations and modern works. The later list put more emphasis than the earlier on two categories: mechanics, mathematics, and the sciences; and modern history and biography. It put slightly less on travel and natural history, and almost none on the broad area of morals, religion, and philosophy, where the percentage of works was three as against seventeen in 1769. Two new categories appeared in 1772, medicine and periodicals, which constituted six and eight percent respectively. The periodicals, with one exception, were clearly not new orders; sets were being brought up to date, and they presented the reader with a choice that ranged from the high seriousness of *The Christian's Mag., or, a Treasury of Divine Knowledge*... to the comparative frivolity of *The Court Miscellany; or, Gentleman and Lady's New Mag.*.... One other item, which stands by itself, was a complete set of the *Journals* of the House of Commons. BF boggled at this: the set cost too much, in his opinion, and was for reference and not for reading; he refused to buy it unless specifically instructed. To the Committee below, Aug. 22.

5. The members of the committee are identified above, respectively, x, 225 n; XII, 125 n; and XVIII, 18 n.

6. The books that Strahan did not send in 1771 were John Ogilvie, *Poems on Several Subjects*..., either the edition ordered before (XVI, 28 n) or the second edition (2 vols., London, 1769); Percivall Pott, either *Remarks on the Disease Commonly Called a Fistula in Ano* (2nd ed., London, 1767) or *Observations on that Disorder... Commonly Called Fistula Lachrymalis* (3rd ed., London, 1769); and [John Gray], *Reflections on Inland Navigations*... (London, 1768), dealing with the Forth and Clyde canal.

From William Henly[7]

ALS: American Philosophical Society

Dear Sir: Sunday Eve. [April?,[8] 1772]

I have this day repeated in the most accurate manner I was able, my experiment with the Bladder gilded with leaf brass, and suspended on an arm of wood turning freely on a needles point. The following is the result of many trials. After giving the bladder a strong spark from the knob of a positively charged bottle; on presenting towards it a smooth round ball 2 Inches diameter, I found it would come towards it, at upwards of two inches distance, and when *within an inch* would throw off its electricity in a full strong spark, (in short as the air was dry, and the silk perfectly good and smooth by which it was suspended,) *as great an one* as it had received from the bottle. After giving the spark as before; upon presenting a fine point towards it, it never acceded to the point in the least, and when it was pushed nearly into contact, (unless it was done very hastily,) no sensible quantity remained in it. I should have observed that if the ball was presented towards the bladder, even if it was swinging in a contrary direction, it would come back and meet it, throwing its electricity upon it at an inch distance as above described.[9]

I suppose Mr. Nairne told you of our ill success, with his batteries, and their having little or no effect on my Electrometer. To prove the goodness of *that* measure, I have this day tried it with your battery setting it upon the prime conductor. I gave the battery 100 turns of my small machine before the index[10] began to move, but it then went on very regularly till it goot $\frac{1}{10}$ Inch above

7. For the electrical experimenter see above, XVII, 259 n.

8. Lightning had struck the Tottenham Court Road Chapel in March, and Henly had been commissioned to fit the building with lightning rods; see Ronayne to BF above, under March 27. Henly began to test the efficacy of pointed as opposed to blunt rods, and the experiment here described was one of a series: *Phil. Trans.*, LXIV (1774), 133, 142–3. We conjecture that Henly reported his findings to BF during the month after the lightning struck.

9. BF had concluded that a pointed rod, unlike a blunt one, would gradually discharge the electricity in an approaching cloud. Above, III, 126–8; IV, 16–19, 23–4; X, 51–2; see also BF's experiments below, Aug. 18. Henly devised his metal bladder to simulate a cloud, and this and other experiments buttressed BF's position when it was later challenged by Benjamin Wilson; see the headnote on the Purfleet committee's report below, Aug. 21.

10. On his electrometer, which measured the intensity of the charge.

right angles, when it made an effort to discharge itself but ended in hissing. At this instant I saw every one of the wooden tops to the bottles beset with loose filaments, I counted 7 upon one of them, and I believe in the whole there might be some 100. Think Sir how this must dissipate that atmosphere which ought to have been confined to the index, and to have regulated its action. On discharging it, the report was amazing, and much melted all the connecting wires. I saw plainly Mr. Nairnes error, and had he been advised by me, he might have prevented it. I have however put him in an easy, and simple way to correct it.[1]

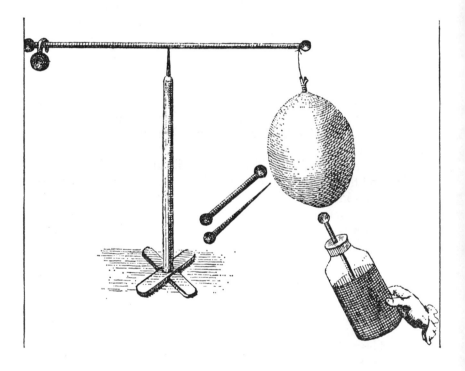

1. Nairne found the electrometer faulty when placed at the usual height, but effective when sufficiently elevated. *Phil. Trans.*, LXIV, 80. Henly may have suggested to him this simple cure, though why it worked we cannot even guess.

I do still aver, that if the apparatus be properly made, *every thing dry, and well connected,* the Electrometer is a just and accurate measurer, a satisfactory and most useful instrument, as with this you are always sure of your force before the discharge.

Some friends of mine being strongly of opinion that the matter of light, and the Electric matter are the same thing, I made an experiment to determine the question (not for my own) but for their satisfaction. I insulated my rubber and collecting the Solar Rays in a burning glass brought it so as to let the rubber be in the focus, I burnt my rubber, (which is wood,) several times, but without producing any Electricity.[2] Believe me Dear Sir to be with real regard yours
                                                                W HENLY

Addressed: To | Dr: Franklin | Craven-street | Strand

2. The rubber or cushion was a wooden block, usually covered with leather, against which a glass globe or cylinder was revolved to generate a static electrical charge; the rubber was customarily grounded. Priestley, *History*, II, 4. Henly insulated the rubber, to determine whether the sunlight could produce a charge. He published a revised version of this experiment in *Phil. Trans.*, LXIV (1774), 419–21. BF, in a reverse experiment, had determined that sunlight would not discharge a charged body: above, III, 128–9.

From Dorothea Blunt

ALS: American Philosophical Society

Three of Dolly Blunt's letters, of which this is the first, can be dated only by what may be considered extravagant guesswork;[3] others cannot be dated at all, and will be published in a supplement at the end of BF's second British mission. His letters to her in this period, to which she occasionally refers, have all disappeared, and with them the clues they might have provided. Dolly rarely mentioned the year in which she was writing; sometimes, as here, she noted the day and the month, sometimes left out the month, and sometimes ignored all such trivial details. The letters appear to belong to the later phase of her friendship with Franklin, after Polly Stevenson's marriage, when she was "paying more attention to you than I have hitherto paid tho not more than I have always been prompted from affection to pay."[4] Our dating of the present one hinges on its subject, a dinner invitation in which she enticed Franklin with the assurance of meeting his old friend Hawkesworth. The two men had had no contact that we know of since January, 1771.[5] On May 7, 1772, Franklin received an urgent request from Hawkesworth for help in a medical problem, which he apparently arranged to provide;[6] our conjecture is that the request grew out of a conversation at the Blunts' dinner table on May 1.

Dear Sir   May the 1st [1772?]
Shoud this be fortunate enough to meet you at home and Shou'd you be disengag'd, I shall think myself in luck for as I cannot persue that pleasing scheme of passing a few days with you, I cannot but desire to see you some where and therefore cou'd you indulge me by dining at Sir Charles Blunts[7] in Ormond Street this Day at 3 o Clock, we hope you will [meet?] Dr. Hawkesworth. I mention'd this as a[n ind]ucement, yet am angry with myself that I did, for your behaviour is always such as convinces me, you are not only ready but desirous to oblige your Humble Servant

Compliments to Mrs. Stevenson   D: BLUNT

Addressed: To / Dr Franklin / in / Craven Street

3. The other letters in this group are below, May 24 and Aug. 14.
4. Above, XVII, 201.
5. Above, XVIII, 6. Hawkesworth and his wife had been, through Polly Stevenson, part of BF's circle for more than a decade; see above, IX, 265 n.
6. See his letter to Hawkesworth below, May 8, and the reply under May 15.
7. For her brother see above, XIV, 93 n.

122

Note on the Walpole Company's Rejoinder to a Report from the Board of Trade

[After May 1, 1772[8]]

After the flurry of activity over the Walpole grant in the spring of 1771, nothing happened for a year.[9] The reason was not only Hillsborough's opposition but also the number and complexity of the problems involved. The land in question included tracts that were claimed by Pennsylvania, by the Ohio Company of Virginia, by the Suffering Traders or Indiana Company, and by the veterans of the French and Indian War whom Washington represented.[1] The Indians, like the whites, had conflicting claims; and the cessions they made to the crown, subject to its approval, were also conflicting.[2] Any line of division between white men and red, furthermore, was subject to the pressure of settlers who were moving across the Alleghenies; confirming such a line when it did not in fact demarcate settlements from hunting grounds would have been an invitation to violence. The many claimants, each in a different

8. The day when the Company was furnished with a copy of the report to which it made its rejoinder. Whether the latter was read at the Privy Council hearing of June 5, or was in rough notes that were later put into finished form, is not clear. The rejoinder and report were published together in a pamphlet, listed in the *Monthly Rev.* the following September (XLVII, 239): *Report of the Lords Commissioners for Trade and Plantations on the Petition of the Honourable Thomas Walpole, Benjamin Franklin, John Sargent, and Samuel Wharton, Esquires, and Their Associates . . . with Observations and Remarks* (London, 1772).

9. For the previous activity see above, XVIII, 75 n, where we were mistaken in saying that the Board of Trade did not respond for two years.

1. Only one of these claims appears in the map above, XVII, [10], which we have found to our embarrassment is erroneous in important respects. The western border of the Walpole claim extended almost twice as far south as indicated, to meet the Wasiotos; from there the mountains run northeast, not east by north, to the New River. But the main error is in the north. The southern border of Pennsylvania ran to a point five degrees west of the Delaware, midway on what we indicate as the northern boundary of the claim. From that point the western Pennsylvania border ran north, either in a straight line or in one that reproduced the course of the Delaware; the charter was open to either interpretation, and claimants chose whichever was to their advantage. In any case the proposed Walpole grant included, between the western frontier of Pennsylvania and the Ohio, a large tract in which many others had claims.

2. For an example, the cessions made at Hard Labor and Fort Stanwix, see WF to BF above, Jan. 6.

way, were asking Whitehall to fix a frontier that was inherently unstable; and Whitehall took refuge in delay.

Hillsborough delayed from policy. He was still adamant against western expansion, and the leaders of the Walpole Company were working hard to undermine his influence. Success seemed in their grasp in December, 1771, when the Cabinet overruled him and ordered an immediate report on the Company's application. But the Board of Trade did not act until the following March, when it held a hearing at which the Company—biding its time—declined to be represented. The Board brought in a report on April 15 that was forwarded to the Committee on Plantations of the Privy Council on April 29; on May 1 the Company requested a copy, which it received.[3] The report raised objections to the grant: part of the land included in it was west of the boundary already established with the Indians at Fort Stanwix and Lochaber, and those legally settled in the territory east of that boundary might properly come under the jurisdiction of Virginia. But the main objection was that stated in the Board's earlier report of March, 1768: creating a new colony remote from the seaboard was mistaken in principle, because such a colony produced nothing of commercial benefit to the mother country to compensate for the cost of defense. The Board therefore advised rejecting the application and reaffirming the Proclamation Line of 1763.[4]

Hillsborough's political strength was waning, for the Privy Council Committee refused to endorse the Board's report out of hand. Instead it held a hearing on June 5, at which the Company took the opportunity that it had declined before the Board, and aired its case at great length. Franklin was present, but the record indicates that he participated only to the extent of answering one minor question.[5] Samuel Wharton unquestionably took the lead in presenting the petitioners' argument, which in its published form was, according to William Knox, Wharton's composition.[6]

A quarter-century later John Almon attributed this rejoinder to Franklin. He had had only five copies printed, Almon added, when

3. Peter Marshall, "Lord Hillsborough, Samuel Wharton and the Ohio Grant, 1769–1775," *English Hist. Rev.*, LXXX (1965) 727–30; *Board of Trade Jour.*, 1768–75, pp. 293–4, 297, 299–300.
4. For the full text of the report see Smyth, *Writings*, V, 467–78.
5. *Acts Privy Coun., Col.*, V, 203–8.
6. The report, the hearing, and Knox's statement are discussed in Clarence W. Alvord, *The Mississippi Valley in British Politics...* (2 vols., Cleveland, 1917), II, 130–6. See also Jack M. Sosin, *Whitehall and the Wilderness...* (Lincoln, Neb., 1961), pp. 199–202; Lewis, *Indiana Co.*, pp. 109–12.

Hillsborough's resignation in August induced him to stop the press.[7] Jared Sparks accepted this attribution, and substantiated it by misreading a letter from Franklin in 1773; later editors followed Sparks.[8] Clarence Alvord disagreed,[9] and so do we. Internal evidence, as well as external, points to Wharton as the principal author. The document is a meandering statement of the case, replete with arguments and historical details that are ill organized, ill written, and sometimes incoherent. Here and there are flashes of reasoning that may be Franklin's, here and there he may have provided the background information; but we can find no ground for believing that the resultant mishmash was his handiwork.

To Joseph Priestley   ALS (draft): American Philosophical Society

Dear Sir,   London, May 4 1772
  I think with you that there cannot be the least Occasion for my explaining your Method of impregnating Water with fix'd Air to Messrs. Banks and Solander, as they were present and I suppose are as well acquainted with it as my self; however I shall readily do it if they think it necessary. I am glad you intend to improve and publish the Process.[1]

7. [John Almon,] *Biographical, Literary, and Political Anecdotes...* (3 vols., London, 1797), II, 237–8. The only truth in the story is that the pamphlet appeared: Almon printed it. For details see Paul L. Ford, *Franklin Bibliography...* (Brooklyn, N.Y., 1889), pp. 139, 141. Ford, although accepting BF's authorship, pointed out that the detail of the five copies was ridiculous.

8. Sparks, *Works*, IV, 302–3, 324–74. BF's letter to WF below, July 14, 1773, mentioned Anthony Todd's remark that Hillsborough could not forgive BF for writing the rejoinder. Sparks ignored what followed, Todd's denial that BF was the author, and in publishing the text of the letter (VIII, 75–6) deleted a statement by a solicitor that he and Wharton and Walpole had produced the document. The editors who accepted Sparks's attribution, apparently without examining it, were Bigelow, *Works*, V, I n, 20–75, and Smyth, *Writings*, V, 465–6, 479–527.

9. Because of Knox's statement, and because Wharton is known to have prepared all such documents for the Company. Alvord, *op. cit.*, II, 134, 317.

1. "Fixed" or "factitious" air often meant any "air," or gas, released by heat or chemical action from its fixed state in a substance, but for Priestley the term meant what we now call carbon dioxide. In the spring of 1772 he explained his method of "impregnating" or carbonating water to Sir George Savile, who put him in touch with the Admiralty. The method might sweeten

You must go half an Inch farther with your Spark to exceed what I show'd here with my Philada Machine in 1758 to Lord Charles Cavendish and others, who judg'd them to be nine Inches. My Cushion was of Buckskin with a long damp Flap, and had a Wire from it thro' the Window down to the Iron Rails in the Yard; the Conductor of Tin 4 feet long and about 4 Inches Diameter. So powerful a Machine had then never been seen in England before, as they were pleas'd to tell me. A Machine was made from mine for Mr. Symmer, and was afterwards in the Possession of Lord Morton. A more convenient Construction I have never since seen, except that of yours.[2]

I intend soon to repeat Barletti's Experiments,[3] being provided with the Requisites, and shall let you know the Result.

I should be glad to see the French Translation of your Book. Can you conveniently lend it to me when you have perus'd it? I fancy it was translated at the Request of Abbé Nollet by a Friend and Disciple of his as I know there was one (whose Name I have forgotten,) that us'd to translate for him Extracts of English Electrical Books.[4] The Abbe's Machine was a very bad one, requiring three

---

water on a long voyage, it was thought, and perhaps reduce scurvy; and the Admiralty wished to use Cook's second circumnavigation, which was about to begin, to test an antiscorbutic. Priestley demonstrated his method to the College of Physicians, which approved; he was then instructed to furnish the ships' commanders and surgeons with details of the process, and on May 7 he did so. Soon thereafter he published his procedure in *Directions for Impregnating Water with Fixed Air*... (London, 1772). F. W. Gibbs, *Joseph Priestley*... (New York, 1967), pp. 57–60; Jack Lindsay, ed., *Autobiography of Joseph Priestley*... (Bath, [1970]), p. 95. Priestley assumed that Banks and Solander would go on the voyage; see his letter, which should be dated May 8, in Schofield, *Scientific Autobiography*, p. 131. In fact they did not go; see the annotation of Hume to BF above, Feb. 7.

2. For Priestley's description of his own machine see his *History*, II, 112–16; BF does not seem to have left any account of his "Philadelphia Machine." Robert Symmer, F.R.S. (d. 1763), had differed with BF on electrical theory, but had asked for and received a copy of his machine; it was in Lord Morton's hands by 1768. I. Bernard Cohen, *Franklin and Newton*... (Philadelphia, 1956), pp. 543–6; above, XV, 93 and n.

3. Carlo Barletti, *Nuove sperienze elettriche secondo la teoria del Sig. Franklin et le produzioni del P. Beccaria*... (Milan, 1771).

4. BF was right. The translator, Mathurin-Jacques Brisson (1723–1806), was Nollet's successor at the college in Navarre; he was indeed a disciple, and

Persons to make the smallest Experiment, one to turn the great Wheel, and one to hold Hands on the Globe. And the Effect after all but weak.[5] Delor had a similar one, and invited me to see him exhibit to the Duchess of Rochefoucault, but the Weather being a little warm, he could perform nothing, scarce obtaining a Spark.[6] This Inconvenience must have occasioned their Making fewer Experiments, and of course his not being so easily convinced. M. Le Roy, however, got early possession of the Truth, and combated for it with Nollet; yet I think the Academy rather favoured the latter.[7] Le Roy will I suppose now confute this Translator, for I have just seen a Letter of his to Mr. Magelhaens, thanking him for sending so excellent an Electric Machine to France; (it is one of the Plate ones) which he has improv'd so as to produce the positive and negative Electricities separately or together at the same time, de façon (says he) qu'on peut faire toutes les Experiences possibles sur l'une ou l'autre de ces deux Electricités. Enfin on etoit si eloigné de connoitre les Phenomenes de ces deux Electricités ici, faute de Machines commodes de les démontrer, que beaucoup des Gens ont été etonnés de voir avec quelle évidence ils etablessent la distinction de ces deux electricités. &c. This Letter is of the 5th Instant.[8] My best Wishes attend you and

by the time of the Abbé's death in 1770, BF later remarked, was the only disciple. *Autobiog.*, p. 244. In his *Histoire de l'électricité traduite de l'anglois de Joseph Priestley...* (3 vols., Paris, 1771) Brisson revived the old feud between his master and BF by arguing in a note (I, 21 n) that the former had first equated lightning with electricity.

5. Priestley had the same opinion of the machine: *History*, II, 107–8.

6. Delor and Dalibard, in 1752, had first publicized BF's electrical theories in France by repeating his experiments. *Ibid.*, I, 381–6; above, IV, 362, 424. We have found no other reference to Delor's failure before the Duchess; it may have happened during either of BF's visits to Paris, in 1767 or 1769.

7. For the long dispute in the Académie des sciences see Cohen, *op. cit.*, pp. 508–9.

8. Jean-Hyacinthe de Magalhaens or Magellan (1723–90) was a former monk turned natural scientist and instrument-maker. *DNB*. He had a wide circle of scholarly friends and correspondents, for whom see Henry Guerlac, *Lavoisier—the Crucial Year...* (Ithaca, N.Y., [1961]), pp. 36–43. The machine that Jean-Baptiste LeRoy received from him provided further means of confirming BF's theories; LeRoy described it at some length in a paper in the *Mémoires* of the Académie des sciences for 1772 (Paris, 1775), pp. 499–512. See also Walsh to BF below, June 21.

yours. I am ever, with great Respect, my dear Friend, Yours most
sincerely   B F.

Dr Priestly

From William Henly   ALS: American Philosophical Society

This letter poses a problem of dating that we are unable to solve. The
internal evidence is as ample as it is conflicting: some of it points to
1772 and some to 1773. The whole tone of the opening paragraph suggests that the Purfleet magazine had not yet been protected by lightning rods, and that Benjamin Wilson's "scheme" for doing so was
being actively considered. His recommendation of a base of brickwork
for the rods was mentioned only in his report to the Board of Ordnance of May 4,[9] which we assume was the scheme. Henly must have
been writing after that date and, to judge by the way he wrote, before
the Purfleet committee overruled Wilson in August.[1] Yet the conclusion of the letter refers to an exploded story about a house in Jamaica;
Franklin, as far as we know, did not hear this story until autumn, or
learn that it was false until the following March.[2] The letter patently
belongs to the period between May and August of 1772, in other words,
and just as patently to the spring of 1773. We have tried elaborate lines of
conjecture to resolve this paradox, but they lead nowhere. Only one fact is
clear, that Henly could not have written the letter before Wilson's report.

Worthy Sir   [After May 4, 1772]
I shall take it as a particular favour if you will be so obliging as
to give the bearer leave to copy out for me the Account of the
damage done by the powder Magazine which was fired by the
Lightening—ever since you mention'd it to me I cannot get it out
of my thoughts.[3] I spoke of it to Mr. Nairne on Saturday, repeat-

9. See the headnote on BF to Dawson below, May 29. Wilson did not mention brickwork, as far as we have been able to discover, in either of his subsequent pamphlets on lightning.
1. See its report below, Aug. 21.
2. See BF to Bache below, Oct. 7, 1772, and March 3, 1773.
3. Henly is undoubtedly referring to the explosion at Brescia, discussed in
the headnote on the letter to Dawson; accounts of the disaster are cited there.
Although Henly might have been asking for one of the brief notices in the
press in 1769, he would have been more interested in the first detailed description, which was in Wilson's pamphlet. If that was what he wanted, he was
writing after its publication in March, 1773.

ing what you observed to me concerning that at Erith,[4] says he I really shudder at the thought. The more I think of Mr. Wilsons scheme for a Conductor the more I dislike it. If I understand the plan aright, it seems not at all unlikely that he would invite a stroke upon his Iron Bar in its full force, and as a Base of Brick work may in dry seasons be looked on as a kind of imperfect insulation, if the Electricity should not be properly dissipated at the bottom who can foresee the consiquence?[5] Should mischief ensue from such an improper apparatus, it might contribute to bring them into disrepute, and so prevent the many good effects which may by proper management be always expected from them.

Mr. Nairne observes to me that the mark made by the spontaneous discharge of a positively charged bottle is only on the inside of the uncoated part of the glass—if the bottle be charged negatively the mark is on the outside only. I intend to try this soon with 2 new Bottles which I shall mark previously to my making the experiment, tis however perfectly consonant to all my experiments made on the surfaces of Glass Ivory &c.

I have written to Dr. Priestley and contradicted the Report of the House &c. in Jamaica. I am Sir faithfully yours   W HENLY
Addressed: Dr. Franklin

To Cadwalader Evans

Extract: Reprinted from Jared Sparks, ed., *The Works of Benjamin Franklin*... (10 vols., Boston, 1836–40), VIII, 4–5 n.

London, 5 May, 1772.

You write, that, besides what was sent here, fifty-four pounds had been reeled at the filature of private persons, who are getting it manufactured into mitts, stockings, and stuffs.[6] This gives me

4. For the use of Erith as a synonym for Purfleet see Robertson to BF below, July 14. During the summer, as Purfleet became more familiar, the synonym tended to disappear; its use here suggests an early date for the letter.
5. BF had long been aware that lightning running through an inadequately grounded conductor might, particularly in dry conditions, produce an explosion. See above, X, 50–1, 57–9; XIV, 263.
6. For the raw silk that had been sent to England see BF to Evans above, Feb. 6. For the small amounts of manufactured silk being produced in Pennsylvania see John F. Watson, *Annals of Philadelphia and Pennsylvania*... (2 vols., Philadelphia, 1855), II, 436–8; *PMHB*, XXXVIII (1914), 123–4.

great pleasure to hear; and I hope that practice will be rather followed, than the sending small parcels to be manufactured here, which are difficult to get done, where all goes on in the great way. Let nothing discourage you. Perseverance will conquer all difficulties; and the contributors will have the glorious satisfaction of having procured an inestimable advantage to their country.

To [John Foxcroft]

ALS (letterbook draft; fragment): American Philosophical Society

[On or before May 5, 1772.[7]]
My Love to dear Mrs. Foxcroft, and to little Sally my grandaughter.[8] My best Wishes attend you all, being as ever, Your affectionate Friend and humble Servant   B FRANKLIN

To Deborah Franklin   ALS: American Philosophical Society

My dear Child,   London, May 5. 1772
    I received your kind Letter of March 2. and am glad to hear that the Ship from Ireland is got safe into Antigua. I hope you will now get the little Token I sent you from thence.[9]
    I have not receiv'd the Letter you mention to have given the young Scotsman, nor that from Mr. Craige.[1]
    I am sorry for the Disorder that has fallen on our Friend Kinnersley, but hope he will get the better of it.[2] I thank you for your

7. The fragment appears in the letterbook immediately before BF to WF below, May 5, and is clearly the end of BF's reply to Foxcroft's letter above, March 2, which mentioned the baby's name.
    8. BF is carrying on to the next generation the whimsy that Judith Foxcroft was his daughter; see Foxcroft to BF above, Feb. 2.
    9. For the misadventures of the ship carrying Irish linen for DF see BF to DF above, Jan. 28. The disappearance of her letter of March 2, to which BF is replying, leaves us in the dark about several matters to which he refers below.
    1. Possibly James Craig (1718–93), a Philadelphia merchant who appears fleetingly in the *PMHB*: IV (1880), 407; XCV (1971), 359.
    2. The disorder, whatever it was, presumably continued into the autumn, when Kinnersley resigned from the College of Philadelphia because his health required wintering in a warmer climate: J. A. Leo Lemay, *Ebenezer Kinnersley, Franklin's Friend* (Philadelphia, [1964]), pp. 105–6.

Advice about putting back a Fit of the Gout. I shall never attempt such a Thing. Indeed I have not much Occasion to complain of the Gout, having had but two slight Fits since I came last to England.

I hope Mr. Bache is with you and his Family by this time, as he sailed from the Downs the latter End of February.[3] My Love to him and Sally, and young Master, who I suppose is Master of the House. Tell him that Billy Hewson is as much thought of here as he can be there; was wean'd last Saturday; loves Musick; comes to see his Gran-ma; and will be lifted up to knock at the Door himself, as he has done while I was writing this at the Request of Mrs. Stevenson, who sends her Love, as Sally does her Duty. Thanks to God I continue well, and am as ever Your affectionate Husband   B FRANKLIN

To William Franklin

AL (letterbook draft): American Philosophical Society

[Dear] Son,   London, May 5. 1772
    [I have rec]eived yours of Mar. 2, with the Bill in[closed] [*torn*] on the Society for £25 Sterling, which is [entered to your?] Credit.[4] I have paid for you lately a [bill in the amount of?] £4 10s. 6d. to one Main's a Shoemaker, [*torn*] by Order of Mrs. Clarke.[5] And on [*torn*] several Sums of which I cannot [now recollect the full?] Particulars.
    [The letter that?] you intended me by Osborne is not [arrived. You?] mention receiving two Letters from me, [written from?] Ireland, but say nothing of one I wrote [to you from?] Glasgow. Perhaps it miscarried. . . .[6]

3. Bache, after an unconscionably long voyage, had reached Philadelphia only a few days before BF wrote. See BF to DF above, Feb. 18.
4. The bill was for Odell (Jour., p. 41). WF had, we presume, paid the salary of his minister in Burlington, Jonathan Odell; in any case the clergyman had drawn a bill in his favor on the Society for the Propagation of the Gospel, which BF credited to WF's account. Three years earlier BF had acted as go-between in the same matter: XVI, 189–90.
5. WF had ordered shoes for his wife (Jour., p. 41), and Miss Mary Clarke often took care of such purchases for her; see above, XIII, 258 n.
6. A brief and mutilated paragraph, omitted here, was apparently intended

This Session of Parliament has been a quiet one, and now draws near a Conclusion. Opposition has made no Figure, and Lord North manages ably. Peace is negociating between the Turks and Russians; and miserable Poland is in a fair Way of being pacified too, if the Entrance of more foreign Armies into it, can produce Peace.[7] There is no present Appearance of any other War likely to arise in Europe, and thence a Prospect of lessening considerably the National Debt.

I continue well, Thanks to God. Sir John Pringle has propos'd to me a Journey for this Summer to Switzerland. But I have not resolv'd upon it, and believe I shall not. I am balancing upon a Wish of Visiting at least, if not returning for good and all (as the Phrase is) to America. If I don't do that, I shall spend the Summer, with some or other of those Friends who have invited me, at their Country Houses.

I am glad to find such a Progress in [the making?] of Silk in Pennsylvania. I hope your Pro[vince will] take a Part in it. I think you sh[ould encou]rage the raising Cocoons in all your Towns. B[etsy should] keep some Worms herself. Her Ex[ample] [*torn*]. The Queen has graciously accepted [*torn*] the first Fruits of Raw Silk from [*torn*] manufactur'd, [*mutilated and torn*] the next Birth Day.[8] [*Mutilated and torn*] I am, Your [*torn*]

I saw Col. Ord[1] the other Day, who kindly enquir'd after you.

for another letter: BF marked it in the margin "To Mr. Galloway I write per Osborn." Most of the paragraph repeats the one to WF that follows, except for mention that the Parliamentary debate on May 1 advanced "no Proposition of further Impositions on America, which some had threatned us with."

7. A precipitating cause of the Russo-Turkish war had been Russian interference in Poland, where Prussia and Austria soon took a hand. A Russo-Prussian treaty of partition had been signed in February, 1772; Austria joined in August, and a year later Poland had lost a quarter of its territory.

8. For the gift of Pennsylvania silk to the Queen see BF to Evans above, Feb. 6.

1. Col. Thomas Ord, R.A., has not appeared before. He was in Philadelphia, where he doubtless met the Franklins, before Braddock's expedition in 1755, and commanded the artillery in that ill-fated campaign; see Stanley Pargellis, *Military Affairs in North America, 1748–1765* (New York, 1936), p. 96 n.

To [John Hawkesworth[2]]   ALS: Yale University Library

Dear Sir   London, May 8. 1772
    Dining abroad yesterday, and not coming home till 12 at Night,
I did not get your Letter in time to answer it by the Return of the
Post as you desired.
    Dr. McBride of Dublin some time since discovered that putrid
Flesh could not only be render'd sweet, but its Firmness restor'd,
by immersing it in Fix'd Air; which is Air that has made part of the
solid Substance of Bodies, and is separated and set at Liberty from
them in their Dissolution, or Fermentation, or Effervescence with
other Bodies.[3] This Air is not fit for Breathing; Flame is extin-
guish'd by it; and, taken into the Lungs, it instantly extinguishes
animal Life: But taken into the Stomach is deemed salutary, as in
Pyrmont Water which contains much of it. Dr. Priestly discovered
that two Sorts of this Air, one produc'd by suffering dead Mice to
putrify under a Glass, the other by the Effervescence of Chalk and
Water with a small Quantity of Acid or Spirits of Vitriol, in either
of which Airs living Mice being put would instantly die, yet the
two being mix'd both became good common Air, and Mice
breath'd in the Compound freely. From his own and Dr. Macbride's Experiments (who thought Fix'd Air would prevent or
cure the Sea Scurvey) he was persuaded it might be of use in
Mortifications. But of this there has yet been only a single Experiment. A Physician of his Acquaintance at Leeds wrote to him
while he was lately in Town, that a Person dying as was thought
of a putrid Fever, with all the Symptoms of a Mortification in the
Bowels, had been suddenly relieved and recovered by the Injec-
tion of fix'd Air as a Clyster.[4] These are all our present Premises;
upon which you can judge as well as I how far one may expect the
same fix'd Air will be of Service apply'd to a Cancer. But since you
ask my Opinion; as the Case may otherwise be desperate and we

    2. The author and teacher, an old friend of BF, for whom see above, IX,
265 n and subsequent volumes.
    3. For Dr. David MacBride (1726–78), a noted medical investigator, see
the *DNB*; "fixed air" is explained in a note on BF to Priestley above, May 4.
The particular experiments to which BF refers are described in MacBride's
Experimental Essays on Medical and Philosophical Subjects (3rd ed., London,
1776), pp. 70–3, 86–7, 130–1, 147.
    4. Pyrmont water, so called from a spa in northern Germany, was a natur-

know of no Danger in the Trial, I should be for trying it.[5] I would first syringe the Sore strongly with warm Water impregnated with fix'd Air, so as to cleanse well the Part. Then I would apply to it a Succession of Glasses fill'd with Fix'd Air, each Glass to remain till the Sore had absorb'd the fix'd Air contain'd in it. It would require a long Description to explain the readiest Methods of obtaining the Air, applying it, and impregnating the Water with it; and perhaps I might not make myself clearly understood. The best Way is *to show it*, which I will do either here, or at Bromley if you desire it.[6] Being ever, my dear Friend, Yours most affectionately

B FRANKLIN

To the Managers of the Philadelphia Silk Filature

Extracts printed in *The Pennsylvania Gazette*, July 29, 1772; ALS (incomplete draft): American Philosophical Society

This letter, to the Managers of the Contributions for Promoting the Culture of Silk, exists in two fragmentary and undated versions. One is extracts that the Managers sent to the press; the other is a draft among Franklin's papers in his hand, with the first page or pages missing. Two of the extracts are from paragraphs that are contained in the draft; the others must have been from an opening section that is now lost. We have no way of telling whether deletions were made in that section, and if so where; we print it as if it were complete, which it probably is not. The composition of the letter can be approximately dated. On February 6 Franklin promised that he and Dr. Fothergill would communicate

ally carbonated water, as distinct from the artificially "impregnated" water that BF referred to in his letter just cited. For Priestley's experiments with mixing the "two Sorts of this Air" produced by putrefaction and effervescence see his *Experiments and Observations on Different Kinds of Air* (2nd ed., corrected; 3 vols., London, 1775–84), I, 98–101. Dr. William Hey (1736–1819), Priestley's acquaintance, was an able surgeon and medical experimenter; see the *DNB*. Hey's letter of the previous February, describing his use of a clyster filled with "fixed air" or carbon dioxide, appeared as an appendix to Priestley's "Observations on Different Kinds of Air," *Phil. Trans.*, LXII (1772), 257–62.

5. The case may or may not have been one of cancer in the modern sense. Cancerous sores, as far as we can discover, were not yet clearly distinguished from cankers, in other words gangrenous or ulcerating sores.

6. For Hawkesworth's reply see below under May 15.

with the committee in about a fortnight.[7] But the two men found it difficult to get together, as Franklin mentions below. When he eventually decided to write alone, some three months had passed; for the letter was sent by the packet that cleared Falmouth for New York on May 10.[8]

[Before May 10, 1772]

The Silk remained long at the Custom-house, before we could get it valued, to ascertain the Bounty. The Valuers opened all the Parcels, and separated the Papers and Marks from them, so that we could by no Means distinguish the Parcel intended for the Queen. We concluded, therefore, to get some skilful Person to pick the proposed Quantity out of the best, which was presented to her Majesty, representing it as the first Fruits of a new Produce in Pennsylvania, humbly offered as a Mark of the affectionate Respect of her Subjects there; and that if she vouchsafed to do them the Honour of accepting and wearing it, they might be the more encouraged to proceed in producing a Commodity, very beneficial to her British Subjects. Her Majesty was pleased to accept it very graciously, and to say, that she would have it woven, and wear it on some public Occasion. I since hear that she proposes it for the King's Birth-day.[9]

While the Silk remained at my House, I had a Number of the Trade to see it, and give their Opinions of it, and I asked their Advice as to any Improvements that might be made. They *all agreed, that the* STAPLE *was as good as any in the World, and that some of it was well reeled.* They objected principally to the Foulness of it.[1]

7. BF to Evans above, Feb. 6.
8. A few weeks thereafter BF told Evans that he had written the committee at length "by the last packet" (below, June 3). This was the *Mercury*, which sailed on May 10 and reached New York by July 20: *N.-Y. Gaz., and the Weekly Mercury*, July 20; *Pa. Gaz.*, July 23. The letter presumably got to Philadelphia as soon as the news of the packet's arrival, in other words by the 23rd, so that the Managers had almost a week to select and publish the extracts in the *Pa. Gaz.* of the 29th.
9. June 4. For the present to the Queen see above, XVIII, 247, and the document following this one. The rest of BF's paragraph repeats what he had written to Evans above, Feb. 6.
1. [*Note to the printed extract:*] The Managers had before observed, that this arose chiefly from Want of due Care in the Reelers to change the Water often enough; a Fault which has been remedied this Season, and they hope their Silk will accordingly be found as clean and glossy as any in the World.

I did not know, till lately, that Silk is sold here by two different Pounds, one of 24 Ounces, and the other of 16 Ounces; and when I informed you last Year, that on shewing some of your first Skains, sent me by Dr. Evans, it might be worth 27s. per Pound,[2] I find that the great or Italian Pound, of 24 Ounces, was meant. You will observe this Distinction in the Paper of Sales herewith sent.

On consulting about the best Method of disposing of the Silk, I was advised to a public Sale by Auction, as the properest to discover its true Value; and as the Quantity was too small to make an Auction by itself, it was agreed to sell it when there should be a sufficient Quantity on Sale from other Countries, *to draw the Trade together*. It was accordingly stored with a great Quantity of different Sorts, which I went to see, and thought the best of ours not much inferior to any there, the Thrown Silk excepted. The Broker had sorted ours, according to his Opinion of its Quality, into five different Lots, as you will see by his Account of Sales. There was about four Hundred Weight of Carolina and Georgia Silk sold at the same Time; and the best Lot of that sold only for 4d. a Pound more than the best Lot of ours, viz. 19s. 6d. the small Pound of 16 Ounces. I am told Silk is just now uncommonly cheap. Along with yours, you will observe, by the Account of Sales sent you, there was some sold from most of the Silk Countries in the World.[3]

The Sample of second Crop Silk was thought as good as any of the others. A great Deal is produced (of the second Crop) in one of the Provinces of China, where the Climate is very like that of North-America. If the Practice of two Crops is not found attended with any great Inconvenience, it might be a great Addition to your annual Quantity.

The Austrian Ambassador, who is an Italian,[4] tells me, that

2. Above, XVIII, 32.
3. An account of the sales, held in London on April 10, was appended to the extracts. Of the five lots of Pennsylvania silk, two sold for 19s. 2d. apiece, one for 18s., one for 17s. 8d., and one for 10s. The prices of Carolina and Georgia silk were in approximately the same bracket, whereas Chinese, Indian, and some Italian were slightly higher and the rest slightly lower. The Pennsylvania product, on balance, stood up well against its competitors.
4. Count Ludovico Barbiano di Belgioioso (1728–1803), of the celebrated Milanese family, was the Austrian minister to St. James's from 1769 to 1783. See his notes to BF below, Sept. 30.

in Italy they have lately found the Reeds or Stalks of Indian Corn to make the best Grates, whereon to feed the Silkworms.[5]

[*Beginning of paragraph missing*] such manner as you may think proper. You will observe that some of the worst, particularly a bundle that was very knotty, sold extreamly low. I think it adviseable never to send any such here, and that it would be better to work it up into Stockings at home.

Some Years since a Silk-Manufacturer here apply'd to me for Encouragement to go to America. He was a poor Man and had a Family, and I could not then advise his going; but he put into my Hands a Paper which I send you as it may afford some Hints. I have forgotten his Name.

One of the Valuers of the Silk at the Customhouse supposing I was to get it manufactur'd here, apply'd (being a Master Manufacturer) to me for the Jobb, recommended by the other, who was a Silk Broker.[6] I learnt from him, that several Americans had sent over small Parcels of 4, 5, or 6 lb. to be manufactered for them here to particular Patterns, which he said was very injudicious, as it was not worth while to set a Loom for a few Yards, and besides most kinds of Manufacture required Silk of different Sorts for the Warp and for the Woof, so that what the People expected was impracticable but at a greater than common Expence, and the Silk after all not entirely of their own Produce. This should be made known, that our People may rather work up their small Parcels at home. The Agent of Rhode Island, Mr. Marchant, had one of those small Commissions from Mrs. Stiles, and was told that 10 ounces were wanting to compleat the Order, which he urg'd me to spare him as, he knew Mrs. Stiles would not like her Silk mix'd with any not American. Knowing Dr. Stiles to be a great Friend to the Design, and who had made many Experiments to improve the Knowledge in raising the Worms I spared him the Quantity desired to be paid for as the rest should sell.[7]

5. The extracts, except for two paragraphs that are noted below in the draft, end here.

6. The master manufacturer was probably the Mr. Patterson, and the broker the Mr. Boydell, mentioned in BF to Evans above, Feb. 6.

7. For Henry Marchant, BF's traveling companion in Scotland, see above, XVIII, 145 n, and his letter to BF below, Nov. 21. Ezra Stiles was much interested in silk culture in America, and was doubtless behind his wife's com-

Dr. Fothergill has some Chinese Prints relating to the Culture of Silk which he purposes to send you. I thought to have written with him a joint Letter to you; but we live remote from each other, have neither of us much time to spare, and the finding him at home is uncertain; therefore I at length concluded to write alone, as I have principally had the Management of the Affair.[8]

I am farther told, what I did not know before and should not have imagined, that there is a vast Difference in the Waste of different Silks when they come to be dyed, viz from 5 to 30 per Cent. and that 'tis therefore a Wonder our Silk, the Waste of which is yet unknown, the Trade having had no Experience of it, would sell so well. But it seems [torn] compar'd with the Carolina Silk, and suppos'd to be of [torn] Quality.

Dr. Pullein, who is now here, approved of your Silk much, but is persuaded his Reel, as lately improved, is better than what you reel with, and advised sending you a Model. I have accordingly got one made under his Direction, which I shall send by Osborne.[9] Your Artists will judge of it, and perhaps find their own preferable.

You will observe in the Account of Sales that there is an Allowance of $\frac{1}{4}$ of a Pound made to the Buyer in every Lot. I do not see the Reason of it, but it seems it is the Custom of the Trade; and also the Custom to allow two Months Credit, and the Payment at the End of that Time is nevertheless called prompt.[1]

You mention about 155 lb. produc'd, but do not say precisely what Quantity you sent. The Weight found here, as you will see by the Broker's Account is 147$\frac{3}{4}$ which with the 10 oz. spared to Mr. Marchant makes 148 lb. 6 oz. and with the 18 lb. in Presents makes 166 lb. 6 oz. This is considerably above the Quantity you mention, as that sold is below it. As you probably, in the 155 lb. did

mission to Marchant; the latter had arranged in February to have the silk woven into a gown for her. Marchant diary (APS typescript), p. 127.

8. See BF to Evans above, Feb. 6.

9. For the Rev. Samuel Pullen or Pullein see above, XVIII, 160 n. Peter Osborne in the *Pa. Packet* sailed from Deal on July 13: *Lloyd's Evening Post*, July 13–15, 1772. The paragraph to this point was printed among the extracts with slight verbal changes; these we have adopted as being closer than the draft to the letter BF sent.

1. The account of the sales, summarized above, mentions that the Pennsylvania silk was sold at two months' credit, and all but one of the other consignments at seven months'.

not mean to include the Presents, there appears a Deficiency too great to be easily accounted for, being 5 lb. 10 oz. Some was probably lost in the Several Drafts of the Lots, which I perceive were weighed only to quarters of Pounds; and in the Presents there was some overweight because we could not divide Skains; but these could [*remainder of paragraph missing*]

Upon the whole, I have not the least Doubt but that, by Perseverance, you may establish this valuable Produce in our Province. And you may believe that Nothing of the Kind can give me more Pleasure than to promote your most laudable Undertaking, by every Service in my Power.[2] I am, Gentlemen, Your most obedient and most humble Servant   B FRANKLIN

To Sir John Pringle   AL (draft): American Philosophical Society

[Before May 10, 1772[3]]

Dr. F. presents his respectful Compliments to Sir J. Pringle, is much oblig'd to him for the Trouble he has so kindly taken in the Affair of the Silk, and is very happy to learn that the Queen has graciously condescended to accept it with a Purpose of wearing it. Her Majesty's Countenance so afforded to the Raisers of Silk in Pennsylvania (where her Character is highly rever'd) will give them great Encouragement to proceed in a Measure the British Parliament seems to have had much at Heart, the Procuring a Supply of that valuable Article from our Colonies, for which at present large Sums are paid yearly to France, Spain, Italy and the Indies.

2. The paragraph to this point was among the extracts, and again we have followed the printed version.

3. The headnote on the preceding document explains why we believe that it should be dated before May 10, and when BF wrote it some time had elapsed since the present to the Queen. If we are right, therefore, this note on the same subject was undoubtedly written well before May 10. Pringle, who had been physician-in-ordinary to Queen Charlotte since 1761, was a natural choice as intermediary to carry her the offer of the silk and to bring her acceptance.

Accounting of Benjamin Franklin's Share in the Walpole Company

AD: American Philosophical Society

⟨May 12, 1772: "Benjamin Franklin Esq., for his Proportion of Expences and Charges incurred from June 1769 to May 1772, on the Application to the Crown for a Grant of Lands on the River Ohio in North America." He had paid £5 5s. in cash on November 6, 1769, and £25 on November 27, 1771. The charge for one share at £44 3s. 4d., dated May 2, 1772, left a balance due to Samuel Wharton and William Trent of £13 18s. 4d. Trent acknowledged receipt of this balance on May 12, 1772, in full settlement of the account.[4]⟩

From Deborah Franklin

ALS: American Philosophical Society

My Dear child   May [14?–]16, 1772
but be fore I can say aney thing I muste Stop to tell who I am writeing to I tell him to Grand papah so then he is gon so I am to tell you that this morning Capt. Loxley is arived but I have not had a letter as yit[5] I have not a lowed my self the libertey to make complaintes to you of aney Sorte but this has bin the moste malleycoley winter that I ever knew in my memery. We air obliged to make fiers in the roome to set by and it is 14 of may.
     Wee had the pleshuer of seeing your worthey friend mr. Small but his stay was so verey Shorte that it cold [could] not be Cold [called] a visit only a vis. When you see him my Compleymentes

4. BF endorsed the account "Wharton and Trent for the Shares of BF WF and J. Galloway pd. May 12th 1772. Entd." What he entered were the three £25 assessments in 1771 and the three later items, which we assume were also assessments, of £13 18s. 4d. (Jour., pp. 38, 41); the £5 5s. payments in 1769 were not recorded. If we are right, these were all charges for expenses rather than for the shares themselves; BF retained WF's and Galloway's receipts from Wharton and Trent, which have since disappeared. In 1773 BF paid £200 for each of the three for further expenses, and this time for purchase money as well. See Foxcroft to BF above, March 2; BF to WF below, July 14, 25, 1773.
     5. The arrival of the *Carolina*, Capt. Benjamin Loxley, was reported in the *Pa. Gaz.*, May 21; the same issue carried an advertisement, dated May 14, of Loxley's intended departure for London.

to him tell him that B Franklin is better recon Sild to his father and
begins to inquier after him and coles him Papey[6] he is a verey
busey lad. I have not heard one word from Capt. Loxley so I
supose he shiped a way with oute you know of it.

I have bin coled to mr. Sumaines as he is verey neare his end it
is a bove seven years [since] he has bin abel to due aney thing to
suporte him selef[7] and I think shee is not halef so big as shee yous
to be. I may goe helpe her and suporte her under her dificalty.

I donte know aney news worthe writeing to you be plesd to
give my beste love and thankes to mrs. Stephenson for all her
kines to my Husband and Son while with her to Mrs. Huson. Kis
her son for me I hear her Son is a fine Lad my love to Salley
Franklin mrs. Strahans famely Mr. and Mrs. Weeste and all that
know me I have not heard of mrs. Sumaines Dafter.[8] I did to a
write another sorte of a letter but it has lefte me at presant. I am
your afeckshonet wife   D FRANKLIN

May 15 1772

I shold a sed sumthing a boute your giveing a power to mr.
Beache.[9] I am verey uncapall of dueing aney bisnes as I am not
abell to walke a boute and my memarey so so poorley and sum
times worse then others. Capt. Folkner has bin hear this day he
will tell you he can poot on speek tickels and look like you. I shold
say sume thing say sume clearly a boute me in regard to her kines
to mr. Beach[1] I will when I am better. As to the Squerels I am
glad thay got Safe and well but I am a fraid as thay air not in the
ground squerel I have maid inquirey after them but it is to soon

6. Alexander Small had returned to New York from Jamaica in April, and
Richard Bache had reached Philadelphia at the end of that month; see above,
Small to BF, April 13, and BF to DF, Feb. 18. Small must have been in Philadelphia soon after Bache's return, when the Kingbird, then two and a half,
was still unaccustomed to a father who had been so long away.

7. Samuel Soumaine had been at death's door since at least 1769: above,
XVI, 213. He died before DF's letter below, June 30.

8. Elizabeth Soumaine Empson had asked BF's help in 1771; see above,
XVIII, 83. That episode doubtless led him to inquire of DF about her.

9. The power of attorney to her and Richard Bache above, Feb. 17.

1. DF was, as she seemed to realize, incapable of saying "sume thing...
clearly," but we believe that she was referring again to Mrs. Stevenson's kindness to Richard Bache, and that he was also the person who with spectacles
on looked like BF; for the resemblance between them see above, XVIII, 258.

but I am told thay air so willd that it is harde to tame them. Let me know wuther thay air a live and is tame and tame and hapey I shold be glad to her [hear] that thay give pleshuer.[2] This is a dul day to me. Salley is writin we have bin expecktin to have Billeys letters down I hope thay will be down in the evening. Benj Franklin ses aske Grand papah Blessme give my Duty to him. I hope I shall be in better sperrites by next opertunety. I am your afeck-shonet Wife   D FRANKLIN

May the 16

Addressed: To / Benjamin Franklin Esqr.

From John Hawkesworth

ALS: Historical Society of Pennsylvania

Bromley Kent Fryday night [May 15?[3], 1772]
Many, many Thanks, my dear Friend, for your obliging favour of the 8th. My Enquiry was on the behalf of a Friend who is very near and dear to me, to whom I have transcribed your Letter, and if she should be inclined to make the Experiment I will claim the kind offer which your humanity has made me. It will not bring you to Bromley, but I hope you will contrive to give me a day now the Days are long and the weather is fine. I have some Expectation of Seeing Mr. Banks and Dr. Solander here with Mr. Fitzmaurice,[4] perhaps you may be of the Party. I will let you know when they come if their warning is sufficient. Perhaps you may hear of it in Town. Adieu I am ever and most affectionately Yours   JNO HAWKESWORTH

2. For the squirrels that DF had sent see BF to DF above, Jan. 28, and below, Aug. 22.

3. Hawkesworth, to judge by BF's letter above of Friday, May 8, was urgent in his request for help; and we presume that he sent this answer on the following Friday. The MS has the notation, as others have in these volumes, that it was given to some one (illegible) by Mr. Sparks.

4. For Banks and Solander see above, XVIII, 209 n, and for Fitzmaurice, Shelburne's brother, X, 348 n and subsequent volumes.

From Richard Bache

ALS: American Philosophical Society

Dear and Honored Sir   Philadelphia 16th. May 1772

A few Days since per Captain Sparks I did myself the Pleasure.[5] I have not much to say at present, more than that we are all well. These are the best Tidings I can send you at this time, I find but slow Sale for my Goods, but what I do sell, is for Cash, so that I am making no bad Debts; I have not sold enough to enable me to reimburse you per this Opportunity the £60. Sterling you were so kind to lend me, I hope to do it soon.[6] I think I mentioned to you in my Letter by Sparks, that the Case of Stationary, lodged at Hugh Roberts[7] his House, is now at Home, but I have not yet opened it. Governor Franklin tells me he has transmitted you Copy of an Account furnished by Mrs. Parker, which differs very materially from the Account I brought over with me, furnished by you,[8] when we have your Sentiments on that Account, I shall endeavor to get the Balance secured to you. I find Steigle on whom Jacob Scroop's Bill is drawn, has not yet been applied to for payment of the Bill, I have wrote to him, and expect his answer daily, if he refuses payment, shall make it my Business to find out the Drawer.[9]

5. He had doubtless written to tell of his arrival, which was announced in the *Pa. Jour.* on the same day, April 30, that Sparks's clearance for London was noted in the *Pa. Gaz.* The letter has been lost.

6. The loan was actually for £65 5s., and the £60 was repaid in September: Jour., p. 39; Ledger, p. 56. BF then asked that the remaining five guineas be invested for young Ben in Jamaica: to Bache below, Oct. 7.

7. For Roberts, BF's old friend, see above, V, 11 n.

8. The accounts are discussed in WF to BF above, Feb. 28. The one that Bache brought with him may have been a duplicate of the "*London* Account" referred to there.

9. Bache, we believe, reworked the name, which should have been Schaub. In June of 1770 BF lent 25 guineas to a Jacob Schaub: Jour., p. 24. A man of the same name immigrated to America in a ship from Rotterdam that stopped in England; he reached Philadelphia in September, 1772. Ralph B. Strassburger, *Pennsylvania German Pioneers: a Publication of the Original Lists of Arrivals in the Port of Philadelphia from 1727 to 1808* (William J. Hinke, ed.; 3 vols., Pa. German Soc. *Proc.*, XLII–XLIV, Philadelphia, 1934), I, 739–40. Steigle, we assume, was Henry William Stiegel (1729–83), the ironmaster and glass-maker, whose ambitious ventures were already leading him down the road to bankruptcy. *DAB*. He was at this time recruiting skilled labor in the British Isles and on the Continent; and BF knew him, if not personally at least

The Money you lent John Schutz is not yet paid, his Brother
Conrad is dead, and he is very poor, however I shall do my utmost to secure this for you.[1] I find Mr. Hall, collects as much as he
can of what is due you, for Newspapers, I mean such Debts as
accrued, before your Connection with him, as well as those, in
which you are concerned with him, but they come in but slowly,
and he is apprehensive a considerable sum will be lost.[2] I have not
had time to look into your other Books of Accounts, shall do it as
soon as possible.

I take the Liberty of troubling you with a Letter for my Mother,
and one for my Sister Lydia, which I beg of you to drop into the
Post Office. Also a Letter for Messrs. Robert and Wm. Alexander,[3]
which you will be pleased to give to the former if he remains in
London, if not, to forward by the post. I am with perfect Esteem
Your most Affectionate Son   RICHD BACHE

I forgot to mention to you, that previous to my return home, Sally
had got fitted up for a Store, the lower part of the Old house next
to Haddock's in Market Street, it is an excellent Stand for a dry
Good Store and answers the purpose very well. I do not think the

---

by reputation. Frederick W. Hunter, *Stiegel Glass* (New York and Boston,
1914), pp. 55, 63, 68–9, 72. What happened, according to our conjectural reconstruction from these data, was as follows: Schaub was one of the laborers
recruited; he stopped off in England on his way to Philadelphia, and asked
for a loan from BF, to whom as the Pennsylvania agent Stiegel might well
have referred him. Schaub gave BF the bill on Stiegel to cover the loan, promised on reaching America to put through a second bill for payment, probably to DF, but then for reasons unknown delayed his crossing more than two
years. BF heard nothing about the bill, and consequently gave Bache the
original and asked him to look into the matter when he reached Philadelphia.
When there turned out to be nothing to look into, because Schaub had not
yet arrived, BF concluded that the "Dutchman" was a rogue: to Bache below,
Oct. 7.

1. Bache was undoubtedly trying to collect the 35 guineas that BF had lent
John or Johann Shütz in England in 1758, at the request of Shütz's brother,
Johann Conrad; see above, VIII, 145 n. Conrad was a Philadelphia paper-
maker, who appears occasionally in vols. II, IV, and v.

2. David Hall was telling Bache much what he had told BF at great length
two years before: above, XVII, 100–1. See also Hall to BF, Feb. 3, 1772.

3. For this banking firm see above, VIII, 444 n.

little North Room of your house would have done at all.[4] I am
Yours &c.   RD BACHE

Addressed: To | Benjamin Franklin Esqr.

A Committee of the Managers of the Pennsylvania Hospital to Franklin, David Barclay, and John Fothergill

Minutebook copy: Pennsylvania Hospital, Philadelphia

Esteemed Friends   Philada 5 mo. 16th. 1772

The Managers of the Pennsylvania Hospital have been expecting to hear from you by every Vessel that has arrived at this place
from London within many months past, but being disappointed of
that pleasure, are apprehensive some Obstacle has occasioned a
delay of your receiving from the Bank, the Monies arising from
the unclaimed shares of the Land Company allotted to the use of
our Hospital.[5]

We are therefore again Nominated to request the favour that
you would inform us by the first Conveyance the real State of this
Affair, in Order that if there remains anything Necessary to be
added or amended by us in the Powers sent you, we may have the
Opportunity of Executing and transmitting them to you in the
most Speedy manner. Our Necessities are so pressing as to make
us very desirous to see an agreeable accomplishment of this business, which, from the information given us by our Friend Daniel
Roberdeau on his return from London last fall, we had promising
Hopes would have been brought to an Issue long since.[6]

Herewith we send you a Duplicate of our last Letter of the 3d.
6 Mo. Earnestly requesting you will be pleased to use your best

4. The store, on the south side of Market between Third and Fourth, had
been open for at least a week; see Bache's advertisement in the *Pa. Gaz.*,
May 7. For "the little North Room" see BF to DF above, Jan. 28.

5. For committee's previous letters about the money from the dissolution
of the defunct Pennsylvania Land Company see above, XVIII, 92–3, 117.

6. Roberdeau had been in England trying to sell his plantation in the West
Indies; see above, XVII, 239 n. David Barclay answered this letter on July 8,
explaining that the technicalities of obtaining a Chancery decree had caused
the delay: Pa. Hospital minutebook. See also BF's reply below, Aug. 28.

endeavours to expedite the transaction of this business and to inform us thereof, whereby you will Essentially Serve the Hospital, which has received indubitable proofs of your benevolent regard, and will greatly Oblige the Managers, on whose behalf we are, Your Respectfull Friends   JOHN REYNELL
        JAMES PEMBERTON
        THOMAS WHARTON

To Benjamin Franklin Esqr. Doctr. John Fothergill and David Barclay In London

From Thomas Foxcroft   ALS: American Philosophical Society

⟨Philadelphia, May 16, 1772: Encloses the bill of lading and other papers for two barrels of "the best Burr Superfine flour."[7] Expects his brother back from Virginia within a few days. Has seen Mrs. Franklin yesterday; she and the family are well. His "Sister"[8] joins in regards. Broke his arm six days ago, but hopes it will mend in three weeks.⟩

From William Smith   ALS: American Philosophical Society

Sir   Philada. May 16th. 1772
I was favoured with your obliging Letter, acknowleging the Receipt of sundry Copies of our Transactions for some learned Societies and Gentlemen in England, and informing us that you had delivered the Books accordingly.

I was then preparing to embark for Carolina, where I was lucky enough to get *One Thousand Guineas* for our College, which is at present in such Repute among them that we have upward of 30 Students from thence, who are Children of the principal Families there.[9] I therefore desired that the other Secretaries might

7. Promised by John Foxcroft in his letter to BF above, March 2. Burr flour was ground by millstones made from a particular kind of rock.
8. His sister-in-law, Judith Osgood Foxcroft.
9. Smith, in his fund-raising in South Carolina for the College of Philadelphia, had triumphed over difficulties which had plunged him in gloom the previous December: Horace W. Smith, *Life and Correspondence of the Reverend William Smith* ... (2 vols., Philadelphia, 1880), I, 468–9.

write to you, and send you the Books for the foreign Societies, as well as the Sheet missing in Dr. Fothergill's Book; but it was neglected, as there were but few good Opportunities during the Winter. The missing Sheet is enclosed herein, which you will be pleased to send to Dr. Fothergill.[1] From Capt. Falconer you will receive a Box, address'd to you containing Copies of our Transactions for the following Societies, with a short Letter on the Blank Leaf before the Title Page for each of them viz 1 The University of Oxford; 2 Cambridge; 3 Glasgow; 4 Edinburgh; 5 St. Andrews; 6 King's College Aberdeen; 7 Mareschal College Do. 8 Royal Acad. of Sciences, Paris; 9 Royal Acad. Stockholm; 10 Imp Soc. Petersburg; 11 Soc. at Gottingen; 12 Soc. Berne in Swisserland; 13 Acad: at Bononia; 14 Acad: at Florence; 15 Royal Acad. at Berlin; 16 Do. at Turin; 17 Academia Naturae Curiosorum; 18 Monsr. Buffon at Paris; with 9 Copies for yourself, making in all 27 Copies.[2]

The Society are sensible that they are giving you a great Deal of Trouble, to find proper and safe Conveyances for these Books; but, besides the Propriety of their Passing thro' your Hands, they know no other Person to whom they could send them, and on whose Zeal for the Credit and Service of the Society they can so well depend.

Should you want any more of the Books, Bradford has sent 50 Copies to the Bookseller Dilly in the Poultry, to whom you can recommend any of your Friends that may want Copies.[3] I am

1. Here and in his opening sentence Smith is replying to BF's letter above, XVIII, 163–4.
2. The British institutions need no identifying; for those in Paris, Stockholm, St. Petersburg, Göttingen, Bologna (Bononia), Turin, and Berlin see *ibid.*, p. 71 n; the Academia Naturae Curiosorum was synonymous with what is there called the Imperial Leopoldine Academy. "Soc. Berne" was probably the Naturforschende Gesellschaft, which in 1771–72 published a 2-vol. *Bibliotheca Botanica*; and the academy in Florence was the Società Botanica, founded in 1739. For Buffon see above, III, 111 n. BF sent the copies for the Italian institutions, plus another for the Grand Duke of Tuscany, by Philip Mazzei, for whom see the *DAB*. In a letter to the Society of Dec. 7, 1773 (APS), Mazzei reported that he had delivered the volumes.
3. For William Bradford, printer of the *Pa. Jour.* and a member of the APS, see above, II, 315 n, and for Charles Dilly and his brother, the famous booksellers and publishers, see the *DNB*. The Poultry connects Cheapside and Cornhill.

sorry more were not sent to London early, as they would have sold, and help'd to make the Society better known. There are now but 40 Copies left in Philada. and those I have sent for to lock up for the Use of the Society; that Number being small enough to keep for Presents to learned Strangers that may come among us and ask for the Book for years to come. The Society, I hope, will still rise in Reputation and Usefulness; but our various Expences at our first Outset, notwithstanding the Assembly's Bounty, have left us near Two Hundred Pounds in Debt to our Printer and others, and I know [not] how we shall get clear, unless the Public *nurse* us a little farther.

Dr. Bond has communicated your last Letter, with the Letters and Presents of Books from Mr. Ludlam, Mr. Foster and others; all which shall be soon answered. Mr. Ludlam does us great Honour by his kind Notice and generous Applause of our Humble Labours. Be so good as acquaint him that Mr. *Rittenhouse* and myself are appointed to write to Him.[4]

I am afraid we have not the proper Titles and Address of some of the foreign Societies, and we had not Time to consult such Books as would [have] given them to us; but perhaps by interlining a Word in any that may be deficient you may set all right. I had drawn up the little Letter for the Blank Leaf before the Title Page in *Latin*; but on further Consultation, we thought as our Book was in English, the Letter should also be English; since whoever could understand the one would understand the other. It was thought also by some that, as a Society, it woud be below our Dignity to use any but our own Language, as the *French* write always in theirs, and we think ours equally good, and that, among the Literati, it is becoming equally *universal*. I am Sir Your most obedient humble Servant   WILLIAM SMITH

P.S. The Acad. Naturae Curiosorum, is that in Germany, but in what Town I do not remember, as Dr. Kuhn who gave the List of German Societies, is not to be found before I must close this; but I believe the Society is at Nuremberg.[5]

4. For Forster's and Ludlam's gifts to the APS see above, XVIII, 274–5, and BF to Bond, Feb. 5, 1772; for David Rittenhouse see XVI, 154 n.

5. He was right. For Dr. Kuhn, professor of botany at the College, see above, XVIII, 164.

The Society have received a Letter from Mr. White, Treasurer I think he is of the Foundling Hospital, with some curious Prints of Animals, part of a great Work he is carrying on, entitled Musaeum Britannicum, and desiring some Assistance from the Society, with respect to American Animals. Please to send him the enclosed after sealing it, with one of the 9 Copies of Transactions sent to yourself, as the Box was sent on board, before the Society ordered the Book for Mr. White. We cannot make out from the Subscription to his Letter whether his Name is John or Thomas, that is J. or T. White.[6]

Dr. Benjamin Franklin

From John Whitehurst[7]   ALS: American Philosophical Society

Dear Sir   Derby 21 May 1772

Perceeiving you were not quite Sattisfied with the Account I gave you of the Clock I made for you,[8] I have now made another with a round Dial. The hour hand of which performs one revolution in 24 hours. Concentric to that, is a hand to Shew the time of high and low water, the hours of flood and ebb. Under the foot of the hour 12, is wrote highwater, at 6 Low water, in Strong characters. I am in hopes Sir that the Simplicity of this method will please you.

If you should approve this Clock the Dial is circular and 13 Inches diameter.[9]

If the London Artist[1] make a difficulty in Executing the Case, I

6. The treasurer of the Foundling Hospital was Taylor White (above, x, 228 n); his work on animals, whatever it was, seems to have vanished without trace at his death, which occurred before Smith's letter reached him. See BF's reply below, Aug. 22.

7. The Derby horologer, whom BF had known for a decade; see above, IX, 42 n, and their correspondence in recent volumes.

8. We assume that this was the "other Clock" ordered by BF the previous summer, and that he had taken exception, in a letter now lost, to something in Whitehurst's description of it above, XVIII, 194.

9. BF presumably did approve, for Whitehurst sent the clock with his letter below of Aug. 4.

1. Probably John Thompson, to whom Whitehurst had referred BF before: above, XVIII, 191.

will Send one along with the Clock. In the Clock now made, Ive made a provision for Seconds, therefore please to Say, whether you choose Seconds or not, as the whole is compleated, and going.

I have Sent Mr. Fitzmaurice a Wheel Barometer, and could wish it to remain unfix, till I come to Town the begining of July as could like to fix it up.[2]

A friend of Mine wants to dispose of an Estate in Virginia. Pray Sir by what means Must it be done? The Estate is left by will. At Your leasure I Shall esteem it favour to receive a line of information. Who am Sir Your Most Obedient Servant

JOHN WHITEHURST

Addressed: To / Benj: Franklin Esqr / Craven Street the Strand / London

From Dorothea Blunt   ALS: American Philosophical Society

My Dear Sir   Saturday May the 23d [1772[3]]

Tho you had never done anything with a design to give me pleasure I shou'd love you for that constant disposition everyone that knows you know you feel to give pleasure to all your fellow creatures. But you have My honour'd friend often given it to me in the very Manner and thing adapted to gratify, and make truly thankful for it. The Piano Forte I ask'd you to lend me and when I did so fully intended answering your wish both by playing on it myself and hearing it play'd on by others; but as I shall not do either in the place it now occupies I came hither this day[4] to ask your permission to have it remov'd to Streatham, where I spend more time, see more Company, and shall oblige the Brother I am

2. Thomas Fitzmaurice, Lord Shelburne's younger brother, was broadening his meteorological interests, for which see above, XVII, 218–19, 247. His ordering a wheel barometer was perhaps related to Alexander Small's "Circular Scheme" (whatever it may have been) for measuring barometric variations in widely separate localities, mentioned in BF to Bond above, Feb. 5. For a description of the wheel barometer see Charles Hutton, *A Mathematical and Philosophical Dictionary...* (2 vols., London, 1796), I, 188.

3. The only year between 1770 and 1775 when the 23rd fell on a Saturday.

4. The only interpretation we can put upon this phrase is that Dolly had come to Craven Street, found that BF was not there, and left him this note.

with when there,[5] by the addition of an Instrument so well adapted to his house. As I propose being in London next Tuesday, I would not trouble you to write to me before, for if you do I shall not receive it till then. Adieu my dear Sir and believe me Your much esteem'd and oblig'd Humble Servant   D: BLUNT

Addressed: Doctor Franklin

From Dorothea Blunt   ALS: American Philosophical Society

Dear Sir   Streatham Sunday 2 o Clock [May 24, 1772[6]]
    I promis'd you to meet your agreable friend on Tuesday in Craven Street, and myself the pleasure of seeing both you and that Lady, but an express arriv'd this day from Odiham with the disagreable news of My Brother Walters little James being ill of a sore throat and fever. My Brother set out to go to him[7] before I cou'd conquer some scruples that held my tongue when I wish'd to say I will accompany you, but the moment it became impossible I overcame them and immediately resolv'd to set out in the machine tomorrow Morning. I shou'd rejoice that it suited you to go the same road so soon, not only because I shou'd like to go with you, but shou'd be inform'd of some little remedy that I might prevail on his father to administer tho not prescrib'd by Dr. Mentrik [?] nor approv'd by him.[8] Do you know where some

5. Dolly had three brothers, Charles, Harry, and Walter. Harry does not appear in her letters to BF until one of March 18, 1779 (APS), when he was living near Bath. Walter (1736–1801) appears only once, in the following document, when he was on his way from Streatham to Sir Charles's house at Odiham. We assume, therefore, that Walter was living at this time in Streatham and was Dolly's host. He later had a house in Kensington, where he died, and a country estate in Hampshire. *Burke's Peerage,* p. 329; *Gent. Mag.,* LXX (1801), 767.

6. We assume, for once with real confidence, that this letter is a postscript to the preceding document, which contained a promise that Dolly found she could not fulfill.

7. James (d. 1832) was at the time Walter Blunt's only child: *Burke's Peerage,* p. 329. The youngster must have been taken ill while visiting his uncle, Sir Charles, whereupon Walter left hastily for Odiham. The Blunt brothers are discussed in note 5 above.

8. In her letter below, Aug. 14, Dolly herself claimed to be knowledgeable about home remedies. She expected BF to produce one, we suggest, because

more of the same sort of american bisquits that you sent to Sir Charles, are to be procured because I am requested to send to a friend in the country? If you do I shall be much oblig'd to you to send Miss Henckell[9] word, who will be in Fenchurch Street. Remember me to Mrs. Stevenson and the family belonging to her and believe me dear Sir your affectionate and oblig'd friend

D: BLUNT

Addressed: Doctor Franklin / Craven Street / Strand

From a Committee of the Library Company of Philadelphia

LS: American Philosophical Society; minutebook copy: Library Company of Philadelphia

⟨Philadelphia, May 28, 1772: They enclose a draft on John Whitmore for £125 from Stocker & Wharton & John Wilcocks at thirty days' sight, dated May 26 in favor of and endorsed by Josiah Hewes, to pay for the books ordered through Sparks for the Library Company. If the amount is insufficient, they will discharge the balance. In a previous letter they had spoken of remitting by Falconer, but the election of directors, the settlement of accounts, and other business prevented them. The letter is addressed to Franklin by Capt. Hood, via Bristol, and is signed by Samuel Rhoads, Josiah Hewes, and Robert Strettell Jones.[1]⟩

---

she knew of his recent correspondence with Hawkesworth, for which see the headnote on her letter above, May 1. Why she imagined that BF might join her on the road to Odiham we have no idea, unless she had heard that he was projecting a trip. He was, but not at the moment or in that direction.

9. This elusive friend of Dolly, BF, and Polly Hewson has appeared before without adequate identification: above, XIV, 275; XV, 245. We now have reason to believe that she was named Elizabeth and was the daughter of the Governor of the Royal Exchange Assurance, James Henckell. Dolly wrote BF on March 18, 1779 (APS), that "Henckell with her respectable parents resides at Hampstead and works in her garden." Mr. and Mrs. James Henckell died soon afterward in Hampstead, where Elizabeth also died in 1787: *Gent. Mag.,* L (1780), 155; LII (1782), 551; LVII (1787), 839.

1. John Whitmore was a merchant of Laurence Pountney Lane, off Cannon St. Anthony Stocker, Thomas Wharton, Jr., John Wilcocks, and Josiah Hewes were Philadelphia merchants: the first two were partners, but we have

To Richard Dawson[2]

ALS: British Museum; French translation by Barbeu-Dubourg: American Philosophical Society

This letter marked the start of an investigation that engaged Franklin's attention intermittently for months to come, and embroiled him in one more dispute about the behavior of electricity. The problem was how best to protect the royal powder magazine at Purfleet against lightning. The magazine was new, and replaced the old one at Greenwich; transfer of powder from one to the other had begun in 1763 and been completed in 1768.[3] A year later a disaster in Italy underlined the danger to all such arsenals: lightning struck the magazine at Brescia, and the resultant explosion destroyed much of the town and killed more than a thousand people.[4] Parliament responded in 1771–72 by passing two gunpowder acts, which established strict supervision of the manufac-

---

no other indication that Wilcocks was a member of the firm; he was the brother of Alexander Wilcocks, the lawyer, and was an organizer of St. Peter's Church. Hewes was the brother of the more distinguished Joseph Hewes of North Carolina. Anne H. Wharton, "Thomas Wharton, Junr., First Governor of Pennsylvania under the Constitution of '76," *PMHB*, v (1881), 428; William J. Potts, "Founding of St. Peter's Church in Philadelphia," *ibid.*, xii (1888), 495; Hubertis Cummings, "Items from the Morris Family Collection...," *ibid.*, lxx (1946), 194–5. The composition of the ¦committee had changed since its letter above of April 27. Samuel Rhoads needs no introduction; for Robert Strettell Jones see above, xviii, 18 n.

2. A captain at the time in the Corps of Engineers, and attached to the Ordnance; he had been commissioned as a lieutenant in the army in 1757, and was promoted to major in July, 1772, and to lieutenant colonel in 1777. *A List of the General and Field-Officers as They Rank in the Army...* (London, [1773]), p. 172; *The Royal Kalendar...* (London, [1770]), p. 168; Whitworth Porter, *History of the Corps of Royal Engineers* (3 vols., London, 1889–1915), I, 181, 188, 202–3.

3. Purfleet, some miles down river from Greenwich and on the north shore, was where men-of-war customarily took on powder. For a brief contemporary description of the village and the magazine see Philip Morant, *The History and Antiquities of the County of Essex...* (2 vols., London, 1768), I, 93–4 of second pagination. For the move from Greenwich see Oliver F. G. Hogg, *The Royal Arsenal: Its Background, Origin, and Subsequent History* (2 vols., London, 1963), I, 109.

4. For accounts of the explosion see the *London Chron.*, Sept. 2–5, 23–26, 1769; *The Annual Register...for 1769* (1770), p. 135 of first pagination; *Gent. Mag.*, xxxix (1769), 457; Benjamin Wilson, *Observations upon Lightning...* (London, 1773), pp. 58–65.

ture and storage of powder in private hands;[5] the government, by implication, would supervise its own establishments.

It began to do so just when the second bill was becoming law. At some time before the beginning of May the Board of Ordnance requested Benjamin Wilson to examine the Purfleet magazine and recommend ways of protecting it. His report, dated May 4, suggested among other things the installation of conductors with blunt tops.[6] The Board, apparently not satisfied, must have asked Franklin for his opinion, because he gave it in the letter below; his recommendation was conductors with pointed tops. This conflict of experts no doubt confused the Board, which on July 1 appealed to the Royal Society for a definitive opinion. By the 14th the Society had appointed a committee, including both Franklin and Wilson, to examine the question and bring in its report.[7]

Sir, Cravenstreet, London, May 29. 1772

Having yesterday at your Request view'd the Magazines of Gunpowder at Purfleet, in order to consider of their Preservation from Danger by Lightning, I am of Opinion

1. That all the Bars of Iron[8] passing down through the Arches of the Roofs towards the Powder, be taken away, as at present they do, with the Copper Hoops on the Barrels, form an imperfect Conductor, more or less compleat as the Piles of Barrels happen to be higher or lower, but such an one as may tend to draw down among the Powder any Lightning that shall happen to strike the Roof, and are therefore dangerous.

5. 11 Geo. III, c. 35, and 12 Geo. III, c. 61.

6. For Wilson, who combined painting with science, see above, IV, 391 n and subsequent vols. He is said to have been portrait-painter to the Board, and to have been commissioned by it as a direct result of the Brescia explosion: Benjamin Vaughan, ed., Political, Miscellaneous, and Philosophical Pieces...by Benj. Franklin... (London, 1779), p. 499 n. Wilson's three-page MS report is in the British Museum.

7. Vaughan (loc. cit.) says that the Board appealed to the Society because of BF's and Wilson's disagreement; Dubourg (Œuvres, I, 282) has a slightly different story. The request itself is in the Royal Soc. MSS; the formation of the committee is mentioned in Lord Barrington to Sir Charles Frederick, July 14, 1772, British Museum. For subsequent developments see below, the committee's minutes under Aug. 12 and its report on Aug. 21.

8. These were vertical bars in the roof of each building, to support a beam on which a crane traveled. Wilson agreed that they were the most dangerous structural defect; see his report in the British Museum.

2. That [the] Building which has a Coping of Lead all along the Ridge from End to End, may be secured by a Pointed Iron Rod erected near each End, communicating with that Coping, and extending down thro' the Chalk Rock on which the Buildings are founded, till it comes to Water. The Rod may be of at least an Inch Diameter (that it may last the longer as well as afford a freer Passage to the Lightning thro' its Substance) and painted to prevent its Rusting.[9] Its upper End should extend ten feet above the Top of the Roof, tapering gradually to a sharp Point; the last six Inches (the better to preserve Sharpness) to be of Copper as less liable to be blunted by Rust.[1] If the Rod cannot conveniently be made all of one Piece, the Lengths of which it is compos'd should be strongly scrued together or into each other by a close Joint, with a thin Plate of Lead between the Shoulders to exclude Moisture (which might occasion Rust) and to make the Joining or Continuation of Metal more perfect.

From all the Electrical Experiments I have made with this View, and all the Instances I have yet known of the Effect of Lightning on these Conductors, it appears to me equally safe (when they are good and compleat down to Water or very moist Earth) whether they are apply'd close to the Wall, and steadied by Staples driven into it, or supported by a Pole or Mast fix'd in the Ground at some Distance from it. The first Method is most convenient, as the Rod may so be bent for avoiding Doors and Windows that are directly under the Pitch of the Roof. Yet as it may be more satisfactory to some Apprehensions, if the Rods are supported in the latter Manner, I should have no Objection to it, provided they can be conveniently posited so as to obstruct no Passage, and are so firmly fix'd as that the Wind may not, by shaking them, break the Iron or Leaden Communication between the Side of the Rod and the Lead that Covers the Ridge.

3. The other four Buildings being, as I understand, to be new-roofed in the same manner with that just mentioned, the same Method will serve for them when so finished. But if it be required

9. The buildings are more fully described in the committee's report. For BF's earlier recommendations about lightning rods see above, v, 76–8; x, 50–2; XIV, 262–3.

1. BF's experiments below, under Aug. 18, buttressed the argument for sharp points.

to secure them in the mean time, then, as their present Roofs are of a different Form, being hipped at the four Corners, and their Hip-joints as well as Ridges Cop'd with Lead extending down to the Eaves, I would advise the immediate boring or digging, near the Ends of each Building, the proposed Passages down to Water, and fixing in them that part of each Conductor which may reach upwards from the Water to the Height of the Eaves: From the Top of this I would extend two Iron Arms reaching to the Corners of the Eaves, where the Leaden Copings of the Hips must be connected with those Bars; and on the Joining of the Hips with the Ridge I would erect Rods nine or ten feet high, pointed as before directed, which, as any Roof is altered may be used as the upper Part of the more upright Conductor. I am, Sir, Your most obedient humble Servant   B Franklin

P s. Leaden Pipe may be used for the underground Part of the Conductors, as less liable to Rust.

Captain Dawson

Notation: 29 May 1772 Ordered that Capt. Dawson cause the same to be executed as above proposed   H.S.C.[2] [*In another hand:*] Letter wrote Copy sent.

From Jonathan Williams, Jr.

ALS: American Philosophical Society

Dear and honoured Sir   Boston May 29. 1772
I have but just Time to acknowledge the Receipt of yours per my Brother, whose Arival we had been long wishing for, but our pleasure was greatly damped by seeing him in such a state of Health; he has not been out since he first entered the House, and is at present very low, we are all fearfull he is consuming fast.[3]
I received per him only three 2d Volumes of Doctr. Priestly

2. Henry Seymour Conway, who became Lieutenant General of the Ordnance in 1767 and after 1770 was its de facto head: Namier and Brooke, *House of Commons*, II, 245–6. Whenever Conway's order was given, BF's advice does not seem to have been carried out in its entirety until after the committee reported: Dubourg, *Œuvres*, I, 282.
3. Josiah was indeed going fast; he died the following August.

Work, when the Setts Arive compleat, I will sell them for the most I can, and pay the whole Money to Aunt Mecom, who is very well, but I believe will not have Time to write by this Oppertunity. I thank You for Poor Richards Advice, and shall endeavour that it shall not be thrown away upon me.[4]

You will please to make my best Compliments to all enquiring Friends; as my Brother is not yet up, he does not know of my writing this, but I think I can take upon me to assure all his old England Friends, of his Esteem and Respect. I must beg you will excuse this hasty Scroll, and believe me to be Your dutifull and Affectionate Kinsman   J WILLIAMS JUNR,

Doctr Franklin

Addressed: To | Doctr Benja Franklin | at M Stevensons | In | Craven Street | Strand | London | per Cazneau

From Samuel Rhoads   ALS: American Philosophical Society

Dear Friend   Philada: May the 30th 1772
   Loxly going early in the Morning to Morrow for London, gives me the Opertunity of Acknowledging thy Favour per Falconer,[5] which with several Canal Papers and Pamphlets came safe to Hand, and I hope will be usefull as I find the Reports of the great Engineers, Smeaton Brindly &ct concerning the Scotch Canal, contain a great deal of Instruction to us unexperiencd Americans. I confess my self much Oblig'd to them, and find by thy sending these Papers, and so far adopting the Project, Canalling grows more into Credit among us, at first it was look'd on as a wild Chemerical Project which all the Strength of America could never execute. Now it is hoped for in time to come. I should have made this Acknowledgment by Falconer, but was then out of Town with the Ingenious David Rittenhouse on an examination of the

4. See the fragment of BF to Jonathan above, under April 2. Priestley's work on color was published in two parts, which are sometimes referred to as two volumes although they are paginated continuously; copies of the second part by itself were therefore not easily marketable.

5. The departure of Benjamin Loxley, Jr., master of the *Carolina*, was not announced until five days later: *Pa. Gaz.*, June 4, 1772. BF's letter by Falconer, who had left London in early February, has not survived.

Ground in order to Judge of the Practicabillity of a Canal between Sculkill and Susquehann to save our Western Trade from total Loss.6 As he was taken sick on the Road, and I was not very well our discoveries are yet too Imperfect to communicate to thee, except that on Levelling the Waters of Schullkill we find that River to Ascend, or the Bed of it to rise, near sixty feet in less than twenty Miles, and suppose it to Continue the same Ascent upwards to Reading. As from its course it approaches the Susquehann, nearer at Reading by twenty Miles than at Philada. and by its Rise approaches the Height of the Middle Ground perhaps more than one hundred feet, Query may it not be best to make it part of the Passage to the back [country7] or will the Difficulties of this Navigation, [subject to all] the Inconveniencies of Innundations and [torn] Ice, be greater than the Expense of Locks Digging [torn] glad [?] of thy Opinion in this Matter and remain [torn]

SL RHOADS

Addressed: To / Benjamin Franklin Esqr: / Agent for Pennsylvania / in / London / per Capt Loxly

6. For John Smeaton (1724–92) and James Brindley (1716–72) see the *DNB*; one was the designer of the Forth and Clyde canal and the other of the Duke of Bridgewater's canal, which BF had visited the year before (above, XVIII, 114–15). BF had provided Rhoads with information about canals early in 1771 (*ibid.*, pp. 93–4), but this time Rhoads was inquiring in an official capacity. Thomas Gilpin had broached his ideas of possible canals in 1769, and had submitted a proposal to the APS. The response had been enthusiastic, both from the Society and from Philadelphia merchants in general, who looked on canals as a way to keep the trade with western Pennsylvania for Philadelphia, against the rising competition of Baltimore; a committee was appointed and brought in a report. See above, XVI, 217–18; XVII, 130; APS *Trans.*, 1 (1771), 293–300 of 2nd pagination; Brooke Hindle, *The Pursuit of Science in Revolutionary America*... (Chapel Hill, [1956]), pp. 210–12. The Pennsylvania Assembly then appointed a committee of its own to survey the Susquehanna, Schuylkill, and Lehigh Rivers, and in January, 1772, added Rhoads to this committee. He apparently persuaded David Rittenhouse, the mathematician, to accompany him on the expedition he mentions. The following September Rittenhouse in turn was added to the committee, which brought in its report four months later. 8 *Pa. Arch.*, VIII, 6609–10, 6748, 6853; Brooke Hindle, *David Rittenhouse* (Princeton, 1964), pp. 94–6.

7. Part of the conclusion has been torn out. We have supplied a few words on the basis of BF's reply below, Aug. 22, in which he advised building a canal instead of trying to make the Schuylkill navigable.

From Jacques Barbeu-Dubourg[8]

ALS: American Philosophical Society

Monsieur   Paris 31e. may 1772

Nous avons icy beaucoup de mauvais Catholiques qui, parce-qu'ils ont manqué une année a faire leurs paques, n'osent plus jamais retourner a confesse. Je ne perds pas courage si aisement, ou je vous suis plus attaché qu'ils ne le sont au st. Siege. Un morne silence de deux ans[9] m'a sensiblement affligé, mais ne m'empe-chera pas de profiter de l'occasion de M M Sutton[1] et de toutes celles qui se presenteront pour me renouveller dans l'honneur de votre souvenir, et vous protester de mon devouement inalterable et a toute epreuve. D'ailleurs Melle. Biheron ne m'a point laissé ignorer les bontés que vous avez eues pour elle, dont je ne vous dois pas moins de reconnoissance que si elles s'etoient epanchées directement sur moi même,[2] et la mention gracieuse que vous avez daigné faire de moi. Je n'en suis point ingrat, et tout ce qui part de vous penetre jusqu'au plus profond de mon coeur.

J'ai vu dernièrement M. Le Roy qui n'a point du tout avancé le remaniement de la traduction de vos ouvrages, pour moi j'aurois craint de les ternir en y portant une main trop maussade;[3] mais au defaut de la sienne, je suis bien tenté de l'entreprendre, mon zele suppléera en partie à ma foiblesse; si vous m'honorez de votre aveu, comme vous m'en aviez flatté, faites moi la grace de m'adresser ce que vous pourriez avoir de nouveau à y joindre, et si vous jugez apropos, je ferai encore repasser le tout sous vos yeux avant de le livrer à nos libraires. J'avois bien etendu mon petit Code de l'humanité, mais on m'a refusé l'approbation neces-

---

8. For BF's French disciple see above, XV, 112–13.

9. A slight exaggeration, for BF had written him in October, 1770: above, XVII, 233–4.

1. Probably John and Richard Sutton, sons of the Rt. Hon. Sir Robert Sutton (1671–1746), a well known diplomat in his day. John died in September, 1772; his brother, who had been an undersecretary of state, thereupon retired from office, succeeded to the family property, and was created a baronet. Namier and Brooke, *House of Commons*, III, 512–13.

2. For Mlle. Biheron's visit to London in 1771 see above, XVIII, 259.

3. LeRoy had agreed to look over the translation that Dubourg was having made; see above, XVII, 127, 236–7.

saire pour le faire imprimer icy, j'y ai eu grand regret, car j'en etois bien plus content que la 1e fois; mais que faire?[4]

Je vous ai adressé les volumes des ephemerides du citoyen[5] a mesure qu'ils ont paru, et que j'ai trouvé moyen de vous les faire passer. Peutetre vous en manque-t-il quelques uns, en ce cas je suis prêt à y suppléer au $1^{er.}$ avis. Mais vous devez savoir que cet ouvrage est toujours fort en retard, par la gene de la presse en ce bon pays cy, où l'on voudroit que tout fût bien, et où l'on craint jusqu'a l'ombre du mal. Adieu, Monsieur et toujours cher Ami, ma femme vous embrasse et vous baise de tout son coeur; et voudroit bien vous tenir encore avec Mr. Pringle que je vous prie d'assurer de mon respect, et de mon devouement. J'ai l'honneur d'être avec des sentimens uniques Monsieur Votre tres humble et tres obeissant serviteur   DUBOURG

From John Walsh: Two Notes

AL: (1) University of Pennsylvania Library; (2) Historical Society of Pennsylvania

The two brief notes below appear insignificant, but they belong to a scientific correspondence that continued intermittently for at least a year, and that chronicled a major advance in the knowledge of animal electricity. The writer, John Walsh (1726–95), was a man who developed his experimental bent late in life. He was the cousin both of Lord Clive and of Nevil Maskelyne, the Astronomer Royal, and moved as he grew older from the world of India to that of science. After serving to good purpose as Clive's secretary in Bengal, Walsh returned home in 1759 with a considerable fortune; in 1761 Worcester returned him to the House of Commons, and continued to do so for almost two decades.[6] But his heart was not in politics. By 1770 he had enough scientific reputation to be elected to the Royal Society, and two years later he was absorbed—for reasons that are as obscure as they are intriguing—with the subject of research that made his name. This was the torpedo fish.[7]

4. The answer turned out to be to have the enlarged *Code* published in London, where it appeared the following year; see above, XV, 115 n.
5. For this periodical see *ibid.*, p. 114 n. LeRoy was supposed to pay for BF's copies, but the arrangement broke down. See BF to du Pont de Nemours below, June 15, Aug. 12.
6. *DNB*; Namier and Brooke, *House of Commons*, III, 602–3.
7. The only slight information we have about how Walsh's interest was

The significance of the research lies in a particular gift of the fish. *Torpedo marmorata*, a sea ray that frequents European coastal waters, is like other members of its family capable of producing at will strong electric shocks from organs on each side of its head.[8] This phenomenon, long attributed to evil spirits, first attracted serious scientific attention in the seventeenth century. A Tuscan physician, Stefano Lorenzini, whose writings were the subject of Walsh's second note below, concluded that the numbing shocks are due to minute particles that pass from the strange organs of the fish into its victim's body. René-Antoine Ferchault de Réaumur (1683–1757), the physicist and naturalist, subsequently amended this hypothesis by substituting for particles the extremely rapid, if equally supposititious, motion of the muscles that compose the fish's organs.[9] Neither theory explained why a fisherman, holding a wet pole or other conductor that came into contact with the torpedo's body, was as effectively numbed as if he had touched it.

The burgeoning of electrical investigation in the mid-eighteenth century brought with it speculation that the shocks from some fish were akin to the discharge from a Leyden jar. Edward Bancroft, the subject of Walsh's first note, carried out a number of experiments with the torpor-inducing or "torporific" eel of Dutch Guiana, and demonstrated that its shocks were indeed electrical. The same had to be true of the torpedo, he argued, unless its physiology was markedly different from the eel's.[1] This was the challenge that Walsh took up. By early 1772 he had met Franklin,[2] who was interested in the problem to the point of borrowing from him Lorenzini's book. In June, Walsh left for

---

aroused is in his letter to BF below, July 1, 1773, in which he speaks of having had many conversations with eminent people in London and Paris about whether electrical principles were involved, and of the encouragement that BF in particular had given him to pursue his research.

8. These two organs, extending vertically through the body, produce charges that often exceed 200 volts. For the fish see Wilhelm Biedermann, *Electro-Physiology* (Frances A. Welby, trans.; 2 vols., London 1896–98), II, 360–469, *passim*, and for a brief treatment specifically of the torpedo J. Frank Daniel, *The Elasmobranch Fishes* (Berkeley, Cal., 1928), pp. 107–10.

9. For the historical background see Sir John Pringle, *A Discourse on the Torpedo*... (London, 1775), pp. 4–19; Biedermann, *op. cit.*, II, 357–8.

1. *An Essay on the Natural History of Guiana*... (London, 1769), pp. 190–9. For Bancroft see above, XVI, 224 n.

2. See George R. Kaye and Edward H. Johnston, eds., *Minor Collections and Miscellaneous Manuscripts* (India Office Library, *Catalogue of Manuscripts in European Languages*, II, part 2; London, 1937), p. 80.

France, the supposed northern limit of the torpedo's range, to search for specimens. He found them off La Rochelle, and proved beyond question that the fish generated an electric charge; its muscles, he concluded, functioned like a Leyden jar. His findings were embodied in a letter to Franklin in 1773 and published in the Royal Society's *Transactions*, and furthered the growing European and American interest in animal electricity.[3] The significance of the torpedo was recognized, and the physiology of its peculiar organs was exposed.[4] Only one mystery remained for later scientists to investigate—how the fish could renew its charges—and this investigation eventually played a part in the discovery of current electricity.

These two notes are impossible to date. Both were written before Walsh's journey to France, and probably not on the eve of departure, because he was still gathering information to prepare himself for his research. Just when he left England is not known, but it must have been early in June; his letter of the 21st, below, suggests that by then he had been in Paris for some weeks. Hence we can only assign the notes to the period before the journey.

Chesterfield Street, Sunday morning [before June?, 1772]
Mr. Walsh presents his Compliments to Dr. Franklyn and requests the favour, if Mr. Bancroft is now in England, to know where he resides, as Mr. Walsh is very desirous of making some enquiries concerning his Torporifick Eel.

Addressed: To Benjamin Franklin Esqr / Craven Street

Chesterfield Street, Thursday [before June?, 1772]
Mr. Walsh presents his Compliments to Dr. Franklin and shall be glad, if Dr. Franklin has no further occasion for Laurenzini,[5] to

3. The letter of July 1, 1773, was published in *Phil. Trans.*, LXIII (1773–74), 461–77. For BF's contact with Walsh in 1772 see below, BF's instructions of Aug. 12 and Walsh's letters of June 21, July 12, and Aug. 27. In America at much the same time David Rittenhouse and BF's friends, Kinnersley and Bartram, were experimenting with the electric eel: Raymond P. Stearns, *Science in the British Colonies of America* (Urbana, etc., [1970]), p. 615.

4. John Hunter, the famous anatomist who worked with Walsh, provided a detailed description of the fish in "Anatomical Observations on the Torpedo," *Phil. Trans.*, LXIII (1773–74), 481–9.

5. Lorenzini's *Osservazioni intorno alle torpedini...* (Florence, 1678) was translated into English as *The Curious and Accurate Observations of Mr. Stephen Lorenzini...on the Dissections of the Cramp-Fish...* (London, 1705).

have it return'd, as he wishes to look into it for some particulers. Mr. Walsh hopes for the favour of seeing Dr. Franklin at Coffee on Friday.

To Deborah Franklin ALS: American Philosophical Society

My dear Child,   London, June 2. 1772
    This just informs you I am well and received yours by the April Packet. I shall write fully to you and all Friends by Osborn. My Love to Sally, Mr. Bache, the Child, and all that love us. I can now only add, that I am ever Your affectionate Husband

B FRANKLIN

Toleration in Old and New England

Printed in *The London Packet*, June 3, 1772; incomplete draft:6 American Philosophical Society

To the PRINTER of the LONDON PACKET.
Sir,
    I Understand from the public papers, that in the debates on the bill for relieving the Dissenters in the point of subscription to the Church Articles, sundry reflections were thrown out against that people, importing, "that they themselves are of a persecuting intolerant spirit, for that when they had here the superiority they persecuted the church, and still persecute it in America, where they compel its members to pay taxes for maintaining the Presbyterian or independent worship, and at the same time refuse them a toleration in the full exercise of their religion by the administrations of a bishop."7

---

6. The draft is addressed to the printer of *The Public Advertiser*.
7. Dissenters, by the spring of 1772, had been encouraged to hope for the removal of their legal liabilities. Several developments encouraged the hope. One was the decision of the House of Lords in the Evans case (above, XVI, 53 n) that nonconformity was no crime; another was an unsuccessful petition to Parliament from a group of Anglican clergy, asking that subscription to the Thirty-Nine Articles be abolished as a requirement for holy orders and for Oxford and Cambridge degrees. Dissenters believed that the time was ripe for redress of their grievances, and a bill was brought in to relieve their ministers and teachers from subscribing to some thirty of the Articles, as re-

If we look back into history for the character of present sects in Christianity, we shall find few that have not in their turns been persecutors, and complainers of persecution. The primitive Christians thought persecution extremely wrong in the Pagans, but practised it on one another. The first Protestants of the Church of England, blamed persecution in the Roman church, but practised it against the Puritans: these found it wrong in the Bishops, but fell into the same practice themselves both here and in New England. To account for this we should remember, that the doctrine of *toleration* was not then known, or had not prevailed in the world. Persecution was therefore not so much the fault of the sect as of the times. It was not in those days deemed wrong *in itself*. The general opinion was only, that those *who are in error* ought not to persecute *the truth*: But the *possessors of truth* were in the right to persecute *error*, in order to destroy it. Thus every sect believing itself possessed of *all truth*, and that every tenet differing from theirs was *error*, conceived that when the power was in their hands, persecution was a duty required of them by that God whom they supposed to be offended with heresy. By degrees more moderate *and more modest* sentiments have taken place in the Christian world; and among Protestants particularly all disclaim persecution, none vindicate it, and few practise it. We should then cease to reproach each other with what was done by our ancestors, but judge of the present character of sects or churches by their *present conduct* only.

Now to determine on the justice of this charge against the present dissenters, particularly those in America, let us consider the following facts. They went from England to establish a new country for themselves, *at their own expence*, where they might enjoy the free exercise of religion in their own way. When they had purchased the territory of the natives, they granted the lands out in townships, requiring for it neither purchase-money nor quit-rent, but this condition only to be complied with, that the

---

quired of them by the Toleration Act. The bill easily passed the House of Commons, but the Lords—thanks in large part to the bishops—threw it out. See Anthony Lincoln, *Some Political & Social Ideas of English Dissent, 1763–1800* (Cambridge, 1938), pp. 196–229; Cobbett, *Parliamentary History*, XVII (1771–74), 432–46. BF's quotation seems to paraphrase part of the Bishop of Bristol's projected speech against the bill: *ibid.*, col. 443.

freeholders should for ever support a gospel minister (meaning probably one of the then governing sects) and a free-school within the township. Thus, what is commonly called Presbyterianism became the *established religion* of that country. All went on well in this way while the same religious opinions were general, the support of minister and school being raised by a proportionate tax on the lands. But in process of time, some becoming Quakers, some Baptists, and, of late years some returning to the Church of England (through the laudable endeavours and a *proper application* of their funds by the society for propagating the gospel[8]) objections were made to the payment of a tax appropriated to the support of a church they disapproved and had forsaken. The civil magistrates, however, continued for a time to collect and apply the tax according to the original laws which remained in force; and they did it the more freely, as thinking it just and equitable that the holders of lands should pay what was contracted to be paid when they were granted, as the only consideration for the grant, and what had been considered by all subsequent purchasers as a perpetual incumbrance on the estate, bought therefore at a proportionably cheaper rate; a payment which it was thought no honest man ought to avoid under the pretence of his having changed his religious persuasion. And[9] this I suppose is one of the best grounds of demanding tythes of dissenters now in England. But the practice being clamoured against by the episcopalians as persecution, the legislature of the Province of the Massachusets-Bay, near thirty years since, passed an act for their relief, requiring indeed the tax to be paid as usual, but directing that the several sums levied from members of the Church of England, should be paid over to the Minister of that Church, with whom such members usually attended divine worship, which Minister had power given him to receive and on occasion *to recover the same by law*.[1]

It seems that legislature considered the *end* of the tax was, to secure and improve the morals of the people, and promote their happiness, by supporting among them the public worship of God and the preaching of the gospel; that where particular people

8. The draft omits the parenthesis.
9. The draft ends here.
1. See Arthur L. Cross, *The Anglican Episcopate and the American Colonies* (New York, 1902), pp. 70–1.

fancied a particular mode, that mode might probably therefore be of most use to those people; and that if the good was done, it was not so material in what mode or by whom it was done. The consideration that their brethren the dissenters in England were still compelled to pay tythes to the clergy of the Church, had not weight enough with the legislature to prevent this moderate act, which still continues in full force, and I hope no uncharitable conduct of the church toward the dissenters will ever provoke them to repeal it.

With regard to a bishop, I know not upon what ground the dissenters, either here or in America, are charged with refusing the benefit of such an officer to the church in that country. *Here* they seem to have naturally no concern in the affair. *There* they have no power to prevent it, if government should think fit to send one. They would probably *dislike*, indeed, to see an order of men established among them, from whose persecutions their fathers fled into that wilderness, and whose future domination they may possibly fear, *not knowing that their natures are changed*. But the non-appointment of bishops for America seems to arise from another quarter. The same wisdom of government, probably, that prevents the sitting of convocations,[2] and forbids, by *noli prosequi*'s, the persecution of Dissenters for non-subscription, avoids establishing bishops where the minds of people are not yet prepared to receive them cordially, lest the public peace should be endangered.

And now let us see how this *persecution-account* stands between the parties.

In New-England, where the legislative bodies are almost to a man Dissenters from the Church of England,

1. There is no test to prevent Churchmen holding offices.

2. The sons of Churchmen have the full benefit of the Universities.

3. The taxes for support of public worship, when paid by Churchmen, are given to the Episcopal minister.

2. After the Glorious Revolution the convocation of Canterbury was torn by quarrels between the two houses, and in the early Hanoverian period was not licensed by the crown to proceed to business; after 1741 it did not meet at all until the middle of the nineteenth century. For the long controversy over establishing bishops in America see *ibid.*, especially pp. 215–25, and Carl Bridenbaugh, *Mitre and Sceptre: Transatlantic Faiths, Ideas, Personalities, and Politics, 1689–1775* (New York, 1962), especially pp. 214–18, 265–70.

In Old England,

1. Dissenters are excluded from all offices of profit and honour.

2. The benefits of education in the Universities are appropriated to the sons of Churchmen.

3. The clergy of the Dissenters receive none of the tythes paid by their people, who must be at the additional charge of maintaining their own separate worship.

But it is said, the Dissenters of America *oppose* the introduction of a Bishop.

In fact, it is not alone the Dissenters there that give the opposition (if *not encouraging* must be termed *opposing*) but the laity in general dislike the project, and some even of the clergy. The inhabitants of Virginia are almost all Episcopalians. The Church is fully established there, and the Council and General Assembly are perhaps to a man its members, yet when lately at a meeting of the clergy, a resolution was taken to apply for a Bishop, against which several however protested; the assembly of the province at their next meeting, expressed their disapprobation of the thing in the strongest manner, by unanimously ordering the thanks of the house to the protesters:[3] for many of the American laity of the church think it some advantage, whether their own young men come to England for ordination, and improve themselves at the same time by conversation with the learned here, or the congregations are supplied by Englishmen, who have had the benefit of education in English universities, and are ordained before they come abroad. They do not therefore see the necessity of a Bishop merely for ordination, and confirmation is among them deemed a ceremony of no very great importance, since few seek it in England where Bishops are in plenty. These sentiments prevail with many churchmen there, not to promote a design, which they think must sooner or later saddle them with great expences to support it. As to the Dissenters, their minds might probably be more conciliated to the measure, if the Bishops here should, in their wisdom and goodness, think fit to set their sacred character in a more friendly light, by dropping their opposition to the Dissenters application for relief in subscription, and declaring their willingness that Dissenters should be capable of offices, enjoy the benefit of education in the universities, and the privilege of appro-

3. See *ibid.*, pp. 317–22; Cross, *op. cit.*, pp. 230–6.

priating their tythes to the support of their own clergy. In all these points of toleration, they appear far behind the present Dissenters of New-England, and it may seem to some a step below the dignity of Bishops, to follow the example of such inferiors. I do not, however, despair of their doing it some time or other, since nothing of the kind is too hard for *true christian humility*. I am, Sir, your's, &c.   A NEW-ENGLAND-MAN.

To Cadwalader Evans

Extract reprinted from Jared Sparks, ed., *The Works of Benjamin Franklin . . .* (10 vols., Boston, 1836–40), VIII, 5 n.

London, 3 June, 1772.

I have at length purchased Stringfellow's right for you, or for you and Mr. James, as you settle it between you. As it was he that immediately recommended the business to me, I have sent the writings to him by this packet. The rights cost £110, and the charges were £5 15s. 6d. There is a letter of the Proprietary to Mr. Tilghman, which it is supposed will remove all difficulties in the office, and I hope the purchase will prove advantageous.[4] Be so good as to acquaint the Silk Committee, to whom I wrote fully by the last packet, that I have since received the bounty from Boydell the broker.[5] The whole sum from government was £35 19s. 6d.; the charges were £5 11s. 6d.; so the net sum received by me was £30 8s. 0d. This, with the £121 5s. 0d., which I am to receive on the 10th instant, will make the whole £152 13s. 0d., subject to the orders of the Committee.[6]

To Abel James   ALS: Yale University Library

Dear Friend,   London, June 3. 1772

Agreable to your Request when in London and what you wrote to me from Bristol relating to the Purchase of Stringfellow's Right,

4. See the following document.

5. For the silk shipped from Pennsylvania see above, BF to Evans, Feb. 6, and to the Managers of the Silk Filature, before May 10.

6. The total, despite the arithmetic, was correct; see BF to Evans below, Dec. 2.

I have attended to the Affair from time to time with Mr. Wheeler, who has been very assiduous in it, and taken a great deal of Pains to bring it to a Conclusion. We could not obtain the Right for less than £110 besides the Charges of Conveyance, and Proof before the Lord Mayor, &c. which amounted to £5 15s. 6d. more, I was obliged to pay the Money down. The Deed is to our common Friend Dr. Evans: But as there is mention in his Letter to you, of which you sent me a Copy, that the Purchase may be for either of you or both, I suppose that to be amicably settled between you, and I send the Writings to you, thro' whom alone I became engag'd in the Business, not having heard any thing from the Doctor immediately concerning it. For greater Safety I took two Setts, lest one should miscarry in the Passage; the other remains with me. I found it was most agreable to Mr. Wheeler that I should leave it to you to satisfy him for his Trouble.[7] Enclos'd you have a Letter from the Proprietary to Mr. Tilghman, a Copy of which, taken by Permission before it was seal'd, is annex'd to the Writings.[8] I hope the Purchase will prove beneficial, as we have done our best. Enclos'd is also a List of the Papers and Letters relating to the Right, which have been deliver'd to me, and shall be sent to you by Osborne, they being bulky and not of immediate Importance. It will be agreable to me to receive the Money I have paid, viz. £115 15s. 6d. Sterling by a Bill as soon as may be. With great Esteem, I am ever, Dear Friend, Yours most affectionately

B FRANKLIN

Abel James Esqr

Notation: London 3rd June 1772 Dr Benjamin Franklin to Abel James

7. For the background of this transaction see BF to Wheeler above, April 3. In May BF had paid £110 for the land and £5 15s. 6d. for related charges to Richard Wheeler, presumably a London lawyer. Jour., p. 41. BF's letter to the Managers of the Silk Filature below, Jan. 6, 1773, shows that they paid Wheeler twenty guineas for his services.

8. The Penns, as proprietors, were giving a written release to James Tilghman, the secretary of their land office; for an explanation of why it was needed see William R. Shepherd, *History of Proprietary Government in Pennsylvania* (Columbia University Studies in History, Economics and Public Law, VI; New York, 1896), pp. 15–16, 72–3.

From William Brownrigg[9]

ALS: American Philosophical Society

Dear Sir   Ormathwaite[1] 12. June 1772.

I have this moment received a letter from Sir John Pringle, in which he is pleased to acquaint me that he shortly intends me the favour of a visit; that you accompany him to Leeds, and may possibly come with him so far as this place. I have great reason to beleive that you will not very willingly part from Sir John on this excursion, or he from you; I should be sorry that either by any accident or business you should be separated; and shall esteem myself highly obliged by the favour of your company along with my good friend, who I have requested to join his more powerful sollicitations to mine on this occasion, and hope he will prevail.[2] I am, with perfect esteem, Dear Sir your very faithful, and most obedient Servant,   W BROWNRIGG.

From William Franklin

ALS: American Philosophical Society

Honoured Father,   Burlington June 12th. 1772

Soon after I received your Letter enclosing a Copy of a Grant of Lands in Pennsylvania to Major Robert Thompson, which you received from Mr. Whately, I happened to meet with our Friend Mr. Galloway, and mentioning the Matter to him, I found he was perfectly acquainted with every Circumstance relative to the

9. A distinguished physician, experimental chemist, and F.R.S. (1711–1800), who was particularly noted for his investigation of firedamp and other gases. *DNB*; Edward H. Davidson, "Franklin and Brownrigg," *Amer. Literature*, XXIII (1951–52), 39–45. He had also published, in 1748, *On the Art of Making Common Salt*, which BF had recommended to friends (above, XI, 88); but this note seems to have been the first contact between the two men. For their subsequent relationship see below, Jan. 27 and Nov. 7, 1773.

1. His family home near Keswick.

2. BF left for his northern tour on or soon after June 17, and was back in London before the middle of July; see BF to DF below, July 14. He and Pringle did visit Brownrigg at Ormathwaite, where the three experimented with the effect of oil on calming the waves of Derwent Water. See Davidson, *op. cit.*, pp. 39, 45–7, 51–4. BF had long been interested in this effect of oil; see above, X, 158–60, and BF to Brownrigg below, Nov. 7, 1773.

Grant, owing to his having been formerly Attorney to the West Jersey Society, who purchased Dr. Coxe's Right to Lands in Pennsylvania, taken up with other Lands granted at the same time to Sir Matthias Vincent and Major Thompson.[3] I therefore requested Mr. Galloway to give me in writing what he knew concerning the Affair, which he has done in the enclosed Letter. It is not improbable, he thinks, but that Major Thompson may have disposed of his Right, as he finds (he says in his Letter) "this Tract is called in a Map of Original Purchasers by the Name of Sir Matthias Vincent, Major Thompson, and Adrian Vrouzen." Here I believe he has inserted, by mistake, *Major Thompson's* Name instead of *Dr. Coxe's*; for I have one of Holmes the Surveyor's Maps of Original Purchases, in which the names on the Tract of thirty Thousand Acres mentioned by Mr. Galloway are placed as follows vizt.

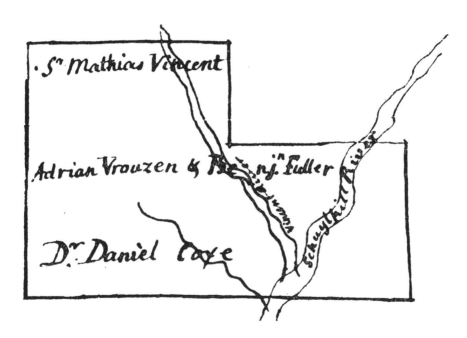

3. Robert Thompson, Matthias Vincent, and Daniel Coxe were all late-seventeenth-century Englishmen who speculated in American lands. Thomp-

On Enquiry, perhaps, it may be found that the Major sold to
Vrouzen and Furlow, or to one of them; and I have heard it suggested that Mr. Peters pretends he purchased the Right of some
Dutchman in Holland, and afterwards exchanged it for Lands
with the Proprietors of Pennsylvania.⁴ However, if there is any
Heir of Major Thompson's living, no Time should be lost in putting in his Claim, as otherwise perhaps the possessors may avail
themselves of the Statute of Limitations. I am Honoured Sir Your
Dutiful Son   WM: FRANKLIN

To Benjn. Franklin, Esqr

<hr/>

son was from Newington Green, Vincent a London merchant knighted in
1685, and Coxe the court physician to Charles II and Anne; the tracts in
question were two townships named after Vincent in Chester Co., Pa.
Charles P. Keith, *Chronicles of Pennsylvania*... (2 vols., Philadelphia, 1917),
I, 131–3; W. A. Shaw, *The Knights of England* (2 vols., London, 1906), II,
261; and the following articles from the *PMHB*: G. D. Scull, "Biographical
Notice of Doctor Daniel Coxe, of London," VII (1883), 317–37; Frederick
Sheeder, "East Vincent Township...," XXXIV (1910), 75; Wayland F. Duna-
way, "The French Racial Strain in Colonial Pennsylvania," LIII (1929),
330–1. Mr. Whately was William, the London banker, who was Thompson's
direct descendant and who had initiated BF's inquiry; see Smyth, *Writings*,
VI, 285, and the headnote on BF to Cushing below, Dec. 2.
    4. "Holmes" was Thomas Holme (1624–95), William Penn's first sur-
veyor. Adriaen Vroesen or Vrouzen (1609–1706), Burgomaster of Rotterdam, acquired five thousand acres in Pennsylvania in 1682. WF's "Furlow,"
who became "Benjn. Fuller" on his map, was Benjamin Furly (1636–1714),
Penn's chief European salesman for American lands. Furly himself acquired
extensive tracts; the one to which WF was referring was in Chester County,
between the present townships of East and West Vincent. See Oliver Hough,
"Captain Thomas Holme, Surveyor-General of Pennsylvania...," *PMHB*,
XIX (1895), 413–27; XX (1896), 128–31, 248–56; *Nieuw nederlandsch bio-
grafisch woordenboek*... (10 vols., Leyden, 1911–37), III, 1365; J. Smith
Futhey and Gilbert Cope, *History of Chester County, Pennsylvania*...
(Philadelphia, 1881), p. 209; Julius F. Sachse, "Benjamin Furly," *PMHB*,
XIX, 277–306. "Mr. Peters" might have been either the Rev. Richard Peters
of Christ Church or his brother William, or possibly the latter's son, who in
1790 claimed a tract originally belonging to Vroesen: *Pa. Col. Recs.*, XV, 481,
485; XVI, 523, 526, 529, 532, 534, 539.

From Joseph Priestley

ALS: American Philosophical Society

Dear Sir   Leeds. 13 June 1772.

You make me very happy by the near prospect of seeing you and Sir John Pringle at Leeds. I shall be intirely at liberty to receive you, and I hope you will contrive to stay as long as possible in this town and neighbourhood.[5] I thank you for the *Native of New England*.[6] I had casually seen the same paper, and was particularly struck with it, without having any suspicion of *Poor Richard* being the author of it. I am obliged to you for your advice with respect to the *dedication*, and shall comply with it, but some other alterations, besides what you noted, must be made in it, if it be addressed to Lord Sandwich only.[7]

I am intent upon the prosecution of my experiments on *air*; and since I wrote to you have observed several remarkable appearances. That very extraordinary kind of air, which Dr. Hales got from Walton Pyrites, and which I had despaired of procuring; I get from all the metals I have yet tried and by means of spirit of nitre.[8] It is quite transparent, but a mixture of it and common air is red for a considerable time, in which the whole quantity is greatly reduced in bulk. A mixture of this and fixed air is not turbid. This air alone is reduced above one half by a mixture of iron filings, and brimstone standing in it, whereas common air is diminished only about one fifth by the same process. When I have the pleasure of seeing you I shall acquaint you with some other

5. BF and Pringle did visit him in Leeds late in June, and witnessed some of his experiments; see Priestley's letters below, July 1 and end of July.

6. "Toleration in Old and New England" above, June 3.

7. We know nothing about BF's suggestions and Priestley's changes. The latter's *Directions for Impregnating Water with Fixed Air . . .* (London, 1772) was dedicated to Sandwich, for whom see above, x, 412 n. The Earl had recently resumed his old post as head of the Admiralty, which he held with more tenacity than distinction until 1782. For the navy's interest in "impregnated" or carbonated water as a possible antiscorbutic see the note on BF to Priestley above, May 4.

8. Walton pyrites were iron, or possibly copper, sulphides named from Walton Heath, Surrey. For the Rev. Stephen Hales see above, IV, 315 n. He discovered that pyrites when mixed with spirit of nitre or nitric acid produce "air," which Priestley called nitrous air and is the modern nitric oxide. Hales, *Statical Essays . . .* (2 vols., London, 1731–33), I, 182–3; Priestley's observations in *Phil. Trans.*, LXII (1772), 210–24.

remarkable properties of this new kind of air.[9] In the mean time, you will do me a very important service by procuring me, and bringing along with you a little of highly concentrated *marine acid.*[10] There is none to be got here; and using a weaker sort in the solution of gold (in order to observe what kind of air came from it) I was obliged to apply a considerable degree of heat, the consequence of which was that the acid menstruum suddenly boiling, my hands, face, clothes, and the walls of the room have been great sufferers by it, as, I am afraid, I shall be able to show you. A pennyweight of gold, which I had bought for the purpose, was also lost. As a reward for this damage, I preserved about three ounce measures of *air* extracted from gold, which, I believe, was never seen before, and have the prodigious satisfaction of finding that it has the very same properties with that which is produced from copper.[1] If I had studied *poor Richard* in time, I should not have indulged myself in these expences, but bad habits are not easily corrected. If, however, the passion be not kept up by considerable success, frugality, and an attention to a growing family will, at length, get the better of experimenting, and then I shall write nothing but *Politicks*, or *Divinity*, to furnish the bishop of Landaff with more quotations for his future invectives against the Dissenters.[2]

The French translation of my History of Electricity I borrowed of M. Walsh; but as it will be of some use to me in a future edition of my work, I think to purchase it. In the mean time, M. Walsh will have no objection to your having it for what time you please, and I can give it you when you are here.[3]

I am suprised that the French electricians should not have been

9. See his letter to BF below, July 1.
10. Hydrochloric acid, which Priestley used to obtain "marine acid air" or hydrogen chloride: *ibid.*, pp. 234–44.
1. Priestley described this experiment at greater length in his *Experiments and Observations on Different Kinds of Air* (3 vols., London, 1774–77), III, 6–9.
2. In a speech in the House of Lords opposing the relief of dissenters, Shute Barrington (1734–1826), Bishop of Llandaff and brother of the Secretary at War, had quoted Priestley and inveighed against his principles. Cobbett, *Parliamentary History*, XVII (1771–74), 441.
3. John Walsh could scarcely object: he had gone to France. See his letters to BF in this volume and, for the translation borrowed from him, BF to Priestley above, May 4.

able to provide themselves with better machines. I am confident that plates will never answer so well as globes or cylinders.[4] I am, with my respectful compliments to Sir John Pringle, Dear Sir, yours sincerely   J PRIESTLEY.

I wish you could bring Dr. Price with you.[5]

From Jonathan Williams, Jr.

ALS: American Philosophical Society

Dear and honoured Sir   Boston June 13, 1772

The Bearer hereof Mr. Adam Winthrop is son to Doctr Winthrop of Cambridge, who you are so well acquainted with, that I need say nothing of the Connection.[6] But with regard to this Gentleman, he is an intimate acquaintance of mine, and a person for whom I have a very great Esteem, therefore beg leave to reccomend him to your Civilities.

Mr. Bancroft's Stay here was so Short that, I had not the pleasure of his Company so long as I wished.[7] I am Your dutifull and affectionate Kinsman   JONA WILLIAMS Junr

Addressed: To / Doctr Benja Franklin / at Mrs Stevensons In / Craven Street / Strand / London / favoured by / Mr Winthrop

4. See *ibid.*

5. For the close relationship, religious and scientific, between Price and Priestley see Schofield, *Scientific Autobiog.*, pp. 105–9.

6. Adam Winthrop (1748–74) had run away to sea in 1768 shortly after graduating from Harvard. He subsequently became the master of the *Lydia*, John Hancock's brig, and died at sea soon afterward. Lawrence S. Mayo, *The Winthrop Family in America* (Boston, 1948), pp. 230–3.

7. This reference was our first inkling that BF's new protégé, Edward Bancroft (above, XVI, 224 n), came to America in 1772. He crossed in company with William Story (above, XVIII, 223 n), and after a seven-week voyage landed in Boston in early June. *Mass. Gaz. and Boston Weekly News-Letter*, June 11, 1772. Why he came or where he went from Boston we have no idea, but he was back in England by autumn: Mary Hewson to BF below, Oct. 22.

From Mary Bache

ALS: American Philosophical Society

Dear Brother   preston June 14 [1772]

Oh with what joy, and pleasure [did] I receive your wellcome letter, with the acoun[t of the] Safe arival of our Dear Son,[8] which he will [*torn*] his Dear family, to think of his, and Dear Sally[*torn*] Makes me quit So. I have been very uneas[y for this?] Month past, and this last week I was quit[e so; not?] hearing any thing of him of So long a time, I fear[ed a?] Missfortune had befallen him, but thank God it is otherwise. I hope I shall have the pleasure of a letter from him soon, or from my Dear Daughter, which will be Equaly the same to Me, so that I hear they are all well and happy. I wonder what our Dear little Grandson wou'd say to his pappa after so long an absance.[9] I do suppose he could Not know him, little fellow if he did how he wou'd rejoyce. I pray god bless them all togather. I heartyly wish you a pleasant Journey, and hope you wont disapoint us, but let us have the happyness of your agreeable Company for Sume time, ware [where] we will do our best indavour to amuse you, and I have a good bed at your Sarvis, and a hearty wellcome to our poor climate [?] the prospects are now delightfull, and I hope you will injoy them.[1] From Dear Brother Your affectionate Sister and humble Servant   MARY BACHE

Addressed: To / Benjamen Franklin Esqr: craven Street Strand / London

To Matthew Boulton[2]

AL: Assay Office, Birmingham

Monday morng. [June 15,[3] 1772]

Dr. Franklin presents his Compliments to Mr. Bolton, and having heard last Night by the Marquis Grisella of Mr. B's intended Call

8. Richard Bache had sailed for home on or about Feb. 18, and did not reach New York until April 24. BF to DF above, Feb. 18.

9. Benjamin Franklin Bache, by the time his father returned, was just over two and a half.

1. BF had obviously written her that he was planning a trip to the north. He and Pringle were at Leeds by the end of the month; see Priestley to BF above, June 13.

2. For the famous manufacturer see above, XVIII, 116 n.

3. Dated by BF's engagement at the Abbey, for which see the next note.

in Craven Street at Ten this Morning, is sorry he cannot be at home to receive him, being oblig'd to be early at Westminster Abby in order to get in.[4] Wishes Mr. Bolton would favour him with his Company at Dinner this Day at 4, or to-morrow if that better suits him. Requests Mr. Bolton would peruse the enclos'd, and add a Line of Permission to Dr. F's Friend L'Abbé Morellet[5] to see his Wonderful Works at Soho.

Addressed: M Bolton

Endorsed: Note of Dr: Franklin —— (no date)

To Pierre Samuel du Pont de Nemours[6]

Reprinted from Albert H. Smyth, ed., *The Writings of Benjamin Franklin*... (10 vols., New York, 1905–07), v, 405–6.[7]

Dear Sir, London, June 15, 1772.

I am much obliged to you for introducing me to the Knowledge of Mr. le Marquis d'Ecrammeville, who appears a very amiable Man, with an excellent Understanding.

4. He was attending the installation of the Knights Companions of the Bath on June 15: *London Chron.*, June 13–16, 1772.

5. A very recent friend. André Morellet (1727–1819) was an abbé only in the broad sense; he was a writer and political economist, who had collaborated with Diderot and d'Alembert on the *Encyclopédie* and was dear to French liberals because a polemic of his in defense of the philosophes had landed him briefly in the Bastille. In 1772 he was sent on a commercial mission to England, where he cemented a friendship with Lord Shelburne that had already begun in Paris, and that greatly influenced the Earl's subsequent views. BF had met Morellet for the first time in the spring of 1772 at a house party of Shelburne's at Loakes, his estate at High Wycombe; Col. Barré, Hawkesworth, and David Garrick were also guests. The Abbé, in talking with BF, steered the conversation away from physics to subjects of mutual interest; and the relationship begun at Wycombe lasted for many years. See Edmond G. Petty-Fitzmaurice, *Life of William Earl of Shelburne*... (2nd ed., 2 vols., London, 1912), I, 428–30; II, 457–8; Claude-Anne Lopez, *Mon Cher Papa: Franklin and the Ladies of Paris* (New York and London, 1966), pp. 284–6.

6. See above, xv, 118 n.

7. The letter, according to Smyth, was in the possession of Colonel H. A. DuPont; but it has not been located in either the Winterthur or Eleutherian Mills collections.

Abraham Mansword's Advice to his Countrymen is very good. I hope they will have more of it.[8]

Pray inform me by a Line, whether M. Le Roy has paid for the Ephemerides in my Behalf.[9] If not, I will upon Sight discharge the amount, by paying your Draft upon me. And I request they may be continually sent me as long as you are concern'd in them.

Go on to do good with your inlighten'd Pen, and by instructing them and inciting them to Virtue deserve well of Mankind and of their common Father. With sincere and great Esteem, I am, my Dear Friend, Yours most affectionately, B FRANKLIN.

From Harvard College

Reprinted from William C. Lane, "Harvard College and Franklin," *The Publications of the Colonial Society of Massachusetts*, X (1907), 238.

⟨June 16, 1772: The President and Fellows vote to extend their thanks to Franklin for the gift of Dr. Priestley's *History and Present State of the Discoveries Relating to Vision, Light, and Colours* (London, 1772), and to request Dr. Winthrop to forward a copy of their vote.⟩

8. The advice was revolutionary. Abraham Mansword was the *nom de plume* of Barbeu-Dubourg, who ostensibly translated two letters from a Philadelphian in the *Pa. Chron.* but actually composed them himself. The first discussed the fundamental laws, the second the constitution, that the American colonies should adopt when they became a federal republic. *Ephémérides du citoyen, ou bibliothèque raisonnée des sciences morales et politiques,* [v] (1771), tome 11, 76–112; tome 12, 7–45. These letters are described and summarized by Alfred O. Aldridge, who resurrected them from obscurity, in "Jacques Barbeu-Dubourg, a French Disciple of Benjamin Franklin," APS *Proc.*, XCV (1951), 366, 369–75. Dubourg's assumption of impending American independence, as Aldridge points out, was remarkable in 1771; equally remarkable was BF's attitude toward it.

9. See Barbeu-Dubourg to BF above, May 31, and BF to du Pont de Nemours below, Aug. 12.

To Francis Maseres[1]

ALS (draft): Library of Congress

Sir   Cravenstreet, June 17. 1772

I thank you for the Pamphlet proposing to establish Life Annuities in Parishes, &c.[2] I think it an excellent one. In compliance with your Wish, pag. 25, 26 I send it back with a few Marginal Notes (perhaps of no great Importance) made in Reading it, requesting it may be return'd to me.[3]

In page 118 of Dr. Price's Book on Annuities, 2d Edition,[4] you

1. Maseres (1731–1824) was a lawyer, mathematician, reformer, and F.R.S. He had served with distinction as attorney general of Quebec, 1766–69; he had then returned home on leave, but retained his office for at least another three years. In 1773 he became, and continued to be for more than half a century, a baron of the exchequer. His writings ranged widely in subject, from mathematics to the American colonies to domestic social and political questions. *DNB*.

2. The pamphlet was first published pseudonymously in the *Public Advertiser*, July 22, 1771, and then anonymously as *A Proposal for Establishing Life-Annuities in Parishes for the Benefit of the Industrious Poor* (London, 1772). It proposed that an act of Parliament should empower the authorities in each parish to purchase Bank annuities, financed by the poor rate, and to use the income thus provided for annuities to be bought by the parish poor. The bill, introduced in 1773, passed the House of Commons but was thrown out by the Lords. Frederick M. Eden, *The State of the Poor: a History of the Labouring Classes . . .* (A. G. L. Rogers, ed.; London, 1928), pp. 67–8.

3. Among BF's papers in the APS is a four-page MS, in an unidentified hand, of remarks upon Maseres' proposal. This document is clearly not the marginalia to which BF refers, but might conceivably be an essay that he wrote after they were returned to him; the style has much of his liveliness and cogency. The argument is that annuities are an unsatisfactory means of relief, and that a better method would be to empower parochial officials by act of Parliament to receive weekly payments from the wages of the laboring poor, to create a fund that would be invested at interest for the use of the contributors in time of need. This scheme does not, as far as we know, have any connection with BF's expressed views on poor relief, and we have found no indication of his authorship except the style and location of the MS. These bits of evidence are too intangible, in our opinion, to warrant accepting the essay even conjecturally as his. A more likely author is Richard Price, for Maseres is said to have published his proposal as a separate pamphlet only after incorporating some "alterations and amendments suggested by the celebrated author of the *Observations on Reversionary Payments, &c.*" *Monthly Rev.*, XLVI (1772), 622.

4. Richard Price, *Observations on Reversionary Payments . . .* (2nd ed., London, 1772). On pp. 380–7 Price commented at length on Maseres' pamphlet.

179

will find mention made of an Institution in Holland. He had that Information from me. Those Houses are handsome neat Buildings with very comfortable Apartments, some form the sides of a Square, with Grass Plats and Gravel Walks, Flowers, &c. and some have little separate Gardens behind each Apartment. Those for Men are called *Oude Mannen Huyƶen,* for Women, *Oude Vrouwen Huyƶen.* I think the different kinds sometimes make different Sides of the same Square. There is a Chappel for Prayers, a common Kitchen, and a common Hall in which they dine together. Two Persons such as best like one another, and chuse so to associate, are generally lodg'd in one Apartment, tho' in separate Beds, that they may be at hand to assist each other in case of sudden Illness in the Night, and otherwise be mutually helpful. The Directors have also a Room to meet in, who form Rules for the Government of the House, hear Complaints, and rectify what is amiss. Gentlemen are Directors of the *Oude Mannen Huys,* Ladies of the *Oude Vrouwen Haus.* A Committee of Two are chosen every Year; who visit often, see the Rules observed, and take care of the Management. At the End of the Year, these are thank'd off, and as an honourable Memorial of their Service, their Names with the Year they served are added to the Gold-letter List on the Walls of the Room. All the Furniture is neat and Convenient, the Beds and Rooms kept clean and sweet by the Servants of the House; and the People appear to live happily.

These Institutions seem calculated to *prevent* Poverty which is rather a better thing than *relieving* it. For it keeps always *in the Public Eye* a State of Comfort and Repose in old Age, with Freedom from Care, held forth as an Encouragement to so much Industry and Frugality in Youth as may at least serve to raise the required Sum, (suppose £50,) that is to intitle a Man or Woman at 50 to a Retreat in these Houses. And in acquiring this Sum, Habits may be acquired that produce such Affluence before that Age arrives as to make the Retreat unnecessary and so never claimed. Hence if £50 would (as by your Table) entitle a Man at 50 Years of Age to an Annuity of £19 3s. 6½d.,[5] I suppose that in such a House, Entertainment and Accommodations to a much

---

5. Maseres' calculation (pp. 15–18) indicated that a £10 investment at three percent interest would buy an annuity yielding £3 16s. 8½d. at the age of fifty; BF multiplied by five.

greater Value might be afforded him; because the Right to live there is not transferrable, and therefore every unclaim'd Right is an Advantage to the House, while Annuities would probably all be claimed. Then it seems to me that the Prospect of a distant Annuity will not be so influencing on the Minds of young People, as the constant View of the Comfort enjoy'd in those Houses, in comparison of which even the *Payment* and *Receipt* of the Annuities are *private Transactions.*

I write this in hopes you will after Consideration favour me with your Opinion whether (in Addition to your Plan, which will still have all its Advantage for small [sums?]) one or more such Houses in every County, would not probably be of great Use in still farther promoting Industry and Frugality among the lower People, and of course lessening the weight of the Poor Tax?

I enclose a little Piece I wrote in America to encourage and strengthen those important Virtues,⁶ of which I beg your Acceptance, and am, with great Esteem, Sir, Your most obedient humble Servant   B FRANKLIN

Mr Maseres.

From William Henly

ALS: American Philosophical Society

Worthy Sir   Wednesday [June?] 17th. [1772?⁷]

Having Received an Account from Dr. Priestley that he could not verify my Experiment of ascertaining the direction of the Electric Matter in its passage through flame, I took the Liberty to call at your House with my Apparatus, in order to shew it you

6. Undoubtedly "Father Abraham's Speech," above, VII, 340–50. BF probably sent one of the English printings, for which see *ibid.*, pp. 330–4.

7. The letter describes one of a series of experiments performed principally in 1771–72: *Phil. Trans.*, LXIV (1774), 389. The only clue to its date is that it was just after Henly found that BF was out of town. Wednesday the 17th narrows the possibilities within the period to three: April or July, 1771, or June, 1772. We have no record that BF was in the country during either of the months in 1771. On June 17, 1772, when he was about to leave on his journey to the north, he drafted the preceding document. If he set out immediately thereafter, Henly could have missed him, gone on to see Nairne, performed and repeated the experiment for him, and written BF about it, all on the same day. This possibility rests on a tissue of conjectures, but we can find no other date that seems as plausible.

both positively and negatively, but I found you was gone into the Country. I then call'd and shew'd it to Mr. Nairne[8] who signed a short Account which I drew up before him, that he was perfectly well satisfied with the Experiment both negatively and positively, and that it was a full and Convincing demonstration of the truth of your Hypothesis,[9] this attested Account I transmitted to Dr. P. I shall be glad of an Opportunity to shew it you at your own House, as I have no Machine.[1] I will not take up more then 10 Minutes of your time—only do me the favour to tell me what day and Hour I shall wait on you, and I will certainly be with you at your Appointment. I hope to get my Cyllender replaced soon, when the Honour of your Company will greatly oblige Sir your most Obedient and Humble Servant   W HENLY

P.S. I was not aware of your going into the Country so soon.

Addressed: To / Dr: Franklin / Craven Street / Strand

From Francis Maseres   ALS: American Philosophical Society

Sir,   Inner temple, June 17, 1772

I am much obliged to you for the favour of your letter and the remarks on my proposal, concerning which this is what I have to say.

In page 46, I think it unnecessary, and rather inconvenient, to limit the expence of these grants in the act of parliament itself. I hope it will be as small as possible, and mean that these grants should be printed with blanks in the manner you propose, and for that reason I inserted the form of the grant.[2]

8. [*Henly's note:*] We had another able witness present, and repeated the Experiment many times both ways, to all our satisfactions.

9. Henly subsequently published his experiment in *Phil. Trans.*, LXIV (1774), 397–8. It substantiated BF's theory (above, XVIII, 19 n) about the direction of flow of electric fluid in the discharge of a Leyden jar, and refuted Benjamin Wilson's hypothesis (*Phil. Trans.*, LI [1759], 320) that flame stored or diminished the charge. See also Priestley, *History*, II, 204–5.

1. His glass cylinder was broken, as indicated below. Our guess is that BF did not arrange a meeting until the evening before Henly's note to him below, under Oct. 28.

2. BF commented, in his letter above of the same date, on Maseres' pamphlet, which contained the draft of an act of Parliament; in the draft was imbedded the form of the deed conferring the annuity.

In page 48; I believe it would be best to keep the parish-book in the church, and suppose it will be kept there.[3] But think it unnecissary to prescribe it positively, as it may happen in some parishes that they keep their registers in some other place made on purpose, and still more convenient than the church: so that this must be left to their discretion.

In page 51. I was inclined to make these annuities unalienable, as you propose, and as the Chelsea pensions to old soldiers are and for the reasons you assign. But some gentlemen of the house of commons who met at Sir George Saville's house to consider this plan, were of a different opinion; particularly Mr. Burke and Mr. Dowdeswell, who alledged that it would be unjust to hinder a man from selling an annuity which he had fairly bought for it's full price, and that it would be a strange thing that a man should go to jail for debt, as might be the case, when he was possessed of an annuity of his own purchasing, by the sale of which he might preserve his liberty. But they directed that the method of assigning it should be pretty formal, as you see, in order to hinder the poor men from selling their annuities for a trifle in fit of drunkenness or folly. And upon the whole I accede to this opinion. But whether I did or no, the directions to me were positive to make it in this manner.[4]

In page 56. The reason of the forfeiture is to make people diligent in demanding and receiving their annuities,[5] whereby the knowledge of them will be continually kept up in the parishes that pay the annuities, and it will be difficult for strangers to per-

3. Each annuity purchased, according to the proposed act, was to be entered in a parish book and signed by the minister, churchwardens, and overseers of the poor.

4. The act provided that a purchaser who wished to sell his annuity must first offer it to the parish officers in a public meeting. If they declined, he had six months in which to sell it elsewhere; the process was then repeated over subsequent six-month periods. This complicated provision was inserted at a meeting of M.P.'s held at the house of one of the most famous of the independent members, Sir George Savile, who represented Yorkshire for many years. He was a friend of Rockingham and had great influence over him. Edmund Burke requires no introduction; William Dowdeswell was Rockingham's chief adviser and led his followers in the House.

5. The act provided that any annuitant who did not collect five or more quarterly payments would be entitled to only the four most recent ones, and would forfeit the others.

sonate them and claim the annuities in their stead either during their (the annuitants) lives or after their deaths, which might perhaps happen now and then if an annuitant was permitted to claim the arrears of his annuity after a neglect of demanding it for eight or ten years.

In page 59. The power of Attorney here mentioned certainly does hazard in the hands of one person the whole stock of the parish.[6] But this is not of necessity. The managers of the parish-fund may, if they please, give their power of attorney to ten persons jointly, if they think proper. 'Tis not therefore the law, but their own choice, that will ever hazard it in the hands of one: and if they chuse to do so, we may suppose that he will be some person worthy of that trust. In general, I suppose, the person so impowered will be some Stock broker, or brokers in partnership with each other, or some banker or bankers, all of whom are every day trusted with more money than any parish will ever probably be possessed of in consequence of these contributions. In truth the main difficulty of the Scheme lies here in getting proper people to manage the fund, which will require a constant open account consisting of many and small articles, and frequent purchases of Stock in the bank annuities with the small sums contributed by the purchasers of life-annuities, and a sale of some of the parish-stock in those annuities four times a year, to make the quarterly payments to the annuitants. However I hope this difficulty will be found to be not insuportable. And the poor men who shall buy these annuities will in all events be sure of receiving them, because of the collateral security given them upon the poor rates of the parishes. Thus much for this proposal. As to the Dutch scheme, I think it obviously useful. Indeed it seems to be no more than what we see often in England by the name of Alms-houses; but perhaps it is more Judiciously executed. However, in general the poor of England are observed to hate confinement, though they have ever so good food and lodging. They like rather to live at large amongst their children and relations and friends. And certainly those charitable institutions best deserve the name of charitable, which gratify the objects of them in the manner they best

6. The act authorized parish officers to appoint an agent with power of attorney to buy and sell the Bank annuities that provided funds for the parochial ones.

like. Therefore I approve most those proposals which leave the poor at liberty to live where they please, and assist them by small donations of a shilling or eighteen pence a week, or so much for each Child in their family. I remain your most Obedient and humble servant, FRANCIS MASERES.

P.S. I desire your acceptance of the copy I herewith send you of a draught of an act of parliament for settling the Laws of Quebec. It has cost me a good deal of time and pains, and has been prepared merely of my own accord, without directions from any body to do so, in order to expedite the Settlement of that province, concerning which the king's advocate, attorney, and Sollicitorgeneral, who were ordered this time last year by the king in council to prepare a plan of laws criminal and civil for the use of that province, have not yet made their report. I have no reason to flatter myself that this draught of mine will be brought into parliament nor do I know any thing to the contrary of it. But every thing relating to that province seems to be in suspense: and nobody knows what to expect.[7] I have read with pleasure your letter in the London packet signed A New-England man.[8] I wish you would publish it in the London Evening, or St. James's Chronicle or the public advertiser.

2d P.S. Upon looking over your letter again, I perceive you dwell very much upon the Dutch scheme, as what you would gladly see

7. Maseres is referring to the complicated discussions and arguments that went on for years before the Quebec Act of 1774. By the time Guy Carleton was appointed lieutenant governor, and Maseres attorney general, of the province in 1766, the temporary system of government adopted after the Peace of Paris was in disarray; and in 1767 the Privy Council ordered a report from the newly arrived officials on what should be done. Maseres wrote the report and, when Carleton disapproved of it and wrote his own, appended his dissent. After Maseres returned to England in 1769 and Carleton followed him a year later, the controversy continued. As part of it Maseres wrote two pamphlets in 1772, both entitled *Draught of an Act of Parliament for Settling the Laws of the Province of Quebec*; the first was printed and circulated among acquaintances for their criticisms and suggestions, which were then embodied in the final form. W. Stewart Wallace, ed., *The Maseres Letters, 1766–1768 . . .* (University of Toronto Studies in History and Economics, III, no. 2; [Toronto, 1919]), pp. 11–12, 20–1, 23–4, 26–7. It is to this first draft that Maseres is referring; if Wallace is correct (p. 27) that it was not printed until August, BF must have received a copy of the MS.

8. See "Toleration in Old and New England" above, June 3.

introduced here. I will therefore say a word or two more about it.
It is perfectly consistent with my proposal, and therefore excites
no Jealousy in me from an attachment to my own scheme. But it
would require a large sum of money, perhaps £10,000, to build
such a county hospital as you describe. And how is this to be
raised? would you wait till the contributions of the purchasers of a
provision in this house should be sufficient to build it? this would
be waiting for ever, I believe: and no one would contribute till the
house was built, and compleatly fitted for the reception of its intended inhabitants. But if the house is once built, whether by
charitable donations, or public money levied upon the county, I
think it would be a very useful institution to permit poor people
to purchase a right of living in it, and being supported by the revenue of it: and in this case their contribution-money should be
laid out in the public fund (as well as in my scheme) in order to
produce the revenue whereby they should be supported in this
house, and the house itself kept in repair. However upon the
whole I think my annuity-scheme more practicable and better
suited to the lower sort of people, who are most likely to come
upon the parish. But I think the principle upon which both are
founded, namely, that of affording industrious people an opportunity of laying out the money they can save in their youth in the
purchase of a provision for their old age, may be applied in many
other instances; and I should be glad to see it so applied. For example, each of the trading, or handicraft companies in London
such as the Skinners, the dyers, the goldsmiths, and so on, (they
being, as I take it, corporations) might receive the money of their
own separate members in the same manner as the parishes do that
of their inhabitants by my scheme, and might grant them equivalent annuities for their lives, not limited to £20 a year, but reaching as far as £100 a year, which would be an encouragement to
industry and frugality in a set of men a degree higher than those
that are the objects of my proposal. The London clergy, who are
likewise, I believe, a corporation, might do the same by their
members to the same amount of £100, or perhaps £200 a year,
and might provide for their widows in this manner. And all other
numerous bodies corporate and politic might do the same.

Further, as to clergymen's widows, it has occurred to me that it
would be no ways unreasonable nor inconvenient to provide for

them by giving them dower of their husbands livings at the rate of one half of the common law Dower, or one sixth part of the husband's living. This to take place only in livings of a certain value, as for instance, £120 a year, or more. The wife to have dower only of one living, though the husband died possessed of two or more. Only two dowers to be allowed at a time upon one living; as thus. Suppose a man A has a living of £300 a year, and dies leaving a widow. She should have a dower out of this living of one sixth of £300, that is, of £50, a year. Afterwards the living is given to B, who dies leaving a widow. She shall have a dower of one sixth of £250 a year or of £41, 13s. 4d. The living is then given to C, who dies leaving a widow, and then to D, who dies leaving a widow, the widows of A and B being still alive. These widows of C and D should have no dower. And no living should ever be reduced by dowers to less than £100 a year. I see no objection to this scheme. The marriages of the clergy are in my opinion greatly beneficial to the public. They in general have many children, and healthy and handsome ones, and educate them better than gentlemen or tradesmen of the same yearly incomes. Why should they not then be encouraged as well as permitted by the State to marry, by making a very moderate provision for the widows out of the public stipends allowed to their husbands, (for in that light only I consider the tythes) in such livings as can bear such a defalcation, and with the precautions abovementioned not to load them with too many dowers at a time. Yours once more,   F: MASERES.

Addressed: To Dr. Benjamin Franklyn / in Craven Street in the Strand / London.

The Sommersett Case and the Slave Trade[1]

Printed in *The London Chronicle*, June 18–20, 1772

It is said that some generous humane persons subscribed to the expence of obtaining liberty by law for Somerset the Negro.[2] It is to

1. This brief but telling assault on slavery shows a development of BF's views; see the headnote on Benezet to BF above, April 27, and Crane, *Letters to the Press*, pp. 221–2.
2. The long struggle that Granville Sharp had waged in the courts to outlaw slavery in England culminated in the case of James Sommersett, a run-

be wished that the same humanity may extend itself among numbers; if not to the procuring liberty for those that remain in our Colonies, at least to obtain a law for abolishing the African commerce in Slaves, and declaring the children of present Slaves free after they become of age.

By a late computation made in America, it appears that there are now eight hundred and fifty thousand Negroes in the English Islands and Colonies; and that the yearly importation is about one hundred thousand, of which number about one third perish by the gaol distemper on the passage, and in the sickness called the *seasoning* before they are set to labour. The remnant makes up the deficiencies continually occurring among the main body of those unhappy people, through the distempers occasioned by excessive labour, bad nourishment, uncomfortable accommodation, and broken spirits.[3] Can sweetening our tea, &c. with sugar, be a circumstance of such absolute necessity? Can the petty pleasure thence arising to the taste, compensate for so much misery produced among our fellow creatures, and such a constant butchery of the human species by this pestilential detestable traffic in the bodies and souls of men? *Pharisaical Britain!* to pride thyself in setting free *a single Slave* that happens to land on thy coasts, while thy Merchants in all thy ports are encouraged by thy laws to continue a commerce whereby so many *hundreds of thousands* are dragged into a slavery that can scarce be said to end with their lives, since it is entailed on their posterity!

---

away slave who had been recaptured and was about to be shipped to Jamaica to be sold. Lord Mansfield's decision to free him was widely interpreted, at the time and later, to mean that any slave arriving in England became free; and this was the purport of the judgment: above, XVII, 38 n. Technically, however, the Lord Chief Justice decided the case on narrower ground, that a slave might not be taken out of the country against his will; if he was resident in England, or willing to leave in bondage, he was not affected. See Jerome Nadelhaft, "The Somersett Case and Slavery: Myth, Reality, and Repercussions," *The Jour. of Negro History*, LI (1966), 193–201, and for a fuller treatment David B. Davis, *The Problem of Slavery in the Age of Revolution, 1770–1823* (Ithaca, N.Y., 1975), pp. 480–501.

3. BF was here drawing on Benezet's letter of April 27.

From John Walsh

ALS and copy: American Philosophical Society

Dear Sir   Paris 21st. June 1772.

After some enquiry I procured the two Copies of Gennete's Book and shall deliver them to Sir John Lambert[4] to forward to you by some one of our returning Countrymen. Your friend M. Le Roy, who presents you his Compliments, has shewn us many Civilities; as has M. Trudaine, the Abbé Morillet's friend[5] for which I must beseech you to make my Acknowledgements to the Abbé. I have been present at two meetings of the Academy des Sciences and have had a polite and obliging reception from the Academicians in general. I have made no Secret of my intentions of prosecuting Experiments on the Torpedo, to which animal by the bye, they are almost Strangers here, Brisson only knows that they exist and in tolerable plenty at La Rochelle, in the neighbourhood of which Reaumur had a Terre.[6] But I have no occasion for academical information on this point, having met at Bologne with two plain sensible Captains of Coasters to La Rochelle and Bourdeaux, who put me out of doubt of their exceeding plenty at

4. Claude-Léopold Genneté (1706–82), a Lunéville physician, wrote a number of books on chimneys, a subject with which BF—Lord Kames's "Smoke Doctor"—had long been concerned, and one on hospitals, a subject of keen interest to Thomas Percival, BF's acquaintance; for this interest see Percival's letter in John Aikin, *Thoughts on Hospitals*... (London, 1771), pp. [85–]98. BF may therefore have asked either for the latest edition of Genneté's *Cheminée de nouvelle construction*... (Paris, 1764) for himself, or for *Purification de l'air croupissant dans les hôpitaux*... (Nancy, 1767) for Percival. Sir John Lambert (1728–99), third baronet, was a Parisian banker; his forebears, before settling in France, had moved from Devon to the Isle of Rhé and back again to England. [Thomas Wotton,] *The Baronetage of England*... (Edward Kimber and Richard Johnson, eds.; 3 vols., London, 1771), III, 31–2; *Burke's Peerage*, pp. 1164–5.

5. For Morellet see BF to Boulton above, June 15. Jean-Charles-Philibert Trudaine de Montigny (1733–77) was an administrator, economist, and scientist, who was responsible for having Priestley's work on fixed air translated into French. Larousse, *Dictionnaire universel* under Trudaine; Suzanne Delorme, "Une famille de grands commis de l'état, amis des sciences, au XVIIIe siècle: les Trudaine," *Revue d'histoire des sciences*..., III (1950), 101–9.

6. For Brisson and Réaumur, his uncle, see above, respectively, BF to Priestley, May 4, and p. 161.

this Season in the neighbourhood of those places. Whether therefore their effect be electrical or not, I persuade myself will be soon
ascertained. I am this instant setting out for La Rochelle and in
three Weeks expect to be in Bourdeaux, possibly in six return'd to
Paris. If you have any Commands for me, which I assure you I
shall ever be proud to receive, you will please to direct them to me
at Sir John Lamberts at Paris and they will be forwarded to me
where ever I may be. I need not remark to you who have lately
been here,[7] the low Ebb of Electricity at Paris. The flatt plates are
the only Instruments now in vogue, which they suppose to be the
strongest and in all States of the Air. The Duke de Chaulne ex-
hibited a Platteau (as they call it, and we a Ramsden's) of upwards of 3 foot Diameter with two Conductors of 12 foot long
and 9 Inches diameter, the Spark from which was insupportable,
striking at full eight Inches Distance. The dry state of the Air here
is certainly favorable to these experiments. The Platteau was
turn'd with great Rapidity and frequently cool'd with Ice to take
off the heat of the Glass by it's violent friction. His whole apparatus was well contrived to produce the strong effects of Electricity; He had as good an apparatus for Kite flying, which we
attempted to make use of but the Wind did not favour us.[8] My next
will convey to you the Event of our Experiments on the Torpedo,[9]
in the mean time I remain with the truest Sentiments of Esteem and
Regard Dear Sir Your obedient humble Servant   JOHN WALSH

I beg my particular Compliments to your fellow travellour Sir
John Pringle

7. In 1769.

8. Marie-Joseph d'Albert d'Ailly, duc de Chaulnes (1741–93), was primarily distinguished as a chemist but was also interested in electrical research.
See Larousse, *Dictionnaire universel,* under Chaulnes. His machine was a development of one invented either by Dr. Ingenhousz or by Jesse Ramsden,
a London optician and instrument-maker (for whom see the *DNB*), or by
each independently. The essence of it was a circular glass plate rotating in
a vertical plane and with cushions against each surface; the plate was a much
more efficient generator, for its size, than a globe or cylinder. Chaulnes had
greatly enlarged the plate over its prototype, and eventually achieved one
five feet in diameter. See Ingenhousz's paper, "Improvements in Electricity,"
Phil. Trans., LXIX (1779), 661–3, 670; Priestley, *History,* II, 111–12. The
Duke's apparatus for kite-flying is illustrated in I. Bernard Cohen, *Franklin
and Newton*... (Philadelphia, 1956), facing p. 489.

9. He sent two reports: below, July 12, Aug. 27.

From William Alexander[1] ALS: American Philosophical Society

Dear Sir   New York June 30: 1772.

It is not perhaps unknown to you that soon after my Arrival in this Country from England[2] I was induced to make several large purchases of Lands with a Veiw of soon disposeing of some of them again to Advantage; you well know the Sudden Change that took place in the Sale of Lands, Vast Quantitys of new Lands Comeing into the Market and a great Scarceity of Cash after the last War render'd lands almost unsaleable; by this means I not only got rid of my ready Money but was left Considerably in debt; I have made many Efforts to extricate my self from so disagreable a Scituation but hitherto in Vain; I am now attempting to do it, by the Sale of a Suffecient quantity of my Lands in this Country by Way of a Lottery, some of the printed Schemes of which are now transmitted to you;[3] the Lottery has already met with very Considerable Success in most of the Colonies in America, I am in hopes it will have some encouragement in G Brittain; I do not a Moment doubt of its haveing your good Wishes; your knowledge of this Country and of the Gentlemen who are Managers of the Lottery enable you to Judge of the honestty of the Scheme; your recommendation of it will be of very Considerable use; I must therefore beg it may have your Countenance among your Acquaintance; such of them as incline to become adventurers in it may be supplied with Tickets by applying to Messrs. Drum-

1. Better known as Lord Stirling, because of his unsuccessful claim to a Scottish earldom. He was born and brought up in America, acquired large landholdings there, and subsequently became a prominent if not distinguished American general in the War of Independence. BF had known him for many years, but their contact seems to have been of the most casual; see above, VI, 244–5; X, 151 n; XIII, 481 n.

2. He had gone to England in 1756 to defend Gen. William Shirley, whose aide-de-camp and secretary he had been; during that visit he had had his title confirmed by a Scottish jury and denied by the House of Lords, but he used it thereafter.

3. Stirling was trying to sell tickets for his lottery not only in England but up and down the American seaboard. The British response was meager to a degree, as BF indicated in his reply below, Nov. 3; and the American response was almost as poor. The whole affair dragged on for another two years and ended in a fiasco. See Alan Valentine, *Lord Stirling* (New York, 1969), pp. 129–36.

mond Charing Cross or to Mr. John Blackburn Merchant in London.[4] The Sale of Tickets is so forward on this side the Water, that if I hear it meets with encouragment in England the Lottery will be drawn by September or October Next. I am Dear Sir Your Most Obedient Humble Servant   STIRLING

Doctor Franklin

From Deborah Franklin   ALS: American Philosophical Society

My Dear child   June the 30 [1772]
    I reseved by the packit which was to a cume by Capt. Laxly I am verey glad to hear that you continew well. I hope your friend Dr. Small is Safe a rived and is well[5] my compleymantes to all that I am obliged to love and respeckt. You may see what blunders by the scratchin oute that I am not capabel of writin so I shall only say that I find my self growing verey febel verey faste. I leve Mr. Beach and Salley to write as I am verey unfitt to due. I have nothing that is good only that I have but verey littel of the head ake nor of the pain that I was so much aflickted for which I am verey thank full to god.
    Mr. Sumain is dead our good old friend Even Evens mr. Gordon you know mr. Bembridg father Polley Pitts[6] and Gorge[7] is a widdower and a dredfull Creyer but is a looking [better a?]gen but shante marry verey soon.

    4. For Drummond and Blackburn see above, respectively, XVI, 269 n; XVIII, 8.
    5. For Capt. Loxley, and Alexander Small's visit to DF earlier in the year, see her letter above, May 14–16.
    6. For Samuel Soumaine's illness see *ibid.* Evan Evans of Norrington had died in the spring; the notice to the executors of his estate in the *Pa. Gaz.*, June 18, 25, makes clear that he had been in far from affluent circumstances, but we have discovered nothing else about him. For Thomas Gordon, a Scots merchant and the stepfather of Henry Benbridge, see above, XVI, 38–9; he had died on June 14: Edward L. Clark, *A Record of the Inscriptions . . . in the Burial Gound of Christ Church, Philadelphia* (Philadelphia, 1864), p. 500. Mary Pitts had died on June 30; she and BF had been involved for years in a complicated matter of a mortgage: above, XIV, 191 n.
    7. George was a slave, or ex-slave, who was DF's servant (above, XII, 45 n); we know nothing about the wife he had lost.

This morning wold aforded you much pleshuer with my king bird he wente in to the water and as soon as he eate his brakefaste he sed he wold go to School and then cume home and play. A littel garle a Schoolmaite ses that Ben Beach is the Commadore over the Maddam but I Supose you will be informd by Salley I am your afeckshonet wife D FRANKLIN

Addressed: To | Benjamin Franklin Esqr.

From William Franklin   LS: American Philosophical Society

Honoured Sir,   Burlington June 30: 1772
    I have recieved your Remarks on our Account[8] on which I have only to observe, That
    The Ten Guineas must have been paid by you for Nelson's Passage, and you expressly say you paid it, I find, in your Letter of the 21st: of Septbr: 1765. which probably you kept no Copy of, as you mention the Vessel to be just upon the Point of Sailing. The 8 Guineas being in Strahan's Account should not be charged. I recollected the Capt: made a Demand for some more Money on her Account after her Arrival, and as you did not charge for the Passage Money, I did not know when I wrote my Remarks on your Account but that I might have paid it, but I since have discovered that it was for Stores.[9]
    I forgot to enquire about the Number of Stoves when I was last in Philadelphia.[1]

8. BF's remarks, unless they are the jottings mentioned below, have been lost. So has the original account, which BF had sent more than a year before. WF had responded with two detailed comments upon it; see above, XVIII, 74–5 and n. These documents, on which BF made a few penciled jottings, and the Memorandum Book cited below, n. 4, are our only source of information for the following notes.

9. WF had undertaken to pay the passage money for Margaret Nelson, a domestic servant (above, XIII, 30 n, 34), and to provide her through William Strahan with eight guineas for expenses. The latter sum, WF thought, had already been taken care of in a settlement with Strahan; BF had agreed.

1. Presumably Franklin or Philadelphia stoves. WF had been charged with six, but wished to be credited for either one or two that he had given to DF; he could not remember which.

The Tea is right as you state it, and I have given myself Credit for the £11 9s. 5d. as an Error.[2]

The Ballance due to me as Comptroller was never settled. The Articles of the Account were not entered in the Post-Office Book till after you returned from Virginia, and I never saw it till long after you went to England.[3] The Bond was given on the 29th: of March 1763, and in the Summer following I purchased the Furniture of Governor Moncton at New York which Mr: Colden paid £330 3s. 9d. for. The Manner the £1000 was made up (as appears by Figures of your Writing which I have on the Back of your Account of Expences on our Journey to Amboy) is thus,[4] vizt

£500 0s. 0d. ⎫	This is for a £500 Sterling Bill	
250 0s. 0d. ⎪	which I remitted to England at 72½	
100 0s. 0d. ⎪	per Cent.	
12 10s. 0d. ⎭		
£862 10s. 0d.		
82 6s. 5d.	Expences to Amboy paid by B. F.	
£944 16s. 5d.		
55 3s. 7d.	Recd. in Cash to make up the Sum	
£1000 0s. 0d.		

2. WF thought that his father had undercharged him for the tea, and was still owed £1 16s.; BF agreed. How and why that sum became £11 9s. 5d. we have no idea.

3. WF was comptroller of the Post Office for some years before 1757; BF inspected the Virginia postal service in 1763. Above, VII, 191–2; X, 252 n. WF must be referring to BF's departure for England in 1764; the accounts took an unconscionable time to settle. WF had been left with a balance of £48 13s. due him from the General Post Office, which BF had presumably collected for him and should have credited to his account.

4. BF's and WF's trip to Amboy was in February, 1763, just after WF and his bride had reached Philadelphia from England; and Gen. Monckton left New York the following June. Above, X, 152 n, 202, 301 n. The newlyweds must have bought the Governor's furniture to set up an establishment worthy of WF's new eminence as a governor himself. He had not yet received any salary, and the Assembly was proving recalcitrant about providing and furnishing an official residence for him. 1 N.J. Arch., IX, 385–6. He obtained the money from Alexander Colden, the New York postmaster; BF presumably credited Colden's account and added the £330 3s. 9d. to WF's account. On March 28, 1763, BF had drawn a bill of exchange on London in WF's favor for £500 sterling, which in local currency amounted to £862 10s.; the next

I have never received any Thing on the Lodge Account since you went away, but I have desired Mr: Bache to enquire of Mr: Swift what is due to us.[5]

Mrs: Franklin wrote to Mrs: Clarke to send her a Cloak, Bonnet, and Cap for this Summer, which I desired you to pay for, but as they are not come, she concludes Mrs: Clarke never got her Letter, which was dated Janry: 6: and we think enclosed in mine to you of that date.[6]

I can't find the Account of the £259 5s. 10½d. which I paid you just before we went to England, but I dare say it is among your Papers, and I am well Convinced that I settled with you for what I received of the Trenton Office,[7] and all other Accounts to the Time of our Departure. Betsy joins in Duty with Honoured Sir, Your ever dutiful Son   WM: FRANKLIN

P.S. I have wrote you 6 Letters by this Opportunity to make up for past Deficiencies.

Notation: To B. F June 30, 1772 (N. 6)

From André Morellet[8]   ALS: American Philosophical Society

ce mardi soir à Whycomb [June 30?,[9] 1772]
Monsieur

Je vous remercie très humblement de votre attention pour moy je me servirai des lettres que vous aves eu la bonté de m'envoyer

---

day his son gave him a bond for £1000 in the same currency. Memorandum Book, 1757–1776 (for which see above, VII, 167–8), p. 13. The bill of exchange, the expenses of the Amboy trip, and the cash from BF made up the amount of the bond.

5. John Swift was a leading member of the Masonic Lodge in Philadelphia: above, V, 236.

6. Mary Clarke often made purchases in London for WF's wife; see BF to WF above, May 5.

7. At the end of WF's term as comptroller the Trenton accounts had been lost or mislaid; see above, VII, 198. Father and son seem to have been equally casual about keeping financial records.

8. See the annotation of BF to Boulton above, June 15.

9. BF had told Morellet that he would be able to be in Birmingham the following Saturday. He actually arrived there on Tuesday, July 7 (to Polly Hewson below, July 8), and we are conjecturing that the Saturday he had in

pour birmingham.[1] J'espere encore que j'aurai le plaisir de vous y trouver. Je pars demain de Whycomb pour oxford ou je passerai 2 ou 4 jours c'est à dire jusques à samedi ou lundi prochain je compte etre à birmingham le dimanche ou le mardi. Vous me dites que vous pourres y etre le samedi c'est une raison qui me decidera à faire tous mes efforts pour partir dès le samedi d'oxford mais je ne suis pas sur de trouver une place dans un stage coach dès le samedi et vous saves qu'ils ne partent pas le dimanche. Je vous supplie toujours de vous souvenir de moy si je n'ai pas le plaisir de vous revoir d'icy à mon retour à londres au commencement du mois d'aoust. Je merite votre amitié par le respectueux attachement et l'estime avec lesquels je suis Monsieur Votre très humble et très obeissant serviteur   L'ABBÉ MORELLET

J'ai fait vos compliments à mylord qui me charge de vous faire les siens et qui vous remercie bien de votre souvenir. Je vous prie de dire beaucoup de choses pour moy à mr. fitzmorris[2] et à mr. le chevalier Pringle. Vous aures la bonté de demander mon addresse à mrs. glover.

Addressed: To / Dr. Franklin / Craven-street in the strand / London.

---

mind was the one before, the 4th; in that case Morellet was writing on the preceding Tuesday, June 30. The Abbé spent only six months in England, and for most of that time, to judge by his memoirs, was led by Lord Shelburne on a whirlwind tour from Wycombe to London to Bowood to Plymouth to Yorkshire; but he unfortunately gave no dates of his itinerary. See Edmond G. Petty-Fitzmaurice, *Life of William Earl of Shelburne*... (2nd ed., 2 vols., London, 1912), II, 457–61. How the Frenchman found time to visit Birmingham, or even whether he did so, we do not know.

1. See BF to Boulton above, June 15.

2. BF had sent his regards to Lord Shelburne, whose brother, Thomas Fitzmaurice, had played host for a time to the house party at High Wycombe. Petty-Fitzmaurice, *op. cit.*, II, 457.

To a French Friend

Extract: printed in Pierre-Joseph-André Roubaud, *Histoire générale de l'Asie, de l'Afrique et de l'Amérique*... (5 vols., Paris, 1770–75), V, 90.

[June, 1772[3]]

Les Américains ne le cédent ni en force, ni en courage, ni en esprit aux Européens.[4]

From Jonathan Williams, Jr.

ALS: American Philosophical Society

Dear and honoured Sir   Boston June 1772

Your Letter of the 14th. April merits my best Acknowledgments, for the kind and affectionate Manner in which you express your Fears of my having appropriated Mr. Warrens Money to other purposes: In the manner this Matter may have appeared to you, those Fears were Just, and I think myself happy in having so good a Friend to forewarn me of even supposed Danger, and be assured Sir that your Advice and informing of what may at any time tend

3. So dated by Roubaud. BF, he says, was writing to a friend in Paris after the appearance of Cornelius de Pauw's *Recherches philosophiques sur les Américains*..., presumably the 3-vol. London edition of 1771. Roubaud adds that he has seen the letter, which has since vanished.

4. It is clear from the context in which Roubaud set the quotation that BF was referring to the American Indians. The sentence we print is in italics, which undoubtedly indicate direct translation of BF. A paraphrase follows: "mais...le fer et autres moyens leur ont manqué pour s'élever au même degré de police." BF was commenting on one of the central points in de Pauw's *Recherches philosophiques*. The book was attracting extraordinary attention, in good part because it was an assault on Rousseau's concept of the noble savage. De Pauw advanced the thesis, buttressed by borrowings from Buffon, Kalm, and others, that the American climate produced degeneracy among the aborigines, and extended his thesis to cover European settlers as well. See Gilbert Chinard, "Eighteenth Century Theories on America as a Human Habitat," APS *Proc.*, XCI (1947), 35–6; Durand Echeverria, *Mirage in the West: a History of the French Image of American Society to 1815* (Princeton, 1957), pp. 10, 12–13.

197

to my disadvantage, will always excite in me the greatest Gratitude and Esteem.

In my last I stated Mr. Warrens Account as it then was with me, the Balance £357[5] since which, I have sent him £170 Sterling and by this Oppertunity I send £100 more, so that there now remains a Balance of but £87 due to him. I also at that time informed you of the Circumstances relating to the Brig, that no part of Mr. Warrens money was appropriated for the payment of her, but only such Goods as came from Champion & Dickason, I therefore in common Justice should remit to them what she neats [nets?], which I shall do in a few Weeks, having sold her for £660 Sterling, by which I have cleared about £40, besides paying the greater part in Goods at a high Advance.[6] This has been a profitable affair to me, but ne'ertheless I do not intend to follow it, I know very well it is a hazardous Business, and therefore shall advance cautiously, under the Advice and Direction of my Father, who I consult upon every Occasion, and without whose Assistance I should not have been able to do so well as I have done, for I came into Business when the Market was glutted with all kinds of English Goods, and every body trying to undersell each other, so that what is at present gained by the Business, must be by steadily preserving, close Attention, and obliging Behavior to Customers, these are things which I have heard you say would never fail; I therefore am not at all discouraged, and endeavour to make the best of bad Times, instead of neglecting the present in hopes for better ones. That you may have a just Idea of the affairs between Mr. Warren and me, it is necessary you should be acquainted with some Circumstances our Agreement was indeed loose, for which I am blameable, but the matter lay in my mind as follows. He was to supply me at the same Credit my other Merchants did, Vizt 9 mo Credit and after that Interest, I told him that I would be as punctual as I possibly could and not appropriate his Money to any other Purpose, but that it might be that I should trespass a little as we cant forsee disappointments, for which Reason Interest was mentioned as a Consideration for such a Trespass, the nine months Credit is

5. See his letter to BF above, April 10.
6. He had originally intended to have Champion & Dickason sell the ship and cargo in Bristol (*ibid.*) but must have changed his mind and disposed of them in America.

not to me near so much, for it is 2½ months before I recieve the
Goods, and almost as much more before the Bills arive. He said it
would not be worth while to enumerate all the Charges that would
arise, but that he would pay them all himself and put 1s. upon each
Yard of Superfine Cloth, and as I understood in *proportion* for the
Rest, which he said would leave about 5 per Ct for his Trouble,
but I am inclined to believe that he has put 1s. per Yd. *indiscriminately*, which makes a very considerable difference, for one
upon 16 is far less than 1 upon 7 or 8, the Superfines and Super
Cloths I find no fault with, I doubt not I shall do well with them,
and flatter myself that in Time I may make a considerable Trade,
but I find that the coarser Cloths come better from the Merchant,
which was the Reason for my Writing my last Order only for
Superfines and Supers, however he did not clearly understand it,
and supposed I should choose some of an inferior Quality assorted,
I accordingly received Yesterday another Supply amounting to
£761 11s. 10½d., which I shall do my best endeavours to remit in
due Time. I have now remitted as much again as I have sold, and
I could not have done it sooner without the most barefaced Injustice to my other Concerns, and you know Sir it is necessary to
support ones Credit uniformly; but 10 mo. is now expired since my
Cloths were Shipped, my Credit was nine, and I have paid all to
£87, great part before due, the remainder I shall pay as soon as
I possibly can, and whatsoever Concerns I may have with him,
I hope always to be influenced by princples of Honour and Honesty, and you may depend upon the utmost exertion of my Abilities,
to give Satisfaction both to You and him. Thus Sir I have explained
my Idea of this Matter, and I should be glad if you could know
whether his and mine correspond, and whether the 1s. per Yd. is
indiscriminately placed, or only on the Superfine. His Letters to
me are very polite and Friendly, and as he says nothing to me in
the complaining Stile, I have wrote nothing in a vindicating one.
He mentions to me that he thinks you would advance me 4 or 500
to enlarge my Trade if I would ask it of you, which is much to the
same purpose with what he mentioned to you, but your goodness
to me has already been more than I have deserved, and I should
look upon such a Request the heighth of presumption, I think an
enlargement of my Trade would be at this present Juncture rather
Imprudent, and I do not see any Occasion for such an Advance to

him, as it will be near 7 mo. before any Money will be due, except the £87.[7] In your letter per my Brother you say you had sent me 6 Copies of Doctr. Priestly's Work, but in the PS you say they could not go with him, but should be sent per the next Ship, ne'ertheless I recieved three per him, but no more neither then nor since, and your not mentioning any thing more about them, makes it difficult to determine whether they have miscarried, or you have omitted sending them.[8]

We are all well and desire to be respectfully remembred to you. My Father has sued Halls Bond and will be glad if you will please to send him a power of Attorney.[9] And also an Account of Cash you have paid for my Brother since his return. With my best Compliments to all inquiring Friends I remain Your dutifull and Affectionate Kinsman   JONA WILLIAMS Junr

To Doctr Franklin

From Joseph Priestley   ALS: American Philosophical Society

Dear Sir   Leeds. 1 July 1772

I presume that by this time you are arrived in London, and I am willing to take the first opportunity of informing you, that I have niver been so busy, or so successful in making experiments, as since I had the pleasure of seeing you at Leeds.[1]

I have fully satisfied myself that air rendered in the highest degree noxious by breathing is restored by sprigs of mint growing in it. You will probably remember the flourishing state in which

7. For the subsequent development of his dealings with Warren see Williams to BF below, Dec. 26.

8. For Priestley's work on color see above, the fragment of BF to Williams, April 2, and the reply, May 29.

9. The attorney in the suit was John Adams, whose law clerk was Jonathan's first cousin, also Jonathan Williams, the son of the customs inspector. Van Doren, *Franklin–Mecom*, p. 138; George Dexter, ed., "Record-Book of the Suffolk Bar," *Mass. Hist. Soc. Proc.*, XIX (1881–82), 151. For the background of the action against Samuel Hall see above, XVIII, 220 n.

1. BF did not return to London until July 14. On the 4th, if we read the date correctly, he was at Preston with the Baches, on the 7th and 8th in Birmingham, and at some time during his trip he was in the Lake District. See below, Bache to BF, Oct. 6; BF to Mary Hewson, July 8, and to DF, July 14.

Joseph Priestley

you saw one of my plants. I put a mouse to the air in which it was growing on the saturday after you went, which was seven days after it was put in, and it continued in it five minutes without shewing any sign of uneasiness, and was taken out quite strong and vigorous, when a mouse died after being not two seconds in a part of the same original quantity of air, which had stood in the same exposure without a plant in it. The same mouse also that lived so well in the restored air, was barely recoverable after being not more than one second in the other. I have also had another instance of a mouse living 14 minutes, without being at all hurt, in little more than two ounce measures of another quantity of noxious air in which a plant had grown.[2]

I have completely ascertained the restoration of air in which, tallow or wax candles, spirit of wine, or brimstone matches have burned out by the same means.[3]

The nitrous air, which I shewed you, I find to be an admirable test of air that is fit for breathing. It makes this air red and turbid, but no other that I have tried. I took air in which a mouse had putrified, which was in the highest degree noxious and fetid and also a quantity of fixed air. The nitrous air admitted to each of these kinds of air separately made no sensible alteration in them but when they were mixd (which I discovered to make a wholesome air) the nitrous air made the mixture turbid, and diminished the bulk of it, as in common air, tho not in the same degree. A mouse put to this mixture lived five minutes without uneasiness, when, if it had been put to either of them separately, a few minutes before, it would have died in a few seconds.[4]

Air that has passed thro' hot charcoal has many, perhaps, all the properties of air that has been diminished by other processes. It

2. Priestley was continuing to investigate the effect that green plants have on the air; see the headnote on the extract of BF's reply below, under the end of July.

3. An awkward sentence: "by the same means" modifies "restoration."

4. For Priestley's earlier observations on "nitrous air," or nitric oxide, see his letter to BF above, June 13. The use of that "air" in the test described here was of great importance, two years later, in his and Lavoisier's discovery of what is now called oxygen. See James B. Conant, "The Overthrow of the Phlogiston Theory: The Chemical Revolution of 1775–1789," *Harvard Case Histories in Experimental Science*, ed. Conant and Leonard K. Nash (2 vols., Cambridge, Mass., 1957), I, 74–7, 82, 88, 98–103.

extinguishes flame, kills animals, and is not diminished or made turbid by a mixture of nitrous air.[5]

But the observation that pleases me more than any I ever made, is the diminution of air by the crystallization (I believe) of quicksilver and the nitrous acid. This effect both precedes and follows the generation of nitrous air from the same mixture. This I suspect to be the case with other crystallizations.[6]

I have observed many other things, which I have not room to mention at present. I am with great respect Dear Sir yours sincerely   J PRIESTLEY.

Addressed: To / Doctor Franklin / at Mrs Stephenson's / in Craven Street, in the Strand / London

From Mary Hewson   ALS: American Philosophical Society

My dear Sir   Broad Street July 6. 1772
As I had the pleasure of receiving your Letter I am bound to answer it. My Mother I must tell you went off last friday week, took our little Boy with her and left Mr. Hewson the care of her House. The first thing he did was pulling down a part of it in order to turn it to his own purpose, and advantage we hope.[7] This Dem-

5. For his experiments with charcoal that produced this "air," which he later called phlogisticated air and is the modern nitrogen, see *Phil. Trans.,* LII (1772), 225–7.

6 In this experiment Priestley, without knowing it, was observing oxidation. Combining liquid mercury and "nitrous" (nitric) acid or spirit of nitre produced the "crystals" that he later called red precipitate (an oxide of mercury), generated "nitrous air" (nitric oxide), and reduced the volume of ordinary air. The first reduction, which pleased him so much, occurred when the mixture gave off nitrous oxide, in modern terms, that combined with oxygen in the air to form nitric oxide. The second reduction doubtless occurred in the test, described in the fourth paragraph of the letter, that produced the "red and turbid" air. If Priestley had heated the red precipitate, as he did in 1774, he would have discovered that it gave off an unknown "air," oxygen. See Conant, *op. cit.,* pp. 94–100.

7. William Hewson, after his breach with Dr. Hunter (above, XVIII, 192–4, 211), was adding a theater to the Craven Street house in which to give a series of anatomical lectures; they proved highly successful. George Gulliver, ed., *The Works of William Hewson...* (London, 1846), pp. xvi–xvii. The Hewsons took over the entire house, and in October Mrs. Stevenson and BF

olition cannot affect you, who ar present are not even a Lodger, your *litterary* apartment remains untouch'd, the Door is lock'd, and the Key in this House. I was commission'd to open any Letter from you, that your orders might be executed, by which means I had the pleasure last saturday of hearing you were well and happy in these middle Regions.[8]

I should have sent your Letter to the Pensilvania Coffee House this Morning if I had not been inform'd by Mr. Rush last night that Capt. Osborne will not sail till thursday or friday.[9] I shall take care to send it.

My Mother said you wish'd the Instrument you commission'd Mr. Hewson to bespeak might be finish'd to go by Capt. Osborne. It is here and if you will favour Mr. Hewson with the proper Directions he will send it on board;[1] as I suppose he can hear from you before the Ship sails.

I can tell you nothing of our little Boy, his Grandmother has taken the charge of him, and Temple writes me word he is well and happy. I have no Occurrence to relate. Mr. Hewson was in Craven Street today therefore I may venture to say you have no Letters.

If you return before friday Dinner time I hope you will favour us with your Company to celebrate the day on which you gave away my Hand.[2] That being one of your many good Deeds, let us all rejoice in the Remembrance, and God grant we may long do so together. I know you will add an hearty Amen to that prayer. Mr. Hewson and my Sister[3] desire me to send their respectful Re-

---

moved to another on the same street. See below, BF to Bache, Oct. 7; Mary Hewson to BF, Oct. 22.

8. The letter from BF that she opened on July 4 has been lost; it was presumably from Preston.

9. For the coffee house see above, XII, 19 n, and for Jacob Rush, who was studying law at the Middle Temple, XVII, 245 n. The *Pa. Packet*, Capt. Peter Osborne, sailed from Deal on July 13: *Lloyd's Evening Post*, July 13–15.

1. The "instrument" was an elastic truss for Cadwalader Evans. See below, the following document and BF to Evans, Aug. 22, 1772, Feb. 10, 1773.

2. Their second wedding anniversary was on July 10.

3. Of the eleven Hewson children four, William and three sisters, were alive in 1767: Gulliver, *op. cit.*, p. xv. The only sister whose name we know is Barbara, who later appeared in Polly's will: Lothrop Withington, "Pennsylvania Gleanings in England," *PMHB*, XXIX (1905), 311.

membrance. I expect Dolly Blunt tomorrow. I am, Dear Sir Your ever affectionate humble Servant   MARY HEWSON

Addressed: To / Dr Franklin / at / Birmingham / to be left at / the Post Office till call'd for

To Mary Hewson   ALS: American Philosophical Society

Dear Polly   Birmingham, July 8. 72

I arrived here yesterday in my Return from the North. This Morning I had the Pleasure of receiving yours of the 6th. I am sorry that my Engagements here will not permit to be in London on your Wedding Day, but I repeat my Wishes of Happiness to you on that Occasion, and pray that you may have many Returns of that Day each happier than its Predecessor, from a Reflection on the constant Felicity the Nuptial State has afforded you.

I must request Mr. Hewson to get the Machine sent by Osborne if possible.[4] The Direction will be the same with that of the enclos'd Letter. [*In the margin:*] Upon second Thoughts I write no letter to Philadelphia from hence. The Direction is *For Dr. Cadwalader Evans, Philadelphia.*

I rejoice to hear of all your Welfares. My Love to all. I hope to be in Town on Sunday. I am, my dear Friend, Yours most affectionately   B FRANKLIN

Endorsed: July 8—72

From John Walsh[5]   ALS: American Philosophical Society

Dear Sir   La Rochelle 12th. July 1772.

It is with particular Satisfaction I make to You my first Communication that the Effect of the Torpedo appears to be absolutely electrical, by forming it's Circuit thro' the same Conductors with

4. The machine, the "instrument" in the preceding letter, could not go by Osborne, who had already cleared for Philadelphia; it was therefore consigned to another ship, but disappeared. BF to Evans below, Feb. 10, 1773.

5. This letter and parts of the one below of Aug. 27 were submitted to the Royal Society, as Walsh requested in his letter to BF of July 1, 1773, and published in *Phil. Trans.*, LXIII (1773–74), 462–6. The printed text has changes in wording and substance, most of which are too minor to deserve notice.

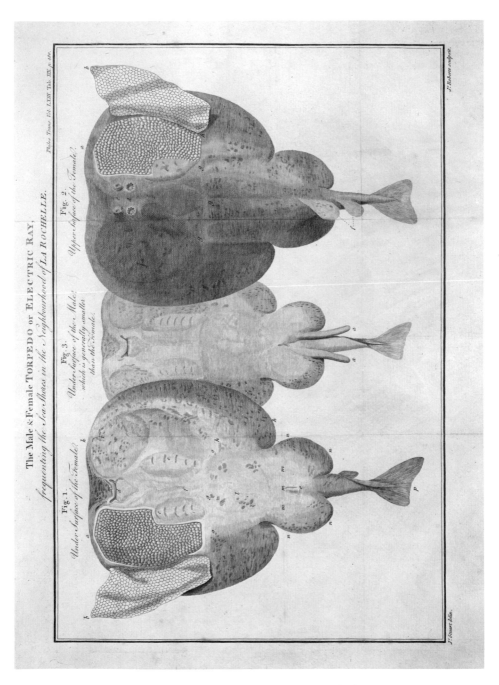

The Male and Female Torpedo Fish
with the Electrical Organs Exposed

Electricity, for instance Metals, Animals, and moist Substances; and by being intercepted by the same non-conductors, for instance Glass and Sealing Wax.[6] I will not at present trouble You with a Detail of our Experiments, especially as we are dayly advancing in them, but only observe that having discover'd the Back and Breast of the Animal to be in different States of Electricity (I speak of that assemblage of pliant Cylinders described by Lorenzini, running perpendicularly from the Back to the Breast, and having some resemblance of the Cells of a Honeycomb[7]) we have been able to convey his Shocks tho' they were very small, thro' a Circuit of four Persons, all feeling it, and thro' a considerable length of Wire held by two insulating Persons, one touching his lower Surface and the other his upper. The Wire exchanged for Glass or Sealing Wax, no effect could be produced. Resuming the Wire, and two Persons were again sensible of the Shock.[8] These Experiments have been varied and repeated without Number, by which the Choice of Conductors is beyond a Doubt determined to be the same in the Torpedo and the Leyden Phial. The Sensation they occasion likewise in the Human Frame is precisely similar: there is not an Engourdissement or Fourmillement of the Torpedo that we do not most exactly imitate with the Phial by means of Lane's Electrometer.[1] We have not yet perceived any Spark or Noise to accompany the Shock, nor that Canton's Balls were affected by it.[2] Indeed all our Tryals have been on very feeble Subjects; whose

6. Substances that transmit but do not store electricity, such as metals, were originally called non-electrics, whereas those that store but do not transmit it, such as glass and wax, were called electrics; BF renamed them conductors and non-conductors. See above, IV, 203–4, 297–8; IX, 350 n.

7. The electric organs of the torpedo, consisting of metamorphosed muscular tissue, are columns of discs or electrical plates, each of which is charged positively on its upper surface and negatively on its lower.

8. Walsh's second report, Aug. 27, gives further details.

1. This sentence was rewritten when the letter was published: "Not only the shock, but the numbing sensation which the animal sometimes dispenses, expressed in French by the words *engourdissement* and *fourmillement*, may be exactly imitated with the Phial, by means of Lane's Electrometer; the regulating rod of which, to produce the latter effect, must be brought almost into contact with the prime conductor which joins the Phial." *Phil. Trans.*, LXIII (1773–74), 463. For the electrometer, which permitted varying the discharges from a Leyden jar, see above, XIII, 459–65.

2. Walsh explains the absence of these effects in his second report.

Shock extended seldom further than the touching finger; I remember it, but once, in above two hundred that I must have taken, to have extended above the Elbow. Perhaps L'Isle de Ré, which we are about to visit, may furnish us with Torpedos fresher taken and of more Vigour,[3] that may give us further insight into these Matters. Our Experiments have been cheifly in the Air, where the Animal was more open to our examination than in Water. It is a Singularity that the Torpedo when insulated should be able to give us, insulated likewise, thirty forty or fifty Shocks from nearly the same part, and this with very little Diminution in their Stre[ngth;?][4] indeed they were all minute. Each Shock is conveniently accompanied by a depression of his Eyes, by which we were ascertained of his Attempt to give it to non-conductors. The Animal with respect to the Rest of his Body is in great degree motionless, but not wholly so. You will please to acquaint Dr. Bancroft of our having thus verified his Prediction concerning the Torpedo[5] and make any other Communication of this Matter you may judge proper. Here I shall be glad to excite the Electricians and Naturalists to push their Enquiries concerning this extraordinary animal, whilst the Summer affords them the opportunity. I am with the truest Sentiments of Esteem and Respect Dear Sir Your most obedient humble Servant   JOHN WALSH

If you favour me with a Line you will please to direct to me at Sr. John Lamberts[6] at Paris: who will forward it to me whether I may [be] here or at Bourdeaux.

Addressed: To Doctor Franklin / Craven Street / London.

Endorsed: Fm J Walsh

3. Rhé, once known in England as the "Isle of Rue" because of a disaster there to English arms in 1627, lies off La Rochelle; limestone reefs north of the island were presumably, at low tide, Walsh's hunting ground for torpedoes.

4. The MS is torn; the printed version reads "Force." Walsh was puzzled, we assume, because he was thinking in terms of analogy with the Leyden jar, in which the charge was reduced or dissipated, whereas the fish could discharge indefinitely.

5. That its shocks were electrical; see above, p. 161.

6. See Walsh's letter of June 21 above.

To Deborah Franklin

ALS: American Philosophical Society

My dear Child   London, July 14. 1772

I am just return'd from a Journey of near a Month, which has given a new Spring to my Health and Spirits. I did not get home in time to write by Osborne, but shall fully to my Friends in general by Capt. All, who sails about the End of the Week. I was charg'd with Abundance of Love to you and Sally and Ben from our Sister Bache and her amiable Daughters. I spent some Days at Preston, visited several Friends in Cumberland, Westmoreland, Yorkshire and Staffordshire. Rachel Wilson sent her Love to you and our Children, as did our remaining Relations at Birmingham, where I likewise staid several Days.[7] In Cumberland I ascended a very high Mountain, where I had a Prospect of a most beautiful Country, of Hills, Fields, Lakes, Villa's, &c. and at Whitehaven went down the Coal-mines till they told me I was 80 Fathoms under the Surface of the Sea, which roll'd over our Heads;[8] so that I have been nearer both the upper and lower Regions than ever in my Life before. My Love to our Children, and all enquiring Friends. I am ever, my dear Debby, Your affectionate Husband

B FRANKLIN

Addressed: To / Mrs Franklin / at / Philadelphia / via New York / per Packet / B Free FRANKLIN

From John Robertson[9]

AL: American Philosophical Society

⟨The Royal Society, July 14, 1772, a note in the third person. The committee appointed by the Society, at the request of the Board of Ordnance, to suggest how to apply lightning rods to the powder

7. Rachel Wilson (1720–75) was a Quaker living in Cumberland. In 1768–69 she had made an extensive tour of the colonies, using Philadelphia as her principal base: John Somerville, *Isaac and Rachel Wilson, Quakers of Kendal . . .* (London, [1924]), pp. 47–80. She had doubtless become acquainted with DF at that time. The relatives in Birmingham were DF's; which ones BF saw we do not know, except that they included the Tylers mentioned above, XVIII, 208.

8. See BF to Barbeu-Dubourg below, under Nov. 12.

9. A mathematician, F.R.S. since 1741 and clerk and assistant secretary of the Royal Society since 1768; see above, XIV, 351 n.

magazine at Erith[1] is requested to meet at the Society's quarters in Crane Court on Saturday, July 18,[2] at seven P.M.; Franklin's presence is desired.⟩

From Thomas Cushing

ALS: Yale University Library

The petition from the Massachusetts House enclosed in the following letter marked another advance in the logic leading toward independence. Whitehall's intention to pay colonial officials out of revenue drawn from America by the Townshend duties was engendering greater and greater opposition in the Bay Colony.[3] In 1771 Hutchinson had exacerbated it by refusing to accept a salary from the House,[4] and by the time the new legislature met in May, 1772, the King was known to have granted him £1,500 per annum. The fat was in the fire. On July 10 a committee of the House brought in a report, adopted by a large majority, which contained six resolves; one of them was that the Governor should ask the crown to rescind its action.[5] On July 14 another committee brought in a petition to the same effect; the House adopted it,[6] and the Speaker forwarded it immediately to Franklin.

It addressed itself solely to the provision of the Townshend Acts that dealt with paying official salaries from the revenues collected,[7] and it broke new constitutional ground. The charter gave the General Court full power to levy money for the support of government, the petitioners argued, and by implication made the Court the sole judge of the amount

1. Erith is on the south side of the Thames, below Woolwich and just across the river from Purfleet. We have assumed that Henly was using the two place names synonymously in his letter to BF above, under May 4; Robertson was clearly doing so because, although a royal magazine at "Erith Level" in Kent is mentioned in 12 Geo. III, c. 61, the committee was charged with investigating Purfleet.

2. The earliest extant minute of the committee's deliberations was dated Aug. 12, and it reported on Aug. 21; see below.

3. See above, XV, 197 n; XVII, 281–2, 303, 312; XVIII, 29, 124–5, 149–52, 177–80.

4. *Ibid.*, p. 149; Bradford, ed., *Mass. State Papers*, pp. 298–9, 324; Hutchinson, *History*, III, 242.

5. *Ibid.*, pp. 245–6; Bradford, *op. cit.*, pp. 325–9. Resolves were a form of protest that BF had encouraged: above, XVIII, 123.

6. *Mass. House Jour.*, 1st session, May–July, 1772, pp. 113, 120–1. The petition itself is in the *Lee Papers*, roll 2, frames 99–101.

7. 7 Geo. III, c. 46; for BF's earlier complaints about this provision see above, XVI, 55, 245.

and means of collection; to deprive it of this power destroyed the
balance between the branches of the legislature, rendered the governor
independent of the people, and exposed them to despotic rule. The
change nullified the form of government established in the charter,
which was a contract between the crown and the people of the province.
By entering into the contract they had agreed to a governor who was
dependent upon them; his independence violated the agreement and
thereby illegitimized his authority. The House therefore demanded a
return to the old practice as a matter of right.[8] Hutchinson rejected the
whole argument as contrary to constitutional theory and practice ever
since the granting of the charter; he refused to address the crown himself, and prorogued the House.[9]

Sir   Province Massachusetts Bay July. 15[–23]. 1772
   The House of Representatives of this Province have directed
me to transmitt to you a humble Petition to his Majesty relative
to the Governors having and receiving a support independant of
the Grants and Acts of the General Assembly, which I accordingly
now Inclose you and they desire you would lay it before his Majesty as soon as may be.[1] They doubt not of your best Endeavors
to get this as well as all their other Greivances redressed. In behalf
of the House of representatives I am with great respect your most
humble servant   THOMAS CUSHING Spk

Benjamin Franklin Esqr

[*In the margin:*] July. 23. 1772 I forgot to Inform you that the
House at their last session made you a grant of six hundred
pounds for Two Years Service ending the 21 Octor. next but his
Excellency has refused his Consent to said Grant.[2] Yours
                                        T CUSHING Spkr.

8. In appealing to the charter as an immutable contract the House was
developing more explicitly the position that it had taken in the earlier dispute
over moving the General Court to Cambridge: above, XVIII, 121 n. For the
contrasting British view of the charter see the headnote on BF to Bowdoin
above, Jan 13.

9. Hutchinson, *History*, III, 257–9; Bradford, *op. cit.*, pp. 331–6.

1. BF received the petition in September but did not present it to Lord
Dartmouth for another two months. BF to Cushing below, Sept. 3, Nov. 4.

2. In the April session the House had voted BF £300 sterling for his services from October to October, 1770–71, to which the Governor refused his
assent; in the new session in July it voted BF £600—again unsuccessfully—
for the period ending in October, 1772. *Mass. House Jour.*, 2nd session,

From Erasmus Darwin[3]   ALS: American Philosophical Society

Dear Sir   Lichfield Jul. 18 —72

I was unfortunate in not being able to go to Birmingham, till a Day after you left it.[4] The apparatus you constructed with the Bladder and Funnel I took into my Pond the next Day, whilst I was bathing, and fill'd the Bladder well with unmix'd Air, that rose from the muddy Bottom, and tying it up, brought it Home, and then pricking the Bladder with a Pin, I apply'd the Flame of a Candle to it at all Distances, but it shew'd no Tendency to catch Fire. I did not try if it was calcareous fixable air.[5]

April, 1772, pp. 185–6; 1st session, May–July, 1772, pp. 121–2. Hutchinson was under instructions to refuse any such grant, because in the eyes of Whitehall BF was no agent. He received no salary from Massachusetts until after his return to America; see above, XVIII, 242 n.

3. Charles Darwin's grandfather, the doctor, scientist, inventor, and poet, whom BF had known since at least 1763: above, X, 227 n. Their relationship had not been close, but they had a number of mutual friends; and Darwin seems to have been stimulated by BF's scientific suggestions. See Robert E. Schofield, *The Lunar Society of Birmingham* . . . (Oxford, 1963), pp. 24, 35, 60–1, 100; Desmond King-Hele, ed., *The Essential Writings of Erasmus Darwin* [London, 1968], p. 15.

4. Although BF's itinerary is not clear, his letter to Mary Hewson above, July 8, indicates that he was in Birmingham on that and the preceding day.

5. This passage, although it leaves many questions unanswered, is significant in the light of Darwin's later development. When BF constructed his apparatus and how it came into Darwin's hands are not clear, but its purpose was to collect in pure form the gas ("unmix'd Air") given off by matter decaying at the bottom of a body of water. Tests had shown that decaying matter released two gases in combination, one inflammable and the other not; see [James Keir,] *A Treatise on the Various Kinds of . . . Gases* (2nd ed., revised, London, 1779), pp. 36, 47, 72, 74. Experimenters in New Jersey years before had set marsh gas alight. In England BF had tried and failed to do so; Priestley had recently succeeded in collecting the gas. See above, XV, 121–2; Smyth, *Writings*, VI, 226–8; *Phil. Trans.*, LXIV (1774), 93. One or the other man's experiments must have accounted for BF's apparatus. When Darwin used it, he apparently concluded that what he had was the incombustible gas, "calcareous fixable air," but did not use the test described in Keir, *op. cit.*, pp. 31–2. His curiosity was starting him on a long path. He had already begun the first of the four works that eventually promulgated his speculative theory of evolution, of which one of the most controversial parts was the spontaneous generation of life from organic matter decaying in water. See Desmond King-Hele, *Erasmus Darwin* (London, 1963), pp. 36, 122–4.

I shall be glad at your Leizure of any observations on the Alphabet, and particularly on the number and Formation of Vowels, as
those are more intricate, than the other Letters.[6] The Welch do
not seem to have the W. Hence they call Woman,'Oman. I suspect
the German W to be a sibilant W, and the same which the Middlesex People or Cockneys use, as in Women and Wine the say
'Vomen and 'Vine, but this Sound I suppose not to be our V. but
the german W, or sibilant W.

It is possible the Welch may have consonat Letters form'd in
the same part of the Mouth with our H, and the Spanish Ch. but I
suspect the Lloyde is no other than the spanish Ch put before the
L. The Northumberland People I think make the R a sibilant
Letter?

I think there are but four Vowels, their successive Compounds,
and their synchronous Compounds. For as they are made by aper-
tures of different parts of the mouth, they may have synchronous,
as well as successive Combinations. *AW* is made like H or Ch
spanish by opening that part of the Fauces[7] a little further. *a* is
made like Sh. or I french. as in ale. *e* as in Eel is made like s or Z.
O as in open, like W. The *u* as in use, is compounded of EU. *i* as in
while is compounded of aw and e. But what is *ah!* as in garter? I
know not. What the french *u*?

I have heard of somebody that attempted to make a speaking
machine, pray was there any Truth in any such Reports?[8] I am Sir
with all Respect your obliged and obedient Servant   E DARWIN

Lichfield Staffordshire

I would return you Dr. Priestley's Pamphlet by the Coach but I
suppose it is to be purchased at the Booksellers. My Friend Mr.

Hence his bathing with BF's bladder and funnel foreshadowed what became
for him a major line of speculation.

6. Darwin shared BF's interest in phonetics and, like him, devised a pho-
netic alphabet. See the analysis of sounds in his additional notes, separately
paginated, to his long poem, *The Temple of Nature*... (London, 1803),
pp. 107–20.

7. The passage from the mouth to the pharynx.

8. Darwin himself had constructed a mechanical mouth, which pronounced
some sounds so precisely that listeners thought a person speaking; and the
invention is said to have been in operation by 1770. *Ibid.*, pp. 119–20; Schofield, *op. cit.*, pp. 109–10.

Day who saw you at Lichfield intends himself the pleasure calling of you in London.[9]

Addressed: For / Dr. Benj Franklin / Craven Street / London.

From Rebecca Haydock

ALS: American Philosophical Society

Doctor Franklin   Philadelphia 20th Inst. [July? 20,[1] 1772]

I am sorry the Silk I have sent will not answer the intend porpose as its out of the common way of trade. I shall be satisfied in haveing it Manufacturd according to the proposal provided its the coular of the pattren.[2] I am sorry to have giving so much trouble but as my kinde Neighbour Docter Franklin is pleas to advise I therefore leave it intirely to you. I think myself greatly Honnour'd an Obliged in receiveing so great a favour from a Gentleman and one so far my soperier, that I may Presume to hope of haveing the pleasure at thy return of thanking the in Person and am with respectful Esteem thy assurd Friend

REBECCA HAYDOCK

Addressed: Dr / Benjaman / Franklin / These

To Ezra Stiles

ALS: Yale University Library

Dear Sir   London, July 22. 1772

This will be deliver'd to you by our common Friend Mr. Marchant. He has had a difficult Negociation here, to obtain Money from a poor Board; to get an old Debt paid by those who are daily put to their Shifts for Excuses to avoid or postpone the Payment of new ones. He has done much more in it than I expected, or indeed than I think almost any other Man could have done, such has

9. The eccentric Thomas Day (1748–89), Darwin's friend and at this time his neighbor in Lichfield, had strong scientific interests, which doubtless accounted for his desire to cultivate BF. *Ibid.*, pp. 51–9 and *passim; DNB.*

1. This was, we believe, the enclosure that DF mentioned a few weeks later; see her letter below under Aug. 6. If we are correct, the most likely meaning of "Inst." is July; about the year there is no question.

2. The "porpose" was undoubtedly outlined in the directions, now missing, that she had sent with the silk. BF had acknowledged them in his reply of Feb. 5, and explained why he had not carried them out but had made other arrangements for manufacture.

been his Perseverance, Assiduity and Address.[3] I write this to you, because I know that what is honourable to your Friends gives you Pleasure. I cannot now write more, nor to any more of my Friends in your Colony, being in a Fit of the Gout which harasses me greatly. I am, my dear Friend, Yours most affectionately

B FRANKLIN

Revd Dr Stiles.

Endorsed: Recd Oct 17. 1772.

From William Watson[4]   AL: American Philosophical Society

Lincoln's Inn fields 31 July 1772.
Doctor Watson presents his complements to Doctor Franklin. He has twice called at his house in hopes of Seeing him;[5] At his convenience if he will call in Henrietta Street, it may be Settled when the expedition to Purfleet may take place; as it Should be, before the Summer is too far advanced. Mr. Cavendish Seldom fails of coming there.[6] Whenever the meeting is fixed, Mr. Burrow, our president[7] is willing to be of the party.

Addressed: To / Doctor Franklin / Craven Street

3. Henry Marchant, the new Attorney General of Rhode Island and BF's traveling companion on his Scottish tour, had come to England with a letter of introduction from Stiles; see above, XVIII, 145. As noted there, part of the reason for Marchant's trip was to obtain reimbursement for Rhode Island's expenses in the Crown Point expedition of 1756; although he also had private business, BF is almost unquestionably referring to his negotiations with the government. Marchant left London on July 24 and reached Newport just two months later: Franklin B. Dexter, ed., *The Literary Diary of Ezra Stiles . . .* (3 vols., New York, 1901), I, 321–2.

4. For the eminent physician, electrician, and naturalist see above, III, 457 n.

5. BF had left town for a visit to John Sargent in Kent; see Cavendish to BF below, Aug. 4.

6. Henry Cavendish was a member, along with Watson and BF, of the Royal Society's advisory committee on protecting the Purfleet powder magazine against lightning; the committee met at Purfleet on Aug. 7. *Ibid.* For its appointment and activities see the headnote on BF to Dawson above, May 29, and the committee's minutes and report below, Aug. 12 and 21.

7. For James Burrow, the ongoing vice president of the Royal Society, see above, XII, 124 n. He served as acting president from the death of James West on July 2 to the election of Sir John Pringle on Nov. 30.

To Joseph Priestley

Extract: printed in Joseph Priestley, "Observations on Different Kinds of Air," the Royal Society, *Philosophical Transactions*, LXII (1772), 199–200.

Priestley's growing sprigs of mint in foul air might not seem like serious science, but it led to one of his major discoveries. A question had long plagued eighteenth-century scientists: how is the atmosphere repurified after being rendered noxious by respiration and by the combustion or decay of vegetable and animal matter, so that it continues to support life? The eventual answer was photosynthesis, the process whereby the action of sunlight permits a plant to absorb carbon dioxide from the air, create organic matter, and release oxygen. Priestley did not glimpse the entire process, but he was demonstrating one important element in it— that plant life (his sprigs of mint) was the purifying agent, which extracted from the air an unwholesome "effluvium," now known as carbon dioxide.[8] He embodied this discovery, along with others, in his "Observations on Different Kinds of Air," which was read to the Royal Society in installments in March and November, 1772. He had sent a first draft of the paper to Franklin the summer before, but continued to amplify it; by the time it was published it contained numerous additions based on work done in 1772.[9]

Franklin was brought into the middle of this experimentation in June, 1772, by his visit to Priestley at Leeds. The older man had long encouraged and assisted his friend in developing from an historian of electricity into a practicing scientist, who was now moving from the study of gases as electrical conductors to the study of the gases themselves.[10] Franklin's role is suggested in the "Observations," where other scientists are alluded to but he alone is quoted.[1] He knew as well as Priestley how important the discovery of the effect of vegetation

8. For the background of his experiments, and later investigation by him and others, see Leonard K. Nash, "Plants and the Atmosphere," *Harvard Case Histories in Experimental Science*, ed. James B. Conant and Nash (2 vols., Cambridge, Mass., 1957), II, 325–434.

9. Priestley's final MS shows a great deal of reworking, and even then does not conform precisely to the printed version. We assume, for reasons explained below, that the extract from BF was among the additions, but when it was added cannot be established. See Douglas McKie, "Joseph Priestley and the Copley Medal," *Ambix*, IX (1961), 1–22.

10. Schofield, *Scientific Autobiog.*, pp. 12–14, 128–37.

1. The extract printed here and another, on p. 234 of the "Observations, from BF's letter to Lining above, VII, 187–8.

would be; "if it holds," he had written almost a year before, it "will open a new Field of Knowledge."[2] After his visit to Leeds he seems to have been convinced that the discovery would hold, and he approached the new field of knowledge in a way that was typical of him. On the theoretical level he fitted it into what was already known; on the practical level he used it to justify the American love of trees.

[July, 1772?[3]]

That the vegetable creation should restore the air which is spoiled by the animal part of it, looks like a rational system, and seems to be of a piece with the rest. Thus fire purifies water all the world over. It purifies it by distillation, when it raises it in vapours, and lets it fall in rain; and farther still by filtration, when, keeping it fluid, it suffers that rain to percolate the earth. We knew before, that putrid animal substances were converted into sweet vegetables, when mixed with the earth, and applied as manure; and now, it seems, that the same putrid substances, mixed with the air, have a similar effect. The strong thriving state of your mint in putrid air seems to shew that the air is mended by taking some-

2. We assume that BF was alluding to this line of investigation in his letter to Canton above, XVIII, 205.
3. The extract consists of two quotations from a single letter. It is impossible to date with complete confidence, because Priestley was vague in his references to the letter from which he took it, and because he ran two series of similar experiments, in August of 1771 and June of 1772, on mice and mint: a mouse was introduced into a jar of noxious air in which mint had been growing for a number of days; if the mouse survived, the mint had purified the air. After the successful August experiment, later ones were unsatisfactory; and Priestley did not resume them, apparently, until June 20, 1772, when he again started the mint growing. On the 23rd or 24th his visitors, BF and Pringle, admired it; on the 27th he introduced the mouse. "Observations," pp. 193–6. The 1771 experiment was reported to BF and elicited the remark to Canton cited above; it may also have elicited the letter, now lost, containing this extract. But the way in which Priestley introduced the extract in his paper, and his placing it at the end of the long passage describing the two sets of experiments, suggest that it was BF's comment on the completed series. If so it was in answer to Priestley's letter above of July 1, with its report on the June experiment. We are therefore assigning the extract, on admittedly shaky ground, to 1772. BF returned to London from the north on July 14, and presumably acknowledged Priestley's letter soon thereafter.

thing from it, and not by adding to it....[4] I hope this will give some check to the rage of destroying trees that grow near houses, which has accompanied our late improvements in gardening, from an opinion of their being unwholesome. I am certain, from long observation, that there is nothing unhealthy in the air of woods; for we Americans have every where our country habitations in the midst of woods, and no people on earth enjoy better health, or are more prolific.

From William Hunter[5] AL: American Philosophical Society

Wind Mill Street. Sunday. [July ?, 1772[6]]
Dr. Hunter's Compliments to Dr. Franklin. He has some preparations which he intends giving away, and if they would be acceptable to Dr. Franklin, he should be glad to see him any morning (except tuesday) from 8 to 10 or 11. for a few minutes.

Addressed: To Dr Franklin / Craven Street

On the Conduct of Lord Hillsborough

Copy:[7] Library of Congress

Because this essay exists only in a copy, it cannot be accurately dated. It was written for the public, to turn it against the Minister and his policies, at a time when Hillsborough's political fortunes were declining and

4. BF is responding to Priestley's conjecture ("Observations," p. 194) "that the putrid effluvium is in some measure extracted from the air, by means of the leaves of plants, and therefore that they render the remainder more fit for respiration." We have deleted the phrase "he adds," which may or may not indicate an excision in the text.

5. For the background of this letter see Dr. Hunter's stipulations about his expiring partnership with William Hewson: above, XVIII, 211.

6. BF later referred to this note as having been written "some time last Summer." To Hunter below, Oct. 30, 1772. We are assigning it to July as the earliest likely month, but in that case it was probably not written before Sunday the 19th, by which time Hunter might well have heard of BF's return the previous week from his trip to the north.

7. In the hand of Lewis or Louis Fevre, for whom see BF to Dubourg below, Dec. 26, n. 7.

before his resignation became known during the first week in August.[8] His replacement by Lord Dartmouth, a happy event for Franklin, led him to withhold the essay in the hope that the American Department would pursue a more enlightened policy. By the following summer his hope was wearing thin, and he published much of the substance of this paper, sharpened by mordant satire, in "Rules by Which a Great Empire May Be Reduced to a Small One."[9] Not long afterward the hope vanished: he concluded that the new Secretary was as uncompromising as the old one, and decided to print the original essay with a preface to explain his reasons.[1] His returning to the same attack indicates that he regarded it as powerful, and it is therefore worth examining as an illustration of his polemical technique.

The essay was propaganda, an attempt to pin the shortcomings of British policy on one man and, by discrediting him, to bring about a more enlightened policy. The Massachusetts House of Representatives led the opposition to the Townshend Acts in 1768, Franklin argues, by petitioning against them and urging other colonies to follow suit; what he does not say, presumably because he wished to avoid controversy on the constitutional point, is that the Massachusetts petition denied Parliament's right to levy the Townshend duties. Hillsborough's determination to prevent concurrent petitions, the argument continues, made him demand that the House rescind its action in calling for them and that the other colonial assemblies refrain from answering the call, on pain of dissolution—an unconstitutional interference with each legislature's freedom of action and right to petition, for which the Secretary should have been impeached. His motives were irrelevant, Franklin adds; only his conduct is at issue.

But his conduct cannot in fact be divorced from his motives. The Americans were ready to believe the worst of him, for since 1767 the fear had been growing, particularly in Massachusetts, that their grievances were not being heard in London. Petitions were sent through improper channels, they were told, or couched in improper language; this stickling for form and ignoring of substance appeared to them to be a mere pretext for keeping their arguments from reaching the King and

8. As BF said later, "just before Lord Hillsborough quitted the American Department": Smyth, *Writings*, VI, 205. For the background of the resignation see the following document.

9. Below, Sept. 11, 1773.

1. The undated preface in Smyth, *loc. cit.*, is printed from BF's draft, addressed to the printer of the *Public Advertiser*, which is with the copy of the essay in the Library of Congress. The draft originally opened with the statement that the essay was "sent to you for Publication" in 1772; BF then amended the quoted words to "written." He later docketed the packet con-

Parliament.[2] They had a case, as Franklin would have been the first to agree; the question is whether he was justified in laying the onus on Hillsborough, by representing his order to rescind a vote and threat to dissolve the colonial legislatures as an attack on their right to petition. If so, the Earl was responsible for denying a basic provision of the Bill of Rights.

The particular petition which started the whole affair did reach the King by way of his Minister, who in receiving and forwarding it ignored technical shortcomings that he might have used for stopping it.[3] Franklin does not mention this concession, but concentrates on the effort to have the vote on the circular letter rescinded in Massachusetts and action on it quashed in other colonies. These two aspects of the Secretary's behavior, accepting the petition and assailing it, seem paradoxical; and as Franklin presents the case they were. They can be reconciled, nevertheless, on the assumption that Hillsborough was acting on the narrow legal grounds so dear to Whitehall, and in the long run so fatal to the empire.

British authorities held that each colonial assembly had power to legis-

------

taining the two documents, "Paper written and printed in England by B. F." This endorsement and the address on the preface would seem to be conclusive evidence that he did eventually publish the attack in the *Public Advertiser*, presumably in 1774 or early 1775. Crane could not find it in print: *Letters to the Press*, pp. 223, 282. We have had no more success, but the search will continue until we decide at what point the preface should appear.

2. Kammen, *Rope of Sand*, pp. 231, 234, 243.

3. See above, XV, 197 n. In that note, *nostra culpa*, we elided Hillsborough's two communications, the circular letter to the governors on April 21 and the letter to Bernard the next day, and described the fate of the petition in England with greater confidence than DeBerdt's ambiguous statements warrant. More important, we agreed with BF that the Secretary had procrastinated; further reflection and research have made us doubt that he did. When the House accused him of delay, he defended himself warmly to Gov. Bernard. He had heard that the petition was in DeBerdt's hands, he said, but did not receive it until eventually Stephen Sayre, an American merchant in London and a business associate of DeBerdt, obtained and sent it to him. The agent's failure to deliver it himself and its lack of authentication precluded forwarding it through regular channels. Neither that consideration, however, nor the indignity offered the crown by not sending it through the Governor and by publishing it before it could reach the throne prevented Hillsborough from presenting it at once. "But His Majesty not considering it as coming properly before him, did not think fit to signify to me any Commands thereupon." Hillsborough to Bernard, Nov. 15, 1768, Bernard Papers, Harvard Library, XII, 12–13.

late, with the assent of the council and governor and the approval of the crown, for its own province alone; it had no power to act in a way that affected other colonies.[4] The resolution calling for other petitions was designed to create the "unwarrantable Combination" of the Hillsborough letter that Franklin quotes, in other words intercolonial opposition to the sovereignty of Parliament expressed in the Declaratory Act. Such opposition was unconstitutional; so also, therefore, was the action that instigated it. Hillsborough required the resolution, not the petition, to be rescinded; and his circular letter to the other governors followed the same line. Each was instructed to prorogue or dissolve his assembly if it insisted on receiving and debating the communication from Massachusetts; nothing was said about acting if the legislature petitioned independently. The Minister and the government believed that collaboration between the colonies would, in his phrase, "subvert the true Spirit of the Constitution."[5] Franklin, intentionally or unintentionally, passed over this issue and attacked Hillsborough for what, strictly speaking, he had not done—but what the reader would naturally assume that he had done.

If the Secretary was technically innocent, he was also politically unwise. The timing of his letters to the governors made him appear to be stifling colonial grievances and curtailing freedom of debate, and his intemperate language greatly strengthened that impression. Appearances, as Franklin pointed out, were all-important, although not to the minds in Whitehall. The whole episode illustrates how little thought was given there to the way Americans would construe British policy, and to the dangers inherent in the letter of the law.

Sir,   [Beginning of August?, 1772]
It is a bad Temper of Mind that takes a Delight in Opposition, and is ever ready to Censure Ministry in the gross, without Discrimination. Charity should be willing to believe that we never had an Administration so bad, but there might be some good and some wise Men in it; and that even such is our Case at present.

4. Colonial assemblies, wrote Grenville's chief lieutenant, "confined as they are within the Limits of their respective Provinces, . . . can never attempt any Measures, which depend for their success upon the concurrence of others. . . ." [Thomas Whately,] *The Regulations Lately Made Concerning the Colonies . . . Considered* (London, 1765), p. 43. See also Sir William Holdsworth, *A History of English Law* (6th ed.; 16 vols., London, 1938–66), XI, 55–6, 248–9.
5. For the full text of his circular letter to the governors see 1 *N.J. Arch.*, X, 14–15.

The Scripture saith, *By their Works shall ye know them*.[6] By their Conduct then, in their respective Departments, and not by their Company, or their Party Connections should they be distinctly and separately judged.

One of the most serious Affairs to this Nation that has of late required the Attention of Government, is our Misunderstanding with the Colonies. They are in the Department of Lord Hillsborough; and from a prevailing Opinion of his Abilities, have been left by the other Ministers very much to his Management. If then our American Business has been conducted with Prudence, to him chiefly will be due the Reputation of it.

Soon after the Conclusion of the last War, it became an Object with the Ministers of this Country to draw a Revenue from America. The first Attempt was by a Stamp Act. It soon appeared, that this Step had not been well considered; that the Rights, the Ability, the Opinions and Temper of that great People had not been sufficiently attended to: They complained, that the Tax was *unnecessary*, because their Assemblies had ever been ready to make voluntary Grants to the Crown in Proportion to their Abilities, when duly required so to do; and *unjust*, because they had no Representative in the British Parliament, but had Parliaments of their own, wherein their Consent was *given* as it *ought to be* in *Grants* of *their own Money*. I do not mean to enter into this Question. The Parliament repealed the Act as inexpedient, but in another Act asserted a Right of Taxing America. And in the following Year laid Duties on the Manufactures of this Country exported thither. On the Repeal of the Stamp-Act, the Americans had returned to their wonted Good Humour and Commerce with Britain; but this new Act for laying Duties renewed their Uneasiness. They were long since forbidden by the Navigation Act to purchase Manufactures of any other Nation, and supposing that Act well enforced, they saw that by this indirect Mode, it was in the Power of Britain to burthen them as much as by any direct Tax, unless they could lay aside the Use of such Manufactures as they had been accustomed to purchase from Britain, or make the same themselves.

In this Situation were Affairs when my Lord H. entred on the American Administration. Much was expected from his supposed Abilities, Application and Knowledge of Business in that Depart-

6. BF misremembered Matthew 7: 20.

ment. The News-papers were filled with his Panegyrics, and our Expectations raised, perhaps inconveniently.[7]

The Americans determined to petition their Sovereign, praying his gracious Interposition in their favour with his Parliament, that the Imposition of these Duties which they considered as an Infringement of their Rights, might be repealed. The Assembly of the Massachusetts-Bay had Voted that it should be proposed to the other Colonies to concur in that Measure. This, for what Reason I do not easily conceive, gave great offence to his Lordship; and one of his first Steps was to *prevent* these concurring Petitions. To this End, he sent a Mandate to that Assembly (the Parliament of that Country) requiring them to RESCIND that Vote and desist from the Measure, threatning them with Dissolution in case of Disobedience. The Governor communicated to them the Instructions he received to that purpose. They refused to obey, and were dissolved! Similar Orders were sent at the same time to the Governors of the other Colonies, to dissolve their respective Parliaments, if they presumed to accede to the Boston Proposition of Petitioning his Majesty, and several of them were accordingly dissolved.[8]

Bad Ministers have ever been averse to the Right Subjects claim of petitioning and remonstrating to their Sovereign: For thro' that Channel the Prince may be apprized of the Mal-Administration of his Servants; they may sometimes be thereby brought into Danger; at least such Petitions afford a Handle to their Adversaries, whereby to give them Trouble. But as the Measure to be complained of, was not his Lordship's, it is rather extraordinary that he should thus set his Face against the intended Complaints. In his angry Letters to America, he called the Proposal of these Petitions, a "Measure of most *dangerous* and *factious* Tendency, calculated to enflame the Minds of his Majesty's Subjects in the Colonies, to promote an *unwarrantable Combination*, and to excite

7. For BF's own expectations see above, XV, 16–19.
8. The "Mandate" was Hillsborough's instructions to Gov. Bernard of April 22 that the vote of the House authorizing the circular letter to the other colonies must be rescinded; the similar orders were his instructions to the other governors of April 21. The latter eventually caused the dissolution of the assembly in New York, South Carolina, and Virginia. See Merrill Jensen, *The Founding of a Nation: a History of the American Revolution, 1763–1776* (New York and London, 1968), pp. 251–64, 300–3.

and encourage an *open Opposition* to and denial of *the Authority of the Parliament*, and *to subvert the true Spirit of the Constitution*; and directed the Governors *immediately* on the Receipt of these Orders, to exert their utmost Influence to defeat this FLAGITIOUS Attempt."

Without entring into the particular Motives to this Piece of his Lordship's Conduct, let us consider a little the Wisdom of it. When Subjects conceive themselves oppressed or injured, laying their Complaints before the Sovereign or the governing Powers, is a kind of Vent to Griefs that gives some Ease to their Minds; the Receiving with at least an *Appearance* of Regard their Petitions, and taking them into Consideration, gives present Hope, and affords time for the cooling of Resentment; so that even the Refusal, when decently express'd and accompanied with Reasons, is made less unpleasant by the Manner, is half approved, and the rest submitted to with Patience.9 But when this Vent to popular Discontents is deny'd, and the Subjects are thereby driven to Desperation, infinite Mischiefs follow. Many Princes have lost Part, and some the whole of their Dominions, and some their Lives, by this very Conduct of their Servants. The Secretary for America therefore seems in this Instance not to have judged rightly for the Service of his excellent Master.

But supposing the Measure of discouraging and *preventing* Petitions a right one, were the Means of effecting this End judiciously chosen? I mean, the threatening with *Dissolution* and the actual dissolving of the American Parliaments. His Lordship probably took up the Idea from what he knows of the State of Things in England and Ireland, where to be rechosen upon a Dissolution, often gives a Candidate great Trouble, and sometimes costs him a great deal of Money. A Dissolution may therefore be both Fine and Punishment to the Members, if they desire to be again returned. But in most of the Colonies there is no such Thing as standing Candidate for Election. There is neither Treating nor Bribing. No Man even expresses the least Inclination to be chosen. Instead of humble Advertisements intreating Votes and Interest, you see before every new Election, Requests of former Members, acknowledging the Honour done them by preceeding Elections,

9. Here and elsewhere in the essay BF is elaborating points that he had raised two years before: above, XVII, 269–70.

but setting forth their long Service and Attendance on the Public Business in that Station, and praying that in Consideration thereof some other Person may now be chosen in their Room. Where this is the Case, where the same Representatives may be and generally are after a Dissolution chosen without asking a Vote or giving even a Glass of Cyder to any Elector, is it likely that such a Threat could contribute in the least to answer the End proposed?[1] The Experience of former Governors, might have instructed his Lordship that this was a vain Expedient. Several of them, misled by their English Ideas, had tried this Practice to make Assemblies submissive to their Measures, but never with Success. By the Influence of his Power in granting Offices, a Governor naturally has a Number of Friends in an Assembly; these, if suffered to continue, might, tho' a Minority, frequently serve his Purposes, by promoting what he wishes, or obstructing what he dislikes. But if, to punish the Majority, he in a Pet dissolves the House, and orders a new Election, he is sure not to see a single Friend in the new Assembly. The People are put into an ill Humour by the Trouble given them, they resent the Dissolution as an Affront, and leave out every Man suspected of having the least Regard for the Governor. This was the very Effect of my Lord's Dissolutions in America, and the new Assemblies were all found more untractable than the old ones.

But besides the Imprudence of this Measure, was it constitutional? The Crown has doubtless the Prerogative of dissolving Parliaments, a Prerogative lodged in its hands for the Publick Good, which may in various Instances require the Use of it. But should a King of Great-Britain demand of his Parliament a Rescission of any Vote they had passed, or forbid them to petition the

1. American electoral practices, although BF exaggerated their bucolic innocence, did differ markedly from British. For the latter see Lewis B. Namier, *The Structure of Politics at the Accession of George III* (2 vols., London, 1929), I, 195–205; Namier and Brooke, *House of Commons*, I, 2–56. For the former see Cortlandt F. Bishop, *History of Elections in the American Colonies* (New York, 1893), and for regional examples Charles S. Sydnor, *Gentlemen Freeholders: Political Practices in Washington's Virginia* (Chapel Hill, [1952]), pp. 11–59; J. Philip Gleason, "A Scurrilous Colonial Election and Franklin's Reputation," 3 *W&MQ*, XVIII (1961), 68–84; Gerard B. Warden, "The Caucus and Democracy in Colonial Boston," *New England Quarterly*, XLIII (1970), 19–45.

Throne, *on pain of Dissolution*, and actually dissolve them accordingly, I humbly conceive the Minister who advised it would run some hazard—of Censure at least,—for thus using the Prerogative to the Violation of *common Right*, and Breach of the Constitution. The American Assemblies have indeed no Means of impeaching such a Minister; but there is an Assembly, the Parliament of England, that have that Power, and in a former Instance exercised it well, by impeaching as great a Man, (Lord Clarendon) for having (tho' in one Instance only) *endeavoured to introduce arbitrary Government into the Colonies*.[2]

The Effect this Operation of the American Secretary had in America, was not a Prevention of those Petitions, as he intended, but a Despair in the People of any Success from them, since they could not pass to the Throne but thro' the Hands of one who shewed himself so extremely averse to the Existence of them. Thence arose the Design of interesting the British Merchants and Manufacturers in the Event of their Petitions, by Agreements not to import Goods from Great Britain till their Grievances were redressed. Universal Resentment occasioned these Agreements to be more generally entred into, and the sending Troops to Boston, who daily insulted the Assembly[3] and Townsmen, instead of terrifying into a Compliance with his Measures, served only to exasperate and sour the Minds of People throughout the Continent, make Frugality fashionable when the Consumption of British Goods was the Question, and determine the Inhabitants to exert every Nerve in establishing Manufactures among themselves.

Boston having grievously offended his Lordship, by the refractory Spirit they had shown in re-chusing those Representatives,

2. Clarendon's colonial policy was only a minor factor in his impeachment. But BF thought otherwise; see his letter to Cushing above, Jan. 13.

3. BF here added the following note: "They mounted a numerous Guard daily round the Parliament House, with Drums beating and Fifes playing while the Members were in their Debates, and had Cannon planted and pointed at the Building." For the sending of troops to Boston in 1768 see above, XV, 187 n, 231, and for contemporary complaints similar to BF's Oliver M. Dickerson, ed., *Boston under Military Rule*... ([Boston,] 1936), p. 109. The complaints appear to have exaggerated: the Court House, where the legislature met, was not under guard or intentionally menaced by cannon, although troops marched past it when the guard was changed.

whom he esteemed Leaders of the Opposition there, he resolved to punish that Town by removing the Assembly from thence to Cambridge, a Country Place about four Miles distant: Here too his Lordship's English and Irish Ideas seem to have misled him. Removing a Parliament from London or Dublin where so many of the Inhabitants are supported by the Expence of such a Number of Wealthy Lords and Commoners, and have a Dependance on that Support, may be a considerable Prejudice to the City deprived of such Advantage; but the Removal of the Assembly, consisting of frugal honest Farmers, from Boston, could only affect the Interest of a few poor Widows who keep Lodging-houses there.[4] Whatever Manufactures the Members might want, were still purchased at Boston. They themselves, indeed, suffered some Inconvenience, in being perhaps less commodiously lodged, and being at a Distance from the Records; but this, and the keeping them before so long prorogued, when the Publick Affairs required their Meeting, could never reconcile them to Ministerial Measures, it could serve only to put them more out of Humour with Britain and its Government so wantonly exercised, and to so little purpose. Ignorance alone of the true State of that Country, can excuse, (if it may be excused) these frivolous Proceedings.

To have *good Ends* in View and to use *proper Means* to obtain them, shows the Minister to be both *good* and *wise*. To pursue *good Ends* by *improper Means*, argues him tho' *good* to be but *weak*. To pursue *bad Ends* by *artful Means*, shows him to be *wicked* tho' *able*. But when his Ends are *bad*, and the Means he uses *improper* to obtain those Ends, what shall we say of such a Minister? Every Step taken for some time past in our Treatment of America, the suspending their Legislative Powers, for not making Laws *by Direction* from hence; the countenancing their Adversaries by Rewards and Pensions paid out of the Revenues extorted from them by Laws to which they have not given their Assent; the sending over a set of rash, indiscreet Commissioners to collect that Revenue, who by insolence of Behaviour, harrassing Commerce, and perpetually accusing the good People (out of whose Substance they are supported) to Government here, as Rebels and Traitors, have

4. For the removal of the Court see BF to Cushing above, Jan. 13. One of the poor widows affected was Jane Mecom: Van Doren, *Franklin–Mecom*, pp. 7–8.

made themselves universally odious there, but here are caressed and encouraged; together with the arbitrary Dissolution of Assemblies, and the Quartering Troops among the People, to menace and insult them; all these Steps, if intended to provoke them to Rebellion that we might take their Lives and confiscate their Estates, are proper Means to obtain a bad End: But if they are intended to conciliate the Americans to our Government, restore our Commerce with them, and secure the Friendship and Assistance which their growing Strength, Wealth, and Power may in a few years render extremely valuable to us, can any thing be conceived more injudicious, more absurd! His Lordship may have in general a good Understanding, his Friends say he has; but in the Political Part of it there must surely be some *Twist*, some extreme *Obliquity*.

A WELL-WISHER TO THE KING AND ALL HIS DOMINIONS.

To Noble Wimberly Jones

ALS: Buffalo and Erie Public Library

Dear Sir,   London,5 Aug. 3[–8]. 1772.

On my late Return from the Country I found your Favour of March 18. which had been left by Mr. Stephens.6 I have not since seen him, but shall be glad of any Opportunity of serving him on your Recommendation.

I see by the Papers that your new Assembly is dissolved.7 I am concern'd at the uncomfortable Train your public Affairs have lately taken, but hope it cannot long continue.

You will see by the enclos'd that the Lords of the Council have not favour'd our Petition. It was difficult to get them to give a

5. Actually May Place, John Sargent's country home in Kent; see Cavendish to BF below, Aug. 4. Our conjecture is that BF had received Jones's letter in mid-July after his tour of the north ("my late Return from the Country") and had taken it with him to Kent to answer; in that case he wrote the body of the letter there, but headed it London for some reason of his own.

6. For William Stephens see the letter referred to.

7. For the old quarrel over the speaker see Jones to BF above, Feb. 2, April 2. The new Assembly was dissolved on April 25, and the news was reported in the *London Chron.*, June 13–16.

Hearing to an Affair which they had before considered and determined.[8]

There is suppos'd to be a Change intended in the American Administration here.[9] If it takes place, I apprehend our Affairs must receive some Advantage, since we can scarce have a Minister less favourable to our Interest than the present. With great and sincere Esteem, I have the Honour to be, Sir, Your most obedient and most humble Servant   B FRANKLIN

PS. Augt. 8. The Paper mention'd as enclos'd, was promis'd me by our Solicitor, but he has not brought it.

Noble Wimberley Jones, Esqr

8. On June 19 the Privy Council had taken final action to uphold Sir William Baker's heirs against the settlers on the lands claimed by the estate. For this long-drawn-out controversy see Jones to BF above, Feb. 2; *Acts Privy Coun., Col.,* V, 296.

9. This is BF's first reference to the impending resignation of Lord Hillsborough, mentioned in the headnote on the previous document. The Bedfordites had long been hoping to get rid of the American Secretary (and through him, it was thought, of Lord North himself), and had used as their lever the Walpole Company's petition for a land grant. On July 1 Hillsborough had sustained a major defeat when the Committee on Plantations of the Privy Council had overruled the Board of Trade, of which he was president, and approved the Walpole petition. On Aug. 1, according to Gipson, the Earl submitted his resignation; on the 3rd Lord North acknowledged it as a *fait accompli*, and rumor of it appeared in the *London Chron.*, Aug. 6–8. As Hillsborough's successor the Bedfordites were pushing Lord Gower, who was a member of the Walpole Company; but North managed to circumvent them and obtain the appointment of his stepbrother, Lord Dartmouth. On the day the new Secretary kissed hands, Aug. 14, the Privy Council endorsed the action of its committee on the Walpole grant. *Acts Privy Coun., Col.,* V, 208; Gipson, *British Empire,* XI, 471–5; Jack M. Sosin, *Whitehall and the Wilderness...* (Lincoln, Neb., 1961), pp. 202–5; Alan Valentine, *Lord North* (2 vols., Norman, Okla., [1967]), I, 256–60.

From Patrick Wilson[1]

ALS: American Philosophical Society

Dear Sir   Monday Augt. 3d 1772

I take my departure for Glasgow in a few Hours, having heard yesterday Evening of an inviting Opportunity of a Ship for the Forth which sails immediately.

Im sorry that Im so much hurried as not to be able to see You before I go. I shall take Care and deliver the Vollume of the American Transactions to the Questor of our Library.[2] I beg the favour of being rememberd to Mr. Small;[3] I ever am most faithfully and most respectfully Your's   PAT. WILSON

Addressed: To | Doctor Franklin | at Mrs. Stevenson's | Craven Street | Strand

From Henry Cavendish[4]

ALS: Historical Society of Pennsylvania

Sir   Tuesday Aug. 4 [1772]

We have agreed to go to Purfleet on friday morning: we propose setting out a $\frac{1}{2}$ an hour past 9; so that I suppose we shall be there about one at latest. I am sorry I could not send you notice sooner; but Dr. Watson was not able to fix on a day sooner. As I imagine friday is about the time you thought of coming to town, you perhaps might like to come back from Purfleet with us.[5] If you

1. The son of Alexander Wilson, the astronomer and type-founder, for whom see above, XVIII, 67 n. Patrick (1743–1811) was obviously connected with the University at this time, and in 1784 he succeeded to his father's chair of astronomy. W. Innes Addison, ed., *The Matriculation Albums of the University of Glasgow from 1728 to 1858* (Glasgow, 1913), pp. 55, 66.

2. BF was carrying out the request in William Smith's letter above, May 16, to present the University of Glasgow with a copy of the first volume of the APS *Trans.*

3. Presumably BF's old friend Alexander Small, who returned to London at about this time from a trip to the Caribbean and America. See BF to Evans below, Aug. 22.

4. The eminent chemist and electrician, for whom see above, X, 41 n, and the *DNB.* He had recently published a paper refining BF's electrical theories: *Phil. Trans.,* LXI (1771), 584–677.

5. BF had left town by July 31; see Watson's letter to him of that date. We assume that he had gone visiting in Kent, where this letter reached him, and

228

should and would write me word, I will take care that there shall be room for you. Your Obedient humble servant

H. CAVENDISH

Addressed: To / Dr Franklin / At Mr Sargents[6] / at May Place / near Dartford / Kent

From Margaret Stevenson   ALS: American Philosophical Society

Dear Sir   Craven Street Tuesday Evening Augt 4 [1772[7]]

I am Hartly glad to hear your so well. I have sent all Leters that ar in my Posstion.

Mr. Alexander and Mr. Small has called, and that is all.[8] News I have none Capt. Falciner I have not seen. Hewsons ar well but Litill Boy is verey Poorly.[9] I my self am, verey so so, I can not write but if aney news should come to my hear your Poly shall Transmit to you for Dear Sir Your Most Oblogied humble Servant

MARGT. STEVENSON

From John Whitehurst   ALS: American Philosophical Society

Dear Sir   Derby 4th Augt. 72

I have this Day deliver'd your Clock to Mr. Clark, who Inn's at the Ball in Wood street[1] and hope it will Arrive Safe and to your Sattisfaction.

---

that he remained there until he went to Purfleet (almost next door) for the committee meeting on Friday the 7th.

6. John Sargent was an old friend; see above, VII, 322 n, and subsequent vols.

7. The only year between the birth of Mrs. Stevenson's grandson, mentioned below, and BF's departure for America when Aug. 4 fell on a Tuesday. She had apparently heard from BF, and forwarded mail to him, while he was staying at May Place.

8. Two of BF's friends fit each of these references: Robert or William Alexander, the brothers who were Scottish merchants and bankers (above, VIII, 444 n); and Alexander Small, the Scottish surgeon, or William Small, the Birmingham scientist (above, IX, 110 n; XI, 480 n).

9. Polly's first child, William, born on April 26, 1771.

1. For the clock see Whitehurst's letter above, May 21, and for John Clark XVIII, 190.

Please to unlock the door, and you will find the Screws, which fasten the Case in the Packing Case. The weights, Ball, Pulley, &c. are Packed between bottom of the Clock and Packing Cases. And please to draw the head of the Case off before you attempt to take the body out.

I've made all the parts of the Case stronger than Common, for the better measurement of time—to prevent any Vibration by the action of the Pendulum. I am Sir Your Most Obedient Servant

JOHN WHITEHURST

Addressed: To | Docr Benj. Franklin | Craven Street Strand | London

From Deborah Franklin

AL: American Philosophical Society

My Dear Child   [August 6,[2] 1772]

I reseved yours by the packit[3] it gives me much pleshuer to hear that you air well and happey. I was in hopes that a packit or a vesill wold [have?] arived before this wente as I saw it in the papers[4] as I was in hopes that wold in forme when you intend to returne agen to your one [own] home. I cante write to you as I am so verey unfitt to expres my self and not a bell to due as I yousd for that illness I had was a polsey all thou I donte shake my memerey failes me I cante expres my self as I yousd to due. I did tell your friend Dr. Small when he was heare[5] that I had thoute it

2. DF mentions noting in the paper "yisterday" the arrival in England of several ships from New York and Sparks from Philadelphia. These arrivals were reported in the *Pa. Gaz.*, Aug. 5, and we are assuming that she read the paper the day it appeared.

3. BF's letter above of May 5 came, we believe, by that month's packet, the *Mercury*, which reached New York about July 20: *ibid.*, July 23.

4. The June packet, the *Lord Hyde*, which in all likelihood carried BF's letter above of June 2, did not reach New York until Aug. 6 (*ibid.*, Aug. 12); we assume that DF saw in one of the Philadelphia papers a notice, which we have not found, that the ship was expected soon.

5. Dr. Alexander Small had arrived in New York from Jamaica in the spring; see his letter to BF above, April 13. When he visited Philadelphia we do not know, but he was back in England by the late summer; see BF to Evans below, Aug. 22.

230

was a polsey my write hand is verey weak some times I am not abel
to try on my close. I am verey Low sperreted that it is verey
trubel sume to tell what I wold say it wold be of servis to ride but
it is not my lot in life but yister day my Nabor Haddock[6] took me
a littel way round a feeld or two for I have bin verey un well for
5 or 6 days I donte make aney complaint to you. I saw yisterday
that several vesils from N york and Sparkes frome this plase air
got to Ingland I beleve Dr. Small was in one of them I hope he is
safe arived att home and well. Mr. Beache ses that he is a good
man. I hope Capt. Folkner is safe arive and well he did take a
hankifchar to Mrs. Stephenson which I hope is got safe to her[7] I
must aske in faver for sume muslim for Salley to worke for her
self I have one my self but have not wore it shee has instruckted
severel of the first ranke hear if you wold let me know if you
shold returne home this fall I heard that Mrs. Write has seen you
but when shee wente I did not know when shee went[8] or I shold
a given her a Letter I send you inclosd Miss Hadock letter to you.[9]
Billey and Mrs. Franklin was [here?] sum weeks this spring and
the widdow and her children and Servantes who is gon home
Agen I supose you had heard her son is a maloncoley obieck to
look on I cante helpe tellin you that I am thankfell that his mother
has taken him home with her for I think it beste for him to be with
his mother[1] if I shold venter to say anything of graite folks I shold
say it greves me much for such maloncoly things that I read of I
wish for better a countes. I ad no more. I observe with pleshuer
you tell me a boute the dear child you tell me and the plesher his
grand mama takes of her and I have bin told with so much plesher

6. For Eden Haydock, DF's neighbor on High Street, see above, XII,
14 n.

7. Falconer, in the *Britannia*, had arrived months before (*London Chron.*,
June 16–18), and Mrs. Stevenson was proud of the "hankifchar" that he
brought her: BF to DF below, Oct. 7.

8. Neither do we know when she went, but she was in England by the end
of March; see BF to Jane Mecom above, March 30.

9. See Rebecca Haydock's letter above, under July 20.

1. We can only hope that BF found this reference more intelligible than we
do. The only widow in DF's circle who might have gone home was, to the
best of our knowledge, WF's sister-in-law, Mrs. Downes, who had lost her
husband the previous autumn (above, XVIII, 195 n). She may have had a son,
and may have returned to Barbados; she seems, insofar as anything in a letter
from DF can be judged in context, the most likely possibility.

of your grand dafter in this place shee is a fine young Ladey shee is the verey pickter of her father a fine Child indead.[2]

To Jonathan Williams, Sr.   ALS: Yale University Library

Dear Cousin   London, Augt. 11. 1772

I received yours of July 4. with the Bill enclosed of £200 for your Brother,[3] which I deliver'd to him accordingly. Calling in here at the N England Coffeehouse,[4] and finding this Ship just upon sailing, I would not miss the Opportunity of giving you this Information, tho' I cannot now write to my other Friends.

It grieves me to hear that poor Josiah is in so bad a State of Health.[5] But being young it is to be hoped he may weather it.

My Love to my dear Sister, and to Cousin Grace and your Family.[6] I shall write to Jonathan per next Opportunity. I am, Your affectionate Uncle   B FRANKLIN

Minutes of the Committee on the Purfleet Magazine

Copy: the Royal Society; partial copy: American Philosophical Society

August 12–21, 1772.

⟨August 12: The Committee agreed to the following:[7] lightning conductors were necessary; they should be placed at each end of each magazine, reaching ten feet above the ridgepole and connecting at the bottom with wells filled with water; the top of the

2. The first grandparent was Mrs. Stevenson, and the child (despite DF's reference to "her") was young William Hewson. BF's "grand dafter" was the Foxcroft baby, for whom see BF to Foxcroft above, under May 5.

3. For John Williams, the customs official, see above, XII, 193 n.

4. At 61 Threadneedle Street, near the Bank of England.

5. Josiah was dying of tuberculosis; see Jonathan, Jr., to BF above, May 29.

6. Grace Harris Williams was actually BF's niece; she and Jonathan had a huge family, seven sons and three daughters.

7. For the names of the committee and details of the recommendations summarized here see the full report below, Aug. 21.

chimney of the Proof House should be connected by lead with the conductor at the end of the adjacent magazine.[8]

August 17: The committee met with Dr. Maty, the secretary of the Royal Society, and agreed that the Board House and Clock House should have conductors. Franklin read a draft of the committee's report, to which all agreed except Benjamin Wilson.

August 18: The committee again met with Maty, Franklin read part of a final draft, and Wilson objected to the use of pointed conductors. Franklin was requested to finish the draft.

August 21. The committee, in Maty's absence, heard Franklin read the final report, in which he inserted a provision for a pointed conductor on the Board House. Wilson protested in writing against the use of such conductors. All the others signed the report, which was to be presented to the Council of the Society.⟩

Instructions for Testing the Torpedo Fish

ADS and incomplete draft: American Philosophical Society

The role that Franklin played in John Walsh's experimentation with the torpedo fish cannot be precisely defined because the evidence is missing. Walsh testified to the older man's encouragement,[9] which may have included something akin to the instructions printed below. But these particular instructions, even though they are endorsed by Walsh, could not have guided his investigation; for they are dated a month after he first reported on it.[1] An undated and incomplete draft among Franklin's papers, entitled "Directions to Discover whether the Power that gives the shock, in touching the Torpedo,. . . is electrical or not," is an early version of the second and third paragraphs below. In his French edition Dubourg translated and printed this draft, with its title; he then followed it with a second document, which he dated August 12 and which is a verbatim translation of the fourth and fifth paragraphs, and explained that it was an addition Franklin made in the light of Walsh's

8. A copy of the minutes of Aug. 12, corrected by BF, is among his papers; it here adds the recommendation embodied in the later report, that the two outermost magazines should each have an extra conductor in the middle of the building to connect the ridgepole with a well.

9. Walsh to BF below, July 1, 1773.

1. See his letter above of July 12, and his fuller report below, Aug. 27.

report of his findings.[2] Did the editor receive the full instructions as printed here? If not, why not? If so, why did he translate part of them and the draft version of another part? Conceivably because that version was what Walsh took with him to France, but this is no more than conjecture. All that can be said with assurance is that the experiments performed by Walsh resembled in many ways those that Franklin suggested.

London, Aug. 12. 1772

It has long been supposed that the Stroke given by the Torpedo was the Effect of sudden violent muscular Motion. It is now suspected to be an Effect of the electric or some similar subtil Fluid, which that Fish has a Power of acting upon and agitating at Pleasure.

To discover whether it be the Effect of a subtil Fluid, or of muscular Motion, let the Fish be touch'd with the usual Conductors of Electricity, viz. Iron or other Metals; and with the known Non-conductors of Electricity, dry Wood, Glass, Wax, &c. If the Stroke be communicated thro' the first and not thro' the latter, there is so far a Similarity with the electric Fluid;[3] and at the same time a Proof that the Stroke is not an Effect of mere muscular Motion.

Let it be observed whether the Stroke is sometimes given on the *near Approach* of a conducting Body without actual Contact; if so, that is another similar Circumstance. Then observe whether in that Case any Snap is heard; and in the Dark whether any Light or Spark is seen between the Fish and the approaching Body.[4] If not, there the Fluids differ.

Let a Number of Persons standing on the Ground, join Hands, and let one touch the Fish so as to receive the Stroke. If all feel it,

2. Dubourg, *Œuvres*, I, 269–71. We note only substantial differences between the draft and the ADS.

3. The draft reads "Fluid, *similar* in *one Property* at least, to that of Electricity."

4. The draft here concludes as follows: "If so, it agrees in *more Properties* with the Electric Fluid.

"Lastly, Touch him with the Wire of a small electrical Phial, and if the Shock can be receiv'd thro' it, observe whether the Wire will afterwards attract and repel light Bodies, and give a Stroke when held in one Hand and the Wire touch'd with the other. If so, the Fluid producing these Effects seems to have *all the Properties* of the electric Fluid."

then let him be laid with his Belly on a Plate of Metal; let one of the Persons so joining Hands touch that Plate, while the farthest from the Plate with a Rod of Metal touches the Back of the Fish; and then observe whether the Force of the Stroke seems to be the same to all in the Circuit as it was before, or stronger.[5]

Repeat the last Experiment with this Variation. Let two of the Persons in the Circuit hold each an uncharg'd electric Phial, the Knobs at the Ends of their Wires touching. After the Stroke, let it be observ'd whether those Wires will attract and repel light Bodies; and whether a Cork Ball suspended by a long silk String so as to hang between the Wires at a small Distance from the Knob of each, will be attracted and repell'd alternately to and from each Knob; if so, the Back and Belly of the Fish are at the Time of the Stroke in *different States* of Electricity.[6]

B FRANKLIN

Endorsed: Franklins Instructions to try if the stroke of the Torpedo be Ellectrical.

To Pierre Samuel du Pont de Nemours

ALS: Henry Francis du Pont Winterthur Museum

Dear Sir   London, Augt. 12. 1772
I am concern'd to understand lately that you have never been paid as I expected for the Ephemerides, and therefore I send you three Guineas by our valuable Friend M. Baudeau, requesting you will let me have the Accompt at your Leisure, and I will take care for the future that the Payment shall be more punctual.[7] You are

5. BF is suggesting the same kinds of experiment as those conducted years earlier with the Leyden jar, for which see Abraham Wolf, *A History of Science, Technology, and Philosophy in the Eighteenth Century* (2nd ed., revised; 2 vols., New York, 1961), I, 221–3.

6. Dubourg for some reason omitted the final clause. In this paragraph BF is designing another test, which Walsh apparently did not make, of analogy with the Leyden jar; the principle is the same as that of his own experiment described above, III, 158, 160.

7. BF had found that his subscription to the *Ephémérides* had been in arrears for months; see his earlier letter to du Pont de Nemours above, June 15. Abbé Nicolas Baudeau (1730–92) had come to Paris at the behest of its archbishop, and had there founded the *Ephémérides* in 1765 to refute the ideas of

doing a great deal of Good to Mankind, for which I am afraid you are not duly rewarded, except in the Satisfaction that results from it to your benevolent Mind. With sincere and great Esteem and Affection, I have the Honour to be, Dear Sir, Your most obedient and most humble Servant   B FRANKLIN

M. Dupont.

From Isaac L. Winn[8]   LS: the Royal Society

Winn was a pioneer in this attempt to apply observations on the aurora borealis to forecasting the weather. His hypothesis was related, no doubt accidentally, to two earlier observations: that high winds follow an auroral display, and that a storm moves in an opposite direction from the winds it creates.[9] His theory, when Franklin had it published and added comments of his own, attracted considerable scientific attention.[1] But it was not, and is not yet, firmly established; evidence of the effect of the aurora on turbulence in the lower air is still slender and conflicting.[2] The ship captain, in short, was formulating a problem that the next two centuries have not settled.

Sir   Spithead 12 August. 1772

I have often wished that somebody would carefully Collate a sufficient number of Meteorological Journals with intent to ob-

the physiocrats. He had been converted, however, largely by the arguments of du Pont de Nemours, who had joined him and Mirabeau to make the *Ephémérides* the principal physiocratic mouthpiece. Baudeau's formulation of his new faith, *Première introduction à la philosophie économique*, had been published in 1771. For his involvement in Polish affairs see Hutton to BF below, Oct. 23.

8. For the merchant captain see above, XVII, 49 n.

9. The first hypothesis was expounded by Henry Beighton in *Phil. Trans.*, XL (1737–8), 263–4; the second was BF's: above, III, 149, 392 n, 463–5; IX, 110–12. For BF's long-standing interest in the aurora see above, II, 185–6; IV, 268, 298–9; VII, 358.

1. The publication was in *Phil. Trans.*, LXIV (1774), 128–32; BF's comments are the following document. For the attention subsequently given the theory see Richard Kirwan, "An Essay on the Variations of the Barometer," Royal Irish Academy *Trans.*, II (1788), 62–5, 70–2; Alexander McAdie, *The Aurora in Its Relations to Meteorology* (Washington, 1885), pp. 13, 15, 18–21.

2. J. Alan Chalmers, *Atmospheric Electricity* (2nd ed., Oxford, etc., [1967]), pp. 45–6, 173–4.

serve and Class the several appearances in the Atmosphere before great Changes in the weather, particularly before great Storms. I am perswaded from my own observation that in general sufficient indications of impending Tempests preceed them a Considerable Time, did we but carefully note them. The phaenomenon which I am going to mention is one of those Indications which not only portend an approaching Tempest, but Ascertain from what Quarter it will come; a Circumstance that may render it of Essential Service to seamen. I believe the Observation is new, that the Aurora Borealis is constantly succeeded by hard Southerly or South West Winds, attended with Hazy Weather and Small Rain. I think I am warranted from Experience to say *Constantly* for in Twenty Three Instances that have occurr'd since I first made the Observation, it has invariably obtain'd. However I beg leave to request you will recommend it to the Notice of the Royal Society, as a matter which when confirmed by Further Observations and Generally known may be of more Consequence than at first Appears. To shew that it may, give me leave to recite the Circumstances which first occasiond my taking Notice of it. Sailing down the English Channel in 1769, a few days before the Autumnal Equinox we had a remarkably Bright and Vivid Aurora the whole Night. In shore the Wind was fluctuating between N.N.W. and N.W. and farther out W.N.W. Desirous of benefiting by the Land Wind and also of taking advantage of earlier Ebb Tyde, I dispensed with the good old Marine Adage (i.e. Never to approach too near a Weather Shore, lest it should prove a Lee Shore) and by short Tacks clung close along the English Coast. Next day the Wind veered to the S.W. and soon after to S.S.W. and sometimes S. We were then in that dangerous Bay between portland and the Start Point and Carried a pressing Sail with hopes of reaching Torbay before dark,[3] but Night fell upon us with thick Haze and small Rain, in so much that we could not have seen the Land at the distance of a Ships Length. The Gale was now increased to a storm. In this dilemma nothing remained but to endeavor to keep off the Shore till the Wind should change. Luckily our Ship was a Stout One and well rigged.

Reflecting sometime after on the Circumstances of this Storm

3. In southerly gales Lyme Bay, near Portland, was exposed, whereas Torbay offered a sheltered anchorage.

and the Phanomena that preceded it, I determined to have particular attention to future Aurora and the Weather that should succeed them and, as I have observed above, in Twenty three Instances have found them uniform except in degree, the Gale generally Commencing between Twenty four and Thirty Hours after the first Appearance of the Aurora. More time and Observation will probably discover whether the Strength of the succeeding Gale is proportionate to the Splendor and Vivacity of the Aurora and the distance of Time between them. I only suspect that the more Brilliant and Active the first is, the sooner will the latter occur, be more Violent, but of shorter duration, than when the Light is languid and dull. Perhaps too the Colour of the Aurora may be some guide in forming a Judgment of the coming Gale. That which preceeded the Storm I have mentiond was exceedingly Splendid. The Tempest succeeded it in Less than Twenty Four Hours, was Violent, but of short (about Eight Hours) Continuance. In June last a little without soundings we had for Two Nights following faint inactive Aurora; the Consequent Gale was not hard but lasted near Three Days, the First day attended with Haze and small rain, the Second with Haze only and the last day Clear.

The Benefit which this observation on the Aurora Borealis when further confirmd and known may be of to Seamen is obvious in Navigating near Coasts which tend East and West, particularly in the British Channel. They may, when warnd by the Aurora Borealis, get into port, and Evade the impending Storm, or, by Stretching over to the Southward, facilitate their Passage, by that very Storm, which might have destroyed them; for no Winds are so dangerous in the Channel as Southerly and South West. In a word, since I have made this observation, I have got out of the Channel, when other Men as alert, and in faster Sailing Ships, but unapprized of this Circumstance, have not only been driven back, but with difficulty have escaped Shipwreck. Perhaps the observation, that Southerly Gales constantly succeed these Phaenomena, may help to account for the Nature of the Aurora Borealis: my own thoughts on that Subject I shall sometime beg leave to lay before you. I am with great Respect Sir, Your Obliged Humble Servant

I L WINN

Addressed: Benjamin Franklin LLD London

Franklin's Conjecture on the Foregoing

Copy:[4] the Royal Society

[After August 12, 1772]

The *Aurora Boreales*, tho' visible almost every Night of clear Weather in the more Northern Regions, and very high in the Atmosphere, can scarce be visible in England but when the Atmosphere is pretty clear of Clouds for the whole Space between us and those Regions, and therefore are seldom visible here. This extensive Clearness may have been produced by a long continuance of Northerly Winds. When the Winds have long continued in one Quarter, the Return is often violent. Allowing the Fact so repeatedly observed by Capt. Winn, perhaps this may account for the Violence of the Southerly Winds that soon follow the Appearance of the Aurora on our Coasts.[5]　　　　B. F.

From Dorothea Blunt

ALS: American Philosophical Society

Weymouth Augt: 14, [1772?[6]]

When and where this may find you my Dear Sir I know not, but I hope soon, and that you [may be] in good health. I fancy my fears

4. The copy, in Fevre's hand, is on the verso of Winn's second letter to BF on the same subject: below, Jan. 22, 1773. The comment could have been on the two letters together, in which case it was obviously written after the later one, or only on the first, the preceding document; we act on the latter supposition because our policy is to assign the earliest feasible date. BF's conjecture, together with an abbreviated version of Winn's second letter, was printed as notes to the first one in *Phil. Trans.*, LXIV (1774), 132.

5. This was not the end of BF's speculations about the aurora; for a continuation of them years later, which embodied this paragraph, see Smyth, *Writings*, VII, 209–15.

6. The letter speaks of Polly Hewson in Broad Street; it was therefore written between Polly's marriage in July, 1770, and her move to Craven Street in the autumn of 1772. In 1770 the Hewsons were visiting his family in late July, and could scarcely have been settled in at Broad Street by Aug. 14; Dolly, furthermore, shows none of the emotion about losing Polly that she did that summer (above, XVII, 201–2). The choice between 1771 and 1772 is a toss-up, but two scraps of internal evidence incline us toward the later year. Dolly alludes in passing to the chance that BF is on his customary "summer flight" from London. If she had been writing in 1771, she would in all likelihood have known that he was setting out in August for his major tour of Ire-

made [me tremble?] more than I believe I ought to have [done. But?] I own I thought you much indispo[sed when last?] I saw you in Craven Street, and I a[llow that] I was conceited enough to think that I cou'd [have] precribd better things than Madeira and ciniamon[?] not that I am an enemy to either in a healthful state, or in some diseases, but you appear'd [to] me to have (at the time you took them) too [much] on your stomach of the nature of sour to [take] any more without being more injured than benefited tho taken with your usual moderation. Be kind enough to believe I am not making any pretentions to knowledge in the nature or mixture of acids or of alkalins, for I have none, but I do remember to have seen my Father (to appearance) in the same state that you was in, and I also remember that such things appear'd to do him harm.[7] I feel also so nearly for you the same degree of affection and respect that I felt for him, that it was natural for me both to think and say the same I shou'd for him, and to him. I know that you must think me very unwise for regretting the loss of pleasure that if I had en[joyed] would now be past and gone, but so unwise [am I] for the knowing that I cou'd have had [more of] your company than I have had [torn] wou'd have been pleas'd with [torn] company. I say my being thus [torn] will make me regrett the loss of [torn] spite of Madam understanding that [torn] by and pronounces it to no purpose.

I must not own that Weymouth does not please me because it is without all controversy [the?] most pleasing place for walking, riding [bath?]ing and going upon the water, and if these are not the most pleasing amusements at this season and in such Italian weather, what are? And why then, it is natural to ask, am I not pleas'd with it? To which I answer, that as much as I can be pleas'd with these amusements, I am, but having been accustom'd to the society of sensible people and finding here either no companonable people or none that have leisure to be such, I shou'd

land and Scotland, which lasted until late autumn; in that case she would scarcely have referred so casually to his leaving town. The second scrap of evidence is her saying that he was indisposed when she last saw him, which might well have been in late July, 1772, during "a Fit of the Gout which harasses me greatly": to Stiles above, July 22. We do not advance any of this evidence as convincing, but merely as feathers to tip the scales of guesswork.

7. Sir Henry Blunt, second baronet (1724–59).

not feel very sorry to set off tomorrow tho by so doing I shou'd Miss seeing the beauxs at the Ball, and dancing withal. If I had not made a vow to keep [in good humour?] I should certainly have been [horrid] cross having been three post days at the office for letters [and] not getting one, there being none there [to get?]. I shall write by the same post that conveys [this to] Broad Street, first because I fear she [may not hear?] of me by you for I hope you have ta[ken your usual sum?]mer flight, and next because I have [reason to?] think that tho I have not been ungrate[ful or un]kind Mrs. Hewson may think me both and [tho' not?] very apt to think the worst of people she may when Will:8 has been cross feel a little inclin'd to think less well of me than I deserve.

Can any living Soul complain of this weather? And yet I dare say Many do. To be sure I being neither a Stable or Cow keeper have no reason so I shall not tho to be sure we ought to have rain if it was only to lay the evil spirit9 in every lane and road and street that is monstrously troublesome even to people of fashion. Dont wonder if I shou'd return a fish, or at least an amphibious animal, as I dwell by the Sea side go in and on it, and feed on the fish thereof. I love dearly to write to you tho I hate you shou'd read my letters. Now as nobody else can pray as youre a wise Man, contrive1 some method of my being pleas'd and not hurt, and this if you can without my being at the trouble or expence of learning to write. About ten days hence I expect to leave this place and to be for a week at Sir Chas: at Odiham Hants. [If] I can love you more I most certainly shall. [If you] feel inclind to write to me, take notice that [I know you] too well to desire *one* unless you are mak [*torn*]. Give my affectionate compliments to Mrs. [Stevenson and?] believe me Dear Sir most heartily and [*torn*] friend and obligd Humble Servant   D: BLUNT

Addressed: Doctor Franklin / Craven Street / Strand / London.

8. Presumably her small son, who had been born in April, 1771.
9. Dust?
1. We dare not impose punctuation on Dolly's prose, which is *sui generis*; but we believe that her meaning is "Now, as nobody else can, pray—as you're a wise Man—contrive," etc.

From Giambattista Toderini[2]

ALS: American Philosophical Society

Monsieur,   Forli, 15 Aoust. 1772.

En vous soumettant mon petit ouvrage, qui a pour titre *Filosofia Frankliniana sopra le Punte preservatrici del fulmine, &c.*[3] c'est le mettre entre les mains d'un Philosophe connu dans le Public pour un des plus illustres, dont les heureuses inventions ont fait faire un si grand Progrès à la Physique. Votre grand esprit, propre de la Nation Angloise, et vos belles lumieres, se sont fait un objet d'attention de defendre de la foudre les batimens, les edifices. Profitant de vos idées, je me suis appliqué a étendre ces preservatifs aux vaisseaux, aux magazins ou reservoirs de poudre. S'il s'y trouve quelque chose digne d'approbation, cette approbation vous appartient. Je propose tout comme le tenant de vous, et comme tel je le reconnois. Quant à moi, je ne souhaite rien tant que de connoitre votre jugement sur ce petit ouvrage. Je profiterai de vos lumiéres. Ce me sera un grand plaisir, Monsieur, si vous auriez bien le temps et la complaisance de me faire savoir, si en Amerique, ou dans votre pays, on a jamais mis en pratique, dans les vaisseaux, des preservatifs contre la foudre, ou si vous, Mr. Watson,[4] ou autres, ont inventés tels preservatifs. Excusez de grace ma curiosité; et si vous avez la bonté de me faire ce plaisir, vous pourrez, Monsieur, remettre la reponse aux mains de Mr. Berlendis, Resident de Venise à Londres.[5] Je suis avec un profond respect, Monsieur, Votre très humble et très obéissant Serviteur

JEAN BAPTISTE TODERINI,
De la Compagnie de Jesus.

2. A Venetian Jesuit and teacher of philosophy (1728–99) at Verona and Forli, near Ravenna, who became in later years a noted Ottomanist. *Nouvelle biographie générale* ... (46 vols., Paris, 1855–66). We have no indication that he had any other contact with BF, or received any acknowledgment of this letter.

3. *Filosofia frankliniana delle punte preservatrici dal fulmine, particolarmente applicata alle polveriere, alle navi, et a Santa Barbara in mare* ... (Modena, 1771).

4. William Watson and BF were serving together on the Purfleet committee; see Watson's letter above, July 31.

5. Baron de Berlendis was the Venetian minister to St. James's: *The Edinburgh Almanack* ... (Edinburgh, [1773?]), p. 45.

To William Franklin

Reprinted from William Temple Franklin, ed., *Memoirs of the Life and Writings of Benjamin Franklin* . . . (3 vols., 4to, London, 1817–18), II, 171.

Dear Son,   London, Aug. 17, 1772.

At length we have got rid of Lord Hillsborough, and Lord Dartmouth takes his place, to the great satisfaction of all the friends of America. You will hear it said among you (I suppose) that the interest of the Ohio planters has ousted him, but the truth is, what I wrote you long since, that all his brother ministers disliked him extremely, and wished for a fair occasion of tripping up his heels; so seeing that he made a point of defeating our scheme, they made another of supporting it, on purpose to mortify him, which they knew his pride could not bear.[6] I do not mean that they would have done this if they had thought our proposal bad in itself, or his opposition well founded; but I believe if he had been on good terms with them, they would not have differed with him for so small a matter. The K. too was tired of him, and of his administration, which had weakened the affection and respect of the Colonies for a Royal Government, with which (I may say it to you) I used proper means from time to time that his M. should have due information and convincing proofs. More of this when I see you. The K.'s dislike made the others more firmly united in the resolution of disgracing H. by setting at nought his famous report.[7] But now that business is done, perhaps our affair may be less regarded in the Cabinet and suffered to linger, and possibly may yet miscarry.[8]

---

6. For the maneuverings that ousted Hillsborough see BF to Jones above, Aug. 3. The Bedfordites, as noted there, were as much interested in attacking North and his protégé as in championing the Walpole Company; but all they succeeded in doing was to replace a protégé by North's relative and close friend. For William Legge, second Earl of Dartmouth, see above, XII, 362 n.

7. BF's monarchical bias seems to be showing. We have no indication that the King disapproved of the Secretary's conduct in office or played a personal part in the ouster; immediately thereafter, on the contrary, he solaced Hillsborough by promoting him to an earldom in the peerage of Great Britain. The "famous report" was from the Board of Trade in April, opposing the Walpole grant; see the note above, under May 1, on BF's purported rejoinder.

8. BF's doubts ran counter to most of the omens. On July 1 the Privy

Therefore let us beware of every word and action, that may betray a confidence in its success, lest we render ourselves ridiculous in case of disappointment. We are now pushing for a completion of the business, but the time is unfavourable, every body gone or going into the country, which gives room for accidents. I am writing by Falconer,[9] and therefore in this only add that I am ever your affectionate father,   B. FRANKLIN.

p.s. The regard Lord D. has always done me the honour to express for me, gives me room to hope being able to obtain more in favour of our Colonies upon occasion, than I could for some time past.[1]

Experiments Supporting the Use of Pointed Lightning Rods

Printed in Benjamin Vaughan, ed., *Political, Miscellaneous, and Philosophical Pieces...by Benj. Franklin...* (London, 1779), pp. 487–99; French translation in Jacques Barbeu-Dubourg, *Œuvres de M. Franklin...* (2 vols., Paris, 1773), I, 289–300; ADS (lacking the conclusion of the published version): Bibliothèque de Genève; AD (fragment of the published conclusion): American Philosophical Society

The following document raises its full share of editorial problems, but none of them greatly affects its substance. The bulk of the paper was

---

Council Committee had considered the results of its hearing on June 5 and recommended, because the area was already being settled, accepting the Walpole petition and establishing a new colony. Lewis, *Indiana Co.*, pp. 112–13. On Aug. 14, the day when Dartmouth took office, the Privy Council endorsed this recommendation. The grant should be made, its report concluded, and the Indian tribes so informed. The Company should be prohibited from settling the portion of the grant between its western border, running south from the Scioto, and the Lochaber line; all previous titles, whether equitable or legal, within the entire tract should be secured in the grant; the colonists should be protected by a proper government. Kenneth P. Bailey, ed., *The Ohio Company Papers, 1753–1817...* (Arcata, Cal., 1947), pp. 257–62. But opposition was already gathering, as BF may have known, and almost immediately made its first attempt to win over Dartmouth; see Lewis, *op. cit.*, p. 122.

9. The two letters, or parts of a single letter, below, Aug. 19.

1. Although the hope was not borne out in the long run, Dartmouth's treatment of him was a welcome change from Hillsborough's. See BF to WF below, Nov. 3.

unquestionably what Franklin read to the Purfleet committee, and what brought the majority of its members to accept his position.[2] When the experiments were first published, in Dubourg's French translation, the editor said that they were read before the committee and dated them August 27; six years later Vaughan published the English text with a note, apparently in the copy from which he was working, that said the same thing.[3] Neither editor knew, however, that Franklin had sent another version to his Swiss friend, de Saussure, in the autumn of 1772. It was, according to him, what he had read to the committee; and he dated it August 18. It shortens the description of the sixth experiment in the printed text and omits that text's concluding paragraph.[4] Both documents, in other words, have Franklin's imprimatur, one indirectly through editions that he supervised and the other in his own hand; yet the two differ in date and in substance. When did he actually read his paper to the committee, and in what form?

On August 12, the earliest meeting of which we have record, Benjamin Wilson objected to the use of pointed lightning rods at Purfleet. On the 17th the committee considered the objection and on the following day, in the light of Franklin's arguments, rejected it and asked the American to complete the draft report. On the 21st the committee met to sign the report, Wilson dissenting;[5] we have no evidence whatever that it met again until December. Hence August 27, despite Franklin's

2. See the headnotes on BF to Dawson above, May 29, and on the committee's report below, Aug. 21.

3. The note is the first of the two below. Vaughan was scrupulous about enclosing his editorial comments in brackets; their absence convinces us that this note was on the MS. Dubourg's comment is that Wilson "proposa les raisons sur lesquelles il se fondoit, et M. Franklin y répondit de la maniere que l'on verra ci-après, qui eut l'approbation des trois autres Commissaires. . . ." *Œuvres*, I, 288. Vaughan always worked from a MS source unless otherwise indicated, and he gave no such indication in printing these experiments. If, then, he was not retranslating Dubourg, yet produced a text virtually identical with his, the two editors must have been using copies of a single MS. Dubourg's copy was presumably dated Aug. 27, and Vaughan's certainly was. We print the English text (without its over abundant italics) as being closer to this original, now lost, than the French translation.

4. BF's letter to de Saussure below, Oct. 8, enclosed this ADS. Both documents have recently been published, with an introduction, by Paul A. Tunbridge, "Franklin's Pointed Lightning Conductor," Royal Soc., *Notes and Records*, XXVIII (1974), 207–19. Tunbridge believes that the ADS was an earlier version of BF's final paper, but adduces no evidence to dissuade us from our guess that it was later.

5. See the committee's minutes above, under Aug. 12, and its report below, Aug. 21.

imprimatur, is an impossible date for the paper. It was presumably written between the 12th, when Wilson first objected, and the 18th, when the issue was settled.

Which form Franklin used to convince the committee is impossible to say, but we are inclined to believe that it was the longer one printed here. Dubourg and Vaughan said so. In its conclusion, furthermore, which chiefly distinguishes it from the shorter version, Franklin rebuts one of Wilson's main arguments, and in polite terms describes it as non-sense; before the committee, it seems to us, he would have been likely to attack all his opponent's points. For these reasons we accept the printed text, but for its date we substitute that of the shortened and slightly altered version that Franklin sent to Switzerland. Why did he shorten it? Perhaps because the full argument seemed unnecessary: de Saussure was so expert in electrical matters, Franklin may have believed, that for him a conclusion arguing against nonsense would have be-labored the obvious.

Aug. 27 [*i.e.*, 18?], 1772.

Experiments, Observations, and Facts, tending to support the opinion of the utility of *long pointed rods*, for securing buildings from damage by strokes of lightning.*

EXPERIMENT I.

The prime conductor of an electric machine, A. B. being supported about $10\frac{1}{2}$ inches above the table by a wax-stand,[6] and under it erected a pointed wire $7\frac{1}{2}$ inches high and $\frac{1}{5}$ of an inch[7] thick, tapering to a sharp point, and communicating with the table; When the point (being uppermost) is covered by the end of a finger, the conductor may be full charged, and the electrometer c,† will rise to the height indicating a full charge: But the moment the point is uncovered, the ball of the electrometer drops, shewing the prime

*Read at the committee appointed to consider the erecting conductors to secure the magazines at Purfleet. Aug. 27, 1772.[8]

†Mr. Henley's.

6. The ADS, which except for the date is virtually identical as far as it goes with the printed text, here reads "Glass Stand."

7. The ADS reads "$\frac{1}{4}$."

8. Notes printed in this manner are not in the ADS (which has only one note, indicated below) and are not, we believe, by Vaughan. Relevant portions of his own notes we identify and incorporate in our annotation.

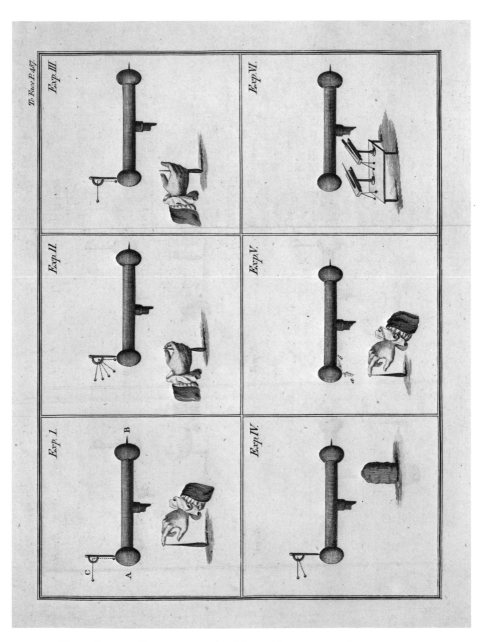

Experiments Supporting the Use of Pointed Lightning Rods

conductor to be instantly discharged and nearly emptied of its electricity. Turn the wire its blunt end upwards, (which represents an unpointed bar,) and no such effect follows, the electrometer remaining at its usual height when the prime conductor is charged.

Observation.

What quantity of lightning, a high pointed rod well communicating with the earth may be expected to discharge from the clouds silently in a short time, is yet unknown; but I have reason from a particular fact to think it may at some times be very great. In Philadelphia I had such a rod fixed to the top of my chimney, and extending about nine feet above it. From the foot of this rod, a wire (the thickness of a goose quill) came through a covered glass tube in the roof, and down through the well of the stair-case; the lower end connected with the iron spear of a pump. On the stair-case opposite to my chamber-door, the wire was divided; the ends separated about six inches, a little bell on each end; [and]⁹ between the bells a little brass ball suspended by a silk thread, to play between and strike the bells when clouds passed with electricity in them. After having frequently drawn sparks and charged bottles from the bell of the upper wire, I was one night waked by loud cracks on the stair-case. Starting up and opening the door, I perceived that the brass ball, instead of vibrating as usual between the bells, was repelled and kept at a distance from both; while the fire passed sometimes in very large quick cracks from bell to bell; and sometimes in a continued dense white stream, seemingly as large as my finger, whereby the whole stair-case was enlightened as with sunshine, so that one might see to pick up a pin.*¹ And

*Mr. De Romas² saw still greater quantities of lightning brought down by the wire of his kite. He had "explosions from it, the noise of

9. The bracketed word is not in the ADS, and a bracketed phrase in the final paragraph is not in the AD; these are presumably Vaughan's insertions.
1. BF devised his apparatus in 1752, and some years later John Winthrop copied it: above, V, 69–71; X, 150. The ball oscillated when the two bells were oppositely charged (indicating a negative charge in the cloud) and rang them in a way that disturbed DF: above, VIII, 94. When the charges were the same (indicating a positively charged cloud) the current flowed across the gap; DF's attitude toward the resultant illumination can be imagined.
2. For Jacques de Romas, the experimental physicist, see above, V, 396 n.

from the apparent quantity thus discharged, I cannot but conceive that a number* of such conductors must considerably lessen that of any approaching cloud, before it comes so near as to deliver its contents in a general stroke: An effect not to be expected from bars unpointed; if the above experiment with the blunt end of the wire is deemed pertinent to the case.

Experiment II.

The pointed wire under the prime conductor continuing of the same height, pinch it between the thumb and finger near the top, so as just to conceal the point; then turning the globe, the electrometer will rise and mark the full charge. Slip the fingers down so as to discover about half an inch of the wire, then another half inch, and then another; at every one of these motions discovering more and more of the pointed wire; you will see the electrometer fall quick and proportionably, stopping when you stop. If you slip down the whole distance at once, the ball falls instantly down to the stem.

Observation.

From this experiment it seems that a greater effect in drawing off the lightning from the clouds may be expected from long

---

which greatly resembled that of thunder, and were heard (from without) into the heart of the city, notwithstanding the various noises there. The fire seen at the instant of the explosion had the shape of a spindle eight inches long and five lines in diameter. Yet from the time of the explosion to the end of the experiment, no lightning was seen above, nor any thunder heard. At another time the streams of fire issuing from it were observed to be an inch thick and ten feet long." See Dr. Priestley's *History of Electricity*, pages 354–6. first edition.
*Twelve were proposed on or near the magazines at Purfleet.[3]

3. BF appended a different note in the ADS: "The Magazines in question are five distinct Buildings each 150 feet long, and 50 feet distant from each other. It was proposed to have a pointed Conductor erected at each End of each Building; in all 10 Conductors, connected by Lead along the Ridge of the Roofs." BF made this proposal after his first visit to Purfleet; see his letter to Dawson above, May 29.

pointed rods, than from short ones; I mean from such as show the greatest length, above the building they are fixed on.

Experiment III.

Instead of pinching the point between the thumb and finger, as in the last experiment, keep the thumb and finger each at near an inch distance from it, but at the same height, the point between them. In this situation, though the point is fairly exposed to the prime conductor, it has little or no effect; the electrometer rises to the height of a full charge. But the moment the fingers are taken away, the ball falls quick to the stem.

Observation.

To explain this, it is supposed, that one reason of the sudden effect produced by a long naked pointed wire is, that (by the repulsive power of the positive charge in the prime conductor) the natural quantity of electricity contained in the pointed wire is driven down into the earth, and the point of the wire made strongly negative; whence it attracts the electricity of the prime conductor more strongly than bodies in their natural state would do; the small quantity of common matter in the point, not being able by its attractive force to retain its natural quantity of the electric fluid, against the force of that repulsion. But the finger and thumb being substantial and blunt bodies, though as near the prime conductor, hold up better their own natural quantity against the force of that repulsion; and so, continuing nearly in the natural state, they jointly operate on the electric fluid in the point, opposing its descent, and aiding the point to retain it;[4] contrary to the repelling power of the prime conductor, which would drive it down. And this may also serve to explain the different powers of the point in the preceding experiment,[5] on the slipping down the finger and thumb to different distances.

Hence is collected, that a pointed rod erected between two tall chimnies, and very little higher, (an instance of which I have seen)

4. Vaughan here commented: "Perhaps their first and principal tendency is, to repel and thereby lessen the influence of the fluid in the *conductor*."
5. For BF's doctrine of points see above, III, 127–8, 472–3; V, 14–20, 23–4.

cannot have so good an effect, as if it had been erected on one of the chimneys, its whole length above it.[6]

EXPERIMENT IV.

If, instead of a long pointed wire, a large solid body, (to represent a building without a point) be brought under and as near the prime conductor, when charged; the ball of the electrometer will fall a little; and on taking away the large body, will rise again.

Observation.

Its rising again shows that the prime conductor lost little or none of its electric charge, as it had done through the point: The falling of the ball while the large body was under the conductor, therefore shows that a quantity of its atmosphere was drawn from the end where the electrometer is placed[7] to the part immediately over the large body, and there accumulated ready to strike into it with its whole undiminished force, as soon as within the striking distance; and, were the prime conductor moveable like a cloud, it would approach the body by attraction till within that distance.[8] The swift motion of clouds, as driven by the winds, probably prevents this happening so often as otherwise it might do; for, though parts of the cloud may stoop towards a building as they pass, in consequence of such attraction, yet they are carried forward beyond the striking distance before they could by their descending come within it.

EXPERIMENT V.[9]

Attach a small light lock of cotton to the underside of the prime conductor, so that it may hang down towards the pointed wire

6. BF had made this point before: above, X, 56; XIV, 263. Wilson disagreed; see the headnote on the committee's report below, Aug. 21.

7. "I.e.," Vaughan elaborated, "drawn for a time, to a different *part* of the conductor, but not *out* of it."

8. For Henly's supporting experiments see the headnote on the committee's report. BF defined striking distance (above, XIV, 262) as the maximum distance across which a discharge will take place from one body to another.

9. BF had performed this experiment more than twenty years before: above, V, 78; see also X, 56.

mentioned in the first experiment. Cover the point with your finger, and the globe being turned, the cotton will extend itself, stretching down towards the finger as at *a*; but on uncovering the point, it instantly flies up to the prime conductor, as at *b*, and continues there as long as the point is uncovered. The moment you cover it again, the cotton flies down again, extending itself towards the finger; and the same happens in degree, if (instead of the finger) you use, uncovered, the blunt end of the wire uppermost.

Observation.

To explain this, it is supposed that the cotton, by its connection with the prime conductor, receives from it a quantity of its electricity; which occasions its being attracted by the finger that remains still in nearly its natural state. But when a point is opposed to the cotton, its electricity is thereby taken from it, faster than it can at a distance be supplied with a fresh quantity from the conductor. Therefore being reduced nearer to the natural state, it is attracted up to the electrified prime conductor; rather than down, as before, to the finger.

Supposing farther that the prime conductor represents a cloud charged with the electric fluid; the cotton, a ragged fragment of cloud (of which the underside of great thunder clouds are seen to have many;) the finger, a chimney or highest part of a building. We then may conceive that when such a cloud passes over a building, some one of its ragged under-hanging fragments may be drawn down by the chimney or other high part of the edifice; creating thereby a more easy communication between it and the great cloud. But a long pointed rod being presented to this fragment, may occasion its receding, like the cotton, up to the great cloud; and thereby increase, instead of lessening the distance, so as often to make it greater than the striking distance. Turning the blunt end of a wire uppermost, (which represents the unpointed bar) it appears that the same good effect is not from that to be expected. A long pointed rod it is therefore imagined, may prevent some strokes; as well as conduct others that fall upon it, when a great body of cloud comes on so heavily that the above repelling operation on fragments cannot take place.

EXPERIMENT VI.[1]

Opposite the side of the prime conductor place separately, isolated by wax stems, Mr. Canton's two boxes with pith balls suspended by fine linen threads. On each box, lay a wire six inches long and $\frac{1}{5}$ of an inch thick, tapering to a sharp point; but so laid, as that four inches of the pointed end of one wire, and an equal length of the blunt end of the other, may project beyond the ends of the boxes; and both at 18 inches distance from the prime conductor. Then charging the prime conductor by a turn or two of the globe, the balls of each pair will separate; those of the box whence the point projects most, considerably; the others less. Touch the prime conductor, and those of the box with the blunt point will collapse, and join. Those connected with the point will at the same time approach each other, till within about an inch, and there remain.

Observation.

This seems a proof, that though the small sharpened part of the wire must have had a less natural quantity in it before the operation, than the thick blunt part; yet a greater quantity was driven down from it to the balls. Thence it is again inferred that the pointed rod is rendered more negative: and farther, that if a stroke must fall from the cloud over a building, furnished with such a rod, it is more likely to be drawn to that pointed rod, than to a blunt one; as being more strongly negative, and of course its attraction stronger. And it seems more eligible, that the lightning should fall on the point of the conductor (provided to convey it into the earth,) than on any other part of the building, thence to

1. This is the one point where Vaughan's text differs markedly from the ADS, but in detail rather than substance. "Supporting the pointed Wire with its Stand," the ADS reads, "on Wax, contrive to suspend a Pair of the larger Pith Balls hanging so freely as that they may separate widely on occasion, when the pointed Wire is under the Prime Conductor. Turn the Globe while the *Point* is uppermost, observing the Distance to which the Balls recede from each other. Then turn up the *blunt End* of the Wire, and again observe the Distance. It will be found small in the latter Case." The experiment was not BF's but Henly's, and had been performed the previous April as part of a series; see the headnote on the committee's report below, Aug. 21.

proceed to such conductor. Which end is also more likely to be obtained by the length and loftiness of the rod; as protecting more extensively the building under it.

It has been objected,[2] that erecting pointed rods upon edifices, is to invite and draw the lightning into them; and therefore dangerous. Were such rods to be erected on buildings, without continuing the communication quite down into the moist earth, this objection might then have weight; but when such compleat conductors are made, the lightning is invited not into the building, but into the earth, the situation it aims at; and which it always seizes every help to obtain, even from broken partial metalline conductors.

It has also been suggested, that from such electric experiments nothing certain can be concluded as to the great operations of nature; since it is often seen that experiments, which have succeeded in small, in large have failed. It is true that in mechanics this has sometimes happened. But when it is considered that we owe our first knowledge of the nature and operations of lightning, to observations on such small experiments; and that on carefully comparing the most accurate accounts of former facts, and the exactest relations of those that have occurred since, the effects have surprizingly agreed with the theory; it is humbly conceived that in natural philosophy, in this branch of it at least, the suggestion has not so much weight; and that the farther new experiments now adduced in recommendation of long sharp-pointed rods, may have some claim to credit and consideration.

It has been urged too, that though points may have considerable effects on a small prime conductor at small distances; yet on great clouds and at great distances, nothing is to be expected from them. To this it is answered, that in those small experiments it is evident the points act at a greater than the striking distance; and in the large way, their service is only expected where there is such nearness of the cloud, as to endanger a stroke; and there, it cannot be doubted the points must have some effect.[3] And if the quantity dis-

2. The objections that follow were Wilson's, made in the committee and outside it; his arguments are discussed in *ibid*.

3. Because they will either draw off the electricity and prevent a stroke, or conduct it safely. The "small experiments" were Henly's the previous spring.

charged by a single pointed rod may be so considerable as I have shown it; the quantity discharged by a number, will be proportionably greater.

But this part of the theory does not depend alone on small experiments. Since the practice of erecting pointed rods in America, (now near 20 years) five of them have been struck by lightning; viz. Mr. Raven's and Mr. Maine's in South Carolina; Mr. Tucker's in Virginia; Mr. West's and Mr. Moulder's in Philadelphia.[4] Possibly there may have been more that have not come to my knowledge. But in every one of these, the lightning did not fall upon the body of the house, but precisely on the several points of the rods; and, though the conductors were sometimes not sufficiently large and compleat, was conveyed into the earth, without any material damage to the buildings. Facts then in great, as far as we have them authenticated, justify the opinion that is drawn from the experiments in small as above related.[5]

It has also been objected, that unless we knew the quantity that might possibly be discharged at one stroke from the clouds, we cannot be sure we have provided sufficient conductors; and therefore cannot depend on their conveying away all that may fall on their points.[6] Indeed we have nothing to form a judgment by in this case but past facts; and we know of no instance where a compleat conductor to the moist earth has been insufficient, if half an inch diameter. It is probable that many strokes of lightning have been conveyed through the common leaden pipes affixed to houses to carry down the water from the roof to the ground: and there is no account of such pipes being melted and destroyed, as must sometimes have happened if they had been insufficient. We can then only judge of the dimensions proper for a conductor of lightning, as we do of those proper for a conductor of rain, by past ob-

4. Tucker we cannot identify; for Raven, Maine, West, and Moulder see above, respectively, x, 53 n, 54 n; IX, 291 n; XVII, 249 n.

5. The ADS ends here, with the date and BF's signature. On the verso is another sketch by him of Henly's electrometer; the only information in it that is not in the sketch above (XVIII, 183) is that the arm may be made of boxwood instead of ivory. BF's fragmentary AD begins with the paragraph following this one.

6. Wilson had raised this objection years before and was still harping on it; see the headnote on the committee's report below, Aug. 21.

servation. And as we think a pipe of three inches bore sufficient to carry off the rain that falls on a square of 20 feet, because we never saw such a pipe glutted by any shower; so we may judge a conductor of an inch diameter, more than sufficient for any stroke of lightning that will fall on its point. It is true that if another deluge should happen wherein the windows of heaven are to be opened, such pipes may be unequal to the falling quantity; and if God for our sins should think fit to rain fire upon us, as upon some cities of old, it is not expected that our conductors of whatever size, should secure our houses against a miracle. Probably as water drawn up into the air and there forming clouds, is disposed to fall again in rain by its natural gravity, as soon as a number of particles sufficient to make a drop can get together;[7] so when the clouds are (by whatever means) over or undercharged [with the electric fluid] to a degree sufficient to attract them towards the earth, the equilibrium is restored, before the difference becomes great beyond that degree.[8] Mr. Lane's electrometer,[1] for limiting precisely the quantity of a shock that is to be administered in a medical view, may serve to make this more easily intelligible. The discharging knob does by a screw approach the conductor to the distance intended, but there remains fixed. Whatever power there may be in the glass globe to collect the fulminating fluid, and whatever capacity of receiving and accumulating it there may be in the bottle or glass jar; yet neither the accumulation or the discharge, ever exceeds the destined quantity. Thus, were the clouds always at a certain fixed distance from the earth, all discharges would be made when the quantity accumulated was equal to the distance: But there is a circumstance which by occasionally lessening the distance, lessens the discharge; to wit, the moveableness of the clouds, and their being drawn nearer to the earth by attraction when electrified; so that discharges are thereby rendered more frequent and of course less violent. Hence whatever the quantity may be in nature, and whatever the power in the clouds of collecting it; yet an accumulation and force beyond what mankind has hitherto been acquainted with, is scarce to be expected.

B. F.

7. See above, XVIII, 154–7.
8. BF's fragmentary AD ends here.
1. Fully described above by its inventor: XIII, 460–2.

To William Franklin

London Augt. 19: 1772

In yours of May 14th, you acquaint me with your indisposition, which gave me great concern. The resolution you have taken to use more exercise is extremely proper, and I hope you will steadily perform it. It is of the greatest importance to prevent diseases; since the cure of them by physic is so very precarious. In considering the different kinds of exercise, I have thought that the *quantum* of each is to be judged of, not by time or by distance, but by the degree of warmth it produces in the body: Thus when I observe if I am cold when I get into a carriage in a morning, I may ride all day without being warmed by it, that if on horse back my feet are cold, I may ride some hours before they become warm; but if I am ever so cold on foot, I cannot walk an hour briskly, without glowing from head to foot by the quickened circulation;[3] I have been ready to say, (using round numbers without regard to exactness, but merely to mark a great difference) that there is more exercise in *one* mile's riding on horseback, than in *five* in a coach; and more in *one* mile's walking on foot, than in *five* on horseback; to which I may add, that there is more in walking *one* mile up and down stairs, than in *five* on a level floor. The two latter exercises may be had within doors, when the weather discourages going abroad; and the last may be had when one is pinched for time, as containing a great quantity of exercise in a handful of minutes. The dumb bell is another exercise of the latter compendious kind; by the use of it I have in forty swings quickened my pulse from 60 to 100 beats in a minute, counted by a second watch:

2. In WTF's hand. We are convinced that this and the following document are both extracts from one and the same letter. Our reason is partly that BF almost never wrote twice to the same correspondent on the same day, and primarily that in WF's reply below, Oct. 29, he acknowledged the receipt of *a* long letter of Aug. 19. If we are right, WTF separated the two when dividing BF's letters into categories by subject matter in the *Memoirs*, II, 10–11, 171–3; later editors, although they printed the extracts next to each other, treated them as distinct. We are compelled to do the same because we do not know which belongs first. WF's quoting in his reply a phrase of his father's and referring to an addition of Aug. 24, both of which are now missing, prove that we have only parts of what BF wrote.

3. Eight years later BF amplified this passage in his famous dialogue with the gout; see Smyth, *Writings*, VIII, 157–8.

And I suppose the warmth generally increases with quickness of pulse.

To Governor Franklin. New Jersey

To William Franklin

Reprinted from William Temple Franklin, ed., *Memoirs of the Life and Writings of Benjamin Franklin*...(3 vols., 4to, London, 1817–18) II, 171–3.

Dear Son,   London, August 19[-22], 1772.

I received yours of June 30. I am vexed that my letter to you, written at Glasgow, miscarried; not so much that you did not receive it, as that it is probably in other hands.[4] It contained some accounts of what passed in Ireland, which were for you only.

As Lord Hillsborough in fact got nothing out of me, I should rather suppose he threw me away as an orange that would yield no juice, and therefore not worth more squeezing. When I had been a little while returned to London I waited on him to thank him for his civilities in Ireland, and to discourse with him on a Georgia affair. The porter told me he was not at home. I left my card, went another time, and received the same answer, though I knew he was at home, a friend of mine being with him. After intermissions of a week each, I made two more visits, and received the same answer. The last time was on a levee day, when a number of carriages were at his door. My coachman driving up, alighted and was opening the coach door, when the porter, seeing me, came out, and surlily chid the coachman for opening the door before he had enquired whether my lord was at home; and then turning to me, said, "My Lord is not at home."[5] I have never since

4. BF had worried about this in his earlier letter above, May 5.

5. Hillsborough told a different story, that BF had repaid his hospitality in Ireland by shunning him in London: WF to BF below, Oct. 13. If BF's account is correct, both his persistence and the Earl's rudeness may seem puzzling. BF doubtless wanted Hillsborough's support in the "Georgia affair," the petition against the land claims of Sir William Baker's estate, which came before the Board of Trade in December. Above, BF to Jones, Feb. 2, April 2; *Board of Trade Jour.*, 1768–75, pp. 274–5. But the primary purpose of BF's calls, we are convinced, was to present the Pennsylvania petition for total repeal of the Townshend duties, for which see his memorandum above, under the end of

been nigh him, and we have only abused one another at a distance. The contrast as you observe is very striking between his conversation with the Chief Justice, and his letter to you concerning your province.[6] I know him to be as double and deceitful as any man I ever met with. But we have done with him, I hope, for ever. His removal has I believe been meditated ever since the death of the Princess Dowager.[7] For I recollect that on my complaining of him about that time to a friend at Court whom you may guess,[8] he told me, we Americans were represented by Hillsborough as an unquiet people not easily satisfied with any ministry, that however it was thought too much occasion had been given us to dislike the present: and asked me, whether, if he should be removed, I could name another likely to be more acceptable to us. I said, yes, there is Lord Dartmouth: we liked him very well when he was at the head of the Board formerly,[9] and probably should like him again. This I heard no more of, but I am pretty sure it was reported where I could wish it, though I knew not that it had any effect.

As to my situation here nothing can be more agreeable, especially as I hope for less embarrassment from the new minister. A general respect paid me by the learned, a number of friends and acquaintance among them with whom I have a pleasing intercourse; a character of so much weight that it has protected me

---

January; and his duty as agent might well have outweighed his indignation at being rebuffed. Hillsborough's attitude can be conjectured. Gov. Wright, who had recently returned to London, may have prejudiced him against the Georgia petition; and the Earl was adamantly opposed to total repeal. If he knew the agent's motives for calling, BF would have been unwelcome.

6. WF must have mentioned, in a letter now lost, the conversation to which he later recurred in that of Oct. 13, between Hillsborough and Frederick Smyth, Chief Justice of New Jersey. The Secretary's letter to WF was presumably the highly critical one in 1768: 1 *N.J. Arch.*, x, 45–8.

7. The King's mother Augusta, Dowager Princess of Wales, had died on Feb. 8. BF may have meant merely to fix the date, or may have meant that her death weakened the Minister's position. If the latter, we are baffled. She had doubtless known Hillsborough as a young man, when she was a widow and he an officer of George II's household; but we have no indication that he was ever her protégé.

8. If we may also, our guess would be Henry Seymour Conway.

9. Dartmouth had been president of the Board of Trade for a year, 1765–66; Hillsborough preceded and followed him in that office.

when some in power would have done me injury, and continued me in an office they would have deprived me of; my company so much desired that I seldom dine at home in winter, and could spend the whole summer in the country houses of inviting friends if I chose it. Learned and ingenious foreigners that come to England, almost all make a point of visiting me, for my reputation is still higher abroad than here; several of the foreign ambassadors have assiduously cultivated my acquaintance, treating me as one of their *corps*, partly I believe from the desire they have from time to time of hearing something of American affairs, an object become of importance in foreign courts, who begin to hope Britain's alarming power will be diminished by the defection of her Colonies; and partly that they may have an opportunity of introducing me to the gentlemen of their country who desire it. The K. too has lately been heard to speak of me with great regard. These are flattering circumstances, but a violent longing for home sometimes seizes me, which I can no otherways subdue but by promising myself a return next spring or next fall, and so forth. As to returning hither, if I once go back, I have no thoughts of it. I am too far advanced in life to propose three voyages more. I have some important affairs to settle at home, and considering my double expences here and there, I hardly think my salaries fully compensate the disadvantages. The late change however being thrown into the balance determines me to stay another winter.

P.S. August 22. I find I omitted congratulating you on the honour of your election in the Society for propagating the Gospel. There you match indeed my Dutch honour. But you are again behind, for last night I received a letter from Paris of which the inclosed is an extract, acquainting me that I am chosen *Associé etranger* (foreign member) of the Royal Academy there.[1] There are but eight of these *Associés etrangers* in all Europe, and those of the most distinguished names for science. The vacancy I have the

1. Congratulations to WF were indeed tardy. He had been elected in 1770 to membership in the Society for the Propagation of the Gospel in Foreign Parts; see the abstract of the Society's proceedings appended to Robert [Lowth], *A Sermon Preached before the Incorporated Society...* (London, 1771), p. 45. BF's honors, with which he was countering his son's meager one, were election to the Batavian Society of Experimental Science and the Académie royale des sciences; see above, XVIII, 100 n, and BF to de la Vrillière below, Sept. 4.

honour of filling, was made by the death of the late celebrated M. Van Swieten of Vienna. This mark of respect from the first Academy in the world, which Abbe Nolet, one of its members, took so much pains to prejudice against my doctrines, I consider as a kind of victory without ink-shed, since I never answered him. I am told he has but one of his sect now remaining in the Academy. All the rest who have in any degree acquainted themselves with electricity are as he calls them Franklinists.[2] Yours, &c.

B. FRANKLIN.

Report of the Purfleet Committee to the Royal Society

Printed in the Royal Society, *Philosophical Transactions...*, LXIII (1773–74), 42–7; AD (draft): Library of Congress.[3]

The Purfleet committee had its first meeting, presumably organizational, on July 18. On August 7 it visited the arsenal, which Franklin had already inspected in May, and then held four meetings in London between August 12 and 21.[4] At the first one the members unanimously agreed on recommending metal lightning rods for the five buildings that constituted the magazine, and on where they should be placed and how fastened, but disagreed on what kind of rod to use.[5] Four of the five men present advocated pointed rods, for reasons that Franklin had made familiar. For almost a decade, however, Benjamin Wilson had been harping on the danger of such rods and the greater efficacy of those that ended in blunt knobs,[6] and he had no intention of changing his mind. On the 17th the committee considered his views, and the next day rejected them. A principal reason was two papers that Franklin read to

2. BF's old scientific antagonist, the abbé Nollet, had left Mathurin-Jacques Brisson as the last remaining survivor of his sect; see Priestley to BF above, May 4. For the opposing sect of Franklinists see the postscript to Bertier's letter above, XVI, 56.

3. The verbal differences in the draft are, with a few exceptions mentioned below, too minor to be worth notice.

4. See above, the headnote on BF to Dawson, May 29; Robertson to BF, July 14; Cavendish to BF, Aug. 4; and the committee's minutes under Aug. 12.

5. See *ibid.* and Benjamin Wilson, *Observations upon Lightning...* (London, 1773), pp. 15–16. Edward Hussey Delaval (above, VIII, 359–60) was appointed to the committee but was unable to attend; he subsequently supported Wilson's position: *Observations*, pp. 19–35.

6. See his paper in *Phil. Trans.*, LIV (1764), 247–53.

his colleagues. One was the experiments and arguments based upon them that are printed above, under August 18. The other was a report of experimental work by Henly that buttressed Franklin's position.[7] Wilson remained totally unconvinced. At the final meeting on August 21, when the committee's report was ready to be signed, he asked Franklin to give up the idea of pointed conductors. "No," came the answer, "I will *never* give it up."[8] Wilson thereupon wrote a formal dissent, which went with the report to the Council of the Royal Society and thence to the Board of Ordnance.[9]

Such controversy over the form of the conductors, although it seems at first glance like that between Big-endians and Little-endians, in fact went to the heart of the question of how lightning behaves. Wilson's position can be briefly summarized.[1] He agreed that points conduct more efficiently than knobs, and hence attract more readily the electricity in an approaching cloud. For that very reason, he insisted, points should not be used: they tended to "solicit" a lightning stroke that otherwise might not occur. No one knew, furthermore, how great a charge might build up in a thunderstorm; points, because they were more effective than knobs, could draw a greater stroke if one did occur.[2]

7. BF mentioned, in the committee's letter below under Dec. 10, that Henly sent him the report (which is now lost) and that it demonstrated the ability of a point to draw electricity from a cloud when twelve times more distant from it than a knob. In *Further Observations upon Lightning . . .* (London, 1774), pp. 2–3, Wilson identified the experiment most damaging to his theories as the fifth in a series that Henly had performed the previous April and later published in *Phil. Trans.*, LXIV (1774), 133–52. In his copy of this pamphlet, acquired by BF and now in the Yale University Library, Henly wrote, "the 5th fully proves that the point would not. . . invite a stroke upon itself at twelve times the distance of the knob. . . ." He presumably meant that the experiment, in which the twelve-to-one ratio does not appear, provided corroboration for another in which it does. The latter was undoubtedly that which he described in the volume of the *Phil. Trans.* just cited, pp. 141–2, 409–10.

8. Wilson, *Further Observations*, p. iv.

9. The dissent was published in *Phil. Trans.* immediately after this report. He expounded it at length in the two pamphlets cited above.

2. Wilson adduced as evidence Henly's experimental work that has just been discussed. It demonstrated, he mistakenly believed, that a point would be *struck* when twelve times as far from the cloud as a knob and also, apparently, that it would receive twelve times the *charge. Observations*, pp. 4–5, 15, 57. Henly's marginal comments on this argument in his copy of *Further Observations* have been badly trimmed, and most of what is left reveals little. But one comment, facing the title page, sums up the controversy. Henly challenged Wilson by letter, to which he received no reply, to "*prove by*

On the same ground he challenged the committee's recommendation that the rods be raised high above the rooftrees: the taller the rods, the greater the likelihood of their coming within the striking distance; hence the shorter the better. Lastly he claimed that the rods his colleagues were recommending were far too small; the larger the conductor, according to him, the greater the chance of its conveying the charge safely. He did not offer, as Franklin did, experimental observations of his own to buttress any of his arguments; and his colleagues found mere assertion unconvincing.[3]

To the PRESIDENT and MEMBERS of the ROYAL SOCIETY.
GENTLEMEN, August 21, 1772.
The Society being consulted by the Board of Ordnance, on the propriety of fixing conductors for securing the powder magazines at Purfleet from lightning, and having thereupon done us the honour of appointing us a committee, to consider the same, and report our opinion; we have accordingly visited those buildings, and examined, with care and attention, their situation, construction, and circumstances, which we find as follows.

They are five in number, each about 160 feet long, and about 52 feet wide, built of brick, arched under the roof, which in one of them is slated, with a coping of lead 22 inches wide on the ridge from end to end; and the others, as we were informed, are soon to be covered in the same manner. They stand parallel to each other at about 57 feet distance, and are founded on a chalk rock, about 100 feet from the river, which rises in high tides within a few inches of the level of the ground, its brackish water also soaking through to the wells that are dug near to the buildings.

The barrels of powder, when the magazines are full, lie piled on each other up to the spring of the arches; and there are four cop-

experiment, that placing a knob, and a point, at an equal distance from a charged body, the point would be struck with the smallest force: or that making the charge exactly the same, the point, could be struck with it, at the greatest distance. . . ." This is substantially what BF had said a decade earlier: above, X, 51–2; see also Henly in Phil. Trans., LXIV (1774), 138, 152.

3. Modern investigation has established that the practical difference between pointed and blunt rods is negligible, but has settled the other questions at issue in BF's favor. See Sir Basil F. J. Schonland, "The Work of Benjamin Franklin on Thunderstorms and the Development of the Lightning Rod," Franklin Institute Jour., CCLIII (1952), 375–92, and The Flight of Thunderbolts (2nd ed., Oxford, 1964), chaps. 2 and 6.

per hoops on each barrel, which, with a number of perpendicular iron bars, (that came down through the arches, to support a long grooved piece of timber, wherein the crane was usually moved and guided to any part where it was wanted) formed broken conductors within the building, the more dangerous from their being incompleat, as the explosion from hoop to hoop, in the passage of lightning drawn down through the bars among the barrels, might easily happen to fire the powder contained in them. But the workmen were removing all those iron bars (by the advice of some members of this Society, who had been previously consulted[4]); a measure we very much approve of.

On an elevated ground, nearly equal in height with the tops of the magazines, and 150 yards from them, is the house where the Board usually meet. It is a lofty building, with a pointed hip-roof, the copings of lead down to the gutters, from which leaden pipes descend at each end of the building into the water of wells of 40 feet deep, for the purpose of conveying water forced up by engines to a cistern in the roof. There is also a proof-house,[5] adjoining to the end of one of the magazines, and a clock-house, at the distance of [blank in text] feet from them, which has a weathercock on an iron spindle, and, probably, some incompleat conductors within, such as the wire usually extending up from a clock to its hammer, the clock, pendulum, rod, &c.

The blowing up of a magazine of gun-powder by lightning, within a few years past, at Brescia in Italy, which demolished a considerable part of the town, with the loss of many lives,[6] does, in our opinion, strongly urge the propriety of guarding such magazines from that kind of danger; and since it is now well known, from many observations, that metals have the property of conducting lightning, and a method has been discovered of using that property for the security of buildings, by so disposing and fixing iron rods, as to receive, and convey away, such lightning as might otherwise have damaged them; which method has been practised near twenty years in many places, and attended with success, in

4. Wilson and BF; see the headnote on BF to Dawson above, May 29.
5. For testing the powder.
6. See the headnote just cited. In his draft BF added, then deleted, a reference to the similar explosion in Jamaica that is mentioned in Small to BF above, April 13.

all the instances that have come to our knowledge,[7] we cannot, therefore, but think it adviseable to provide conductors of that kind for the magazines in question.

In common cases, it has been judged sufficient; if the lower part of the conductor were sunk three or four feet into the ground, till it came to moist earth; but this being a case of the greatest importance, we are of opinion that greater precaution should be taken. Therefore, we would advise, that, at each end of each magazine, a well should be dug in or through the chalk, so deep as to have in it at least four feet of standing water. From the bottom of this water should arise a piece of leaden pipe, to or near the surface of the ground, where it should be strongly joined to the end of an upright iron bar, an inch and half diameter, fastened to the wall by leaden straps, and extending ten feet above the ridge of the building, tapering from the ridge upwards to a sharp point, the upper 12 inches of copper, the iron to be painted.

We mention lead for the under-ground part of the conductor, as less liable to rust in water and moist places; in the form of a pipe, as giving greater stiffness for the substance; and iron for the part above-ground, as stronger, and less likely to be cut away. The pieces, of which the bar may be composed, should be screwed strongly into each other, by a close joint, with a thin plate of lead between the shoulders, to make the joining or continuation of the metal more perfect. Each rod, in passing above the ridge, should be strongly and closely connected by iron or lead, or both, with the leaden coping of the roof, whereby a communication of metal will be made between the two bars of each building, for a more free and easy conducting of the lightning into the earth.

We also advise, in consideration of the great length of the buildings, that two wells, of the same depth with the others, should be dug within twelve feet of the doors of the two outside magazines; that is to say, one of them on the north side of the north building, the other on the south side of the south building; from the bottom of which wells, similar conductors should be carried up to the eaves, there joining well with a plate of lead, extending on the roof

7. BF heard, a few months later, of an example to the contrary, but it proved to be unfounded: to Bache below, Oct. 7. Some years earlier BF had recommended protecting a powder magazine with a single rod placed near but not on the building: above, x, 183–4.

up to the leaden coping of the ridge, the said plate of lead being of equal substance with that of the coping.

We are further of opinion, that it will be right to form a communication of lead from the top of the chimney of the proof-house to the lead on its ridge, and thence to the lead on the ridge of the corridor, and thence to the iron conductor of the adjacent end of the magazine; and also to fix a conductor from the bottom of the weather-cock spindle of the clock-house, down on the outside of that building, into the moist earth.[8]

As to the board-house, we think it already well furnished with conductors, by the several leaden communications above-mentioned, from the point of the roof down into the water, and that, by its height and proximity, it may be some security to the buildings[9] below it; we therefore propose no other conductor for that building, and only advise erecting a pointed iron rod on the summit, similar to those before described, and communicating with those conductors.[1]

To these directions we would add a caution, that, in all future alterations or repairs of the buildings, special care be taken that the metalline communications be not cut off or removed.

It remains that we express our acknowledgements to Sir Charles Frederick, Surveyor-general of the Ordnance, for the obliging attention with which he entertained and accomodated us on the day of our enquiry. With very great respect, we are, Gentlemen, Your most obedient, humble servants,   H. CAVENDISH,
WILLIAM WATSON,
B. FRANKLIN,
J. ROBERTSON.

8. The draft here adds a sentence that was later deleted, either by BF or some one else: "For tho' the Proof-house and Clock-house have not generally any Gunpowder in them, yet as Lightning sometimes rends large Stones out of Buildings, and throws them about with Violence, so as to penetrate and damage other adjacent Buildings, to avoid any Danger, however unlikely to happen, from such Collision, we think it adviseable to secure them."

9. So in the draft; the printed text reads "building," which must be a misprint.

1. Most of the committee thought this rod redundant, but apparently agreed to it to meet Wilson's charge that they were being inconsistent; see his *Observations*, pp. 5, 15–17.

From Arthur Lee AL: Historical Society of Pennsylvania

Monday. 21. Augt. 1772.
Mr. Lee's Compliments to Dr. Franklin. The Gentleman who deliverd him the inclosd Letter, having informd him, that the Bearer of it from Mr. Cushing was under an express injunction to deliver it to Dr. Lee in the absence of Dr. Franklin, as the Contents requird immediate attention; Mr. L. took the Liberty of opening it.[2] The Contents however appear to Mr. L. to be such, as may well wait for Dr. Franklin's better judgment.

From William Strahan ALS: American Philosophical Society

Dear Sir   New Street August 21. 1772.
As you will probably write to Philadelphia by some of the Vessels now about to sail thither, may I request the favour of you to remind Mr. Galloway of the Money due to me for Types and Newspapers sent to Mr. Goddard by his Order above four Years ago, and which, as stated in my Letter to him of the 6th. Decr. 1770. amounted then to £172 15s. 2d.? I wrote him the 7th. of August last Year to which I have had no Answer. It is surely high time this Money was repaid, which I beg your Interposition to procure me without farther Delay. It is hard I should suffer by the Madness and Ingratitude of Goddard whom I never had the least Concern with. It was Mr. Galloway's Order that I obeyed; and to him I look for my Reimbursement.[3]

2. For Lee's association with BF in the Massachusetts agency see above, XVII, 257–8; this is the first extant communication between them. We have no idea who carried Cushing's letter, but it was undoubtedly that of July 15 above; BF replied below, Sept. 3.

3. Galloway had placed the order in 1767, when he and Thomas Wharton had been Goddard's silent partners in starting the *Pa. Chron.*: above, XIV, 147 n. They had subsequently quarreled with the printer, and defaulted on their share of the partners' obligations. Goddard, as a result, was in prison for debt, but was managing to carry on his bitter vendetta against Galloway in the pages of the *Chron.* Benjamin H. Newcomb, *Franklin and Galloway: a Political Partnership* (New Haven and London, 1972), pp. 213–17, 219–21. BF was contemptuous of Goddard's attacks; see his letter to WF above, Jan. 30. In these circumstances Strahan's request may well have embarrassed him. He seems to have ignored it, for he wrote Galloway the next day, when he had

I will do myself the Pleasure of waiting upon you in a Day or two, and in the mean time remain, with the warmest Respect and Esteem Dear Sir Your faithful and affectionate humble Servant

WILL: STRAHAN

Dr. Franklin

Addressed: To / Dr Franklin / at Mrs Stevenson's / Craven Street

To Richard Bache

ALS (letterbook draft): American Philosophical Society

Dear Son,   London Augt. 22. 1772

I have not had time to look over the Remarks sent me on Parker's Account, but shall do it shortly.[4]

I am glad you received the Box safe that went by Loxley.[5]

I do not wonder that Dry Goods are at present as you say a miserable Concern. After the Non Importation Agreement ended, People crowded in their Goods expecting a lively Demand, and it seems they have overdone it. Vendues and Credit are the Consequence, where you say People can buy what Goods they please under the prime Cost. And Credit at 75 per cent Advance. But it is easy to see that such a Trade cannot hold. Numbers will be discourag'd by it, some will break, and Trade will return to its due Course and regular Profits, of which those who follow it steadily will reap the Advantage.[6]

Tell Sally I receiv'd her pleasing Letters of May 16 and June 30. Mrs. Stevenson says the Bedstead is not to have a Cornice, and therefore no Covering it with Calico. She sends the Silks by Capt. Falconer, and Mr. Bache's Picture,[7] and some Patterns and Thread

presumably received this note, without mentioning its contents: below, Aug. 22. We have no proof that he ever did raise the matter, but see his letter to Bache below, Dec. 1.

4. For Parker's accounts see above, WF to BF, Feb. 28, and Bache to BF, May 16; the Remarks, we assume, were the memorandum enclosed in the former.

5. For Loxley's arrival see DF to BF above, May 14.

6. For the credit crisis see Jonathan Williams, Jr., to BF, above, April 10.

7. Sally's letters have not survived; the bedstead reappears in BF to DF below, Feb. 14, 1773. The picture was doubtless one that Richard had commissioned in England, perhaps of his father or brother.

for Tambour Work. Mrs. Stevenson, Mr. and Mrs. Hewson, and Sally, join Love to you and yours, with Your affectionate father

B Franklin

Mr Bache

To John Bartram

ALS: Central Library, Salford, England; draft: American Philosophical Society

My dear old Friend,   London, Aug. 22. 1772

I received your kind Letter of May 10. I am glad the Rhubarb Seed got safe to hand. I make no doubt of its Thriving well in our Country, where the Climate is the same with that of the Chinese Wall, just without which it grows in plenty and of the best Quality.[8] I shall be glad to know how you find the Turnips. I ask'd Solander about the Lucern Seed you wrote for. He could give me no Account of it, nor can I learn any thing of it from others. You may rely on my Friendship in recommending your Seeds. I send all that enquire of me about American Seeds to Mr. Freeman.[9] He should advertise them when they come. I hear nothing lately of Young, and think him not of much Consequence.[1] With Love to Mrs. Bartram and your Children, I am ever, my dear Friend, Yours most affectionately   B F

Addressed: To / Mr John Bartram / near / Philadelphia / per Capt Falconer

8. For BF's and Bartram's interest in the cultivation of rhubarb see above, XVI, 173, 261; XVII, 22. Chinese rhubarb was particularly esteemed: above, IX, 398.

9. James Freeman, Dr. Fothergill's nephew, had assumed responsibility for distributing the seeds that Bartram was sending to England. See above, XVI, 250.

1. William Young was in Bartram's opinion an upstart rival, who was trying to supersede him in royal favor; and BF was repeating a reassurance that he had given the year before. See above, respectively, XVII, 290; XVIII, 180. Reassurance was needed, for Young had come to England the previous autumn with a collection of botanical specimens for the King and Queen. *Pa. Gaz.*, Nov. 21, 1771.

To Anthony Benezet

ALS (letterbook draft) and copy: American Philosophical Society; copy: Haverford College Library

Dear Friend,   London, Augt 22. 1772

I made a little Extract from yours of April 27. of the Number of Slaves imported and perishing, with some close Remarks on the Hypocrisy of this Country which encourages such a detestable Commerce by Laws, for promoting the Guinea Trade, while it piqu'd itself on its Virtue Love of Liberty, and the Equity of its Courts in setting free a single Negro. This was inserted in the London Chronicle of the 20th of June last. I thank you for the Virginia Address, which I shall also publish with some Remarks.[2] I am glad to hear that the Disposition against keeping Negroes grows more general in North America. Several Pieces have been lately printed here against the Practice, and I hope in time it will be taken into Consideration and suppress'd by the Legislature. Your Labours have already been attended with great Effects.[3] I hope therefore you and your Friends will be encouraged to proceed. My hearty Wishes of Success attend you, being ever, my dear Friend, Yours most affectionately   B F.

Mr Antho Benezet

2. Benezet's letter and BF's communication to the *Chron.* (June 18–20) are above. BF apparently never wrote his remarks on the Virginia address, which was an extract of an open letter—anonymous, but by Arthur Lee—to the members of the House of Burgesses in 1767, urging the abolition of slavery. Benezet reprinted the extract in the book he had sent BF with his letter of April 27. He considered Lee's brief statement (it is only six pages) "one of the most compendious and weighty declarations on the subject." George S. Brookes, *Friend Anthony Benezet* (Philadelphia, 1937), p. 332.

3. Benezet's book, *Some Historical Account of Guinea*..., was reprinted in London in the spring; see the publication notice in the *London Chron.*, May 2–5. The other attacks on the slave trade that BF had in mind were probably one in June in *The Scots Mag.*, XXXIV (1772), 297–303, and Thomas Thompson, *The African Trade for Negro-Slaves*... (Canterbury, [1772]), which was noticed in May in the *Monthly Rev.*, XLVI (1772), 541.

To a Committee of the Library Company of Philadelphia[4]

ALS: Harvard University Library; letterbook draft: American Philosophical Society;[5] minutebook copy: Library Company of Philadelphia

Gentlemen,   London, Augt. 22. 1772

I received your Bill on Whitmore for £125 Sterling, which is carried to the Credit of the Library Company. With this you will receive the Books, of which inclosed I send the Invoice. I hope they will come safe to hand, and please. The Journals of the House of Commons are not to be had at present under 25 Guineas, or £25, therefore I did not think it adviseable to send them, as at Auctions or Sales one has frequent Opportunities of purchasing them much lower. Besides they are Books rather to be consulted on Occasion than read, and any one having such Occasion may find them in the Assembly's Library. I will however send them if you direct me to do it. With great Regard, I am, Gentlemen, Your most obedient humble Servant   B FRANKLIN

Messrs. Robt. Strettel Jones, Saml Rhoads, and Josiah Hewes

Addressed: To / Messrs. Robt. Strettel Jones / Samll Rhoads, & Josiah / Hewes, a Commte. of the Di- / rectors of the Library Company. / Philadelphia / per Capt. Falconer

Endorsed: London August 22 1772 Letter from B Franklin per Capt. Falconer.

4. In answer to the committee's letter above, May 28, where the members are identified, and to the earlier letter of April 27 with an order for books. The committee did not resume the correspondence until Dec. 28, 1773.

5. The draft contains a note omitted in the final version, that five percent is to be deducted from the prices on the invoice; the remainder of the note, badly torn, seems to refer to books that were not in the main consignment.

270

To a Committee of the Managers of the Pennsylvania Hospital

ALS (letterbook draft): American Philosophical Society

Gentlemen   London, Augt. 22. 1772.

I suppose Mr. Barclay has acquainted you from time to time with the Difficulties that have attended our obtaining the Money for the Hospital. He communicated to me the other Day the enclos'd Note left for him by the Solicitor. Dr. Fothergill is now out of Town, which we fear will prevent our being able to receive it till his Return about the End of next Month: I hope the Affair may be finished soon after to your Satisfaction.[6] I am, very respectfully Gentlemen, Your most obedient humble Servant

B FRANKLIN

Messrs Reynell, Rhoads and Pemberton

To Thomas Coombe[7]

ALS (letterbook draft): American Philosophical Society

Dear Friend,   London, Augt. 22. 1772

I rejoiced to hear of your safe Arrival and happy Meeting with your Friends. I hope every other Circumstance there will prove agreable [to?] you, if you chuse to continue at Philadelphia. [The?] Letter you intended me by Loxley[8] did not come, so I shall expect that Pleasure. Things remain here much in the State you left them. Mrs. Stevenson, Mr. and Mrs. Hewson, Miss Dolly Blunt and Sally, continue to respect and Love y[ou as] does no less Your affectionate Friend and [Servant]   B FRANKLIN

Revd Mr Coombe

6. See BF's second letter to the committee below, Aug. 28.

7. The young Philadelphia clergyman who had become an habitué of Craven Street, and had officiated at Polly Stevenson's marriage; for his return to America see BF to WF above, Feb. 3.

8. The *Carolina*, Capt. Benjamin Loxley, had cleared Philadelphia in early June and reached London in late July: *Pa. Gaz.*, June 4; *Lloyd's Evening Post*, July 20–22.

To Cadwalader Evans

ALS (letterbook draft): American Philosophical Society

Dear Friend, London, Augt. 22. 1772

I hope you received the Elastic Truss, and that it answered and gave Satisfaction.[9] It gives me great Pleasure to understand by yours of Apr. 30 that the Assemblies have shown a Disposition to encourage the Produce of Silk.[1] You can never overdo the Market here, and will soon be able to manufacture what you want for yourselves. Mr. Small speaks highly of our Country, and of your Civilities to him.[2] I have long since sent over Accounts of the Sale of your Silk, and of the Money in my Hands, which is ready to be paid to the Managers Order.[3] With great Esteem I am, Dear Friend, Yours most affectionately   B FRANKLIN

Dr Evans

To John Foxcroft

ALS (letterbook draft): American Philosophical Society

Dear Sir, London, Aug. 22. 1772

I received your Favour of June 29. and was glad to hear of your safe Return from Virginia, and that you were determin'd to observe a strict Regimen for the Preservation of your Health.[4]

You have no doubt receiv'd a surprizing Demand from the Office for Letters sent per Packet. It is a very unjust one as great Part of

9. See above, Polly Hewson to BF, July 6, and his reply of the 8th. Evans had presumably asked for the truss in his missing letter of April 30.

1. In the previous September the managers of the silk filature had requested support from the Assembly, which in March had agreed to contribute £1,000 as soon as private subscribers had raised the same amount; this condition was subsequently met and the money paid. 8 *Pa. Arch.*, VIII, 6684–6, 6846, 6886. In April the N.J. Assembly was expected to take similar action in that colony (*Pa. Gaz.*, April 30, 1772); we assume that the Assembly did so, although no records of that session are in print.

2. Dr. Alexander Small had a brief stay in Philadelphia: DF to BF above, May 14. He must have packed a lot into it.

3. See BF to the managers of the silk filature above, before May 10.

4. Foxcroft's illness had begun the previous winter; see his letter to BF above, Feb. 2. For his trip to Virginia see his brother to BF above, May 16.

it has been accounted for in our last general Settlement; and the rest will be so in future Settlements: How a particular Account can be render'd of those Letters I confess I am not able to say. On a former Demand of the same kind I wrote a Letter to Mr. Todd (of which I think I sent you a Copy) wherein I explain'd the Difficulty of keeping such separate Accounts by so many Offices, and I thought I had given Satisfaction, because I heard no more of it. Now it is revived I cannot conceive for what Reason but that our Accounts have been so long delayed, which makes me very uneasy, and therefore I beg you would make it an immediate Business to hasten them[5]. I have been several Times to the Office to talk with Mr. Todd about it, but have not yet met with him.

As to the Mistake in our private Account I think it cannot take you above an Hour at any time to examine and settle it. I have explain'd it in former Letters; and as we are both mortal, and the Sum is considerable I am not satisfied to have it remain unsettled. So I hope you will be so good as to excuse my mentioning it so often.[6]

I shall be glad to see Mr. Finlay and render him any Service in my Power relating to his Office.[7]

Mr. Wharton thinks little of the Information relating to the Virginians Proceedings. I am afraid they will engage us in Disputes if we succeed. But we have not yet kill'd the Bear.[8]

5. The Post Office bore the cost of packet ships, and letters sent by them consequently paid higher postage rates than those by private ships. Todd's desire for a strict accounting of receipts from the packet service may have been motivated by more than official zeal, for the service provided him with lucrative fees; see above, x, 217 n. BF succeeded, however, in having this particular demand withdrawn: to Foxcroft below, Nov. 19. "Our Accounts" were the annual ones for the American post office from April to April, 1771–72. They did not arrive until a month later: *ibid.*

6. BF harped on this theme in his letters to Foxcroft above, Feb. 4, and below, Oct. 7, Dec. 2. His concern is in marked contrast to his indifference about his accounting with David Hall, for which see above, XVII, 172 n.

7. Hugh Finlay, the Quebec postmaster (above, x, 223 n), arrived in England in the autumn, and soon afterward was appointed the first surveyor general of the American postal system; see BF to Foxcroft below, Nov. 3, 19, Dec. 2.

8. BF, in a missing portion of his letter to WF of Aug. 19, had said much the same about Wharton's views; see WF to BF below, Oct. 29. The information on which those views were based, unless BF is referring to some later news of which we have found no record, was that sent months before in Foxcroft's

I am sorry to hear that your Brother has not fully recover'd his broken Arm. I receiv'd the Flour he sent me in good Order; and shall be glad to have four Barrels more of the same, with 20 Kegs of Hopkins Biscuits and 5 of Massey's Ditto.[9]

My Love to my Daughter and to yours,[10] with best Wishes for your Prosperity. I am ever, my dear Friend, Yours most affectionately   B FRANKLIN

Mrs. Stevenson, with Mr. and Mrs. Hewson, are pleas'd with your Remembrance of them, and present their Compliments.

Mr Foxcroft

To Deborah Franklin

ALS: American Philosophical Society; letterbook draft: Library of Congress

My dear Child,   London, Augt. 22. 1772

I wrote to you by Sutton that I was pretty well recovered of my Gout, but it return'd upon me that Day, and has handled me pretty severely for some Nights past, tho' now I am something better.[1]

Mrs. West has another Son to whom I am Godfather.[2] That Family is well, as is Mr. Strahan's and Mr. Hewson's. They always desire to be affectionately remember'd to you. My other Godson, Billy Hewson, grows a fine Boy, runs about every where, goes into the Cold Bath like a Man. I hope our dear little Benjamin does the same; to whom I will write a Letter as soon as he can read.

---

letter to Todd and, more important, Galloway's to Jackson; see above, WF to BF, Jan. 6, BF to Galloway, Feb. 6. WF, as he made clear in writing to BF below, Oct. 29, took the opposition from Virginia much more seriously than Wharton did.

9. For the contents of this paragraph see Thomas Foxcroft to BF above, May 16, and BF's reply to that letter below, Dec. 2.

10. Foxcroft's wife and their new baby.

1. The attack seems to have lasted intermittently for at least a month; see BF to Stiles above, July 22.

2. Benjamin West, Jr. In June BF had, as godfather, spent five guineas in fees: Jour., p. 42.

The Squirrels are still alive, and great Favourites in the Bishop's and Lady Spencer's Families.[3]

Mr. Small came well home, and is full of the Praises of our Country. I thank you for your Civilities to him as my Friend. He desires to be kindly remembred to you and yours.[4]

I am happy to hear that your Headach and other Pains have left you. I hope you will yet be favoured with a good Measure of Health.

You mention several Deaths of our Friends, as Mr. Sumaine, Mr. Hugh Evans, and Mr. Gordon. Then you mention Polly Pitts, but in a manner that I do not know whether you mean that she too is dead.[5] I hope not. Pray tell me.

I rejoice that you have so much Pleasure with your King-Bird. Give him a Kiss from me with my Blessing. Mrs. Stevenson and Polly present their Love to you and yours. I am ever, my dear Debby Your very affectionate Husband   B FRANKLIN

Addressed: To / Mrs. Franklin / Philadelphia / per Capt. Falconer

To Joseph Galloway   ALS (draft): New York Public Library

Dear Friend,   London, Augt 22. 1772

I acknowledged before the Receipt of your Favour of May 14, since which I have no Line from you. It will be a Pleasure to me to render any Service to Mr. Tilghman[6] whom you recommended.

3. Margaret Georgiana Poyntz, a relative of Mrs. Shipley, had married John Spencer (1734–83), who since 1765 had been first Earl Spencer: Namier and Brooke, *House of Commons*, III, 460. They seem to have been notable for little more than their lineage. But their children, for whom the squirrels were clearly meant, were destined for fame. Georgiana (1757–1806) became, as Duchess of Devonshire, one of the most distinguished women of her day; see *DNB* under Georgiana Cavendish. George, second Earl Spencer (1758–1834), later headed the Admiralty during the most critical years in the struggle against revolutionary France. *DNB*.

4. For Alexander Small's brief visit to DF see her letter above, May 14–16.

5. She was. For her death and those of Samuel Soumaine, Thomas Gordon, and Evan Evans see DF to BF above, June 30. Hugh Evans had also died that spring, at the age of ninety: above, XIV, 139 n.

6. Doubtless Edward Tilghman (1751–1815), later a famous lawyer; he had graduated from the College of Pennsylvania in 1767 and was admitted to the Middle Temple in June, 1772. *DAB*.

The Acts pass'd in your Winter and Spring Sessions I have not yet receiv'd, nor have I heard from Mr. Wilmot that they have been presented.[7]

Lord Hillsborough, mortify'd by the Committee of Council's Approbation of our Grant in Opposition to his Report, has resigned. I believe when he offer'd to do so, he had such an Opinion of his Importance that he did not think it would be accepted; and that it would be thought prudent rather to set our Grant aside than part with him. His Colleagues in the Ministry were all glad to get rid of him, and perhaps for that reason join'd more readily in giving him that Mortification. Lord Dartmouth succeeds him, who has much more favourable Dispositions towards the Colonies.[8] He has heretofore express'd some personal Regard for me, and I hope now to find my Business with the Board more easy to transact.

Your Observations on the State of the Islands did not come to hand till after Lord Rochford had withdrawn his Petition. His Lordship and the Promoters of it were so roasted on the Occasion, that I believe another of the kind will not very soon be thought of. The Proprietor was at the Expence of the Opposition; and as I knew it would not be necessary and thought it might be inconvenient to our Affairs I did not openly engage in it, but I gave some private Assistance that I believe was not without Effect. I think too that Mr. Jackson's opinion [was of?] Service.[9] I would

7. For Henry Wilmot, the agent of the Proprietors, see above, IX, 16 n. The Governor had assented to the laws in March, but royal confirmation was not forthcoming until April, 1773, and did not reach Philadelphia until October. 8 *Pa. Arch.*, VIII, 6847–8, 7028–31.

8. For the maneuvering behind Hillsborough's resignation and Dartmouth's appointment see BF to Jones above, Aug. 3. BF was mistaken that all Hillsborough's colleagues were glad to see him go; he was one of the closest associates of Lord North, who was extremely reluctant to part with him but not strong enough to resist the attack of the Bedfordites. See Bradley D. Bargar, *Lord Dartmouth and the American Revolution* (Columbia, S.C., 1965), p. 56.

9. The status of the islands in the Delaware River and Bay had long been in doubt. Both Pennsylvania and New Jersey had claimed them by their charters; early in the century, however, the king's law officers had decided that they belonged to neither but were still crown land. *Board of Trade Jour.*, 1718–22, pp. 283, 294–5; *Acts Privy Coun., Col.*, II, 772–3. The Earl of Rochford, Secretary of State for the Southern Department, had recently petitioned

lodge a Copy of your Paper in the Plantation Office, against any similar future Application, if you approve of it. I only think the Island Holders make too great a Concession to the Crown when they suppose it may have a Right to Quitrent. It can have none, in my Opinion on the old Grants from Indians, Swedes and Dutch where none was reserved. And I think those Grants so clearly good as to need no Confirmation, to obtain which I suppose is the only Motive for offering such Quit Rent. I imagine too, that it may not be amiss to affix a Caveat in the Plantation Office, in Behalf of the Holders of Property in those Islands, against any Grant of them that may be applied for, till they have had timely Notice and an Opportunity of being fully heard. Mr. Jackson is out of Town, but I shall confer with him on the Subject as soon as he returns.[1]

I thank you for your Care in obtaining and transmitting the Bill Willing & Morris on James Snedel for £500 which is paid. Your friendly Attention in these Affairs is extreamly obliging.[2]

I acquainted Mr. Jackson with the Intention of the Assembly that he should receive the Votes and Laws free of Expence, and offered to reimburse him what he had paid as Postage for them. But he would not receive it as he had Money of theirs in his Hands, and said he could charge it. He tells me that you did not know of that Money. I remember the sending it when I was last

for a grant of some of them; the Penns, through counsel, opposed the petition before the Board of Trade. After long debate the Board reported favorably, on the ground that the islands were uninhabited and at the disposition of the crown. Richard Jackson, as counsel to the Board, may have suggested legal objections to its report; in any case further testimony before the Privy Council's Committee on Plantations established that several of the islands in question had de facto owners and were highly cultivated, whereupon Rochford withdrew his petition. *Ibid.*, v, 332–5; *Board of Trade Jour.*, 1768–75, pp. 278, 282, 284, 289–91. See also below, 1773: Trustees of the Burlington Free School to BF, Jan. 5, and BF to Galloway, Jan. 6.

1. The first editor to publish this letter omitted everything from here to the final clause. WTF, *Memoirs*, II, 174. Subsequent editors followed suit.

2. The affairs were the annual payments to BF as agent of Pennsylvania. This payment had been received in June: Jour., p. 42; Ledger, p. 45. For Thomas Willing and Robert Morris see the *DAB*; "Snedel" was James Shedel, a London merchant at 65 Carpenter's Hall, London Wall. *Kent's Directory*... (London, 1770).

in America; the Sum I forget, but think it was about £400. It must be mentioned in the Votes of 1762, 3, or 4.[3]

I beg Leave to propose as a Member of our Philosophical Society Monsieur Jean LeRoy, Vice Directeur de l'Academie Royale des Sciences à Paris. He is a Person of great Merit, a Friend to America, and who will be pleas'd with the Honour of being chosen.[4]

Don't let us yet be too sanguine about[5] Expectations of the Grant. There is a great dea[l to do?] before the Business is compleated, and many Things happen between the Cup and Lip. I am ever, my dear Friend, Yours most affectionately   B FRANKLIN

Mr Galloway

To Samuel Rhoads

ALS: Yale University Library; letterbook draft: American Philosophical Society

Dear Friend,   London, Augt. 22. 1772

I think I before acknowledg'd your Favour of Feb. 29. I have since received that of May 30.[6] I am glad my Canal Papers were agreable to you. If any Work of that kind is set on foot in America, I think it would be saving Money to engage by a handsome Salary an Engineer from hence who has been accustomed to such Business. The many Canals on foot here under different great Masters, are daily raising a number of Pupils in the Art, some of whom may want Employ hereafter; and a single Mistake thro' Inexperience, in such important Works, may cost much more than the Expence of Salary to an ingenious young Man already well acquainted with both Principles and Practice. This the Irish have learnt at a dear Rate in the first Attempt of their great Canal, and now are endeavouring to get Smeaton to come and rectify their Errors.[7]

3. It was. See above, XI, 358 n.

4. The APS responded promptly: Jean-Baptiste LeRoy, BF's friend and correspondent, was elected on Jan. 15, 1773. APS, *Early Proceedings...* (Philadelphia, 1884), p. 75.

5. BF deleted the word; the MS is defaced at this point, and whatever he substituted has been lost.

6. Only the letter of May 30 survives.

7. The Irish "great Canal" was to run from Dublin to the Shannon, across

With regard to your Question, whether it is best to make the Skuylkill a part of the Navigation to the back Country, or whether the Difficulty, of that River, subject to all the Inconveniencies of Floods, Ice, &c will not be greater than the Expence of Digging, Locks, &c.[8] I can only say, that here they look on the *constant Practicability* of a Navigation, allowing Boats to pass and repass at all Times and Seasons, without Hindrance, to be a Point of the greatest Importance, and therefore they seldom or ever use a River where it can be avoided. Locks in Rivers are subject to many more Accidents than those in still-water Canals; and the Carrying-away a few Locks by Freshes or Ice, not only creates a great Expence, but interrupts Business for a long time till Repairs are made; which may soon be destroyed again; and thus the Carrying-on a Course of Business by such a Navigation be discouraged, as subject to frequent Interruptions: The Toll too must be higher to pay for such Repairs. Rivers are ungovernable Things, especially in Hilly Countries: Canals are quiet and very manageable: Therefore they are often carried on here by the Sides of Rivers, only on Ground above the Reach of Floods, no other Use being made of the Rivers than to supply occasionally the Waste of Water in the Canals. I warmly wish Success to every Attempt for Improvement of our dear Country; and am with sincere Esteem, Yours most affectionately   B FRANKLIN

I congratulate you on the Change of our American Minister.[9] The present has more favourable Dispositions towards us than his Predecessor.

S. Rhoads, Esqr

Addressed: To / Samuel Rhoads, Esqr / Philadelphia / per Capt. Falconer.

----

a great bog and several rivers. Work on it was halted in 1770 for further surveys, after the expenditure of £77,000, and a series of engineers thereafter failed to solve the difficulties; John Smeaton was apparently not among them. By 1790 the venture had cost more than £500,000, was still incomplete, and was notorious as a canal for draining public money. John Phillips, *A General History of Inland Navigation...* (London, 1792), pp. 330–1, 340, 344.

8. See the conclusion of Rhoads's letter above, May 30.

9. The appointment of Dartmouth on Aug. 14 as Hillsborough's successor; see the annotation of BF to Jones above, Aug. 3.

To Benjamin Rush[1]

ALS:[2] Yale University Library; letterbook draft: American Philosophical Society

Dear Sir,   London, Augst 22. 1772

I am favoured with yours of June 24. and shall as it is my Duty endeavour to obtain the Royal Assent to every Act passed by our Assembly; and to that you recommend, the more particularly as I think it reasonable in itself, and connected with Liberty of Conscience a Fundamental of our Constitution.[3] But I am doubtful of its Success when I recollect that an Act of the same kind about twenty or twenty-five Years ago was repealed here, as introducing new Modes of Swearing unknown to the English Laws.[4] I shall however try what can be done.

I imagine I should thank you for a little Piece on preserving Health which I have read with Pleasure.[5] I wish you all Prosperity, being, with great Esteem, Dear Sir, Your most obedient humble Servant

1. For BF's old friend, the Philadelphia physician and humanitarian, see above, XIII, 387 n.

2. Some autograph-hunter has cut off the signature.

3. The Pennsylvania act, passed the preceding March, to legalize an oath taken by raising the hand instead of kissing the Bible. *The Statutes at Large of Pennsylvania from 1682 to 1801* (15 vols., Harrisburg, 1896–1911), VIII, 239–40; J. Thomas Scharf and Thompson Westcott, *History of Philadelphia, 1609–1884* (3 vols., Philadelphia, 1884), II, 1269. For an exhaustive, not to say exhausting, dissertation upon the relationship BF mentions between the act and liberty of conscience see Marshall to BF below, Oct. 30. We have found no other evidence of Rush's concern with this particular issue, but he was a lifelong opponent of statutory oaths; see Lyman H. Butterfield, ed., *Letters of Benjamin Rush* (2 vols., Princeton, 1951), I, 527–8.

4. BF was presumably referring to an act for naturalizing foreign Protestants who were not Quakers, and who refused to take any oath; but he was wrong about its fate. It was passed in 1743 and approved in 1746. *Pa. Statutes at Large* (cited above), IV, 391–4; *Acts Privy Coun., Col.*, IV, 21–3.

5. Rush's *Sermons to Gentlemen upon Temperance and Exercise*, published in February, 1772: *Pa. Gaz.*, Feb. 6. Rush sent a copy to Edward Dilly, the London bookseller, who republished the pamphlet in May under an amended title. Lyman H. Butterfield, "The American Interests of the Firm of E. and C. Dilly, with Their Letters to Benjamin Rush...," Bibliographical Soc. of America *Papers*, XLV (1951), 308–9.

I have lately heard from our Friends Dubourg and Dupont at Paris, who were well.[6]

Dr Rush

Addressed: To / Dr Rush / Philadelphia / per Capt. Falconer

Endorsed: Benjn. Franklin August 22 1772

To William Smith

ALS and letterbook draft: American Philosophical Society

Sir,   London, Augt. 22. 1772

I received yours of May 16.[7] with the Box of Books, and have already delivered and forwarded most of them as directed. I supply'd Dr. Fothergill with the wanting Sheet. I approve much of the Letter's being in English. I forwarded your Letter to Mr. White, Son of *Taylor* White, Esqr late Treasurer of the Foundling Hospital (now deceas'd) but he has not call'd for the Book. I am glad to hear of your Success at South Carolina, and that the College flourishes. I send inclos'd a Pamphlet on a new Discovery that makes some Noise here.[8] With my best Wishes of Prosperity to the Society, and Thanks for the Number of Books they have sent me, which I shall endeavour to dispose of to their Credit, I am, Sir, Your most obedient humble Servant   B FRANKLIN

Revd Dr Smith

Endorsed: To D Smith relative to 1 Vol of Transactions

6. During his stay in Paris in 1769 Rush had been introduced, through BF, to Jacques Barbeu-Dubourg and Pierre Samuel du Pont de Nemours. Butterfield, *op. cit.* in n. 3 above, I, 77 n.

7. Where the matters that BF is discussing are explained.

8. Probably Joseph Priestley's *Directions for Impregnating Water with Fixed Air...* (London, 1772).

To Robert Towers and Joseph Leacock[9]

ALS (letterbook draft): American Philosophical Society

Gentlemen,   London, Augt. 22. 1772
   I received yours and should readily have afforded the Assistance in my Power you desire, to Mr. Crafts, in sending Hands to you for the Glass-house, if he could have found any willing to go on reasonable Terms. It is always a Difficulty here to meet with good Workmen and sober that are willing to go abroad.[1] I heartily wish you Success in your laudable Undertaking to supply your Country with so useful a Manufacture, and am, Your most obedient Servant   B FRANKLIN

Messrs Towers and Leacock

To John Tyler[2]

ALS (letterbook draft): American Philosophical Society

Loving Kinsman   London, Aug. 22. 1772
   I received yours of May 16. and am glad to hear you are well. I hope your Nailing Scheme may answer.[3] I was lately in Birming-

9. Towers (d. *c.* 1779) was a Philadelphia tanner, who served for a time during the War of Independence as Pennsylvania commissary of stores. *Pa. Col. Recs.*, X, *passim*; 3 *Pa. Arch.*, XIV, 500. Joseph Leacock (F.2.2.9: above, VIII, 140) was David Hall's brother-in-law and DF's cousin. In the fall of 1771 Towers and Leacock had started a glass factory on what is now Richmond Street; a few months later they advertised for workmen (*Pa. Gaz.*, Jan. 23, 1772) and presumably asked BF's help at about the same time; the letter to which he is replying has been lost. Their venture was not a success, and before the end of 1772 the property was sold. Harrold E. Gillingham, "Pottery, China, and Glass Making in Philadelphia," *PMHB*, LIV (1930), 125–6; Rhea M. Knittle, *Early American Glass* (New York and London, [1927]), p. 144.
   1. BF had already had trouble with a man whom Stiegel was trying to recruit for his glassworks; see Bache to BF above, May 16. We have been unable to identify Crafts.
   2. A young relative of DF, who had emigrated from Birmingham to Philadelphia in 1771 with a letter of introduction from BF to DF. See above, XVIII, 208, and BF to DF, Jan. 28, 1772.
   3. It did not. At about this time Tyler, by his account, invested some £300 in an iron foundry with another man, who promptly ousted him, kept his

ham, and saw your Friends there who are well. A Box has been committed to my Care for you, which I send herewith. I should have been glad of an Opportunity of rendring any Service or Pleasure to the young Man you recommended to me, wishing as I do Success to all new Manufactures in America. I am, Your Friend and Servant   B FRANKLIN

Mr Tyler

From Peter Timothy   ALS: American Philosophical Society

My dear Sir,   Charles-Town, Aug. 24. 1772.

It is almost sufficient to discourage any Man from continuing to write, who has sent so many Letters as I have to you since the 16th of August last Year, without receiving an Answer to any one besides the first, and that after Six Months had elapsed.[4] But I will suppose they have miscarried: I can not believe that Doct. Franklin will withdraw his Friendship from any Man, while it may be in his Power to serve him, merely because he has been *unfortunate*. I have been so, but never willfully wrong'd any Man. I have suffered, by never being lukewarm in any Cause.[5] I must be active, and I never did set that Value upon Money, which the prudent Part of the Mankind generally does: In that Respect I have been imprudent; and if I have been unjust, the World says, it is to myself and Family. You have already been made acquainted with many Particulars of my Situation, tho' in a very confused Manner.

My natural Eyes being almost worn out, I have declined the Printing Business, and am now employed in putting my Affairs in order for a Settlement.[6] In the mean Time I am ready for any Employment in His Majesty's Service, that will not degrade me,

---

money and tools, and eventually brought suit against him. Tyler to BF, June 6, 1787, APS.

4. No letter from BF in 1771 has survived, and only one from Timothy: above, XVIII, 233–5.

5. But he had suffered from not being warm enough against the Stamp Act to satisfy the radicals: above, XV, 200–1.

6. The settlement was short-lived: Timothy left the business in the hands of partners from March, 1772, to November, 1773; he then resumed control and maintained it until his death in 1782. Hennig Cohen, *The South Carolina Gazette, 1732–1775* (Columbia, S.C., 1953), pp. 4–5, 248–9; above, I, 342 n.

which any Friend may think me fit for or can procure by his Interest. The Naval Officer's Place here is not of any considerable Value, the Duty is easy; it is held by one Stephenson, and executed by Mr. Raper his Deputy:[7] I could be satisfied with a Reversion of that Office. I know your Disposition from Mr. Hughes, whose Loss I shall ever lament; if you say you will serve me if you can, I am sure you will do it.[8] The Manner must be left to you.

My Son Benjamin Franklin has just happily got thro' the Measles, and a fine promising Boy; but as I have lost eight Sons in Teething, my Apprehension for him will not be over till he has all his Teeth.[9]

When I began this Letter it was with an Intent to say nothing of myself—but *Self*, somehow or other, even in unmercenary Minds will always prevail; and I find myself as apt to wander as other Men. I took up my Pen, only to recommend to your Notice and Friendship, a very worthy and intimate Friend of mine, Capt. Elias Vanderhorst, by whom this will be handed to you—a Gentleman, who can perhaps give you as good an Account of this and the Southern Colonies as any you ever yet have met with. He is

7. The position of the naval officer was an old one. He was responsible jointly to the governor and the British Board of Customs, and by this time was appointed by the crown; among his various duties were those of enforcing the navigation acts and overseeing the clearance of ships from Charleston. South Carolina was one of the few colonies in which the office was commonly discharged by a deputy. Charles M. Andrews, *The Colonial Period of American History*... (4 vols., New Haven, 1934–38), IV, 187–9, 420; Leonard W. Labaree, ed., *Royal Instructions to British Colonial Governors, 1660–1776* (2 vols., New York and London, 1935), II, 657, 664, 760–2, 773–4; Thomas C. Barrow, *Trade and Empire: the British Customs Service in Colonial America, 1660–1775* (Cambridge, Mass., 1967), pp. 118–19. The naval officer at the time was one Benjamin Stevenson: *The Royal Kalendar*... (London, 1772), p. 280. His deputy, we are convinced, was Robert Raper (1709–79), a Charleston lawyer who was clearly connected with the customs service and must have been the naval officer of that name who turned up in Newport in 1769. See Philip M. Hamer and George C. Rogers, Jr., eds., *The Papers of Henry Laurens* (3 vols. to date; Columbia, S.C., 1968–), I, 38 n; Carl Bridenbaugh, "Charlestonians at Newport, 1767–1775," *S.C. Hist. and Geneal. Mag.*, XLI (1940), 45.

8. For BF's services to his old friend John Hughes, and the latter's death in Charleston the previous January, see above, XVII, 157 n; XVIII, 235 n.

9. The baby was nine months old at the time; he managed to survive, and eventually went into his father's printing business. Douglas C. McMurtrie, *A History of Printing in the United States*... (2 vols., New York, 1936), II, 327.

modest and sensible, of unquestionable Honour and Veracity; has enjoyed a good Fortune, but sunk it in Trade, by Ill-Usage, not Misconduct.[1] In short, he is such a Man, that I am persuaded, when you know him, you will not regret his having been recommended by Your most affectionate oblig'd and very obedient humble Servant.   PETR. TIMOTHY.

From William Strahan   ALS: American Philosophical Society

Dear Sir   New Street Thursday, Augst. 27. [1772?[2]]
    Inclosed is the Receit for the Books. They told me at the Coffeehouse yesterday, that the Captain takes his Bag away tomorrow. Please to remember your Engagement to dine with me tomorrow at 4. I am ever Dear Sir Your affectionate humble Servant
                                                WILL: STRAHAN
Addressed: To | Dr. Franklin | Craven Street

From John Walsh   ALS: American Philosophical Society

Dear Sir   Paris, 27th. Augt. 1772.
    I will not let this Post slip without making to You my hearty congratulations on your being elected by the French Academy of Sciences to be one of it's eight foreign Members, a truely illustrious Society; and I will freely say it, even to You, because I

1. Elias Vanderhorst (1735–1816), the son of John and Mary Elizabeth Vander Horst, was a Charleston merchant who had commanded a company during the Cherokee war of 1760–61. He remained in England for the rest of his life. By 1775 he was established as a merchant in Bristol, where after the Revolution he served as the American consul for many years. See Alexander S. Salley, *Marriage Notices in the South-Carolina Gazette*...(Albany, 1902), pp. 24–5; *S.C. Hist. and Geneal. Mag.*, III (1902), 204; Mabel L. Webber, ed., "Josiah Smith's Diary...," *ibid.*, XXXIII (1932), 103; *Sketchley's Bristol Directory*... (Bristol, 1775), p. 99; *Gent. Mag.*, LXXXVI, pt. I (1816), 567.
    2. Aug. 27 also fell on a Thursday in 1767, but in that year BF would scarcely have had a dinner engagement on the 28th, when he left for Paris: above, XIV, 241. The books also point to 1772: they were either those for the Library Company (see BF's letters to its committee above, Aug. 22, and below, Aug. 28) or some that Strahan furnished BF at this time for WF: Jour., p. 43.

think it, that Your Election does honour to the Judgement of the Academy.[3]

On my Arrival here the 21st. I found your favour of the 28th. July, having order'd my Letters to be detained at Paris during my Journey from La Rochelle; to which I was engaged by Circumstances, that agreably arose, to give more time than I at first proposed: Among the Rest that of seeing my Nephew well settled at the Academy of Angers.[4] The hope of seeing you soon in England, which I always entertained, and do now, is the reason you have not had a full account by Letter of my further Experiments on that wonderfull Animal the Torpedo.

I spent a compleat week at the Isle de Ré in my Experiments and had every convenience there for prosecuting them, except that I was something restricted by the Jealousy of the Governour from making them where the Animal was caught. At my Return to La Rochelle, I communicated to the Gentlemen of the Rochelle Academy and to many of the principal Inhabitants all that I had observed concerning the Torpedo, in the Intention of stirring up a Spirit of Enquiry both as to it's Electricity and general Oeconomy, and I shall be glad to find that this has produced other effects than meer Surprize. I did hope that three days of very general Exhibition in this manner would have left me nothing more to do in France, but finding by an absurd Paragraph in the french Papers that those present are not very capable of relating of what they heard saw and felt;[5] and being a good deal pressed by your Con-

3. For the choice of BF as a foreign associate of the Academy see his letters below, to de la Vrillière, Sept. 4, and to the Academy, Nov. 16.

4. The nephew was Arthur Fowke (c. 1756–75), the son of Walsh's sister Elizabeth and Joseph Fowke, who like Walsh had been in the service of the East India Company. After Elizabeth's death and Joseph's return to India in 1771, Walsh took charge of their children. Arthur lived with him in London, met BF there and pronounced him agreeable, and then went to France with his uncle and shared in his experiments. In mid-August Walsh, apparently on the spur of the moment, enrolled him for a few months in the famous Académie d'équitation at Angers. The young man returned to England the following February; in 1774 he followed his father into the Company's service in India, where he soon died. George R. Kaye and Edward H. Johnston, eds., *Minor Collections and Miscellaneous Manuscripts* (India Office Library, *Catalogue of Manuscripts in European Languages*, II, part 2; London, 1937), pp. 64–5, 68, 71–2, 80–3.

5. For the trip to Rhé see Walsh's letter above of July 12. The experiments

freres of the Academy to communicate a Fact so interesting and singular, I shall endeavour to conquer my Indolence and Aversion to stepping forth on the publick Stage because indeed I feel that it will be ridiculous in me if I do not. You must therefore allow me to address a short Letter to You on this Subject. As the Coasts of France abound with this Animal and as it is denied to us,[6] with your Leave I will publish the Letter here with a french Context, by either your friend LeRoy or Du Bourg. This cannot be affected entirely during my Stay here, especially as a plate must accompany the publication, therefore I shall probably be able to converse with you on this Matter, however I hope that will not prevent my hearing from you first. It is now high time for me to acquaint You with the Result of my Experiments on the Isle de Ré and I must do it in a Word if I mean to use this post. The Vigour of the fresh-taken Torpedos there was not able to force the Torpedinal Fluid across the most minute Tract of Air, not from one Link of a small Chain to another, not even thro' a Separation made by the Edge of a Knife in a Slip of Tinfoil pasted on Sealing Wax. The Spark therefore and snapping noise attending it were denied to all our Attempts, either in the Light or compleat Darkness.[7] I observed to you in my Last the Singularity of the Torpedo being

---

before the La Rochelle Academy were reported in the *Gaz. de France* of Aug. 14. The secretary of the Academy, it seems, agreed with Walsh's view of the report, for two months later he sent the newspaper a lengthy description of what had happened. An extract of that description is included in Walsh's letter to BF below, July 1, 1773; see also Jean Torlais, "L'Académie de la Rochelle et la diffusion des sciences au XVIIIe siècle," *Revue d'histoire des sciences...*, XII (1959), 119–20.

6. It was not denied, Walsh later discovered; he found torpedoes off the English coast, and reported to the Royal Society on his experience with them: *Phil. Trans.*, LXIV (1774), 464–73.

7. The spark and noise were proof of an electrical discharge, and their absence raised doubt about Walsh's analogy between the torpedo and the Leyden jar; see BF to Ingenhousz below, Sept. 30, 1773. Walsh later demonstrated that an electric eel could make sparks: John Nichols, *Illustrations of the Literary History of the Eighteenth Century...* (8 vols., London, 1817–48), I, 156. The full solution to the problem came not from Walsh but from Henry Cavendish, who showed that an electrical discharge might occur without spark or noise: "An Account of Some Attempts to Imitate the Effects of the Torpedo by Electricity," *Phil. Trans.*, LXVI (1776), 200–4, 216–23; Arthur J. Berry, *Henry Cavendish: His Life and Scientific Work* (London, [1960]), pp. 113–14.

able when insulated to give to an insulated Person a great number
of successive Shocks: In this Circumstance I have taken no less
than fifty Shocks from him in the Space of a Minute and half. All
our Experiments confirmed that the Torpedinal fluid was concentrated in the very instant of it's Explosion by a sudden Energy of
the Animal; and as there was no gradual accumulation and Reten-
tion of this elastick fluid as in the Case of charged Glass, it is not
surprizing that there should be no effect on Canton's Balls of Attraction or Repulsion.[8] In short the Torpedinal Shock appears to
arise from a compressed elastick fluid restoring itself to it's former
State by the same Conductors as the elastick fluid compressed in
charged Glass. The Skin of the Animal, bad conductor as it is, appears to be a better conductor of the Torpedinal elastick fluid than
the least Tract of the likewise elastick fluid Air. Notwithstanding
the weak Spring of the Torpedinal fluid I was able to convey it in
the publick Exhibitions at La Rochelle thro' two Brass Wires of
twelve feet each and thro' 4 to 8 Persons, at different times, the
Wires and Persons communicating with each other by the medium
of Water, in Basins placed between each. The Torpedo laid on a
wet Napkin was placed on a Table six feet distant from the Table
on which the Basins stood. One End of One of the Wires was
wrapt in the Wet Napkin and the other End went into the first
Basin in which the first Gentleman put a finger of one hand, with
a finger of the other hand in the next Basin. The Circuit was in
this manner continued to the last Basin. One End of the other
Wire was put into this last Basin and with the other End I just
touched the Back of the Fish, when all the Persons in the Circuit
were affected, but I, the toucher, being out of it felt nothing.[9] The
effect in Air, on many repeated Experiments, is about four times
as strong as it is in Water.[1] I have only Room to wish you a Return

8. For Canton's balls, a form of electrometer, see above, IX, 351 n. Cavendish's experiment, just cited, modified Walsh's conclusion by showing that
the discharge was too rapid and complete to make the balls separate; see
Berry, *op. cit.*, p. 114.

9. This experiment was similar to one that BF suggested in his instructions
above, Aug. 12; for a more detailed discussion of it see Walsh to BF below,
July 1, 1773.

1. Walsh later elaborated this sentence into several paragraphs: *ibid.* The
principle involved, the same as that of Henly's experiment with different
circuits the previous October (above, XVIII, 229–31), was that most but not

of Health[2] and to assure you that I am with the greatest Esteem and Respect Dear Sir Your obedient humble Servant

JOHN WALSH

To a Committee of the Library Company of Philadelphia

ALS (letterbook draft): Library of Congress

⟨London, August 28, 1772: Encloses a bill of lading of the books for the Library Company. Endorsed to Robert Strettell Jones, Samuel Rhoads, and Josiah Hewes.[3]⟩

To a Committee of the Managers of the Pennsylvania Hospital

ALS (letterbook draft): Library of Congress

Gentlemen,   London, Aug 28. 1772
    Mr. Barclay writes to you fully, but I cannot refuse myself the Pleasure of congratulating you on our having at last obtain'd the Money for the Hospital, viz £7634 11s. 1d. 3 per Cent Bank Annuities, with £909 1s. 4d. Interest.[4] This Sum will be a great Help

---

all of the charge passes through the circuit that has the greatest conducting power.
    2. From his severe attack of gout, which he must have mentioned in his missing letter of July 28, and did mention to Stiles on the 22nd and DF on Aug. 22.
    3. For the list of books see the letter above of April 27 from the committee, which then had a different composition; the new group wrote to BF on May 28.
    4. For the money from the Pa. Land Co. see the Hospital Managers' letter to BF et al. above, May 16. On Aug. 27 David Barclay had written to inform the Managers that the Bank of England, on a Chancery order, had transferred to him, Fothergill, and BF for the use of the Hospital the annuities and interest that BF mentions; Fothergill would return from Cheshire within four to six weeks, Barclay added, and the agents would then dispose of the annuities whenever directed to do so. Their value fluctuated, and at the moment was 89 per cent of par; they had originally been purchased for only £6,451 4s. (Pa. Hospital minutebook.) Barclay apparently handled the transaction, which does not appear in BF's accounts. For the eventual disposition of the annuities see the Manager's letters below, Oct. 20, Nov. 4, 1772; Jan. 1, 1773.

to our Institution. With my best Wishes for its Success and sincere Esteem for its benevolent Managers and Physicians, I am, Gentlemen Your most obedient humble Servant   B FRANKLIN

Messrs John Reynell S. Rhoads and I Pemberton[5]

From William Bowden[6]   ALS: Historical Society of Pennsylvania

Sir   St. Thomas's Hospital 29th. August 1772
The great regard I have for my friend M Skey the bearer of this, engages me to take the liberty to introduce him to you.[7] He wants some information with respect to the new Settlement intended at the Ohio, and as I am very sensible your opinion will be of great use, I presume to ask your favoring him with your sentiments on that head, for a guide to him in pursuing his scheme. I hope you will excuse this freedom, and believe me to be with great regard Sir Your most Obedient humble Servant
                                        W. BOWDEN

Addressed: To / Dr Benjamin Franklin / In / Craven Street / Strand

From Jonathan Williams, Sr.

ALS (incomplete and mutilated): American Philosophical Society

[August?, 1772]
[*Beginning mutilated*] advice, because I [*torn*] I think afterward indeed I am [*torn*] fearing that he is Spending his [*torn*] nought his

5. BF seems to have confused the two Pemberton brothers: James had signed the letter to him and others above, May 16.
6. A London merchant trading with America, and a prominent dissenter. He had just been elected governor of the New England Co., and was a member of the Presbyterian Board and a trustee of Dr. Williams' charity; he was also a director of the Bank of England and the treasurer of St. Thomas's Hospital. See William Kellaway, *The New England Company, 1649–1776: Missionary Society to the American Indians* ([London, 1961]), pp. 171, 173.
7. No Skey appears in *Kent's Directory...* (London, 1770). A George Skey was a Russia merchant in London, but all we know about him is that he had a son, born in 1798, who later became a famous surgeon; see the *DNB* under Frederick Carpenter Skey. If the father married late in life, he might have been in his younger days a business acquaintance of Bowden.

Situation puts me in [mind of a quotation?] I have somewere seen [*illegible*] the God if the [*torn*] to hold attendance and Dependence be [*torn*].8

Agreeable to your Orders Some [*torn*] your account for the Cost and Loss on the Tic[ket?] [*torn*] another £20 Prize but Whether [*torn*] it or your I now Cant tell however [if you will take the?] Troble Please to Let me know what [*torn*] Will Send a Bill to Discharge it.9 With my most [*torn*] thanks for all favours shew'd to my Belov'd Son Who got home Just time enought to take Leave of his Friends and bid them a Long farewell, in him we mourn the Loss of a good Son, a most affectionate Brother, agreeable Compainion and Faithfull Friend.1

I have obtain'd an Execution against Hall Returnable next Feby. he has given Personal Security So that the money must be paid or he must Go to Goal at Present its verry unsartain Whether he Will Live or Die Polliticaly tho' I Wish he may Live for more Reasons then one.2 Aunt Mecom and Daughter are Well my Wife and Children Desire to be Respectfully Remember'd to you. I am with the greatest Esteem your Dutyfull Nephew and Humble Servant   JONA WILLIAMS

[*In the margin:*] [All the money from?] Hall, is it your order that I Deliver it to Aunt Mecom—Please to Say [*remainder missing*]

Addressed: To / Doctr Benjamin Franklin / at Mrs Stevenson's in / Craven Street / Strand / London / per the Argo / Capt Folger

8. Our guess, from these remaining fragments, is that Williams was talking about the business dealings of his son Jonathan, for which see BF's correspondence with the two above, Jan. 13, April 10.

9. Williams' lottery tickets figured prominently in his correspondence with BF in the two previous volumes.

1. The blind Josiah had returned from England in May and died in Boston on August 15. *Mass. Gaz. and Boston Weekly News-Letter*, Aug. 20, 1772.

2. The suit against Samuel Hall had been a theme of BF's correspondence with the Williamses; see, for example, the letter to BF from Jonathan, Jr., above, end of June. The settlement dragged on into 1774. Williams presumably hoped for Hall's political survival because of the latter's *Essex Gaz.*, which was taking a strong anti-ministerial stand: Philip Davidson, *Propaganda and the American Revolution, 1763–1783* (Chapel Hill, 1941), p. 228.

From Nathaniel Falconer[3] ALS: American Philosophical Society

Dear Sir   Downes September the 2d, 1772

I am Sorrey to Trouble you with aney Triflings matters of mine but as it is uncertain that I shall Return Directly to London or go Elswhere I must beg the Favor of you to Call on mr. Samuel wharton when the Grant is made for my Right for Forty Thousand acres for which he has already Received Fifty pounds Sterling of mildreed & Roberts where his order to Trent and Trents Recpt Lays[4] if aney more on my part is Nessarey on my part you will be So Good as to pay it your Frendly assistance in this matter will much oblige your most obident Humble Servant

NATH FALCONER

Addressed: To / Docter Franklin / in / Craven Street / in the Strand / London

3. BF's old friend, at this time master of the *Britannia*.
4. Falconer was anxious to secure his interests, we assume, because he had heard while in England of the Privy Council's recent decision in favor of the Walpole grant; he was now outward bound, carrying a number of BF's letters written on Aug. 22. The firm of Mildred and Roberts, Quaker merchants in London, was connected with two other friends of BF: it was part owner of James Sparks's ship, the *Mary and Elizabeth*, and Daniel Mildred (above, XVI, 169 n) was associated with Dr. Fothergill. *PMHB*, XXVII (1903), 495; Betsy C. Corner and Christopher C. Booth, eds., *Chain of Friendship: Selected Letters of Dr. John Fothergill* ... (Cambridge, Mass., 1971), pp. 258, 263. For William Trent, Wharton's associate, see above, XIV, 266–7; XVI, 38 n, 133 n. Once these details are disposed of, the question remains of how or whether Falconer was involved in the Walpole Company. The easy answer, that he had a whole or fractional share, is suspect. A share did not at this stage entitle the holder, as far as we know, to any specific acreage; if the Company had obtained the 20 million acres for which it was applying, each of the 72 shareholders would have acquired not 40,000 but 277,777. By 1772 even fractional shares were selling at fantastic prices: Peter Marshall, "Lord Hillsborough, Samuel Wharton and the Ohio Grant, 1769–1775," *English Hist. Rev.*, LXXX (1965), 733. Falconer could scarcely have afforded to buy at that time, and his name was not on the list of original shareholders in Lewis, *Indiana Co.*, p. 88 n; even if he had been one of the group, his assessments to date would not have come to £50. The most likely explanation, though we have no supporting evidence, is that Wharton was selling rights in advance to parcels of the land that he expected to obtain for his five shares.

To Thomas Cushing AL (letterbook draft): Library of Congress

Sir,   London, Sept. 3. 1772

I write this Line just to acknowledge the Receipt of your several Favours of July 15 and 16, enclosing the Resolves of the House relating to the Governor's Salary, and the Petition to the King.[5] Lord Dartmouth, now our American Minister, will probably not be in Town till the Season of Business comes on, I shall then immediately put the Petition into his Hands, to be presented to his Majesty.[6] I may be mistaken, but I imagine we shall not meet the same Difficulty in transacting Business with him as with his Predecessor, on whose Removal I congratulate you most heartily. I shall write fully per some of the next Boston Ships. At present can only add, that with the sincerest Esteem and Respect, I am, Sir, &c.

Honble. Thos Cushing, Esqr[7]

5. For the resolutions and the petition that grew out of them see Cushing's letter above, July 15. The resolutions were presumably enclosed in his second letter, of the 16th, which has now been lost.

6. Dartmouth returned to town at the beginning of November, when BF presented the petition: to Cushing below, Nov. 4. Parliament reconvened on Nov. 26.

7. BF made a note to himself in the margin that by the same packet he had written Colden to acknowledge bills for £372 10s., and had sent some "small Letters" to other friends. All these have been lost; that to Colden is mentioned in BF's letter to him below, Oct. 7.

To the Duc de la Vrillière[8]

AL (draft): American Philosophical Society

[September 4, 1772[9]]

It was with the greatest Pleasure I received the Information your Grace has condescended to give me of my Nomination by the King to fill a Vacancy in the Academy of Sciences as Associé etranger. I have a high Sense of the great Honour thereby conferr'd on me, and beg that my grateful Acknowledgments may be presented to his Majesty. With the greatest Respect I have the Honour to be &c.

Endorsed: M. Garnier Translation of my Letter to the Duc de la Vrilliere[1]

To John Huske[2]

ALS (letterbook draft): American Philosophical Society

Dear [Sir]   London, Sept. 6. 1772

I have deferred Writing to you agreable to the Caution you gave me, till this safe Opportunity offered. America is infinitely

8. Louis-Phelypeaux, comte de Saint-Florentin and duc de la Vrillière (1705–77), was a minister of the crown and president of the Académie royale des sciences; see Larousse, *Dictionnaire universel*, under Saint-Florentin. On Aug. 16 he had written the secretary of the Academy that after the death of Baron van Swieten, the Austrian doctor (above, XVIII, 165 n), the King had nominated BF to succeed him as a foreign associate: archives of the Academy, Paris. BF's election was announced in the *London Chron.* of Aug. 22–25. He sent this acknowledgement on the advice of Pringle and LeRoy (below, p. 307), and later thanked the Academy itself: below, Nov. 16.

9. The date, absent in the draft, is supplied from the French translation on the back, to which BF's endorsement refers.

1. Charles-Jean Garnier (1733–83?) probably succeeded de Francès as secretary to the French Ambassador, and in any case held that position for many years; see Butterfield, ed., *John Adams Diary,* II, 298. BF must have sought Garnier's help because he was unsure of his own French, and then presumably copied the translation as his finished letter. It went by the abbé Morellet, who was returning from a whirlwind visit to England. See LeRoy to BF below, Sept. 30, and Morellet to BF above, under June 30.

2. BF is replying belatedly to Huske's letter above, March 10, which recommended the Chevalier O'Gorman and his scheme for making wine in America.

oblig'd to you for your continual good Wishes and Schemes for her Advantage: But I am sorry to tell you that she is here become an Object of Jealousy, and that the obtaining Money from our poor Treasury to forward such Schemes, tho' at the same time equally beneficial to this Country, is out of all Expectation. A new Colony however is forming, where good Land may be had cheap, and where your Friend may probably find an Opportunity of serving himself and Family, while he is at the same time useful to the Publick wherein I shall be glad [to] serve him.[3] Of this I shall write more fully when Things are riper. In [the mean] time, I am, with great Esteem, Dear Sir, Your most obedient humble Servant

BF

Mr Huske

To John Walsh

ALS (letterbook draft): American Philosophical Society

Dear Sir,   London, Sept. 6. 1772

I am glad to find by your Favour of the 27th past, that you are return'd safe and well to Paris after your Expedition to the Sea Coast, and that you intend to publish an Account of your Experiments. Your doing it as you propose in a Letter to me I shall esteem a very great Honour.[4] Nothing new in the philosophic way has occur'd here since my last, in which I think I mention'd Dr. Priestly's Experiments whereby he found that growing Vegetables restore Air that has been spoilt by Putrefaction.[5] Your Friends here expect your Return with some Impatience.[6] I am,

3. BF seems to have discussed with O'Gorman, before the latter's return to France, the possibility of viticulture in the new colony that the Walpole Company expected to create from its land grant. See the postscript to the Chevalier's letter to BF below, Jan. 4, 1773.
4. Walsh had mentioned that he intended to publish the letter in France, but changed his mind and sent it to the Royal Society the next year. It is printed below, July 1, 1773.
5. See Priestley to BF above, July 1.
6. They had not long to wait; Walsh returned to London on Sept. 17. *The Public Advertiser*, Sept. 18.

with sincere Esteem and Respect, Dear Sir, Your obliged and most obedient humble Servant   BF

Mr Walsh

Reply to a Defender of Lord Hillsborough

AD (incomplete draft): American Philosophical Society

Sir,   [After September 7, 1772[7]]

In your Paper of the 7th Instant, one M.S. attempts to defend Lord Hillsborough's Conduct, attack'd it seems, by some preceding Piece which I have not seen. To defend a Friend is honourable but could not M.S. do this without abusing the New Englanders?[8] If Calumny is so bad a thing when level'd at a single Man, that he ranks the Writer of it among "*real Villains*," what must it be when pour'd upon a whole People, and intended to set them in a Light that must render them odious to their Sovereign? The "Principles of that Colony, he says, will never be reconciled to monarchical Government," the People have "republican Views," and adds, that "the Proceedings of Fanaticks and Republicans, under the Conduct of Cromwell, is so fresh in our Minds, that there is not one honest and sober thinking monarchical Englishman, but thinks the Bostonians have been governed rather by too slack than too tight a rein; and that the Administration cannot keep too vigilant an Eye over them."[9] To turn the Mind of a Father against his Children by false Insinuations, is wicked; because it may destroy the Peace and Happiness of a Family: But the Father's natural Affection may operate against the malevolence of Slander: while the Anger of a Prince once excited, having no such Counterpoise, may be attended with the most fatal Consequences, to his Subjects and possibly to himself. Jealousy breeds Severity, and that destroys Affection. Thereby not only the

7. The letter to which this was a reply appeared in the *Gazetteer* of that date. See Crane, *Letters to the Press*, pp. 223–4. We have been no more successful than he was in finding BF's reply in print, and conclude with him that it remained in MS.

8. BF originally wrote, then deleted, "Bostonians."

9. BF began the following sentence with "A Backbiter who writes," and then deleted the phrase.

Hands of Government but the general Force of the Empire is weakened. Detestable therefore is the Employment of either Tongue or Pen in that kind of Leasing-making[1] as our Ancestors call'd it. With regard to that People, and their Principles, I shall speak what *I know*, There was never Joy greater, more universal or more sincere than theirs on the Accession of the present Family; nor a more perfect and uninterrupted Loyalty in any Subjects to all the Princes of it. A Jacobite is unknown among them. But they are Whigs, and whenever the Crown assumes Prerogatives it has not, or makes an unwarrantable Use of those it has, they will oppose as far as they are able. This Whiggism of theirs it seems is now out of Fashion, Toryism being at present here the Courtly Principle. Hence the Persecution they suffer'd during Lord Hillsborough's Administration, and which perhaps they will still suffer; for tho' it is easy to throw Dust in the Eyes of a good King it is not so easy to get it out again. Hence such Slanderers as M.S. were listened to, believed and caressed: and every one who distinguished himself by oppressing or abusing the New Englanders has been honoured and rewarded. Time however will convince all sound Understandings, that they are Subjects worth cherishing, and that their Friendship to this Nation is worth Securing; not by Violence, for that will destroy it; but by Justice and Kindness. And what "tighter Rein" would this "honest sober thinking monarchichal Englishman" advise our Administration to use than that which they have used? Is it not enough that[2] upon every groundless Rumour, their Capital should be invested by a Fleet, and Regiments pour'd in to dragoon them? Is then this "sober thinking Englishman" of Opinion with that humane Lord who said, when he heard the Soldiers had killed 5 Bostonians [*remainder missing*]

1. Uttering untrue and slanderous speeches, a phrase of Scots law.
2. BF here wrote and then deleted "The Commerce of the Country is daily harassed by a mad Board of Customhouse Clerks under the name of Commissioners, that and Men of War's Men in the dirty Employment of Customhouse Officers."

From Marie Catherine Biheron[3]

ALS: American Philosophical Society

Monsieur   de Paris ce 10 Septembre 1772

Je suis tres sensible à l'honneur de votre souvenir et vous remercie de votre grasieuse lettre; je saisis avec empressement l'occasion de Mr. Walsh pour vous envoyer le discours de notre Cour
des Aides fait par notre Celebre Magistrat Mr. Malherbe. Jaurois
souhaité qu'il fut imprimé tel qu'il est[4] je desire qu'il vous soit
agreeable. Je suis bien faché que Madame Stevenson n'ait pas
encore eue son fil il a été donné au capitaine Guilbée maître du
vaisseau nommé Laigle par Madame Bosse [à] Calais. J'ay l'honneur de la remercier et la prie d'agréer mes particuliers compliments ainsy que sa chere famille elle voudra bien me pardonnée
de lui adresser quelque chose [qui] poura etre à son Usage et le
recevoir des mains de l'amitié [que] je vous ait voué de tout mon
coeur à tous. Je ne scais si Monsieur Walsh serra content de nous
mais nos savans [l'ont] tres considerée pour son merite et grande
connoisance. Jay eté bien flaté de pouvoir parler de vous avec lui
ayant eue l'honneur de le recevoir plusiers fois que ne puisje me
procurer ce plesir plus souvant ou de vous aller reiterer de vive
voix au mois de Novembre combien jay l'honneur de vous etre
avec la plus grande Consideration Monsieur Votre tres humble et
obeisante servante   BIHERON

Ozerai'je suplier Madame Steveson de remetre le petit paquet de
poudre à un marchand de toille qui doit l'aller prendre chez elle,
c'est un pauvre infortunée que jay eue le bonheur de soulager d'un
mal qu'il a à un oeil et jespert quil vera passablement dans quel-

3. See above, xv, 115 n. She had recently returned to Paris from her visit
to England.
4. For John Walsh see above, pp. 160–2, and his later letters to BF; and for
Lamoignon de Malesherbes XVI, 207 n. Among BF's papers in the APS is a
translation of Malesherbes' speech in defense of the Cour des aides in 1756, but
what Mlle. Biheron sent him was almost unquestionably the remonstrances
in February, 1771, against the suppression of the parlements in Maupeou's
coup d'état that is discussed above, XVIII, 113 n. The remonstrances,
although widely circulated, were not published; see Pierre Grosclaude,
Malesherbes, témoin et interprète de son temps... (Paris, [1961]), pp. 237,
779. Mlle. Biheron may well have been hinting that BF should give them to
the press.

que mois. Je connois l'exelance de votre coeur et l'amour que vous avéz pour le bien public ainsy que Madame de Stevenson c'est ce qui m'a engage à vous prier de ce service.

Madame St. Cydoin à l'honneur de vous remercier et vous presente comme à Madame Stevenson ses compliments.

To Joseph Priestley

ALS (letterbook draft) and copy: Library of Congress

In July, 1772, Lord Shelburne asked Priestley to be his librarian. The offer, although both financially and personally appealing, put the scientist into a quandary. On the one hand, the Earl was as attractive as the salary: "for ability and integrity together, the very first character in this kingdom," a friend of dissenters and one who would be an influential patron. On the other hand, Priestley's life in Leeds was so comfortable and productive that he had not contemplated moving, except perhaps to America.[5] He wrestled long with the decision, and did not accept until December.[6] Meanwhile he consulted Franklin, who suggested a solution to the problem by way of "prudential Algebra."[7]

Dear Sir,   London Sept. 19. 1772

In the Affair of so much Importance to you, wherein you ask my Advice, I cannot for want of sufficient Premises, advise you *what* to determine, but if you please I will tell you *how*. When these difficult Cases occur, they are difficult chiefly because while we have them under Consideration all the Reasons *pro* and *con* are not present to the Mind at the same time; but sometimes one Set present themselves, and at other times another, the first being out of Sight. Hence the various Purposes or Inclinations that alternately prevail, and the Uncertainty that perplexes us. To get over this, my Way is, to divide half a Sheet of Paper by a Line into two Columns, writing over the one *Pro*, and over the other *Con*. Then

5. Schofield, *Scientific Autobiog.*, pp. 105–6. Priestley, it should be added, was one of the few people in the kingdom who took this view of "the Jesuit of Berkeley Square."

6. *Ibid.*, pp. 105–6, 108, 111–12; John T. Rutt, *Life and Correspondence of Joseph Priestley...* (2 vols., London, 1831–32), I, 187–8.

7. BF later urged the same system on Jonathan Williams, Jr.: Smyth, *Writings*, VII, 281–2.

during three or four Days Consideration I put down under the different Heads short Hints of the different Motives that at different Times occur to me for or against the Measure. When I have thus got them all together in one View, I endeavour to estimate their respective Weights; and where I find two, one on each side, that seem equal, I strike them both out: If I find a Reason *pro* equal to some two Reasons *con*, I strike out the three. If I judge some two Reasons *con* equal to some three Reasons *pro*, I strike out the five; and thus proceeding I find at length where the Ballance lies; and if after a Day or two of farther Consideration nothing new that is of Importance occurs on either side, I come to a Determination accordingly. And tho' the Weight of Reasons cannot be taken with the Precision of Algebraic Quantities, yet when each is thus considered separately and comparatively, and the whole lies before me, I think I can judge better, and am less likely to make a rash Step; and in fact I have found great Advantage from this kind of Equation, in what may be called *Moral* or *Prudential Algebra*. Wishing sincerely that you may determine for the best, I am ever, my dear Friend, Yours most affectionately

B FRANKLIN

Dr Priestly

From Georgiana Shipley[8] ALS: Yale University Library

Dear Sir   Chilbolton Tuesday 22d September [1772[9]]

I have the Misfortune to acquaint you that last week poor Mungo got out of his Cage and was killed by a Dog. I was really very much concerned for it, as I am remarkably fond of all Squirrels, and particularly valued Mungo as being the Gift of my good Friend. I perfer'd it to the European Squirrels for being more Gentle and Goodhumored and full as lively.[1]

8. For the Shipley's fourth daughter, who was about sixteen at the time, see above, XVIII, 200 n.

9. The one year during BF's acquaintance with the Shipleys when the 22nd fell on a Tuesday. The family had gone to Chilbolton, Hants., the only living that the Bishop had not resigned on his transfer to St. Asaph, because their principal residence at Twyford was being remodeled.

1. For the gift of squirrels see BF to DF above, Jan. 28, and below, Feb. 14, 1773.

Papa and Mama are gone to spend a week at Bevismount. The Bow Windows at Twyford go on but Slowly.² I believe we shall not be able to remove there this year, but we all hope you will still hold yourself engaged to spend some part of the Autumn at Chilbolton all this Family desires their best Compliments and I remain Your Obliged humble Servant   GEORGIANA SHIPLEY

Addressed: To / Benjamin Franklin Esqr / at Mrs: Stephensons / Craven Street / Strand / London

Endorsed: The Answer is on the other Side.³

To Georgiana Shipley   ALS (draft): Yale University Library

Dear Miss,   London, Sept. 26. 1773 [1772⁴]

I lament with you most sincerely the unfortunate End of poor *Mungo*: Few Squirrels were better accomplish'd; for he had had a good Education, had travell'd far, and seen much of the World. As he had the Honour of being for his Virtues your Favourite, he should not go like common Skuggs⁵ without an Elegy or an Epitaph. Let us give him one in the monumental Stile and Measure, which being neither Prose nor Verse, is perhaps the properest for Grief; since to use common Language would look as if we were not affected, and to make Rhimes would seem Trifling in Sorrow.

2. Bevis Mount, on the outskirts of Southampton, had been the seat of Mrs. Shipley's uncle, the third Earl of Peterborough, who had entertained there Swift, Pope, and other literary figures; see the *DNB* under Charles Mordaunt. At this time the estate was in the hands of the Earl's nephew and Mrs. Shipley's cousin, the elderly General Sir John Mordaunt, for whom see also the *DNB*. The bow windows at Twyford that were a major part of the remodeling are shown in the illustration of the house in the *Autobiog.*, following p. 44.
3. In BF's hand; his answer is the following document.
4. BF misdated the draft by a year. He wrote on the inside of the four-page sheet that Georgiana used for the preceding document, to which he was clearly replying; five months later he sent the correspondence to DF: below, Feb. 14, 1773.
5. The "Name by which all Squirrels are called here, as all Cats are called *Puss*": *ibid.*

Alas! poor *Mungo*!
Happy wert thou, hadst thou known
Thy own Felicity!
Remote from the fierce Bald-Eagle,
Tyrant of thy native Woods,
Thou hadst nought to fear from his piercing Talons;
Nor from the murdering Gun
Of the thoughtless Sportsman.
Safe in thy wired Castle,
Grimalkin never could annoy thee.
Daily wert thou fed with the choicest Viands
By the fair Hand
Of an indulgent Mistress.
But, discontented, thou wouldst have more Freedom.
Too soon, alas! didst thou obtain it,
And, wandering,
Fell by the merciless Fangs,
Of wanton, cruel Ranger.[6]
Learn hence, ye who blindly wish more Liberty,
Whether Subjects, Sons, Squirrels or Daughters,
That apparent *Restraint* may be real *Protection*,
Yielding Peace, Plenty, and Security.

You see how much more decent and proper this broken Stile, interrupted as it were with Sighs, is for the Occasion, than if one were to say, by way of Epitaph,

Here Skugg
Lies snug
As a Bug
In a Rug.

And yet perhaps there are People in the World of so little Feeling as to think, *that* would be a good-enough Epitaph for our poor Mungo!

If you wish it, I shall procure another to succeed him.[7] But perhaps you will now chuse some other Amusement. Remember me

6. BF has christened the dog that Georgiana mentioned as the culprit.

7. BF did so, and the successor apparently lived to a ripe old age. See DF to BF below, Oct. 29, 1773; Georgiana to BF, May 1, 1779, APS.

respectfully to all the [*torn*] good Family; and believe me ever,
Your affectionate Friend   B FRANKLIN

To Richard Price   ALS: American Philosophical Society

Dear Sir,   Cravenstreet, Sept. 28. 1772
  Inclos'd I send you Dr. Priestly's last Letter, of which a Part is
for you, he says, but the whole seems as proper for you as for me.
I did not advise him *pro* or *con*, but only explain'd to him my
Method of Judging for my self in doubtful Cases, by what I called
Prudential Algebra.[8]
  If he had come to town, and preach'd here some times, I fancy
Sir John P. would now and then have been one of his Hearers; for
he likes his Theology as well as his Philosophy. Sir John has ask'd
me if I knew where he could go to hear a Preacher of *rational*
Christianity.[9] I told him I knew several of them, but did not know
where their Churches were in Town; Out of Town, I mention'd
yours at Newington, and offer'd to go with him. He agreed to it,
but said we should first let you know our Intention. I suppose, if
nothing in his Profession prevents, we may come, if you please
next Sunday; but if you sometimes preach in Town, that will be
most convenient to him, and I request you would by a Line let me
know when and where. If there are dissenting Preachers of that
Sort at this End of the Town, I wish you would recommend one
to me, naming the Place of his Meeting. And if you please give me
a List of several, in different Parts of the Town; perhaps he may
encline to take a Round among them. At present I believe he has
no View of attending constantly anywhere; but now and then only
as it may suit his Convenience. All this to yourself. My best Respects to Mrs. Price and Mrs. Barker.[1] With sincere Wishes for

8. Priestley's letter, now lost, must have discussed his uncertainty about
Lord Shelburne's offer to make him his librarian; see BF's reply above, Sept.
19. Price appears to have conveyed the offer, and Priestley wrote him a number of times for his advice: Schofield, *Scientific Autobiog.*, pp. 105–6, 108, 111.
  9. Rational Christianity was the contemporary term for what came later to
be known as Unitarianism. Pringle, who was much interested in theological
questions, did eventually find his home among the Unitarians: *DNB*.
  1. We cannot improve upon our predecessors' guess (above, XIV, 220 n)
that Mrs. Barker was Mrs. Price's companion.

your Health and Welfare, I am ever my dear Friend, Yours most affectionately   B FRANKLIN

Dr Price

Endorsed: Dr. Franklin 1772

From Sir John Pringle   AL: American Philosophical Society

For some nine years William Hewson and Dr. William Hunter were partners in a course in anatomy that they gave for medical students, until Hunter dissolved the partnership.[2] Hewson then decided to give a course of his own, and accordingly spent the winter and spring of 1772 in making anatomical preparations to be used in his lectures, which began on Sept. 30, 1772, in a theatre that he had built next to his house in Craven Street. Before then, doubtless as advance publicity, he gave a lecture on the spleen and thymus, to which he invited notables in the medical world.[3] He also invited prominent friends before the opening of the course, to judge by the letter that follows, to view the materials that he had prepared as demonstrations.

Wednesday morning [before September 30?, 1772]
Sir John Pringle presents his Compliments to Dr. Franklin, and desires the favour of the Doctor's letting him know at what hour he can most conveniently meet Sir J. P. at Mr. Hewson's this morning from 11 to 3, inclusive, Sir J. P. being engaged only till 11.

Sir J. P. presumes that Mr. Hewson has already bespoken the favour of Dr. Franklin's company for seeing his preparations some time this day.

If 11 will answer Sir J. P. will wait at home till Dr. F. call him, as lying little out of his way.

Addressed: Dr Franklin / at Mrs Stevenson's / Cravenstreet

2. See above, XVIII, 192–4, 211.
3. Thomas J. Pettigrew, *Memoirs of the Life and Writings of the Late John Coakley Lettsom...* (3 vols., London, 1817), I, 143–4 of second pagination.

From the Count of Belgioioso:[4] Two Letters

AL: American Philosophical Society

Portmansquare Septr the 30th [1772[5]]

The Count of Belgioioso presents His best Compliments to Dr. Franklin and would take it as a particular Favour if He'd please to inform Him where the Person lives who makes the Glasses for the Harmonica according to His Invention: as the French Embassadour[6] who is a great Lover of Musick and is desireous of having One enquired to The Count about this said Person; but he not being able to satisfy him in this particular, has recourse to Dr. Franklin's Goodness for an Information.

Addressed: To / Dr. Franklin / in / Cecil Street / near the Strand

Portman Square Sepr the 30th. [1772]

The Count of Belgioioso presents His best Compliments to Dr. Franklin with many thanks for the new Token of Friendship He is pleased to give him in His obliging offer:[7] but the French Embassador being at present in Scotland whence He will not return till the latter end of next November; the Count is obliged to differ [defer] giving Dr. Franklin a particular Answer in this Respect.

Addressed: To / Dr. Franklin / in Craven Street / Strand

4. Count Ludovico Barbiano de Belgioioso (1728–1803) had recently turned from a military to a diplomatic career. He was Ambassador to St. James's from the court of Vienna, 1769–83, and during his stay in London developed a wide circle of acquaintances, from the King to scientists and writers. He was subsequently the instrument for putting into effect in the Low Countries the disastrous reforms of Joseph II. *Dizionario biografico degli Italiani* (15 vols., to date, Rome, [1960–]), VI, 211–13.

5. This and the following document were clearly written on the same day and on the same business, a favor requested by the French Ambassador. The second note speaks of the Frenchman's being in Scotland, and his tour of the British Isles was in 1772: *London Chron.*, Sept. 17–19, Nov. 17–19, 1772.

6. For Adrien-Louis de Bonnières, comte de Guines (1735–1805), the French Ambassador to St. James's from 1770 to 1776, see Larousse, *Dictionnaire universel*, under Guines.

7. BF had clearly replied to Belgioioso's written inquiry, perhaps by giving the bearer an oral message; in all likelihood he had offered to order the armonica.

William Henly: Note on the Electrical Phenomena of a Thunderstorm[8]

AD: American Philosophical Society

Wednesday Sepr. 30. 1772

At 10 Minutes past 2: p.m. I heard what I thought (but was not certain) was a Clap of Thunder. However on putting out my Rod, I observed the balls to diverge 1½ or 2 Inches.[9] Presently I heard *a very distinct and loud clap*, when the Electricity *which before was positive*, instantly changed to *negative* and the balls (having first closed,) diverged to 3 Inches distance. The approach of excited wax would now nearly double the[ir distance?] of divergence, which I observed near a dozen times; and what is remarkable the end of the Rod, which I held in my hand, *without the wax* had the same effect when brought between the strings.[1] This effect I also observed many times. The Electricity continued *constantly negative* near half an Hour, when the balls *gradually closed*, and all appearances thereof *finally ceased*.

From Jean-Baptiste LeRoy

ALS: American Philosophical Society

aux Galeries du Louvre ce Mercredy 30 7bre [1772]

J'aurois repondu plutot Monsieur et cher confrère, à la lettre que vous m'avez fait l honneur de m'écrire; si je n'avois voulu vous parler de celle que vous m'avez fait remettre, par LAbbé Morellet, pour M. Le Duc de la Vrillière.[2] J'ai conçu, par là, que vous

8. We include this document, although it is not strictly within our rubric, because it was without doubt sent to BF, and is part of a line of experimentation in which he was much interested.

9. Henly was using, with slight modifications, the apparatus and procedure developed by Thomas Ronayne for the observations that he forwarded to BF with his note above, Feb. 15. For a description of the rod see *Phil. Trans.*, LXIV (1774), 428–9.

1. [*Henly's note:*] The end of this Rod must therefore be affected in the same manner as the balls themselves.

2. BF's letter has been lost; for his acknowledgement of his election to the Académie des sciences, sent via Morellet and LeRoy to la Vrillière, see above, Sept. 4.

desiriez que je la remisse en main propre à ce Ministre, et ce n'est que depuis quelques Jours, que j'ai pu le voir, et m'acquitter de votre commission. Il m'a paru sensible à cette attention de votre part; ainsi vous avez bien fait de suivre le conseil du chevalier Pringle, et vous avez vu par ma derniere lettre que c'étoit aussi mon avis.

Si vous ne saviez pas mieux calculer en Physique qu'en Monnoye, ou que vous ne fussiez pas plus instruit dans l'une que dans l'autre partie; Vous n'auriez pas fait toutes les belles découvertes que vous avez faites. Comment vous imaginez que nôtre livre de france, vaut 20 sols d'angleterre? Un francois, qui le voudroit pourroit bien abuser de votre erreur. Sachez donc Monsieur et cher confrère, que votre guinée vaut 24 de nos livres, et que le shilling qui en est la 21me partie vaut de notre monnoye 22 sol + 10 deniers,[3] c'est à dire, très près de 23 sols, qu'en conséquence la livre Sterling vaut 22 livres 17 sols, plus ou moins, selon le cours du change, et que partant le prix de la lunette se monte à 94 livres 17 de notre monnoye. Or comme ce que j'ai donné à M. Du Pont avec ce que j'ai mis pour la lampe Oeconomique, et quelques autres petits articles peut aller à 50 livres il se trouvera que je vous serai encore redevable de 44 ou à peu près. Car la dessus, je n'ai aucune certitude. Nous n'avons comme vous le dites fort bien pas plus d'ordre l'un que l'autre. Au reste Vous voyez par là que loin d'être mon débiteur c'est moi qui suis encore le votre sans parler de ce que je vous dois pour le Nouvel Electromètre. Quant à vos ports de lettres je vous prie de ne me pas parler de ces misères là.

M. Walsh m'a fait voir l'Electrometre de M. Henley[4] il peut être utile dans beaucoup d'Occasions mais je doute fort qu'il donne une grande précision dans l'estimation de la force Electrique. Cependant je vous suis très obligé des Offres que vous me faites à ce sujet et en consequence j'en ferai usage si vous le trouvez bon dans l'Occasion. Pourvu toutes fois que mes commissions ne vous donnent pas trop de peine.

3. Twelve deniers made a sol and twenty sols a livre.
4. John Walsh's visit to France to study the torpedo fish has been mentioned in numerous letters earlier in the volume. For Henly's electrometer see above, XVII, 260; LeRoy's phrasing suggests that it was different from the "Nouvel Electromètre" mentioned above, but in that case we have no guess about the latter.

Les Experiences de M. Priestley ont paru intéressantes ici cependant nos meilleurs chymistes ne regardent pas ce qu'il appelle de *l'air fixe* comme un véritable air. Ils croyent que les propriétés de cet air là tiennent à quelques particules étrangeres qui se trouvent mêlées avec l'air pur et que n'appartenant point à cet air pur elles ne peuvent être que l'effet de la combinaison avec ces parties étrangeres.[5] Le temps developpera qui aura raison!

Quelques chymistes de notre Académie se sont associés ici pour faire des Experiences avec le Verre ardent du Palais Royal et un autre du même genre ils ont déja observé plusieurs Phenomenes curieux et entr'autres que malgré ce qu'a avancé autrefois M. Homberg l'or est absolument *invitrifiable* ou inalterable au Verre ardent.[6] J'ai dit autrefois quen Physique on devroit imiter Locke (qui voulut prevoir dans ses loix pour la Caroline qu'on les examinat tous les 50 ans pour voir s'il n'y auroit pas à les reformer[7]) c'est a dire qu'il faudroit de temps en temps repéter les Experiences principales. On va toujours et on regarde, sur parole, des faits, comme constants, ou comme certains, qui ne sont rien moins.

La frégate la Flore, en mer depuis un an, pour essayer les montres marines de mon frère et d'autres horlogers vient d'arriver à Brest de son voyage ou au moins on compte qu'elle y est. Mais on n'a encore aucun détail certain sur la marche des montres.[8] Comme on se plait ici à dire des choses extraordinaires on a fait courir

5. Priestley's small pamphlet, *Directions for Impregnating Water with Fixed Air*... (London, 1772), had appeared in August in *Introduction aux observations sur la physique*..., II (1772), 323–31. It keenly interested French chemists in general and Lavoisier in particular, and helped precipitate a major investigation of the nature of gases. See Henry Guerlac, *Lavoisier—the Crucial Year*... (Ithaca, N.Y., [1961]), especially pp. 55–9, 71–2, 193.

6. Willem Homberg (1652–1715), a Dutch physician and scientist settled in Paris, became director of the chemical laboratory of the Académie des sciences, and contributed to its publications. See his "Éclaircissemens touchant la vitrification de l'or au verre ardent," Académie des sciences, *Mémoires* (for 1707; Paris, 1708), pp. 40–8.

7. John Locke's Fundamental Constitutions of Carolina, which fortunately were never put into effect, contained a provision that all acts of parliament should lapse after a hundred years. Bartholomew R. Carroll, *Historical Collections of South Carolina*... (2 vols., New York, 1836), II, 382.

8. During the voyage of the *Flore* a number of chronometers were tested, and Pierre LeRoy's was found to be even more accurate than expected. Académie des sciences, *Mémoires* (for 1773; Paris, 1777), pp. 283–97.

le bruit que M. Le Comte de Lauragais s'étoit fait Quaker. Je ne sais trop si vos quakers voudroient de nos Ducs pour confrères.[9]

Je vois par les Papiers anglois que M. Walsh est de retour à Londres. J'espere que vous l'encouragerez à publier ses experiences sur la Torpille il a besoin que vous le pressiez un peu car je crois que content de s'assurer des faits par lui même il est peu empressé de les publier et nous y perdrions trop. J'espere que vous voudrez bien lui dire mille choses pour moi ainsi qu'à M. Le Chevalier Pringle.

Recevez tous mes remercimens Monsieur et cher confrère de l'Electrometre et de l'Amalgamme, et de nouvelles assurrances des sentimens distingués destime et d'attachement que je vous ai voués pour la vie   LeRoy

Je n'ai pas besoin de vous redire que je suis toujours à vos ordres pour tout ce que vous desirerez de ce pays cy.

From Richard Price   ALS: American Philosophical Society

Dear Sir   Newington-Green Sept 30th 1772

I have Sent you enclosed Dr. Priestley's letter to you, together with another which I received from him last night. Indeed I don't know whether to be glad or Sorry on account of his rejection of Lord Shelburne's proposal.[1] I love him and am heartily concerned for him and wish he was better provided for.

I think myself extremely obliged to you for mentioning me to Sir John Pringle. I am afraid you will both of you be disappointed in me, Should you ever honour me in the manner you propose. My principal congregation is at Hackney. I preach there every Sunday morning at the meeting in the Gravel-Pit field near the Church, beginning at half an hour after ten. In the Afternoon I

9. For the witty and amoral Comte de Lauraguais, a son of the Duc de Villars-Brancas, see LeRoy to BF above, March 5.

1. Price was returning the Priestley letter, now lost, that BF had enclosed in his to Price above, Sept. 28, and was reciprocating with another letter that he himself had received, in which Priestley indicated that he was about to turn down the invitation to be Lord Shelburne's librarian: Schofield, *Scientific Autobiog.*, p. 108. The invitation was in fact accepted some months later. See the headnote on BF to Priestley above, Sept. 19.

preach at Newington-Green and begin at three.[2] Next Sunday at Hackney is Sacrament day. A member of the congregation also was buried this week. This will limit me to one Subject, and therefore you would probably hear me there to more disadvantage next Sunday than on any of the following Sundays. But I refer myself entirely to Sir John Pringle's and your candour. Both places are so distant from your end of the town that I can hardly expect to see you. I sometimes exchange with some of my brethren in the city; but I have at present no prospect of doing this soon. Dr. Kippis you are acquainted with. He is a worthy and ingenious man of very liberal principles, and preaches pretty near you, or at Long Ditch near Crown-Street in Westminster. Dr. Amory in the afternoon, and Mr. White in the morning at the Old Jewry, Dr. Jefferies at Pinners-Hall Old Broad-Street in the afternoon and Dr. Flemming in the morning; Mr. Radcliffe in the morning and Dr. Calder in the afternoon at Poor-Jewry-Lane Aldgate; Dr. Prior in Goodman's-Fields; Mr. Palmer both parts of the day at New-Broadstreet; Mr. Pickard at Carter-Lane near St. Pauls in the morning, and Dr. Furneaux at Clapham are all likewise preachers of Christianity on the rational plan.[3] But the congregations of many of them are very thin, partly perhaps for this very reason.

2. For BF's inquiry in behalf of Pringle see his letter above, Sept. 28. Price had accepted a call to be the morning preacher at the Gravel-Pit Meeting House in Hackney, then a fashionable London suburb, but had retained his connection with his old church at Newington Green. See Roland Thomas, *Richard Price, Philosopher and Apostle of Liberty* (London, 1924), pp. 28, 40, 47.

3. *I.e.*, what came to be known as Unitarianism, of which Price discerned preachers in a variety of denominations. Dr. Kippis (above, xv, 85 n) was more eminent, according to one historian, as a writer and clerical politician than as a preacher: Herbert S. Skeats, *History of the Free Churches of England* (London, [1891]), p. 362. Thomas Amory (1701–74), a product of Taunton Academy, the dissenters' chief cultural center in western England, was pastor of the Presbyterian church in Old Jewry; his sermons were reputedly dry in content and dull in delivery. *DNB*. Nathaniel White (1730–95) had studied with Dr. Doddridge at Northampton, and was associated both with Amory as morning preacher in Old Jewry and with Price as afternoon preacher at the Gravel-Pit; his sermons were serious, ingenious, and evangelical. Dr. Joseph Jeffries (d. 1784) and Dr. Caleb Fleming (1698–1779) were Baptist ministers of the Pinners' Hall congregation; Fleming had few admirers, though warm ones. For Jeffries see Joseph Ivimey, *A History of the English Baptists...* (4 vols., London, 1811–30), III, 344–5, 408; *Gent. Mag.*, LIV (1784), 73; for Fleming see the *DNB*. Ebenezer Radcliffe (above, XIV, 219 n) was pastor of

I have not yet heard when our Club is to meet.[4] Mrs. Price sends her best respects to you. I allways think with much pleasure and gratitude of your friendship, and am, Dear Sir, with great regard your obliged humble Servant   RICHD: PRICE

P.S. I forgot to mention Mr. Farmer who preaches in the afternoon at Salters-Hall near the Post-office. He is one of the most admired preachers we have; but he is going to leave Salters-Hall at Christmas. He is the author of a Dissertation on miracles published two years ago; and also of an Enquiry into the account of Christ's temptation in the wilderness; and I have just read an Essay of his in manuscript on the Demoniacs the design of which is to prove that they were only Epileptics and madmen. Dr. Foredice also is well-known.[5]

---

the Presbyterian congregation in Aldgate until it dissolved in 1774, and John Calder, a Scot, was his assistant; after 1774 Calder devoted himself to writing. William Prior (d. 1774) had a congregation in Goodman's Fields and also preached weekly at Salters' Hall. John Palmer (1729–90), a Presbyterian, had the reputation of being a sensible and broad-minded preacher. Edward Pickard (1714–78), pastor of the Presbyterian congregation in Carter Lane, was a leader among the dissenters. So was Dr. Philip Furneaux (1726–83), pastor of the independent congregation at Clapham and, like Prior, a preacher at Salters' Hall, who was famous for his weighty, well composed, and badly delivered sermons; he and Amory were chief movers in the effort to emancipate dissenters (for which see above, p. 163 n): *DNB*. Information about all these men is derived from the sources cited and, with the exception of Jeffries, from Walter Wilson, *The History and Antiquities of Dissenting Churches and Meeting Houses, in London, Westminster, and Southwark* (4 vols., London, 1808–14), I, 125–7; II, 5, 154–9, 227–9, 283–90, 385–98; IV, 315.

4. The Club of Honest Whigs, which included among its members not only BF and Price but also a number of the clergymen just mentioned: Amory, Calder, Jeffries, and Radcliffe. Verner W. Crane, "The Club of Honest Whigs: Friends of Science and Liberty," 3 *W&MQ*, XXIII (1966), 218–19.

5. Hugh Farmer (1714–87) was a theologian and pastor of a church at Walthamstow, Essex, where Radcliffe also preached weekly. Farmer, like other independents, delivered sermons to the Presbyterian congregation at Salters' Hall; his pulpit style was marked by clear exposition and fresh delivery. The works of his to which Price referred were *A Dissertation on Miracles*... (London, 1771), *An Inquiry into the Nature and Design of Christ's Temptation*... (London, 1761), and, not yet published, *An Essay on the Demoniacs*... (London, 1775). *DNB*. James Fordyce (1720–96), a Scot, was pastor of the Presbyterian church in Monkwell Street; his great popularity as a preacher declined some years before his retirement in 1782. For the two see Wilson, *op. cit.*, II, 60–1; III, 209–14.

311

I have read the Scheme you gave me, and think it deficient; but I will consider it farther and send you a more particular account.[6]

Endorsed: Dr Price's Directions about Prrs.

From Jacques Barbeu-Dubourg

ALS (incomplete): American Philosophical Society

[September, 1772?[7]]

[*Beginning lost.*] Je ne vous dirai rien de Mademoiselle Biheron qui a l'honneur de vous ecrire elle même, et qui aime autant a peu pres que moi a s'entretenir de vous. Mais je vous proteste que ma femme est si eprise de la même passion pour vous que nos Pretres, et nos Moines perdent tous les jours de leur credit sur son esprit, cecy soit pourtant dit entre nous sous le secret. Il est certain que si sa santé etoit plus ferme, elle se laisseroit volontiers mener a Londres pour vous embrasser encore une fois, aussi bien que Mr. Pringle qu'elle honore aussi tres particulierement. Pour moi je redoute le printems prochain plus que l'on n'a jamais redouté la saison des frimats; et de tems en tems je me berce de la douce esperance qu'un plus long sejour de votre part a Londres pourra etre necessaire à vos Compatriotes et qu'ils vous y retiendront, et que vous repasserez encore une fois le pas de Calais. Dieu le veuille, et me fournir l'occasion de vous temoigner efficacement combien je vous suis parfaitement et inviolablement attaché, Monsieur et cher Ami Votre tres humble et tres obeissant serviteur

DUBOURG

6. The scheme was one that WF had sent from New Jersey. In all probability it was the proposal of local Presbyterians, which was eventually approved, to establish an incorporated fund for ministers' widows and orphans (1 *N.J. Arch.*, x, 339–51, 353–5); this is just the sort of plan on which BF would have consulted Price as an authority. The latter's comments, now lost, were eventually sent to BF and forwarded to Burlington; see BF to WF below, Dec. 2.

7. This fragment can be dated only by guesswork. The one gossamer clue is that Mlle. Biheron is about to write BF. (Dubourg's sadness at the prospect that BF will return home next spring is no clue, because that prospect was perennial in the latter years of BF's mission.) Only three letters from la Biheron survive, and none refers to Dubourg's communicating with BF. We are arbitrarily selecting the earliest one (above, Sept. 10), according to our practice, and are assuming that Dubourg wrote shortly before or after that date.

From Joseph Smith

ALS: American Philosophical Society

Esteemed Friend   Burlington October 1. 1772

I reciev'd thy Letter of the 6. Feby. but not till after the dissolution of the late Assembly which I believe was in consequence of a request they made at the close of their last Session after they had granted the money requested for the supply of the Troops and were on good terms with the Governor, the matter in dispute being amicably settled.[8]

The present Assembly met last month at Amboy. I understand they have continued thee Agent, but who the Committee are appointed to correspond with thee I have not heard.

I have agreeable to thy request reciev'd this day for thy use Two hundred and seventy five pounds, being two years and nine months Salary as Agent and shall follow thy directions in the application of it as soon as I have them[9] being with great Esteem Thy Respectful Friend   JOSEPH SMITH

Doctr. Franklin

Addressed: To / Benjamin Franklin Esqr / Agent for the Colony of / New Jersey / London / via New York / per Capt Laurence

From Richard Bache

ALS: American Philosophical Society

Dear and Honoured Sir   Philadelphia 6th. October 1772

Since my last I am favored with yours of the 4th [?] 14 and 16 July by the Captain's Osborne All and Sparks, the first dated at Preston, where I find you have been making happy by your Presence a good Old Woman and her four Daughters. Captain All told us he never saw you look better than when he left London so [that] we were pleasing ourselves with the agreeable Thoug[ht that?] your Journey had contributed greatly to your Hea[lth

8. Two issues had been in dispute, the manner of appointing an agent and the payment of the troops; see above, XVIII, 134, 218 n, 260–1, 270 n. Both had been resolved before the end of 1771, and in the following February the Assembly had been dissolved at its own request, to permit elections in which three newly enfranchised counties would be represented. The Assembly so elected had convened on August 19. 1 *N.J. Arch.*, XVIII, 279, 297–8.

9. BF had promised further instructions in his letter above, Feb. 6.

until?] the other day the Packet's Arrival, brought us some accounts of your having had a fit of the Gout, attended with an intermitting Fever, but that you were getting better. I hope this will find you quite well. I purpose writing you by Capt. All, who will sail in a few days, as does [your daughter?]. We are all thank God very well at present. Ben has had the Meazles very favorably. Mr. and Mrs. Franklin who are now in Town; my Mother Sally and Ben join me in Love and Duty to you. My Love to Mrs. Stevenson and other friends. I am Dear Sir Your most Affectionate Son

RICHD: BACHE

Addressed: To / Benjamin Franklin Esqr. / Craven-Street / London

To Richard Bache ALS (letterbook draft): Library of Congress

Loving Son, London, Oct. 7. 1772

I receiv'd yours of Sept. 1. and am rejoic'd to hear you are all well. Your good Mother and Sisters were so about a Fortnight ago, when I heard from them. The Bill you sent me for £60 Whinney on Smith, Wright & Grey, being good, I return your Note enclos'd and correct'd.[1] There remains Five Guineas unpaid, which you had of me just on your going away, so I suppose you forgot it. Send it in a Venture for Ben to Jamaica. By the way, it has been reported here that some Years since a very long Building in that Island, which had a Rod or Conductor at each End was nevertheless struck by Lightning in the Middle and much damaged.[2] Did you hear of such a Thing while you was there? If so, pray enquire and learn the Particulars from thence, what kind of Rods, how plac'd, how high above the Roof, how deep in the Ground, and other material Circumstances with regard to the Building and the Damage. If you heard of no such Event while you was there, I suppose the Story is not true. But a Mr. Smith, who was there in some Business, and now here a Merchant, I think, relates it, as what he heard spoken of when there.

1. See Bache to BF above, May 16.
2. In Bache's reply below, Jan. 4, 1773, he acknowledged the gift to his son. The report about the house turned out to be erroneous: BF to Bache below, March 3, 1773.

I am surpriz'd to hear that the Dutchman I assisted with 25 Guineas turn'd out a Rogue, and that Sheets has paid nothing of what I furnish'd him when here.[3] I am afraid I do not grow wiser as I grow older. Pray let me know whether the Dutch Printer Armbrüstor has paid any thing, or is solvable or not.[4] And also how the Affair stands of the Mortgage I had on my Friend Maugridge's Plantation:[5] No intelligible Information has yet [been] given me of it.

We are moving to another House in the same [Street] leaving this to Mr. Hewson.[6] As soon as I am settled in my new Apartments I shall examine Parker's Accounts and write to you on them.

You hope I was not a Sufferer in the late general Wreck of Credit here.[7] My two Banking Houses, Browns & Collinson, and Smith, Wright & Grey, stood firm, and they were the only People here in Debt to me, so I lost nothing by the Failure of others; and being out of Debt my self my Credit could not be shaken by any Run upon me: Out of Debt, as the Proverb says, was being out of Danger. But I have since hazarded a little in using my Credit with the Bank to support that of a Friend as far as £5000, for which I am secur'd by Bills of the Bank of Douglas, Heron & Company accepted by a good House here; and therefore I call it only hazarding *a little*, tho' the Sum is large enough to ruin me if I were to lose it.[8] Our Friends the Alexanders went on again immediately, being supported by great Houses here and thro' them by

3. For the elusive "Dutchman," Jacob Schaub, and the loan to John Shütz see Bache to BF above, May 16.

4. For Anthony Armbruster and his debt see above, V, 421 n; X, 289 n; XII, 342 n.

5. See above, XIV, 135 n; XV, 227–8.

6. See Mary Hewson to BF above, July 7.

7. The banking crisis began when Alexander Fordyce (d. 1789), a principal partner in Neale, James, Fordyce & Downes, absconded in June with large sums belonging to the bank. It closed. Others were forced to follow suit, and the panic spread to Scotland and eventually to the Continent. *London Chron.*, June 9–11, 20–23, 1772; *Scots Mag.*, XXXIV (1772), 304–18, 547–52; W. Marson Acres, *The Bank of England from Within...* (2 vols., London, 1931), I, 200–3; Sir William Forbes, *Memoirs of a Banking-House* (London and Edinburgh, 1860), pp. 39–44; Andrew W. Kerr, *History of Banking in Scotland* (4th ed., London, 1926), pp. 83–94.

8. This sentence was lightly deleted, either by BF or one of his editors.

315

the Bank, their Bottom being manifestly very great and good, tho' they had embarrass'd themselves by assisting the Adams's and others.[9]

The Affair of the Grant[1] is in good Train, and we expect it to be compleated soon after the Boards meet; if no new Difficulties start up unexpected. My Love to Sally and the Boy. I am Your affectionate Father   B FRANKLIN

Mr Bache

To John Bartram

ALS: Haverford College Library; letterbook draft: American Philosophical Society

My dear old Friend,   London Oct. 17. [*i.e.* 7?[2]] 1772
I received sometime since the enclosed Letter from Dr. Hope, and lately the Gold Medal it mentions was delivered to me for you. By the first Ship directly to Philadelphia I shall send it in the

9. The friend whose credit BF shored up was William Alexander. He and his brother Robert (for whom see above, VIII, 444 n) were deeply involved in the affairs of Douglas, Heron & Co., known as the Ayr Bank. One of its investments was in the Adelphi, the building speculation of the famous architect Robert Adam and his brothers, which the panic in June brought to a halt. *London Chron.*, June 20–23, 1772. The bank closed its doors at the same time, but reopened in September. It was unlikely to fail, BF originally wrote in the draft, "though at present a little embarrass'd." He was wrong on the first point: the bank survived only until August, 1773. The Alexanders were also near the end of their tether. Robert died in 1774 and William, after taking care of his debt to BF, was forced into bankruptcy in October, 1775. Kerr, *op. cit.*, pp. 89, 91–3; Henry Hamilton, "Failure of the Ayr Bank," 2 *Economic History Rev.*, VIII (1956), 405–17; Jacob M. Price, *France and the Chesapeake: a History of the French Tobacco Monopoly, 1674–1791 . . .* (2 vols., Ann Arbor, Mich., [1973]), II, 697–8.

1. To the Walpole Co.

2. BF certainly wrote "17". But in the draft in his letterbook (Library of Congress) he seems to have written "17" and then clearly overwrote "7"; the draft appears, furthermore, between that to Priestley above, Sept. 29, and that to Colden below, Oct. 7. From the 8th to the 24th BF was visiting in the country (to WF below, Oct. 7, Nov. 3–4). He may have taken his letterbook with him to copy out and dispatch his correspondence, in which case all his letters dated the 7th from the drafts were actually sent later; but a simpler hypothesis is that in this one case his pen slipped.

Care of some safe Hand, thinking it not so well to hazard it with this Letter round through New York. Mr. Hope's Letter to you is not yet come to my hands.[3]

I hope the Rhubarb you have sown and distributed will be taken care of.[4] There seems to me no doubt of its doing as well with us as in Scotland. Remember that for Use the Root does not come to its Perfection of Power and Virtue in less than Seven Years. The Physicians here who have try'd the Scotch, approve it much, and say it is fully equal to the best imported.

I send you enclos'd a small Box of Upland Rice, brought from Cochin China. It grows there on dry Grounds, and not in Water like the common Sort. Also a few Seeds of the Chinese Tallow Tree. They have been carefully preserv'd in bringing hither, by Mr. Ellis's Method. I had them from him, and he tells me they are in good Condition fit to vegetate.[5] I hope they may grow under your skilful Care. My Love to Mrs. Bartram and all yours from Your affectionate Friend   B FRANKLIN

Mr Bartram

Addressed: To | Mr John Bartram | near Philadelphia. | via New York | per Packet | B Free FRANKLIN

3. See Hope to BF above, Jan. 23.

4. BF had said much the same thing in his previous letter to Bartram above, Aug. 22.

5. BF was adhering, as so often before, to the long-standing tradition of sending plant seeds to America for experimentation, naturalization and selection. Vietnamese or upland rice, because it did not need flooding, was easier to grow and healthier for the cultivators than common rice; the Chinese tallow tree, which grew in many warm countries, yielded a vegetable tallow used in making candles and soap. John Ellis (*c.* 1710–76), the well known naturalist and F.R.S., had been importing the rice into England for many years; he had received a shipment in 1772, of which this gift was doubtless a part. See BF to Jones below, Oct. 7, and the Bell pamphlet cited there; for Ellis see also the *DNB.* His "Method" he had explained in *Directions for Bringing over Seeds and Plants from the East-Indies and Other Distant Countries, in a State of Vegetation...* (London, 1770).

From Mr. Jesser[6]   AL: American Philosophical Society

College hill.[7] 7th: October. 1772.
Mr. Jesser presents his Compliments to Dr. Franklin and is sorry
he had not the Pleasure of finding him at home at any of the times
he called.

The Governors of the London Hospital will be much obliged
to the Doctor if he will write to Mr. Colden and Mr. Dixon by
this day's Mail what the Dr. thinks to be necessary on the State
of the Case which Mr. Jesser left for [the] Dr. last Monday.

Addressed: To / Dr. Franklin.

Endorsed in Franklin's hand: Wrote accordingly the same Day BF

To Alexander Colden

ALS (letterbook draft): Library of Congress

⟨London, October 7, 1772. Has acknowledged in previous letters
the receipt of bills amounting to £372 10s. and another of
£56 12s. 5½d.; has since received three totaling £328 2s. 3d., one
of Mackie on Molleson and two of Carr on James Russell, and by
the last packet, with Colden's letter of September 3, four more:
Boylstone on Lane, Son & Frazer, Hothersall on Frederick Russell, Williams on Boddington, and Godard on Todd, which add up
to £545 0s. 8d. Is glad to hear that the accounts may be expected
by the next packet.[8] Inquires in a postscript about the advertising

6. An agent, probably an attorney, for the London Hospital; he had been
working for several years on the disappearance of Elizabeth Holland (above,
XVIII, 157), the matter that elicited this note. We print it out of the usual
order because it accounts for part or all of the two letters from BF that follow.

7. On Upper Thames and Cannon Streets: Henry B. Wheatley, *London
Past and Present* (3 vols., London, 1891), I, 444–5.

8. Colden's letter of Sept. 3 is missing; it must have contained a promise
to send the annual accounts for 1771-72. The merchants on whom these
bills for postal receipts were drawn, all Londoners, we presume were the
following: either John or Thomas Boddington, one an agent in the Tower
and the other a linen draper in Cheapside; Lane, Son & Fraser, a firm at
11 Nicholas Lane; William Molleson in Gould Square, Crutched Friars;
Frederick Russell at 3 Watling St.; either the James Russell who was a
merchant of Hylord's Court, Crutched Friars, or the agent of the same name

318

for Mrs. Holland; asks for copies of the printed advertisements, and Colden's affidavit stating whether or not they have elicited any knowledge of her whereabouts.⁹⟩

To John Dixon¹   ALS (letterbook draft): Library of Congress

[Dear] Sir,   London, Oct. 7. 1772
I was duly favour'd with yours of March 8. 1771. accompany'd by the Gazettes containing the Advertisements relating to Eliz Holland, and the Mayor's Affidavit; for which I am much oblig'd to your kind Care.² But it seems there is still wanting an Affidavit from you expressing what you express in your Letter, that "notwithstanding all the Enquiry that has been made by means of those Advertisements, no such Person can be found or heard of in your Colony." If you will send me such an Affidavit, certify'd by the Mayor it will add to the Obligation, and I shall take care the additional Expence be paid to your Order. My Compliments to Mrs. Dixon and Mrs. Davenport, with Thanks for their kind Remembrance of me.³ I am glad to hear they are well. I am, with great Regard, Sir, Your most obedient humble Servant

B FRANKLIN

Mr Dixon

in Noel St., Soho. *Kent's Directory. . .* (London, 1770); see also, for the second James Russell, *The Royal Kalendar. . .* (London, [1772]), p. 170. Todd was doubtless Anthony Todd, the secretary of the Post Office. Four of the Americans who drew the bills were in all likelihood the following: Thomas Boylston, the prominent Boston merchant; Norris Goddard of New York; Ebenezer Mackie, a Baltimore trader who was leaving the country and whose bill was protested (*Pa. Gaz.*, March 26, 1772; BF to Colden below, Nov. 3); and Jonathan Williams, Sr. or Jr. Carr and Hothersall we cannot identify. For the postal accounts see BF to Colden below, Dec. 2.
9. See the preceding and following documents.
1. The postmaster at Williamsburg, and co-publisher with Alexander Purdy of the *Va. Gaz.*; see above, XIII, 108 n.
2. The search for Mrs. Holland, mentioned in the two preceding documents, had been active in Virginia and New York in 1763–64 and was then apparently abandoned; why it now revived we do not know.
3. Both were sisters of BF's old colleague in printing and the Post Office, William Hunter. Rosanna Dixon's first husband had been Joseph Royle (d. 1766), Hunter's successor as publisher of the *Va. Gaz.*: Douglas C.

To John Foxcroft   ALS (letterbook draft): Library of Congress

Dear Sir,   London, Oct. 7. 1772
    I had no Line from you by this last Packet, but find with Pleasure
by yours [to] Mr. Todd that you and yours were well.
    The Affair of the Patent is in good Train, and we hope, if new
Difficulties unexpected do not arise, we may get thro' it as soon
as the Board meet. We are glad you made no Bargain [about]
your Share, and hope none of our Partners there [will] do any such
Thing; for the Report of such a Bargain here before the Business
is compleated might overset the whole.⁴
    Mr. Colden has promised by this Packet that we shall certainly
have the Accounts per the next.⁵ If they do not come, I think we
shall be blam'd, and he will be superseded: For their Lordships
our Master, are incens'd at the long Delay.
    I hope you have by this time examin'd our private Account as
you promis'd, and satisfy'd yourself that I did, as I certainly did,
pay you that Ballance of about £389 in my own Wrong. It would
relieve me of some Uneasiness to have this Matter settled between
us, as it is a Sum of Importance, and in case of Death might be not
so easily understood as while we are both in being.⁶ With Love
to my Daughter and best Wishes of Prosperity to you both, and
to the little one, I am ever, my dear Friend, Yours most affectionately   B FRANKLIN
    Our Friends here are easy about the Virginia Grants, Mr. W.
assuring us that they are mostly out of our Bounds.⁷
Mr Foxcroft

McMurtrie, *A History of Printing in the United States*... (2 vols., New
York, 1936), II, 288. Mary Davenport's husband, the Rev. Joseph (1732–88),
was rector of Charles Parish, York Co., Va.: "Old Virginia Editors,"
I *W&MQ*, VII (1898–99), 17.
    4. Foxcroft, on his return to America, had heard such discouraging reports
about the affairs of the Walpole Company that he had thought of selling his
share; see his letter to BF above, March 2.
    5. See BF to Colden above, Oct. 7, and below, Dec. 2.
    6. See BF to Foxcroft above, Feb. 4, Aug. 22, and below, Dec. 2.
    7. For the potential conflict between Virginia land grants and the ambitions
of the Walpole Company see WF to BF above, Jan. 6, and below, Oct. 29.

To Deborah Franklin

ALS and letterbook draft: American Philosophical Society

My dear Child   London, Oct. 7. 1772

I receiv'd yours per the August Packet,[8] but had no Line from you by that of September. I was glad however to learn by Mr. Bache's Letter that you were all well.

I have had several Touches of the Gout lately, but am otherwise very well.

Mr. and Mrs. West, Mr. and Mrs. Strahan, Mrs. Stevenson, Mrs. Hewson, and Sally Franklin, have at different Times enquir'd after your Welfare and desired to be affectionately remember'd to you and Sally. My Love to her and Benny boy.

I shall write more fully per next Ship, and send what you desire. Mrs. Stevenson is very proud of her Handkerchief.[9] Mrs. Hewson has written for her to Sally. I am ever, my dear Debby, Your affectionate Husband   B FRANKLIN

Addressed: To / Mrs Franklin / at / Philadelphia / viâ N York / per Packet / B Free FRANKLIN

To William Franklin

ALS (letterbook draft): Library of Congress

Dear Son,   London, Oct. 7. 1772

I received yours of Sept. 1. with one enclos'd for Mrs. Clarke, which I immediately forwarded to Bristol; but she call'd on me two Days after to enquire how you did. She returns into Oxfordshire for the present, and after some time to Bristol again.[1]

I am glad you have satisfied Hayne that he went on a Fools Errand. There is no convincing those People here. His Wife was mad in a manner, and whoever said a Word of doubt about the Circumstances of the Story, she immediately suspected them to be concerned in the Plot with the wicked Americans to cheat her

8. Above, under Aug. 6.

9. See *ibid.*

1. Mary Clarke often did errands in London for WF's wife; what her connection was with Bristol and Oxfordshire we have no idea.

of her Right. At the same time I saw she could lie abominably for her Story at different times was quite inconsistent and Contradictory.[2] There are certainly some Villains who go about the Country imposing upon People with these Stories of great Estates left them in America; for I have had many Applications of the sort equally groundless. And I believe the same Game is plaid in America, for we have every now and then Fools that come from thence to look for Estates in the Clouds here. The Informer always gets some little Consideration for his Trouble in coming out of his way to give the Information.

The Affair of the Grant is in Train to be compleated as soon as the Boards meet, if no sinister Accident prevents. The Board of Trade is to draw the new Articles that are to be inserted by our Proposal; such as that of our maintaining the Government, &c. I hope to hear of no Land-Jobbing among our Partners in America till the Grant [is] pass'd.[3] It may hurt us extreamly.

I am very well. But we are moving to another House in the same Street; and I go down tomorrow to Lord LeDespencer's to

2. Richard Hayne of Shoreditch and his wife, Mary, were searching for an inheritance that turned out to be a will-o'-the-wisp. The wife claimed to be the only daughter and heiress of Richard Saltar or Salter of Burlington Co., N.J. He was unquestionably Judge Saltar (c. 1699–1762), a member of the New Jersey Supreme Court and Council; three daughters survived him, but none was named Mary. *Dartmouth MSS.*, II, 177–8, 249; I *N.J. Arch.*, XXXIII, 370; John E. Stillwell, *Historical and Genealogical Miscellany...* (5 vols., New York, 1903–32), IV, 187–8, 194–5. Mary Hayne insisted, nevertheless, that the estate was rightfully hers. Her husband went to New Jersey to investigate and returned empty-handed; he later contended that the true will had been concealed from him. The pair continued for more than a year to pester BF and Lord Dartmouth. BF concluded that the man was a fool and the woman insane, but Dartmouth was sufficiently impressed with her claim to have it investigated in America. See BF to WF below, Feb. 14, April 6, and July 14, 1773.

3. BF's "sinister Accident" echoes his earlier fears after the Privy Council had approved the Walpole grant: to WF above, Aug. 17. The Board of Trade did not give serious consideration to the matter again until April, 1773: *Board of Trade Jour.*, 1768–1775, pp. 351–4, 356. BF, despite his hope, may have heard of land-jobbing in America, which was certainly going on. In 1771 George Croghan, one of the most active American partners, had begun to advertise and sell land south of Fort Pitt and within the Company's proposed grant: Charles H. Hart, ed., "Letters from William Franklin to William Strahan," *PMHB*, XXXV (1911), 450–1.

[stay a] Week till things are settled.[4] Love to Betsey. [I am] ever
Your affectionate Father   B FRANKLIN

[*In the margin:*] Mr. Small presents his best Respects[5]

Addition to W Franklin.

I am glad your Healths are restor'd, and think as you do that
Amboy Air may possibly agree better with you both than that of
Burlington. I would have no Consideration of my Coming home
or staying, weigh with you against Considerations of Health,
which are of all others the most *important*. If Franklin Park is as
you say a fine healthy situation, and you are besides fond of Farming, I should think you would find most Happiness there, and have
enough of Town Life and Company during your Sessions at Amboy and Burlington.

You ask me how we shall reconcile Lord H.'s Conduct at different times relating to the Ohio Affair. It is irreconcileable.[6]

To Noble Wimberly Jones

ALS: Mrs. Craig Barrow, Wormsloe, Savannah, Ga. (1961)

Sir,   London, Oct. 7. 1772.

In my last[7] I acquainted you with the Change of Ministry in the
American Department, as then expected. It has since taken Place:
And from the Character of Lord Dartmouth we may hope there
will be no more of those arbitrary Proceedings in America that
disgrac'd the late Administration.

Inclos'd I send you a small Quantity of Upland Rice from
Cochin China. It grows on dry Ground, not requiring to be over-

4. BF actually stayed more than a fortnight: below, Mary Hewson to BF,
Oct. 22, and BF to WF, Nov. 3.

5. Alexander Small had presumably seen the WFS during his recent visit to
America.

6. Hillsborough had suggested that the promoters ask for vastly more land
than they had at first intended (above, XVII, 8) and, when they did so, had
changed his stand and opposed them. His purpose was consistent, it has been
argued, because he thought that enlarging the scheme would destroy it; see
Peter Marshall, "Lord Hillsborough, Samuel Wharton and the Ohio Grant,
1769–1775," *English Hist. Rev.*, LXXX (1965), 721–2.

7. Above, Aug. 3–8.

flow'd like the common Rice. I hope it will grow with you, and that it may be useful to your Country, as you already are acquainted with the manufacturing of the Article. Mr. Ellis, who imported the Seed, tells me it has been carefully and well preserved on the Voyage; and requests me to send a small Quantity to Mr. Jonathan Bryant. If he be in your Province, as I think he is, please to give him some out of your Box. I send also a few Seeds of the Chinese Tallow Tree, which will I believe grow and thrive with you. 'Tis a most useful Plant.[8] With great Respect, I am, Sir Your most obedient and humble Servant   B FRANKLIN

Noble W. Jones Esqr

Endorsed: Dr. B. Franklin datd. 7th. October 1772

To Horace-Bénédict de Saussure[9]

ALS: Bibliothèque de Genève; draft: American Philosophical Society

Sir,   London, Oct. 8. 1772

I was not in England when your Favour of Oct. 28. 71. arrived in London, and it was not till many Months after its Date that I receiv'd it. In the meantime, the Philosophical Transactions of our Royal Society were published, containing the Letter of the Dean and Chapter of St. Paul's, and the Report of the Committee

8. For the rice and the tallow tree and John Ellis see BF to Bartram above, under Oct. 7. James Habersham had suggested to Ellis that Jonathan Bryan (1708–88), a South Carolinian who settled in Georgia and had a plantation on the Savannah River, would make good use of the rice seed. It was not a success in Georgia, but the tallow tree was: it spread widely throughout the south. Malcolm Bell, III, *Some Notes and Reflections upon a Letter from Benjamin Franklin to Noble Wimberly Jones...* (Darien, Ga., 1966), pp. 3–8. For Bryan see also Mary Granger, *Savannah River Plantations* (Savannah, Ga., 1947), pp. 43–4, 394–404; Isabella R. Redding, *Life and Times of Jonathan Bryan* (Savannah, 1901).

9. The letter is among the papers of de Saussure (1740–99), the celebrated Swiss physician, geologist, electrical experimenter, and mountaineer, who in 1772 was a founder of the Genevan Société pour l'avancement des arts. He had visited England in 1768 and been elected an F.R.S.; BF doubtless became acquainted with him at that time, but this is the first extant communication between them. For de Saussure's career see Douglas W. Freshfield, *The Life of Horace Benedict de Saussure* (London, 1920).

324

appointed by the Society to consider of the Means of Securing that Edifice from Lightning,[1] which I thought would fully answer the End of your Letter, by authenticating the Fact in a fuller Manner than anything from me could do, as I knew the Transactions go to your Country. This, with a Multiplicity of Business that press'd upon me at my Return, together with a blameable[2] Backwardness in Writing that grows upon me with Years, occasion'd me to postpone answering from time to time, till I am now asham'd you should know I am alive. But, they say, *it is never too late to mend*, and I will endeavour to mend this Fault if you are, as I hope you are, good enough to forgive me.

Pointed Conductors to secure Buildings from Lightning have now been in use near 20 Years in America, and are there become so common, that Numbers of them appear on private Houses in every Street of the principal Towns, besides those on Churches, Publick Buildings, Magazines of Powder, and Gentlemens Seats in the Country. Thunder Storms are much more frequent there than in Europe, and hitherto there has been no Instance of a House so guarded being damaged by Lightning: for wherever it has broke over any of them, the Point has always receiv'd it, and the Conductor has convey'd it safely into the Earth, of which we have now five authentic Instances. Here in England the Practice has made a slower Progress, Damage by Lightning being less frequent, and People of course less apprehensive of Danger from it; yet besides St. Paul's Church, St. James's Church, the Queen's Palace, and Blenheim House,[3] a number of private Gentlemen's Seats round the Town are now provided with Conductors; and the Ships bound to the East and West Indies and the Coast of Guinea begin to supply themselves with Chains for that purpose made by Mr. Nairne,[4] especially since the Return of Messrs. Bankes and Solander, who relate that their Ship was, as they think, saved by one of those Chains from Damage, when a Dutch Ship lying

1. See above, XVI, 146–51.
2. "Inexcusable" in the draft.
3. St. James's, Piccadilly, was the work of Christopher Wren and the Queen's House at Greenwich of Inigo Jones; Blenheim House was presumably Blenheim Palace, Vanbrugh's vast pile in Oxfordshire.
4. The instrument-maker, for whom see above, X, 171 n; he has appeared frequently in recent volumes. For an example of a chain conductor see above, XVII, 49–52.

near them in the Road of Batavia was almost demolished by the Lightning.[5]

Of late too, the Board of Ordnance here have applied to the Royal Society for their Advice how to secure the great Magazines of Gun powder at Purfleet from Lightning; the Society appointed a Committee to visit the Magazines and report their Opinion thereupon, which is done, advising the Securing them by Conductors; and you will see the Report in the next Vol. of Transactions,[6] wherein the manner of doing it is directed. But as that Volume will not be published till next Summer, I will send you immediately a Copy of the Report if you desire it. On this Occasion I was induc'd, by a difference of Opinion in one of the Committee, to make some Experiments which I communicated to them in Writing, to show more clearly the Effect of *pointed* Rods, and the Advantage of making them extend as high as possible above the highest Part of the Building. Inclos'd I send a Copy of it.[7]

I hope you have removed the Prejudices of your Fellow-Citizens relating to your Conductor, and that you have long since compleated it,[8] so as to make the Experiments with it that you had in View. I wish to hear how it succeeded with you.

I am much oblig'd by the curious Experiments of which you gave me an Account. I suspect that the Light remaining on the Card, is common Light, which had been imbibed by it, and was conceal'd in it till driven out by the electric Fluid.[9] Accept my

5. For the voyage of the *Endeavour* see above, XVIII, 214. The episode at Batavia is described in John C. Beaglehole, ed., *The Journals of Captain James Cook on His Voyages of Discovery* (3 vols. in 4, Cambridge, 1955–67), I, 433.

6. It is printed above, Aug. 21.

7. See the headnote on BF's experiments above, under Aug. 18.

8. De Saussure had erected a lightning rod, said to have been a hundred feet high, above his home in Geneva; his neighbors were so disturbed that he published a pamphlet to reassure them, *Exposition abrégée de l'utilité des conducteurs électriques* (Geneva, 1771). See Freshfield, *op. cit.*, p. 130. Here and in the final paragraph BF is replying to the letter, now lost, of a year earlier.

9. De Saussure's letter must have contained an account of experiments, presumably his own, with some luminescent substance. Whatever the experimenter's purpose, the result apparently revealed a phenomenon now known as electroluminescence: a body stimulated by an electric charge emits previously absorbed light. Controlled scientific exploration of this phenomenon did not occur until the nineteenth century; see E. Newton Harvey, *A History of Luminescence from the Earliest Times until 1900* (Philadelphia,

best Thanks, and believe me, with sincere Esteem and Respect,
Sir, Your most obedient humble Servant   B FRANKLIN

From Jacques Barbeu-Dubourg

ALS (incomplete): American Philosophical Society

[Before Oct. 9. 1772?[1]]

[*Beginning lost.*] Il est arrivé icy depuis environ un mois un Abbé
qui a eté Professeur de Philosophie à Perpignan et que l'on
certifie qui a gueri radicalement six paralytiques par le moyen de
l'electricité.[2] Les Magistrats l'ayant adressé a la faculté de Medecine pour constater le succès des nouvelles experiences qu'il de-
voit faire icy, ell' a nommé a cet [*torn:* examen quelques?] membres du nombre desquels je suis. Il a commencé a [*torn:* électrifier
des?] malades depuis 15 jours, le 1er. des trois s'en trouve tres
bien et les progrès sont considerables d'un jour a l'autre. Les
2 autres n'ont qu'à s'en louer jusqu'icy mais les progrès sont lents.
Nous dressons chaque jour une espece de procès verbal dont je
vous ferai part à la fin, au moins si cela tourne bien. Il ne leur fait
recevoir aucune sorte de commotion, il se contente de leur faire
recevoir la matiere electrique par le moyen d'une chaine de fer
attachée au côté sain. Il joint à cela avec un air de mystere quelques petits secours appropriés au mal. Au reste il paroit plustôt un
bonhomme qu'un genie transc[endant]. Il vous honore sur votre

---

1957), pp. 396–8, 404. BF's brief reference is tantalizing because it is his
earliest comment, as far as we know, on the absorption and re-emission of
light, a subject to which he did not return until 1784: Smyth, *Writings*, IX,
227–30. But he had long been interested in the nature of light, and had suggested years earlier a wave theory that conflicted with the prevailing New-
tonian view of moving corpuscles. See above, III, 128–9; IV, 299–300; I.
Bernard Cohen, *Franklin and Newton*... (Philadelphia, 1956), pp. 320–3.
    1. In his letter of Oct. 9, the following document, Dubourg enclosed the
new volume of the *Ephémérides*; in this letter he promised to send the new
volumes by the first opportunity. The periodical ceased publication in March,
1772; it was not revived until the end of 1774, and then under a new title.
Hence we assume that Dubourg was referring to the volume or volumes for
1772.
    2. In all likelihood the Abbé Sans, whom Dubourg mentioned in his letter
below, Oct. 28.

327

renommée, et connoit peu vos [*torn:* ouvrages?] mais il va se mettre à les etudier.

Un jeune homme de merite et de talens peu communs m'a prié de vous consulter sur l'Amerique et sur un honneur rendu à Newton. Je prens la liberté de joindre icy sa petite note, et vous repons qu'il ne fera point mauvais usage de vos instructions, c'est un poete philosophe, qui a autant de goût que de feu.[3]

[Je vais vous?] envoyer par la 1e. occasion les nouveaux volumes des [Ephémérides] du citoyen, mais il ne m'est pas possible de les inserer dans ce paquet. Je tâcherai d'y joindre quelques autres nouveautés, s'il y en a qui en vaillent la peine.

Le paquet deposé chez MM. Dilly de la part de M. Rush ne m'est point encore parvenu.[4] J'espere cependant pouvoir l'en faire bientôt retirer par un ami, car j'ai grande impatience de le voir.

Quant aux lettres et petits paquets comme celui cy, on m'a assuré que nous pouvions moyennant l'adresse cyjointe ne nous en pas gener de part et d'autre, quelque frequente que dût etre notre correspondance; c'est a mon confrere M. Poissonier[5] que j'ai cette obligation, et il me flatte même que nous pourrons continuer ainsi d'un hemisphere à l'autre, [avec] la même franchise.

J'ai mille complimens a vous faire de tous ceux qui ont eu l'honneur de vous connoitre icy, pour moi je ne vous en offre que pour Mr. Pringle, votre digne et respectable ami que j'honore de toute mon ame. S'il m'eût été possible de passer dans votre isle, j'aurois eu bien à coeur d'etre presenté de votre main a Mr. Maty dont vous me faites l'honneur de me parler, regrettant bien de n'avoir

3. The young man is unidentifiable; the honor done to Newton that appealed to him, as a "poete philosophe," may possibly have been one of the rhymed epitaphs in *Poor Richard*: above, III, 251; VI, 327–8.

4. The packet, we assume, contained Benjamin Rush's *Sermons to Gentlemen upon Temperance and Exercise* (Philadelphia, 1772). Edward Dilly, the famous bookseller, had republished the pamphlet in London with an altered title; see the annotation of BF to Rush above, Aug. 22.

5. Pierre-Isaac Poissonier (1720–98) was a doctor and chemist, who had served with the French army and, as reward for carrying out a secret mission to Russia, had been made a counselor of state. By this time he was a leading figure in French public health. Larousse, *Dictionnaire universel*. To judge by references to him in Dubourg's correspondence with BF, Poissonier was traveling frequently between London and Paris; in Oct., 1773, he was elected an F.R.S., and BF was one of his nominators: above, VIII, 359.

pas eu le plaisir de le voir lorsqu'il est venu en france. Je suis avec un sincere et respectueux attachement, Monsieur et cher Ami Votre tres humble et tres obeissant serviteur DUBOURG

From Jacques Barbeu-Dubourg

ALS: American Philosophical Society

Monsieur et cher Ami Paris ce 9e. 8br. 1772

J'arrive de la campagne ou j'ai passé deux jours, et j'ai enfin trouvé a mon arrivée le manuscrit de la traduction de vos oeuvres par M. Lesqui (le premontré) qu'il avoit depuis si longtems egarée, et pour quoi je l'avois beaucoup harcelé surtout depuis une quinzaine de jours. En consequence, vous pouvez compter que je vais dès aujourd'huy me mettre à l'ouvrage, et ne le quitterai point que je ne l'aye terminé autant bien que je le pourrai faire, soit que je puisse tirer plus ou moins de parti de ce qui est fait, soit qu'il me faille recommencer tout à neuf.[6] J'ai pris à cette intention un jeune homme pour ecrire sous ma dictée, afin d'accelerer d'autant; et je vous ferai passer ma besogne lettre à lettre, à mesure que j'avancerai.

Il me paroit que vous avez eprouvé beaucoup plus de difficultés qu'il n'etoit naturel de prevoir pour faire imprimer avec exactitude mon petit Code en françois a Londres, et moi de mon côté j'ai decouvert qu'il m'auroit eté plus facile que [je] ne l'esperois de le faire imprimer en france, clandestinement à la verité, mais qu'importe? Si donc les memes difficultés subsistent chez vous, je vous supplie de me renvoyer mon manuscrit par la 1e. occasion (car je n'en ai point conservé de copie) et on me le fera imprimer secretement à Paris.[7]

J'ai l'honneur de vous envoyer cyjoint le nouveau volume des

6. "Lesqui" was a slip of the pen; the translator was the Abbé l'Écuy, for whom see above, XVII, 237. Years later the Abbé claimed that Barbeu-Dubourg had had no part in the translation except to supervise it and make a few additions and corrections; see l'Écuy's translation of John Watkins, *Nouveau dictionnaire universel*... (Paris, 1803), p. 426.

7. Barbeu-Dubourg had hoped to have his *Petit code* printed in London through BF's good offices; when it appeared there, apparently, he abandoned his idea of a clandestine printing in Paris. See his letters to BF above, May 31, and below, Nov. 28.

OCTOBER 9, 1772

Ephemerides du Citoyen, qui est appellé le 3e. de la 6e. année, parceque les auteurs se sont trop laissé arrierer pour ne pas rougir d'intituler volume de mars celui qu'ils donnent a la fin de 7bre ou au commencement d'octobre; quoique ce retard ne vienne pas de leur faute, mais plustôt des tracasseries qu'ils ont eprouvées de notre gouvernement peu commode à son ordinaire.[8]

Melle. Biheron s'est non seulement occupée de la commission de Madame Stevenson, mais ell'a consulté sur cela les persones les plus au fait et du meilleur goût; ainsi j'espere que la commission sera bien faite quoiqu'en s'ecartant un peu des termes de la commettante; Melle. Biheron est pourtant bien aise de l'en prevenir. Elle me charge de vous assurer de ses civilités, et de toute la reconnoissance qu'elle conservera toujours de vos bontés.

Ma femme, qui me detourne souvent de toute autre sorte de travail que je voudrois entreprendre, est, et sera toujours la 1ere. à m'aiguilloner à celui qui peut vous faire plaisir, et contribuer a repandre votre gloire. Elle me charge de vous faire mille amitiés pour elle. J'ai l'honneur d'etre avec un inviolable attachement Monsieur et cher Ami Votre tres humble et tres obeissant serviteur

DUBOURG

Mes respectueux complimens a M. Pringle

From Joseph Galloway

ALS (mutilated): American Philosophical Society

Dear Friend   Philadelphia Octr. 12. 1772.
I inclose three Bills of Exchange the Amount of your last Years Salary drawn by   Sterlg.

John Wilcocks on Alexr. and Jas. Baillie for		£142 9s. 6½d.
Do	Do for	166 15s. 3½d.
Daniel Roberdeau on John Trevanion Esqr.[9]		190 15s. 2d.
		£500 — —

which I hope will be duly honor'd.

8. In its first year, 1765–66, the *Ephémérides* appeared in six issues; in the next four, 1767–71, it appeared in twelve; and in its final year under this title, 1772, it appeared in only three.

9. For John Wilcocks see the Library Committee to BF above, May 28, and for Daniel Roberdeau XVII, 81. John Trevanion was doubtless the partner in

330

Joseph Galloway

Our annual Election is now over, and I am again returnd to a Seat in the House, but whether with or against my Inclination I really cannot inform you. The Opposition I met with was the only Matter which gave Rise to a Wish to be elected, while my [health,] which has been long wasting in the Public Service, added to the [impossibility?] I find of pleasing an envious and discontented People by [*torn*] Endeavors to serve them, with an Abundance of un[*torn*] operated on the other side to render me [*torn*] situation, I gave my self no Trouble [*torn*] that all the reputable Part of the [*torn*] Election. The feeble Opposition [*torn*] giving me dayly [*torn*] State [*rest of page missing*] sending Men of Property and Character to the Legislative Council, and left it to be managed by the very Dregs of the People. To convince you of this I need only mention that Goddard wanted but a few Votes to constitute him a Representative for the County of Philadelphia. Mr. Fox who has served them 20 Years and Mr. James one of the most active and sensible Members the City ever had they have ungratefully rejected. Converse with the old Friends of good Order and Government and they express much Uneasiness and Alarm at the wicked and base Conduct of these mad People and yet they do not lift a finger to prevent it. Can you beleive that the Proprietary Friends principally obstructed Goddards Election while those whom we used to call ours woud not take the Trouble to walk to the State House? Indeed, my good Friend, shoud it ever be my Lot to stand in Need of Friendship, I shoud not know where to look for it among the latter, while I have a moral Assurance of meeting [it although?] unaskd among the former.[1] Such is the [*torn*] since you left us!

Wood & Trevanion, a firm with which Roberdeau dealt (*ibid.*, p. 88), and may well have been the man of that name who was later M.P. for Dover: Namier and Brooke, *House of Commons*, III, 562. The Baillies we cannot identify, but one of Wilcocks' bills was not drawn on them; see BF's reply below, Dec. 2.

1. Galloway's party in Philadelphia had dissolved in the electoral catastrophe of 1770, and he had retained his place as speaker of the Assembly only by winning a seat, at the bottom of the poll, from Bucks County. He never succeeded thereafter in restoring his popularity with the Philadelphia voters. The mechanics and small merchants, influenced by William Goddard's diatribes in the *Pa. Chron.*, turned against him; and in the election of 1772 they ousted two other conservatives who have often appeared in these vol-

A little Difference in [torn] Branches of the Legislature on [torn] at length given up by the [torn] has existed between [torn] Continuance [rest of page missing] by the Grantees, the Proprietors of the new Grant will receive very little Advantage from their Purchase.

This will be deliverd by my very Worthy Friend Doctor Denormandie, with whom, if I mistake not, you have some Acquaintance. He is on his Way to Geneva on Business relating to an Estate left him by a Relation. He may stand in Need of some Advice and perhaps recommendations [on?] his Travels.[2] Any Act of Friendship which you may do him, will be esteemed as done to My Dear Friend, Yours most Affectionately   Jos. GALLOWAY

Addressed: To / Benjamin Franklin Esquire / Deputy Post Master General of / North America in / Craven Street / London / favor'd by Doctr Denormandie

From William Franklin   ALS: American Philosophical Society

Honoured Father,   Philada. Octr. 13th. 1772

I informed you by the Packet which sailed a few Days ago, that I had received yours of the 14th. and 15th. of July, and 8th. of August, but that the one you mention to have wrote to me on the 3d. of Augst. at Mr. Sargent's was not come to hand. My Mother, however, has I find received one of that Date from you by the

---

umes, Joseph Fox in the county and Abel James in the city. Galloway, shorn of allies, began to conciliate his old enemies in the Proprietary faction. See Benjamin H. Newcomb, *Franklin and Galloway: a Political Partnership* (New York and London, 1972), pp. 217–25.

2. John Abram Denormandie (1721–1803) was a physician and justice of the peace in Bristol, Pa., and a member of the APS. The family was Swiss, and an uncle who died in 1771 had left his residuary estate to his American relatives. Arthur Sandys, *Annals of De Normandie...* (Cambridge, Mass., 1901), pp. 145–50; see also APS, *Early Proceedings,...* (Philadelphia, 1884), pp. 19, 44, 65, 75. De Normandie's stay in London was brief, for he left on Dec. 2 for Geneva with a letter of introduction from BF; see BF to WF below, Dec. 2.

Packet, which makes me suspect that mine has been intercepted and kept by the same Person who broke open my Letters to you.[3] Who that Person is I would give a great deal to know. I do not think it is any one who lives on this Side the Water. My Packets to you are always sent under Cover to the Postmaster at N. York, and put into the Mail at Bristol. I can hardly imagine that any of the Postmasters on the Road would have a Curiosity to open them, nor can I believe that Mr. Colden, or Mr. Antill his Son-in-law, would be guilty of so base an Action. I have some times thought that it might possibly be done by Lord Hillsborough's Directions, but as my Letters have often contained pretty free Animadversions on his Lordship's Conduct, I think he would not, if he had seen them, wrote so complaisantly to me as he has done of late. He has besides spoke handsomely of me to our Chief Justice, not long before he left England, and said at several other Times that I was a sensible Man, made a good Governor, understood my Business well, and wrote well. He likewise told the *Chief* of the Civilities he had shewn to you in Ireland, and the Invitation he had given you to visit him in London, but that you had called at his House but once since your Return and that was at a Time when you must have been morally sure of not seeing him, though you knew he had a Day in every Week set apart for seeing the Agents and Gentlemen from America.[4] However, he said, that he look'd upon you as a Man of great Abilities, and of uncommon Knowledge in American Matters, and that he liked to hear you talk on the Subject, tho' you differed from him in Sentiments respecting some particular Points.

Sometimes I cannot help suspecting that Wharton, who I have Reason to think has obtained an uncommon Influence over Mr. Todd, has prevailed on him to open my Letters, in order that he

3. None of these letters has been found. Here and in BF's reply below, Dec. 2, both men are worried about invasion of their private correspondence —at just the time when BF was in process of acquiring the private letters of Thomas Hutchinson.

4. Alexander Colden was the New York postmaster, and John Antill was acting for him; see *Journal Kept by Hugh Finlay...* (Brooklyn, 1867), pp. 46–7. Frederick Smyth, Chief Justice of New Jersey, had recently returned from a visit to England with Hillsborough's comments on the Franklins. For BF's quite different story about trying to call on the Minister see above, p. 257.

might discover what I wrote to you concerning the new Colony, or relative to my Dissatisfaction with his Conduct. Or, perhaps, he has, thro' Mr. Todd, obtained the Letters on the Arrival of the Packet, under Pretence of forwarding them to you, and has taken that Opportunity to break them open. He is capable of doing that and worse to my Knowledge. Mr. Foxcroft tells me that Mr. W. took up his Letters sometimes which came by the Packet, and forwarded them to him, while in London.[5] Do enquire whether he forwarded my Letters to you by the July Packet, and [?] who they were delivered to at the Genl. Post-Office.

Your Letters to me by the Packet are never defaced, nor do you mention that those you receive from others by that Conveyance are. I took uncommon Pains in doing up the Packet which contained the Letters I sent you down to June 30, and put all the Papers referred to in regular Order, agreeably to their Numbers, so that there coming to you in such Disorder is an evident Proof that the Letters had been purposely broke open. That you may know whether any of them were taken out and kept, I inclose you a List of them.

As Capt. All purposes sailing Tomorrow, and I am a good deal engaged in Company here I cannot write fully by this Opportunity. Enclosed are three Letters I received from Mr. Foxcroft when I was at Amboy, which when you have read please to return. If Mr. Todd has not shewn you the *certified List of the Virginia Grants on the Waters of the Missisipi*, and the *Extracts from the Proceedings of the Virginia Assembly*, which Mr. Foxcroft sent him by the September Packet, I wish you would ask to see them. The List goes down no farther than 1754, at which Time there was above 3 Millions of Acres granted; but I am told that there have been many Grants since (exclusive of the 200,000 Acres to the Provincials) but, Query Whether any of them are valid, tho' the Assembly of Virginia have resolved that they all are? The *Proceedings* will shew you that the Virginians were authorised by His Majesty to extend their Boundary to Holston's River, and from thence to the Mouth of the Great Kanawa, which will take in the

5. WF had for some time been at odds with Wharton, whom he blamed for the rumors circulating in Philadelphia that BF was useless in obtaining the grant. Foxcroft was also suspicious, about much more than the interception of letters; see BF to Foxcroft above, Feb. 4.

greatest Part of the new Colony. Query if that Line was ever countermanded by Government?[6]

Mr. Todd writes to Mr. Foxcroft (Augst. 8th) that after many Delays the Affair was finally determined in our Favour, and that Lord H. went out upon it, but without intending to join the Opposition. And a Boston Paper says that Lord Dartmouth has succeeded to his Office.[7] We are impatient for the Arrival of Falkener, by whom we may expect a certain Account.

I have this Moment heard that Govr. Spry of Barbados is dead, and that Capt. Williams the Engineer has taken his Passage in Capt. All in hopes of getting to England in Time to be appointed Captain of Needham's Fort, an Office which has been generally given to the Person who officiated as private Secretary to the Governor, but which Capt. Wms. had Interest enough to obtain an Order or Recommendation for when Spry was first appointed Governor, and, soon after he had receiv'd the Commission re-

6. In November, 1769, the Virginia House of Burgesses ordered a list of all parcels of land between the Alleghenies and the Ohio that had been granted by the province since the 1740's but not actually settled; the latest date on the list when compiled was 1754, when Whitehall had limited the size of grants. John P. Kennedy, ed., *Journals of the House of Burgesses* . . . *1766–1769* (Richmond, 1906), p. 302; the list itself is printed in Kenneth P. Bailey, ed., *The Ohio Company Papers, 1753–1817* . . . (Arcata, Cal., 1947), pp. 232–40. The extracts of the proceedings were from the journals of the House and perhaps the Council; WF discusses them at greater length in his letter below, Oct. 29. They all had to do with the drive to extend Virginia's border westward, the first fruit of which was the treaty of Lochaber. For details and for the "200,000 acres to the Provincials," veterans of the French and Indian war, see WF to BF above, Jan. 6. The answer to WF's final query is no, because the government did not have time to approve or countermand before the Lochaber line was revised in the Donelson line to the mouth of the Kentucky. Gov. Dunmore forwarded this revision, together with a map doctored to make it seem less sweeping than it was, to London in the spring of 1772; Hillsborough and Dartmouth refused to accept it without further investigation. By the time it was approved in May, 1773, Dunmore and his Council had already started making grants in the area. John R. Alden, *John Stuart and the Southern Colonial Frontier* . . . (Ann Arbor, 1944), pp. 283–9. WF, here and in his letter of the 29th, shows no knowledge of the Donelson line, or of the Privy Council's action on Aug. 14 upon the Walpole grant.

7. Dartmouth succeeded Hillsborough on Aug. 14, the day when the Privy Council gave preliminary approval to the Walpole Co.'s grant; see the annotation of BF to Jones above, Aug. 3.

335

signed it, because Spry was offended at his being forced upon him, and did not ask him to Dinner. However, if he gets it once more he will not, I fancy, be such a Fool as to quarrel with his Bread and Butter again. I wish I could succeed Govr. Spry,[8] but I stand no Chance for any Promotion or Enlargement of my Salary, I imagine, while Lord H. is at the Head of the American Department, and is so much displeased with your Conduct, tho' I am now the oldest Governor in all His Majesty's American Dominions.

Captn. Williams brought over with him from England some Mahogany Chairs with Hair Bottoms, which cost him about 22 s. Sterling a Piece, and 3 s. Sterling a Piece for Matts, packing and Frieght to Philada. I wanted the Workmen here to make me a Dozen like them, but tho' Mahogany is considerably cheaper here than in England, I could not get anyone to undertake to make them under 55 s. Currency a Piece, and they would probably not be so well finished. I shall therefore be obliged to you if you would send me a Dozen of such kind of Chairs, made in a fashionable Taste, by Captn. All. If you should see Capt. Wms. he will tell you who made those he has, and what kind they are. But I leave the Form entirely to your Direction. I want them for a Parlour.

I must likewise beg you to send me a handsome Tea Urn. I can't afford a Silver One, and therefore must be contented with a plated One, or a Copper One with Silver Spout and Handles, of which I have seen some that look'd elegant enough. Send me that which you think best.[9]

I have been here for a Week past, and have dined at Govr.

8. Dr. William Spry had been governor of Barbados from February, 1768, till his death on Sept. 4, 1772; he was succeeded by Edward Hay. Sir Robert H. Schomburgk, *The History of Barbados...* (London, 1848), pp. 332–3. All we know about Capt. John Williams of the Engineers is that he was commissioned in 1766: *A List of the General and Field-Officers...* (Dublin, 1774), p. 174. Needham's Fort commanded the approaches to Bridgetown.

9. WF presumably wanted the chairs and the urn for Franklin Park. BF commissioned the urn from Matthew Boulton, who among other things was the largest manufacturer of Sheffield plate, and plate of unequaled quality. See BF to WF below, Feb. 14, March 3, July 14, 1773; Seymour B. Wyler, *The Book of Sheffield Plate* (New York, [1949]), pp. 36–7.

Penn's, with whom I am become very sociable.[1] Betsy joins in Duty, with, Honoured Sir, Your dutiful Son   WM: FRANKLIN

P.S. Since writing the above, I have agreed with a Workman for the *Chairs*, so that you need not send them.

From Jonathan Williams, Jr.

ALS: American Philosophical Society

Dear and honoured sir   Boston October 13. 1772
    I received your favour dated July 22 and am very happy that my Letter gave you satisfaction: I am only concern'd that the length and frequency of them, will be tedious and troublesome to You.[2]
    I am glad to find by your Letter just received for my Father,[3] that you are well enough recovered from the Gout to be in the N England Coffee House.
    In my last I acquainted you with the Death of my Brother, and in the same Letter gave you an Account of Henry's unfaithfulness; I have now the pleasure to acquaint You, that he is still content with his Situation, and his Master seems satisfied with him, when I recieve my Indentures and your approbation, I shall take care to fix him with every customary Advantage: as I thought best not to bind him, till I heard from You.[4] My Father is Just re-

1. Richard Penn was technically lieutenant governor; his uncle Thomas and brother John were the governors and proprietors, and John replaced Richard in 1773.
2. The disappearance of BF's letter precludes identifying which one of Jonathan's gave him satisfaction. They were indeed frequent: four, from April through June, are printed above.
3. Above, Aug. 11.
4. For Josiah's death see his father to BF above, end of August. The letter from Jonathan, Jr., has been lost, and with it the explanation of how Henry Walker (A.5.2.3.3.1.2) had been unfaithful. The young man—he was fifteen at the time—was fond of Josiah and had gone with him to America in the spring, apparently to be a servant of his and his brother's. After Josiah's death Henry misbehaved, perhaps because he was not fond of Jonathan. The latter decided against keeping him, and proposed to apprentice him to some one else. BF must have agreed, for the arrangement was made and worked well. See below, Hannah Walker to BF, Dec. 22, 1772, and June 20, 1773; BF to Jonathan, Jr., July 7, 1773.

turned from a Journey in the Country, and if he has time will write by this Oppertunity but as the Ship is just going to sail he may be disappointed. With my most respectfull Compliments to all enquiring Friends I remain Your dutifull and affectionate Kinsman

J WILLIAMS JUNR

Aunt Mecom and all Friends are well, the Year 73 is now so near at hand without the prospect of seeing You, that we begin to fear you will break through your Intention of visiting every ten Years.[5]

Addressed: To | Doctr Franklin | London

From the Pennsylvania Assembly Committee of Correspondence
LS: Library of Congress

Sir, Philadelphia Octr. 16. 1772

We transmit inclosed the Resolves of the House appointing us their Committee of Correspondence, and you their Agent to transact the Affairs of this Province in Great Britain.[6]

The Instructions given by former Assemblies, respecting the Trade and Commerce and other general Rights, and Liberties of America, have been so full and explicit, that nothing material occurs in Addition to them. We have therefore only to desire, in case any Measures should be pursued that may by any means affect them, that you would exert your utmost Endeavours in Opposition; and that, on the Contrary, should any thing offer which may seem likely to restore that Harmony between Great Britain and her Colonies, so necessary to their mutual Safety and Happiness, that you will promote it by every mean in your Power.

We are also ordered to inform you that the House, taking into their Consideration your Salary for the ensuing Year, have resolved, that you shall be allowed at the Rate of five Hundred Pounds Sterling per Annum for the first Six Months, and after-

5. For these decennial visits see above, XVII, 165, and BF to Jane Mecom, April 13, 1772.

6. At its first meeting, on Oct. 14, the new Assembly had re-elected Galloway as speaker, and on the following day had chosen this committee of correspondence and reappointed BF as agent. 8 *Pa. Arch.*, VIII, 6896, 6898–9.

wards at the Rate of three Hundred Pounds Sterling.[7] We are
your Assured Friends[8]   Jos. GALLOWAY Speaker
                                SAML RHOADS
                                SL SHOEMAKER.
                                WM. RODMAN
                                ISA: PEARSON

Benjamin Franklin Esqr.

Endorsed: Pennsylvania Committee of Correspondence 1772
Salary reduced from £500 per Annum to £300

A Committee of the Managers of the Pennsylvania Hospital to Franklin, David Barclay, and John Fothergill

Minutebook copy: Pennsylvania Hospital, Philadelphia

Esteemed Friends   Philadia. 10th. Mo. 20th. 1772

It is with much satisfaction we received Intelligence from our
Friend David Barclay, by his Letter of the 27th Augst. That, "by
Order of the Court of Chancery there is transferred to you, for the
use of the Pennsylvania Hospital, Seven thousand, six hundred
and thirty four pounds 11s. 1d. three per Cent reduced Bank Annuities, Also that the Court has directed the payment of Nine
hundred and Nine pounds 1s. 4d. the Amount of dividends due
thereon", which transfer we conclude you will have accepted,
and received the said Dividends long before this can come to
your hands.

The Managers have therefore agreed to dispose of Bills of Ex-

7. The action of the House, taken at the time of BF's reappointment (*ibid.*,
p. 6899), is mysterious. The committee's letter and the endorsement, which
appears to be in BF's hand, mean that his salary was cut by £100 for 1773; and
we can find no record that the action was rescinded. Galloway and Samuel
Rhoads seem to have opposed it; see BF to Galloway below, Jan. 6, 1773. If
so they failed, for BF entered only £400 as his 1773 salary. Yet by the end of
1774 he had apparently received a total of £2,000 from the province for the
past four years. Jour., pp. 52, 57; Ledger, p. 3.

8. For Samuel Shoemaker see above, XII, 344 n; all the others had been
members of the previous committee: above, XVIII, 232–3.

change to the Amount of Three thousand pounds Sterling, which they expect to be able to Effect in a Short time, in such manner as to have the money immediately placed out here on good real securities at our Legal Interest.[9]

You are therefore requested to sell out so much Capital Stock, as with the Payment for the dividends will Enable You to discharge our Drafts to the Amount above mentioned, the particulars of which you will hereafter be duly advised of, and we hope you will have it in your Power to make Sale of the Stock at the rate mentioned viz. 89 per Cent or in case of any emergency reducing the Value of them below that rate, that you act therein with such precaution, as to provide against any material Loss.[1]

Expecting to have the further pleasure of hearing again from you soon, agreeable to the intimation of our Friend David Barclay; and to receive the Solicitors Bill for transacting the Affair We are respectfully Your Obliged Friends

The Managers for the present year are[2]

Israel Pemberton	Jacob Lewis	And it is agreed that the
Samuel Rhoads	Thomas Wharton	Bills to be drawn be
John Reynell	Daniel Roberdeau	Signed by at least,
Isaac Jones	Isaac Cox	Eight of us
Joseph Morris	William Logan	

To Docr. John Fothergill Benjamin Franklin and David Barclay Agents in London for the Pennsylvania Hospital

9. See BF to the Managers above, Aug. 28, and their letter below, Nov. 4.

1. Barclay answered on Dec. 2 that the rate of 89% he had quoted was on the eve of a semiannual dividend, and that the annuities had now fallen to 87%; there was also, he added, a solicitor's bill of £38 8s. 6d. Pa. Hospital Minutebook.

2. The form of the MS makes it impossible to tell whether this paragraph was part of the letter or of the minutes, but we are inclined to think the former. Four of the managers—Pemberton, Rhoads, Roberdeau, and Wharton—have appeared so often in these volumes that they need no introduction. For Jones, Logan, Morris, and Reynell see above, respectively, XI, 339 n; III, 456 n; IX, 274 n, 372 n. Isaac Cox was a sea captain who was a manager from 1770 until his death five years later, and who left the Hospital £50 in his will; Jacob Lewis (1714?–74), a Quaker merchant, had been an original contributor and a manager since 1759. Thomas G. Morton and Frank Woodbury, *The History of the Pennsylvania Hospital*... (Philadelphia, 1895), pp. 367, 405–6; *PMHB*, XXIX (1905), 100–1; above, V, 328; *Pa. Gaz.*, April 6, 1774.

From Mary Hewson

ALS: American Philosophical Society

Dear Sir   Broad Street Oct. 22. 1772

My Mother hopes you receiv'd a Letter from Mr. Collinson, for she desir'd him to write to you one evening about a Bill which he told her was not accepted. The enclos'd are all that came since you heard last from us.[3] Mr. Strahan presents his Respects to you and begs the Favour of your Company at Dinner next Tuesday to meet Sir John Pringle and some body else, whose name was dropt before the message arriv'd to me. Your Apartment in Craven Street will be ready for you on monday; if you wish to be in Town sooner we shall have a Bed at your Service on Saturday, and you will make us happy by accepting it; you need not leave us till Tuesday if you find it convenient to stay. I think you had better accept my offer, as it will afford you an opportunity of seeing your things mov'd, without being more in my Mother's way than she would like. She is to sleep in her new House tonight, and I hope she will now take a little rest, for she has fatigu'd herself very much and is far from well.

Lectures go on briskly; a fresh Pupil to day who makes up the half hundred whose names are enter'd, besides some others who have promis'd, among whom are your Friends Mr. Walsh and Mr. Bancroft.[4]

Your Godson (that is his Mother for him) is much oblig'd by your kind mention of him. He is very well, improves every day

3. The writer was Peter Collinson's nephew Thomas, for whom see above, IX, 211 n. He had joined his father-in-law, Henton Brown, in the firm of Brown & Collinson, one of BF's bankers. See Norman G. Brett-James, *The Life of Peter Collinson* [London, 1926], p. 220. The protested bill of exchange was Mackie on Molleson, remitted by Alexander Colden; see BF to Colden above, Oct. 7, and below, Nov. 3. Polly was forwarding BF's mail because he was visiting Lord Le Despencer at West Wycombe; he returned on the 24th.

4. Hewson was inaugurating his anatomical lectures, for which he had reconstructed the Craven Street house; his family was in the throes of moving into it from Broad Street, while Mrs. Stevenson supervised the transfer of her things and BF's to another house on Craven Street. John Walsh, back from France and his investigation of the torpedo fish, presumably wanted more anatomical knowledge to help his research. Edward Bancroft must have just returned from his flying visit to America, for which see Williams to BF above, June 13.

"in wisdom and in stature," and I might conclude the scripture sentence, for those improvements are the Favour of God, and his little engaging manners procure the favour of man.[5] But not a word does he speak.

As I know you want a great deal of courting I repeat my Invitation to you for next Saturday Sunday and Monday; if you can resolve to leave the Paradise you are in, you will give us Pleasure by making your abode here. I am, my dear Sir, with unalterable affection your faithful and obedient Servant   MARY HEWSON

From James Hutton[6]   ALS: American Philosophical Society

Dear Sir   Oct. 23. late at night. [1772]

I hope you will excuse my troubling you in the Country, if I could have found you in Town I had not. Yet I hope this will give you some pleasure as well as Trouble. I call'd in Craven Street found them busy in moving and Mrs. Stevenson much engaged.[7] I have just received the inclosed printed Paper from Paris, and as I have but this one, beg the favour of you to return it me in a frank as soon as you can. By this you will see that the time for Subscribing is lengthend, and that a general Introduction to the work will now appear soon: by which means his Plan will be better understood.[8] He was mightily pleasd with the Proposals I sent him of

5. "And Jesus increased in wisdom and stature, and in favor with God and man." Luke 2: 52.

6. The Moravian leader; see above, XVII, 223 n.

7. On Oct. 8 BF had gone to Lord Le Despencer's country estate.

8. Two advance notices were printed of Antoine Court de Gébelin, *Monde primitif, analysé et comparé avec le monde moderne* . . . (9 vols., Paris, 1773–82). One was an eight-page prospectus dated April 15, 1772, the other a one-page "programme" dated Oct. 17; we believe that Hutton was referring to the latter, fresh from Paris, and that the former was the enclosure mentioned in his postscript. Court de Gébelin (1725–84) had been educated for the Protestant ministry but had abandoned it for the literary and scholarly life; his vast opus, never finished, was intended to throw new light on the ancient world, especially its languages and literature. He subsequently collaborated with BF in France in producing the periodical *Affaires de l'Angleterre et de l'Amérique.*

Mr. Bryant (late Secretary to the late D. of Marlbro') which if you have not seen are really worth your sight and may be had at Elmsleys.9 The Introduction of my Paris friend will consist of 12 sheets in 4to. This He has causd to be carefully examined by several of his learned friends both as to matter and form; and He has attended to my Request to be as careful as possible to have his work appear in a manner worthy of Him. He enquires of me if I know any thing of a Letter to Martin Folkes concerning the Rise and Progress of Astronomy among the ancients London 1746. Farther Account in three Letters Oxford 1748 on the Astronomy of the Chaldeans, the Constellations of Job and the Astronomical Mythology.1 If you can recollect any thing of those two pieces or if any one where you are could tell me any thing of them I should be glad.

He mentions also a new Etymology. *Artemis* in Greek is the name of Diana or the Moon. Now *Ar-temis* are two words of the Primitive Language which signify exactly regle de la Terre and the prim[itive] word *Ar* is your English word E*ar*th and of *Tem*is the Greeks made *The*mis, Goddess of Order, of Justice. On ne pouvoit mieux definir cet Astre. It was for the same reason the name given to Apollo or the Sun.

You see by the Leaf I send you to day that the work is forward and hastens, I long to see it and I wish him more Subscribers. You and Dr. Moreton2 were the first in England that gave him Encouragement. If but a few of his Discoveries are real, among the many He imagines, I think much is gained, as real Knowledge in

9. Jacob Bryant (1715–1804), secretary to Charles Spencer, Duke of Marlborough (1706–58), had devoted himself to scholarship after the Duke's death; at this time he was writing *A New System or an Analysis of Ancient Mythology*... (2 vols., London, 1774). *DNB*. For Peter Elmsley, one of the best known London booksellers of the century, see Henry R. Plomer *et al.*, *A Dictionary of Printers and Booksellers...from 1726 to 1775*... ([Oxford], 1932), pp. 83–4.

1. Hutton was looking for two works by George Costard (1710–82). The title and date of the first are as given; the second is *A Further Account of the Rise and Progress of Astronomy amongst the Antients, in Three Letters to Martin Folkes*... (Oxford, 1748), which deals with the subjects Hutton mentions. For the author and Folkes, the antiquary to whom Costard addressed his learned works, see the *DNB*.

2. Charles Morton, the secretary of the Royal Society, for whom see above, x, 71 n.

any thing is well worth getting and can afterwards be made use of to good and curious purposes.

It is some thing curious that Mr. Bryant here and He in France agree in many things which they most certainly could not steal from one another. Bryant and He treat Semiramis, Cadmus, the Argonauts Minos &c as Allegorical Personages. He is charmed that while He is digging at Paris in the Mines of Antiquity an Englishman is doing the same thing here, and as they both take different routs, it will give a certainty to what shall be proved by both; it is very remarkable He says que ce genie Allegorique presqu'inconnu jusques ici, ou qu'on traitoit de vision se soit fait sentir tout à la fois à des Personnes si eloignées et qui ne pouvoient se concerter.

I learnt to day that the Bishop of Vilna is gone from France towards Poland and as his great family Estates (those of the Massalsky) are included in that part which the voracious Austria has seized, it is thought He is gone by way of Vienna; the Ecclesiastical Estates the Russian Code maker has taken chiefly under its Dominion. Abbé Baudeau was at Paris still Oct. 18.[3] The Marquis de Pezay return'd last night from his Tour, I have not seen him yet, but I hear My Lord Lyttleton whom He has twice visited was much pleasd with him: to please such a Man non ultima laus est.[4] You know that I am extremely your   HUTTON.

P.S. As it may give pleasure where you are I send you inclosed

3. Ignacy Jozef Massalski (1729–94), Bishop of Vilna since 1762, has been characterized as a loathsome scoundrel: Robert N. Bain, *The Last King of Poland and His Contemporaries...* (London, [1909]), pp. 101, 104–5, 147; see also *Wielka encyklopedia powszechna PWM ...* (13 vols., Warsaw, 1962–70), VII, 100. Nicolas Baudeau (for whom see BF to du Pont de Nemours above, Aug. 12) had gone to Poland at Bishop Massalski's invitation, and produced as a result of the visit his *Lettres historiques sur l'état actuel de la Pologne et sur l'origine de ses malheurs* (Amsterdam, 1772).

4. In this sentence Hutton apparently shifts away from Polish affairs. Alexandre-Frédéric-Jacques de Masson, Marquis de Pezay (1741–77), was returning to France, we conjecture, from an English tour. He was a minor literary figure, protégé of Maurepas, for a time tutor to the Dauphin, and a man of vast self-esteem; see Mrs. Paget Toynbee, ed. *Lettres de la Marquise du Deffand à Horace Walpole...* (3 vols., London, 1912), III, 277 n. Pezay's literary pretensions were presumably what attracted him to Lord Lyttleton, for whom see above, VIII, 145 n.

one of the printed Proposals for Monde Primitif, in case any one in the Company wanted to know more of this Plan.

I may possibly go at the latter End of next week towards Bath and Bristol, in which case if you could tell me of any body in either of those places who resembles my Craven Street friend and whom you would wish me to salute in your Name I should be glad.

Once more begging your pardon for any Interruption of pleasure this may occasion, I will only add that the Letter on foreign Travels in the London Chronicle the other day was mine:[5] the Printer took the Liberty to mutilate it.

Endorsed: Mr Hutton

From Jacques Barbeu-Dubourg

ALS: American Philosophical Society

Monsieur et cher Ami   A Paris ce 28e. 8bre. 1772

Je travaille autant qu'il est en moi à remplir mes engagemens, en refondant en entier la traduction de vos excellens ouvrages;[6] mais je sens trop ce qui me manque pour esperer de rendre la copie digne de l'original. Trouvez bon que je vous demande quelques eclaircissemens à mesure que j'avancerai.

Je ne trouve point dans le dictionaire le mot *orreries* page 34, je conjecture qu'il signifie *cadrans*.[7]

Non plus que les mots *surf* and *spray* page 41,[8] que je ne devine pas, et qui m'arrêtent.

Ni *jostled*, page 47,[9] qui cependant m'embarrasse moins.

Votre experience avec la fumée de resine pour rendre visible

5. A letter signed "S.N.," *London Chron.*, Oct. 15–17; it dealt with the benefits that young men could derive from the Grand Tour.
6. See Dubourg's earlier letter above, Oct. 9.
7. The page references are to the 1769 edition of *Exper. and Obser.*; for convenience we have provided references to our edition of the *Papers*. *Cadran* is scarcely the French for orrery, a mechanical planetarium, for which see above, III, 361.
8. *Ibid.*, p. 367.
9. *Ibid.*, p. 372.

l'athmosphere electrique me satisfait beaucoup.[1] En avez vous tiré tout le parti que vous auriez pu? Je m'en rapporte à vous.

Je voudrois savoir ce qu'entend le Dr.——par *my old theme*, et par *your Doctrine of the Origin*, &c.[2]

Les experiences sur le froid produit par les corps evaporables[3] ne vous engagera-t-il point à en faire quelques unes sur le chaud produit par les corps *deliquescens*, c'est a dire qui attirent l'humidité de l'air, et s'y liquefient, comme l'alkali fixe du tartre, d'où provient l'huile de tartre par defaillance (*per deliquium*)? Par rapport à l'electricité medicale, les experiences de l'Abbé Sans, (il y a deux ans) n'eurent pas les grands succès qu'il en promettoit.[4] Je vous envoye cyjoint le detail d'une autre expe[rience] assez singuliere que suit un simple artiste; a qui j'ai donné une petite consultation à ce sujet, où vous verrez une idée peu commune que j'avois depuis longtems sur l'epilepsie.

Je reviens à vos lettres sur les refroidissemens, page 347, est-il bien exact de dire que le ver a soye est vétu de sa soye dans son etat d'embryon?[5] Le changement du ver en chrysalide se fait dans le coucon de soye, mais le veritable etat d'embryon est, à mon avis, dans l'oeuf avant que le ver en eclose.

Ne manque-t'il pas à votre quarré magique de 8, de faire par ses diagonales 260?[6] Je me suis amusé à en faire un qui remplit toutes vos conditions et quelques autres difficultés de plus, comme de pouvoir en transposer des moitiés, ou des quartiers sans y causer aucun prejudice et qui de tous les sens fait toujours 11000 en l'honneur des 11000 vierges de nos legendes. Dans votre quarré magique de 16, il y a au moins un nombre repeté (241) et au moins une ligne fautive qui est la 1e. comme je m'en suis tenu a cette

1. Above, IV, 13–14.

2. Dr. Perkins wrote "Origins": *ibid.*, p. 337. The reference, which was to waterspouts, Dubourg expanded in translation into "Origines des trombes." *Œuvres*, II, 135.

3. Above, VII, 184–5; VIII, 108–9.

4. Probably the experiments described in Sans's *Guérison de la paralysie par l'électricité, ou cette expérience physique employée avec succès dans le traitement de cette maladie* (Paris, 1772). The author was a canon and professor of physics at the University of Perpignan: Joseph Marie Quérard, *La France littéraire*... (12 vols., Paris, 1827–64), VIII, 440.

5. Above, VII, 188.

6. Above, IV, 394–6.

tres legere inspection que le hazard m'a procuré, je desirerois que vous revoyiez s'il n'y en auroit pas d'autres.

Coals page 362,[7] est à ce qu'il me semble ce que nous appellons du charbon de terre, mais nous le regardons comme un fossile d'origine vegetale, et non de la 1e. antiquité de notre globe faites y attention.

Avez vous repeté votre jolie experience sur le mouvement des liqueurs[8] avec 3 liquides de pesanteurs differentes et de couleurs assez distinctes comme l'huile de gayac, l'eau et l'huile commune? Comme j'avois eu l'honneur de vous le proposer?

Ne vous sembleroit il pas interessant de chercher à determiner le *maximum* et le *minimum* des rapports de la profondeur des canaux navigables aux bateaux qu'ils doivent porter?

Je n'ai point trouvé dans le dictionaire le mot *track-schuyt* page 492.[9] Mais voilà assez de questions à la fois. Si vous pouvez vous faire à mes importunités, elles seront suivies de beaucoup d'autres.

Voulez vous que je vous envoye quelques cayers traduits, avant d'aller plus loin? Ils peuvent bien faire actuellement la 8e. partie du total. Je vous en ferai passer au moins quelques uns par Melle. Biheron, si elle retourne a Londres vers la fin du mois prochain, comme elle s'y dispose; mais je crains 1°. pour sa santé qui n'est pas encore trop bonne. 2°. Pour ses fraix, qui ne sauroient manquer d'etre grands, et qu'elle ne retirera peutetre pas encore. Au nom de Dieu, si vous ne voyez pas jour à un meilleur succès de ce voyage que du precedent, faites moi la grace de me le dire entre nous, j'insisterois sur des motifs de santé pour la retenir.[1]

Je vais songer aussi à faire regraver les planches necessaires pour l'edition prochaine; ainsi je vous prie 1°. de revoir le grand quarré magique, pour le rendre absolument correct, 2°. de songer si vous n'auriez pas quelques nouvelles figures à ajouter auxdites planches, et de m'en faire part sans delay. Il faut faire en sorte que vous puissiez emporter avec vous, quand notre Europe vous reperdra, une paquotille de la traduction complette de vos ouvrages.

7. Above, VII, 357.

8. Probably the experiment described above, x, 158–9. See also Brownrigg to BF above, June 12.

9. For this and the preceding paragraph see above, xv, 115–18.

1. Mlle. Biheron was in London again by the end of the year, still in bad health; see BF to Dubourg below, Dec. 26. We have no idea what the purpose of her trips was, or why the first one had been a failure.

Par rapport à mon petit Code de la Raison, je m'en tiens a ce que j'ai eu l'honneur de vous marquer par ma derniere. Si vous trouvez trop d'embarras à le faire imprimer en françois a Londres, faites moi la grace de me le renvoyer; je pourrai le faire imprimer secretement en province.[2]

Ma femme, et ses voisines et tous vos amis et amies de ma connoissance m'ont chargé de mille amitiés pour vous sans oublier votre digne ami M. Pringle. J'ai l'honneur d'etre avec un inviolable attachement, Monsieur et cher Ami, Votre tres humble et tres obeissant serviteur   DUBOURG

From William Henly   ALS: American Philosophical Society

Sir: Wednesday 2 OClock [October 28, 1772?[3]]

I have this morning received the [enclosed] Letter from a friend at Lewes, and though it may contain nothing that is new or very material, yet I take the liberty of sending it to you thinking it may employ a few leisure minutes if you have any such.[4] I this morning left at Mr. Nairnes a drawing for an instrument to shew your beautiful experiments with the point.[5] I think I have given it every convenience you can wish, and in as simple a manner as possible. In short I flatter my self that it will meet with your approbation, as I think I have much improved upon the sketch I produced last night at your house.

2. See Dubourg's earlier letters above, May 31, Oct. 9.

3. This is another letter that can be dated only by guesswork. Henly speaks of showing BF, the evening before, the drawing for an instrument that he is having made, presumably the one described in his quasi-letter below, Nov. 28. If that was the approximate date when he received it, and if the job took a month or so, work on it began in late October. BF returned to London on or about Oct. 24 (BF to WF below, Nov. 3); the next Wednesday was the 28th. We conjecture that Henly visited him on the 27th and wrote this letter the following day.

4. The enclosure, which has disappeared, was probably from William Chapman (1749–1832), the engineer and canal-builder, for whom see the *DNB*. Chapman was in Brighton the following February, when he wrote Henly about lightning. APS.

5. Presumably those that BF described above, Aug. 18. For a sketch and description of the completed instrument see Henly to BF below, Nov. 28. For Edward Nairne see above, x, 171 n and subsequent volumes.

I hope Sir you will some day give me leave to take a copy of your experiments and observations, which are certainly exceedingly clear and satisfactory and such as I cannot but think will prove really beneficial to the public.[6] I have the Honour to be Dr. Franklins obliged and very Humble Servant   W HENLY

Addressed: To / Dr. Franklin / Craven-street / Strand

From William Franklin   ALS: American Philosophical Society

Honoured Father,   Burlington Octr. 29th. 1772

I writ to you on the 13th. Inst. by Capt. All, and informed you that yours of the 3d. of Augst. was not come to hand; since which I have received it by the Septr. Packet. What prevented it from coming by the Augst. Packet, as my Mother's of the same Date did, I know not. I have likewise received yours of the 17th. of Augst. by Sutton (I believe,) and your long Letter of Augst. 19, with Additions to the 24th. by Falkener also yours of Septr. 2 and 3 per the Packet.[7]

At present I can only take notice of the first Paragraph of yours dated Augst. 19, wherein you mention that Mr. Wharton told you, on your beginning to mention the Intelligence I had sent you respecting the Virginia Claim, "that he had all that Intelligence long before, that there was little or nothing in it, since the Grants being made contrary to Proclamation, and the Surveys without Authority, they were all void." I doubt not but he has had all that Intelligence before, and that he does not think it prudent, as you say, to talk of those Grants lest our most influential Partners should be discouraged.[8] However, as I did not think it just that they should,

6. Henly is referring, we conjecture, to BF's recent writings on electricity, for which see above under Aug. 12, 18, and 21. This material was included in Barbeu-Dubourg's *Œuvres*, which was then in process of translation, but not in the fifth edition of *Exper. and Obser.*, published in 1774. Henly did receive at least part of what he asked for; see his letter below, Dec. 30.

7. The surviving letters, above, are BF's of Aug. 17, parts of that of the 19th, and WF's of Oct. 13.

8. The quotation from BF is in neither of the extracts printed above. Wharton was presumably referring to the statement of Virginia's case in William Nelson's letter to Hillsborough in 1770, of which Wharton had seen an extract in February, 1771, and to which he had produced a rebuttal: above,

349

for the Sake of carrying a present Point, be deceived to their Loss, I thought it my Duty to acquaint you, from time to time, that you might inform them, what Opposition we are likely to meet with in getting Possession of our Lands, even if we should obtain our Grant. The Virginia Claims to the Land on the Ohio may possibly prove on Examination to be not well founded, but I think, such as they are, they ought to be made known beforehand to the Gentlemen who are to pay their Money for a Colony in that Country. If you have read the *Extracts from the Journals* of the Virginia Assembly, which I mentioned in my last as sent to Mr. Todd by the Septr. Packet, you will there see that the Virginians found their Claim on a Report of the Board of Trade in 1769, the King's Approbation of it, and a Requisition made in pursuance thereof for £2500 Sterling, which the Assembly accordingly advanced.9 Lest those *Extracts* may not have been shewn to you, I now send you a Copy of a *State of the Virginia Claim*, which I made out from them, together with some *Remarks* thereupon. These cannot fail giving you a proper Idea of the Matter, and I must beg you, let Mr. Wharton say what he will, to make it an Object of your particular Attention. If there has been such a Report of the Board of Trade, with the King's Confirmation sent to Virginia, it may pos-

---

XVIII, 75 n (where March 5 should be March 7); Kenneth P. Bailey, ed., *The Ohio Company Papers . . .* (Arcata, Cal., 1947), p. 255. BF had apparently confided his suspicion that Wharton was concealing the strength of their opponents' case to avoid discouraging his partners, a suspicion that was subsequently confirmed in a long interview with Wharton and Trent: to WF below, Feb. 14, 1773.

9. WF mentioned the extracts in his letter of Oct. 13, and this passage permits a guess about what they were. One was in all likelihood Botetourt's speech to the House of Burgesses on Nov. 7, 1769, informing it that the Board of Trade's report of the previous April, moving the Hard Labor line westward, had been approved if the colony would bear the expense; another the memorandum from the House of Dec. 13, urging the extension of Virginia's southern border, as the Cherokee frontier, westward to meet the Ohio; and a third the appropriation of £2500 for negotiating with the Indians. See John P. Kennedy, ed., *Journals of the House of Burgesses . . .*, 1766–69 (Richmond, 1906), pp. 226–7, 335–6, 346, 353; the Board of Trade's report may be found in *N.Y. Col. Docs.*, VIII, 161–2. It is probable, for reasons noted below, that the resolves of the House on June 15, 1770, reversing its previous stand and accepting the Lochaber line, were also included: Kennedy, *op. cit.*, 1770–72, p. 74. For details of these negotiations see the annotation of WF to BF above, Jan. 6.

sibly account for Lord H's late Opposition to the Grant of a new Colony. He might be apprehensive of that Transaction being thereby brought to light, and that his Character would suffer for having at first encouraged the Design of a new Colony, at the very Time he was authorizing the People of Virginia to take Possession of the Country for themselves in which it was to be established. If these Things are so, how can we account for Mr. Jackson, Mr. Cooper, Govr. Pownall, cum multis aliis, being ignorant of them?[1] If they are not so, to let us here know the Truth, and to let the Virginians know it, who rely much upon them, ought certainly to be done, otherwise the worst of Consequences may happen. Should the Extent of Country claimed by Virginia as their Boundary be confirmed, you will easily see by looking at Evans's Map, that the small Tract which will be left for the Proprietors of the new Colony, will not be worth their Purchase Money.[2] One Reason, therefore, why I think our influential Friends ought to be particularly informed of the real State of this Matter is, that they may use their Influence, in case those Claims can't be set aside, to obtain for us a proportionably valuable Tract lower down the Ohio. But common Honesty, I think, requires they should know the whole Truth, let the Event be what it may. At any Rate, I was determined to clear my Conscience, which I think I have fully done by the Letters I have sent you on the Subject, and by writing the enclosed State.

I likewise send you a Copy of a Letter from Mr. Hooper to me, enclosing one from Mr. Tilghman, respecting [Mr.?] Penn's Western Boundary, which I think of Consequence [torn] Boundary

1. For WF's earlier complaint about Hillsborough's inconsistency see the annotation of BF to WF above, Oct. 7. Richard Jackson and Grey Cooper, respectively counsel for the Board of Trade and secretary to the Treasury, should have known well what was going on, as should Gov. Thomas Pownall, whose brother was secretary of the Board of Trade.

2. The relevant portion of the Evans map of 1755 is reproduced in Gipson, *British Empire*, IV, facing 188. What "Extent of Country" was WF talking about? If he meant everything north of the Virginia border projected westward, not even a small tract would have remained for the Company. He must therefore have known, it seems to us, that that grandiose scheme of projection had died aborning and that the Lochaber line had been accepted, but must not have known that the latter had been redrawn by Donelson in 1771. Only the Lochaber line, to the east of and roughly parallel to the border of the Walpole grant, left a tract to the Company.

certainly ought to be, if we may ju[dge by the] Words of the Charter, a *crooked Line* according to the *Curves of the Delaware*; and such a Line, as it happens, will be *most advantageous* to the Proprietors of the new Colony; at least in the Opinion of Mr. *Hooper*, who has taken a great deal of Pains in his Enquiries, in hopes of being the Surveyor General.³ It was him I recommended to you to propose for that Office, and not Mr. *Hutchins*, as you seem by your Letter to understand. The latter is an Officer in the Regulars at Pensacola.⁴

I write this in a Hurry, in hopes of reaching Capt. Sutton, who I hear is to leave Philadelphia Tomorrow. By Capt. Falconer I shall answer all your Letters fully. In the mean Time, I am, as ever, Honoured Sir, Your dutiful Son   WM: FRANKLIN

P.S. Pray observe the Caution with regard to Mr. Tilghman's Letter, as requested by Mr. Hooper.

Addressed: To | Dr Franklin | Craven Street | London

3. James Tilghman, the father of Washington's aide-de-camp, was secretary of the Penns' land office. Robert Lettis Hooper (d. 1797), a future deputy quartermaster general of the Continental army, had been a surveyor in western Pennsylvania for George Croghan and WF. As early as February, 1771, according to Hooper, WF had promised to help him become surveyor general of the new government on the Ohio; later that year the Governor had commissioned him to survey the grant. How much he covered is not clear; he probably surveyed the borders, and certainly concentrated on the panhandle between the Pennsylvania frontier and the Ohio. See James Sullivan *et al.*, eds., *The Papers of Sir William Johnson* (14 vols., Albany, 1921–65), VII, 1132–3; VIII, 294; Charles H. Hart, ed., "Letters from William Franklin to William Strahan," *PMHB*, XXXV (1911), 450; Hooper to WF, [March, 1772,] APS; Bache to BF below, Nov. 3. For the two interpretations of the western Pennsylvania border—whether it ran straight north or reproduced the contours of the Delaware—see above, p. 123 n. The second interpretation would have added considerably to the lands claimed by Virginians and by the Walpole Company.

4. For Thomas Hutchins see BF to Galloway above, Feb. 6. The army engineer was in Philadelphia at the end of 1771 and in Pensacola by the following March. See the introduction by Frederick C. Hicks to the reprint of Hutchins' *A Topographical Description of Virginia...* (Cleveland, 1904), pp. 19–20.

To William Hunter
ALS: Royal College of Surgeons

The partnership between Dr. William Hunter and Polly Hewson's husband was dissolved, after much recrimination, during the winter of 1771–72. Dr. Hunter had stipulated that the "preparations," in other words the demonstration material for the anatomy course that they had been giving jointly, should remain his sole property. But in the summer of 1772 the irascible Doctor relented somewhat: although he could not bring himself to give the material to Hewson directly, he did give it to Franklin, who assumed that it was meant for Polly's husband.[5] Hunter then seems to have repented of his generosity; at least he queried Franklin about what he had done with the gift, and evoked this answer.

Sir,   Cravenstreet, Oct. 30. 1772

I should sooner have answered your Questions but that in the Confusion of my Papers, occasioned by removing to another House, I could not readily find the Memorandums I had made during the unpleasant Time in which, as a common Friend, I was obliged to hear your and Mr. Hewson's mutual Complaints. I have now found one of those Memorandums, dated Augt. 23, 1771 the same which I afterwards read to you, containing your Idea as then express'd of the Terms on which you were to proceed together. The following is an Extract from it....[6]
⟨He expects Hewson to continue, while they are associated, to make preparations at Hunter's direction and expense and, once these are done, others of his own if he wishes; all that are made become Hunter's property, to dispose of as he pleases.⟩
Some time last Summer, after your Parting, you wrote me a Note, which I cannot at present find,[7] but I think the Purport of it was, that you had some Preparations which you could spare and were dispos'd to give me, desiring I would call and look at them; I did so, and accepted them. I apprehended it to be your Supposition in giving them to me, that as I had no Use for them, I should probably give them to Mr. Hewson, which I immediately did. Having said this, I must add, in Justice likewise to Mr. Hewson, that his

5. See above, XVIII, 211; Hunter to BF, end of July, 1772.
6. The extract has already been printed under its date: XVIII, 211.
7. The note eventually turned up, and is that just cited at the end of July. "Your Parting" refers to the end of the Hunter-Hewson partnership.

Conception of the original Agreement between you was, that he had a Right to make such Preparations for himself, your Business and the common Interest of the Partnership not being neglected. Here you had differ'd in Opinion; but came to a kind of Compromise express'd in a Paper that I handed between you, a Copy of which I have obtain'd from Mr. Hewson to send you. I am, Sir, Your most obedient and most humble Servant

B FRANKLIN

Dr Hunter

From William Marshall[8] ALS: Library of Congress

Sir.   Philadelphia October 30th. 1772

I beg leave to lay before you an affair very interesting to all in our Communion and to some thousands of other religious denominations in this extensive province. Ten petitions from sundry parts of the province were laid before our Legislative body last winter Setting forth the complication of grievances we labour under arising from our Conscientious Scruples about the mode of swearing by kissing the Gospels; and praying for an indulgence in swearing by an uplifted right hand the mode practised in Scotland Holland and Germany where the most of the Scruplers did originally come from.

The prayer of our Petitions has been granted with the greatest unanimity.[9] Our petitions were enforced by sundry others from persons who tho they did not scruple the common mode themselves yet saw the difficulty we laboured under did pray for this indulgence to us as being for the good of the community; many of this last class of Petitioners were magistrates and other persons in some of the most important Stations in the Colony.

8. The Rev. William Marshall (c. 1740–1802) was a Scot, sent to Pennsylvania in 1763 as a missionary of the Anti-Burgher Associate Synod of Scotland. In 1769 he moved to Philadelphia, where in 1771 his congregation built a church in Spruce Street. A decade later he was involved in acute controversy with his flock, which split apart. One faction denied him the pulpit; the other seceded with him, and built a new church on Walnut Street. William B. Sprague, *Annals of the American Pulpit* (9 vols., New York, 1859[–73]), IX, pt. 3, 7–15.
9. For the Pennsylvania act see BF to Rush above, Aug. 22.

The mode of swearing by lifting up the hand and swearing by Almighty God is innocent in itself and in our opinion most agreable to his word the only rule of faith and manners among protestants; it is influential upon the wellfare of Government and agreable to the British Constitution particularly the Constitution of this highly favoured Colony which breathes so much tenderness to the Sacred rights of Conscience and is absolutely inimical to evry species of persecution for Conscience sake. It has been always used in Scotland and the New England Colonies without any inconvenience; Yea it is practised by our Sovereigns themselves when they take the Coronation oath for the protestant Establishment in North Britain pursuant to the union. It was allowed by Judges in England to be valid in the case of some Scots men who were called thither to give Evidence against the Rebels after the last Rebellion.[10]

We can assure you Sir that our Scruples about kissing the Gospels in swearing do not arise from the want of Loyalty to our Soveregn king George or regard to the Laws of our Country, we can produce as triumphant Evidence of our Loyalty as any of our fellow subjects, nor from an affection of Novelty (for the mode now allowed us is not new), far less from any stubborness of Temper, but from a conscientious persuasion that lifting up the hand and swearing by God is most agreable to his revealed will in that solemn act of adoration. This is an affair very interesting to us and our posterity since it affects our religious Liberty and so nearly concerns our conscience which is exempted from human jurisdiction.

Tho' some may view our conscientious scruples as groundless they are however invincible while we are not possessd of evidence that this is the case. We hope they will not be deemd a whimsical novelty, or having a tendency to injure Government by weaking the Solemnity of an oath or opning a door for unnecessary innovations; it is the very opposite to these we aim at. The weaknesses of subjects when not injurious to the interests of Community are

10. In the summer of 1746, after the collapse of the Jacobite rebellion, a crowd of Scottish prisoners was indicted at Carlisle. Witnesses against them refused to swear in the form prescribed by English law, and after some delay the judges permitted them to take the oath according to the Scots form. *Gent. Mag.*, XVI (1746), 494.

tenderly provided for in our excellent Constitution. Moreover the mode of swearing by kissing the Gospels is not essential to the oath but is a circumstance which may be dispensed with when the investigation of Truth renders it necessary. The indulgence now granted us and which only wants the royal assent to render it permanent is not so much as has been granted to others which makes us hope that we shall be successfull. Quakers Menonists and Moravians are allowed the affirmation in lieu of an oath and Jews to swear by the Pentateuch, we are his majesty's natural born subjects who only want the mode which takes [place?] already in different parts of the British Empire and in no place can indulgences of this kind be granted with greater propriety than in Pennsylvania; This Dr. Franklin well knows.

If this Law now made in our favour shall be reversed, I tremble to paint the consequences then upwards of six thousand sober and industrious inhabitants of this province must be reduced to a very disstressing alternative; Either they must violate the sacred rights of Conscience, or suffer in their persons and properties and be debarred from serving their Country in ev'ry case where an oath is required, an alternative very opposite to that Constitution erected by the great Sir William Penn and maintaind hither to inviolate by his Illustrious posterity yea to that Spirit which we found breathing in our legislative body when we laid our case before them. The speaker of the house and sundry of the Representives of this County pushd the affair in our favour with all the ardor as if it had been in behalf of Quakers. Our rising Community must be nipt in the bud if the royal assent is denied and that yoke of superstition wreathed again about our necks. May it therefore please you Sir to use your influence With our Gracious sovereign king George and the members of his honourable privy Council to prevent this Law made in our favour from being repealed and thereby you will more eminently serve a religious denomination, than in any other earthly concern. In their name I now address you, and having nothing more to add but best wishes for your health and prosperity, and that I am Sir your most obedient most humble Servant.   WILLIAM MARSHALL.

If you are pleased to favour me with a Letter informing me how this matter that we are so anxious about: and so impatient to know the fate of, direct to, minister to the Scotch presbyterian Cong. in Philada. The members of our Presbytery who are six in number in this Province (and all of us Scotch-men) would have all signd this letter could it have suited to waite till our next meeting: for we are so far sccaterd that it is difficult to meet together frequently and I apprehended no time was to be lost in applying as above. If money be necessary in pursuance of this affair please to inform us (as we are quite ignorant of affairs of this nature) and it shall be remitted.

Endorsed: Revd Mr Marshall about the Mode of Swearing. Oct 30. 72

To Jacques Barbeu-Dubourg

ALS (draft; incomplete): American Philosophical Society

[Early November, 1772[1]]

[*First part missing*] in this Foggy Climate and smoaky City without too much Hazard, I will do my utmost when she comes to promote her Interest.[2]

It is true that many English People go to Paris, but I do not often know of their going, and therefore must sometimes make use of the Post, or wait long for an Opportunity of Writing to you.[3]

About two Weeks since when I was in the Country a Letter from you was left at my House, which by its Date might have come round by the Way of China, for it is of May 27, 1771. There were left with it another Letter for Dr. Rush, and two Parcels of the Ephemerides, one for him the other for me, containing nine Books each. The Person who left them said he would call again to explain to me the Reason of their being so long detain'd; but he

1. The letter is in answer to one of Oct. 28 from Dubourg, and another received about a fortnight earlier during BF's absence in the country, which ended about Oct. 24: BF to WF below, Nov. 3. In a sentence deleted from this draft BF promised Dubourg another letter soon, which was doubtless the one from which an extract is printed below under Nov. 12.

2. He is answering Dubourg's letter above of Oct. 28, which referred to Mlle. Biheron's impending trip to London.

3. Here and in what follows BF is touching on subjects raised in Dubourg's letter (above, XVIII, 110–13) that "might have come round by Way of China."

has not since called; and I have no Conception where they can possibly have been all this time. My Set is now compleat except Tom. XII. for the Year 1771. my last is Tom. III of the Sixth Year.

Salute Mad. Dubourg most affectionately in my Behalf, with Madelle. Biheron, and our other Friends. My best Wishes attend you all. I promise myself the Happiness of seeing them and you once more; for I think of returning home (when I do return) thro' France and Italy, taking my Passage at Leghorn in some of our Ships that go thither with Corn, or Fish. I am ever, my dear Friend, with the sincerest Esteem, Your most obedient humble Servant   B FRANKLIN

The Code is now printed as far as Chap. LXXXVI, *Intérêts generaux*. I inclose a Leaf, as a Specimen of the Type.[4]

To William Alexander

ALS (letterbook draft): Library of Congress

My Lord,   London, Nov. 3. 1772
On my Return to Town I found your Favour, with the Schemes of your Lottery,[5] to which I wish Success, and besides ordering some Tickets for my self, I have spoken well of it on every Occasion; but I find little Inclination among my Acquaintance to engage in Lotteries at such a Distance, and one cannot be very open in promoting them, it being contrary to express Acts of Parliament, as well as offensive to Administration here, which would avail itself of all that is to be gain'd that Way.[6] With great and sincere Esteem, I am, My Lord, Your Lordship's most obedient and most humble Servant   B F

Lord Stirling,

4. For BF's printing of the *Petit code* see Dubourg's letter to him below, Nov. 28.

5. See above, June 30.

6. Lotteries were illegal in Britain unless authorized by act of Parliament. But the difficulty in suppressing them, which BF suggests between the lines, is apparent from the succession of statutes on the subject, among which were 5 Geo. I c. 9, 8 Geo. I c. 2, and 12 Geo. II c. 28. For the attitude of the government toward the colonial lotteries see John S. Ezell, *Fortune's Merry Wheel: the Lottery in America* (Cambridge, Mass., 1960), pp. 47–50.

To Alexander Colden

ALS (letterbook draft): Library of Congress

Dear Sir,   London, Nov. 3. 1772

Inclos'd I return to you Mackie's Bill on Molleson for £294. 5s. 2d. with a Protest; the same being refus'd Payment for want of Effects.[7]

The Packet of last Month is not yet arriv'd. I hope she will bring the Accounts so long expected.[8] I am, Dear Sir, Your most obedient humble Servant   B FRANKLIN

Mr Alexr. Colden.

To John Foxcroft

ALS (letterbook draft): Library of Congress

Dear Sir,   London, Nov. 3. 1772

I received your Favour of June 22d per Mr. Finlay, and shall be glad of an Opportunity of rendring him any Service on your Recommendation. There does not at present seem to be any Disposition of the Board to appoint a Riding Surveyor, nor does Mr. Finlay seem desirous of such an Employment.[9] Every thing at the Office remains as when I last wrote, only the Impatience for the Accounts seems increasing. I hope they are in the October Packet now soon expected, agreable to Mr. Colden's last Promises.[1]

7. See above, BF to Colden, Oct. 7; Mary Hewson to BF, Oct. 22. BF is saying that Mackie had exhausted his credit with Molleson.

8. If the accounts did not come by that packet, BF expected Colden to be dismissed: to Foxcroft above, Oct. 7.

9. The power of decision rested with Anthony Todd, the secretary of the Post Office. The Postmasters General attended occasional meetings of their Board, which was largely a ratifying body; most business was done at frequent meetings of senior officials, called Ordinary Boards, which were presided over and dominated by the secretary. Kenneth Ellis, *The Post Office in the Eighteenth Century: a Study in Administrative History* (London, 1958), pp. 16–17, 24–5. In this particular case both the Board and Hugh Finlay changed their minds: he was appointed within the month. BF to John Foxcroft below, Dec. 2.

1. The accounts arrived on the packet but were unacceptable; see *ibid.*, the letter preceding this one, and below, BF to Foxcroft, Nov. 19; to Colden, Dec. 2.

I spent a Fortnight lately at West Wyecomb, with our good Master Lord Le Despencer, and left him well.[2]

The Boards have begun to act again, and I hope our Ohio Business will again go forward.[3] My Love to my Daughter, concludes from Your affectionate Friend and humble Servant

B F

Mr Foxcroft

To William Franklin

ALS (letterbook draft): Library of Congress

Dear Son,   London, Nov. 3[-4]. 1772

I wrote to you per the October Packet, and have not since had any Line from you. I spent 16 Days at Lord Le Despencer's most agreably, and return'd in good Health and Spirits. Lord Dartmouth came to town last Week, and had his first Levee on Wednesday, at which I attended. He receiv'd me very politely in his Room, only Secy. Pownal present; expressing some Regret that he happened to be from home when I was near him in the Country, where he had hop'd for the Pleasure of seeing me, &c.[4] I said I was happy to see his Lordship in his present Situation, in which for the good of both Countries I hoped he would long continue; and I begg'd Leave to recommend my Son to his Protection, who, says I, is one of your Governor's in America. The Secy. then put in, *And a very good Governor he is*. Yes, says my Lord, he has been a good Governor, and has kept his Province in good Order, during Times of Difficulty. I then said, that I came at present only to pay

2. For BF's visit to the Postmaster General see Mary Hewson to BF above, Oct. 22.

3. On Nov. 2 the Board of Trade received an order, pursuant to the Privy Council's action on Aug. 14, to report on the terms of the Walpole grant and to draw up plans for civil government in the vast tract; but the report was not forthcoming until May, 1773. *Board of Trade Jour.*, 1768–75, pp. 316, 351–2, 354, 356.

4. John Pownall, an inheritance from Hillsborough, was both undersecretary of the American Department and secretary to the Board of Trade. BF had been in Birmingham in early July; Dartmouth's country estate, Sandwell Park, was nearby in Staffordshire.

my Respects, and should wait on his Lordship another Day on Business; to which he said he should always be ready to hear me and glad to see me. I shall attend his Levee again to day, on some N England Affairs, and hope we may now go on more smoothly;[5] but Time will show. As the Boards are met again, the Ohio Affair will again be put forward as soon as Mr. Walpole comes to [Town?], who went lately into Norfolk. I am almost settled in my new Apartment; but Removing, and sorting my Papers and placing my Books and things has been a troublesome Jobb.[6] I am amaz'd to see how Books have grown upon me since my Return to England. I brought none with me, and have now a Roomfull; many collected in Germany, Holland and France; and consisting chiefly of such as contain Knowledge that may hereafter be useful to America. My Love to Betsey, concludes at present from Your affectionate Father   B FRANKLIN

Postscript to W F.

Nov. 4 I was this Day again at Lord Dartmouth's Levee who show'd me particular Respect in sending for me out of the Crowd long before my Turn, and apologizing for having kept me so long by Means of Mr. Maseres's detaining him on Canada Affairs.[7] He receiv'd my Business too very properly not making any Objection to my Acting as Agent for the Massachusetts without the Governors Approbation of my Appointment as his Predecessor had done. Whether this will continue or not is now the Question; for as he has the same Secretaries, Pownall and Knox, probably they will remind him of the later Measures, and prompt him to continue them.[8]

5. BF's business was to present the petition from Massachusetts against the Governor's being paid his salary from Whitehall. See Cushing to BF above, July 15, and BF to Cushing below, Nov. 4.

6. See BF to DF below, Nov. 4.

7. For those affairs see Maseres to BF above, June 17.

8. The long controversy, often mentioned in the previous volume, over BF's status as agent of the Massachusetts House had quieted after Hillsborough's resignation; and BF no longer talked, as he had before that event, of refusing to continue. See his letter to WF above, Jan. 30.

To Peter Timothy ALS (letterbook draft): Library of Congress

Dear Sir, London, Nov. 3. 1772

I received yours of Aug. 24. by Capt. Vanderhorst, to whom I should willingly have shown any Civilities in my Power, but I being gouty of late seldom go into the City, and he has not called on me since he delivered your Letter. I am sorry you talk of leaving off your Business with a View of getting some Post.[9] It is so difficult a matter to obtain any thing of the kind, that I think to leave a good Trade in hopes of an Office, is quitting a Certainty for an Uncertainty, and losing Substance for Shadow. I have known so many here dangling and soliciting Years for Places, till they were reduc'd to the lowest Poverty and Distress, that I cannot but pity a Man who begins to turn his Thoughts that way: The Proverb says, *He who has a Trade has an Office of Profit and Honour*;[1] because he does not hold it during any other Man's Pleasure, and it affords him honest Subsistence with Independence. I hope therefore you will alter your mind and go on with your Business. I assure you it is not in my Power to procure you that Post you mention or any other, whatever my Wishes may be for your Prosperity. I am now thought here too much an American to have any Interest of the kind.

You have done me Honour in giving a Son my Name. I wish he may live to be an Honour and Comfort to you. With Compliments to Mrs. Timothy, I am ever, Dear Sir, Your faithful and most obedient Servant   B F.

Mr Timothy

To Jonathan Williams, Sr.

ALS (letterbook draft): Library of Congress

Dear Cousin, London, Nov. 3. 1772

My Sister, to whom I have not now time to write, acquainted me in her last Letter, that there was some Expectation her

9. The various matters that BF discusses in this letter are explained in the one from Timothy to which he is replying.
1. *Poor Richard*: above, VI, 321.

Daughter would soon be married with her Consent. If that should take Place, my Request is, that you would lay out the Sum of fifty Pounds, lawful Money, in Bedding or such other Furniture as my Sister shall think proper, to be given the new-married Couple towards Housekeeping, with my best Wishes: And charge that Sum to my Account.[2] I can now only add that I am ever Yours most affectionately   B FRANKLIN

Mr Jonathan Williams,

From Richard Bache   ALS: American Philosophical Society

Dear and Honoured sir   Philad[elphia, Nov. 3, 1772[3]]
     I have to acknowledge Receipt [of your letter of?] 22 August per Falconer. Captain Falconer has left his Ship, as she is going to Carolina for a Frieght of Rice, he purposes staying at Home this Winter.[4]
     At the Request of Mr. Baynton, I send you an Extract of a Letter from Mr. Hooper a surveyor, to him, respecting the Western Boundary of this Province &c. with his sentiments thereon. Also a number of Remarks of Mr. Morgan, which may be usefull to the Proprietors of the new Colony (should it take Place) in regard to the Mode of Settlement, granting of Land &c.[5] I would have had Mr. Baynton to have sent them himself, but he [was afraid?] of being troublesome, therefore has put the Matter upon me. I cant help mentioning one thing to you, as a Matter [that?] will greatly impede the Settlement of the new Colony, and which has already alarmed and discouraged many People from setling to the Westward, and that is, the demolishing and abandoning, Fort Pitt, for which, it is said, Orders are issued. I am told that Governor Penn has applied to General Gage for a Respite of these Orders, 'till

2. Jane Mecom's daughter Jane (Jenny) married Peter Collas in the following March; she acknowledged the wedding present in a letter to BF below, Jan. 9, 1773.
     3. BF referred to the letter by date in his reply below, Feb. 3, 1773.
     4. See Falconer to BF below, Nov. 15.
     5. John Baynton and George Morgan were Samuel Wharton's partners; see above, respectively, XI, 187 n; XIII, 400 n. For Robert L. Hooper, Croghan's surveyor, see WF to BF above, Oct. 29.

[he can hear again from?] Home respecting the Matter.[6] If so [torn] the Proprietors of the new Colony to back [torn] that Pitsburg may be continued a Garrison Town.

My Mother, Sally and Ben are all well, they join in love to yourself, Mrs. Stevenson, Mrs. Hewson &c. with Dear sir Your truly Affectionate son   RICHD: BACHE

Permit me to congratulate you on your late honorary Appointment in France.[7]

Dr. Franklin

To Thomas Cushing

> ALS (letterbook draft): Library of Congress; AL (copy): Public Record Office

Sir,   London, Nov. 4. 1772

Lord Dartmouth our new American Minister came to Town last Week, and held his first Levee on Wednesday, when I paid my Respects, acquainting him at the same time that I should in a few Days wait upon him on Business from Boston, which I have accordingly since done and have put your Petition to the King into his Hands, that being the regular Course.[8] His Lordship receiv'd me very obligingly, and made no Objection to my acting as Agent without an Appointment assented to by the Governor, as his Predecessor had done; so that I hope Business is getting into better Train.[9] I shall use my best Endeavours in supporting the Petition,

6. Gage had corresponded with Lord Hillsborough during the winter of 1771–72 about abandoning Fort Pitt, and in the following August ordered it evacuated. In late October Lieut. Gov. Penn asked him to leave part of the garrison until the Assembly could provide for raising provincial troops to replace the regulars. Gage acquiesced, but his countermanding order arrived too late; in early January, 1773, the soldiers of the garrison showed up in Philadelphia. Carter, ed., *Gage Correspondence*, I, 319, 335, 341, 344; II, 138.

7. For BF's election to the Académie royale des sciences see above, the second extract from BF to WF, Aug. 19, and BF to de la Vrillière, Sept. 4; below, BF to the Académie, Nov. 16.

8. For the petition about the Governor's salary see Cushing's letter above, July 15, and BF's reply, Sept. 3, as well as BF's letter below of Dec. 2.

9. For Hillsborough's objection to BF's status see above, XVIII, 9–16, 153 n, 242 n, and the Cushing letter just cited. Dartmouth, unlike his predecessor,

and write to you again and more fully by the next Ship to Boston.[1]
In the mean time I remain with great Respect, Sir, Your most
obedient and most humble Servant   B Franklin

Mr Cushing

To Deborah Franklin

ALS (letterbook draft): American Philosophical Society

My dear Child,   London, Nov. 4. 1772
I have been much in the Country this Summer, at the Houses of
different Friends, and am now returned in good Health, Thanks
to God. We are removed to a more convenient House in the same
Street, Mrs. Stevenson having accommodated her Son-in-Law
with that we lived in. The Removing has been a troublesome
Affair, but is now over.[2] My Love to our Children and Grandson.
Tell our good Neighbour Miss Haddock, that her Silk is done, and
shall be sent by the first Ship directly to Philadelphia.[3] I am ever,
my Dear Debby, Your affectionate Husband   B Franklin

The Managers of the Pennsylvania Hospital to Franklin, David Barclay, and John Fothergill

Minutebook copy: Pennsylvania Hospital, Philadelphia

Pennsylvania Hospital 11 Mo. 4th.[–7] 1772
Esteemed Friends
This accompanies duplicate of our last since which we have re-
ceived Benja. Franklin's favour of the [*blank*].[4]

---

worked for some time with BF as if he were a duly constituted agent; see
subsequent volumes. The fact that the legal question remained unresolved
does not seem to have disturbed BF, but it did Bollan; see the latter's comments to the Massachusetts Council in Mass. Arch., XXII, 586, and in 6 Mass.
Hist. Soc. *Coll.*, IX, 316–17.

1. See his letter below, Dec. 2.
2. The move was troublesome for Mrs. Stevenson but not for BF: he escaped
to Lord Le Despencer's at West Wycombe until the domestic crisis was over.
Above, BF to WF, Oct. 7, and Mary Hewson to BF, Oct. 22.
3. BF changed his mind; see his letter to DF below, Nov. 19.
4. See above, their letter of Oct. 20 and BF's of Aug. 28.

In pursuance of what we proposed, we have since drawn on you the following Bills at thirty days sight vizt.

No. 1 payable to James Pearson for £100.
    2 ditto to ditto   100.
    3 ditto to ditto   175.   £375.
    4 ditto to Joseph King sign'd by all ⎫
      the same as above Except Israel ⎬   200.
    Pemberton   ⎭
    5 ditto to John Bull   500.
    6 ditto to ditto   300.
    7 ditto to ditto   250.
    8 ditto to ditto   200.
    9 ditto to ditto   150.
   10 ditto to ditto   200.
   11 ditto to ditto   275.   1875.
                              £2450. Sterling

And we intend in a few day to draw for £550. more, having the opportunity of selling the Bills at 60 per Cent Exchange, and of placing the Money on Interest at 6 per Cent, with Land Security.

We hope you will have the money in your hands before the Bills appear and become due, but that you may not be subjected to any inconvenience or our fund to any disadvantage in the Sale of the Stock, we have by the Tenor of the Bills contracted that they shall not be liable to any further damage, than the Payment of our Lawfull Interest after they become due, untill it suits you to discharge them. The Bills are printed in the like manner and Terms with the blank herein Inclosed. We are with much Respect Your asssured Friends[5]

                                   11 Mo. 7th. 1772

We have further drawn on you Two Setts Bills as follows.

One Sett N. 12 payable to Cornelius Corsen for £200.
    ditto 13 ditto to ditto   for   200.
                              £400. Sterling[6]

5. The minutes record that all the Managers present were signers. They were much the same group listed in the letter to BF above, Oct. 20; but Cox, Jones, and Lewis had disappeared, and been replaced by James Pemberton and Thomas Mifflin, neither of whom needs introduction.

6. The Managers were investing part of their recent windfall in 6% land mortgages to Pearson, King, Bull, and Corsen, who received bills of ex-

From John Bartram

ALS: Historical Society of Pennsylvania

My dear ould worthy Friend   November the 11th. 1772

I have here before me thy kind letter of august 22 1772. I sowed the Rhubarb seed in two places the one in the sun the other in A shady cool place. That which was in the cool place growed the leaves was as big as the palm of my hand but not palmated perhaps it may be next year.

The Tarnup seed came up well growed large and tasted well and is by some admired and expects it may be A fine improvement.

I here no more of the medal from Edenboro nor from Dr. Hope.[7]

---

change in sterling in the amounts listed. The sample bill enclosed, dated Oct. 31 (Pa. Hospital Minutebook), was at thirty days' sight but, in lieu of damages, carried 6% interest thereafter until discharged. This provision did indeed save BF from "inconvenience"; without it he would have been liable, if the bill had been protested at the end of the thirty days, to heavy costs and even to arrest. For the procedure involved see Wyndham Beawes, *Lex Mercatoria Rediviva; Or, the Merchant's Directory*... (London, 1752), pp. 415, 444.

The mortgager first mentioned was James Pearson (1735–1813), a Philadelphia carpenter and builder and long a manager of the Carpenters' Company; see J. Granville Leach, "The Record of Some Residents in the Vicinity of Middle Ferry, Philadelphia...," Geneal. Soc. of Pa. *Pub.*, IX (1924–26), 56–7. Joseph King was probably the early member of the Library Company and contributor to the Hospital (above, II, 347; V, 320, 328), who was serving as its treasurer at the time of his death; see the Managers to BF below, Oct. 29, 1773. John Bull (1730–1824) lived in Limerick, Montgomery County, and was for a time a justice of the county court; he owned an extensive tract of land that he offered as part of the security for his mortgage. Theodore W. Bean, ed., *History of Montgomery County* (Philadelphia, 1884), pp. 756, 1005; Pa. Hospital Minutebook, Nov. 3, 1772; see also William H. Egle, "The Constitutional Convention of 1776...," *PMHB*, III (1879), 197. Cornelius Corsen was one of two, father or son. The father (1714–74) was a large landholder in Northampton township; the son (b. 1751), who had a sizable tract in Bucks County, later served in the War of Independence. Orville Corson, *Three Hundred Years with the Corson Families in America*... (2 vols., [Burlington, Vt.], 1939), I, 113–17, 130.

The suggestion that the money be invested in securities, particularly land, seems to have come from the man who had been the prime mover in obtaining the funds in the first place, Dr. Fothergill. See his letter of Aug. 29, 1772, to James Pemberton in Betsy C. Corner and Christopher C. Booth, eds., *Chain of Friendship: Selected Letters of Dr. John Fothergill of London, 1735–1780* (Cambridge, Mass., 1971), p. 388.

7. See above, John Hope to BF, Jan. 23, and BF to Bartram, Aug. 22.

We have had several bright Arora Borealis last summer and in the heat of harvest which is very uncommon at that season and we had two slight shoks of an earthquake very little thunder or rain but much hail in several parts distant from Philadelphia.

A late cold dry spring, temperate summer, and now A warm dry fall very few troubled with agues some bad nervous fevers but not very mortal but the favourablest Measels I ever knew and as yet the slowest in spreading. Perhaps when cold weather approaceth it may be more severe and spread more. I remain dear friend with much love and respect thy sincearly wellwisher as formerly

JOHN BARTRAM

PS can hardy see to write or read.

To Jacques Barbeu-Dubourg

Translated extract: printed in Jacques Barbeu-Dubourg, ed., *Œuvres de M. Franklin*... (2 vols., Paris, 1773), II, 199.[8]

[November 12–16, 1772[9]]

Je suis persuadé, comme vous, que le charbon de terre est d'origine végétale, et qu'il a été formé vers la surface de la terre;[1] mais comme de précédentes convulsions l'avoient enterré fort avant en plusieurs endroits, et recouvert de plusieurs couches fort épaisses, nous avons obligation aux convulsions suivantes d'avoir remis sous nos yeux les extrêmités des lits de charbon, afin de nous mettre à portée d'y fouiller. Je visitai l'été dernier une grande mine de charbon de terre à Whitehaven dans le Cumberland; et en suivant la veine, et descendant peu-à-peu vers la mer, je parvins jusqu'au-dessous de l'océan, où le niveau de sa surface étoit à plus de 80 brasses au-dessus de ma tête;[2] et les mineurs m'assurerent que leurs ouvrages s'avançoient jusqu'à quelques milles au-delà, en descendant toujours par degrés au-dessous de la mer. La pierre d'ardoise qui forme le toit de la mine de charbon, est empreinte en

8. For an English retranslation see Smyth, *Writings*, V, 552–3.
9. The extract is clearly from the missing letter of these dates that Dubourg acknowledged in his reply below, Nov. 28.
1. See Dubourg to BF above, Oct. 28.
2. We have changed the depth from 800 fathoms, which was Dubourg's error. BF pointed it out in his letter to him below, June 29, 1773, and it was noted in the corrigenda of the *Œuvres*. But it remained in the text, and in the retranslation that later editors printed.

plusieurs endroits de feuilles et de branches de fougeres, qui
croissoient sans doute à la surface, lorsque l'ardoise étoit encore
dans un état de sable sur les bords de la mer. Ainsi il paroît que ce
charbon a souffert un affaissement prodigieux.

From Frederik van Westerholt[3]

ALS: American Philosophical Society

Monsieur,   Hacforth, ce 12 Nov. 1772
   La lecture de votre projet d'un voyage par Souscription pour
porter les commodités de la vie et tous nos avantages et jouis-
sances Européennes aux contrées éloignées qui en sont privées,[4]
que j'ai trouvé traduit litteralement dans le Tome Second des
Ephemerides du Citoyen de cette année 1772, qui ne m'est parvenue
que depuis quelques heures, ma tellement frappé d'admiration,
que saisit de votre esprit de bienveillance universelle je n'ai pu
resister a la tentation de profiter de la permission que vous avez
bien voulu annoncer a toutes les personnes qui desirent favoriser
votre projet louable et fraternel de vous communiquer leur sentiment, ainsi permettez, Monsieur, que quoique je n'ai pas l'avantage d'être *Anglois*, d'être Citoyen de votre illustre et respectable
Nation a qui seul il semble que vous daigné vous addresser pour
pouvoir cooperer a vos belles actions, permettés que j'ai l'honneur de vous representer que le bien qui doit en resulter infaillible-
ment sur toutes les nations de l'univers leur donne en quelque
façon droit de vous offrir leur services, et de pretendre contribuer
de leurs moyens a vos louables desseins, que quoique je suis de la
Province de Gueldre, une des Provinces Unies des Pays-Bas, ou
les richesses ne peuvent deborder comme chez vous en Angleterre, que j'ai d'ailleurs le malheur d'être un pauvre Gentilhomme
Campagnard, oberée et chargé d'une grande famille d'enfants,
qu'étant cependant un de ceux qui pensent qu'il est de leur devoir

---

3. For a few uninformative biographical details about this Dutch baron,
Frederik Borchard Lodewijk van Westerholt (1726–75), see *Nederland's
Adelsboek*, XLVI (1953), 334–5. We know little more about him than BF did,
but this letter shows that he was a genuine if obscure devotee of the Enlighten-
ment.
4. See above, XVIII, 214.

de demander au ciel leur pain quotidien et les autres bénédictions divines, pensent aussi qu'il est également de leur devoir de montrer leur gratitude envers leur grand bienfaiteur de communiquer cordialement pour autant qu'ils en ont reçus ces mêmes bienfaits sur ces autres enfans.

Que quoiqu'un pauvre ne laisse pas d'être charitable en n'offrant que son obole,[5] puisque Dieu l'a destiné de vivre en Société il a droit de s'unir a la grande chaine de Bienfaits reciproque, que Dieu a formé pour le bonheur du monde, qui doit réunir les hommes de tous les partis, de toutes les religions; que c'est par elles qu'il a droit de tenir a ses voisins, et a sa patrie. Que puisque c'est de l'utilité des actions privées, et multipliées que nait l'utilité publique, que c'est a elle que tout doit se rapporter; que c'est pour elle que l'intérêt bien entendu travaille; que c'est dans l'avantage de tous que chaque Citoyen trouve le sien propre que le bien qu'on fait au monde augmente chacun sa part. Ces antiques vérités, jamais peut-être assez bien senties, me persuadent que quoique pauvre j'ai droit de m'associer avec mon obole a la grande société, que je ne sauroit mieux employer quatre ducats d'Hollande[6] que j'espère vous ne mépriserez pas, car si tous les coeurs sensible de l'Europe oberée en faisoit de même, vous vous trouverez, Monsieur, Amiral de la plus belle flotte qui jamais a été equipée, infiniment plus respectable que la detestable Armado Espagnole, et plus nombreux que les vaisseaux de transport des Croisades. Ainsi je vous prie faite moi l'honneur, Monsieur, de me faire savoir à mon addresse ci-joint par quel canal je pourroit faire remettre franco a Amsterdam mes quatre oboles ou quatre ducats d'Hollande pour vous les faire parvenir, quelque peu d'influence que je doive avoir, permetté qu'un coeur sensible se berce dans la pauvreté, que peut-être arrivera-t'il qu'il touchera quelque roue, selon Pope, dont l'effet surpassera ces esperances,[7] qu'il aura en

5. Mark 12: 42–4.
6. Some thirty years later the ducat, a gold coin, was worth 9s. 4d.: Christopher Dubost, *The Elements of Commerce...* (2 vols., London, [1805]), II, 344.
7.   "So man, who here seems principal alone,
          Perhaps acts second to some sphere unknown,
          Touches some wheel, or verges to some goal;
          'Tis but a part we see, and not the whole."
Alexander Pope, *An Essay on Man*, I, 57–60.

attendant l'honneur de votre reponse, le loisir et le bonheur d'y pouvoir joindre, les offrandes de ces amis et fournir ensemble une espèce de directeur, ce qui n'est cependant pas de notre ambition. Soyez assuré, Monsieur, que personne n'est avec plus d'admiration et plus réellement Monsieur, Votre très humble et très obeissant Serviteur   F. DE WESTERHOLT.

Mon addresse est, a Monsieur le Baron de Westerholt, Seigneur de Hacforth, Membre du Corps des Nobles de la Province de Gueldre en Hollande par Zutphen à Hacforth

From Nathaniel Falconer   ALS: American Philosophical Society

Dear Sir,   Philadelphia Novr. 15th. 1772

This serves to acquaint you I have sent you by Captn. Sutton[8] one barrel of Newtown Pippens, one Cask of shell Bark Hickory nutts and two Kegs of bread which I hope will come safe to hand as the ship is going a voyage that was very disagreeable to me. I have concluded to stay at home this Winter, so that I shant have the Pleasure of keeping Christmas with you this year. I was a few days ago at Burlington, and spent some hours with your Son. He read me that part of your Letter where you mention'd receiving my Letter from the Downs for which I return you many thanks for your kind offer.[9] If Mr. Wharton shoud, as I am not like to return to London, say he has not Received any mony on my account which I can hardly think he will Mr. Daniel Mildred who paid the money will at any time make it appear.[1] I am very sorry Sir to give you any trouble about this matter but you know how the matter is and unless your kindness obtain it for me, it is very plain I shall neither get Land or my money back again, your son shew'd me the Claims made by the Virginia Company and

8. James Sutton, master of the *Catherine*, cleared for London a day or two later: *Pa. Gaz.*, Nov. 18, 1772.

9. BF's letter to WF has been lost, but it doubtless contained an assurance that he would advance Falconer money if need be, as the latter had asked when writing from the Downs (above, Sept. 2). BF repeated the assurance in replying to the present letter, but the Captain sold his right to the Whartons. See below, BF to Falconer, Feb. 14, and Falconer to BF, May 13, 1773.

1. See Falconer's letter above, Sept. 2.

his Remarks thereon if their Claime is good the remaining part of the grant will not be worth half the purchas'd money.[2] My best Compliments to Mrs. Stevenson, Mr. and Mrs. Hewson, and Miss Hewson, Sally Franklin and Master Temple. I am Dear Sir, with great Regard Your most humble Servant

NATH FALCONER

Addressed: To / Doctor Franklin / in / Craven Street, Strand. / London / per favor / Cap. Sutton

To the Académie Royale des Sciences[3]

Photograph of ALS: Académie des sciences, Paris

Gentlemen, London, Nov. 16. 1772

A Place among your foreign Members is justly esteemed, by all Europe, the greatest Honour a Man can arrive at in the Republick of Letters: It was therefore with equal Surprize and Satisfaction that I learnt you had condescended to confer that Honour upon me. Be pleased to accept my grateful Acknowledgements, and believe me with the greatest Esteem and Respect, Gentlemen, Your most obliged and most humble Servant B FRANKLIN

Royal Academy of Sciences at Paris.

2. See WF to BF above, Oct. 13, 29.

3. BF had already sent his thanks to de la Vrillière, the President of the Academy: above, Sept. 4. A roster of the membership was published in the *Connoissance des temps, pour l'année commune 1774...* (Paris, 1772), 291–318; in BF's copy he made notes by the names of the eleven members whom he knew. That copy is in the APS, but his marginalia have been mutilated by later trimming. Only one is of major interest: of Lamoignon de Malesherbes he wrote, "A particular Friend, president de la Cour des Aides, fort eloquent, actuellement exilé 1773." The rest of the note appears to say that BF dined with some one at Malesherbes' house, and conversed a good deal with him at Mme. Somebody's in Compiègne in 1769; the last three words are clear. This snbstantiates our conjecture above (XVI, 207 n) that BF's visit to France in 1769 first brought him into touch with the celebrated Frenchman.

From Deborah Franklin

ALS: American Philosophical Society

My Dear Child   November 16 1773 [*i.e.*, 1772[4]]

I did resevef yours by Capt. Folkner but as he dus not Saile to London I have sente to you by Capt. Suttun who was so verey obliging as to Cole to see me two Barrels of apels which I hope will provef good.[5] I Cold not get sume Indea meel and Buck wheet flower but I shall by next opertunety. Salley and the Child is gon up to stay with mrs. Franklin while Billey is to stay sume days in town Mr. Beache is gon up to stay sume days and then returne with Billey when he Cumes to toune and what a taske it is to write a line. Give my love to everey one that knows me our Polley and her Son to Salley Franklin Mrs. Weste and her Sones[6] Love them for me. Mr. Strahan and famely my friend our fine I shold say hes bin verey ill severel week I hold Mr. D Hall severel week I have bin to see him several times I hope he will be spaird for his famely sake and for maney others.[7] I am your Afeckshonet wife   D FRANKLIN

Addressed in another hand: To / Benjamin Franklin / Esq. / London

From a Committee of the Managers of the Philadelphia Silk Filature

LS:[8] American Philosophical Society

Dear Friend   Philadelphia 17th: Novr. 1772

The new Elected Managers of the Filature met last Evening with a View of acknowledging thy late letters but found the Catharine Captain Sutton would depart so suddenly,[9] that there was not Time, and therefore requested us to ask their excuse for the delay. And to forward said Captain Sutton's Bill of Loading for two Trunks of Silk, the Produce of this Year, with a Certificate

---

4. The references to Falconer, Sutton, and David Hall prove that DF mistook the year.

5. BF must have had a surfeit of apples; see Falconer to BF above, Nov. 15.

6. Elizabeth Shewell West, Raphael, and Benjamin, Jr., who was BF's godson. See BF to DF above, Aug. 22.

7. David Hall, BF's old friend and partner, died on Christmas Eve. *DAB*.

8. The letter is not in James's hand; it may be in Morgan's.

9. See Falconer to BF above, Nov. 15.

from our Custom House to recover Bounty. Their request is that thou will Employ our Friend Freeman, in Gracious Street,[1] or any other Person thee may think will transact the business in the best way. Also "The Managers request thy Acceptance of four pounds of the Silk now sent of such a quality as will suit the purpose thee may chuse to put it to best."

We are sensible how much the promoters of the Culture of Silk are Obliged to Doctor Franklin for the trouble he has taken in the business; in their behalf, we thankfully Acknowledge it, and remain with perfect Esteem, his Assured ready Friends[2]

ABEL JAMES
BENJN. MORGAN

Benjamin Franklin Esquire.

To John Foxcroft

ALS (letterbook draft): Library of Congress

Dear Friend, London, Nov. 19. 1772

I received yours and Mr. Colden's with the Accounts, and Bills, per Packet, concerning which shall be more particular in my next. This Line is only to inform you, that in my Opinion you are likely to obtain from the Board the Addition you desire to enable you to live at New York; that probably Mr. Finlay will be appointed Riding Surveyor; and that the extraordinary Demand made on us for the Packet Letters is withdrawn I having settled that matter

1. A pleasing variant of the reality, Gracechurch Street. For James Freeman, Fothergill's nephew, see above, XVI, 250 n.

2. Abel James has appeared too frequently in recent volumes to need identification. Morgan needs it but eludes it. All we can say with assurance is that he was elected twice in 1770 as one of the twelve Managers of the Silk Filature and was re-elected, this time with James, in 1771: *Pa. Gaz.*, March 22, Nov. 8, 1770; Nov. 14, 1771. A Benjamin Morgan was read out of the Philadelphia meeting in 1772 for marrying a non-Quaker, was chosen in the same year as a manager of the Corporation for the Relief and Employment of the Poor, was elected to the APS in 1774, was a manager of the Philadelphia Almshouse and House of Employment in 1776, and in 1791 was an iron merchant living on South Front Street. Hinshaw, *Amer. Quaker Genealogy*, II, 601; *Pa. Gaz.*, May 14, 1772; APS, *Early Proceedings*... (Philadelphia, 1884), p. 87; Robert J. Hunter, "The Origin of the Philadelphia General Hospital," *PMHB*, LVII (1933), 47; Clement Biddle, *The Philadelphia Directory* (Philadelphia, 1791), p. 91. We cannot determine whether these were appearances of several Benjamin Morgans or of a single person.

with the Office.[3] On these Things I hope I shall be able by the Packet fully to congratulate you. On the other hand I am desired by Mr. Todd to tell you that the Accounts are by no means satisfactory, as the Money receiv'd from the Offices is *lump'd*, without any Accounts to support or vouch it: That always heretofore the separate Accounts of each Office were copied and sent over with the general Account; and these are now for the present Account expected from you without Delay.[4] And when you send the Accounts of this Year to April next, the same are to accompany it, and so on from year to Year; otherwise the Accounts will not be accepted at the Auditor's Office. He will write to you on this Head per Packet: But in the mean time I wish you would forward it immediately.

I will now only mention farther, that the Account of Bills sent me since our last Settlement is right; but that Credit should have been given me for two Bills return'd protested to Mr. Parker, as you will see by the enclos'd State of my Account copied from that I have delivered in. I can now only add my Love to my Daughter &c. Yours affectionately　　　　　　　　　B FRANKLIN

[*In the margin:*] On Cunningham　£20
　　　　　　　Prot.　　　　　　　25*s*. 8*d*.
　　　　　　　　　　　　　　　21　5*s*. 8*d*.
　　　　On Milligan　　52
　　　　　Prot　　　　　　　5*s*. 9*d*.
　　　　　　　　　　　　£73　11*s*. 5*d*.[5]

3. For the Board see BF to Foxcroft above, Nov. 3. Law required the headquarters of the American post office to be in New York, and London had been trying for almost a decade, without success, to see that the deputy postmasters general lived there; see above, XII, 89 n. For Hugh Finlay's appointment and the affair of the packet letters see BF to Foxcroft above, Aug. 22, Nov. 3, and below, Dec. 2.

4. Colden, with no experience of the postal accounts, had made up those for 1771–72 under the direction of Foxcroft, whom BF clearly held responsible for their being so slovenly. See his letters to Colden and Foxcroft above, Oct. 7, and below, Dec. 2.

5. The only way we can interpret this transaction is that BF, on handing in Comptroller Parker's accounts, had made good the protested bills out of his own pocket; see his letter to Foxcroft below, Dec. 2. For the bill on Cunninghame see above, XVII, 137; this is the first information that the bill on Milligan (*ibid.*, p. 133) was protested.

To Deborah Franklin

ALS (letterbook draft): American Philosophical Society

My dear Child,   London, Nov. 19. 1772

I had no Line from you per last Packet, but hope to receive Letters of yours per Capt. All when he arrives. Thanks to God I am at present in very good Health and Spirits; which however I must not flatter myself will continue much longer, as the Course of Nature usually brings on with Age many Infirmities. As this Ship goes in a hazardous Season, I do not send Miss Haydock's Silk by her, especially as being for Summer Wear it will be in time by the Spring Ships.[6] Nor do I write now any other Letters but one to Mr. Foxcroft. My Love to Mr. Bache, Sally and the Boy. Ever yours I am affectionately   B FRANKLIN

From Henry Marchant

ALS (letterbook draft): Newport Historical Society

Dear Sir,   Newport Rhode Island Novr. 21. 1772

Hurried by one Circumstance and another since my Return, I have not been able till now to sit down to acknowledge my Obligations to my London Friends, and particularly to you Sir. However late, I do most sincerely acknowledge myself highly Obliged for the many Marks of Politness and disinterested Friendship conferred upon me. It was my Mortification that I was not a fitter Subject for Them. I will however still boldly hope for the Continuation of your Friendship, and I will strive for a small Share of your Esteem.

We had rather a disagreable Passage of Eight Weeks much wet Weather, and frequent pretty smart Gales. The most disagreable Circumstance, was the great Danger we were one Day put in, of being consumed by Fire, thro' the shocking Carelessness of the Carpenter, who had set a Pot of Pitch upon the Fire and left it.

---

6. He had had recent experience of the hazardous season: a gift that he had sent to DF the previous autumn had not reached her until the following April; see BF to DF above, Jan. 28. For the silk see BF's correspondence with Rebecca Haydock above, Feb. 5 and July 20; BF to DF, Nov. 4.

It soon boiled over, took Fire and put the Caboose in a Blaze. The Flames burst out at every Crevice and reached up often above the Mizzin Staysail. Thro' great Spirit and Dexterity of all Hands We happily extinguished it. This happened one Day just as we were a going down to Dinner about five Weeks After we left England.[7]

Upon my arrival at Boston, my Spirits you'l imagine were much abated. The first News I had was the Death of a much honored Friend Mrs. Trowbridge the Wife of Judge Trowbridge of Cambridge, with whom I had lived near five years while he was Att: Genl. She was One of the best Women in the World, She called me Her Son. Mr. Hubbart next informed me of the Death of my Third and only Son a Child of Three years old. He died with the Effects of the Measles, the Day after I left London. My two Daughters had been very ill with the same Disorder but are since happily recovered. I had scarcely heard this most distressing Account, when Mr. Williams came in. I saw He was in Mourning but not suspecting the Cause I pulled out my Letters for his Son. The good Man could scarcely utter the Cause of his apparent Greif. His Son was no more. That unfortunate good youth Sir, lived but to speak again to his Parents.[8] Here were two Fathers that could well sympathize with each other. I know the good Mrs. Stevenson whose Bowells yearned toward Him, will feel most pungent Greif. All that well knew him will pay the Tribute of Tears to his memory. He was *a good Lad.* I went to Cambridge

7. Marchant and Edward Church, traveling companions in Scotland the year before, left London on July 24 and sailed on the *Hayley*, Capt. James Scott; she was almost two months on the voyage, July 28 to Sept. 20, and the fire broke out in mid-Atlantic on Aug. 21. Franklin B. Dexter, ed., *The Literary Diary of Ezra Stiles*... (3 vols., New York, 1901), I, 304, 321–2.

8. Martha Remington Trowbridge was married to the well known lawyer and judge, Edmund Trowbridge, for more than thirty years. *DAB.* Marchant's first son died at two months; his second, born in 1768, lived for only two years, and his third, William, for only three. Meanwhile two daughters arrived, Sarah and Elizabeth. James N. Arnold, *Vital Record of Rhode Island*... (21 vols., Providence, 1891–1912), IV, pt. 2, 104; VIII, 434. Tuthill Hubbart, the Boston postmaster, who broke the sad news about the third boy, needs no introduction. The deaths all occurred within less than a month, while Marchant was on the Atlantic: young William on July 25, Martha Trowbridge on the 31st, and Josiah Williams on Aug. 15. Dexter, *op. cit.*, I, 256; *Mass. Gaz. and the Boston Weekly News-Letter*, Aug. 6, 20.

the first Evening to see my afflicted Friend Mr. Trowbridge, and in three or four Days having finished some necessary Business I set out for Newport. The meeting a kind Wife in Affliction and Distress, after so long an Absence, is perhaps the tenderest and most feeling meeting that we can have an Idea of. Mrs. Marchant Herself thro' a Series of Sickness in the Family and this Afflicting Stroke, with the Anxiety She was under at my Absence, was reduced very low in Health and Spirits: I hope She is better. I have carried Her over with me into the Country once since I came Home, And She is sensible of Advantage from the exercise and change of Air. She desires Her Regards to you Sir, and Mrs. Stevenson and her Thanks, as she is pleased to say, for those Friendly Services bestowed upon One in whom She has so great an Interest. I consider Mrs. Stevenson as claiming an Equal Right in this Letter, or I should have wrote one particularly to Her. I shall be proud ever to retain a Place in Her affections, and to be in the Remembrance of all Her Family and such of Her Friends, as I had the Happiness of being known to. You will be pleased not to forget me to Mrs. Bache and the young Ladies[9], And any Friends who may make mention after me.

Dr. Stiles tells me he means soon to honor himself by writing to you. He has had and still has much Sickness and Distress in his Family[1] which I presume hinders him this opportunity.

You will see by One of the Papers inclosed I have marked the Passage, how honorably Mr. Otis has waved the advantage of the Pecuniary Damages he recovered of Commissioner Robinson, and how meanly he has condescended to get rid of them. The Concessions R——n has made are such as no man of Honor or Spirit could make, because They amount to a Confession of a most unmanly attack and assault.[2]

9. Marchant and Church, during their tour of northern England, had visited Richard Bache's mother and sisters at Preston. See above, XVIII, 257.

1. Smallpox was raging in Newport, Stiles's daughter was thought for a time to be down with it, and his son had been inoculated. Dexter, *op. cit.*, I, 297, 300, 303.

2. In 1769 John Robinson, the customs commissioner, quarreled with and injured James Otis, who sued him. The suit was settled in August, 1772: Robinson paid the costs, and to escape damages "meanly condescended" to give Otis a written apology. For a balanced account of the case see *Sibley's Harvard Graduates*, XI, 277–80.

378

The News of the burning the Gasspee Schooner in our River near Providence arrived in England just before I came away by an Express for that very notable Purpose. It made some Noise there at first; The Colony have heard nothing from Home since, but the Papers tell us, a Commission had passed the great Seal appointing the Governors of this Colony and Connecticut, and the Cheif Justice of New-Jersey, New York and Boston to try such Persons as may be discovered that were concerned in that Transaction.

I cannot yet give Credit to this News Writer; a Commission of that kind would be an annihilating Stroke to the very being of our Civil Constitution, and they had better proceed boldly than by such side Strokes. Besides there never was less Cause for such an unprecedented Measure. The burning that Scooner was done by a few not thirty at most unknown disguised rash men. The Authority upon the first Notice shew their highest Disapprobation of the Act, took the tenderest Care of the Master who was wounded. And a Proclamation was instantly issued by the Governor for the Apprehending the Concerned, all that Government, or that Majestracy could do has been done.[3] But, by all accounts the Master was a very dirty low fellow. He had suffered his People to commit many outrages upon the Possessions and Property of the Inhabitants on Shore, and had so harrassed all the woodmen that they were afraid to go up or down the Rivers. The Price of Wood was

3. The affair precipitated by the destruction of H.M.S. *Gaspee* is too well known to need detailed explanation. In June the schooner, on patrol against smugglers, ran aground; during the night she was boarded and burned, and her commander wounded. When the news reached London in July, the law officers of the crown gave their opinion that the crime was high treason; the government created a commission to apprehend the culprits and send them to England for trial. The commission, which eventually brought in an inconclusive report for want of evidence, consisted of the Governor of Rhode Island, the Chief Justices of New York, New Jersey, and Massachusetts, and the judge of the Boston Vice-Admiralty Court. Their appointment was known in Newport a day or two before Marchant wrote; the news produced a vociferous reaction in the local press and throughout the colonies, and was a factor in the formation of the intercolonial committees of correspondence. John R. Bartlett, *A History of the Destruction of His Britannic Majesty's Schooner Gaspee...* (Providence, 1861); Gipson, *British Empire*, XII, 24–37; Bradley D. Bargar, *Lord Dartmouth and the American Revolution* (Columbia, S.C., 1965), pp. 74–81.

raised a third more than usual, many could not get it at all, and suffered greatly thro' one of the severest Winters We have had for forty years past. Those little Scooners are daily committing such Acts amongst us, as in England, would meet with severe Chastisment. Bullets from the man of War laying in Our Harbour, often whistle along across our Wharfs to the Danger of the Lives of the Inhabitants, and this has I am informed been done only at firing a Gun as a Signal to his Own Boat to come on Board &c. The Bullets have not been taken out, but the Guns fir'd pointed at the Town. Such and many more are the Indignities which Americans must yet suffer.

We have just the News by a Letter from the Governor of Boston, of a Piracy committed near Cape Cod upon a fishing Scooner, by a large armed Topsail Scooner, who killed all on Board, except one Man who let himself down into the Water by a Rope, and hung by her Quarter the whole Time of the Piracy. It is said that the Ad——l Himself suspects one of those Scooners fitted Out for the Protection of Trade. Time will soon discover.[4] Two men of War have sailed in Quest of the Pyrate, one from Boston and one from this Port. Pyracy in this Transaction is only a little more bold and hardy than Common.

I Question whether it will be thought to send off an Express with the News of the Murther of five or six or more American Fishermen. It may perhaps hereafter be said that it was done by Command of an officer. The officer may deny he gave the Command, and so all escape. But more of this hereafter. I have I reflect been already tedious. I must conclude just observing that the Province of the Mass. Bay never were in such a Ferment since the Stamp Act as at present. The Occasion is their Judges being made

4. Time did not discover. No trace was found of the topsail schooner, if indeed she ever existed except in the imagination of the one survivor of the massacre, on whose word the whole story depended. The authorities concluded that he was lying, and had murdered his crew mates. He stood trial for piracy and was acquitted for lack of evidence; but his counsel, John Adams, was never convinced of his innocence. Wroth and Zobel, eds., *John Adams Legal Papers*, II, 335–40; Butterfield, ed., *John Adams Diary*, III, 297. Marchant's unquestioning acceptance of the story as he heard it tells something of the mood in New England that autumn. Many others believed as he did (though Admiral John Montagu was presumably not among them) that the crime had been committed by a patrol ship like the *Gaspee*.

independant of the People, and that too out of Their Own Monies, raised upon Them without their Consent.[5]

When will British folly and madness end? I am dear and honored Sir Your ever obliged Friend and Servant   H: MARCHANT

Addressed: To Benjn: Franklin Esqr. DD:F.R.S: / Craven Street / at Mrs. Stevensons / London / per the Tristram / capt. Shand

To [a Member of the Royal Society][6]

ALS: American Philosophical Society

Sir   Cravenstreet, Nov. 26. 1772

The Council of the Royal Society having put Sir John Pringle, Bart. in nomination for President; and being myself persuaded

5. The issue of judicial salaries, coming hard upon that of the Governor's salary, precipitated an upheaval that eventually brought the government of Massachusetts to a standstill. What was at stake was the independence of the judiciary. In America, unlike Great Britain, demands for judicial tenure had failed. The executive might dismiss a judge at will, but the assembly paid him, so that he was under some measure of control by both authorities and could not, at least in theory, become completely the tool of either. Now this traditional balance was being upset in Massachusetts, and the Bostonians were quick to react. On Sept. 28 the *Boston Gaz.* published a report that the judges of the Superior Court were to be paid out of receipts from the remaining Townshend duties; a month later the Boston town meeting asked the Governor to confirm or deny the report, and he refused. As excitement mounted, the meeting appointed a committee, the later Boston Committee of Correspondence, to draw up a statement of the colonists' rights and circulate it throughout the province. The issue of judicial salaries was lost for a time in the welter of other grievances, but did not vanish; it reappears time and again in BF's later correspondence. For the general background see Bernard Bailyn, ed., *Pamphlets of the American Revolution, 1750–1776* (1 vol. to date; Cambridge, Mass., 1965), pp. 249–55; Leonard W. Labaree, *Royal Government in America: a Study of the British Colonial System before 1783* (New Haven and London, 1930), pp. 389–400. For the developments in Boston see Richard D. Brown, *Revolutionary Politics in Massachusetts: the Boston Committee of Correspondence and the Towns, 1772–1774* (Cambridge, Mass., 1970), pp. 52–7; Gipson, *British Empire*, XII, 47–50.

6. The letter is clearly one that BF sent to an indeterminate number of members on the eve of the presidential election. Sir John Pringle's candidacy was under attack from an elderly and eccentric physician, Sir William Browne (1692–1774), for whom see the *DNB*. In two speeches to the Society Browne

from what I know of his Learning in general, his thorough Acquaintance with Experimental Philosophy, his constant Attendance at our Meetings, and his extensive Reputation in the Republick of Letters throughout Europe, that he would fill that Office with great Propriety, and to the Honour and Advantage of the Society, I beg leave to request your Vote and Interest in Support of that Nomination. I am, very respectfully, Sir, Your most obedient humble Servant   B FRANKLIN

From William Henly   ALS: American Philosophical Society

Worthy Sir: Thursday mor[ning, November 26?[7], 1772]
I have Received your very obliging favour, and take the first opportunity of returning you my most sincere thanks for the trouble I have given you. I have done very little in Electricity since I had the pleasure of seeing you,[8] one appearance however I beg leave to trouble you with, as I have never met with one of the kind before. Having charged my 6 Gallon Jar so as to repel the Index of the Electrometer to about 75 degrees, I insulated it, with a view to discharge it by giving it the contrary Electricity, but finding the Electrometer very damp, and much disposed to throw off the Electric matter, I applied the Ball of a long Rod (which I had in my hand) to the top of the stem, when the whole charge seem'd to fly off in a very fine stream almost instantaneously, and the index came directly into contact with the Ball of the Jar wire. As this happen'd so suddenly and every thing was kept at such a distance from the coating, I suspected that the outside could not

argued that only mathematicians should be chosen to the Council and the presidency, and that Pringle specifically was disqualified because he had declined a less exacting office for reasons of health. John Nichols, *Literary Anecdotes of the Eighteenth Century*... (9 vols., London, 1812–16), III, 320–3. Pringle was elected on Nov. 30, at the same time that BF was chosen for the Council. *Gent. Mag.*, LXII (1772), 590–1. Browne, we believe, went on to more outrageous attacks on the new President, which elicited BF's diatribe printed below at the end of the year.

7. The letter mentions a machine that will be finished within a few days; it was probably the new conductor described by Henly below, Nov. 28. We assume that he was writing on the previous Thursday.

8. Presumably a month before: see Henly to BF above, under Oct. 28.

have Received its natural quantity so fast as it had been drawn off from the inside, and on presenting my finger towards the Coating, when it had come within an Inch distance of it, a most beautiful and large pencil flew off from my finger, finely diverging towards the coating of the Jar much resembling one of those towards a very large Excited stick of sealing Wax. Probably this Sir may be no new appearance to you, but should that be the case, I flatter myself you will excuse the trouble I give you by laying before you an Account of it.[9]

I now venture to give my 2 large Jarrs their full charge, even so as to cause a Cascade of Fire to flow over the Neck of the thickest of them which repels the Index of the Electrometer, the whole thickness of the Rod above right Angles or 90 degrees.

With this charge, I have procured a large quantity of those Balls Mr. Canton was so obliging as to shew me, and a great number of large vitrified pieces, perfectly visible to the naked Eye; I have preserved both, for your inspection. I have never fail'd with this charge to fire a quil of Gunpowder, fill'd with the whole grains, and without at all drying or preparing them, tho the weather had made them very damp.[1] Mr. Nairne thinks to finish my new Machine by the latter end of this week, when I receive it, I intend myself the pleasure of waiting on you, to request the Honour and favour of your Company to spend another Evening with me in the Electrical way. I beg your excuse for this long interruption, and that you would believe me most sincerely your obliged, and very Humble Servant   W HENLY

Addressed: To / Dr. Franklin / Craven Street / Strand

9. The jar, Henly is saying, had been discharged in such a way that the electricity inside had returned to its natural level while the outer surface retained a strong negative charge. This was contrary to BF's fourth observation on the electrical action in a jar, above, III, 158. The second part of the experiment conformed to a recognized principle, however, that a negatively charged conductor (the exterior of the jar) induced a positive charge in a grounded conductor (Henly's finger) to the point of producing a spark: Priestley, *History*, I, 359; II, 7. See also Edward W. Gray, "Observations on the Manner in Which Glass Is Charged with the Electric Fluid, and Discharged," *Phil. Trans.*, LXXVIII (1788), 121–4.

1. For Canton's "glass" balls see above, XVIII, 182 n. BF had pioneered in exploding gunpowder by an electric spark: above, IV, 145, 202.

From Jacques Barbeu-Dubourg

AL (incomplete): American Philosophical Society

Monsieur et tres cher Ami   A Paris ce 28e. 9bre. 1772

J'ai reçu la lettre dont vous m'avez honoré en date du 12e. 9bre. avec un p.s. du 16.

Je suis au moins à la moitié de ma traduction de votre in 4°. et j'espere l'achever sur la fin de l'année, ou dans les commencemens de l'autre. *Non laboratur ubi amatur*, disoit st. Augustin.

Vous ne sauriez douter que je ne reçoive avec plaisir, que je n'attende même avec impatience le supplement que vous m'annoncez, vos nouvelles experiences sur les verges foudroyables, et vos instructions pour diriger les faiseurs d'experiences sur l'anguille de Surinam, sur la torpille &c.[2] Vous sentez bien aussi que je ne serois pas fâché de recevoir quelque exemplaire de mon petit Code imprimé sous vos heureux et glorieux auspices;[3] mais je voudrois bien tâcher d'eviter les frais enormes de la poste. Votre derniere lettre m'a eté taxée à cent sols; que seroit-ce d'un paquet un peu fort? S'il ne se rencontre point d'occasion favorable (comme il y en a peu de ce genre) vous pourriez, s'il y a des messageries en Angleterre comme en france, m'envoyer par cette voye (tant soit peu plus lente mais beaucoup moins coûteuse) tous les paquets un peu gros, mais non pas deux exemplaires à la fois d'un même ouvrage quelconque, parceque les visites tant à la douane qu'a la chambre de la Librairie de Paris entraineroient des tracasseries et des vexations desolantes.

En attendant je vous prie de vouloir m'adresser un exemplaire du petit Code sous une 1e. envelope a mon adresse, cette envelope simplement arrêtée avec un peu de cire d'Espagne (sans cachet) puis une 2e. envelope (pareillement arretée avec un peu de cire sans cachet) avec cette suscription *pour la gazette de france* et en-

---

2. BF's instructions concerned only the torpedo fish, not the electric reel: above, pp. 233–5.

3. Dubourg was asking for his *Petit code de la raison humaine: ou, Exposition succincte de ce que la raison dicte à tous les hommes, pour éclairer leur conduite, & assurer leur bonheur.* BF was having the anonymous pamphlet printed for him in London, and must have told him that advance copies were already available. Publication was not until 1773; see Luther S. Livingston, *Franklin and His Press at Passy* (New York, 1914), p. 70.

fin une 3ᵉ. envelope cachetée et adressée a Monseigneur, Monseigneur le Chancelier de france A Versailles.

Non seulement, j'espere que cet exemplaire pourra me parvenir par ce moyen, franc de port, mais si vous aviez par hazard quelques papiers publics d'Amerique qui vous fussent devenus inutiles, ou quelques autres paperasses imprimées sur la politique, sur le commerce, sur les arts, &c., &c., pas trop vieilles, du même pays surtout, mais aussi d'Angleterre, au defaut des autres, dont vous voulussiez bien glisser de tems en tems une piece sous les mêmes envelopes pour l'auteur de la gazette de france, vous pourriez me faire passer en même tems par cette voye, autant de petits paquets qu'il vous plairoit; chaque paquet pour moi de 4 à 5 feuilles au plus sous la 1ᵉ. envelope interieure, quelque feuille, demifeuille (ou feuillet complet dans certains cas) sous la 2ᵉ. envelope pour la gazette, et le tout toujours recouverte d'une 3ᵉ. envelope exterieure a M. Le Chancelier. Et cela pourroit se repeter une ou 2 fois par semaine, au besoin. Je vous prie aussi d'en vouloir adresser un exemplaire sous une 1ᵉ. envelope a Madame la Duchesse de fitzjames, cette 1ᵉ. arretée avec de la cire sans cachet, et recouverte d'une 2ᵉ envelope adressée a Monseigneur Monseigneur le Duc d'Aiguillon, Pair de france, Ministre d'Etat, a Versailles.

Enfin je vous prie aussi d'adresser dabord la 1ᵉ. feuille seulement d'un exemplaire du même code a Son Altesse Serenissime Madame La Duchesse de Chartres, au Palais royal A Paris.[4] Et

---

4. We are at a loss to explain either the purpose or the operation of Dubourg's complicated system of delivery. Did he devise it merely to save postage, or because he thought the pamphlet might be confiscated? In his second set of instructions, for papers from BF, he seemed to be providing a quid pro quo, absent in the first set, to assure that copies reached him: the editor of the *Gazette de France*, François-Louis-Claude Marin (1721–1809), was also public censor and hence subordinate to Chancellor Maupeou (above, XVIII, 113 n); tidbits from BF for the *Gazette* might have induced Marin to forward an enclosure to Dubourg. But why the duchesse de Fitzjames should receive a copy by way of the duc d'Aiguillon, or the duchesse de Chartres should wish to have only the first sheet, we cannot conjecture. Victoire de Goyon de Matignon, duchesse de Fitzjames, was a lady-in-waiting to the Dauphine, Marie Antoinette; Armand de Vignerot Duplessis de Richelieu, duc d'Aiguillon (1720–82), was a relative of Maupeou and Minister of Foreign Affairs. Louise de Bourbon-Penthièvre, duchesse de Chartres, was the greatest heiress in France, and the wife of the famous or notorious prince

garder le reste de cet exemplaire pour quand vous aurez de mes nouvelles à ce sujet.

Madame La D[uches]se de fitzjames [m'a promis?] de me rapporter quelques torpilles vivantes de [*torn*] où elle est actuellement, mais je crains bien [qu'elles n'arrivent?] mortes.

Voicy comment j'ai traduit *and the silk by which the silk-worm, in its tender embrio state is first cloathed: et la soye qui a eté donnée à un insecte delicat, pour passer son etat critique.* J'ai preferé à dessein le mot d'*insecte* à celui de ver, par la raison q'un ver proprement dit n'ayant point de membres distincts et n'etant point sujet a diverses metamorphoses, c'est abusivement que la chenille qui file la soye est appellée ver à soye. En ecrivant cecy, je me ravise; il me semble qu'il vaudra mieux mettre *une chenille delicate.*

Je vous envoye cy joint mon quarré magique des 11000 vierges puisque vous etes curieux de le voir. En même tems je prens la liberté de vous representer que vos diagonales coudées ne doivent point vous dispenser des diagonales entieres plus simples, et plus à portée de tout le monde. J'ai verifié en entier votre grand quarré magique de 16, et je n'y ai trouvé que les 2 seules et mêmes fautes que le hazard m'avoit fait rencontrer au 1er. coup d'oeil, par une singularité qui m'etonne encore.[5]

J'ajouterai en note au dessous de votre texte dans la lettre sur les couches de terre ce que vous [racontez?] de votre descente dans les mines de charbon fossile de Whit[ehaven.[6] *Remainder missing.*]

of the blood whose role in the Revolution, as Philippe Égalité, brought him to the guillotine.

5. For this and the preceding paragraph see Dubourg to BF above, Oct. 28.
6. See *ibid.*, and BF to Dubourg above under Nov. 12.

From [William Henly]

AD and draft: American Philosophical Society; printed in the Roya Society, *Philosophical Transactions...*, LXIV (1774), 403–6.[7]

Novr. 28. 1772.
The Description and use, of a new Conductor for *Experiments in Electricity*,[8] contrived by Mr. H—— and executed by Mr. Edward Nairne.

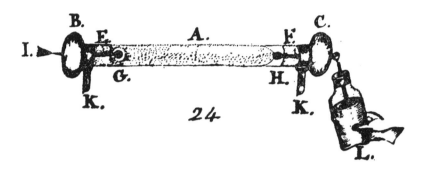

7. The three versions were written in the order in which we list them, and differ with each other in some details. Henly altered the design of his conductor as he worked with it, and a plate in the *Phil. Trans.* shows the fully developed instrument. We publish the AD with its illustration, and silently supply from the printed text, where possible, words that are missing in the original. It and the later draft, both in Henly's hand, are badly damaged.

8. The novelty of the conductor was that it was transparent, so that the apparent direction of flow of the electrical fluid could be observed. Henly's brain child may well have been descended from the apparatus devised by Canton and others, for which see above, XVI, 112 n, and Priestley, *History*, I, 349–54. BF had discussed with his friend the plans for the instrument; see Henly's letter above, under Oct. 28.

A.   A Tube of Glass 2 feet in length, 2 Inches diameter.

B. C.   Balls with a ferril of Brass (2 Inches long, to each) which are to be cemented to the ends of the tube, and made *Air tight*. One of the plates which are solder'd to the ferrils, hath a small hole dril'd through it, by which the Air is to be exhausted; it is cover'd by a strong valve well secured, and conceal'd by the brass ball.

[E.] F. A Coating of Cement from the Brass caps, 3 Inches upon the glass at each end, to prevent the moisture from adhering to the tube, and conducting the Electricity over its outer surface.[9]

G. H.   Balls of Brass ½ Inch diameter fixed upon wires which project into the tube 5/2 Inches from the plate at the end of it.[1]

I.   A fine point to collect the Electricity from the globe [*in the margin:*] or to disperse it in the Air as in the above experiment.[2]

K. K.   Supporters of sealing wax, upon which the Glass Conductor is to be mounted for experiments.

L.   A Bottle properly prepared for electrical experiments and charged positively.

N.B. The dots in the tube are intended to represent the appearance of the Electricity in it.

The use of the Glass Conductor

The Glass tube thus furnished and mounted, being *properly exhausted*, *and perfectly dry*, will Act in all respects like one of Metal: and the Electrometer being placed upon the Brass ball C. will answer to the charge of a Jar or Battery exactly. But the principal use

9. In the *Phil. Trans.* version the cement, and therefore this sentence, are omitted.

1. In the *Phil. Trans.* version the diameter of the balls is increased to ⅜″ and 5/2 (or 5½; the numerals are obscure) becomes 2½.

2. This experiment is probably the "beautiful analysis of the Leyden phial" that Henly described in his published paper (pp. 400–1); in that case the AD must originally have been part of a longer document.

of this Instrument is *to ascertain the direction of the Electric matter, as it passes through it*; which end it compleatly answers in the manner following. Place the collecting point before the Globe, and sit a bottle with its Knob in contact with the Ball C. of the Conducductor, or hang a chain &c. from thence to the table, and the Ball H. *in the Tube* (on working the Machine,) becomes entirely enveloped in *a dense white Atmosphere of Electricity*. If the point I. of the Conductor be brought nearly into contact with an insulated Rubber, and a communication be made from the opposite end to the Earth; the ball G. *in the tube*, will be surrounded with the Atmosphere. If the bottle L. be charged *positively* and its Knob be applied as in the figure the Atmosphere will be upon G. But charge the Bottle *negatively* and apply it as before, and the Atmosphere will then appear upon H.

CONJECTURES on these phenomena.

It is supposed that the impelling power of the Globe, or the Knob of a positively charged bottle, drives the particles of the Electricity through the substance of the Ball, wire &c. (with which they are in contact,) with great velocity, and [moving?] in a straight Line; But the Electricity having enter'd the vacuum, the repulsion of its particles immediately takes place, and the tube is instantly fill'd with Light.[3] The dense white Atmosphere upon the opposite Ball is imagin'd to proceed from this cause, for as every particle is supposed to be in a state of repellency with respect to its next neighbour, and as the Vacuum gives them a free liberty of expanding themselves, or standing at their greatest distance from each other: they will not enter *the opposite ball in the tube* in a point or small space as they do in the open Air, but (as before observed,) having free liberty to expand themselves, their natural property of repelling each other, causes them *actually to do so*, and thus *the Wire and ball*, becomes illumin'd with a very dense Atmosphere of the particles of Electricity, which they enter *in all parts, at the same time*, in order to their conveyance into those bodies, placed to receive them at the end of the Brass work.

3. From this point to the end of the paragraph the *Phil. Trans.* version is markedly different; the principal change in substance is that the light is attributed to the small portion of air remaining in the tube.

By this simple and easy process, may an ocular demonstration be at all times given, of *the truth and propriety* of Dr. Franklins hypothesis of the Leiden Bottle &c.[4] And if his Doctrines are but embraced, till his Opponents bring as good proofs of their being erroneous; I flatter myself *that Learned, Candid and Ingenious Gentleman,* will scarcely wish them to be retained longer.

Mr. Henly sends his most grateful acknowledgments of Dr. Franklins favour of this day, and assures him the injunctions in his Card shall be stric[tly complied?] with. Mr. H. earnestly hopes to hear o[f the health?] of his worthy Friend and the whole family.

From David Colden[5]   AL (draft[6]): New-York Historical Society

Dear Sir   Novr. 30th. 1772

The attention you pay to every Invention that promises either utility or amusement to Mankind induces Me to communicate to you a very simple Machine which I have made this Year for sowing

4. The *Phil. Trans.* text ends here, presumably because the following sentence, which was included in Henly's later draft as well, was considered too provocative.

5. For the son of Cadwallader and brother of Alexander Colden see above, V, 135 n.

6. With the draft is another, undated, which is similar in subject matter but not in wording to the first two paragraphs of this letter, and explains the drill plough or seed drill in great and confusing detail; the confusion is heightened by the fact that an accompanying page of sketches does not correspond to the explanation. Colden presumably sent BF two letters at the same time. One was that which we publish here from draft. The other was a detailed description of his plough and how it operated, also in letter form but meant for publicizing the invention in England. This detailed description is not informative enough to be worth printing. But in its final version, since lost, it was comprehensible; for in his reply below, March 5, 1773, BF spoke of laying it before the Royal Society of Arts. Colden may have hoped to win a gold medal that the Society offered for the best drill plough, and BF was the natural intermediary: he had been involved in the Society's work since 1755, and is said to have attended regularly the meetings of its agricultural committee. Above, VI, 275–6; IX, 321–2; Derek Hudson and Kenneth W. Luckhurst, *The Royal Society of Arts, 1754–1954* (London, [1954]), p. 63.

Seeds in Rows. I am happy in haveing an opportunity of address-
ing you upon any Thing that may be worth your Notice; If it
shall prove of no real value to others, it gives me a very great
pleasure by introduceing Me again to one I so greatly Esteem and
Admire.

I know nothing of Drill Ploughs, or of the Drill Husbanday but
what I have learnd from Books. I find it a general Complaint of
the best Machines that have been invented for this Work, that they
are so Complex, so Gimcrak so easily put out of Order, and so
difficultly repaird, and with all so high Priced, as to be entirely
unfit for the uses of common Farmers. That which I have contrived is quite simple, may be made by any common Workman,
and at a very triffling Expence. It has answerd my Expectations
in sowing Pease, Wheat Turnips and Lucern; it may however
very possibly fall so much short of the best Drills, as to dissappoint
those who are acquainted with Them. Should it be so I hope to be
excused for I have it not in my power to make a Comparison,
haveing never seen the work of any other Drill but my own, nor
indeed a Drill-Plow of any kind. It is in your power to determine
whether this Contrivance is worth communicating to the World;
should you think that it is, I beg the favour of you to do it for Me
in the Way you think best. I have avoided giving the Dimensions
of any Part, because it is not essential in any part of the Contrivance, and by multiplying words would lengthen and obscure the
Description. No workman can be at a loss to know the proper size
of the Parts to give the necessary Strength. I likewise think it
quite needless to mention the manner of fixing the Parts together.

I have lately got the Annual Register for 1771. One of the first
things I fell upon was the Abstracts from Mr. Kalms account of
his Travels in America. I was much surprised with a wonderfull
Story he tells from my Father, of a black Snake that attacked one
of our Servants, for I never heard the Story in the Family, indeed
the date he gives it is within my own Memory. My Father cannot
immagine how Mr. Kalm came to father such a Story upon him,
for as no such Thing ever happend in our Family, or to any one
that he ever heard of, the Traveller could not have got it from
him. However my surprise vanishd when in the next page I found
him telling on his own knowledge that the Indians at Sir W. John-
sons could out run the swiftest Horses. And a Frog out run the

NOVEMBER 30, 1772

Indians.⁷ I had two opportunities a Year or two agoe, of examining the black Snake facinating a Bird; of which Mr. Kalm does not omit some wonderfull Tales. In both the Cases which I saw, I found that the Bird was far from being in Love with the Snake, that She was doing her utmost to drive him away from her Nest, puting her own Life into his Jaws to save her young Brood. I calld several Persons to examine the first of these Encounters which I saw; they all agreed that the Bird must be enchantd but alterd their Opinion as soon as I shewd them the Nest and young Birds. I really beleive there is nothing more in all the Tales we are told of these Inchantments. I gave our worthy Friend Peter Collinson an account of what I had observed upon these occasions, some Time before he dyed.⁸

My Father presents his Compliments to You. He longs to have your Remarks upon his Papers.⁹ He enjoys a great share of Health and surpriseing Spirits for a Man at 85. He has much more Strength now than he had two Years agoe.
I am

Endorsed: Decr. 8th. 1772 Drill Plow

7. For Peter Kalm see above, III, 300 n. The tidbits from his travels, which Colden had encountered, were in *The Annual Register . . . for 1771* (1772), pp. 93–102 of second pagination; for the particular passages referred to see pp. 95–6, 99.
8. The letter has not survived, but Collinson referred to it in writing to David's father in 1768: *The Letters and Papers of Cadwallader Colden* (N.Y. Hist. Soc. *Coll.*, LVI [1923]), p. 144.
9. BF had in all probability received Colden's paper, "An Inquiry in the Principles of Vital Motion," the previous winter; he had then made excuses for not reading it, and more than a year later was still making them. See Collinson to BF above, under the end of March; BF to Alexander Colden below, June 2, 1773.

To Joseph Galloway

Extract: minutes of the American Philosophical Society

[November?¹ 1772]

I must now beg Leave to recommend to your Society *Baron de Kliengstadt*² of Petersburg who has lately travelled thro' England to collect Improvements in Husbandry &c. Being acquainted with him I took the Liberty of requesting his Care of our Book directed to the Academy of Sciences at Petersburg and I gave it to him open as he expressed a Curiosity to read it. He was so pleased with it and conceived so high an Opinion of the Society that he desired the Honor, as he politely expressed it, of being a Member, offered to correspond with the Society and send them from Time to Time any Information, Seeds or other things they might want from Russia.³

To Richard Bache

ALS (letterbook draft): Library of Congress

Loving Son,   London, Dec. 1. 1772

I have received yours of Oct. 6 and 13. and Sally's of Oct. 25.⁴ It rejoices me to hear that you are all well, and that Benja. is re-

1. Perhaps earlier but not later, for the letter was acted upon in Philadelphia in mid-January, 1773.

2. Timotheus Marzahn von Klingstädt (1710–86) was termed in the APS minutes "Counsellor of State to the Empress of Russia, Member of the Commission of the Law, of the Oeconomical Society at Petersburg &c." He was both a legal and an agricultural expert. For a number of years he served in judicial and administrative offices, until dismissed in 1771; he then embarked on his travels. He was a member of the Russian Academy of Sciences and a founder of the Free Economic Society and of its transactions, and he wrote extensively on commerce and husbandry. Christian G. Jöcher, *Allgemeines Gelehrten-Lexicon...* (11 vols., Leipzig, 1750–1897), VII, 508–9; *Ruskii biograficheskii slovar...* (25 vols., St. Petersburg, 1896–1918), VIII, 741.

3. Klingstädt was elected on Jan. 15, 1773 (at the meeting when this recommendation was read), in company with three of BF's old friends: Jean-Baptiste LeRoy, Dr. Alexander Small, and the Rev. Thomas Coombe. APS MS minutes.

4. Only the first is extant, and the loss of the other two leaves in mystery some of the matters that BF is discussing.

covered of the Measles. I will write him a little print Letter, as soon as I hear that he can read Print.[5]

Thanks to God, I am perfectly well at present, but being so far advanced in Life, I cannot expect a long Continuance of Health free from the usual Infirmities of Age.

The Mr. Coombes to whom you wrote, was burnt out a few Days before your Letter came to hand, but sav'd enough of his Stock to come within his Insurance. He will pay the Charge you mention, tho' he has not yet.[6]

I am pleas'd you follow'd the Advice of your Brother, relating to the Money due from Goddard; for tho' I think with you that the Company is bound in Honour to make it good, I suppose there may be reasons for not making the Demand at present, which your Brother may be acquainted with tho' I am not.[7]

Mrs. Stevenson is pleas'd that her Care in procuring the Things for Sally, has given Satisfaction: and I am glad they proved agreable. My Love to your Wife and Son. If I hear that he continues a good Boy, I shall love him very much, and send him something by Capt. All.[8] I am, my dear Children, Your affectionate Father

B F

Mr Bache

Decemr Packet.

5. BF as a grandfather expected precocity: the boy had just turned three. He was lucky to be alive; William Marchant's son of the same age had died of measles. See Marchant to BF above, Nov. 21.

6. The unfortunate merchant was William Combes, a mercer in Chandos Street, Covent Garden: *Public Advertiser*, Nov. 17, 1772.

7. Richard had consulted Theophylact Bache, we assume, about some debt left over from one of William Goddard's two partnerships, with Galloway and Thomas Wharton or with Benjamin Towne. The reference is too oblique to establish that this was the debt from Galloway about which Strahan had written BF: above, Aug. 21.

8. For Isaac All, master of the *Richard Penn* and BF's nephew by marriage, see above, XII, 31 n.

To Deborah Franklin

ALS (letterbook draft): American Philosophical Society

My dear Child   London, Dec. 1. 1772

I received yours of Oct. 14. and one without Date, which I suppose to be written since. Capts. All, Osborne, and Sparkes, are arrived; and a Barrel of Apples with another of Cranberries are come, I know not yet by which of them.

I am glad to hear you continue so well, and that the Pain in your Side and Head have left you. Eat light Foods, such as Fowls, Mutton, &c. and but little Beef or Bacon, avoid strong Tea, and use what Exercise you can; by these Means, you will preserve your Health better, and be less Subject to Lowness of Spirits.

It seems Polly Pitts is really dead. I suppose you know that we have a Mortgage on her Lotts. Mr. Galloway took it for me. You do not tell me whether any thing has been done about it; or whether any Interest was ever paid. Nor have you ever told me, whether Mr. Maugridge's Executors have paid off his Mortgage to me, and that to the Insurance Office.[9] I wish you would.

Give my Love to Mrs. Montgomery and all enquiring Friends. Mrs. Stevenson and Polly Hewson, and Sally Franklin present their Love, the latter adds her Duty. She is about to be married to a Farmer's Son.[1] I shall miss her, as she is nimble-footed and willing to run of Errands and wait upon me, and has been very ser-

9. The complicated affair of Mary (Polly) Pitts' mortgage was not settled until after BF's return to Philadelphia: above, V, 16; X, 250–1; XIV, 191 n. BF's mortgage on the Maugridge property had presumably been paid off in full by 1771; that held by the insurance company, the Philadelphia Contributionship, was not settled until 1772. Above, XV, 227–8, 288; J. Bennett Nolan, "Ben Franklin's Mortgage on the Daniel Boone Farm," APS *Proc.*, LXXXVII (1943–44), 397.

1. For Mrs. Montgomery see above, XVII, 167. Sally Franklin (A.5.2.3.1.1.1.) married James Pearce in the spring of 1773, when BF gave her twenty-five guineas as a wedding present. BF to DF below, April 6, 1773; Jour., p. 47. Pearce was himself a substantial farmer, a sober and industrious young man, "and I think it likely to prove a good Match." BF to Samuel Franklin below, July 7, 1773.

viceable to me for some Years, so that I have not kept a Man. I am ever, my dear Debby Your affectionate Husband   B F.

P.S. Have just opened the Apples and Cranberries, which I find in good order, all sound. Thanks for your kind Care in sending them.

Mrs Franklin

To John Hughes, Jr.[2]

ALS (letterbook draft): Library of Congress

Dear Sir,   Dec. 1. 72

I received yours of Oct. 12. and in answer to your Enquiries acquaint you, that when I was in Ireland I went to the proper Office, and received the Information noted in red Ink on a Paper enclos'd; I then wrote the Letter of which I now send you the rough Draft, together with the Answer I received. I wrote also to the other Gentleman, but received no Answer. I am afraid there is little Expectation of obtaining any thing from Government here, and as little from the Drawers of the Bills: But of that you will judge on perusal of Mr. Grant's Letter. I return also the Protests.[3]

I am enclin'd to think the Land mention'd in your Father's Will as what he was concern'd in with Baynton, Wharton & Co. is not that in which I propos'd to interest him; but another, by some Agreement between them before Mr. Wharton came over. For I think I have heard there was some such Agreement. And as I never received any Answer from him to my Proposal, I apprehend his

2. The son of BF's old friend of the same name. The father had died in Charleston, S.C., in January, and the son soon followed him to the grave: his will was probated at the end of 1773. William O. Sawtelle, "Acadia: the Pre-loyalist Migration and the Philadelphia Plantation," *PMHB*, LI (1927), 279 n.

3. The disappearance of the relevant documents leaves this paragraph almost incomprehensible. The senior Hughes, our conjecture is, received or bought two bills of exchange drawn by Irishmen. When both were protested, he asked BF to look into the matter. During his Irish tour in 1771 BF did so, located the drawers, and subsequently wrote them. One, Mr. Grant, replied unsatisfactorily. As for the government, young Hughes perhaps hoped that it owed his father arrears of salary as customs collector.

Name has been omitted;[4] but I shall enquire; and shall be glad if I can serve his Children in that or any other Affair, having no doubt of your carefully reimbursing me what I may advance for the Family. By my Accounts here, your Father was not in my Debt, but in Advance with me £4 2s. 0d. How the Account may stand in Philadelphia I know not.

Present my respectful Compliments to your Mother,[5] with whom and all of you I condole sincerely, on the Loss of so valuable a Husband, Father and Friend. I am, with great Regard, Your most humble Servant   B F

Mr John Hughes, jun.

To Alexander Colden

ALS (letterbook draft): Library of Congress

Dear Sir,   London, Dec. 2. 1772
    I duly received yours of Oct. 10. with the Accounts, accompanied by Bills of Exchange as follows,[6]

Walker on Cunningham for	£82 11s. 5½d.
R N. Colden on Meyrick for	400 0s. 0d.
These from you as your Ballance	482 11s. 5½d.

4. For Baynton, Wharton & Morgan see above, XI, 187 n. BF had apparently suggested to the elder Hughes that he take a share in the Walpole Company, and nothing had come of the idea. Hughes had been associated with BF in securing land grants in Nova Scotia some years before, but had never achieved a clear title: above, XII, 345–7. At the time of his death he was working through Baynton and Samuel Wharton to obtain another Nova Scotia grant; part of his claim to it he bequeathed to his son John, who passed it on in his will. PMHB, loc. cit.

5. Sarah Jones Hughes, who had married John Hughes in 1738: Ellwood Roberts, Biographical Annals of Montgomery County, Pennsylvania... (2 vols., New York and Chicago, 1904), I, 282–5.

6. The accounts were for the American post office, 1771–72. Cunningham was William Cunninghame & Co.: above, XVII, 55 n. Some of the others on whom the bills were drawn can be identified from Kent's Directory... (London, 1770) as, in order of appearance, James Meyrick, agent, in Parliament St.; John Buchanan in Little Tower St.; Barnes & Ridgate and Long, Drake & Long, two firms in Bishopsgate St.; William Molleson in Gould Square, Crutched Friars; Perkins, Buchanan & Browne in Fowkes Bldgs., Tower St., and West & Hobson in Catherine Court, Tower Hill. Meyrick was

And the following from Mr. Foxcroft as his
Ballance, viz

Leitch on Buchanans	150	0s.	0d.
Dick & Steward on Buchanans	61	14s.	2d.
Walker on Cunningham	257	16s.	4d.
Turner on Barnes & Ridgate	72	7s.	5d.
Sandys on Sandys	15	0s.	0d.
Dunn on Long Drake & Long	100	0s.	0d.
Edlin on Molleson	20	0s.	0d.
Taylor on Perkins, Buchanan & Browne	15	0s.	0d.
Blair on Cunninghame	100	0s.	0d.
Belt on West & Hobson	50	0s.	0d.
	841	17s.	11d.

The Account of Bills remitted to me by Mr. Parker and yourself
was right; but I should have had Credit for protested Bills return'd
to him, viz

Bill on Cunningham & Co.	£20	0s.	0d.
Charges	£1	5s.	8d.
Do on Milligen	52	0s.	0d.
Charges		5s.	9d.
In all	73	11s.	5d.

And you will also give me Credit for Mackie on Molleson return'd
to you protested per Packet Nov. 3. the Sum £294 5s. 2d.[7]

---

undoubtedly a partner in Meyrick & Porter, regimental agents: *The Royal
Kalendar*... (London, [1772]), pp. 170, 184–6. Two of the partners in Long,
Drake & Long were probably Beeston and Samuel Long, for whom see
Lillian M. Penson, "The London West India Interest in the Eighteenth
Century," *English Hist. Rev.*, XXXVI (1921), 383; Drake we cannot identify.
Of those who drew the bills only one can be definitely placed: Richard
Nicholls Colden, Alexander's son. Others may have been Alexander Dick,
London merchant and insurer, and William Taylor, a ship chandler
(Lucy S. Sutherland, *A London Merchant*... [London, 1933], pp. 61, 118,
141, 152); George Walker, a Barbadian planter who was resident in London
and agent for the colony (Lillian M. Penson, *The Colonial Agents of the British
West Indies*... [London, 1924], pp. 155, 165, 203); Zeph[aniah] Turner (see
BF to Colden below, Jan. 6, 1773), who may well have been connected with
John Turner & Sons of Amsterdam, a firm trading with America, for which
see James B. Hedges, *The Browns of Providence Plantations*... (Cambridge,
Mass., 1952), pp. 255, 257.

7. For the protested bills see above, BF to Colden, Oct. 7, Nov. 3, and to
Foxcroft, Nov. 19.

I am now to tell you by Order of the Board that the Accounts are not regularly stated and render'd as usual, and therefore not satisfactory. All the Receipts are lump'd in one Sum, without particularizing how much from each Office, when receiv'd and by whom. It is therefore required and expected that you immediately make out and send the Accounts in that Form; together with a Copy of the separate Accounts as they stand in your Books with each Postmaster, all ballanced; that it may be seen how much is due from each, as well as what has been received from them. This is to be done directly for the Accounts to 1772. and the same is to accompany the Account for 1773, and so for every succeeding Year; each separate Office Account to commence with the Ballance of the preceding Year. I beg you will do this without Delay, as the Account is rejected at the Office, and I can make no Settlement, with the Office, nor the Office with the Treasury till it arrives. With my best Respects to your good Father, to Mr. and Mrs. Nicholls,[8] and to Mrs. Colden, I am, with great Regard, Dear Sir, Your most obedient humble Servant   B FRANKLIN
Mr Colden

To Thomas Cushing

ALS and incomplete copy: Public Record Office; letterbook draft: Library of Congress[9]

The interview described in the first part of this letter involved Franklin further in the developing crisis in Massachusetts, and the enclosure he

8. Colden's father- and mother-in-law. For Richard Nicholls see above, II, 407 n; XII, 229 n.
9. The incomplete copy, which is otherwise identical in wording with the ALS, omits the discussion of the Hutchinson letters; the draft has some variations, and because of the letter's unusual importance we have noted all that are not picayune. The ALS is headed by BF's copy of his previous letter to Cushing (above, Nov. 4), and also has two later notes by Thomas Moffat, the Rhode Island Loyalist. The first mentions BF's conference with Dartmouth and the revelation of the correspondence "purloind from the Collection of the late Mr. Whatley." The second remarks that Bernard or Hutchinson can understand and explain this letter, "more especially with regard to the Character Conduct and Property of Persons therein mentioned and referrd to." In the circumstances Moffat's comments were surprisingly mild: some of his own letters to Whately, as mentioned below, were in the purloined correspondence that was published in Boston.

described in the second part inflamed that crisis and deeply affected the remainder of his English mission. The importance of the letter is obvious, and so are the problems that it raises.

The subject of the interview was a petition from the Massachusetts House against the crown's paying the Governor's salary, on the ground that the House controlled it as a matter of right.[1] Franklin had presented the petition in November. The Secretary, in accepting it, had tacitly acknowledged what his predecessor had denied, the American's position as agent of the House;[2] but the document itself was scarcely designed to inaugurate an era of reconciliation under the new regime. Dartmouth faced a dilemma. The right claimed by the House was sure, he knew, to meet angry rejection, which would further heat the atmosphere in Massachusetts; yet his refusing to forward the claim would reinforce the colonists' grievance that they were denied access to the throne.[3] His solution was to delay, obviously in the hope that time would cool tempers in Boston, moderate open defiance, and so permit him to use his good offices. In the interview he agreed to transmit the petition if the agent insisted, but urged him to withhold it pending consultation with his constituents. Now that they had a friend in the American department, the Minister implied, they might change their tune. Franklin had little hope that they would, and said so; but in the end he reluctantly agreed.

The interview was a promising moment, it might seem, for two influential men of intelligence and good will, if they wanted reconciliation, to search together for possible means. But the search did not go far. Dartmouth, if he was quoted aright,[4] advanced nothing immediately constructive; all he offered was delay, which would be constructive only if Massachusetts gave him room to maneuver. Franklin accepted the offer, which he clearly believed would not change his constituents' stand, and stopped there. He could not have done more, it may be argued, without compromising his own stand. In January, writing to Cushing, he had opposed a royal salary for the Governor,[5] and to Cooper he had explained why: only through financial control of the chief executive could the House prevent implementation of illegal in-

1. See the headnote on Cushing to BF above, July 15.
2. See BF to Cushing above, Nov. 4.
3. See above, p. 217–18.
4. BF's account of the interview, like his report of the very different but equally unproductive conversation with Dartmouth's predecessor almost two years before (above, XVIII, 9–16), is the only one we have, and may not accurately reflect the Minister's attitude.
5. See above, p. 23.

structions from the crown.[6] When the agent first saw the petition, and found that the House claimed such control by constitutional right, he showed no sign of uneasiness.[7] When he agreed to withhold the petition until it was reconsidered, he touched on the possibility that in doing so his constituents might wish, not to retreat from their claim, but to add to it all their other grievances. What he seems to have hoped was that they would be sufficiently mollified by Hillsborough's removal to change the tone rather than the substance of their demands. He, like Dartmouth, was buying time. He had no way of knowing that the purchase would prove useless because the House, far from being mollified, was becoming still more intransigent.

His desire to lessen that intransigence was the motive he gave for sending the packet of correspondence that he enclosed with his letter. The motive has been impugned and defended from that day to this; his decision to forward the packet was probably the most controversial act of his career. What he sent were private letters written some years before by Thomas Hutchinson, Andrew Oliver, and others to a mutual friend in London, Thomas Whately. How he acquired the correspondence is a question still wrapped in mystery, and hence open to fascinating if inconclusive conjecture; so is the much more crucial question of why he sent it. The mystery is worth examining even if it cannot be solved, but first a sketch of the background.

Thomas Hutchinson and his wife's brother-in-law, Andrew Oliver, were scions of distinguished Boston families and had long been prominent in the provincial government. Prominence did not mean popularity; neither one had held elective office for many years, and both had numerous enemies. At the time the letters were written, between 1767 and 1769, Oliver was secretary of Massachusetts and Hutchinson was chief justice and lieutenant governor. Oliver managed extensive local property of an English family related to Whately, and in this way got into correspondence with him. Hutchinson's correspondence was probably arranged through the other Bostonian who figures largely in the affair, John Temple.[8]

Temple has appeared frequently in earlier volumes, for he was an old acquaintance of Franklin and his son. He was also a distant relative of Earl Temple and his brother, George Grenville, and used this connec-

6. See above, pp. 13–14.
7. See his brief letters to Cushing above, Sept. 3 and Nov. 4.
8. In 1765 Whately asked Temple for an introduction to Hutchinson, who was intending to come to England but did not; it is reasonable to assume that Temple suggested a correspondence between the two. See Bernard Bailyn, *The Ordeal of Thomas Hutchinson* (Cambridge, Mass., 1974), pp. 225–6, and for a thorough discussion of the whole mysterious affair pp. 221–38.

tion for all it was worth. In 1761 he was appointed Surveyor General of the Customs for the northern colonies, and soon afterward stretched his authority by appointing Timothy Folger customs collector of Nantucket. Folger was eventually dismissed.[9] Temple married the daughter of James Bowdoin, Franklin's old friend, and became as popular with the mercantile community as he was unpopular with his fellow officials. When he was named to the Board of Customs Commissioners in 1767, his bias toward the Americans outraged the other members; and his conduct was a theme of Hutchinson's and Oliver's letters. In 1770 Temple was recalled, and he arrived in England at a time when he could have purloined the letters.

So much for the chief American dramatis personae. The chief known protagonists in England, aside from Franklin himself, were George Grenville and Thomas Whately. Grenville, after having been the King's first minister for the two fateful years that culminated in passage of the Stamp Act, became a leader of opposition until his death in 1770, and worked consistently against any policy that might be construed as surrender to colonial demands. His lieutenant, protégé, and confidant was Whately, an M.P. who during the years in power had been a secretary of the Treasury, and during the years of opposition was the manager and principal strategist of the Grenville faction in the House of Commons.

For any one who wished to maintain a firm line with the colonies, Hutchinson and Oliver were useful correspondents. Their letters were full of violence and threats of violence against royal officials in Boston, and hence were fuel for British resentment. The writers indicated that the members of the Board of Customs Commissioners, John Temple excepted, went in fear of their lives, and that public order was breaking down under pressure of the mob. Oliver argued in 1767 that royal officials must be paid by the crown, an argument that had already been accepted by the framers of the Townshend Acts; he also proposed altering the charter to create an order of patricians, from which the Council would be chosen. Hutchinson insisted that the only way to avert disaster was to remove government gradually from popular control, and to secure the dependence of the province at the cost, much as it pained him, of abridging "what are called English liberties"; for no distant colony could be so governed as to give its inhabitants the same liberty as those of the mother country. In general, although both men clearly wanted an uncompromising ministerial policy, they did not say what it should be. They viewed with alarm, as might be expected of conservatives in power and threatened by violence, and they waited hopefully

9. See above, XVI, 207 n.

for the administration to act. They did not, in short, instigate repressive measures, as Franklin says they did; they argued that such measures were necessary, but in these letters they did not specify any.[1]

At some time after the beginning of 1770 a packet of the correspondence, perhaps a random sample, began the wanderings that brought it into Franklin's hands. By the time it reached him Grenville and Whately had died, the first in November of 1770 and the second in June of 1772. Either man may have lent the letters to some one who failed to return them, or they may have disappeared after Whately's death, when his papers came to his brother and executor, William Whately, a London banker. All that can be established is that they vanished, and that Franklin had them by the beginning of December, 1772; he always kept silent about when and from whom he obtained them. He sent the originals to Cushing, with strict injunctions against publicizing them. Whether or not he was naïf enough to believe that the injunctions would be respected, they were ignored; the letters were printed in Boston, and the recriminations began.

The man most strongly suspected, then and since, of having purloined the correspondence was John Temple. By the time he reached London from America, Grenville had died and left his papers—which may or may not have included the letters—to his brother and executor, Lord Temple; even a distant relative might have had access to them. If, on the other hand, the letters remained with Whately, John Temple also had access to them. He was frequently in touch with Thomas and, four months after his death, called on William Whately to look for correspondence of his own, and for a time was left alone with the papers. After the letters became a *cause célèbre*, word of this October visit got around. Temple and William Whately were under a cloud, each as a possible culprit, and in trying to exonerate themselves they quarreled

1. See *The Representations of Governor Hutchinson and Others, Contained in Certain Letters Transmitted to England, and Afterwards Returned from Thence, and Laid before the General Assembly of the Massachusetts-Bay...* (Boston, 1773), especially pp. 16, 22, 30–2. This is the most complete of the early editions. It contains, like the others, six letters from Hutchinson, four from Oliver, one apiece from Charles Paxton and Nathaniel Rogers, and one enclosure of Robert Auchmuty to Hutchinson; it also includes three letters and an enclosure from Thomas Moffat and one letter from George Rome. For the various American and British editions and reprints in 1773–74 see Thomas R. Adams, *American Independence: the Growth of an Idea...* (Providence, R.I., 1965), pp. 72–5. The letters have not been republished for more than a century, but they will appear as an appendix to Volume xx, below.

publicly with one another. The result was a duel in December, 1773. At that point Franklin broke his silence. He announced in the press that he alone had obtained and transmitted the letters, that they had never been in William Whately's possession, and that Temple therefore could not have taken them from him.[2] Whately later sued Franklin in Chancery to force him to reveal how he had acquired them. Unfortunately for the historian, however, the defendant left the country before the suit was concluded, and little record of it remains.

This is all of the story that can be reconstructed with reasonable assurance. What little more Franklin had to say is not enlightening. The letters, according to him, were being handed about in England to discredit the colonists; but he apparently did not know of their existence until at some point he was in conversation with "a Gentleman of Character and Distinction," who assured him that colonial grievances arose from policies proposed to the government "by some of the most respectable among the Americans themselves." The gentleman, whom we shall have to call X, found Franklin incredulous, offered to convince him and through him his countrymen, and returned a few days later with the letters in question; eventually he consented to have the originals sent to Boston, on condition that they be kept from the public and that his name be concealed.[3] Franklin's only other significant statements were two: that Thomas Whately delivered the letters to some one;[4] and that Grenville, "the Centre to which flow'd all the Corres-

2. See BF's statement below, Dec. 25, 1773. Note that he denied, not that Temple had taken the letters, but only that he had taken them from William Whately. Almost as soon as the writers knew that their letters had been returned to Boston, they suspected Temple: Oliver to Robert Thompson, June 3, 1773, Oliver Letterbook II, Mass. Hist. Soc.; Hutchinson to Israel Mauduit, Aug. 23, 1773, Mass. Arch., XXVII, 536–7. Years later, in 1779, Samuel Adams, Bowdoin, Charles Chauncy, Cooper, and Cushing—who called themselves knowing—testified to their belief that Temple had been the means of procuring the letters, had consequently lost a lucrative post in England and another post in America, and should be compensated. 6 Mass. Hist. Soc. *Coll.*, IX (1897), 434–6. In a letter to BF in 1781 Temple explained that he had elicited support from these men, which they had hesitated to give to his unsubstantiated statement; but he *had* procured the letters, he reminded BF, and had imposed the restrictions on their use. *Ibid.*, pp. 461–2. If BF answered, his reply has been lost, so that we have only Temple's word for the part he played; and in 1779–81 he was trying so hard to rebuild his reputation in Boston that his word is open to question. He remains by far the likeliest suspect, in our opinion, but no more than that.

3. From BF's apologia in 1774: Smyth, *Writings*, VI, 262–4.

4. *Ibid.*, p. 286. The some one could of course have been Grenville.

pondence inimical to America," lent them to some one and died before they were returned, whereupon they started on their wanderings.[5] If either statement is true, the some one could have been X, who showed the packet to a number of people before bringing it to Franklin. Or it could have been taken by a quite different person, who passed it on to another, so that it went through many hands before coming to Craven Street; in that case X need not have had any connection with Grenville or Whately, or any opportunity to get at the papers of either one.

Motive, rather than opportunity, may give some ground for conjecturing X's identity. Two possible motives come to mind, a dislike of Hutchinson and a desire, if Franklin is to be believed, to demonstrate that some of the most respectable Americans had asked for and obtained the measures, now branded as grievances, that they considered necessary for the welfare of the colonies. Any one familiar with the situation in Boston must have known that the letters would arouse particular fury against the Governor. If that was X's purpose, he may have intended his ban on publication to be ignored, as it was. But who in England had reason for such an attack? Certainly John Temple, who blamed his dismissal from the customs post on Hutchinson;[6] Temple knew Boston, and Franklin knew him. Thomas Pownall seems at first glance to be another possibility, because he had ambitions to return to his former governorship. He was on good terms with leaders in Boston, and on good enough terms with the ministry to be a candidate for the position if it fell vacant. But he must have known that undermining the incumbent's position in Massachusetts might well strengthen it in Whitehall, where governors were made and unmade, and hence was no sure way to create the vacancy; ambition gave Pownall at best a questionable motive for acting as X did. The search for that faceless person among Hutchinson's possible ill-wishers turns up nothing conclusive.

X's desire to put the onus of past British policy on American shoulders reveals little about his motives. He may have been trying to exculpate the Pitt–Grafton administration and smooth the path of the present one by diverting colonial bitterness elsewhere; he may equally well have realized that he was stirring up more trouble. But in either case why the strict injunction to keep his name secret? If he purloined the letters, he had every reason to conceal his part in the affair. If he came by them

5. BF to Cushing below, July 7, 1773.
6. Peter O. Hutchinson, ed., *The Diary and Letters of His Excellency Thomas Hutchinson* (2 vols., London, 1883–86), I, 207, 209. What Temple told Hutchinson is again hearsay evidence, but reliable because it was against Temple's interests by the time he produced it.

honestly, he was perhaps so situated that he could not afford to have the part known. All that can reasonably be conjectured about him is that he was less oblivious than the Grenvillites to American opinion, and that he had a guilty conscience or a delicate position or both. These supposititious clues do not identify him, but they do invite further speculation.

Temple again is a strong candidate. He was bitter against Hutchinson, and presumably against the North administration because it had recalled him. But it had also reimbursed him with an English customs post;[7] he was therefore a placeman who, if his taking the letters should ever transpire, stood to be ruined again. No one else is known to have had such a good opportunity for taking them, and he fulfills our other conjectural criteria for X.

Another candidate, intriguing though less likely, is William Strahan. In late 1769 and early 1770 he was doing what he could to circulate Franklin's statement on the colonial question among politicians in London.[8] Assume for the moment that one of them was Grenville, whom Strahan respected as a pillar of the opposition;[9] assume that the former minister responded to Franklin's views by insisting that the Bostonians must be brought to heel because they were defying all authority, and by giving Strahan the letters to prove his point. Such assumptions droop without support, and here there is only a little. In the early months of 1770 Strahan spoke of accounts from America that were working against conciliation, and commented on the difference between Franklin's and his opinions and sources of information;[1] what his own sources were he did not say. We have no evidence that the two men were in close touch again until August, 1772, when they apparently met at least twice within a few days.[2] These could have been the two crucial meetings that Franklin, according to his story, had with X: at the first the conversation ranged over the colonial issue, and at the second the letters changed hands.

But at that point conjecture runs into difficulties. If Strahan produced

7. Late in 1771 he was appointed Surveyor General of the Customs in England: 6 Mass. Hist. Soc. *Coll.*, IX, 280, 357. He lost the position in 1774 because, he later claimed, of his part in the affair: above, p. 404 n. BF disagreed. He could find no reason for the dismissal, he wrote Temple's father-in-law early in 1775, except that the Surveyor General had criticized the administration in the public press. Smyth, *Writings*, VI, 311.

8. See above, XVI, 233–5, 243–9.

9. "Correspondence between William Strahan and David Hall, 1763–1777," *PMHB*, XI (1887), 354.

1. *Ibid.*, p. 229; J. E. Pomfret, ed., "Some Further Letters of William Strahan, Printer," *PMHB*, LX (1936), 478.

2. See Strahan to BF above, Aug. 21, 27.

the packet, why did he do it then? Dartmouth had just succeeded Hillsborough, and the hope of reconciliation was brightening; also the ambitions of the Walpole Company, in which Straham was involved, seemed about to be realized. Why did he not let well enough alone?

The answer may lie partly in his political views and partly in his character. His position on the colonial question was between Franklin's and the Grenvillites': although he consistently supported the principle of Parliamentary taxation, he had favored partial repeal of the Townshend duties.[3] In 1771 he had concocted a plan for Anglo-American union, to be presented to those in power; he boasted of knowing "some of our Great Men, who are in the Secret of Affairs."[4] He had, as this suggests, a high if unwarranted opinion of his political connections, and preened himself on his sources of information. If he told Franklin that British policy had been based on advice of prominent Americans, and was challenged for proof, he might well have produced it without weighing the consequences for any one but himself. A pledge to keep his name secret would have been a natural precaution, not so much because of his conscience—he could be cavalier about private letters[5]—as because of his position: a printer doing business with the government was open to reprisals. He may even have taken the further precaution of securing the pledge in writing, for in later years he is said to have had in his possession an extract in Franklin's hand of this letter to Cushing.[6] But hearsay and supposition add up to nothing more than a possibility. The secret that Franklin kept is still as safe as it was with him; X, like Junius, remains unknown.

The question of his identity is much less important than the question of why Franklin sent the letters. The reasons that he gave are clear enough: his resentment of the British government decreased, he said,

3. *PMHB*, XI, 355–7; LX, 477 n.

4. *Ibid.*, XI, 489.

5. For examples of his disclosing such letters and being criticized for it by Thomas Wharton and Hutchinson see *ibid.*, XXXIII (1909), 447–9; Hutchinson, *op. cit.* (above, p. 406 n), II, 324–5.

6. Strahan twice mentioned the extract to Hutchinson, who apparently never saw it. *Ibid.*, pp. 118, 248. Strahan may have obtained the pledge, if it was part of the extract, for other reasons than self-protection; the evidence is only suggestive. A large number of other men, most of them obscure, have also been suspected of stealing the correspondence. We have been unable to find evidence against them, even as tenuous as that against Strahan, and have therefore left them out of consideration. For a discussion of them see Bernhard Knollenberg, "Benjamin Franklin and the Hutchinson and Oliver Letters," Yale University Library *Gaz.*, XLVII (1972), 1–9; see also the references in Gipson, *British Empire*, XII, 59 n.

on discovering that its policies had been instigated by Americans; and he assumed that the discovery would have the same effect on his Boston friends. His aim was to reconcile them to the mother country, in short, at Hutchinson's and Oliver's expense. But if this was his real aim he was not thinking clearly. He knew, and had a petition from the House of Representatives to prove it, that the Governor was at loggerheads with the legislature because he had followed instructions from Whitehall. Directing anger at him, as instigator of the policies behind the instructions, could not conceivably divert it from the government that had made those policies its own, but could only exacerbate the quarrel. Franklin admitted as much later. He had been glad to accept X's condition of keeping the letters secret, he said, because he feared that publishing them would produce violence in Massachusetts.[7] That fear runs counter to his claim, to which he consistently adhered,[8] that he was hoping to improve Anglo-American relations.

He later added another point that must be taken into account. Disclosing the letters gave the government the chance to seek reconciliation, he asserted, by laying the blame for the quarrel where it belonged, on the writers, and shifting to a more liberal policy; but Whitehall ignored the opportunity.[9] The furor against Hutchinson and Oliver, in other words, could and should have led to their replacement by more conciliatory officials backed by a more conciliatory minister.[1] Dartmouth seemed ready to inaugurate a new era if given an opening, which Franklin may have believed that he was providing. In that case, however, his miscalculation was spectacular, and does small credit to his acumen.

If the promotion of harmony is ruled out as an implausible motive, Franklin's relationship with his constituents remains. Their increasing opposition to royal authority was revealed in their petition, which the interview he describes with Dartmouth had just dissuaded him from presenting; and that opposition must have disturbed him because it threatened his concept of the empire. In an unreflecting moment he may

7. Smyth, *Writings*, VI, 263–4.
8. See, for example, his apologia in 1774: *ibid.*, p. 263.
9. *Ibid.*, pp. 196, 204, 282–3.
1. BF may conceivably have misread the furor over Gov. Bernard's letters as substantiation for this hope. They were sent to Boston and published in 1769, and shortly afterward the Governor was allowed to resign: above, XVI, 222 n. But his resignation was not the result of the disclosure, and had no effect on ministerial policy. Hutchinson himself believed that his local enemies were soliciting their correspondents in England for copies of his letters, in order to distort them and enrage the people against him. To Dartmouth, March 20, 1773, Mass. Arch., XXVII, 468.

really have believed that he could improve the situation by shifting the focus of argument from theories to personalities. About the former he was not yet fully decided; about the latter he was. His anger at the writers, if it was as genuine as it seems, doubtless made their exposure appear to be a service to Massachusetts.

At that particular moment such a service was timely, for his handling of the petition laid him open to criticism in Boston. He had earlier castigated his predecessor, Dennys DeBerdt, for delay in presenting a petition.[2] Now he himself was not only delaying one but referring it back, at Dartmouth's behest, for reconsideration. His announcement to Cushing that he had reluctantly agreed to do so was followed immediately by his announcement of the letters. This juxtaposition may have been more than coincidence, or it may not. All we know of his reasons for sending the correspondence is what he tells us, and that may be interpreted as anything between deception or self-deception at one extreme and the truth at the other. The verdict of history may perhaps be the one that John Dryden gave on another controversial episode:

> Succeeding times did equal folly call
> Believing nothing or believing all.

Sir,   London, Dec. 2. 1772

The above is a Copy of my last,[3] and no Ship has since sailed for Boston. A few Days after my leaving your Petition with Lord Dartmouth, his Lordship sent for me to discourse with me upon it. After a long Audience he was pleas'd to say, That notwithstanding all I had said or that could be said in Support[4] of the Petition, he was sure the Presenting it at this time could not possibly produce any Good; That the King would be exceedingly offended, but what Steps he would take upon it was uncertain; perhaps he would require the Opinion of the Judges or Government Lawyers, which would surely be against us; perhaps he might lay it before Parliament, and so the Censure of both Houses would be drawn down upon us; the most favourable thing to be expected was, a severe Reprimand to the Assembly by Order of his Majesty; the natural Consequence of which must be, more Discontent and Uneasiness in the Province. That possess'd as he was with great Good-will for New-England, he was extreamly unwilling that one

2. See above, xv, 196–9.
3. Of Nov. 4, as explained above, p. 399 n.
4. The draft inserts "and Justification."

of the first Acts of his Administration with regard to the Massachusetts should be of so unpleasant a nature: That Minds had been heated and irritated on both sides the Water, but he hoped those Heats were now cooling, and he was averse to any Addition of fresh Fuel: That as I had delivered the Petition to him officially, he must present it if I insisted upon it; but he wished I would first consult my Constituents, who might possibly on Reconsideration think fit to order its being deferred. I answered, that the great Majority with which the Petition, and the Resolves on which it was founded, were carried thro' the House, made it scarce expectable that their Order would be countermanded; that the slighting, evading or refusing to receive Petitions from the Colonies on some late Occasions by the Parliament, had occasioned a total Loss of the Respect for and Confidence in that Body, formerly subsisting so strongly[5] in America, and brought on a Questioning of their Authority: That his Lordship might observe, Petitions came no more from thence to Parliament, but to the King only; That the King appeared to be now the only Connection between the two Countries; and that, as a continued Union was essentially necessary to the Well-being of the whole Empire, I should be sorry to see that Link weakened as the other had been: That I thought it a dangerous thing for any Government to refuse receiving Petitions, and thereby prevent the Subjects from giving Vent to their Griefs. His Lordship interrupted me by replying, that he did not refuse to deliver the Petition; that it should never be justly said of him that he intercepted the Complaints of his Majesty's Subjects, and that he must and would present it, as he had said before, whenever I should absolutely require it; but from Motives of pure Good will to the Province, he only wish'd me not to insist on it, 'till I should receive fresh Orders. Finally, considering that since the Petition was ordered, there has been a Change in the American Administration; that the present Minister was our Friend in the Repeal of the Stamp-Act, and seems still to have good Dispositions towards us; that you had mention'd to me the Probability that the House would have remonstrated on all their other Grievances, had not their Time been taken up with the difficult Business of a general Valuation; and, since the Complaint of this Petition alone was likely to give Offence, it might perhaps be judg'd adviseable to

5. In the draft "so strongly" is omitted.

give the Offence of all our Complaints at once, rather than in Parts and after a Reprimand received; I say, upon the whole[6] I thought it best not to disoblige him in the Beginning of his Administration, by refusing him what he seem'd so desirous of, a Delay at least in presenting the Petition, till farther Directions should be received from my Constituents. If after Deliberation they should send me fresh Orders, I shall immediately obey them: And the Application itself may possibly derive greater Weight from the Reconsideration given it, while the Temper of the House may be thought somewhat calmed by the Removal of a Minister who had render'd himself so obnoxious to them. Accordingly I consented to the Delay desired, wherein I hope my Conduct will not be disapproved.[7]

On this Occasion I think it fit to acquaint you that there has lately fallen into my Hands Part of a Correspondence, that I have reason to believe laid the Foundation of most if not all our present Grievances. I am not at liberty to tell thro' what Channel I receiv'd it; and I have engag'd that it shall not be printed, nor any Copies taken of the whole or any part of it; but I am allow'd and desired to let it be seen by some Men of Worth in the Province for their Satisfaction only. In confidence of your preserving inviolably my Engagement, I send you enclos'd the original Letters, to obviate every Pretence of Unfairness in Copying, Interpolation or Omission. The Hands of the Gentlemen will be well known. Possibly they may not like such an Exposal of their Conduct, however tenderly and privately it may be managed. But if they are good Men,[8] and agree that all good Men wish a good Understanding and Harmony to subsist between the Colonies and their Mother Country, they ought the less to regret, that at the small

6. The whole passage from "that you had mention'd" to this point is omitted in the draft.

7. The draft inserts here: "I shall not on this Occasion presume to advise; but only add, That tho' I thought I could perceive that his Lordship was not, after all, convinc'd himself of the Reasonableness of the Petition, yet his Unwillingness to present it at this time did not proceed so much from his own Opinion of it, as from his Knowledge of the Sentiments of others, whose Judgment upon it would be rely'd on and follow'd." Massachusetts reacted by sending a second petition and instructing BF to submit them both; see Cushing's letter to him below, March 24, 1773.

8. The draft inserts "or pretend to be such."

Expence of their Reputation for Sincerity and Publick Spirit among their Compatriots, so desirable an Event may in some degree be forwarded. For my own Part, I cannot but acknowledge, that my Resentment against this Country, for its arbitrary Measures in governing us, conducted by the late Minister, has, since my Conviction by these Papers, that those Measures were projected, advised and called for by Men of Character among ourselves, and whose Advice must therefore be attended with all the Weight that was proper to mislead, and which could therefore scarce fail of Misleading; my own Resentment, I say, has by this means been considerably[9] abated. I therefore wish I was at Liberty to make the Letters publick; but as I am not,[1] I can only allow them to be seen by yourself, by the other Gentlemen of the Committee of Correspondence, by Messrs. Bowdoin, and Pitts, of the Council, and Drs. Chauncey, Cooper and Winthrop,[2] with a few such other Gentlemen as you may think it fit to show them to. After being some Months in your Possession, you are requested to return them to me.

As to the Writers, I can easily as well as charitably conceive it possible, that a Man educated in Prepossessions of the unbounded Authority of Parliament, &c. may think unjustifiable every Opposition even to its unconstitutional Exertions, and imagine it their Duty to suppress, as much as in them lies, such Opposition. But when I find them bartering away the Liberties of their native Country for Posts, and negociating for Salaries and Pensions, for which the Money is to be squeezed from the People;[3] and, conscious of the Odium these might be attended with, calling for Troops to protect and secure the Enjoyment of them; when I see them exciting Jealousies in the Crown, and provoking it to Wrath against a great Part of its faithful[4] Subjects; creating Enmities

9. The draft reads "exceedingly."

1. The draft, from the beginning of the sentence, reads: "But as I am not, as I have said at liberty to make the Letters publick."

2. For Councillor James Pitts, a wealthy Boston merchant who was Bowdoin's brother-in-law, and the Rev. Charles Chauncy, minister of the First Church since 1727, see respectively *Sibley's Harvard Graduates*, IX, 76, and the *DAB*. The progressive breakdown of BF's restrictions are described in Cushing's letters to him below, March 24, April 20, and June 14, 1773.

3. The draft reads "Salaries and Pensions extorted from the People."

4. The draft reads "so great a Part of its most faithful."

between the different Countries of which the Empire consists; occasioning a great Expence to the new Country for the Payment of needless Gratifications to useless Officers and Enemies; and to the old for Suppressing or Preventing imaginary Rebellions in the new; I cannot but doubt their Sincerity even in the political Principles they profess; and deem them mere Time-servers, seeking their own private Emolument thro' any Quantity of Publick Mischief; Betrayers of the Interest, not of their Native Country only, but of the Government they pretend to serve, and of the whole English Empire. With the greatest Esteem and Respect, I have the Honour to be, Sir, Your most obedient and most humble Servant

B FRANKLIN

To Cadwalader Evans

ALS and letterbook draft: American Philosophical Society

Dear Doctor, London, Dec. 2. 1772

I am much concern'd to hear of your Illness, and hope that long before this time you have been able to execute your Intentions of Riding, and have recovered your usual Health and Vigour.

I received your Favour of Oct 21. with the Bill enclos'd drawn by Order of the Managers for promoting the Culture of Silk, on me, for £152 0s. 9d. in favour of James & Drinker and yourself: and am glad the Purchase I made was satisfactory. As this Sum exceeds my Disbursement, the Overplus will wait your Orders; and particularly I wish to have Directions what I am to pay Mr. Wheeler for his Diligence and Trouble in the Transaction, which really was considerable.[5]

The Truss was sent; I am vex'd that it did not come to hand, and

5. BF's purchase was the £115 15s. 6d. he had spent for the city lot in Philadelphia; the £152 was what he had received for the silk; the "Overplus" was slightly more than £36. See above, BF to Wheeler, April 3, to Evans and to James, June 3; BF to James below, Dec. 2; Ledger, p. 59. What the Managers were doing, if we reconstruct the bookkeeping correctly, was transferring the proceeds of the silk from their account with BF to Evans' account with him (though why the firm of James & Drinker was involved we have no idea); the purpose was to cancel Evans' debt to BF for the lot. Out of the £36 surplus BF subsequently paid Wheeler £21 for his services: loc. cit.; Jour., p. 46; BF to the Managers of the Silk Filature below, Jan. 6, 1773.

413

must enquire what became of it.[6] With great Esteem, I am ever, my dear Friend, Yours most affectionately B FRANKLIN

Dr Cadr Evans

Addressed: To | Dr Cadwalader Evans | Philadelphia | viâ N York | per Packet | B Free FRANKLIN

To John Foxcroft ALS (letterbook draft): Library of Congress

Dear Friend, London, Dec. 2. 1772

I am sorry to acquaint you that the Account Mr. Colden sent over from New York by the Octr Packet is look'd upon at the Office as no Account at all, the Receipts being lump'd in one Article of £5649 2s. 3½d. without any State of the Accounts of the several Offices to support that Article. It is therefore rejected, and I can make no Settlement till you send it me in the usual Form, viz. giving Credit to G.P.O. for every separate Sum receiv'd and of what Office, and accompanying the General Account with a Book of the particular Accounts as they stand between the several Offices and the American G P Office stated clearly as they stand in the Comptroller's Book, and ballanced. To do this, it is not necessary to wait till every Officer has remitted his Ballance. It is enough to show what was due from him when the Accounts were made up. I wrote to you on this Head about the Middle of last Month,[7] and to day Mr. Todd call'd on me, and earnestly desired I would urge it on you, for no Account can be settled by me, or render'd to Government by the Office, till this arrives. And I wonder at its being omitted, since it has always been the Practice. By a Letter Mr. Todd show'd me, dated Nov. 4. from Mr. Colden, he seems sensible that the Account he render'd was imperfect; for he excuses him self by saying, that he had no Precedent to show him how the Accounts had been heretofore stated, and that he therefore followed your Direction, you having assur'd him that was the usual Form, which Mr. Todd wonder'd at. I beg therefore

6. See BF to Evans above, Aug. 22, and below, Feb. 10, 1773.

7. Above, Nov. 19, where BF discusses not only the accounts but also a number of other matters mentioned later in this letter. See also BF to Colden above, Dec. 2.

that you would immediately urge him to get them done and send them over in the manner mentioned.

The Account of Bills charg'd to me is very right; excepting that I had no Credit for two return'd to Parker protested, but I had overpaid into the Office before the Accounts arrived, supposing I should have been charged with what the Philadelphia Office has paid on my Account to Mrs. Franklin. Full Credit is given me for my Salary, and no mention of those Payments. Perhaps you have taken them into your private Account with me, by Way of discharging what I overpaid you here; but you mention nothing of it.[8] Will you not take it amiss if I once more mention that I am uneasy at the long continuance of that Account unadjusted?

I congratulate you most cordially on the Allowance now made you of £100 a Year for House Rent in New York; and on Mr. Finlay's Appointment as Riding Surveyor (which you seem'd to desire) with a Salary of £200 a Year, and an Allowance to continue in his Quebec Office besides. He goes over in the Feby Packet and will immediately enter on Business: So that I now hope all will soon be in good Order. But pray don't let the Accounts wait for him. I can now only add my best Wishes of Happiness to you and Yours, from Dear Friend, Yours most affectionately

B FRANKLIN

Mr Foxcroft

8. For the protested bills, totaling £73 11s. 5d., see the letter to Foxcroft just cited. BF had apparently paid this amount to the post office, assuming that Foxcroft would credit him with it against the monthly allowance of £30 Pennsylvanian that DF was receiving from the Philadelphia post office (above, XVIII, 91). When he discovered that he was not being so credited, and that the allowance was not being debited against his salary, he wondered whether Foxcroft was paying DF himself to discharge the £389 that BF, in his letters above of Feb. 4 and Oct. 7, had pointed out were due him in their personal accounting. Foxcroft was not; the post office was providing the allowance on credit. In Oct., 1776, BF settled for £1042 5s. 7¼d. sterling that the Philadelphia post office had paid DF between Sept., 1769, and March, 1774. Jour., p. 61; Ledger, p. 11.

To Thomas Foxcroft   ALS (letterbook copy): Library of Congress

Dear Sir,   London, Dec. 2. 1772

I received yours of Oct. 23. with Invoice and Bill of Lading for the Bread and Flour you shipt per Osborne, and am much oblig'd by your Care in procuring and sending it so readily. I hope you have recovered your Health.[9] Present my best Respects to your good Brother and Sister, and believe me with sincere Regard, Your most obedient humble Servant   B F.

Mr Thos. Foxcroft,

To William Franklin   ALS (letterbook draft): Library of Congress

Dear Son,   London, Dec. 2, 1772

I have received yours of Oct. 4. 8. and 13. I cannot imagine what became of my Letter of Augt. 3. from May Place.[1] It was however of no great Importance. Mr. Denormandie is gone this Day to Geneva. I gave him a Letter of Recommendation to a Friend there.[2]

I am persuaded that your Packets were not open'd at the Office; for tho' a Secretary of State has the Power of ordering Letters to be opened, I think it is seldom used but in times of War, Rebellion, or on some great publick Occasion; and I have heard they have Means of copying the Seal so exactly, as that it cannot be discovered that the Letters have been look'd into. It is plain therefore, that whoever rubb'd your Packets open, had not the Use of such Means. And yet as you are satisfy'd it was not done on your side the Water, I suspect the Letter Carrier might be corrupted and the Business done between the Office in Lombard Street and my House. When a Packet arrives, a special Messenger goes directly from the Office with the publick Letters, before the Sorting is finished. Mine have been sometimes sent by the same

9. These matters were covered in Foxcroft to BF above, May 16.

1. Of the letters he mentions, only WF's of Oct. 13 is extant. For BF's visit to May Place see Cavendish to BF above, Aug. 4.

2. For Dr. John Denormandie see Galloway to BF above, Oct. 12. The friend in Geneva was, we conjecture, de Saussure, to whom BF had recently written; see his letter above, Oct. 8.

416

Messenger, who call'd on me in his Way to Lord H.'s and sometimes in his Return. And as he[3] told Mr. Strahan that his Letters to you were often return'd to me from America, and yours to him sent thro' my Hands, to be seen he suppos'd by me before Delivery; and since his Resignation your Packets do not appear to have suffered the least Violation, I fancy the Rubbing them open may possibly have been the Ingenuity of Mr. Secry. Knox.[4] By the List you have sent me I find none of the Papers missing. Another Circumstance in favour of this Opinion is, that no Letters to me were thus abused but yours and those from the Assembly of Boston. This I think clears the Person you suspected,[5] and rather fixes the above Conjecture.

I have not seen your Speech at the Opening of your last Session: but I hear it has been commended by the Ministry.[6]

I return Mr. Foxcroft's Letters as you desire.[7] I make no Remarks on the Reports he mentions. I know not who is meant by the *Hero of your Speech*. Nor will I say more at present of the Ohio Affair, than that it is not yet quite secure, and therefore I still advise Discretion in speaking of it.

Dr. Price has been so good as to give me his Opinion of your Scheme, which I send; hoping it may be of Use. I suppose you have his Book, referr'd to in the Paper.[8] Some Acknowledgement or Thanks should be sent him for the Trouble he has taken.

I continue very well, Thanks to God. On Monday last, I was

3. Lord Hillsborough.

4. WF frequently submitted his official letters to his father for approval and forwarding; see above, XVI, 36 n. We pointed out there that the arrangement was difficult to conceal, but this is the first evidence that Hillsborough knew of it. For William Knox, Undersecretary of the American Department, see above, XV, 94 n.

5. WF had voiced suspicion of Samuel Wharton in his letter of Oct. 13 above.

6. In his speech WF asked for appropriations for public works, and for bounties on flax, hemp, and silk. He also urged that officials' stipends be raised to meet the increased cost of living, and suavely implied what would happen if they were not: poverty had forced the Chief Justice to apply to the crown, which had assumed his whole salary. 1 *N.J. Arch.*, XVIII, 298–300.

7. Enclosed in WF's letter of Oct. 13 and now missing.

8. See Price to BF above, Sept. 30. If the scheme is correctly identified there, the book referred to was unquestionably Price's *Observations on Reversionary Payments*... (London, 1771).

chosen into the Council of the Royal Society for the 4th time. Our Friend Sir John Pringle was elected President, which is very agreable to him.[9]

I shall send you a Tea Urn by the first Ship.[1]

Just now comes to hand yours of Nov. 3. whereby I find mine of Aug. 3. is received. I am glad to learn that you and your neighbouring Governors are so sociable. I shall communicate what you write about the Virginia Grants.[2] At present I can only add that I am, with Love to Betsey, Your ever affectionate Father

B FRANKLIN

To Joseph Galloway ALS (letterbook draft): Library of Congress

Dear Friend, London, Dec. 2. 1772

I am favoured by your kind Letter of October 12.[3] inclosing three Bills of Exchange, viz.

Wilcocks on Baillie for	£142 9s. 6½d.
Do. on Col. Johnstone[4] for	166 15s. 3½d.
Roberdeau on Trevanion for	190 15s. 2d.
In all	£500 0s. 0d.

being the Amount of my last Year's Salary. I am much obliged to the House for their Punctuality, and to you for your friendly Care in the speedy Remittance.

I am glad you are returned again to a Seat in the Assembly, where your Abilities are so useful and necessary in the Service of

9. And to BF, who had canvassed for his friend among the membership; see his letter above, Nov. 26.

1. WF had requested the urn in his letter of Oct. 13. BF added at this point: "I just now hear that the November Packet is arrived, so I stop here till I receive the Letters that come by her." The sentence was deleted, probably by him because the next sentence replaced it.

2. WF's missing letter presumably amplified what he had said in those of Oct. 13 and 29.

3. Q.v. for the matters that BF raises in the first three paragraphs.

4. BF first indicated, as Galloway had, that the bill was on Baillie, and then amended this to Johnstone. Alexander Johnstone (1727–83) was lieutenant colonel of a regiment stationed in the West Indies but, like many officers of the day, was an absentee living in London. See *Burke's Peerage*, p. 1409; Richard Cannon, *Historical Record of the Seventieth, or Surrey Regiment of Foot...* (London, 1849), pp. 2–3; BF to Galloway below, Feb. 14, 1773.

your Country. We must not in the Course of Publick Life expect *immediate* Approbation, and *immediate* grateful Acknowledgement of our Services. But let us persevere, thro' Abuse and even Injury. The internal Satisfaction of a good Conscience is always present, and Time will do us Justice in the Minds of the People, even of those at present the most prejudic'd against us.

I have given Dr. Denormandie a Recommendation to a Friend in Geneva, for which Place he set out this Morning; and I shall be glad of any Opportunity of serving him when he returns to London.

I see by the Pensylvania Gazette of Oct. 21. that you are continued Speaker, and myself Agent, but I have no Line from you or the Committee relative to Instructions.[5] Perhaps I shall hear from you by Falconer. I find myself upon very good Terms with our new Minister Lord Dartmouth, who we have every reason to think means well to the Colonies. I believe all are now sensible that nothing is to be got by contesting with or oppressing us. Two Circumstances have diverted me lately. One was, that being at the Court of Exchequer on some Business of my own, I met there with one of the Commissioners of the Stamp Office, who told me he attended with a Memorial from that Board, to be allowed in their Accounts the Difference between their Expence in endeavouring to establish those Offices in America, and the Amount of what they received, which from Canada and the W India Islands was but about £1500, while the Expence, if I remember right was above £12,000 being for Stamps and Stamping, with Paper and Parchment return'd upon their Hands, Freight, &c.[6] The other is the present Difficulties of the India Company and of Government on their Account. The Company have accepted Bills which they find themselves unable to pay, tho' they have the Value of Two Millions in Tea and other India Goods in their

5. The *Pa. Gaz.* must have crossed the Atlantic faster than the committee's instructions; for the latter see above, Oct. 16.

6. The Commissioners were responsible for collecting the stamp duties that had been imposed, primarily upon legal documents, since 1694. By this time the annual yield was approaching £400,000; the total receipts from America were slightly more than £3,000. Stephen Dowell, *A History of Taxation and Taxes in England . . .* (2nd ed., 4 vols., London, 1888), III, 287–91; Dora Mae Clark, *The Rise of the British Treasury: Colonial Administration in the Eighteenth Century* (New Haven, 1960), pp. 160–1.

419

Stores, perishing under a Want of Demand. Their Credit thus suffering, and their Stock falling 120 per Ct. the Bank will not advance for them; and no Remedy is thought of but lowering their Dividend from 12½ to 6¼ per Cent. whereby Government will lose the £400,000 per annum it having been stipulated that it should no longer be paid if the Dividend fell to that Mark.[7] And altho' it is known that the American Market is lost by continuing the Duty on Tea, and that we are supply'd by the Dutch,[8] who doubtless take the Opportunity of Smuggling other India Goods among us with the Tea, so that for the 5 Years past we might probably have otherwise taken off the greatest Part of what the Company have on hand, and so have prevented their present Embarrasment, yet the Honour of Government is suppos'd to forbid the Repeal of the American Tea Duty; while the Amount of all the Duties goes on decreasing, so that the Ballance of this Year does not (as I have it from good Authority) exceed £80 after paying the Collection; not reckoning the immense Expence of Guarda Costa's,[9] &c. Can an American forbear smiling at these Blunders? tho' in a national

7. For the financial crisis of 1772 see BF to Bache above, Oct. 7. Because of it the East India Company was slow in realizing cash from its sale of imports; it also grossly underestimated the financial demands upon it. Cutting its dividend rate would have saved the annual payment of £400,000 due the government by statute (9 Geo. III, c. 24), but at the price of a catastrophic fall in the Company's stock. The Directors temporized until autumn, when they confessed themselves unable to repay their customary loan from the Bank of England and the Bank refused to extend it. See Sutherland, *East India Co.*, pp. 223–8; Benjamin W. Labaree, *The Boston Tea Party* (New York, 1964), pp. 58–62. Lord North intervened early in 1773, and pushed through Parliament three remedial measures: a loan, a regulating act, and the Tea Act that led directly to the Tea Party.

8. The smuggling of tea into America, from the Netherlands and elsewhere, had been thriving for some years; and by 1772 the legal importation of tea was only thirty percent of what it had been in 1768. *Ibid.*, pp. 52–7, 331; see also Gipson, *British Empire*, XII, 17–18.

9. Revenue from the duties as a whole, with tea a notable exception, was not declining but increasing; so was the cost of collection. See Clark, *op. cit.*, pp. 186–8. The war against smuggling, part of the new era inaugurated by the Townshend Acts, involved turning the crews of private ships into customs officers, paid from whatever they seized. Oliver M. Dickerson, *The Navigation Acts and the American Revolution* (Philadelphia, 1951), pp. 216–17. The name of guarda costas derived from the notorious Spanish patrols in the Caribbean that had helped to precipitate the War of Jenkins' Ear in 1739.

Light they are truly deplorable. With the sincerest Esteem, and
inviolable Attachment I am, my dear Friend, ever Most affectionately yours   B FRANKLIN

Mr Galloway

To Abel James

ALS (letterbook draft): Library of Congress; copy: Historical Society
of Pennsylvania

Dear Friend,   London, Dec. 2. 1772

I duly received your Favours of Sept. 22 and Oct. 9. and am
glad the Purchase proves acceptable. Our Friend Dr. Evans has
remitted me the Bill you mention, drawn for the Produce of the
Silk. It exceeds what I paid, and I wait Orders for the Disposition
of the Overplus, particularly what I am to pay Wheeler for his
Services in the Business.[1]

I do not at this Distance understand the Politics of your last
Election, why so many of the Members declin'd the Service, and
why yourself and Mr. Fox were omitted (which I much regret)
while Goddard was voted for by so great a Number. Another Year
I hope will set all right. The People seldom continue long in the
wrong when it is nobody's Interest to mislead them. It must be
very discouraging to our Friend Galloway, to see his long and
faithful Services, repaid with Abuse and Ingratitude; but let him
persevere in well-doing and all will end well, and to his final
Satisfaction.[2] And tho' it may be inconvenient to your private
Affairs to attend Publick Business, I hope neither you nor Mr. Fox
will thro' Resentment of the present Slight, decline the Service
when again called upon by your Country. With great and sincere
Esteem, I am ever, Dear Sir, Your affectionate Friend and most
obedient Servant   B F.

Mr Abel James

1. See above, BF to Wheeler, April 3, to James, June 3, and to Evans,
Dec. 2.

2. For Galloway's description of what had happened see his mutilated
letter above (which BF had presumably received by this time) of Oct. 12. BF's
optimism emphasizes how little he understood the shift of political power in
Philadelphia.

To Jacques Barbeu-Dubourg

Translated extract:[3] printed in Jacques Barbeu-Dubourg, ed., *Œuvres de M. Franklin*... (2 vols., Paris, 1773), II, 215.

De Londres, 8 Décembre 1772.
Lorsque les verres sont rangés sur le fuseau horisontal, ou pour me servir de votre expression, *enfilés*, et que chacun est arrêté à demeure, on voit la totalité du plus grand verre qui est tout à l'extrêmité à main gauche; le suivant entrant dans le premier ne montre qu'environ un pouce de sa bordure qui s'avance en-dehors du bord du plus grand; ainsi successivement chaque verre contenu déborde le verre contenant, laissant par ce moyen à découvert une bordure sur laquelle on peut appuyer le doigt. Les verres ne se touchent pas l'un l'autre, mais ils sont trop serrés pour laisser passer le doigt entre deux, de sorte que la bordure intérieure n'est pas susceptible de frottement. On applique le doigt à plat sur la bordure du plus grand verre, sur le bord du plus petit, en partie sur la bordure et en partie sur le bord des verres des grandeurs intermédiaires. Il n'y a que l'expérience qui puisse bien instruire en pareil cas, parce que les différens verres demandent à être touchés différemment: les uns un peu plus sur le bord, et les autres un peu plus sur la bordure. Il ne faut qu'une heure ou deux d'exercice pour apprendre cela.

Je fais graver une figure de l'Armonica, et je compte pouvoir vous l'envoyer bientôt.

To Lord Dartmouth   AL (draft): Dartmouth College Library

Cravenstreet, Dec. 8. 72
Dr. Franklin presents his best Respects to Lord Dartmouth, and believing it may be agreable as well as useful to him, to receive other Information of the Sentiments and Disposition of Leading

3. Dubourg translated this passage from a long letter, now missing, to which BF referred in writing him below, Dec. 26. In the discussion of his armonica BF is amplifying what he had said to Beccaria a decade earlier: above, X, 127–30. The extract was retranslated into English, so badly that BF would have spurned it (WTF, *Memoirs*, III, 359); subsequent editors have used that text.

422

People in America, besides what Ministers are usually furnish'd with from the Officers of the Crown residing there, takes the Liberty of communicating to his Lordship a Letter just received from the Speaker of the Assembly of the Massachusetts Bay, written not as Speaker, but in his private Capacity. Dr. F. purposes to wait on Lord D. at his Levee to-morrow, and shall be happy if he may bring from thence any thing proper to write in Answer, that should tend to compose the Minds of People in that Province, at present greatly disquieted and alarm'd by some late Measures of Government.[4]

Endorsed: Note to Lord Dartmth with Mr Cushing's Letter of Oct. 27 72

From Theophylact Bache[5]

ALS: American Philosophical Society

Sir,   New York 10th decemr. 1772.

Your much esteemed favor of 19th Sepr. was handed me by Mr. Alexander Chysholm. I shall pay due attention to this stranger, and shall be happy in doing him service.[6]

He has been to Phila: and is much disappointed in his expectations of setling there. He intends waiting here until Spring, before he determines what to do: We hope to get him well fixed at Woodbridge.

I am much obliged to you for your kind information of the state of my Mothers family at Preston. I have not heard from them in a long time. Mrs. Franklin, and the family were all well the last Ac-

4. Speaker Cushing's letter of Oct. 27, which has not survived, dealt with the sources of unrest in Massachusetts and the ways in which they might be eliminated. For the letter and Dartmouth's reception of it see BF to Cushing below, Jan. 5, 1773. The effect of BF's action was to inaugurate a friendly correspondence between the Secretary of State and the Speaker: *Sibley's Harvard Graduates*, XI, 386.

5. For Richard Bache's older brother see above, XIV, 174 n.

6. BF's letter of introduction has disappeared; in his reply below (Feb. 3, 1773) the name is Chysholme, but we can find no trace of the man under any spelling.

counts I had from my Brother, and hope it [will not now?] be long before I have the pleasure to see [you? *Torn*]. With great respect and esteem [I am?] Sir Your most obedient humble Servant

THEOPHYLACT BACHE

Addressed: To | Benja: Franklin Esqr | London | per Cap Winn

Members of the Purfleet Committee to the Royal Society

AL (incomplete draft): American Philosophical Society

On December 8 Benjamin Wilson, the vocal minority of one on the Purfleet committee, amplified his views in a long letter to the Surveyor General of the Ordnance, Sir Charles Frederick, in which he took sharp issue with the other members. On the 10th Sir Charles forwarded the letter to the Royal Society and asked for an opinion on it; the matter was urgent, he pointed out, because the Board of Ordnance needed to know at once what the best means were of safeguarding the magazine. The letter was consequently read at the Society's meeting later that day, before the report that it criticized; Wilson hoped to persuade the meeting to reject the committee's recommendation of pointed rather than blunt lightning rods, but he was disappointed. On the 17th his colleagues on the committee responded in a letter to the Society's President, Sir John Pringle, that ignored his arguments and brusquely reaffirmed their stand.[7]

This chronology indicates that the draft below was composed during the week between the 10th and 17th. What happened, we believe, was that the committee members were so incensed at being attacked before the membership that they commissioned Franklin to write a reply to be read at the next meeting. He did so, elaborating the arguments for pointed rods; and this incomplete draft is what remains of his answer. As the days passed, we conjecture, the angry scientists realized that such

7. The committee's report is above, Aug. 21, and its letter to Pringle below. Wilson's dissent from the report and his letter to Frederick were published in *Phil. Trans.*, LXIII (1773–74), 48–65. For Frederick's communication to the Royal Society and Wilson's reason for wanting his letter read before it see the latter's *Observations upon Lightning . . .* (London, 1773), pp. [iii–v]. For Frederick (1709–85), an M.P. and F.R.S. and a man of considerable influence, see Thomas Thomson, *History of the Royal Society . . .* (London, 1812), app., p. xxxix; Namier and Brooke, *House of Commons*, II, 472–3.

a detailed rebuttal would lead only to an unseemly and unprofitable wrangle, and decided to content themselves with a curt letter to Pringle.

Gentlemen,   [After Dec. 10 and before Dec. 17, 1772]
The Committee appointed by you in July last on an Application from the Royal Ordnance to consider of the most proper Means of securing the Powder Magazines at Purfleet from Danger by Lightning, made their Report to the Council during your Recess, agreable to your Instructions, who immediately transmitted it to the said Board. That Report together with the Committee who sign'd it, having since been censured by Mr. Wilson in a Letter to Sir Charles Frederic, Surveyor of the Ordnance, which Letter was read at Sir Charles's Request to the Society, and before the Report it self, with the Reasons on which it was founded could in the usual Course be laid before them, apparently tending to prejudice the Society against their Committee, especially as Mr. Wilson has stated his Objections with all the Strength they are capable of, and has passed over very slightly the Answers made to them in the Committee, and the Reasons on which it proceeded, only intimating his Ability and Intention of examining and invalidating those Reasons at some future time: We can not but think it a Piece of Justice due, not to ourselves merely, but to the Philosophical Part of the Question, that the Grounds of our Report in the Point controverted should be more fully explained than it could properly be in the Report itself. We therefore take the Liberty of acquainting you, that Mr. Wilson's Objections to the Use of Pointed Conductors were heard and considered in the several Meetings of the Committee with Patience and with Candour; that they were all answered and obviated to the Satisfaction of every one of the Committee but himself; and the Substance of what was said on the Occasion being contained in a Paper of Experiments, Observations and Facts, drawn up by Mr. Franklin, and read to the Committee in the Presence of Mr. Wilson, several of the Committee having seen the Experiments themselves, we here present the Society with that Paper.
(Here insert the Paper.)[8]

8. We earnestly wish that the paper had been inserted, because it would have indicated which version of his experiments BF read to the committee;

The Committee had also before them an Experiment of Mr. Henley's, related in a Letter from that Gentleman to Mr. Franklin, which as it seems to have been misapprehended by Mr. Wilson, is also here inserted, viz.

(Here insert it.)[9]

By this Experiment in which the Prime Conductor [is] suppos'd to represent a Cloud, it appeared, that the Point would operate at 12 times the striking Distance in drawing off and lessening the Quantity of Electric Fluid, before the Cloud could approach within that Distance; that a blunt Body drew off none of it till it came within that distance; that therefore if it struck on the blunt Body it would strike with its whole Force undiminish'd; on the Point it would either not strike at all or with a diminish'd Quantity for what is drawn off by a pointed Conductor, is at the same time convey'd away into the Earth. But these Consequences did not strike Mr. Wilson; to him, as he says in his Letter, "it appeared that the Difference in the Effects upon this Fluid, between pointed and blunted Metal, is as 12 to 1." And thence he seems to conclude that in a Stroke upon a Point 12 times the Quantity must be discharged, that would have fallen on a Body which had no Point:[1] For being persuaded from some Circumstances observed by the Verger of St. Pauls, in and about the Conductors upon that Building, the morning after the Thunder on March last; and examined by himself and Mr. Delaval about a Week after, that "a Bar of Iron near 4 Inches broad and about $\frac{1}{2}$ an Inch thick," had been "made considerably *hot* if not absolutely *red*; by a Stroke of Lightning;"[2] he says, he "thinks it a happy Circumstance that there was no Point fixed upon the Top of the Church to solicit a greater Quantity;" for "the Difference in the Effects between blunted

see the headnote on those experiments above, under Aug. 18. BF's references to numbered experiments, later in the draft, are to this paper; most of the other matters he deals with are explained in the headnotes on the committee's report above, Aug. 21, and on its letter to Pringle below, Dec. 17.

9. The experiment or experiments discussed in connection with the committee's report above, p. 261 ns.

1. For Wilson's misinterpretation of Henly see *ibid.*

2. During the storm on March 22, according to Wilson, St. Paul's was struck: *Observations*, pp. 13, 22. Henly visited the Cathedral soon afterward, and could find no indication of the effects of lightning. He so informed the Royal Society: *Phil. Trans.*, LXIV (1774), 148–51.

and pointed Ends, in causing a Discharge in our Electrical Experiments appearing to be as 12 to 1, it is easy to comprehend the very great Danger this noble Fabric has probably escaped, by having no pointed Apparatus upon it." To your Committee this Deduction still appears quite unconnected with the Premises, which they conceive afford Conclusions directly contrary; and that, supposing the Fact tho' a doubtful one, that so great a Quantity fell as to heat such an Iron Bar to the Degree imagined, yet if there had been a pointed Apparatus to have operated on the approaching Cloud while it was at 12 Times the Striking Distance, drawing off continually and conveying into the Earth Part of the Quantity it contained, all the Time of its Approach till within the Striking Distance, the Remainder must be less than the original Quantity, and strike therefore with less Force. And For another Reason, drawn from Exp. iv. it seems rather likely that for Want of Points on so great and lofty a Bulk of Metal as the leaded Roof of that Edifice presents to a Cloud, the electric Atmosphere of that Cloud might have been drawn from its more distant Parts, and accumulated over the Building before the Stroke, so as to afford an Explosion much larger than it could have done if such Accumulation had been prevented, or its Quantity previously drawn off and convey'd away by pointed Conductors.

Three of your Committee who signed the Report in question, were also on the Committee you appointed to consider of the securing St. Paul's.[3] They are now charg'd with Inconsistency, for advising *Pointed Conductors* in the present Case, and not in the former. "It is worthy of Note," says Mr. Wilson, "that those Conductors did not terminate in a Point; nor was any Point put upon the Cross at the Top, and yet Dr. Franklin was of that Committee. If Points are *so essential* to our Safety, why was not the reason enforced at the Committee for having them on that capital Edifice?"

To explain this, it may be proper to observe, that the Advantages expected from Pointed Conductors have been three, viz. 1.

3. For the membership of the committee to examine St. Paul's see above, XVI, 151. Four men were appointed to, and three served on, both committees: BF, Watson, and Wilson. Delaval took no part in the Purfleet committee; see above, p. 260 n. BF seems to have written originally "Two of your Committee"—meaning himself and Watson—and then for some unknown reason changed it to three.

427

To prevent a Stroke as in Exp. v. by creating a greater Distance between the striking Parts of a Cloud and the Building. Or, 2dly. if the Cloud should come on so fast that a Stroke could not be prevented, then to lessen its Quantity and Force, by previously drawing off and conveying away into the Earth silently a Part of it. And 3dly. to direct the Lightning precisely upon the Conductor prepared to receive and convey it away without Damage, rather than suffer it to fall on any other Part of the Building, which it might damage in its Way from thence to a low unpointed Conductor. Those who have a Pleasure in Disputation are sometimes apt to make their Opponents say more or less, or something different from what they have really said, in order to obtain a little Advantage in Argument. No one of the Committee has ever asserted that Points were *essential to our Safety*. Dr. F. who first proposed them, and may therefore be supposed most fond of them, has, as quoted by Mr. Wilson, mentioned a Case in which a House might be safe without them, [that] is, to wit, "when the Roof is *covered* with Lead or other Metal, and Spouts of Metal are continued from the Roof into the Ground to carry off the Water." Now this was precisely the Case of St. Pauls. The Dome and the whole Roof of the Church were *covered* with Lead, from whence a Number of large leaden Pipes descended into the common Sewers; but some Connections of Metal were wanting to unite the different Leaden Coverings with each other, and make the Communication with the Earth compleat. This being agreed to, none of the Committee thought it necessary to propose Points. Dr. F. would not propose them for a Dwelling House so covered, unless where some timid Inhabitant dreaded the Noise of an Explosion, which a Pointed Conductor might give a Chance of Preventing. For it being indifferent on what Part of such a Roof a Stroke should fall, the Conductors being compleat from all Parts, there would be no Reason for desiring to draw it to a particular Quarter. This too was in a great degree the Case of the Board House; another Instance given of our Inconsistency: for tho' not intirely covered with Lead, yet every Angle of the Roof being well cop'd with broad Plates of that Metal, all communicating with the Leaden Gutters within the Parapet, and thence by large leaden Pipes quite down into the Water of two Wells one on each side the Building, it was thought sufficiently safe as a Dwelling House; and being

428

no Powder Magazine itself, and plac'd at a considerable Distance from them, some of the Committee conceiv'd it not to be within our Charge, and therefore were [remainder missing]

To the ROYAL SOCIETY.

Members of the Purfleet Committee to Sir John Pringle

Printed in the Royal Society, *Philosophical Transactions...*, LXIII (1773–74), 66.

The letter below was the laconic response of the majority of the Purfleet committee to Benjamin Wilson's attack on their report.[4] The rest of the story is soon told. When Wilson discovered that he could not undo the committee's decision in favor of pointed lightning rods, he publicized his arguments against them in a pamphlet the following March.[5] Its appearance put Franklin under considerable pressure to reply, and for a time he intended to do so.[6] Then he changed his mind, and decided merely to include the paper that he had read to the committee in the forthcoming edition of *Experiments and Observations*.[7] Even this, he may have decided, was more disputatious than he cared to be; in any case he eventually limited his rebuttal in the new edition to a brief footnote, which did not mention Wilson by name but cited his pamphlet as an example of misrepresentation.[8]

Franklin's failure to counterattack doubtless chagrined his supporters. William Henly took on himself to defend the committee's findings, which were based in part on his own experiments, in a paper before the Royal Society at the end of 1773. Wilson's reply was read to the Society but not accepted for publication, and then became a second pamphlet.[1] Throughout the protracted debate Franklin held his peace, for he considered Wilson's objections "too trifling to deserve further

4. See the headnote on the preceding document.

5. *Observations upon Lightning...* (London, 1773); for its publication see BF to LeRoy below, March 30, 1773.

6. *Ibid.*

7. To Ingenhousz below, Sept. 30, 1773; Dubourg, he added, had already printed the paper in *Œuvres*.

8. The note is printed above, VI, 99 n.

1. Henly's paper is in *Phil. Trans.*, LXIV (1774), 133–52. Wilson discussed the failure to print his reply when he published it as *Further Observations upon Lightning...* (London, 1774), pp. iii–iv.

notice."[2] Years later, when the controversy boiled up again, he stayed out of it because, as he said, he had already expressed his opinion fully in the committee report of 1772. "I have never entered into any controversy in defence of my philosophical opinions," he added; "I leave them to take their chance in the world. If they are *right*, truth and experience will support them; if *wrong*, they ought to be refuted and rejected. Disputes are apt to sour one's temper, and disturb one's quiet."[3]

Sir, December 17, 1772.

Having heard and considered the objections to our Report, concerning the fixing pointed Conductors to the Magazines at Purfleet, contained in a letter from Mr. Wilson to Sir Charles Frederick, and read to the Royal Society, we do hereby acquaint you, that we find no reason to change our opinion, or vary from that Report. We have the honour to be, Sir, Your most obedient, humble servants,

H. CAVENDISH,
W. WATSON,
B. FRANKLIN,
J. ROBERTSON.

From Jacques Barbeu-Dubourg

Extract: printed in Jacques Barbeu-Dubourg, ed., *Œuvres de M. Franklin*... (2 vols., Paris, 1773), II, 129–33; ALS (incomplete): American Philosophical Society

The document that follows is in two parts, a printed extract and the conclusion of a letter in manuscript. The two are quite different in subject matter; neither contains any evidence of precisely when it was written, or of its belonging with the other. We have joined them and dated them, nevertheless, for reasons that seem plausible though far from conclusive. The printed extract was part of Dubourg's ongoing colloquy with Franklin about translating *Experiments and Observations*: the Frenchman sent comments, in the form of embryonic notes, on the American's "Observations Concerning the Increase of Mankind." When Franklin, in his letter below of December 26, acknowledged receiving Dubourg's of the 19th, and went on to say that he would welcome the translator's notes in the published work, he seems

2. Henly's marginal note on his copy of *idem*. BF acquired this copy, which is bound with other pamphlets of his in the Yale University Library.
3. Smyth, *Writings*, VII, 65.

to have been responding to these comments. He then mentioned Mlle. Biheron, perhaps because Dubourg had assigned her a complicated errand at the end of his "*longissime* lettre". If the letter was that of the 19th and ranged from comments on the "Observations," and perhaps other Franklin essays, to instructions for wrapping peppermint water in printed matter, it was indeed long. All that survives of it, we conjecture, is these two disconnected parts.

[December 19, 1772?]

On peut considerer en grand la population de l'univers entier, ou fixer spécialement ses regards sur la population de quelqu'état en particulier.[4] La premiere considération n'est point inutile, pourvu qu'on ne s'y arrête pas trop; la seconde est la plus nécessaire, parce qu'il importe sur-tout de voir autour de soi, et qu'il est plus aisé d'y bien voir. C'est ce que vous avez fait, Monsieur, et je vous en loue; mais il seroit à desirer que vous ne vous en tinsiez pas là: puissé-je vous aiguillonner à pousser vos méditations plus loin.

I. L'intention manifeste du Créateur est que l'homme croisse et se multiplie, et qu'il remplisse la terre; puisqu'il l'a doué d'une fécondité plus que suffisante pour compenser sa mortalité.

II. Tant que la population de la terre n'est pas portée à son comble, c'est entrer dans les vues de la Providence que d'en favoriser l'accroissement.

III. Mais les hommes ayant besoin de nourriture et de vêtement, la terre ne comporte qu'autant d'habitans qu'elle en peut nourrir et vêtir. Telles sont les limites naturelles de la population.

IV. Le point important pour favoriser la population est donc de pourvoir à la subsistance du plus grand nombre d'hommes qu'il soit possible.

V. Le mariage étant le seul moyen de population dans l'univers, doit sans doute être encouragé; mais rien n'est plus propre à l'encourager que la perspective d'une subsistance assurée.

VI. La voix puissante, qui appelle tous les hommes au mariage, se fait sur-tout entendre dans l'âge que la Nature a spécialement adapté à ce grand sacrement. Les mariages prématurés, les mariages tardifs, les mariages mal assortis étant moins conformes à l'ordre éternel, sont moins bénis de Dieu, et contribuent moins à

4. Dubourg is commenting, as noted above, on the text of BF's "Observations Concerning the Increase of Mankind..." in *Exper. and Obser.* (1769), pp. 197–206; for a slightly different version of the text see above, IV, 227–34.

la population. Mais, je le répete, rien n'invite tant à se marier en tems opportun, que l'assurance d'une subsistance aisée, qui semble appeller des consommateurs.

VII. Quel est le moyen de pourvoir à la subsistance du plus grand nombre d'hommes? C'est 1°· de tirer du sein de la terre tout ce qu'elle est capable de produire à leur usage: 2°· de faire de ses productions la meilleure application possible.

VIII. Pour remplir le premier objet, il faut non-seulement recueillir toutes les productions naturelles de la terre, sans en laisser rien perdre mal à propos; mais encore travailler à la fertiliser de plus en plus, en faisant servir l'art à seconder la nature. La recherche des fruits sauvages, herbes, et racines comestibles a fait les premiers fonds de la subsistance des hommes: la chasse et la pêche y ont bientôt concouru: l'agriculture est venue enfin, qui a multiplié, et ne cesse de multiplier annuellement ces fonds, à proportion de l'application qu'on y donne.

IX. L'instinct et l'expérience ont fait connoître l'usage des productions de la terre: des arts émules de l'agriculture ont étendu et multiplié ces usages.

Ces arts précieux à l'humanité ont rendu comestibles des matieres qui ne sembloient pas propres à nourrir des hommes, ou ont approprié à leur vêtement ce qui, dans l'état où la nature l'offroit, n'y pouvoit aucunement convenir; ou ils l'y font servir mieux, ou plus long-tems, ou à un plus grand nombre d'hommes à la fois.

X. La meilleure culture est celle qui peut tirer du même fonds de la terre, les productions les plus abondantes. La meilleure oeconomie est celle qui peut, avec la même quantité de matieres, faire subsister aisément le plus grand nombre d'hommes. Le plus sage gouvernement est celui qui sçait réunir la meilleure culture avec la meilleure oeconomie.

Ces principes posés, essayons d'en faire l'application à quelques articles de votre Mémoire.[5]

Quand vous dites (n°· II.) *que le peuple s'accroît en raison du nombre des mariages*, il est évident que cela doit s'éntendre particulierement des mariages faits à tems et bien assortis.

---

5. The references that follow are to BF's numbered paragraphs, 1 through 10, in *ibid*. Paragraph 11 was omitted in *Exper. and Observ.* with no change in numbering. Dubourg changed to consecutive numbers, so that his 11 is 12 in the English text, and so on.

Ce que vous dites (mêmes n⁰· II.) *que ce nombre augmente à pro-*
portion de l'aisance et des moyens de soutenir une famille, demande
une petite explication; car l'aisance étant le résultat de l'abon-
dance et de l'oeconomie, l'un par l'habitude du luxe se trouve mal
à son aise là où plusieurs se trouveroient fort à l'aise par l'habitude
de la frugalité.

Ce que vous dites (n⁰· V.) *que l'artisan est celui de tous à qui il faut*
le moins de terrein pour en tirer sa subsistance, ne doit pas être pris à
la lettre: car le travail de l'artisan n'étant qu'accessoire au travail
productif, il tire de ceux pour qui il travaille les matieres propres
à sa subsistance. On peut donc bien dire combien il lui faut de
terrein pour son habitation et son atelier, mais non pas combien il
lui en faut pour sa subsistance, qu'il attend d'ailleurs.

Parcourez l'Amérique: un peuple chasseur ne sçauroit entretenir presque aucuns artisans sur un territoire immense, tandis
qu'un peuple agricole en fait subsister un grand nombre sur un
territoire très-borné.

Vous dites (n⁰· XI.) que *tout esclave est voleur, par une conséquence*
assez naturelle de son esclavage. Cela est bien vrai au fond, mais ce
terme de *voleur* ne vous paroît-il pas trop fort? J'aurois dit simplement que tout esclave est pillard; car le mot *vol* suppose une at-
teinte portée aux loix d'une juste propriété: or il n'y a aucuns rapports d'équité entre le tyran et l'esclave.

Ce que vous dites du commerce (no⁰· XII. et XIII.) mériteroit
d'être développé et discuté avec soin; mais ce n'étoit pas ici le
lieu. Prenons cependant garde d'oublier qu'il y a entre l'agriculture
et le commerce la même disparité qu'entre une source et un canal.

Tous ceux que vous appellez (n⁰· XIII.) *les Peres de leur nation,*
ne doivent pas être mis sur une seule et même ligne. En effet, ceux
qui encouragent et perfectionnent des arts particulierement utiles
à leur patrie sont les peres de leurs nations respectives; mais ceux
qui encouragent et perfectionnent l'Agriculture, cet art des arts,
dont l'utilité est universelle, sont en quelque sorte les peres de
l'humanité.

Vous parlez (n⁰· XV.) *de fortifier doublement un pays, en augmen-*
tant sa population, et en diminuant celle de ses voisins. Permettez-moi
de vous représenter que les avantages qu'on peut tirer du mal de
ses voisins, ont souvent plus d'apparence que de réalité. Les principes de la justice et les sources de la félicité sont les mêmes, tant

pour les nations que pour les particuliers. Commençons par chercher et faire ce qui est honnête et équitable; et quand nous l'aurons
fait, nous ne tarderons peut-être pas à reconnoître que la prudence
la plus consommée n'auroit pu nous dicter rien de plus utile. Ceci
paroitra un paradoxe à bien des gens; parce que peu de personnes
ont assez réflechi sur cette matiere, toute importante qu'elle est. Je
me suis appliqué à la développer dans un petit ouvrage que je pourrai peut-être faire imprimer un jour, et dont je prens la liberté de
vous envoyer une copie en attendant, pour en avoir votre sentiment.

Tous nos Philosophes oeconomistes vous sçauront bon gré du
soin que vous avez eu (n°· XVI.) de bien distinguer l'intérêt des
marchands de celui de leur nation: deux choses très-différentes, et
quelquefois même tout-à-fait opposées, quoique la plupart des
politiques modernes ayent presque toujours confondu l'une avec
l'autre.

Vous comptez (n°· XXI.) sur plus d'un million d'ames Angloises
dans les Colonies du continent de l'Amérique Septentrionale en
1751. M. Dickinson a compté sur environ trois millions d'ames
dans ces mêmes Colonies à la fin de 1767; c'est-à-dire, 16 ans après.[6]
Je cherche à vous concilier. La différence vient apparemment 1°·
de ce que vous ne parlez que des naturels Anglois, et qu'il y joint
tous les Irlandois, François, Vaudois, Saltzbourgeois, Palatins,
Moraves, Juifs, &c, établis parmi eux; 2°· des progrès de la population dans ces heureuses régions en 16 à 17 ans.

Dans ce même paragraphe (XXI.) j'admire le ton modeste avec
lequel vous voulez bien supposer que la population de votre pays
ne double qu'une fois seulement en 25 ans. Nous prendrions bien
un autre ton, si nous pouvions en dire autant ici.

Vous prévoyez qu'en moins d'un siecle il y aura plus d'Anglois
en Amérique qu'en Europe. Non-seulement il seroit peu étonnant
que l'Angleterre fût un jour à l'égard de ses Colonies, ce que fut
Tyr à l'égard de Carthage; mais la postérité pourroit voir sans
miracle toute la Grande-Bretagne, ce Chef-lieu, cette Mere-
patrie, à peine équivalente à l'une de ses provinces d'outremer, et
Londres, cette superbe Métropole, éclipsée par votre humble
Philadelphie.[7]

6. John Dickinson, *Letters from a Farmer in Pennsylvania*... (Boston,
1768), p. 46.
7. The printed extract ends here; the MS conclusion follows.

Lorsque Melle. Biheron sera un peu reposée,[8] je vous prie de lui dire qu'elle me feroit grand plaisir et encore plus a un de nos amis, si elle vouloit bien nous faire l'emplette a Londres de bonne eau de menthe poivrée (*peper menth water*) au moins une douzaine de bouteilles de pintes mesure de Paris, en grandes ou petites bouteilles, mais par preference en petites bouteilles, et plustôt encore 24 pintes que 12. d'en faire faire 2 ou 4 ballots bien emballés, et de me les adresser par les voitures publiques avec les precautions d'usage, un seul ballot à la fois, mais tous successivement de semaine en semaine.

S'il y avoit moyen d'enveloper chacune de ces bouteilles d'une feuille de vos notes et matereaux divers, ou d'une feuille de mon petit Code,[9] cela feroit bien mon affaire mais en ce cas, il faudroit 1°· que cela fut si bien emmailloté que ces feuilles ne fussent pas excessivement gâtées, 2°· qu'elle eut attention à n'y employer dans chaque ballot que des exemplaires de la même feuille du Code pour toutes les bouteilles, ou tout au plus que des exemplaires de 2 feuilles, par exemple dabord de la 1ᵉ· et de la 3ᵉ· et l'ordinaire suivant des exemplaires de la 2ᵉ· et de la 4ᵉ· afin que si on fouilloit avec le plus grand soin, comme il faut s'y attendre, cela n'eut l'air que de feuilles de rebut, et qu'on ne put pas se douter que l'on pourroit icy les rassembler successivement et en refaire a deux tems des exemplaires complets. Que pensez vous de cette idée?

Au reste si cette eau, *peper menth water*, est un peu chere à Londres, fut ce à 6 livres argent de france la pinte de france, cela ne doit pas arreter Melle. Biheron; on lui en tiendra un fidele compte.

Mais il est tems de finir cette *longissime* lettre. Ma femme vous embrasse de tout son coeur, je ne suis point jaloux. J'ai l'honneur d'etre avec un parfait et constant attachement, Monsieur et cher Ami, Votre tres humble et tres obeissant serviteur   DUBOURG

Mes respectueuses civilités a Mr. Pringle

8. See Dubourg to BF above, Oct. 28.
9. See Dubourg to BF above, Nov. 28.

From Hannah Walker   ALS: American Philosophical Society

Most Honoured Sir   Westbury Decem 22 1772
   I have received your kind Present for which I return you a
thousand thanks for such great Benevolence and hope your
Charitable Distributations will be Doubly restored from above
and I have sent my sons Indentures as Mrs. Stevenson Informed
you Desired I should. I am Extremly sorry to hear of Mr. Williams Death and that my Son is removed because he seemed so
firmely attached to his Masters that I dare to say it would not have
been a little as would have persuaded him to Part from them for
he seemed so chearfull about going and told me his Master said as
soon as he had got a little Money he would buy somthing for him
to try his Luck as his seeming so willing and chearfull made me
Part with him a great Deal Comfortableer then I Expected I
should.[1] I hope Honoured Sir you will Please to do me the Favour
to Direct Henerys Letters when I write to him for Perhaps he
may not have Nothing to Pay for them if his good Master had
lived I should not have been so thoughtfull about him as Now I
am being in a strange Countery but hope he will Prove a very
good Boy to gain Friends. My Family all joyns me in Humbly Begging the accepance of all our Duties, from your most Humble and
most obedient Servant   H WALKER
P S   Sir I wish you the compliments of the approching season.
Addressed: To / Doctor Franklin / at Mrs Stevensons / Craven
Street the Strand / London

   1. She had parted with her son Henry in early spring; he had sailed for
Boston with Josiah Williams at the beginning of April, and Josiah had died
in August. Henry's subsequent difficulties remain obscure; see Jonathan
Williams to BF above, Oct. 13.

To Jacques Barbeu-Dubourg

ALS (draft): American Philosophical Society

Dear Sir,   London, Dec. 26. 1772[2]

Last Night I received your Favour of the 19th per Post,[3] which
I think is the best Conveyance for our Letters without any direct
Address; for I perceive that not only the little Piece which I sent
on the 4th Inst. but a long Letter of the 8th. have miscarried.
With the first I only thank'd you for the Square of 11000,[4] and
made a short Remark of some Imperfection I observ'd in it, and
told you I had somewhere a Square of 8, with the Diagonals you
requir'd which I would send you if I could find it. I also mentioned that I deferr'd sending the other Pieces you directed, till I
should hear from you that the first was correct. Nevertheless they
went the Week following, and I suppose have likewise miscarried.
I shall write over again the Purport of my Letter of the 8th. and
send it with this.[5] And as I pay no Postage here, I would request
that for the future you would keep a little Account of what you
pay there, and we will divide that Expence between us. Only I
wish you to let me know how I may make my Letters cheapest,
i.e. whether Letters are paid for in Paris according to their
Weight, or according to the Number of Pieces of Paper as
here.[6]

Page 179 *Binnacle*, Boyer explains this under the Word *Bittacle*,
which is the same thing, tho' the first is more agreable to the common Pronunciation.

P. 209. It ought to be 1756, and not 1754.

2. Dubourg's acknowledgment below, Jan. 13, 1773, indicates that BF's
letter was finished on the 30th, perhaps with a postscript that is now
missing.

3. Fragments of what we conjecture is this letter are printed above.

4. See Dubourg to BF above, Oct. 28.

5. BF's "little Piece" of the 4th has been lost. His long letter of the 8th has
survived only in the extract printed above, which Dubourg may have translated either from the original, if it eventually arrived, or from the recapitula-
tion of it that BF promised to enclose with this letter.

6. Dubourg had suggested in his letter above, Nov. 28, an elaborate
method of communicating with him, apparently designed for economy as
well as security. BF clearly wanted to save him postal charges but was un-
interested in his method.

P. 219. *Acrement-close*, is a proper Name, the Name of a particular Field.

P. 225. It should be, *a Point as at P in Fig. 2.*

P. 231. What you say on the Fixing of Salt, may be put in a Note of the Translator.

P. 253. *after a warm* SPELL. Spell is a vulgar English Word, therefore improper. It should have been, *after a warm Season.*

P. 266. Here make another Note of the Translator.

P. 278. A Surveyor's *Chain*, meant here, is four Pole, or 66 feet.

P. 311. *Outward Warmth*—It is not a "chaleur exterieure que l'on eprouve en entrant dans une Chambre pour y prendre le bain froid," that would indeed be unintelligible. As the Passage seems difficult, I have got my Clerk who is of French Extraction, to put it into his French, which perhaps you will understand better than my English.⁷

I will as you desire send to Messrs. Dilly and enquire for the American Transactions.⁸ If it is not come there, I shall send you another by the first Opportunity. I am sure the President of that Society can have but one Objection to your translating their Book, which is, an Apprehension that the Sale of it will not pay for the Trouble and Expence of printing; and the Society must esteem it

7. BF was using Abel Boyer, *Dictionnaire royal, françois-anglois et anglois-françois. . .*, probably the 2-vol. edition (London, 1752). The page references to the 1769 edition of *Exper. and Obser.*, in the order in which BF lists them, may be found above as follows: IV, 270, 369 (BF is correcting the date when the letter was read at the Royal Society), 431, 434, 440–1 (Dubourg did append a note: *Œuvres*, II, 36), 474, 300 (Dubourg again appended a note, at the colon of the sentence beginning "The Chymists have analys'd Sulphur. . .": *Œuvres*, I, 174); V, 258; II, 440. The clerk who translated this last passage appears only as L. Fevre; see his two letters to BF below, Aug. 4, 5, 1773. We have little certain information about him. He was apparently first employed in the spring of 1772, for in the following March BF paid him £10 for a year's wages (Jour., p. 47); subsequent payments suggest that he kept his position throughout BF's English mission. He then joined Lord Shelburne's household, and Priestley wrote of him approvingly to BF in 1776. Sparks, *Works*, VIII, 173. Twenty years later a Lewis "Favre," who we are convinced was the same person, died at fifty-seven; he was by that time the Marquis of Lansdowne's old and confidential servant, a gentleman esteemed for his simple manners and frugal life. *Gent. Mag.*, LXVI (1796), 971.

8. The APS had sent fifty copies of its *Trans.* to Charles and Edward Dilly, the London booksellers and publishers. Smith to BF above, May 16.

great Honour to them to enroll you among their foreign Members.[9]

I have not the least Objection to your making what Notes you please in the Translation. I only wish I could have the Advantage of seeing them before my new Edition is printed in English.

Melle. Biheron has been indispos'd, but is now well again. We join in the Wishes of the Season for you and Madame Dubourg. I am ever, Yours most affectionately   B F

M Dubourg

From Jonathan Williams, Jr.

ALS: American Philosophical Society

Dear and honoured Sir   Boston Decemr 26. 1772

This being the last month in the Year, I have been 'till now busily employed in casting up and settling my affairs, and as I never form'd very great Expectations, I find myself very content with the result. It appears that I have good enough to pay all I owe, and £300 Sterling left being the clear profits of last years Business. In the last Account I gave you of my Affairs with Mr. Warren[1] the Ballance in his favour was   £87
since I have received Goods which become due
    not till Janry next   761 12s.
                   Ballance 848 12s.

I have paid him as follows
Bill Holder on Smith   £100
Higington on Elton   119
Saunders on Hog   160
Hodge on Newman   86 2s. 8d.
Newman on Newman   62 6s. 8d.

9. This implied promise was not fulfilled until January, 1775, when Dubourg was elected to the APS; see its *Early Proceedings*... (Philadelphia, 1884), p. 95.
1. In his letter above, under the end of June.

Brooks on Brooks[2] $\underline{32\quad 5s.}$

                                             559 14s. 4d.
Ballance Due Janry next $\underline{288\ 17s.\ 8d.}$

                                             848 12s. 0d.

                                    please to turn over

I have had Goods since to the amount of   £295 10s.
Which become due in May next.
    Ballance on the other side $\underline{288\ 17s.\ 8d.}$
the whole sum I stand indeted to Mr. Warren $\underline{584\quad 7s.\ 8d.}$

You will please to excuse my troubeling you with such Circumstances but I think it my duty to inform you of the State of my
Affairs.

As this is the Season of the Year, when Business is almost entirely stagnated, and my Father having some Accounts in Phila.
which require the presence of one of us, I shall set out next week,

2. None of the names on the list can be positively identified, but some are
worth conjecture. Bill Holder was probably a young man from Bristol who
later became a tobacco merchant there, trading with Virginia: Walter E.
Minchinton, ed., *The Trade of Bristol in the Eighteenth Century* (Bristol
Record Soc. *Pub.*, xx; Bristol, 1957), p. 65, and *Politics and the Port of Bristol
in the Eighteenth Century*... (Bristol Record Soc. *Pub.*, xxiii; Bristol, 1963),
p. 216. Higington was perhaps Paul Bevan Higgington, "a very eminent
Dutch Merchant" who died in London in 1774 (*Public Advertiser*, June 17,
1774); Elton was in all likelihood Isaac Elton, father or son, both Bristol
bankers, for whom see Minchinton, *Trade of Bristol*, pp. 185–6; Charles H.
Cave, *A History of Banking in Bristol*... (Bristol, 1899), pp. 9, 44–5, 232–3.
Hog may have been Robert Hogg of Hogg & Campbell, Wilmington, N.C.:
Charles C. Crittenden, *The Commerce of North Carolina, 1763–1789* (New
Haven, 1936), pp. 96 n, 142; but a more likely candidate is Thomas Hogg
(d. 1784), the Edinburgh banker: George W. Corner, ed., *The Autobiography
of Benjamin Rush*... (Princeton, 1948), p. 47. Hodge could have been Capt.
Michael Hodge (1743–1816), a prominent citizen of Newburyport: John
Quincy Adams, *Life in a New England Town*... (Boston, 1903), p. 98 n;
Benjamin W. Labaree, *Patriots and Partisans: the Merchants of Newburyport,
1764–1815* (Cambridge, Mass., 1962), pp. 75, 78, 85. One of the so-called
Newmans might have been Samuel Newnam, partner in a Bristol bank (Cave,
op. cit., pp. 11, 87–8), and the other a son or brother traveling on business in
the colonies. The same applies to the Brookses: Robert was a tea-dealer and
Samuel a broker, both at 69 Watling Street, London: *Kent's Directory*...
(London, 1772).

and hope soon to pay my Respects to your good Lady and Family. Please to remember me to all enquiring Friends and believe me to be your Dutifull and affectionate Kinsman

J WILLIAMS junr

Addressed: To / Doctr Benja Franklin / at Mrs Stevensons In Craven Street / Strand / London

From William Henly ALS: American Philosophical Society

Dear Sir: [December 30, 1772³]

I send you herewith the paper of your experiments, and shall think myself under great obligation for the addition.⁴ I am quite at a loss what to think or say about the Bell. The effects are so contrary to the notions I [had] entertained of Electricity; and yet I scarse know how to disbelieve my Friends relation, for though by his Letter he appears to be no Schollar at all, yet [he] is as sensible, and as clever a Man in Conversation as you would wish to converse with.⁵

Mr. Nairne Mr. Lane⁶ and I were yesterday from [about?] 3 O Clock at St. Pauls. I took my fishing Rod.⁷

Going up. In the Stone Gallery Thermometer 28. no Ch[arge⁸].

3. Henly, when he published these experiments, dated them between Dec. 24 and 29: *Phil. Trans.*, LXIV (1774), 427. His letter mentions Monday (which in that week was the 28th) and "yesterday" as if they were different days; we assume that his experiments were performed on the 29th and that he was writing on the 30th.

4. Our conjecture is that Henly had received part of the material he had requested in his letter above, under Oct. 28, and a promise from BF to send more.

5. The bell is undoubtedly a reference to BF's first experiment described above, Aug. 18, and therefore the friend is BF. Henly is parodying Benjamin Wilson, whose letter opposing BF's theories had been read before the Royal Society on Dec. 10; see the headnote above, p. 424, on the Purfleet committee's letter.

6. For Timothy Lane, F.R.S., the apothecary and electrical experimenter, see above, XIII, 288 n, 459 n.

7. For Henly's rod, which was in effect an electrometer, see his note above, Sept. 30.

8. The only word that makes sense in context: there was no electricity in the air.

Wind very troublesome quite round the Building. In the Golden Gallery Thermometer 31. Balls diverged 1 Inch full. In the Lanthorn *a very warm Room* Thermometer 35. The Rod being projected through a Hole its whole length, on the side opposite to that, from which the Wind blew: the balls diverged I think 1¾ Inch and *were nearly stationary.*

Coming down. In the Stone Gallery Thermometer 29. Balls diverged ½ Inch. The Wind *while we were there* got round more to the Southward, and the Air grew more hazy, which I believe brought on, or increased the Electricity.⁹

Monday Evening 5 O Clock Mr. Bell¹ went there, and observed that in the Stone Gallery Balls diverged when held at Arms length² ¼ Inch, Thermometer 34. In the Golden Gallery, held in the same manner they diverged ½ Inch Thermometer 33. In all these cases the Mercury had time to subside before observation. I am Dear Sir sincerely yours   W HENLY

From Jacques Barbeu-Dubourg: Dedicatory Epistle

Printed in [Jacques Barbeu-Dubourg,] *Petit code de la raison humaine; ou Exposition succincte de ce que la raison dicte à tous les hommes, pour éclairer leur conduite, et assurer leur bonheur (London, 1773), pp. [v–]vi.*

Monsieur,   [Late 1772³]

Vous reconnutes dans la premiere esquisse de ce Petit Code,⁴ l'effusion simple et naïve de votre propre coeur; j'ai achevé de le

9. Henly was investigating the relationship between altitude, temperature, and electrical charge in the atmosphere; he believed that fog on a frosty day was strongly and positively electrified: *Phil. Trans.,* LXIV (1774), 425–6.

1. Possibly George Bell (1755–85), the Scottish physician and botanist; he and BF had a number of friends in common, through any of whom Bell and Henly might have met; see the Literary and Philosophical Soc. of Manchester *Memoirs,* II (1785), 381–93. Whoever this Bell may have been, he and Henly often collaborated in electrical experiments: *Phil. Trans.,* LXII (1772), 134; LXIV (1774), 137, 417.

2. [*Henly's note:*] from the Ballustrade.

3. A bill from William Strahan, among BF's papers in the APS, contains an entry for printing and binding the *Petit Code* in December, 1772.

4. BF had been interested in the work ever since its first appearance in 1768, and had had Polly Stevenson translate it into English: above, XV, 115 n; XVII, 185–6, 291.

developer autant que je l'ai pu, et j'espére que vous ne vous y reconnoitrez que mieux. S'il m'étoit échappé quelque chose de moins exact, daignez le rectifier; c'est pour vous le soumettre que je vous l'ai dedié, ayant été assez heureux pour trouver réunis en vous un grand maître et un bon ami. Vous allez vous éloigner de cet hemisphere, et je ne puis vous suivre dans l'autre; mais l'immense océan que vous avez à traverser ne separera point les meilleures parties de nous-mêmes, nos ames seront toujours unies, comme elles l'ont toujours été; je me fais honneur de le publier, et vous ne rougirez pas de l'avouer; vous pouvez avoir de plus nobles emules, mais vous n'avez point de plus fidele serviteur.

J B. D.

To Sir William Browne

AD (draft): American Philosophical Society

This blast shows Franklin at his most abusive and least witty. His anger had been aroused by the vagaries of Sir William Browne, an old and wealthy physician and former President of the Royal College of Physicians, and an F.R.S. since 1739. Sir William had strongly opposed the election of Sir John Pringle, as noted above,[5] to the presidency of the Royal Society. Browne's speeches on that occasion had aroused a small furor, but they had clearly not exhausted what the octogenarian had to say: he had written and published further attacks on Sir John. They elicited the following counterattack from Franklin. It was presumably intended for whatever newspaper had published Browne's polemics, but we have no indication that it ever saw print.[6]

[1772]

People are sometimes *too young* to take Advice. They have not yet Sense enough to see its Propriety and feel its Value. Possibly a

5. BF to a Member of the Royal Society, Nov. 26.
6. A search of the pamphlet literature and of all available London newspapers of the period has failed to turn up either Browne's further harangues against Pringle after the election, although BF refers to them as in print, or the latter's reply. It is conceivable that the reply was a private rather than a public attack, and even that it was sent to Browne; but in that case would BF have concealed his authorship?

Man may also be *too old*, when that Sense begins to fail him. I hope it is not quite your Case, and therefore I take the Trouble of giving you a little Admonition.

Your Years have a Claim to some Respect, if you did not forfeit it by your Misbehaviour. Buffoonery and Tavern-Bawling can not possibly become a Physician and Philosopher. If People laugh, 'tis a Laugh of Contempt which they find hard to be restrain'd even by their Pity. But when you think to entertain them with malicious Libels on the most worthy Characters in miserable Verse and more wretched Prose, which manifest the Badness of your Heart as well as Head, their Contempt gives Place to their Indignation.

A learned Society many Years since when your Character was not so much impair'd did you the Honour of chusing you a Member. Unhappily indeed: For that Choice has never been an Honour to the society. You owe it however some Respect, though the Members should never on any Vacancy, once think of you for their President. Your Ambition may be excusable, but not your Resentment. They may know, tho' you do not, your extreme Unfitness for the Station. And you ought to have had more Regard for the Reputation of the Body you are connected with, than to endeavour rendering the Members ridiculous to the Publick, by framing absurd Harangues of your own, and printing them as delivered by the Person chosen, at the time of his Election. The Endeavour indeed is impotent. No Reader can even believe what you wish him to believe that the Speech you have written and twice published as the President's, was ever spoken by him or heard by them; or that they could possibly have elected a Man capable of making it: But every one who knows Sir W. B. may readily believe it yours; for he who can with such Facility make silly Speeches for himself, can easily forge them for other People.

Hitherto, therefore, your Malevolence has done no great Mischief. But for your Life, stir not a Foot farther, in this dangerous Road. When a Man once gives the Devil leave to guide him, there is no knowing how far he may be led. From forging a Speech to rob another of his Reputation, 'tis any easy Step to forge a Bond to rob him of his Money. Aged as you are there may be several Sessions at the Old Bailey, before you are call'd upon by a natural Death; One of these may afford you a real Occasion for the Exercise of your Speech-making Faculty; and perhaps your *last* Per-

444

formance of the kind, may be that which will give your Hearers the highest Satisfaction. I am, Sir Wm. among many others,

AN OFFENDED FELLOW OF THE R. SOCIETY

To Sir Wm Browne

From William Henly   ALS: Historical Society of Pennsylvania

Sir: [1772?7]
I think myself exceedingly obliged to you for your intended favour of a Visit some Evening, but hope you will so far oblige me as to give me previous notice by a Line, when I shall with a high pleasure accommodate my time to your convenience. I am with the utmost Respect Sir your obedient and Humble Servant

W HENLY

To Dr. Franklin
Addressed: To / Dr. Franklin

From Francis Maseres   AL: American Philosophical Society

[17728]
Mr: Maseres presents his compliments to Dr: Franklyn and sends him two more copies of the collection of Quebec instruments and the draught of a toleration-act;9 of which he desires the doctor to

7. This was the year when BF was most closely associated with Henly, who was giving experimental support to the Purfleet committee's conclusions; see the headnote on the committee's report above, Aug. 21. Henly's first sentence is presumably acknowledgment of some written word from BF, perhaps a delayed answer to the letter from Henly above that we conjecturally assign to June 17. In that case this note was after BF returned to town in mid-July, which was the first time he could have received and responded to that letter.

8. This note was clearly written some time after BF's letter to Maseres above, June 17, but how long a time we cannot say. Maseres refers to Father Abraham's speech, which BF had enclosed in that letter, and himself encloses the draft of a lengthy toleration act that he wrote, he says elsewhere, in the summer of 1772: *Additional Papers Concerning the Province of Quebeck...* (London, 1776), pp. 258–9.

9. *A Collection of Several Commissions, and Other Public Instruments,...Relating to the State of the Province of Quebec in North America, since the*

transmit one set to his son, Governour Franklyn of New Jersey, and the other to Mr: Galloway, of Philadelphia, the speaker of the house of Assembly, with Mr: Maseres compliments, by the first convenient opportunity. He desires the doctor would send him another copy of his tract called Squire Richard, if he can spare one, for a friend of Mr: M's, who was much pleased with it, and desires to have one.

Addressed: To / Dr: Franklyn, in Craven Street / in the Strand.

From [Johann David Michaelis?[1]]

Copy:[2] American Philosophical Society

⟨1772? In Latin with no date, salutation, or signature. Has decided, because of Franklin's "most noble occupations" and involvement in public affairs, to consult him as little as possible. Wishes

---

Conquest of It by the British Arms in 1760 ... (London, 1772) and *A Draught of an Act of Parliament for Tolerating the Roman Catholick Religion in the Province of Quebec, and for Encouraging and Introducing the Protestant Religion into the Said Province* ..., no place or date.

  1. Michaelis (1717–91), a professor at Göttingen, was a noted Biblical scholar and the foremost teacher of Semitic languages in Europe. Pringle and BF had met him during their German tour in 1766; see Michaelis' *Lebenbeschreibung* ... (Leipzig, 1793), pp. 102–3, 110–11. The German had corresponded with Pringle, who in 1769 had sent BF's regards to him and the other members of his learned society. This was the local Königliche Gesellschaft der Wissenschaften, of which Michaelis was director from 1761 to 1770. In February, 1772, Pringle acknowledged receiving two copies, for himself and BF, of the first volume of the Society's transactions "renewed," in other words the *Novi commentarii Societatis regiae Gottingensis* (Göttingen and Gotha, 1771); an earlier series had ended in 1755. For Pringle's letters see Johann G. Buhle, ed., *Literarischer Briefwechsel von Johann David Michaelis* (3 vols., Leipzig, 1794–96), II, 230, 310. We conjecture that BF wrote Michaelis to thank him for the transactions and to ask for twelve more copies to take with him to America (in the spring of 1772 he referred several times to returning home), and that this letter was Michaelis' reply.

  2. The copy is almost unquestionably in BF's hand. Why he should have gone to the trouble we have no idea, unless the letter appealed to him as an exercise in torturing Latin. The language is so verbose and convoluted that a literal translation is unintelligible; we have therefore resorted to a résumé that we hope does justice to the central points.

first to thank him for favoring the Society by taking with him twelve copies of its revived[3] work; has arranged to have the volumes bound and sent to Hamburg at the Society's expense (in excess of twelve thalers) in the hope that through them more buyers will be attracted; although the Society is not interested in making a profit, neither does it wish to lose money. Asks Franklin to select, perhaps with the advice of the illustrious Watson,[4] the names of outstanding people who have recently died, particularly physicians, professors, and members of the Royal Society, and to have their biographies compiled and sent to ornament future volumes of the transactions. Encloses a few small literary gifts, to refresh Franklin's memory of the Göttingen circle. May God return him unscathed to his fatherland. "Embrace in your friendship and favor those who love you and wish you well.">

From Jonathan Shipley   AL: University of Pennsylvania Library

⟨Monday evening, [1772?[5]], a note in the third person and in the Bishop's hand. He and his family will call upon him with Lord and Lady Spencer[6] tomorrow evening between seven and eight.⟩

3. The adjective is *recusi*, which in context makes no sense. We suggest that it was BF's misreading of *renati*.

4. For William Watson, F.R.S., the noted physician and scientist, see above, III, 457 n.

5. Our guess about the year is based on the slender clue of squirrels. DF had sent some as pets; they arrived in January, and by August were great favorites in the Shipley and Spencer households. BF to DF above, Jan. 28, Aug. 22. We are conjecturing that the gift was the reason for the Shipleys' and Spencers' call.

6. For the Spencers see the August letter just cited.

Index

Compiled by Mary L. Hart and Joy G. Sylvester

INDEX

Colden, Alexander (*cont.*)
359, 374, 375, 397–9, 414–15; and search for E. Holland, 318–19; and opening of wf–bf mail, 333; writes Todd, 414; letters to, 318–19, 359, 397–9
Colden, Mrs. Alexander, mentioned, 399
Colden, Cadwallader: "An Inquiry in the Principles of Vital Motion," 94, 392 n; story of, in Kalm's *Travels...*, 390; mentioned, 399
Colden, David: invents drill plough, 390–1; on alleged hypnotism of birds by snakes, 392; letter from, 390–2
Colden, Richard Nicolls, bills of exchange by, 397
Collas, Peter, marriage to Jenny Mecom, 363 n
Collection of Original Papers Relating to the History of...Massachusetts-Bay (Hutchinson) Randolph papers printed in, 13
Collection of Several Commissions... Relating to the State of the Province of Quebec... (Maseres), for wf, Galloway, 445–6
College of Physicians, Edinburgh, Sir Alexander Dick president of, 5 n
College of Physicians, London, sees Priestley method of carbonating water, 126 n
Collinson, Michael: wants books, Colden essay, 94; letter from, 94–5
Collinson, Peter, mentioned, 94 n, 341 n, 392
Collinson, Thomas, and protested bills of exchange for bf, 341
Colonies, North America: dispute with Britain, xxxi, 8, 23, 27, 71, 96, 220, 259, 338, 413; Hillsborough's attitude, policies toward, xxxi, 21, 219, 227, 243, 258; Dartmouth's attitude toward, xxxi, 244, 276, 279, 400, 408, 410, 419; crown as "legislator" for, 11; Irish support for, 12, 21, 71; and impeachment of Clarendon (1667), 18, 224; silk culture in, 20, 137 n; as possible rival to Irish beef, butter trade, 22; flaxseed exported from, 22; possible linen trade of, 22; British attitude, policies toward, 27, 103 n, 217, 220, 225–6, 295; agriculture in, 49; Scottish exports to, 71; plan for viticulture in, 86–7, 295; attitude of, toward Britain, 96, 220, 406; and British imports, 101 n; depressed economy of, 101 n; rumored Hillsborough bill on, 103; climate of, 136; opposition in, to appointment of Anglican bishops, 167; projected federal laws, constitution of, 178; Lord Stirling's large land purchases

in, 191; ignorance of, in Britain, 225; seeds sent to, for experimentation, 317 n; use of lightning rods in, 325; thunderstorms in, 325; price of mahogany in, 336; Strahan plan for union with Britain, 407; and British Stamp Office expenses in, 419; Dutch tea smuggled, legally imported into, 420, 420 n; English population in, 433–4; Britain's future relationship to, 434. *See also* Agents, colonial; America; Americans; Animals; Assemblies, colonial; Boundary; Bounties; Charters, colonial; Committee of Correspondence, intercolonial; Constitution, imperial; Currency, paper; Declaratory Act; Elections; Governors; Judges; Lottery; Manufacturing, colonial; Navigation Acts; New England; Nonimportation; Petitions and remonstrances; Proclamation of 1763; Post Office, North American; Requisitions, royal; Secretary of State for the American Colonies; Slavery; Slave trade; Sovereignty; Stamp Act; Taxation without representation; Townshend Acts; Trade, colonial; *and individual colonies by name.*
Colors, Priestley book on, 91, 156–7, 178
Combes, William: shop burns, 394; debt to R. Bache, 394
Commerce. *See* Trade.
Committee of Correspondence, Boston, to circulate declaration of rights, 381 n
Committee of Correspondence, Mass.: to see Hutchinson-Oliver letters, 412; letter to, 26–8; mentioned, 103, 104
Committee of Correspondence, Pa.: bf urged to write to, 71; instructs bf, 338–9; members of, 339; letter from, 338–9; mentioned, 419
Committees of Correspondence, intercolonial, *Gaspee* affair and formation of, 379 n
"Common" air, in Priestley's experiments on airs, 133, 173, 201, 202 n
Commons, British House of: and governors' reports on colonial manufactures, 19, 48–9; and bounty on silk, 20 n; presentation to crown of speaker of, 95–6; passes Royal Marriage Bill, 103 n; *Journals* wanted by Lib. Co., 118 n, 270; and bill on dissenters (1772), 164 n; and bill on annuities for laboring poor, 179 n; Grenville faction in, 402; mentioned, 160, 183
Commons, Irish House of: bf admitted to, 21–2, 49–50; Pery speaker of, 48 n

Conductors: BF's terminology, 205 n; gases as, 214; and tests on torpedo fish, 234; of Henly, 348, 387–90, 383. *See also* Chain conductor; Lightning rods.
Connecticut, governor of, mentioned, 379
Connoissance des temps, pour l'année commune 1774..., prints roster of French Academy, 372 n
Connolly (brig): stormy Dublin-Phila. voyage, 45 n, 90 n, 130; BF fears lost, 90
Conservation, BF urges, 216
Constitution, imperial: colonial charters in, 8, 9; role of governors and governors' commissions in, 8, 9, 219; British concept of, 8–10; role of royal instructions in, 8–10, 12; Bostonian concept of, 8, 10; colonial assemblies in, 8, 10, 217, 219; BF's concept of, 8, 10, 408; crown's role in, 8, 219; right of petition in, 9–10, 217, 224; and 19th-century empire, 10; and Townshend Acts, 23; colonial councils in, 219; royal prerogative in, 223–4; and modes of taking oaths, 355; Hutchinson on, in governing distant colonies, 402; mentioned, 222, 356
Continental Congress, mentioned, 18 n
Contract, Mass. charter as, 209
Contributions for Promoting the Culture of Silk. *See* Silk Filature, Phila.
Conway, Henry Seymour: and protection of Purfleet powder magazine, 156; mentioned, 258 n
Cook, Capt. James: voyage to Antarctic (1772–5), 75 n, 126 n; *Endeavour* voyage, 85 n
Cook, John, and land title for Phila. Silk Filature, 98
Coombe, Thomas, Jr.: carries mail, 55, 56; BF recommends, 56; returns to Phila., 56, 271; impressions of BF, 56 n; and Polly Stevenson's marriage, 271 n; elected to APS, 393 n; letter to, 271
Cooper, Grey: BF's possible introduction of, to Story, 24 n; and BF's "Wagon Affair" accounts, 74; and Va. claims, 351
Cooper, Samuel: and crown's payment of governor's salaries, 13–14; and J. Temple's role in Hutchinson letters affair, 404 n; to see Hutchinson-Oliver letters, 412; letter to, 13–16
Copper, in Priestley experiments on air, 174
Corbyn, Thomas, Benezet sends tracts on slave trade to, 113–14

Corn, Indian, and feeding of silkworms, 137
Corporation for the Relief and Employment of the Poor (Phila.), mentioned, 374 n
Corsen, Cornelius: bills of exchange to, 366; Pa. Hospital mortgages to, 366 n
Costard, George: *A Further Account of the Rise and Progress Of Astronomy amongst the Ancients...*, 343; *A Letter to Martin Folkes...*, 343
Cotton, Robert, speech on Suffolk's impeachment, 18 n
Council, Mass.: and return of Mass. General Court to Boston, 17 n; and proposed compromise on Maine eastern lands, white pines, 26; act on slave importation (1771), 155 n; Oliver urges change in, 402; mentioned, 10, 412. *See also* General Court, Mass.
Council, N.J., and appointment of colonial agents, 3 n
Council, Pa., mentioned, 331
Council, Va.: and Va. land grants, 4 n, 335 n; Abercromby agent for, 12; opposes appointment of Anglican bishop, 167; mentioned, 335 n
Councils, colonial: and appointment of colonial agents, 3 n; constitutional role of, 219
Cour des aides (France), Malesherbes' defense of (1756), 298 n; mentioned, 372 n
Court Miscellany; or, Gentleman and Lady's New Magazine, for Lib. Co., 118 n
Cowper, Lancelot, mail, seeds for BF, 88, 92; letter to, 88
Cox, Isaac: Pa. Hospital manager, 340; mentioned, 366 n
Coxe, Dr. Daniel, Pa. land grant to, 171
Crafts, Mr., and workers for Phila. glass factory, 282
Craig, James, mentioned, 130 n
Craige, Mr., mentioned, 130
Cranberries, for BF, 395, 396
Crane, Stephen, letter to, 67–8
Craven Street: Hewsons take over No. 36, 202–3 n, 239 n, 304, 315, 341, 365; BF, Mrs. Stevenson move to No. 1, 202–3 n, 315, 322, 341, 342, 361, 365
Credit: BF's "ready money" plan as substitute for, 34, 97, 100, 101, 157; and crisis of 1772, 101 n, 267, 315–16, 419–20
Croghan, George: sells Walpole Co. lands, 322 n; mentioned, 352 n
Cromwell, Oliver, mentioned, 296

Hutchinson, Gov. Thomas (*cont.*)
17 n; prorogues Mass. House, 17 n, 209; Story seeks aid from, 24 n; vetoes Mass. act on slave trade (1771), 115 n; and Boston town meeting's protest on judges' salaries, 381 n; T. Whately wants introduction to, 401 n; BF's, Bostonian hostility to, 405; and dismissal of J. Temple from Customs Board, 405; mentioned, 380, 399 n. See also Hutchinson-Oliver letters; Instructions, royal.

Hutchinson-Oliver letters: BF's role and motives in affair of, xxxii, 333 n, 401, 403, 404–5, 407–9, 411–13; W. Story in affair of, 24 n; printed in Boston, 399 n, 403; written to T. Whately, 401, 402, 403, 404; contents of, 402–3, 412–13; possibly in possession of Grenville, 402, 403, 404–5, 406; suspects in affairs of: John Temple, 403–4, 406; T. Pownall, 405; W. Strahan, 406–7; others, 407 n; Temple duel with W. Whately over, 404; W. Whately's suit against BF over, 404; British ministry's action on, 408; list of Bostonians allowed to see, listed, 412

Hutton, James: calls at Craven St., 342; letter from, on Grand Tour printed, 345; letter from, 342–5

Hydrochloric acid, for Priestley, 174

Hydrogen chloride, in Priestley experiments, 174 n

Iceland, Banks, Solander voyage to, 75 n, 85 n, 126 n

Immigrants, to New England for religious reasons, 164

Impeachment: of Earl of Suffolk (1386), 17–18; of Lord Clarendon (1667), 18, 224; Parliamentary power of, 224

Independence, for colonies, 178 n

India: silk from, 136 n; mentioned, 30

Indiana Co., claims of, and Walpole Co. grant, 123

Indians, Indian affairs: boundary with, 4 n. 123, 124; BF on, 197; and Walpole Co. grant, 244 n; grants of Delaware islands, 277; stories on, in Kalm's *Travels...*, 391; mentioned, 164. See also Cherokees; Six Nations.

Ingenhousz, Dr. Jan: visits Paris, 84 n; dines with Pringle, 84 n; electrical machine of, described, 190 n

Inoculation, of B. F. Bache, 4, 90

"Inquiry in the Principles of Vital Motion" (C. Colden), Ms. sent to BF, 94 n, 392 n

Inquiry into the Nature...of Christ's Temptation... (Farmer), mentioned, 311 n

Instructions, royal: constitutional role, 8–10, 12; views on, as binding on governor, 8, 9, 10, 11–12, 17 n, 408; as "law of the land" in colonies, 11–12; on royal officials' salaries, 14, 21, 400–1; and tax exemption of customs commissioners in Mass., 14, 49; and removal of General Court to Cambridge, 17, 18, 49; and appointment of colonial agents, 49; and placing of Castle William under royal jurisdiction, 49; and governors' acceptance of colonial assembly speakers, 96 n; to Hutchinson, on BF's Mass. salary, 209–10 n; Hillsborough's, on Mass. circular letter (1768), 219, 221

Introduction aux observations sur la physique..., Priestley's work published in, 308 n

Ireland: BF's trip to, 5, 7, 12, 13, 16, 23 n, 25, 26, 28, 32, 42, 44–5, 46, 48, 53 n, 56, 59, 61, 65, 67, 71, 75 n, 82, 94 n, 95, 103, 131, 239–40 n, 324, 396; beef, butter, linen trade of, 7, 22–3, 71; economic conditions in, 7, 22–3, 71; aristocracy, gentry in, 7, 71; support for colonies, 12, 21, 71; Parliamentary regulation of trade, manufactures, 19, 22, 48–9, 71; effect on, of absentee pensioners, landlords, 22; imports American flaxseed, 22; rack-rents in, 22; "great canal" of, 278–9 n. See also Commons, Dublin, Irish House of.

Iron foundry, of J. Tyler, in Pa., 282

Italy: silk culture and trade, 136 n, 137, 139; BF may visit, 358

Jackson, Mr. and Mrs. Charles, mentioned, 40

Jackson, Richard: and Va. claims, 3, 351; Galloway writes, 3 n, 59 n, 274 n; travels with BF, 18–19, 47–8, 217–18; admitted to floor of Irish Parliament, 21–2, 50; borrows, comments on *Zend-Avesta*, 31 n, 36–7; may dine with BF, Morton, 37; forwards Galloway letters, map, papers, to BF, 37, 70; and ownership of Delaware islands, 276, 277; Pa. *Votes, Laws* for, 277; and Pa. Assembly money, 278; letter from, 36–7; mentioned, 52 n

Jacobites, mentioned, 297, 355 n

Jamaica: powder magazine in, exploded by lightning, 106, 263 n; house in, purportedly struck by lightning, 128, 129, 314

James, Abel: and purchase of Stringfellow's right for Phila. Silk Filature, 98, 168–9;

Persecution, religious, BF on, 164
Pery, Edmond Sexton: dines with BF, others, 48; and admission of BF to floor of Irish Parliament, 50
Peterborough, Lord, mentioned, 301 n
Peters, Mr., and Pa. land originally purchased by R. Thompson, 172
Peters, Richard, mentioned, 172 n
Peters, William, mentioned, 172 n
Petit code de la raison humaine (Barbeu-Dubourg): London publication, 329, 348, 358, 384–5; copies to go to France, 435; dedicated to BF, 442–3; Polly Stevenson translates, 442 n. *See also* "Code de l'humanité...."
Petitions and remonstrances: from Mass. to crown, on governor's salary, xxxii, 208, 209, 219, 221, 293, 361 n, 364, 400–1, 408, 409–11; constitutional right of, 9–10, 217–18, 221; from Pa. against Townshend Acts, 53, 257 n; Rogers' to Privy Council, 80; on Baker's Ga. land claims, 95, 226–7, 257 n, 258 n; from Md. Quakers on slave trade, 115–16; from Walpole Co., 124, 227 n, 243–4 n, 322, 335; from Anglican clergy to Parliament, 163 n; from Mass. to crown on Townshend Acts, 217, 218, 221; BF on danger of government's refusal to hear, 222, 410; by Rochford, on Delaware islands, 276; to Pa. Assembly, on mode of taking oaths, 354
Pezay, Alexandre-Frédéric-Jacques de Masson, marquis de, English tour of, 344
Philadelphia: glass factories in, 43 n, 282; original land purchases for, 98 n; trade of, threatened by Baltimore, 158; British troops in, 364 n; aurora borealis visible in, 368; measles, other diseases in, 368; shift of political power in (1772), 421 n; possible future eclipse of London by, 434; mentioned, 50, 254, 266. *See also* Mechanics, Phila.; Merchants, Phila.; Pennsylvania; Silk Filature, Phila.
Philadelphia, College of: medical school of, 64, 65; Kinnersley resigns from, 130 n; funds, students from S.C., 146, 281
Philadelphia Almshouse and House of Employment, mentioned, 374 n
Philadelphia Contributionship, claim on Maugridge estate, 395 n
Philadelphia County: Stringfellow land in, 98 n; in 1772 Pa. elections, 331; mentioned, 356
Philippe-Egalité. *See* Chartres, duc de.

Philips, Mr., and land title for Phila. Silk Filature, 98
Philosophical Transactions: for Winthrop, 35; for APS, 63; Ronayne paper in, 78 n; Henly papers in, 78 n, 93 n, 121 n, 182 n, 261 n, 429 n; prints Walsh reports on torpedo fish, 162, 204 n; prints Winn's paper, BF's conjectures on aurora borealis, 236 n, 239 n; Wilson's papers, letter in, 260 n, 424 n; prints report on lightning rods for St. Paul's, 324–5
"Phlogisticated air." *See* Nitrogen.
Phonetics, E. Darwin's study of, 211
Phosphorescence, of the sea, described, 108
Photosynthesis, Priestley's role in discovery of, xxx, 214
Physiocrats, mentioned, 236 n
Pianoforte, BF lends to D. Blunt, 150
Pickard, Edward, recommended as dissenting preacher, 310
Pitt, William. *See* Chatham, Lord.
Pitt, Fort: to be abandoned, 363; Pa. provincial troops may garrison, 364 n; mentioned, 322 n
Pitts, James, to see Hutchinson-Oliver letters, 412
Pitts, Mary (Polly) Yeldhall: death of, 192, 275, 395; BF's claim on estate of, 192 n, 395
Plants: for Hope, from Bartram, 41; in purification of "noxious" air, 201–2, 214, 215–16, 295
Plough, drill, invented by D. Colden, xxx, 390–1
Poems on Several Subjects... (Ogilvie), ordered but not received by Lib. Co., 118
Poissonnier, Pierre-Isaac: biog. note, 328 n; and BF-Dubourg mail system, 328
Poland, partition of, 132
Political, Miscellaneous and Philosophical Pieces, Vaughan edits, 245, 246
Pomlin(?), Gov., mentioned, 80
Poor: English, 71; Maseres' plan of annuities for, 179, 183; BF on support of, 179 n, 180–1; suggested fund for relief of, 179 n; and proposed homes for aged, in England, 180–1, 186
Poor Richard's Almanack: advice from, sent to J. Williams, Jr., 97; rhymed epitaphs in, 328 n; proverb from, 362; mentioned, 157, 173, 174
Pope, Alexander: *An Essay on Man*, 370 n; mentioned, 301 n
Population: in colonies, 115 n, 433–4; natural, economic and political influences on, 431–4; Dickinson on, 434

Spencer, George, Lord, mentioned, 275 n
Spencer, Georgiana, mentioned, 275 n
Spencer, John, Lord: squirrels for family, 275, 447 n; to visit BF, 447
Spencer, Margaret Georgiana Poyntz: to visit BF, 447; mentioned, 275 n
Sports, Charles I's proclamation on, 16
Spruce Street (Phila.), mentioned, 354 n
Spry, Gov. William: death, 335; Barbados governor, 336 n
Squirrels: DF sends, for Shipleys and Spencers, 43–4, 141–2, 275, 447 n; death of, epitaph for, Mungo, 300, 301–2
Staffordshire, Eng., BF visits, 207
Stamp Act (1765): passed, 104, 220; colonial opposition to, 220, 283 n; mentioned, 51, 380, 402
Stamp Act, repeal of (1766): Dartmouth supports, 410; mentioned, 220
Stamp Commissioners, British, and income, expenses in colonies, 419
Stanwix, Fort, treaty of, 4 n, 123, 124
[Statement of the Petitioners in the Case of the Walpole Company] (Wharton), mentioned, 349 n
Stavers, Bartholomew: Boston-Portsmouth postrider, 60; payment to, 60 n
Stephens, William (Gov. of Ga.), mentioned, 89
Stephens, William (Gov.'s grandson), recommended to BF, 89, 226
Stevenson, Benjamin, S.C. naval officer, 284
Stevenson, Margaret: moves to No. 1 Craven St., xxix, 202–3 n, 315, 341, 342, 365; to visit Vinys, 39; Mrs. Viny writes to, 39–40; dines with BF, others, 43; and BF's grandsons and hers, 43, 231; health of, 45, 229, 341; apples for, 87 n; and curtains for DF, 90; and cask of porter for BF, 99; sends cod sounds and tongues, 99; trip of, 202; forwards BF's mail, 229; DF sends handkerchief to, 231, 321; buys goods for S. Bache, 267, 394; and Mlle. Biheron, 298–9, 330; affection for Josiah Williams, 377; letter from, 229; mentioned, 29, 36, 46, 54, 55, 66, 112, 122, 131, 141, 152, 241, 268, 271, 274, 275, 299, 314, 321, 364, 372, 378, 395
Stiegel, Henry William: bill of exchange on, 143; Mannheim glass works of, 282 n
Stiles, Elizabeth Hubbard, silk for, 137
Stiles, Ezra: recommends Marchant, 30, 213 n; Zend-Avesta for, 30–1; interested in ancient Eastern religions, 31; and

colonial silk culture, 137; illness in family of, 378; letters to, 30–1, 212–13
Stirling, Lord. See Alexander, William (Lord Stirling).
Stocker, Anthony, mentioned, 152 n
Stocker & Wharton, draft from, 152
Storms: Winn's observations on aurora borealis and, xxx, 236–8: BF's conjectures on, 239; at sea, described, 107–8; BF's theory on, 236 n; Henly on electrical charge in, 306; frequency of, in colonies and Europe, 325
Story, William: and N. Wheelwright bankruptcy, 23–4; seeks official appointment, 23–4; and the Hutchinson letters affair, 24 n; possibly introduced to G. Cooper, 24 n; returns to America with Bancroft, 24 n, 175 n
Stoves (BF's invention). See Pennsylvania fireplace.
Strahan, Margaret Penelope: BF, others dine with, 43; mentioned, 141, 321
Strahan, William, BF, others dine with, 43, 285, 341; political differences of, with BF, 91; corresponds with Hall, 91 n; and books for Lib. Co., 117, 285 n; and M. Nelson's voyage, in BF-WF accounts, 193; Goddard's debt to, 266, 394 n; and books for WF, 285 n; circulates queries on Townshend Acts and answers, 406; and Hutchinson letters affair, 406–7; plan of, for Anglo-American union, 407; political views of, 407; and extract of letter to Cushing, 407; in Walpole Co., 407; prints Barbeu-Dubourg's Petit code, 442 n; letters from, 266–7, 285; mentioned, 47, 274, 321, 373, 417
Stringfellow, John, right of, in Phila. land: bought for Silk Filature, 97–9, 168–9, 413 n, 421; papers, letters on, forwarded to A. James, 169
Struensee, Dr. Johann, overthrown in Denmark, 73 n
Sturgeon, for BF, 44
"Suffering Traders." See Indiana Co.
Suffolk, Lord, impeachment of (1386), 18 n
Sulphuric acid, in Priestley's experiments on airs, 133
Sunlight: Henly's, BF's experiments on electricity and, 121, 121 n; role in photosyntheis, 214
Sunspots, Marshall's observations on, sent to BF, 92
Susquehanna River: possible canal from, to Schuylkill, 157, 279; survey of, 158 n
Sutton, Capt. James: carries mail, goods for BF, 274, 349, 371, 372, 373; commands Catherine, 373

INDEX

Wilkes, John, mentioned, 12 n
Williams, Grace Harris: sends cod, 99 n; family of, 232 n; mentioned, 34, 291
Williams, John: and debt to BF of J. Williams, Jr., 34; in financial difficulties, 34 n; debt to BF, 100; bill of exchange for, 232
Williams, Capt. John, wants command of Barbados fort, 335–6
Williams, Dr. John, charity of, 290 n
Williams, Jonathan, Sr.: and S. Hall's debt to BF, 28, 200, 291; bills of exchange from, 32–3, 232, 319 n; debt to BF for sons, 33, 34, 100, 200; and goods for J. Williams, Jr., 100; desires Josiah's return to Boston, 102; and business affairs of J. Williams, Jr., 198, 291 n; wants BF's power of attorney, 200; family of, 232 n; lottery tickets for, 291; and death of Josiah, 291, 377; and BF's wedding gift to niece, 362–3; letter from, 290–1; letters to, 32–4, 232, 362–3; mentioned, 337, 440
Williams, Jonathan, Jr.: carries gifts for J. Mecom, 28; returns to Boston, 32 n; debt to Warren, 33, 34, 100, 101–2, 197–200, 439–40; debt to BF, 33, 100; business affairs, 33–4, 97 n, 100–2, 291 n, 439; BF advises on "ready money plan," 34, 45 n, 97, 100, 157; Priestley's work on vision, light and colors sent to, 97, 156–7, 200; elastic gum for, 100; shipping venture of, 100, 198; bills of exchange from, 101, 439–40; WTF writes, 112; age of, 112 n; and financial aid for J. Mecom, 157; sees Bancroft, 175; recommends A. Winthrop, 175; possible BF loan to, 199; and BF's "prudential algebra," 299 n; and H. Walker's apprenticeship, 337; trip to Phila., 440; letters from, 100–2, 156–7, 175, 197–200, 337–8, 439–41; letters to, 34, 97; mentioned, 232
Williams, Jonathan (son of John), mentioned, 200 n
Williams, Josiah: studies music, 33 n; returns to Boston, 33 n, 94, 102, 104, 156, 200, 436 n; death, 33 n, 94 n, 156 n, 291, 337, 377, 436; BF's loan to, 33, 34, 200; to bring copies of Priestley's new book, 97, 200; illness, 156, 232; H. Walker attends, 436 n; mentioned, 157
Williamsburg, Va., Dixon postmaster of, 319 n
Willing & Morris, bill of exchange by, 277
Wilmot, Henry, and Pa. acts (1771, 1772), 276

Wilson, Alexander, mentioned, 228 n
Wilson, Benjamin: on Purfleet committee, xxx, 154, 427 n; dispute with BF on pointed vs. blunt lightning rods, xxx–xxxi, 119 n, 154, 233, 245, 250 n, 252–4, 260, 261–3, 326, 424–9, 429–30, 441 n; BF's portrait by, 62–3; report to Board of Ordnance by, 128, 129; electrical experiments and theories of, 182 n; dissents from Purfleet committee report, 233, 245, 261, 424, 429; theories on lightning, 261–2; *Further Observations upon Lightning . . .*, 261 n, 429 n; Henly challenges by letter, 261–2 n; letter from, to Sir C. Frederick forwarded to Royal Soc., 424, 425; inspects St. Paul's for lightning damage, 426; and Henly's experiment on pointed rods, 426–7; on committee on lightning rods for St. Paul's, 427 n; *Observations upon Lightning . . .*, 429
Wilson, Patrick: and APS *Trans.* for Glasgow University, 228; letter from, 228
Wilson, Rachel, BF visits, 207
Wind: BF's interest in physics of, 110 n; Beighton theory on aurora borealis and, 236 n; and Henly's electrical experiments in St. Paul's, 442
Wine: possible Parliamentary bounty on, 20, 49; and lead poisoning from vessels, 71. See also Viticulture.
Winn, Isaac L.: observations by, on aurora borealis and storms, 236–8; BF's conjectures on, 239; letter from, 236–8; mentioned, 424
Winthrop, Adam: biog. note, 175 n; recommended to BF, 175
Winthrop, John: *Phil. Trans.* for, 35; report on transit of Venus, aberration of light, 35, 105; electrical experiments of, 247 n; to see Hutchinson-Oliver letters, 412; letter to, 35; mentioned, 175, 178
Wood & Trevanion, mentioned, 331 n
Wool manufacture, regulated in Ireland, 19
Wren, Christopher, builds St. James's Church, 325 n
Wright, Gov. James: dispute with Ga. Assembly over Jones as speaker, 55 n, 95, 96 n; BF not call on, 95; and appointment of BF as Ga. agent, 95; in England, 95 n; and Ga. petition on Baker's land claims, 258 n
Wright, Patience Lovell: wax models by, 93; recommended to BF, 93, 104; visits BF, 93, 231; wax model of BF, 93 n; visit to England, 231 n

494